GUSTAVE **COURBET** HIS LIFE AND ART

Jack Lindsay

GUSTAVE **COURBET** HIS LIFE AND ART

JUPITER · LONDON · 1977

First published in 1973.
Second impression April 1977.
JUPITER BOOKS (LONDON) LIMITED
167 Hermitage Road, London N4 1LZ.

ISBN 0 904041 92 I HARDBOUND
ISBN 0 904041 93 X LIMP EDITION

Composed in Monotype Ehrhardt, Series 453,
and printed and bound in Great Britain
by W & J Mackay Limited, Chatham.

Contents

List of Illustrations

To Roy Noakes

The earth is ours to love; but love
brings conflict in its harmony.
I seek to change the loved one; she
has her ideas of changing me.
So we in Nature seek to find
the image of ourselves; instead
a difficult mistress she turns out,
quick with surprises when abed.
And what results, in steadfast love,
is something not narcissistic at all,
nor a mere mirror-image baring
a ghost delusively at our call.

I say this since our Courbet was
a man who hugely loved the earth.
He sought to give all things their rights
and art a clear harmonious birth.
He achieved the thing he sought, and yet
it turned out different from his thought,
different every living moment
and yet the very thing he sought.
Thus, mastered in his mastering,
he went his Heraklean Way.
The artist has no other choice
in our more deadly deceitful day.

JACK LINDSAY

FOREWORD

No artist of high stature can have received so much abuse as Courbet did in his lifetime; the attacks were made not merely on aesthetic grounds, but saw him as a vile debaser of moral values as well. He could hardly complain, since from 1848 to 1849 he set himself up in conscious antagonism, artistically and politically, to all the established standards of his day. But the denigration of his role did not halt with his death in 1877; as late as 1921, when Léonce Bénédite, Curator of the Luxembourg, was invited to represent the State at the unveiling of the tablet at Ornans, he declined to attend on the ground that he had 'received counter-instructions'. And I think that this book of mine shows how the abuse during his lifetime has fixed his image and determined much of the perspective by which his work is still viewed. In the issue of the *Figaro Littéraire* of 19 March 1971, Dominique Jamet, dealing with the Commune, describes Courbet as an 'infamous dauber [*barbouilleur*]'.

Courbet lived a very full life and much of it is well documented; he himself was a voluminous letter-writer. Under the banner of his Realism, he made the decisive break with all established standards, in theory as in practice; and though this break was made possible by the work of many artists ranging from Hogarth and Goya to David and Gros, from Turner and Constable to Géricault and Delacroix, the decisive blow was struck by Courbet. Modern Art with its multiple potentialities of integration and disintegration was founded; the individual artist was thrown strongly back on his own resources at the same moment as the social relations of art were grasped with a new fullness. We find this conflict acutely present in Courbet and his work; and that is why his life has a peculiarly rich significance for us.

A word here may not be amiss on the function of an artist's biography. Such a biography, it seems to me, is sometimes seen as hardly distinguishable from a study of his art – though at the other end we meet lives which are merely a chronicle of events and pictures painted. It seems to me that each type is equally far from what the work should be. It must be primarily an account of the artist's life, but it must be permeated by an understanding of just what his artistic contribution was, what was the creative aim driving him on. Thus, though it may make lengthy analyses of certain pictures important in his development, its value will lie in the central conception of the man, which shows how his art-aims have links in varying degrees with all his actions and how his total personality, his total experience, shapes his art. If the book truly achieves this unity, then the reader will always afterwards find himself making a radically new approach to any picture by the artist, seeing it more clearly in itself and in its relation to his whole development.

On the biographical side there is abundant material. There are many accounts, extended or slight, of Courbet during his lifetime, which vary very much in value. For long he had considerable journalistic value, so that frivolous as well as serious commentators wrote of his art, his behaviour, his creed. Two critics, Champfleury and Castagnary, were closely connected with him at different phases of his life; and though neither man can be said to have deeply understood him, their writings are often useful. There are only two largescale Lives: that by Riat in French (1906) and that by Gerstle Mack in English (1951). Riat had access to much family material, but has to be critically used; Gerstle Mack wrote with more scholarship, but contributed nothing essentially new in his more ordered account. Courbet's letters, despite their great interest and range, have never been collected. There is a two-volume collection of biographical material by Courthion (1948 and 1950); Charles Léger in several works also put together much more material; and Robert Fernier in his *Bulletins* of the *Amis de Gustave Courbet*, has provided yet another valuable collection of documents, facts, and discussions. Troubat, Borel, Bonniot and others have dealt with various important relationships of the painter. On the biographical and personal side there is thus a large amount of details, trivial or highly significant, to be sifted through, collated, and put coherently together. But the book by Gerstle Mack remains the sole work, still at all up to date, which tries to tell the story of Courbet's involved life at anything like the necessary length; and though it provides a good structure for the main events, it makes no attempt whatever to penetrate inside the man and his art.

When we turn to the body of critical work on the art, the material is much poorer. Occasionally, in the many accounts of his personality and art written during his life, there are acute comments; but in general the argument remains within narrow limits. Courbet is seen as the apostle of a very restricted 'realism', a naturally gifted painter with strong animal spirits, but with a low plebeian vision. In the twentieth century Meier-Graefe made a good start, but almost all that has followed has been desultory, unable to break from the early preconceptions. Important interpretations, bringing out the links with popular art, have however been made by Schapiro and Nochlin. Here was the first break-through to a fresh perception of Courbet's aims and achievements; and a serious attempt to discard the old superficial judgments and see the real social bases of his art has been made by Clark. Slowly there has been emerging a realisation of Courbet as a painter with a deep poetic vision, a man who thought hard about his art, thought steadily, consistently, and coherently, with genuine passion, as few painters have done, an artist who massively embodied in his forms the great energy that appeared in the events of his life. We see in him the first artist who fully broke through the conventions of academic art and insisted on thinking everything out again from the ground up, and who thus acted as a great liberator; the first artist who made a clear and conscious unity of personal life (the revolt against romantic love), artistic aims (the treatment of every object with entire respect, as an embodiment of energy in a specific form), and social and political views (his socialism, which is Proudhonian and yet goes far beyond Proudhon). Only a man of strong powers of thought as well as of painting skills and aptitudes could have achieved such a unity.

In this perspective the old ideas of him as bull of a man who happened to be a fine spontaneous painter show up in their hopeless inadequacy. The first effective expression of the changing attitude to Courbet appears in the Catalogue of the 1969–70 exhibition at the Villa Medici in Rome, with its preface by Bucarelli. The reader of my book will be able to estimate how far I justify in my detailed analysis the claims made above.

There are many points of similarity between the careers of David and Courbet. I have not laboured these as I have written a book largely about David, *Death of the Hero*, and anyone interested enough to read that book together with this will not need to be reminded of the kinship.

JACK LINDSAY

Acknowledgement is made to the following who have supplied photographs: Photographie Giraudon, Photographie Bulloz, Lauros-Giraudon and Denise Bourbonnais.

1 EARLY YEARS 1819-37

A landscape-painter can hardly but be strongly affected by the sort of scenery amid which he grows up. Constable, Courbet, Cézanne are clear examples. Each was deeply influenced by the earth of his childhood and youth, and each kept returning to that earth with fuller understanding and penetration. Courbet was born at Ornans in the province of Franche-Comté, close to the Swiss frontier. The region is mountainous, cut with Alpine foothills. The higher levels consisted of wooded slopes and steep cliffs; the rough face of the grey stone was warrened with caves and grottoes, from which burst wild streams. Some of the streams came from long underground passages, then rushed headlong down the channels they had cut in the rock. Lower down were broad open valleys, with scattered villages. Ornans stood, in the department of Doubs, on the highway between Besançon and Pontarlier, with a population of some three thousand. The river Loue flowed through in a broad channel; and the houses were built of local stone, with the steep roofs of a town that could expect heavy snow in winters. Their style was a mixture of French and Swiss elements, with some German touches intruding from Alsace.[1]

The inhabitants included many *vignerons*, vine-growers, men with the sturdy independence of the mountaineer, tall men with square shoulders, prominent cheekbones, heavy jaws. They were organised in a fraternity under the protection of St Vernier, and celebrated his yearly festival. They formed a majority in the elections and in effect ruled the town. Clannish, they had great pride in their region. The rains brought much soil down the slopes, and the *vigneron* had to carry it up again in a basket hung on his back; he had assiduously to build walls and dig channels. The basket became part of his insignia, worn even when he had nothing to pick up. Lean and hard-living, these peasants relaxed with good cheer in the winter; and they spent much spare time in hunting or fishing. Proudhon, born at Besançon, was proud of his 'rustic blood', and boasted, 'I am pure Jurassic limestone'.[2] The folk spoke in a thick guttural accent all their own; Courbet inherited it and in later years often deliberately stressed it.

Max Buchon, Courbet's close friend, collected and published *Popular Songs of the Franche-Comté*. They bring out the hearty down-to-earth humour of regional jollity. One song tells of a Goat that eats up the cottages, is arrested by twenty-four sergeants and taken to the *Parlement*. As she enters, she gives 'one fart in the nose of the judges and two at the lieutenant. She knows a thing or two, my nannygoat, she knows a thing or two!' Then, 'She raised up her tail on a bench for to sit; at that moment she loosed a whole basket of shit.' And so on. Buchon comments: 'There is a song that does not lack the *franc-comtois* damn-all', and adds that he does not need to defend the song's inclusion, 'for I have heard it sung so heartily and so often by the ladies, nay, even by churchmen, that I have no way of forgetting it here. Why are these bawdries so well received among us, at all merry meetings, if not because they harmonise with the old basis of our bantering temperament . . . against the *parlements*?' Victor Hugo wrote to Buchon, 'I owe to you the revelation of my native land', and 'I love this old earth which is both French and Spanish'.[3] The earthy directness and humour of the songs is wholly in the key of Courbet's character, and the ditties he used to improvise have their clear link with the regional folksongs.

Courbet was born on 10 June 1819 at Ornans. His full names were Jean-Désiré-Gustave. His father, Eléonor-Régis-Jean-Joseph-Stanislas Courbet, was a well-off landowner with fields and vineyards in the area of Flagey, a village some eight miles south of Ornans; the farmhouse was plain but comfortable. At Ornans, Gustave's maternal grandfather, Jean-Antoine Oudot, had a slightly larger house, in the rue de la Froidière, overlooking the river. A family tale declared that Mme Courbet, after leaving Flagey in a carriage, was overtaken by her pangs and bore Gustave under an oaktree by the roadside, at a spot La Combe-au-Rau. Such a birthplace would have befitted Gustave, but more likely he was born at the Oudot house. The official record is dated 11 June 1819, his father making a deposition before the mayor.[4] The stock was old *franc-comtois*. His paternal grandfather, Claude-Louis Courbet, was born in 1751 and died at Flagey on 12 April 1814; the grandmother, born as Jeanne-Marguerite Cuinet, died there on 23 June 1806. The grandparents on the mother's side were of more interest, and they survived into the child's early years. Jean-Antoine Oudot was born at Ornans in 1767; his wife, Thérèse-Josèphe Saulnier, was also of Ornans.[5] She was 'a good housekeeper, industrious, economical'. He was 'a man without pretentiousness but extremely enlightened, who had read the works of Voltaire and other philosophers, assertive, brusque, even coarse in argument, whose integrity and goodness were acknowledged by everyone'.[6] A staunch Republican of 1793, he had a profound effect on his grandson. On his knees Gustave read the *Almanach des Républicains* edited by Sylvain Maréchal, a follower of Babœuf, in which he found among other things the tale of William Tell.[7] Thus Gustave absorbed at an early age an enthusiasm for the Revolution. He wrote in 1861: 'My grandfather, a Republican of '93, had invented a maxim which he repeated to me again and again: *Shout loudly and march straight ahead!* My father always followed this advice, and I have done the same.'[8]

Régis Courbet, though not badly off, was no member of the gentry; he had no wish to rise in the world, though now and then he played his part in municipal affairs, holding various offices at Flagey, and no doubt enjoyed the petty politics of the area, where he knew everyone and everyone knew him as a respected landowner. His holdings were small scattered parcels, but they added up to a large enough figure to gain him a vote under Louis-Philippe before universal suffrage came in. He worked the land by hired labourers, and was intelligent enough to want to try improved methods without knowing enough to do it effectively.

He was intensely interested in agricultural improvements. He made many attempts at large scale farming without success; he tried to put in a drainage system; he invented a harrow and improved other farm equipment. But he grew quickly bored. I've seen a store room at Flagey packed with his devices; all sorts of implements, unused and unusable, lay there in the dust. . . . Tall, thin, tireless, he was forever on the move, on foot, on horse, in a carriage. . . . He frequented fairs and markets where he could be noticed far off in the crowd, boisterous, jovial, shaking hands, haranguing the bystanders, shouting, laughing, gesticulating. . . . As a young man, he possessed unusual strength and good looks. He kept both for many years. . . . His education was better than one would have expected to find in a peasant born towards the end of the Revolution. . . . Endowed with a merry disposition and a caustic tongue, he was always ready to jest. . . . He was certainly the most unconscionable chatterbox I ever met in my life.[9]

Born 10 August 1798 at Flagey, on 4 September 1816 he married Sylvie Oudot, born at Ornans on 11 July 1794. We can see how many of his characteristics – his *bonhomie*, his restless activity, his assertiveness, his amiable egoism – were carried on by his son, who, however, gained from his mother and the other Oudots his qualities of intellectual and moral tenacity and probably much of his sensibility. Gustave, indeed, in his life showed a ceaseless struggle between tenacity of purpose and out-turned boisterousness, but on the whole the struggle was enriching and helped to drive him on his creative quests. Max Buchon wrote:

From his mother and his maternal grandfather, *le père* Oudot, Courbet got his personal tenacity; from his father, a born constructor of agricultural theories, the adventurous disposition of his spirit. All Courbet's works in major mode proceed from his grandfather, all those in minor mode from his father. You have seen the household at Ornans and at Flagey. If grandfather and grandmother Oudot had survived there, you would have dissected your Courbet without anyone's aid.[10]

As an example of the way in which these mountaineers were interrelated, we have Buchon's excited discovery that in the will of an ancestor of his, François Buchon, of Dournon, domiciled at Flagey in 1702, the wife was 'la Catherine Courbet', of the same place.[11]

Mme Courbet was, said Buchon, 'a tenacious woman, affirmative, of good sense, affectionate, simple and good'. Later the Comte Albert de Circourt, a friend of Wey, met her in a diligence and said that he found her 'of correct attire, endowed with modesty, a fine tact, a delicate spirit, much disturbed at the excessive praise with which her son was troubled'.[12] But even if she was not one of the *dames* chanting 'The Goat', she had a more energetic character than she displayed before the Comte. These tough mountain-folk, who produced *le père* Oudot, Gustave, Max Buchon, Proudhon, had an extreme sense of independence. Among the relations who inspired Proudhon was a cousin, Melchior, who abandoned holy orders in 1789 to become a leader of the Revolution in Besançon; he presided over the local Jacobin club, was jailed after the Terror, and carried on as a prominent Freemason. Then there was the grandfather, Jean-Claude Simonin, nicknamed Tournesi for his service in the Tournay regiment during the Hanoverian war, who was famed for his boldness in resisting the pretensions of the landlords and for his war with their foresters. In a quarrel over firewood he mortally wounded one of the latter, and the man, so the tale went, died repentant of his oppressions of the poor, recognising 'the instrument of heavenly justice in Tournesi's hand'. Tournesi himself died through a fall on an icy road in the 1789 winter as he went round preaching rebellion. 'I place him on a level with the men of Plutarch', said Proudhon.[13]

Four sisters followed Gustave. The first, Bernardine-Julie-Clarice, born on 9 September 1821, died at Ornans on 29 December 1834. We know nothing of her; but Gustave was fifteen at her death, and in so closely knit a family he must have been strongly affected. But exactly how, we can only guess. On 26 August 1824 came Jeanne-Thérèse-Zoé, an impetuous vehement character, as restless and ambitious in her own way as was Gustave; then, on 1 August 1828 Jeanne-Zélie-Mélaïde, who at an early age seems to have developed an uncertain health that turned her to sentiment and piety; finally, Bernardine-Juliette, born 14 December 1831, tough and assertive, living with intense emotion the closed family life from which Gustave and Zoé broke. He was twelve when she was born, and she always remained his faithful young sister.

The first references are to Gustave as a small boy making good progress at school and hopefully praised and guided. Cousin Oudot wrote on 2 January 1823, 'You'll tell Gustave not to cut his fingers making lanterns.' He was then about three-and-a-half. With a jump we come to 7 January 1830:

Kiss your little writer on both cheeks for me; his little letter is a pleasant surprise, better than the bonbon of New Year's Day. His hand is firm; his words are well formed; I, his pedant of a cousin, would like to write as well. . . . It's eight years since he jumped on my knees; I see him still as I left him, and I'll be quite astonished on meeting him again to see his head reach up to my chin. For the rest, if he's grown, it's not only in height, he must be as good as he was a fine child.

Mme Oudot goes further. 'I thank you, my dear Gustave, for having thought of telling me about your progress; I congratulate you. You could already be the secretary of the Mairie. Courage; keep it up; don't waste your time; when you're bigger you'll have nothing to regret.'[14] He was soon to tire of such well-meant exhortations.

In 1831 he was sent to the little seminary at Ornans, a subordinate diocesan institution administered by the archbishop of Besançon, which catered for the laity as well as for the theologically inclined. He was there for six years, gaining poor marks.[15] Max Buchon, who had begun attendances in 1830, later recalled those days:

We were in the same class, both stammerers, I a boarder, he a day-pupil; I sedate, quiet, and retiring; he lively and boisterous. I got prizes at the end of each year; he got nothing of the sort. I left at the close of 1833; he stayed on. Up to that point our relations had been less than nothing; it was in the following years that Courbet began to find himself. Carving his walking-stick head with a knife must have been, according to Cuénot, his first exploit. At my times at the seminary there were no drawing lessons. Only after I left, under the direction of the abbé Oudot, another of Courbet's relations, did *le père* Baud, a poor devil, come to make the pupils draw with the pencil.
There was in the approach to the chapel, unattached, a religious picture, which, in Cuénot's account, Courbet wanted to copy straight off. He took a porcelain palette from his sister, found colours at a building painter's, and on with it! Refractory to all other branches of learning, Courbet distinguished himself by his French essays, always so comical that the teacher regularly put off the reading of them till the last for grand finale. On Thursdays it was he who by his ascendancy had the last word in determining the direction of our walk.[16]

From early he had come to know and love the countryside over which he rambled. Proudhon sets out what must have been also Gustave's experiences.

1 Courbet by Thibouet

2 Courbet leaning on a tree or creeper
(H. Tournier)

3 Courbet talking to himself

4 Courbet based on a photograph by Léger
Mansell Collection

5 Ornans

6 Proudhon: photograph by Nadar

7 Courbet's world by Félicien Rops

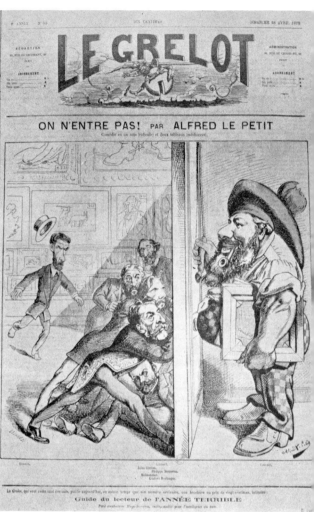

8 'On n'entre pas' by Le Petit
in *Le Grelot*

UNE BAIGNEUSE, par M. Courbet

Femme de 45 ans sur le point de se laver
pour la première fois de sa vie, dans
l'espoir d'apporter un soulagement à ses
varices.

LA FILEUSE, par M. Courbet

La fraîcheur de cette villageoise tend à
nous prouver que la malpropreté n'est pas
aussi nuisible à la santé qu'on le croit
généralement en société.

9 From *Art Bulletin* XLIX

Plate 13

0 Woodcut from *The Wandering Jew* (Champfleury)

Projet de tente conçu par Courbet pour son Exposition de 185

11 Pavilion by Courbet
from *Art Bulletin* XLIX

A L'EXPOSITION

**Leçon de politesse donnée par M. Courbet
à deux bourgeois**

A la vue de M. Courbet, les bourgeois n'ôtent
que leurs chapeaux. A la vue des bourgeois,
M. Courbet ôte son chapeau, sa veste et son gilet.

12 'Le Rencontre' by Courbet
from *Art Bulletin* XLIX

La Fileuse de Courbet.

— Pendant que Courbet la peignait, on voit bien qu'elle ne se peignait gué
—Quand elle se réveillera, ça ne lui ferait pas de mal de filer au bain a

13 'La Fileuse de Courbet' by Nadar
in *Le Journal pour Rire* 1853

14 'Siesta' (Léger)

15 'Democritisation de l'art'

16 'Les Vaches à M. Courbet'

17 'Le Retour du Marché'
from *Le Journal pour Rire* 1851

18 Courbet by Le Petit
from *Le Hanneton*

Courbet by Baudelaire

20 Courbet and two canvases (Léger)

21 Courbet by Manet

22 Courbet's teaching studio

23 Daumier's joke

24 Caricature of 'Les demoiselles' (Léger)

What pleasure in those days to roll in the high grass, which I would have liked to browse as my cattle did! To run with naked feet on the smooth paths and along the hedgerows! To sink into the fresh deep soil as I hoed the green maize! And often in the hot June mornings I would throw off my clothes and bathe in the dew that drenched the turf. . . . I could hardly distinguish Me from Not-Me. Me – it was all I could touch with my hand, all I could embrace in my vision, all that seemed good for some purpose; Not-Me was all that could hurt or resist me. The idea of my personality was confounded in my mind with that of my well-being, and I had no anxiety to search above for unextended and immaterial substance.

These words express precisely the underlying sense of rich direct physical contact between the self and nature in Courbet's paintings, the element of early experience which he carried forward into his art.[17]

At times Gustave went with his mother gathering berries, sometimes no doubt with Clarice or even Zoé, but often alone. The countryside was close at hand. If he crossed the old arcaded bridge of Nahin and climbed the rock Founèche, he could look down from its grey mass on the Salins highway and the town below. Also he could walk under the Rocks, leaving Ornans by the gate of the Îles-Basses which leant against his house. He went a short way up the main road and then along a side turn to the right by a meadow – here he later built a studio. Going up a steep path among vines, he skirted a drinking-trough cut in stone and came at last to the rock on which stood the remnants of the Château d'Ornans, an old residence of the Dukes of Burgundy. Round about were the typical rocks of the Loue which he so often painted, bare, rounded, hanging sheer, their grey tones contrasting with the brown slopes ribbed with vines or the lower grounds of grass or orchard. After the rocks came an easy walk for a couple of hours and then a sharp descent. Or else, going by a winding path, amid blackberries, honeysuckle, walnuts, beeches and hornbeam, with a stream brawling below and continual glimpses of Ornans, he reached the Rock of Eight Hours, used by the *vignerons* as a meridian, and below it the valley of Mambouc. Passing other well-known rocks, each with its name – the Mont, the Garenne, the Saut Chevalier – he returned home or pushed on to the village of Saules with a fine view of the surrounding plateau. Or again, he might climb to another plateau, where the Courbet lands lay, taking the highway that dominated the val de Chauveroche, on to Chassagne. Here he could see wide commons with stone outcrops, sparse long grass, heath, junipers, and oaks often stunted. Indeed there was an endless series of choices for his walks. He enjoyed the effect of a vast sky spreading out as he climbed up from the valleys, or the exhilarating sense of solitary power as he sat on a rock-edge and looked down at the Valbois cascade. Through the little wood of Flagey he could then pass on, across the commons, where grew a splendid old oaktree, to the family house. Later he made his way to the domainal forests where he learned to hunt.[18]

These wanderings were of more value to him in later life than most of what he learned at school. In time the fine script on which he had been complimented fell into a careless scrawl; and in his usual way he insisted on making a virtue out of a failing. In 1873 in an argument with the picture-dealer Hollander of Brussels, he wrote one of his furious letters; Hollander got his own back by publishing the letter in a Leipzig periodical with comments on its spelling errors. Dr E. Ordinaire wrote to Castagnary that Gustave

feels no shame at all for the mistakes in his letter. In the first place he says that one does not need to take the trouble to conform to spelling rules when writing to such a shady character, and further he refers to great men who made similar errors, and prides himself on his resemblance to them in this matter. When I remarked that a painter should at least spell the word *toile* [canvas] correctly, he insisted that there were no rules for the middle of a word but only for its two ends, and that he had a perfect right to spell *toile* with a double *l*.[19]

He was, however, still far from such casuistical excuses. It was some time before his stammer left him, but he was developing the bold front with which he covered up many fears and uncertainties. Writers on him agree in declaring that he disliked intellectual activity, that the dislike grew stronger with the years, and that he found no pleasure in reading. He was later, states the shallow and emphatic Gros-Kost, 'so lazy that he read nothing but the newspapers in which he was mentioned, while he mocked and poked fun at culture'. The sight of a book 'threw him into a rage; the appearance of an inkstand made him shudder'. In fact, he had an unusually active intellect and was passionately interested in almost all questions of culture. What the critics mistook for laziness or aversion was his rejection of one type of intellectual activity in favour of another; and they got quite out of focus the bravados of his self-defence.[20] We have seen that he was early outstanding in his French essays; he remained volubly eloquent with pen and tongue throughout his life, often with a finely original turn of phrase.

In 1834 his sister Clarice died and he must have experienced a great shock. An alien force had broken into the secure family circle, which no doubt had the effects of making that circle all the more significant and absorbing, and at the same time of intensifying the sense of what Proudhon called the Not-Me, all that hurt and resisted the Me. The Me had nourished itself on the strong family union and on the movement of discovery, of enjoyment, into the surrounding world of nature – a movement in which the sense of expanding personality was one with that of abounding well-being. At any rate about this time there began in him the assertion of independence, of sturdy revolt, which was to grow ever more powerful, without any weakening of the family bond and the trust in nature. Its first manifestation seems to have appeared in his resistance to religious instruction, perhaps aided by comments which he had heard his Voltairean grandfather make. It was not inability to learn the catechism, it was a deliberate piece of childish devilment, which made the preparations for his first communion abortive. Castagnary, repeating what Gustave had told him, says that no matter how often he came up with other students before the ecclesiastical examiners, he was always deferred.

The sins he revealed to his confessor so monstrously exceeded, in number and in kind, the iniquities appropriate to his tender age that nobody was willing to give him absolution. . . . These successive rejections began to affect his reputation. The Ornans housewives gossiped and wondered what would happen to him. Then Cardinal de Rohan, archbishop of Besançon, came to Ornans and was informed of the situation. The cardinal, a sensible man, decided to clear up the matter in person. 'Come to see me,' he told Courbet, 'we'll have a chat.'

The boy asked nothing better; he presented himself to the cardinal, who received him kindly . . . and persuaded him to confess. Courbet fell on his knees and began to tell his sins. Suddenly the cardinal, who had been looking in another direction, heard the confession of some outrageous wickedness, quickly turned his head and saw that the boy was reading from a large notebook. To make sure he had forgotten nothing, Courbet had compiled a list of all the sins it would have been possible to commit, from the most trifling peccadillo to the darkest of crimes. It was this litany he had read to his other confessors, who had failed to notice the fraud in the gloom of the confessional. The archbishop understood at once and burst into a roar of laughter. So Courbet had the honour of receiving his first communion from the hands of the cardinal who, wishing to make the most of an almost miraculous event, delivered a sermon to the astounded housewives on the text: *Quomodo fiat istud?* – How was this wrought?[21]

By oft telling, the story has doubtless grown more and more impressive, but we may assume it had a basis in fact and that Courbet was already constructing his defiant mask.

About this time he discovered the possibilities of art. There was no drawing class till 1833–4, when the headmaster, Abbé Gousset, later archbishop of Rheims and a cardinal, had been replaced by the former professor of rhetoric, the abbé Oudot whom Max Buchon mentioned, another cousin of Mme Courbet. Now elementary lessons in drawing and painting were given by Claude-Antoine Beau, known as *le père* Baud, reputed to be an old pupil of Gros.[22]

Le père Baud has left in the church of Ornans a portrait of Courbet young, set up for the devotion of the faithful under the name of St Vernier. *Le père* Baud did not have a great talent, but he had excellent teaching principles. He led his pupils out into the open country, in the midst of a picturesque site, and initiated them, by pencil or by brush, into reproducing what was before their own eyes. He himself would set to work like a student, an older student.[23]

Two of his works, kept at Ornans, are long landscapes, very naïve in style, in one of which we see his pupils painting away at the local scene, with Courbet in the front row. Beau seems to have been educated at the art school in Besançon, then to have studied under Baron Regnault (rather than Gros) at Paris. In 1834 he showed at the Salon *Portrait of his Daughter at the Piano*; he sent in two works in 1835 that arrived too late: *Portraits of Children on Foot* and *An unfortunate Family succoured by a Charitable Lady*. (Later Courbet painted his sisters giving alms to a poor girl and the *Beggar's Alms*.) Beau made copies of Mignard, Vernet, Guérin, Picot, Sigalon. His *Saint Vernier* shows Courbet at eighteen years with long flowing hair and large ecstatic eyes; but the execution is feeble.

The important thing was that Courbet had now found an activity which enthralled him and into which he could pour himself. He filled sketchbooks with studies of people, flowers, but not of landscape. The episode of the religious painting, mentioned by Buchon, must have occurred about this time. He also painted his friends, for instance a schoolmate Bastide, who, later a chaplain in the French army at Rome, recalled that he still had at Ornans 'a horrible portrait of myself painted by my friend Courbet at the age of fifteen'. A self-portrait, done about the age of fourteen, is still extant.[24]

2 BESANÇON COLLÈGE 1837-40

Régis Courbet simply could not imagine art as a career; he wanted his son to rise in the world by becoming a lawyer or the like. He insisted that Gustave must go on to the Collège Royal at Besançon. The obdurate resistance to the college that Gustave set up as soon as he entered it is proof enough that there were difficult and stormy moments before he was driven off from Ornans. Besançon, some fifteen miles away, was the capital of the department of Doubs; with its houses of grey stone it lay neatly within a large U-shaped bend of the Doubs river; over the bridge at the base of the U was the suburb of Battant, a quarter then peopled by 'vine-growers, workmen, and industrious, honest and caustic petty landowners', where Proudhon had been born.[1] Balzac remarked, 'No town offers so dull and dumb a resistance to progress', and added that the 'sad, devout, scantily lettered town of war and garrison' well deserved the trouble of having its 'manners and behaviour, its physiognomy' painted. The journalist Pelloquet commented, 'They are all clockmakers and nothing but clockmakers'. Stendhal used it in *Le Rouge et le Noir* for Julien Sorel and his seminary; but he did not know it well, building up his picture out of many towns of the region. However, he too called it a 'war town'.[2]

At the college Gustave was entered as a boarder for the study of philosophy: and at once he bombarded his parents with complaints. He later described his experiences with a resentment that did not lessen with the years.

I went to the Collège de Besançon where I learned to despise teaching. However it was necessary to carry on with Greek and Latin and mathematics, three things precisely for which I had no propensity. I learned the least I could so as not to burden my head with things useless to me. I really ought to have been learning French and foreign languages, history and geography, the liberal and mechanic arts, but no – I had to learn Latin and Greek and mathematics, so as to become a soldier, a profession that horrified me (under the Empire and still later, pupils used to drill with rifle and drum; luckily all that was over when I entered there).

In considering this condition of things, I told myself in my stubborn innards: Since all these fine chaps do Latin, they are strong enough without me, in this line there's too much competition. I turned my thoughts towards art.[3]

His account ends with the words 'I must confess that in prison where I am . . .'. So he was writing in Ste-Pélagie, and it seems that the experience of being in a jail made him think again of boarding-school.

After the passage about resolving to learn as little as possible, he tells how his dreams were all of escape into the free landscapes he had known. They were dreams of oxen, horses, meadows, of 'houses in rocks with a hearth for cooking potatoes that were eaten with the milk of goats'. He goes on:

But the bell rang. I had to go to the study where one slept on one's desk. Here is the programme

8

drawn up by the rebels among ourselves: (1) not to go to confession, (2) to make the classes impossible, (3) to do drawing and music, write verses, novels [*romans*] and love-letters to the girls of the Sacré-Cœur, (4) to use all one's ingenuity to find food, (5) to establish gymnastics and fights at night, (6) to try out dodges on the censor.

I won't describe here the means we used to arrive at our ends, to get some profit out of the sad education given to youth. Only I must say that our band later on distinguished itself in the world. One became a ship's captain, the other a general in Africa, others were engineers of bridges and highways, poets, literary men; one was president of the law-court in Brazil, another an agriculturist, and me, I was a painter. . . . As for those strong in Greek, who got first prizes, they were swallowed up in the offices of society or filled some sort of holes. Their names were never heard again.[4]

He insists that the experiences had a permanent effect on him. They must have gathered together all the resistances he had been developing, and thus represented his first consistent and prolonged assertion of independence. In his family life as we have noted, and will have to keep on noting, there was the contradiction between an extreme dependence on the bond and a sheer repudiation of it. Every attempt by Régis Courbet to exert his paternal authority led to flat rebellion on his son's part, and yet this rebellion did not in the least negate the attraction of the family hearth. The experiences of the college had their deep effect because they set him in a total opposition to authority and because in them he first underwent the deprivation of family warmth and security. They foreshadowed the jail experiences after the Commune which had such a shattering effect on him.

When nightmares agitate my sleep, it's seldom they are not college memories. We were hungry and cold in winter. We slept in dormitories where the air came in through the window-frames by grooves big enough for one's hand to go in. After putting all one's clothes on top of one's meagre coverlet, one finished by adding the portmanteau which was stowed under the bed. At 5.30 a.m. the drum was beaten. We got up, shivering, and the basins were frozen. We went to study, then at 8 we ate a bit of dry bread with water; at noon, soup, a little piece of beef and vegetables, always the same, a sort of dessert, nuts or cheese, a glass of watered wine, all of which had to be got down in twenty minutes. Then we went back to study at 1.30. And so on. I beg you to believe it wasn't the attractive work talked of by Fourier.

After the rising at 5.30 came two hours' study, then half an hour of recreation, then two hours of philosophy lectures, the students having to 'take notes as fast as the teacher talked'. Another hour of study; then from 11 to noon a drawing lesson; a lunch lasting fifteen minutes with all talking forbidden; recreation till 1 o'clock, study till 2, then two hours of mathematics which he found so incomprehensible he had to pay twelve francs a month for private lessons in order to get even the lowest marks; from 4 to 5 more recreation; then two-and-a-half hours' study; supper; bed at 8.30. Twice a week there was an additional class in physics.

He begged for an extra blanket. The wintry chill of the class-rooms made the students pool their pocket-money to rent a small stove and buy firewood. The teachers were always sourfaced and 'never spoke a word to the pupils during the whole year'. The students themselves were 'much more spiteful than at Ornans; they thought of nothing but teasing, making mischief and playing practical jokes'. Even the art classes were bad; 'There is no passable model.' But what Gustave complained most about was the food. After the bit of bread for breakfast came at noon a bowl of soup and a plate of fried potatoes or cabbage or some other vegetable 'always watery'. For supper a slice of meat with salad and apple; and so little time was allotted that even this scanty provender had often to be stuffed in part into his pocket. 'I long to see Ornans and all of you; that should be forgivable the first time I've been away from you all.'[5]

Perhaps the obsession he felt later with regard to food and drink was in part derived from the acute sense of deprivation now bitterly forced upon him. The idea of home and security was linked with the feeling of a well-filled belly, with warmth. A few days after the first complaints he was suffering from colic through the awful 'cold mutton they give us every evening'. He was denied the pipe which had already become habitual. When he tried to smoke, he was caught; and if he didn't smoke, he insisted that he felt 'dizzy and faint'. Even the pleasures of drawing were spoiled. 'There are a hundred of us in the large room that's so cold one can't hold a pencil.' Also, 'everyone shouts and talks and makes so much noise one can't hear oneself. If only I could go somewhere else. I could copy some bits of painting.'[6]

He kept up his complaints in a steady stream of furious letters. If he wasn't to be let leave the college, at least let him be boarded out. His father refused. Gustave lost his temper. 'Perhaps you think I wrote to you for my own amusement? Not at all. I've already sold my college suit for 33 francs; according to the estimate of the tailor who told me it cost 35.' He threatened. 'Since in everything and every place I must always be an exception to the general rule, I'll continue to follow my own destiny.' Finding appeals of no use, he increased his threats. On 4 December 1837 he wrote, 'If you won't let me be an *externe*, I'll go off, for I'm accomplishing nothing at the college; this is ridiculous, it's impossible.'[7]

Régis seems to have bidden him be patient; for on 9 December he wrote:

I want you to know I've come to a definite decision and I don't need two more months in my present situation to come to it. Since you've shown yourselves so obstinately set against me, I'm totally disgusted. You have tried to force me, and in all my life I've never done anything through force; that is not my character. You put me in college against my will, and now I've become too antagonistic to do any work here. I give up my classes with regret, especially as I have only one more year to go and I know very well I'll be sorry for this later; but no matter. I couldn't finish my studies here, and all I have done so far is absolutely worthless, because in these classes one must do all the work or none of it; and now, in whatever employment I may decide to take up, my studies will be of no more value than if I'd never done them; for all these classes are directed to the award of a bachelor's degree, without which they are pointless, and now any profession I choose will need a completely fresh start.

Had I been able to foresee this kind of opposition I should have long past given up my classes. They've been dragged out too long, for by this time there are many occupations and many schools into which I can no longer enter as too old. I'll do the best I can. But to stay two months more at this college is absurd, impossible. I've already too little time ahead of me to waste two months in a barracks like this. I beg you to try to come next Sunday, you two and my grandfather, if the weather allows, because I refuse to stay here much longer. I shall run away. You've already made me waste enough time by your procrastination. . . .

I am longing to see Ornans again. . . . Be sure to tell my grandfather not to worry. I hope you're all well. As for myself, I vomit only once in a while when hunger drives me to eat their mutton.[8]

But despite all the bluster and protest, Régis refused to yield. Gustave kept on threatening actions from which he flinched when the time came. He wrote that he'd had his trunks packed for a week and that he'd be back in Ornans on New Year's Day; but he didn't go. On 5 January 1838 he declared that the headmaster approved of his departure and that he'd be home next Sunday – 'whether you write to me or not. . . . I was determined to leave the other day, but when the headmaster heard of it, he sent word it'd be better to wait for a letter from you. I am no longer attending classes; I have stopped that altogether.' Régis was unmoved. Gustave raged, but stayed on at the college. For a month or two he gave up writing home.[9] Then on 19 March he sent a more vehement letter than ever. He was doing no work; the teachers no longer paid him any attention and indeed didn't even speak to him. The physics professor had punished the twenty more backward pupils by ordering them to copy out ten extra pages every week; another teacher made his life unbearable by sneers and curses; the headmaster had caught him smoking and hoped to get rid of him in a few days. Once more he begged his father to relent and not force him to run away.[10]

At last Régis agreed to let him become an *externe*. Before Easter we find him in a small room in the house of Arthaud in the rue du Rondot-Saint-Quentin: the house where in 1802 Victor Hugo had been born. Castagnary tells us:

A new term began. An old friend of the family, Mlle Beffort, once Ursuline of Ornans, housekeeper of the abbé Riduet, ex-priest *assermenté* [who had accepted the Constitution] of the diocese of Besançon, had declared in his favour. The appeals of the old lady, seconded by the grandfather, finally gained complete success. It was decided the student should finish the term already begun and after that would be restored to a free life. This promise gave him back his courage. He began to work and follow the courses: 'As for my classes, I work as I promised to do. I have had a candle bought for me and I keep awake like most of the philosophers till ten o'clock. . . . I follow always the course of M. Lacaze, we are doing geometry. Now what embarrasses me is Greek and history, for we have no teacher for these things.'[11]

He certainly studied philosophy; for Castagnary adds that Juliette[11] had kept his notebooks with the customary summaries and analyses.

As *externe* he was much happier. He was taking mathematical lessons from the coach Meusy and tried to keep his promises. But the examinations scared him. Soon he was writing home that the number and the difficulty of the courses were much worsened; he was expected to pass tests in

Greek translation, geography, and astronomy: subjects we have not studied in our classes, as well as chemistry, algebra, Latin, all the wellknown writers; also a composition to begin with, and if that isn't well done one isn't let go on. All that, added to the prodigious number of subjects we were already studying, throws me into a frightful panic.[12]

When he left in 1840 he had never presented himself for these examinations and had no bachelor's degree.

But he had not wasted his time. He had spent more and more time with local artists. The painter Jourdain lived in the same house, a mediocre artist, but a man with a studio, smelling of linseed oil and turpentine, and ready to talk of art. Even more useful were two friends of Gustave's own age, the son of the landlord Arthaud, and Édouard Baille, later a moderately successful painter of religious subjects. Both these friends studied at the École des Beaux-Arts in Besançon; and soon Gustave was going with them to class under the director Charles Flajoulet.[13] A drawing by Baille, dated 1840, shows Gustave as a slight elegant young man, with a faint down on his cheeks. Castagnary says:

The broad sweep of the eyebrow-arch shelters eyes of a great beauty. He has the tranquil look of a lion that feels his force. The mouth is bantering and positive; the jutting cheekbones and the compact build of the head accentuate energy and willpower. He wears long hair, curling to the level of the collar. Seated, with crossed legs, he has the clothes of the elegants of the time: tailcoat, trousers with fly, and holds already in hand that pipe which will never leave his lips and with which he'll go through life.[14]

Flajoulet was then about sixty, eccentric and likeable, 'good as bread, naïve as a child, adored by his pupils'.[15] He called himself a pupil of David and Gros, though his name has not been found in the lists of their pupils. He ardently admired Greek and Roman art as well as Raphael, and painted a series of thirty-seven pictures of the loves of Eros and Psyche. 'My compositions are not as good as those of the divine Sanzio, but I have produced two more than he did.' He wrote verses and sang them to his own accompaniment on the lyre, and when pleased with a pupil would promote him to the rank of a god. There was a god of colour, a god of drawing, a god of harmony. 'Marvellous, sublime you are, my friend, the king of colour. Take care, take care, don't look in at the Temple of the Arts through the keyhole.' He called himself the god of drawing, but gave to Gustave, his favourite pupil, the title of god of colour.[16] He had grandiose concepts but lacked skill. He sketched out, says Wey, 'on his canvases, which soon became smudged with confused scrawls in charcoal, vast compositions which he visualised in his mind and displayed with enthusiasm, believing them to be already executed. A strange teacher, this slightly crazy fellow.'[17] But he seems also to have been a good teacher in that he carried his enthusiasm over to his pupils and encouraged them, despite his fantastic ideas, to draw directly from life. Gustave filled sketchbooks with drawings of eyes, ears, legs, arms, feet, torsos, as well as street-scenes of Ornans and Besançon, and attempted portraits of his friends, Adolphe Marlet and Urbain Cuénot. He made some crude paintings: *Ruins by a Lake* (1839), *A Monk in a Cloister* (1840), landscapes near Ornans, including the Roche du Mont, the approach to Ornans, his grandfather's house, the Valley of the Loue, the Islands of Montgesoye where he set himself with a gun under his arm against a hilly background of poplars and willows.[18] He also tried his hand at lithography.

He made no effort to hide his artwork from his family. He wrote, probably in 1839,

I've recently taken up a kind of drawing that'd suit me perfectly if my money resources would allow me to practise it a bit more often. It's lithography. I'm sending you some examples with which I'm well pleased. Give one to Adolphe Marlet, the one with his name on it; you may give the others, which aren't so good, to anyone you like, telling them these samples are provisional and I'll exchange them when I print other copies, for I'm sending all I have. Tell *père* Beau [Baud] these are merely proofs.

He didn't forget to ask for ten francs to cover the printing costs.[19]

We may note that the effort to grapple directly with nature is at this phase linked with a strong romantic streak: the monk leads a young nun to a staircase, with a monastery, chapel, and poplars at the back; a woman stabs herself in a wood while her lover goes off with another girl. Castagnary assumes that Gustave was keenly interested in poetry in these years, affected by Lamartine, Hugo, de Musset.

At the college of Besançon as at the Little Seminary, Courbet must have been one of the party of the new movement. I see him bury himself in the countryside, on a holiday, with a volume of Victor Hugo or of George Sand, then, stretched out on the strong-smelling grass, in the midst of the valley of the Loue, in the shade of great trees, intoxicate himself with poetry and sentimentality.[20]

In view of the fact that he later in art carried on and matured certain realistic elements of the tradition begun by David and expanded by Gros and Géricault, it is of much interest that the two teachers of his early years seem to have been connected in some way with the studios of Gros and David, and to have inherited aspects of the Davidian outlook and method.

Max Buchon had now re-entered Gustave's life. In 1833 he had gone to study in the Jesuit seminary at Fribourg in Switzerland; returning to France in the autumn of 1938, he joined Gustave at the Besançon college. Now their friendship became firm and lasted till Max died some thirty years later. Maximilien Buchon had been born at Salins, some twenty-five miles from Ornans, on 8 May 1818. His father, Jean-Baptiste Buchon, had fought under Napoleon and retired as captain; he was in 1818 aged 41, and his wife, Jeanne-Louise Pasteur, was 25. Max's first memories, like those of Gustave, were of the Loue, together with the fir forests around Salins, the smithy and the market, and the fire that burned his home down. The Buchons were well enough off to let him carry on as a writer without the need of living on his books. Champfleury wrote truly of him:

Son of a former soldier, Max Buchon kept the imprint of authority; a sort of gash, furrowing one of his cheeks, seemed the old scar of a sabre-blow, and the resolute physiognomy of the man made one think of some infantry captain retired to his hearth in early years; but this impression came only from the first glimpse. His eyes which were good, pure, with an intent look, and despite everything, dreamy, held traces of the melancholies of a child whose youth has been sadly repressed. The poet, early deprived of his mother, had never known the tendernesses of family life; his father reared him in a hard way; however, Max Buchon, enclosed in appearance, had on the contrary a heart abundantly open, and was all love for his friends, for nature, as well as for intellectual and artistic matters. Letting himself go only rarely, unless to his intimates, he was born a confidant. He became in effect the devoted confidant of our works, of our struggles.[21]

He became a friend of the whole Courbet family as well as of Gustave; and, deeply affected by the writings of Victor Considérant of Salins and Proudhon of Besançon, he soon began to work as an ardent republican-socialist:

Max Buchon was not much of a talker. He lent a willing ear to the endless chatter of the Courbet family. . . . When they did ask him to speak, he would come to life and they'd listen attentively to his narration, with a grave expression, of droll stories told with a clever aptitude for mime. Enraptured by new ideas and inspired by a vision of happiness for all previously oppressed humanity, this apostle preached by setting an example and gathered in groups, in the countryside at a place called Les Engoulirons between Arbois and Salins, all the republican-socialist partisans in the area. . . . Completely honest, he had a bold and fearless mind, an unfaltering conviction. His upright character and his kind heart attracted to him all the wretched folk toiling on the land. He used to wander, with knapsack on back and staff in hand, in quest of old songs in the Doubs and the Jura. . . .

His prose as well as his poetry, without flamboyance, was the painting in small brush-strokes of the men, habits, and customs of his corner of the Jura. . . . A realist, a collector of popular songs, a French forerunner of Naturalism, Max Buchon wielded an influence superior to his written works. There was so little of the typical man of letters about him.[22]

Much of this development was yet to come; but Max was already expressing his humanist views. He drew Courbet in to illustrate his first work, *Essais poétiques*, with four lithographs. These immature works show a conscript bidding farewell, with tears, to his sweetheart at a wayside shrine on a tree; two Negroes ministering to an injured white man by the sea; a wayfarer at the edge of a lake; and two lovers (Gustave and one of Max's cousins as models) seated in a big room by a window.[23]

The summer holidays of 1840 were spent at Ornans and Flagey. Gustave was painting and sketching, and pestering his father for permission to go to Paris. Régis, obstinate as he was, and reluctant to see his one son abandon all hopes of a legal career for such a dubious trade as that of an artist, was forced to recognise that his son was even more obstinate. He gave in, apparently saving his face by insisting that Gustave was to make some sort of trial of the law courses.

Though such glimpses as we have of the Courbets in the intimacies of their family life come later on, we had better anticipate some of them here; for the effects of those intimacies on Courbet were profound and lasting. Certainly one of the reasons why he never married was because he could not outgrow the bond with his mother and his sisters. The odd tension which we have found in his reactions to the Besançon college between extreme home-dependence and extreme personal independence continued to dominate him all his life. In one sense that life was a flight from the family as the sole means of establishing himself as an individual against its ubiquitous claims; in another sense it was a ceaseless return to the family for renewal of strength in order to continue his flight and his assertion of individual rights.

Castagnary has left us an excellent picture of the family.

I have seen later this interior at Flagey and at Ornans, when the grandfather and grandmother Oudot no longer were alive, and when the *demoiselles* were grown up. It was a household of country bourgeois, which, in the midst of the cares and roughnesses of rural life, has not given up every kind of intellectual preoccupation. It exhaled a rustic perfume hard to define, with a wholly penetrating charm. There was a great love of one another; Gustave has always been the best of sons and the most devoted of brothers. His folk adored him and he adored his folk. The affection felt for him at home overflowed on to his Ornans comrades and on to the friends he sometimes brought from Paris. The family tastes had nothing vulgar. Prolonged easy circumstances had allowed refinement and the extension of the children's education.

Also, in the evening, the big room that served both as living and dining room, was transformed gladly into a reading or concert hall. When there had been enough talk, when the father, Régis Courbet, had shatteringly defeated the ladies at cards, music was played. Gustave's sisters sang with a great accuracy of feeling, while accompanying themselves on the piano. Gustave made his pleasant head-voice heard. Sometimes Promayet, son of the organist, who was the girls' teacher, took up his violin. When Max Buchon was there, literature also came on. Max Buchon recited verses. But, what was remarkable, what Gustave and his sisters sang was not the modish romances or the grand airs of the latest opera; it was some song of the country, badly rhymed, but of exquisite sentiment; the verses that Buchon spoke were not a lyric or dramatic piece of some poet with a great range, it was a humble scene of daily life that he had laboriously put in verse, concerning himself throughout with exact detail. It seemed that there lay the mark of the house; those who lived there and those who frequented it had an equal taste for the simple and the natural.[24]

Castagnary idealises a little; things were rougher and tougher than he allows for; but on the whole he conveys truly the spirit and the manners of the Courbet household. The mother played the flute, Zélie the guitar, Juliette the piano at Ornans and the harmonium at Flagey. Zoé no doubt sang; but as she developed she seems to have rather dissociated herself from the home-concerts and taken to reading. Champfleury, who visited the Courbets in 1856 and used his impressions for a novel on the three girls, *Les Demoiselles Tourangeau*, shows them at a later phase. The father has not changed; he is agitated with continual activities that lead nowhere. He is 'a man of ideas who alarms his wife with schemes that ceaselessly float through his brain, schemes that for forty years have inspired him to cry: I have made my fortune! – without having in fact succeeded in anything but squandering his patrimony.' The wife is 'an excellent woman, who adores her son, imagines that students live at Paris like princes, and fears we'll find her cooking modest'. She and Julienne [i.e. Juliette] attend to the cooking and household work. Julienne is always busy, always smiling. But the other sisters, with less work on their hands, are not so satisfied. The eldest, Christine [i.e. Zélie], has dark languid eyes that now and then illuminate her sickly face; she finds it an effort to smile and she seems to envy her active younger sister. 'The poor girl suffers from her inability to display the treasures of goodness that are in her. . . . Her gentle sad voice veils all the delicacy of a melancholy soul turned in upon itself.' She is like a flower that the gardener has forgotten to water, a bird with clipt wings. But the strangest of the trio is Émelina [i.e. Zoé]: 'A brain muddled [*embarbouillé*] by foolish reading. I hadn't crossed the threshold before Mlle Émelina began to pester me with a thousand questions about Paris, where nothing exists for her but drama and romance. What interests her most of all is the romantic lives of famous men and women.' Still, 'in spite of her romantic notions Mlle Émelina is really an amiable person.' She is shown as an ardent feminist, arguing that women are downtrodden and prevented from developing.[25] Though Champfleury clearly embroiders the facts, especially perhaps with regard to Christine-Zélie (who in the novel ends by committing suicide), his picture is generally supported by all we know of the girls. In view of the difficulty of penetrating inside the closed and secretive family world of the Courbets, his novel is of much importance.

In November 1840 Gustave at last left for Paris – on exactly what terms we do not know, but he was certainly expected to study law. Perhaps he had promised to try his best in that sphere before he finally went his own way. In a document he drew up in 1873 he stated, 'Arriving in Paris to study law, he lived there for several years on the four or five thousand francs that his father allowed him. Accepted at the Salon Exhibition in 1842 he continued to paint with the approval of his parents.'[26] He is here making the best possible case for himself, and he may be overstressing his work as a law student; but he must have had a brief career in the Faculté de Droit. He carried with him several letters of introduction to Paris acquaintances of the family and the farewell good wishes of a host of relatives and friends. He must have been saddened to some extent, despite his excitement, by the death of Flajoulet on 15 September; but whatever he had sworn to Régis, we can be sure he had no intention whatever of persevering as a law student.

His first lodgings were in the rue Pierre-Sarrazin, a short road linking the rue Hautefeuille with the Boulevard St-Michel; but he soon moved to a small hotel, 28 rue de Buci, where, paying twenty francs monthly, he lived in an attic for about two years. The room was reached by 'only 104 steps'.[1]

Max Buchon called on him there: 'under a very lofty attic-roof lit by a skylight; he wore an immense head of hair and a big collarless coat.'[2] Snow fell on the roof so heavily in the winter he couldn't paint in the dim light and had to climb out with pails of hot water to melt the snow; he asked his parents for extra mattress, blanket, sheets. As throughout his life, he had little furniture. He liked the left bank and never moved from it. The area that pleased him was the tangle of crisscrossing streets through which the present Boulevard St-Michel was driven.

Régis had arranged for a firm of colour merchants, Panier, of 75 rue Vieille-du-Temple, to act as bankers and pay out his remittances. The firm wrote on 20 August:

It will always be a pleasure for us to pay out to your son such sums as he may require; but we shall call upon you regularly for repayment within a month and a half on each occasion, it being impossible for us to maintain unproductive resources, since we need them constantly for our own purchases, which are all on a cash basis.[3]

The main family connections in Paris were on the Oudot side. The Oudot grandfather had a brother who, after becoming a colonel and then camp-marshal, died at the head of his brigade in 1814 under the walls of Paris; he left a son and two daughters. The son, François-Julien, studied at the Collège Charlemagne and became professor of civil law at the Law School in Paris.[4] He welcomed Gustave, who however did not find the household to his liking. Oudot wanted to supervise and direct, and Gustave did not want to repeat the struggle with his father. He was soon complaining to his parents that Oudot treated him discourteously; he would call on him no more than was necessary. Oudot had accepted his choice of career, but wanted him to take the conventional roads to success. He had backed Régis up about the Besançon college: 'I trust Gustave understands that he is and should be a reasonable man, and that the future is a matter on which he should always think.' Now he wrote on 18 December 1842 after one of Gustave's visits:

We have had a talk . . . with your big sturdy boy, who has brought back to us a lungful of Ornans air. May he meet great success! May he become an artist to the glory of his native town. Is he following the best path towards achievement? Is he right to insist on attaining success through his talent alone, without lessons from a master? I have some doubts about it, but in any event it is courageous of him.[5]

Courbet must have seen quite a lot of Oudot when he first arrived. Oudot was the most important relative in Paris; he was also at the School of Law, where we may assume Courbet went through some preliminaries as an intending law student. Oudot's character may be read in his book, *Conscience et science du devoir* (1855) in which he sets out his views. Life has as collective end the continuous improvement or perfection of the species on earth, and as individual end the aspiration to another life; the means in both cases is the enlightened devotion of the individual towards the species. Despite the pietistic slant, there is much stress on social relations; a study of the relations of man with the rest of creation is held to show that for him the social state is the state of nature. 'As soon as the conscience has said in an absolute manner: *assistance due by every being to every being*, the role of the science at once begins.' Oudot appears as a man who had thoroughly thought out his positions, however little some of the formulations would appeal to young Courbet.

Whatever slight links the latter had with the School of Law, they were soon broken; and he turned wholly to art. No opposition appears to have been made. Oudot's pressure seems to have been solely directed towards getting Courbet to embark on his career in the correct and orthodox way. He wanted Gustave to register at the art school under the Baron von Steuben; but the lad could not bear its academic attitudes and went along only four or five times. No doubt he had sounded out Baille, who had had time to learn about the Parisian art world; and he knew of less formal institutions, such as the Atelier Suisse, on the Île de la Cité, which, a decade later, Cézanne, also an anti-academic student, was to frequent.[6] Suisse, once a model for David, gave no instruction or criticism; he merely provided nude models for artists to draw or paint at a small fee. Gustave spent many evenings at the Atelier during the next five years, and amassed a number of nude studies that were of much use to him later. In 1861 he painted Suisse himself with his hair white against a dark background. He remarked of the old man that he had 'become a great connoisseur of painting through the simple habit of watching the artists at work'.[7] He also frequented the Atelier run by *le père* Lapin in the same rough-and-ready way. Schanne, who also worked there, said that he was never seen 'to draw the entire figure; he merely made studies of details'.[8]

Besides Baille there was another boyhood friend, Adolphe Marlet of Ornans. Marlet introduced him to his master Auguste Hesse, who had a studio of the same sort as Steubens. Though Gustave did not work under him, Hesse had the intelligence to realise that he had an unusual talent, and took interest in his work. His praise certainly helped Gustave in these early years. He seems to have been still a stammerer when he left for Paris; for he was suffering from the disability at the Besançon college as at the Ornans seminary. He had written home from there, 'Because of my difficulty in speaking, I have warned my teachers not to make me read out aloud in class'.[9] However, we do not hear of it in any of the accounts of him at Paris. Perhaps he gained more confidence now that he was on his own, definitely removed from his father's control; perhaps he developed his way of speaking slowly with an exaggerated rustic accent in order to counteract the stammer, and thus in time eliminated it.

Not that his father gave up trying to control and badger him. Perhaps the Oudot remonstrances against Gustave's decision to ignore the academies worried him; but even without that he wasn't likely to abandon his fussy authoritarian ways. He decided that Gustave had gone to Paris to indulge in wild dissipations that would impoverish the family; that he was doing nothing useful and was merely wasting time and money. Gustave retorted bitterly at his father's incessant querulous complaints.

I always like to receive your letters, even with the unfailing little sermon which I've known by heart ever since I've been old enough to think, for I seem to have heard it even before that. You see, I'm not behaving like the youth of today who will listen to nothing that's said to them. Unless you take me for a madman, I do not see what good these lectures can do me any longer – because you must understand that I am thinking seriously, a hundred times more seriously than you yourself, about all these matters. Further, all this discourages me more than it encourages, for it's just like the jab of a spur to an animal that's already pulling too hard. You are the opposite of those who surround me here and try to distract me from my work from time to time out of fear I'll injure my health. . . .[10]

No doubt he exaggerated the extent to which he was avoiding all pleasures and ruining his health; but his main point – that he was devoted to his work – was abundantly true. His father's obtuseness irritated him intensely, but he could not help writing the same rebuttals to the same old complaints and counsels.

I have received your letter in which, as usual, you pile up reproaches on me. I don't understand how you can always say the same things when you have no facts on which to base them. Some people are entranced at my amazingly frugal way of life; others cling to their doubts. If I didn't know this old habit [of yours], it would be disheartening.[11]

Indeed, after he paid his rent and the bills for canvas and paint, he could have had little cash left for food, let alone wild dissipation. For breakfast he had some dry bread in the studio; his next meal was at 5 p.m. in a cheap restaurant near by which had fixed prices.[12]

He seems to have dropped Baille and found a more congenial friend in a young painter, François Bonvin, met at the Suisse. Bonvin's father had an inn, a *guinguette*, in the suburbs, at Vaugirard; and François, the eldest son, could only paint at night; by day he worked at a minor job in the Assistance Publique, a charitable State-agency. Gustave painted him, dressed in a blouse, in 1846.[13] He seems to have liked him for his enthusiasm, though they often disagreed. Gustave said Bonvin painted on too small canvases; Bonvin replied that Gustave's canvases were too big. Once they reached the point of quarrelling, but François Wey brought them together again.[14] Gustave was not interested in most of the Italian painters of the Renascence; he looked down on Leonardo, Raphael, and (oddly) Titian, for he admired the other great Venetians, especially Veronese. Certain Spaniards, such as Velásquez, Ribera, Zurbarán, he also liked for their weight of form, as well as many Dutch and Flemish masters. Rembrandt most of all attracted him, the painter who 'charms the intelligent but confounds and annihilates imbeciles'.[15] These early judgments remained with him all his life. While he was always keen to visit Holland and Belgium, he never thought of Italy; at the Louvre he copied Rembrandt, Hals, Van Dyck, Velásquez, and he tried some pastiches in Flemish or Venetian style.

But his ideas were not as clear or mature in the early 1840s as these predilections suggest.

He still held confusedly romantic ideas and had not at all found where he stood in the conflict of styles in contemporary art. He must have heard the gossip about Ingres returning from Rome in April 1841, with his follower Schnetz going to take his place in the Rome Academy, and about the jailing of the critic Théophile Thoré (later to be one of his defenders) for an inoffensive pamphlet on behalf of the democratic party. At the 1841 Salon he saw three splendid works by Delacroix (*The Taking of Constantinople by the Crusaders*, *The Shipwreck of Don Juan*, *The Jewish Wedding*), but does not seem to have been impressed. Most of the other works were of the usual tame academic kind, a *Leda* by Riesener, an *Andromeda* by Chassériau, naval fights by Gudin, a *Siesta* by T. Johonnot, a *Martyrdom of St Polycarp* by Chenavard, Meissonier's *Chess-Players*, highly praised by Théophile Gautier. A Corot was lost among mediocre landscapes.[16] In 1842 Ingres did not show, as also Vernet, Ary Scheffer, Robert-Fleury, Delaroche and many other famous academics; the popular works were two tiny laboured works by Meissonier, Isabey's picture of Napoleon's coffin being brought aboard its ship, two heroic drawings by Decamps together with a watercolour of a comic Turkish scene, *Coming out of School*. Certainly, apart from the Delacroix of 1841, there was not much that deserved the attention of a rebel; but it is odd that in all the early letters and recorded comments of Gustave we find no sign of interest in what was going on in the art world. Castagnary, indeed, does say he used to remark of the bourgeois Salons of the 1840s that he there had seen 'the last examples of those famous types of romanticism: the thin woman and the pallid man'. But that was probably a witticism compounded long after the event. We have to turn to Gustave's own work, scanty as are the remnants from these years, to find out what he was thinking. Apart from portraits of friends like U. Cuénot, copies of works by Géricault and Delacroix (*Dante and Virgil*) as well as of Schnetz's *Prisoner* (wrongly called *Job*) and Robert-Fleury's *La Sainte-Barthélemy*, he put much effort into an allegorical Faustian picture, *Walpurgis Night*, in which the Alchemist pursues a woman, Nature – a big work, 2.60 m. high and 1.95 wide – and a conventional History-Painting with a Biblical theme, *Lot and his Daughters*. Perhaps he had heard at the 1842 Salon that Decamps was working on the latter theme, but did not have the work ready for exhibition. In his painting, one daughter was in the act of exposing herself naked to her father while the other lay on the ground at a grotto-entry and poured wine into his cup. In a modified form this work still exists, but he later painted his *Wrestlers* over the *Walpurgis Night*. He also painted an allegory of *A Man delivered from Love by Death*, using himself for the bereaved lover struggling with Death. But this work probably came late in the progress of the love-affair we shall soon encounter. He also painted an *Odalisque* inspired by the poem of Hugo, which begins, 'If I were not a captive, I'd love this land . . .'; and two stanzas of this poem are found written in a notebook of the period. Odalisques were common enough in these years, but he may have been moved by Pradier's statue, *Odalisque*, in the 1841 Salon.[17] Further, he showed an interest in the novels of George Sand by a *Lélia*, which suggests the novel of 1833. He did not forget landscape, painting in the Fontainebleau Forest during a brief stay there in 1841.

Burty gives a description of him in these years:

He was slim, tall, supple, wearing long black hair with a black silky beard. He was never met with-out an escort of friends, as one tells of Italian masters coming out of their studios. His long lan-guorous eyes, his straight nose and low brow, with his superb profile, his projecting lips mocking at their corners as the eyes were at theirs, his smooth and bulging cheeks, gave him the closest resem-blance to the Assyrian Kings who are set on bodies of bulls. His drawling and melodious accent . . . added a peasant charm to his words, very caressing and very fine.[18]

He also had very fine hands. (Gros-Kost later denied the common comparison with an Assyrian profile and said that Courbet resembled the old portraits of François I.)

One of the Ornans faithful who had come to Paris about the same time as he, was Proma-yet the musician, who often returned to Ornans on visits but who worked for poor pay in Paris in the orchestra of the Cirque de l'Impératrice, the Jardin d'Hiver, and the Hippo-drome. He failed to rise in the musical world though Gustave 'tried to find him employ-ment and exerted himself to persuade the Parisians to share his enthusiasm for him without success. The musician's excessive touchiness was one of the causes of his failure to win recognition'. When unemployed or hard up, Promayet camped in Gustave's studio. We find him later in the rue Hautefeuille, sleeping in a hammock behind a screen. He repaid Gustave with 'all the devotion one could demand from a member of the canine family'. Gustave with his boisterous display, in which it is sometimes difficult to distinguish genuine conceit from mere high-spirits, insisted on giving the musician lessons. 'Every morning he forced Promayet to practise as he swayed in his hammock, insisting that this training would enable him to play with greater facility when he was quietly and comfortably seated.'[19] Gustave himself tried to imitate the noise of the north wind in the countless chimneys of Cuénot's house at Ornans, which was built at the mountain-base, the *bise* coming in with an organ-roar. Schanne cites his song *Mother Evrard*:

> When I smoke my pipe, at Mother Evrard's place,
> That nice girl Adèle brings me in my beer.
>   *Tra, la la lou, la la la la, lou, la!*
> O bring a drink to me here
> And then I'll drink, I'll drink, I'll drink;
> With an old friend I'll smoke my pipe
> Together and we'll sing this song:
> Pish to money and pish to all greatness,
> Pish to those people who call themselves the world.
>   *Tra, la la lou, la la la la, lou, la!*

Bonvin says that when music was mentioned, his antelope's-eye lighted up; and we may note that his image of himself as a musician issues in pictures where he is shown as a 'cellist and as a guitarist.[20]

It is hard to sort out the events of these early Paris years in any sequence or to give an effective chronology to what we know or possess of his works. But we learn that he went in 1841 with Urbain Cuénot to Le Havre and had his first glimpse of the sea. 'I was enchanted with this trip, which has greatly developed many ideas about various things I needed for my art. We have at last seen the sea, the horizonless sea; how odd it seems to the valley-dweller. We saw the fine buildings that line it. It is too tempting; one feels carried away, one would like to sail off to see the whole world.'[21] But he does not seem yet moved to put on to canvas the new sense of immensity born within him.

Self-portraits deeply interested him all his life. He had probably made some at Ornans and he resumed the practice in Paris. About 1841 he did the *Man in Despair*, in which he depicts himself with his hands clutching his luxuriant hair in an attitude of romantic despair; he stares wildly out of the canvas. The work shows the influence of the studies he made in the Spanish gallery of Louis-Philippe, where there were at least 82 works painted by, or attributed to, Zurbarán. The treatment of the flesh and of the white shirt with its harsh folds and clear shadows derives from that master, as also perhaps the attempt to achieve an intense expression. There were seven versions of *St Francis in Ecstasy* in the gallery, and Courbet was perhaps remembering them when he painted his half-open mouth, while thinking of the *Seven Martyrs* as he drew the anguished tightening hands. Though in thus secularising religious motives he probably did not yet have any intention of deliberate parody or transformation, the use made of them is none the less significant.

In 1842 he painted his other early work which can be called successful, *Self-portrait with the Black Dog*. This was painted in Paris, but shows him seated on the ground in front of the entry to the grotto of Plaisir-Fontaine near Ornans. The area was impressed on his memory, but he may have carried studies of it to Paris. We see him with the long dark curly hair of the period, which is covered by a broad-brimmed hat; his dress and pose is that of a dandy. He wears a loose pink-lined painting-jacket of some dark materials, and green-striped trousers of grey; a cane and sketchbook lie behind him on the left. On the right, outlined against a far-off sunny landscape, is a black droopy-eared spaniel. The general effect is romantic, and yet the studied elegant pattern has a note of Ingres–classicism. A few touches with the palette-knife show that he had already begun the experiments with handling paint which were to be so fruitful for him.[22]

A letter of May 1842 to his parents tells how he got the dog. 'Now I have a wonderful little English dog, a pure-blooded spaniel, given to me by one of my friends; it is admired by everyone and welcomed by my cousin [Oudot] much more enthusiastically than I am.'[23]

In the autumn of this year he went back to Ornans, the first of his long series of returns which lasted sometimes for a few weeks, sometimes for several months, but which he could not do without. During this visit he painted at least two landscapes: *Founèche Rock*, showing Ornans and the road to Salins, and *Winter Woods*, which seems the first of his snow scenes. He also painted Juliette, now about eleven years old: she is dressed in brown and leans against a wall; she looks a little distant and not so childish as in a little portrait painted when she was about ten, in which, seated against the sky, she holds an album with a sly merry look.[24] It may have been this year rather than in 1840 (before leaving for Paris) that he painted his father. The work shows a classic sobriety of treatment and design, reminding us of both David and Ingres. Régis's astute, tense and lively face is quiet for once as he poses in his cap, rather formally, with his hand thrust into his waistcoat, against an empty background. It is hard to believe that Gustave painted this work before he had seen the canvases of Ingres and the Davidian school in Paris.[25]

On 8 January 1843 he moved from the rue de Buci to 89 rue de la Harpe, once the chapel of the Collège de Narbonne, then remodelled into a studio for Gati de Gramont, a painter, and later used as a music-room by Habeneck, conductor of the orchestra of the Opéra. This was a good-sized studio with vaulted ceiling; on the first floor, it had a window opening into a courtyard as well as a skylight; and it could be kept warm in winter. He was delighted and considered he would be 'splendidly installed for work; for this is a fine large house, very quiet'. The rent was 280 francs a year.[26] Habeneck had left a bottle of blue ink; and for a year Gustave's letters to his parents were in blue. He worked alone till noon; then in the evening he went to the Suisse. 'He remembered *père* Baud, who had more than once demonstrated to him the uselessness and danger of a master.'[27]

We know little of what he did in 1843, but 1844 is better documented. On 21 February he was still irritably seeking to ward off his father's complaints and suspicions.

If you think I am trying to deceive you, I am much offended. One thing is certain: I can't work any harder. And yet my father has the effrontery to write me letters which, far from encouraging me, are extremely depressing, and they always arrive at the most inopportune moments – just at the times I am most pressed. I thank him for his remonstrances, but he shouldn't always say the same thing. I believe that I give more thought to my future than anyone else, and I'm proving it. I live in so economical a fashion that it might soon be regarded as ridiculous. My father ought to have a son who squanders money as young people usually do in Paris.

He goes on to try to make Régis understand something of the way he lives and what his hopes are:

I've just done a picture, which is big enough and has given me so much work that for a month I've been at my wits' end. And still I haven't done as I'd like to, for I was so pressed that I didn't know what to do, and was incapable of thinking of anything else. If you think I'm amusing myself, you're wrong. For more than a month I haven't really had a quarter of an hour to myself. This is how it is. I have models that cost a lot, with whom I work till 5 p.m., the hour of my dinner. In the evening I have to get in the necessary supplies for my work, run after models from one end of Paris to the other; then I have to go and see people who can be useful to me, if I'm not to pass as a bear. . . .

The persons round me who are in a position to grasp what I'm doing, for example, M. Hesse, Marlet's teacher, to whose house I often go to show what I've done, and who has visited me: for he takes a great interest in me . . . and many others agree in the prediction that if I keep on working as I do I'll ruin my health.[28]

Later he writes:

I've just sent my picture to the show; I had only up to the 20th of this month. M. Hesse said the strongest things to me about it, and has predicted the most flattering things; he has made such compliments to me on what I've done, and on the works here in my studio, I didn't know what to answer; he wants me also to send a portrait . . . which I did two years ago. If I've not been accepted, I'm unlucky.[29]

He had become enough known to pick up some commissions, which made a useful addition to his allowance. He told his parents:

The other day I got a little money from ——. These people are only mildly honest. They tried to bring down the portrait's price, though we had definitely agreed on it. They offered me 100 francs, to which I replied that I'd rather give it to them as a gift. I think that shamed them a little. At last with the tone of people unable to pay, they asked me if I'd be satisfied with 150; not wanting to quarrel with them on that score, I replied coldly enough that I was well satisfied; they paid me 150 francs altogether in two instalments. There's no need to go to their father's burial in a carriage or put on such swank as they do, in order to behave like this.[30]

In March he was able joyously to announce that the jury had accepted the *Self-portrait with the Black Dog*, but rejected the more recent work.

At last I have been accepted at the Exhibition, which gives me the greatest pleasure. The accepted picture is not the one I would have most liked to show, but that doesn't matter. I can ask for nothing better, for the painting they refused wasn't really finished. I didn't have the time; I'd started off too late. They have done me the honour of giving me a very good place in the show, which is some compensation.

To his grandfather he wrote that the portrait had been hung in the gallery of honour reserved for the best works in the Salon, and that if larger it would have been awarded a medal, 'which would have been a magnificent start'. There were many compliments, but he expected all the same to earn no money that year, as he meant to devote himself 'to more important work; nothing is so prejudicial to that as a need to earn money too soon'.[31] He didn't want the family to think they could now drop his allowance.

The Salons at this time were paid for out of the Civil List; in effect the King invited the artists to show in his Louvre, and he alone could modify the statute of invitations. The great importance of the Salons for the artists through the nineteenth century cannot be overstressed. Only in the later decades do private exhibitions become at all effective. The Salons were great social events, mass-spectacles, attended by vast numbers of people; they were extensively discussed in the journals and in pamphlets; they formed a main theme of conversation for many weeks; they enabled a new artist to make an impact on the public and gain patrons, who thereafter would call at his studio. They thus could not be ignored by even the most dissident of artists, as we see from the careers of Delacroix, Corot, Courbet, the Impressionists, Manet, Cézanne. Also, they provided a solid basis of established art against which the rebel could react, moving away into his new formulations and techniques. To conquer the Salon without accepting the conventional norms meant triumph for the rebel. Through the Salons the successful artist had been able to rise to the same level as that of his bourgeois patrons, shedding the last remnants of his old status as craftsman and becoming respectable with his wealth and his recognition by the State. This respectability of the successful artist in turn begot the bohemianism and loose living of the dissidents.

Courbet had arrived in Paris at a moment when, under Louis-Philippe, there had been considerable expansion in commercial and industrial developments. As the textile industry grew, a demand was created for machinery and fuel; new markets were offered for the metal industries. The areas affected were those where textiles were combined with availability of coal and ores on which an iron and machine-making industry could be based. In turn, railways were needed for these areas. Such developments had little direct effect on Courbet's Franche-Comté, but they were generally beginning to upset old ways of life and to generate new forces of resistance. Thus, impacting in multiple ways on his mountaineer's-independence, they drove him into revolt as they did his fellows, Proudhon, Considérant, and Max Buchon.

The Salons began from 1841 to become more intolerant; the academic monopoly sought to strengthen itself. But in 1843 the reactionaries over-reached themselves and went so far that even Ingres, in no way a liberal, was troubled. As a result an exhibition of the rejected was held in the Bazar Bonne-Nouvelle; an *Alliance of the Arts*, initiated by Thoré and P. Lacroix, sought to find new ways for the sales of books and pictures, but had a brief life. *Sylphide*, directed by de Villemessant, accused the Salon:

What could have been foreseen has happened; there have been decisions of ignorance, there have been those of envy. . . . The Institute is made up of men who were educated under the Empire; they are the evil tail of the Davidian school, the opaque residue of what, in its most perfect state, produced Gros, Guérin, Girodet, Gérard, the most false, the most impotent of all the schools. Happily for art, it has been destroyed by M. Ingres in the domain of drawing, by M. Delacroix in the domain of colour.

The jury of 1844 was thus somewhat demoralised; it allowed Corot's *Burning of Sodom*, with a changed name, to slip in, though it had been rejected in 1843; it indeed passed so many works that they overflowed untidily over the Louvre. This was the Salon that accepted Gustave's *Self-portrait*. But the young artist who attracted general attention was T. Couture with his *Love of Gold*.[32] Meanwhile the third of the five-yearly Expositions of Industry had been prepared in the Champs-Elysées, and opened in May; and the artists found that popular attention had been drawn away to a considerable extent from art to industrial and commercial matters. This Exposition was far larger than those of 1834 and 1839, and marked the sharp industrial expansion that had been going on.[33]

Gustave returned to Ornans this year. He painted Juliette in a striped dress of blue and yellow, in an armchair by a window, against a background of figured drapery. He may also have done a portrait of grandfather Oudot this year, and one of Zélie in a blue dress with white collar and cuffs, her cheek on her right hand, her dark hair parted in the middle and drawn smoothly over the ears – though this work may date from 1846.[34]

A more important work of this period was *Lovers in the Country*, probably painted in 1843 or early 1844; it was refused in the Salons from 1844 to 1847. Riat describes it:

It is a painting full of poetry. The painter has depicted himself full-length, showing his left profile, his long hair flowing in the wind. An extremely pretty girl leans against him, inclining her delicate and poetic profile towards his right shoulder, softly undulating golden tresses covering her ears and temples, setting off the paleness of her complexion. Holding hands, they tenderly contemplate the setting sun among the trees. The young woman is apparently Joséphine, who was for a long time the artist's model and mistress.[35]

But though Gustave seems to have had a mistress named Joséphine at one time, the girl here is certainly Virginie Binet, of whom we shall have more to say. The picture may be taken to celebrate the full flowering of her love-affair with Courbet. She has a full face with lips slightly turned up at the corners; and while he is shown looking up and out at the sunset scene, she looks downwards, her head slanted. They may be happy lovers, but they do not seem to share the same thoughts. (As often, Courbet stresses a certain fleshiness of the under-chin and throat: perhaps to show his disdain of conventional standards of beauty, perhaps because he likes all fullnesses of the female body.)

In December, after returning from Ornans, he replaced 'the bad little iron-stove' with one in faience, which cost ten francs, to heat the studio; and he congratulated himself on his new system of living. To his breakfast of dry bread he has added a bowl of milk daily, delivered for four sous by a suburban dairyman; and is surprised to find the milk better than that at Ornans. Finally his hunchbacked concierge makes him a pot of coffee, which is brought up by her hunchbacked husband – 'an incredible pair'. But he put the milk and coffee on the stove to warm, often forgot them in his obsession with work, and they boiled over. In the letter detailing these amenities he adds a request for the denial of the Ornans rumour that he is about to marry Mlle C. He insists that he has no more idea of marrying than of hanging himself.[36]

In February 1845 he told the family that he had been working every day without any rest, even on holidays and Sundays; he was physically and mentally exhausted. He had just sent five paintings to the Salon: *A Young Girl's Dream*, (*The Hammock*); *Guitar-player*; *Chess-players*; portrait of a man; portrait of Juliette. The latter was the work he had done the previous year, 'which I have entitled as a joke, *Baronne de M*. The frames cost me a great deal of money, but one can't do otherwise. I am now awaiting the result.' Probably the family had remarked that Juliette looked quite an elegant young lady, full of self-confidence, in her portrait, and Gustave was carrying on the pleasantry; perhaps he also hoped to impress the jury. *The Hammock* showed a young girl in a striped dress asleep in a hammock slung between two trees in a shady forest-glade with a brook in the foreground. No doubt the theme had been suggested by one of his models lying in the hammock which Promayet used in the studio; the mixture of grace and realism in the girl's pose, the casual angle and the rich solidity of form, combine to provide the first definite signs of what was to come in his mature style. And it is characteristic that he transported the studio-study into the heart of nature, the forest – thus opening the way to his own *Baigneuses* and to many works like Manet's *Déjeuner sur l'Herbe*. The use of a girl asleep is also deeply characteristic. Sleep as a moment of total relaxation, of entry into oneself and into nature without the obstructions and defences of the everyday waking consciousness, recurs as one of Courbet's central themes. The lack of a complete correlation between the studio-study and the deep woodland setting even increases the effect of a dream-relation between the girl and the life of nature, with its dark flow, its obscure recesses. The contrast between the two sloping segments of the hammock, large and simple in their diagonal lines (with opposing inner curves), and the relaxed body of the girl, horizontal with an upturn at the head and a downturn at the knees, has a rich sensuous effect, which is in turn contrasted with the complex patterns of leaves and boughs. The girl is suspended securely and yet precariously over the dark flow which her tresses and her soles almost touch; the patch of light at the back is the waking life from which she has withdrawn into her cavern of sleep, which is also the deep sensuous life of her own body. This, then, is a work in which at last a number of the deepest elements in Courbet's sensibility come together.

Perhaps it was the forest-fantasy of *The Hammock* which gave him the idea of painting a nude in woodland-shadows by a stream. About this time he produced *Woman Sleeping near a Stream*. Clothes cover one leg and the part of an arm, but the stress is on the nudity. Here we have the complete sleep-union with nature. The nudity brings out the sexual motive. The woman sleeps after an embrace or has bared herself in the wild privacy of a daydream (she seems to be Virginie). The entry into the waters and the following surrender to nature in sleep is thus merged with the encounter of love. For Courbet's notion of sleep we may take an aphorism of his: 'When one has succeeded in being a man, one returns to the earth for the great sleep. One survives only in one's works, and the men who have not arrived (whether by nature or by lack of ancientness of breed) survive only in their progeny: thus history ends.' Castagnary says, 'He was in love with the light of life; he was afraid of death; he never painted death apart from the uncompleted *Wake of the Dead Woman*; he never went further than sleep, Life, always life.' (He forgets the *Burial*, but his point is sound.)

Chess-players has not been identified. *Guitar-player* is a self-portrait, showing him languorous-eyed, scarlet-booted, and chestnut-haired, at the foot of a tree against rocks and woods. We see how strongly he was still held by romantic posturings, which appear even more affectedly in *Le Sculpteur* (also called the *Poet*) of this period. The male portrait may have been of Paul Ansout (painted 1844) or of Paul Blavet (1845); it may even have been a first version of the *Wounded Man* we shall consider later. The jury took what must have been the feeblest work, *Guitar-player*; the fine *Hammock* was thrown out. Gustave wrote to his parents in March 1845, 'I have no right to complain, for they also rejected a great many famous men who certainly have better claims than I.' (One out of the five pictures sent in by Delacrox was rejected; but Gustave seems to be exaggerating in order to cover up his own discomfiture.) He is happy to report that *Guitar-player* has attracted two would-be buyers, a banker and a picture-dealer; Hesse advises him to ask 500 francs, but Gustave thinks that too high for a small work done in a fortnight: 'That's also what the banker said; as for dealers they don't always pay up.' However, nothing came of the overtures.

The Ansout portrait is worth glancing at. It is a fine example of Courbet's work at this period; its touch is fluid and careful, but the form is not cramped or tight. Already the shadows are gaining transparency; the design of the body, leant loosely on the right arm, is well realised. But as with the early portrait of his father, we see a strong Ingres-influence in the general system. The work is also of interest because of the role that Ansout seems to have played in Courbet's life, as we shall see when we come to Virginie Binet and her son. Ansout, born in 1820 at Saint-Valéry-sur-Somme, son of a merchant draper at Dieppe, had been sent to study law in Paris, and it was perhaps at the École de Droit that he met

Courbet. When the latter came to paint him, he didn't like his trousers and persuaded him to change into the light-coloured striped pair he himself wore proudly in *Self-portrait with the Black Dog*.

Important for his future development was the decision that he reached at all costs to paint big works. He is perhaps recalling how his *Self-portrait* had been lost in 1844 among the mass of pictures; but more likely he is reacting to the endless gossip that went on about the vast painting by Vernet, *Smala d'Abd-el-Kader*. In May 1844 Vernet had announced that it would cover 70 feet by 15. Delayed by three commissions from the king, he was allowed two extra months to finish the work; and the problems of bringing it to the Louvre and installing it were considerable. Vernet, nervous and small, turned up ten times, on foot or on horse in his brilliant uniform as staff-officer of the National Guard, glittering with medals. Gustave must have heard all about it and seen the painting.

Small pictures don't make a name. I must paint a large picture that will make me decisively known at my true value. I want all or nothing. All these little pictures are not the only things I can do. I want to do things in a bigger way. What I am saying is not mere presumption; everybody I meet who knows anything about art predicts an assured future for me. The other day I made a study of a head, and when I showed it to M. Hesse, he told me in front of everyone in his studio that there were very few masters in Paris capable of equalling it. Then he added that if I could produce a picture painted like that during the next year it would win me a high rank among painters. I admit there's some exaggeration in his words. But what's certain is that I must make a name for myself in Paris before five years. There can be no middle course and I must work with this aim. I know it'll be difficult to attain; there are few, sometimes only one in thousands, who comes through. Since I've been in Paris, I've scarcely seen two or three truly strong and original. To make more rapid progress I need but one thing, money, in order to carry out my ideas boldly.

We see that, apart from a natural wish to show his career in as favourable a light for Ornans, the main purpose in his letters is to convince his father that the allowance should not be stopped or curtailed. He goes on:

I won't earn a penny this year, one cannot work and make money at the same time. This is the worst possible assumption. The little I might earn would retard my progress enormously, especially during those years most vital to my advancement. You should understand this.[37]

Here, as always, we find him a very shrewd special-pleader, driven by a strong emotion which enables him to work up his case with much effect. The family knew the way he talked; he had to keep on pitching things higher and higher. And this method of presentation and argument that he had to use with his family, especially Régis, ended by powerfully affecting the way he set out his own case for everyone. But his father was deaf as usual to his appeal for an increased allowance which would enable him to build as quickly as possible on the gains already made. He felt sure that he knew his Gustave all too well, and discounted much of what he said.

Gustave, however, had a stroke of luck when J. van Wisselingh, a young dealer from Amsterdam, visited Paris to buy pictures. He bought two Courbets for 420 francs and commissioned a portrait of himself. More, he declared that he could and would create a market for such works in Holland, where he predicted a big success. And he kept his word. A few years later, moving to The Hague, he introduced a rich collector, Mesdag, to buy seven Courbets, Thus began Courbet's long and successful links with Dutch dealers, artists and collectors; from the outset he was popular in Belgium and Holland, with a reputation that steadily increased.[38]

He began on the big picture he wrote about: 10 feet wide by 8 high. But his strength failed him. He perhaps tried to work too fast on it, as he wanted to get away for another summer at Ornans. He hoped to get through with enough of the work so that it would be in a good dry condition for him to resume work when he returned. He warned his father that he would spend most of his holiday at Ornans, with his grandparents and various friends, rather than at Flagey with his parents and sisters. And that is what he did. With Promayet, Cuénot and other young friends he drank wine and beer, hunted and fished, wandered on the hills, and got together evening concerts where he sang with his usual verve. Some years later, when a stereotyped picture of Courbet had developed and most people saw in him what they had been brought to expect, Silvestre wrote down one of his songs with the following comment:

It is by this burlesque independence that he wipes out questions, he amuses, he wants to astonish; and he repeats himself like a clock. His persuasive *bonhomie* and his lack of ceremony will always make him the friend of the observer of odd types and the jovial bourgeois. He professes, for the rest, like the bourgeois, the love of the positive, the fear of imagination, scorn of the poet. He has however made verses, but blank ones, and composed songs, words and music, which he sings at the gatherings of good fellows. Here is a fragment of these realist poesies:

> All the lads were singing
> When they gathered in the evening at the pub,
> All the lads were singing,
> Repeating this refrain,
> > *Tra la la la la, lou lou lou, la,*
> > *Tra la la la la, lou lou lou, la,*
> > *Trou lou lou lou lou lou.*
>
> When I lived at home with father
> I had a girl in love with me.
> Jeannette, who lived next door,
> Had got my heart from me, she had.
> When evening came, then all the time
> I spent close at her side.
> Of love spoke our eyes,
> A love with no twists or lies.
>
> A mayor with lots of money
> Came up and tried to win her
> > *Tra la la la la, lou lou lou, la.*
> With no nonsense he remarked:
> We must get married at once,
> Lovely one, give me your love,
> In return all my goods I'll give.

On the night of the betrothal
I wept for my unfaithful girl.
But nightly to my room
She dodges off to find me.
She says, My darling love,
I bring my heart to you
So if you didn't get the girl
you'll get her making love.[39]

When he returned to Paris he did not take up the project of a big work afresh. He said there wasn't enough light in the short winter days. But in fact he couldn't yet tackle the task. Probably he didn't really know what to paint. He couldn't take up one of the conventional classical, biblical or romantic themes; he couldn't inflate his self-portraits in a way that would make the large scale relevant. He waited.[40]

About this time the poet Armand Barthet, future author of *Lesbia's Sparrow*, when hard up, used to come into the studio to get warm. 'You can't make up poems without fire', he explained. Courbet was amiable and generous in giving such shelter to penniless poets and artists. A January letter seems to show him discouraged; but knowing how quickly he developed an emotional heat when arguing his own case, and how he then felt the point he was making to be of supreme importance, we may discount his remarks as perhaps warning his father that a certain amount of success didn't mean a position with immediate cash rewards: 'There is nothing in the world more difficult than to practise art, especially when nobody understands it. Women want portraits without any shadows; men want to be painted in their Sunday-best; there's no way to avoid these attitudes. It'd be better to turn a wheel [in some mechanical job]; at least one wouldn't have to abdicate from one's views.'[1]

However, he was painting enough pictures to send eight into the Salon. Only one was accepted, an unidentified self-portrait, and that was so skied that it was hard to make out, though three or four journals of Paris had promised to review it. 'It's true', he wrote in March, 'that it was, as art, the main item; but in the opinion of many people and of artists of my acquaintance, what they've rejected wasn't inferior.' The judges, old idiots in taste, are maliciously disposed towards him. They can't do anything themselves, so they seek to 'stifle the young folk who could move on over their bodies'. Rejection was an honour. How could they do otherwise with 400 pictures to deal with daily, two a minute? 'Everyone complains. The greatest names have also been thrown out; it's a true lottery.'[2] What he says has some truth. Some 2,600 works had been rejected, including pictures by Decamps, Diaz, Corot, Riesener, Flers, Mottez.[3] One wonders if Courbet read what Baudelaire published about this Salon, especially the conclusion 'On the Heroism of Modern Life'.

. . . The life of our city is rich in poetic and marvellous subjects. We are enveloped and steeped in it as though in an atmosphere of the marvellous, but we do not notice it. The *nude* – that darling of the artists, that necessary element of success – is just as frequent and necessary today as it was in the life of the ancients; in bed, for example, or in the bath, or in the anatomy theatre. The themes and resources of painting are equally abundant and varied; but there is a new element – modern beauty.[4]

And he compares the heroes of the Iliad with those of Balzac; the former are mere pygmies next to the latter.

A fine self-portrait, *The Man with the Pipe*, was painted about this time. A comparison of the man here shown with the sleek unruffled dandy of the *Self-portrait with the Black Dog* gives some clue as to the extent to which Courbet had grown in the last four or five years. He himself has changed from the immature elegant into a dishevelled fellow, with thick matted hair and shaggy beard; and a new strength and sensitivity is apparent, communicated by a considerable growth in technical power. The modelling of the face with its fine nose, sensuous mouth, dreamy yet intent eyes, has become plastic, with an assured grasp of the whole form and of its local subtleties. (His love of the pipe went far back, but he may have been stimulated in his esteem for it by reading Baudelaire's 1845 epigram aimed at Meissonier: 'A Fleming minus the fantasy, the charm, the colour, the naïvety and the pipe'.[5]) *The Man with the Pipe* seems to have been rejected by the 1846 jury, and again by that of 1847. We must look, however, at the portrait of van Wisselingh to see how he had now managed also to paint other people sensuously; we see a first synthesis of his romantic and realist sides, expressed by merged elements from Delacroix and Ribera.

His March letter enables us to get behind the thoughts of the Courbet who musingly puffs at his pipe:

There's nothing more difficult than to gain a reputation in painting and make oneself accepted by the public. The more one becomes different from the others, the more difficult it is. Realise that to change a public taste and way of seeing is not a small task; for it's nothing less than to overthrow what exists, and to replace it. You can be sure there are always jealous persons and offended interests. Despite my objections I'm always badly hung at the show. But what do I care for them? That's not what will discourage me. Painting, when one conceives it, is a state of fury. It's a continual struggle. It means going mad, upon my word. Despite that, I'm going to do a picture, or several, for next year.[6]

The word used for 'mad' is 'fou'; for 'fury' it is 'enragé', a word hard to translate. It conveys madness, possession, determination; and so was used for extreme devoted revolutionaries, *Les Enragés*. These words of 1846 belong to the period when Courbet still had many direct romantic traits; he would not later have used them. And yet they express something in him which persisted at all phases. His attack on life and art did not cease to own this dedicated passion when he became a Realist. The comments on the problem of changing public taste shows that he had already measured calmly and thoroughly what he was up against, even if he still did not know just how he meant to make the changes.

Again he spent several months at Ornans and the neighbourhood, returning to Paris in December. A letter written on the first day of 1847 tells how he has rented a small room opposite his studio, and how he has worked on a portrait of Urbain Cuénot. Hesse and others like it, but he doubts if it will enter the Salon, as it is 'completely outside the ideas of the examiners'. He consoles himself with a project mooted once more for a show of the rejected.[7]

Sure enough, the portrait was thrown out, with two other works of his. On 23 March he reported to the family. For the officials he felt only contempt. 'Their judgment doesn't matter; but one must exhibit to become known, and unfortunately there's no other exhibition. In former years, when my own style was less fully developed and I still painted a little as they do, they accepted me; but now that I've become myself, I must henceforth abandon hope.'[8] But once again the jury had gone too far. They offended so many artists that many of the more liberal-minded, even if they were among the accepted, formed an association of protest, with the aim of putting on an independent show in a private gallery. The rebels included Delacroix, Daumier, Decamps, T. Rousseau, Ary Scheffer, and the sculptor

Barye, in whose house they met on 15 April to draw up a resolution in legal form in favour of yearly independent shows. (The scheme was never carried out, as the revolution of 1848 intervened.)[9]

Courbet visited Holland this summer, his first foreign trip.[10] Van Wisselingh welcomed his decision and promised to help, supplying letters of introduction to 'a certain Van den Bogaert, chief Cupbearer to the King of Holland, a very influential person and one of the leading figures in Amsterdam'.[11] Courbet had been an enthusiast for Rembrandt and other Dutch masters ever since he saw their paintings in the Louvre; now, seeing much more of their work, his admiration was intensified.

I have been in Amsterdam for two days. I've already become acquainted with two or three artists; I'll call on them today. I'll also visit the Museum, which will be open. I'm already enchanted with everything I've seen in Holland, and it's truly indispensable to an artist. A voyage like this teaches one more than three years of work. At The Hague, a charming city, I saw the finest collections. The king lives there. I don't yet know the day when I leave, for I might be commissioned to do a portrait here. People assure me that if I were to stay on two or three months, so as to become known, I could make money. My style [*genre*] is agreeable to them. I brought with me only one small landscape, which they like very much in terms of craftsmanship [*comme façon*]. Nobody here paints in that manner.[12]

We feel in these letters both his need to keep in touch with home and his need to report and defend himself in his father's eyes: a mixture of strong affection and self-justification. Nothing seems to have come of the suggestion about a portrait. The rate of exchange made living expensive, and Courbet had to leave Amsterdam a week later. He told van Wisselingh, 'I bless the stars that made us know one another.'[13]

He was back in France by September; his presence there was indeed called for. On 17 September 1847 Virginie bore him a son, who was given the name of Désiré-Alfred-Emile Binet. Perhaps he had gone off to Holland in order to escape the problems of her childbed. We know very little of this important relationship of his, apart from the pictures in which Virginie appears, the collapse of their union late in 1851, the deep effect that the break had on him, and the way in which remorse later haunted him. Virginie seems to have been strong-minded, and we can imagine that Courbet with his bohemian habits, his ingrained fear of the least assertion of discipline or control from outside, must have soon come into prolonged and painful conflict with her. He could not settle down with her in any form of normal household; she could not accept his need to live a roving life of talk and booze. As he now was in Ornans in early September he does not even seem to have stayed in Paris in order to be with her at the time of the birth. Virginie could not but have deeply resented such behaviour; but we cannot interpret the events with any certainty.

In Ornans he was grieved to find that his grandmother Oudot had died on 16 August. Under the influence of what he had seen in Holland, he turned again to landscape with a keener eye and painted several canvases, including *Evening Shadows*; *The Valley of Scey*; and a pencil drawing, *Within the Forest*. An important step forward had been taken. He also painted Promayet, and, strangely, a large religious work for the parish church at Saules, an upland village about four miles from Ornans where the curé was the abbé Claré. He used Urbain Cuénot, dressed up in bishop's vestments, for the patron saint in the theme (popular in medieval days) of *St Nicholas Raising the Children from the Dead*. Though his heart wasn't much in the work, he did his best to follow Zurbarán and produce a canvas rich in colour. Probably he was drawn in by his friend, the architect Victor Baille of Besançon. Baille had drawn up the plans and devised the ensemble of the choir, thus creating the space necessary for the painting, which replaced an old one according to a vow made by the archbishop of Besançon, Cardinal Mathieu, after a pastoral visit in 1836. The congregation must have been somewhat surprised to find their rites now presided over by a saint with the familiar features of Cuénot, president-founder of the choral union of Ornans and boon companion of Courbet on hunts and evenings of song. If Courbet did the job to get money, he had to wait; for the village authorities did not complete the purchase till January 1848 and did not pay over the price, 900 francs, till 1850. However, despite his anti-religious convictions he probably did the work to show the locals that he was indeed a painter, and out of a general wish to support regional ventures.[14]

He also made a drawing of a *Girl in a Reverie* (also called *Guitarist*) which shows Zélie in a dreamy mood playing her guitar. The painting of his three sisters at Flagey farm must have been done about this time, but they show no sign of mourning for their grandmother; the work, then, may be of 1846, though we should expect it from its confident style to be of this year. (In 1848 the grandfather died, so that then there would also have been a reason for mourning.) The girls are chatting with an old woman who 'knew a lot of stories, *racontotes* as they are called in Comté'. She faces the girls on the right. On the left is Zoé, brunette with big eyes and fine profile; she wears a wide-brimmed hat of straw; her hand rests on the shoulder of Zélie, who is seen from the back, her hair plaited, in a black bolero. Her sleeves, like Zoé's, are rolled back to the elbow; her right hand rests, open, on her hip; her chestnut-coloured skirt, drawn back, shows her grey-blue petticoat; and she holds a pitchfork, the tip of which is being examined. Juliette is seen three-quarters on the further side of her sisters.[15] This work is important in showing Courbet coming effectively down to direct everyday themes.

A letter of 21 December 1847 shows him back in Paris, taken up with the problem of pictures for the next Salon. He has only just found a model, who arrives at 9 a.m.; after that he works till dusk, then dines and goes to see various people.[16] Probably about this time he painted *Marc Trapadoux Examining an Album of Prints*. This character deserves a few words, as he illustrates the sort of eccentric dissident with whom Courbet was friendly in these years. Bearded and dressed in a rough labourer's blouse, he sprawls with the book in his lap. The foreshortening of his out-thrust legs has something of the effect of a photograph's distortion, and the caricaturists seized on this point to show the feet vastly enlarged. Trapadoux had written a biography of St John of God (Portuguese founder of the Brothers of Charity in the sixteenth century), and in 1861 he published a study of the Italian actress, A. Ristori. In 1876 Courbet described him to Ideville (who had bought the painting):

a very studious man with a distinguished mind and learned in philosophical studies. He presented himself to me as also to Champfleury and to Baudelaire with a book he'd written on the Life of St Jean-de-Dieu. He came from Lyon where he was born. He changed his principles through our acquaintanceship and became a realist (though you used to say that this way of being is unconscious in me) and romantic through his own past and other acquaintances. He believed that asceticism was an inebriation and helpful to thought [*conception*]. He wrote several very remarkable articles on painting, making for this purpose some trips to Belgium. He wrote letters for the newspapers and returned to Paris where he died in poverty eight or nine years ago. He was an original, even eccentric character who gave himself up to extraordinary exercises in the belief that he thus increased his bodily forces and those of his intelligence; for the rest, a sincere and devoted man. He was known in the artistic circles of Paris.[17]

Frequenting the Café Momus, he was close to Henri Murger, whose *Scenes of Bohemian Life* (1848) merged him with Jean Wallon (a rich young provincial from Laon) to produce the character of Colline. Schanne, who appears in the novel as Schaunard, says that Trapadoux was 'tall and nervous, with unkempt hair and bushy beard; his nose was perceptibly bent to the left as if scorning conventional symmetry. His skin was swarthy, an Arab's skin. He wore a high hat with narrow wavy brim; as to his overcoat, it had once been green.' Hence his nickname 'the Green Giant'. Nobody knew how he kept himself; Baudelaire, says Schanne, could alone lift a corner of the veil surrounding his life; but in fact he knew little of the recluse. Once, when it was too late for him to go home, he was admitted to Trapadoux's shabby lodging in the Boulevard du Montparnasse, a room with iron bed and piles of dusty books, and spent a restless night during which he saw him going through a series of violent convulsions, using as dumb-bells a pair of bottles filled with buckshot.[18]

Courbet spent the winter of 1847–8 in preparing for the next Salon. In January 1848 he wrote to his parents:

My picture is getting on fast. I hope to finish it for the show. If accepted, it will help me a lot and secure me a big reputation. In any event I'm on the threshold of success; for I'm surrounded by people very influential in the press and the arts, enthusiastic about my work. At last we are able to found a new school, of which I'll be the representative in painting.[19]

The problem of estimating how far such letters represented his everyday attitudes arises from the fact that he felt compelled to write home only reports of success, and with his volatile temperament, once he started saying how well he was doing, he completely convinced himself. It seems likely that the need to send glowing reports to Ornans, combined with an aggressive buoyant outlook, had much to do in creating the mask of extreme confidence and self-glorification with which he came to meet the world and which was taken by superficial observers to represent the whole man. In this case, was he exaggerating in his remarks about the New School, with himself as the leader in art? We have seen that while he had been making some important advances in his art, he had by no means yet reached a clear and settled viewpoint.

It is uncertain just when he moved his lodgings to 32 rue Hautefeuille, where he stayed till 1871. Probably it was in 1848; and it was after that move that he became such a frequenter of the Brasserie Andler. However, he may well have already found that brasserie and helped to build it up as a rendezvous of artists. He needed to have some regular haunt where he could meet and discuss art and politics. When the Brasserie Andler was opened is not sure, but it was some time round 1848. At this date Courbet had probably not yet met Champfleury, his first champion, or at most knew him slightly. Probably he and various young artists and writers who were dissatisfied with the Salon, the Institute, and the cultural establishment in general, had been talking together for some time, and he had been developing his particular kind of wit, dominating the discussions, and in this way appearing at least in his own eyes and those of a few close friends as the leader of a New School.

Now, before the Salon could open, the February Revolution of 1848 broke out. The year was one of general European unrest, with Chartism coming to a head in England and with France producing the most politically mature upheavals. Insurrection appeared in Paris on 24 February. The people stormed the Chamber of Deputies and compelled the proclamation of a Republic; the king fled to England. But the groups that now took charge represented the higher bourgeoisie; they were pleased to see a Republic which they could control and manipulate, but they had no intention of making concessions to the radicals and socialists, whom they excluded from any share in the government. Courbet, with his impetuous nature, must have been very excited, though as yet his political ideas were vague and general, a reflection of his grandfather's archaic republicanism. We cannot take at its face value what he wrote to the family at this moment, since his main aim was clearly to pacify Régis. In February he wrote with assurances that he was not at all interested; nothing was emptier than politics; he had played his part in 'destroying ancient errors', and if new ones cropped up again, he'd repeat his performance. But painting was the essential thing; and he'd been working away all the last fortnight, 'in spite of the Republic, which is not the most favourable form of government for artists, at least not according to history'. He thus trotted out a reactionary cliché in which he could not have believed.[20]

All his seven pictures were accepted at the Salon: *Walpurgis Night*, *Cellist* (himself), *Sleeping Girl*, a portrait of Cuénot, and three landscapes (*Morning*, *Noon*, *Night*); there were also three drawings; *Girl in a Reverie* and two portraits. But the acceptances were hardly a triumph. Scared by the previous year's discontents and the general political uncertainty, the jury passed almost everything: 5,500 works.[21] However, at last Courbet gained some notices, and good ones at that. Champfleury in a pamphlet said that the painter of the *Walpurgis Night* would be a great painter; P. Haussard in the *National* on 15 June praised the *Cellist* as reminding him of Caravaggio and Rembrandt.[22] Still, nothing was sold. For a while he hadn't a sou and had to invite himself to dinner with friends, a pleasant Parisian custom. He had to beg for money. If only his father could turn from his struggle to invent the perfect harrow! He owed for two terms, 200 francs; a third would soon come up. His clothes were in rags; to economise he was going to put on the uniform of the National Guard. 'I'll be superb in that, and I'm to be taken for a *citoyen enragé*.' But he declared the demonstration of 16 April a joke. Some wags spread the rumour that the Communists with Blanqui and Cabet would overthrow the provisional government and share out goods.

25 *Self-portrait with a Black Dog.* 1842. 46 × 55 cm.
Musée du Petit Palais, Paris (see page 24).

26 *Portrait of a Man with a Leather Belt. c.* 1844. 101 × 83 cm.
National Gallery, London (see page 54).

27 *The Wounded Man.* 1844. 81 × 97 cm.
Louvre, Paris (see page 27).

28 *The Bather asleep near a Brook.* 1845. 82 × 64 cm.
Museum of Modern Art, Detroit (see page 27).

29 *The Happy Lovers* (author's title: *Lovers in the Country*).
1844. 77 × 60 cm.
Musée des Beaux-Arts de Lyon (see page 25).

30 *Young Girls from the Village*
(author's title: *Young Women of the
Village*). 1851. 53 × 66 cm.
Art Gallery of Temple Newsam
House, Leeds (see page 91).

31 *The Sleeping Spinner.* 1853.
91 × 115 cm.
Musée Fabre, Montpellier
(see pages 102–105).

32 *Portrait of Juliet Courbet.* 1844. 77 × 60 cm.
Musée du Petit Palais, Paris (see page 26).

33 *Portrait of Hector Berlioz*. 1850.
61 × 48 cm.
Louvre, Paris (see page 75).

34 *Portrait of Baudelaire*. 1847.
82 × 64 cm.
Musée Fabre, Montpellier
(see pages 49–50).

35 *After Dinner at Ornans* (author's title: *The Afterdinner at Ornans*). 1849. 195 × 217 cm.
Musée Courbet, Lille (see page 39).

36 *Funeral at Ornans* (author's title: *Burial at Ornans*). 1849. 314 × 665 cm.
Louvre, Paris (see pages 60–72).

Throughout the day there were shouts: 'Death to the Communists! Down with Blanqui!' All very ridiculous and meaningless. At bottom nobody knew why he was demonstrating. He hoped that the provinces would send true republicans to the Chamber; otherwise they'd be thrown out of the windows, 'always without doing them any harm'. As for the Assembly sitting elsewhere than in Paris, it was as grotesque as wanting to 'place a man's head in his stomach; not that that's surprising on the part of the provinces, which only think of the stomach'.[23] A competition was announced for an allegorical painting of the Republic to replace a portrait of the dethroned king. Courbet decided to have a try but soon gave up. So he and Bonvin called on Daumier on the Île St Louis to urge him to compete. Daumier did submit a sketch, but failed. Courbet wrote home that he himself would enter instead 'the competition for popular songs, open to musicians'. This was probably a half-joke, though he liked to imagine that he had the elements of a great musician.

But we can get behind this façade which he set up for the family. He had recently come to know Baudelaire, who fought on the barricades in the first days of the February insurrection and who, together with Champfleury and Charles Toubin had founded *Le Salut Public*, a radical sheet of four pages, with the first issue on 27 February. Toubin says the three editors began with a capital of 100 francs, writing their articles at a table in a café near the École de Médecine, and patching the paper together in less than an hour. If Courbet had already moved, they were working right under his studio, and he was certainly in close contact with them. For when it was found that another sheet with the same name was being circulated, Baudelaire asked Courbet to draw a vignette to distinguish their journal from the other. Courbet promptly produced a drawing of a barricade scene: a young rebel in blouse and top hat stands on a heap of stones, brandishing a musket and holding a tricolour inscribed: 'Voice of God, Voice of the People'. The woodcutter added a crowd with muskets and bayonets as a background. The third issue failed to appear. 'The two numbers sold well, but the vendors forgot to bring back to us the proceeds of their sales.' On the night of the 27th Baudelaire put on his blouse and cried the journal in the rue Saint-André-des-Arts.

The contents are not signed, but the more vivid passages are no doubt by Baudelaire:

For three days the population of Paris is admirable for its physical beauty. . . . Whoever wants beautiful men, men of six feet, let him come to France. A free man, whoever he is, is more beautiful than marble. . . .

The painters have bravely thrown themselves into the Revolution! They have fought in the ranks of the People. At the Hotel de Ville artists bore on their hats, written in letters of blood, the title of 'Republican Artists'. Two of them climbed on a table and harangued the People. One spoke of a demonstration that must be made at the Louvre against the Academy of Painting, which, for eighteen years, has drunk so many tears, has killed off so many young talents by hunger and poverty. But the silly old men, architects, musicians, surveyors and geometricians are down today. Don't give them the kick of the ass-hoof . . .

After three thousand years of slavery, Right is going at last to make its entry into the world. French People, you are the redeemer of mankind.

The Revolution of 1848 will be greater than that of 1798; besides, it starts where the other left off.[24]

Can we imagine that Courbet, even when his political ideas were still immature, could have failed to be moved by such words, written as they were by his recent friends Baudelaire and Champfleury? Even if we did not have the evidence of his collaboration with *Le Salut Public*, we could guess that what he wrote to the family was only camouflage. We must also add the fact that within a couple of years he emerged as a convinced socialist and that the experiences of 1848-9 were clearly crucial in his development, turning him from a brilliant and promising young artist into a great one.

We have two imprecise recollections from later years. After the Commune he prided himself that he had carried on his grandfather's work.

My grandfather was a *sans-culotte*; in 1848 he was eighty-three. As he couldn't eat without me, one day as we dined I said to him, 'Grandfather, we are in a Republic.' 'In a Republic!' he replied. 'I warn you that you won't keep it for long, and besides you won't make as much of it as we did.' For me those words were wounding; for what's the use of life if men don't make more of it than their fathers? I kept those words in my heart. So for twenty years I was at a loss how to find out ways of making more of it than grandfather. Pride aside, I believe that we arrived at it, and, despite the general anguish of France, the principles professed by the minority of the Commune [to which he belonged] were, whatever one says of them, superior to those of 1793 by their generosity, their humanity, and their universality.

Also, in a profession of faith addressed to Vallès, he declared:

In 1848 I opened a Socialist Club in opposition to the clubs of Jacobins, Montagnards, and others whom I qualified as 'republicans without the true [*propre*] nature, historical republicans'. The Republic, one, indivisible, authoritative, begot fear; socialism, not having sufficiently elaborated, was rejected; and the rejection of 1849 carried the day to the profit [later] of a monstrous regime.

He does not say whether the Club was in Paris or Ornans; but the context suggests Paris. However, these reminiscences at least make nonsense of the letters to the family.

Then after the exhilaration of February and the hopes of the following months there came the agony of June. A second uprising led to the defeat of the radicals by the armed forces, with a ruthless suppression of all democrats. Large numbers were shot, jailed, deported. What Courbet was doing during the decisive days, we do not know. But now he was too shocked to hide his emotion in the report-to-home (dated 26 June), though he hastened to insist truly enough on his own pacific attitudes. (In the large number of anecdotes about him there is no record of his really losing his temper or using in anger his considerable strength; yet with his often aggressive and provocative manner there must have been many times when he was goaded by heated opponents.)

This is the most distressing spectacle one could possible imagine. I don't think anything like it has ever happened in France, not even the massacre of St Bartholomew. . . . I won't fight for two reasons. First, because I have no faith in war with rifles and cannon, it is not in line with my principles. For ten years I have been fighting a war of the intelligence. So I'd be untrue to myself if I acted otherwise. The second reason is that I have no arms, so can't be tempted. Hence you have nothing to fear on my account.[25]

We can now deal with his move and his establishment of Andler's restaurant as his base, and with the important contacts he set up or strengthened this year. The house to which he moved was at the corner of the rue Hautefeuille and the rue de l'École de Médecine:

An old house of austere aspect, a remnant of what was the College of the Premonstratensians [an order of Augustinian canons]. After the suppression of the monasteries in 1790, the priory became secular property and the chapel was turned into a private house. The Café de la Rotonde on the ground floor, and Courbet's studio on the floor above, occupied what had been the chapel's apse. It was a vast room, lofty, with the roofing as ceiling-beams, recalling the roof of an ancient church as they traverse it high up, giving it an unusual look. The furniture seemed very inadequate: a divan covered with worn-out rep, half a dozen dilapidated chairs, an old dresser with rounded front, a small table littered with pipes, empty beer glasses, and copies of newspapers. All this was half-buried under an avalanche of paintings of all kinds and sizes, some framed and hung on the walls, others merely standing on the floor with their backs to the room. In the middle, an empty space and an easel with an unfinished portrait. In the corners, huge rolls of canvas resembling reefed sails. No luxury whatever, not even ordinary comfort.[26]

In one corner was a wooden partition closing off a small bedroom; there was a big skylight and a small window looking over the rue de l'École. The approach was by a splendid Louis XIII staircase.

Francis Wey records a visit made late in 1848.

During the winter of 1848 one afternoon I met M. Champfleury near the bottom of the rue de la Seine, and as we were chatting away on the pavement, he discoursed on a young painter of immense merit, still quite unknown, and who, a native of my own Franche-Comté, had the right to a visit. He added that his artist was wholly self-taught and without support, without any connections. At last he asked me to go and see him, and I acquiesced in his wish, a little thoughtlessly, I admit.

'Then,' replied Champfleury, with reasonable suspicion, 'why not go at once? It's not far from here and you won't carry away any regrets.'

I took his arm and we reached the rue Mazarine, to cross at last the Place de l'École de Médecine. On our arrival at our destination, there condescended to come out in front of us a large young man, pale, sallow, bony, ungainly – he was so then. He saluted me with his head without a word, then resumed his stool before a canvas that I got a glimpse of by passing behind the artist.

I recall getting a surprise also unexpected. The canvas revealed to our glances was treated with a lack of ceremony, as rustic as the subject, and attested a masterly insouciance, an experimental ardour. The profound tonality of the picture, its method of execution, did not recall any known school. 'With a gift so rare and so marvellous,' I said to the young man, 'how is it you aren't already celebrated? Nobody has ever painted in that way.'

'*Pardié,*' he replied with a thoroughly provincial Franc-Comtois accent, 'me, I paint like the good God.'

These were the first words with which Gustave Courbet favoured me. In two words he had defined his method. This canvas, which made his first appearances famous, was *The Afterdinner at Ornans.*

Courbet had now broken through into the kind of art that expressed his whole being, and he had achieved the manners which were to make him one of the best-known figures in the Paris world of art and letters.

To recover the text, the sense even, of the comments that we exchanged by fits and starts at this first meeting, is something I won't try to do. Enough to know that this young man seemed to me indeed bizarre, as if in revolt at times against most theories, and impregnated with a deliberate ignorance which sought to create an effect. Everything, again, was uttered with a rough *bonhomie,* sometimes with the accent, even with certain phrases, of his native province. I asked him in what studio he had studied. In none, said he; 'I know what I want. I see it in too much independence to be, like a herd of slaves, submitted to masters. We must indeed change all that.'

The proofs of his exceptional quality were before us, and I perceived close at hand a portrait of a man in shirt-sleeves, his cutty-pipe between his teeth: the brow and the eyes of an extraordinary beauty were spoiled by the vulgarity of the mouth and the heaviness of the jaws. The model could be recognised without hesitation; he was there with his life-story told. He showed these two masterpieces a few weeks later; the *Man with the Pipe* caused as much astonishment as the other work.[27]

Wey, we must realise, was an aesthete, a man of good education, one of the gentry: against such a man Courbet would bring out all his defences. He had been born at Besançon in 1812; and C. Nodier, also a Bisontin, had him admitted to the School of Chartres in 1834. He published tales and novels; travelled in Belgium, Holland, Switzerland, Italy, then turned to philology. He was waiting to become (in 1852) Inspector General of Departmental Archives; he was erudite, classically-minded, but ready to welcome the new if it didn't go too far and outrage his ideas of good taste.

The Brasserie Andler was only two doors from Courbet's studio, 28 rue Hautefeuille. Many of his old friends lived thereabouts; it was a perfect place for him as a centre for eating, drinking, talking, holding court. For some fifteen years he used it as his club. Schanne says it was 'very modest in looks, a real village-tavern'. Andler was Swiss, 'and the pronunciation of our language always remained a mystery to him. More, he was slow-witted; and if he grasped our jokes, it was only after a week of meditation.' Others declared that Mme Andler was the Swiss member of the family, Andler a Bavarian.[28] Certainly the place had a hearty Teutonic note. Champfleury speaks of 'hams hanging from the ceiling, garlands of sausages, cheeses as big as millwheels, barrels of savoury sauerkraut', which 'seemed to belong in a monastic refectory'.[28] Castagnary tells how it looked in 1860:

A room shaped like a tunnel, long and dark, with no furniture beyond wooden tables and benches on which the patrons sat back to back. It was a brasserie run in the German style: beer, sauerkraut, ham. A central aisle was kept open for service, for which M. Andler was sufficient. Mme. Andler, whose rotund figure was ill adapted for walking, and Mlle Louise [her niece], a young woman blonde and mild as beer. . . . At the back a billiard table that was amicably shared. On one side a bright cheerful room lighted by a skylight like a studio. It was completely filled by an immense table of unpainted wood. There meals were served to the regulars; there were fought out the philosophical, aesthetic, and literary discussions, intermingled with paradoxes, laughter, and witticisms. The meal took a long time. Courbet ate slowly, like peasants and cattle. We talked of a thousand things. As soon as he realised that I didn't expect him to speak only of painting, he relaxed, became gay and charming. After the meal, pipes were lighted, coffee was taken. Then, some friends having come up, a request was made for a *moss* [big beer-pot], which Mme Léonie brought smoking.

Realism may have been born in Courbet's mind in his studio . . . but the brasserie held it over the baptismal font. Here it was that he established contact with the outside world. From six to eleven in the evening we ate, argued, coined phrases, laughed, and played billiards. Courbet held court. The brasserie was merely an extension of his studio. People eager to see him came there. . . . He held forth on all the arts, all the sciences, even those he knew nothing about. . . . Great was the number of Parisians attracted to this manger where, they were told, a new god had been born. . . . The fame of the brasserie spread, its praises were sung in prose and poetry.

Thursday was the most crowded day. The intellectuals and artists gathered at the big table where Courbet presided. Among the artists were Bonvin, Daumier, Corot, Chenavard, Decamps, F. L. Français, A. Gautier, Jean Gigoux (of Besançon), the animal sculptor Barye. And there were the musicians Promayet and Schanne; the writers Baudelaire, Champfleury, Max Buchon (when in Paris), F. Desnoyers, E. Montégut who translated Shakespeare; the art critics T. Silvestre and G. Planche. Proudhon and Jules Vallès also came at times, and, after 1860, Castagnary.[29] Champfleury, calling the place the Temple of Realism, says that well-known painters came to see 'how was shod the man who made such an uproar with his big *sabots*,' critics, 'sounding line in hand, to gauge the degree of the doctrine's profundity,' disillusioned folk who wanted to regain a faith, if only for a moment; clever fellows who wanted to get into a New School; beginners in letters and arts; idlers, curious people, *bons viveurs*.[30] Champfleury relates: 'One day a billiards game was played between Decamps, Corot, Courbet and me. Who marked the points? It must be said at once, Gustave Planche, old Planche, who had himself chosen the job of declaring the score without disturbing aesthetic discussions that were going on near him between Chenavard and Baudelaire.'[31]

But the most serious discussions were usually enlivened with much laughter. Castagnary describes Courbet's portentous laugh, which

started like a rising rocket. Hearing wheezes mingled with popping noises, one would look at Courbet who seemed to be having convulsions; he wriggled, stamped on the floor, lowered and raised his head while his stomach heaved and shook violently. As soon as he had quieted down and seemed to have stopped laughing, off it would go again as if he were gurgling into his beard. Certain fireworks throw off similar showers of sparks. At last, after several alternations of silence and noise, he would subside, and calm would return. The fit would have lasted two or three minutes.[32]

Such a laugh, however spontaneous in its earlier forms, has an element of deliberate stimulation and could have reached the degree of virtuosity here described only after Courbet's bulk had much increased.

Delvau, for whose book on the Cafés of Paris (1862) Courbet did a drawing of the brasserie, opened with an account of Andler-Keller, which he found to be like the beer-cellars of Munich. It was, he said, the oldest one in Paris, certainly the best known.

One evening – a dozen years ago – I found myself leaning on my elbows before a pot of beer, in the Andler-Keller. I mused and smoked, watching the others muse and smoke. Sleepiness was already getting hold of me, because I was alone, because I wanted to sleep, and also because my neighbours were carrying on delightful conversations, which I didn't understand in the least.

It might have been ten o'clock. The double rows of oaken tables, with benches of the same wood, were crowded with frenetic drinkers of hops: students and engravers on mixed woods. The kitchen, at the back, was mute. Mme Andler slept at her counter, and by the repeated oscillations of her goodnatured head one could suppose, without calumny, that she aspired to the tomb – that is, to the conjugal bed. Mlle Louise – pronounce it *Luisse*, to sound like Mme Andler – imitated her in a corner, with oscillations more discreet but just as significant. As for M. Andler, he played his usual hand of piquet at a table next to me and from time to time made violent assaults on a *moss* next to him.

Conversations were besides being carried on at every point of the hall, and there was scarcely a table without its 'speaker' [he uses the English word]. It was animated, but devilish noisy. The billiard balls of the one table, placed beside the kitchen, added their contribution and knocked one another with a remarkable fury. I couldn't hear myself dream.

At this time Realism was already flourishing, that incestuous fruit of a carp and a rabbit. And in this Temple of Realism, where M. Courbet was then the sovereign pontiff and M. Champfleury the cardinal officiating, there were then, as the public of boozers, students and wood-engravers understood, only realists and non-realists. I have neither time nor space enough to give an exhaustive catalogue. But what I can and will say is that since I came into the world and my ears were attached to each side of my head, they have never been shocked with so many different jargons. The jargon of enthusiasts, sceptics, innovators, apostles of the idea, missionaries of art, friends of progress, friends of liberty, theologians, metaphysicians, art students, men of letters – and the jargon, yet more barbarous, of lawyers – has often tormented them. But, of all the jargons, none has appeared to me so formidably boring as that of the realists.

Probably because the realists can't or won't speak French. Yet M. Courbet is a master-painter and M. Champfleury a man of talent.[33]

From this diatribe it would follow that Courbet and his friends had introduced a new full-ness of discussion, a new attempt to attain theoretical precision. Delvau describes Courbet's entry, followed by an uproar, a *brouhaha*; and even those who didn't know him at once recognised him on account of the many caricatures; the billiard-players stopped and raised their cues respectfully 'like so many exclamation marks'.

He moved on, carrying his head high – like Saint-Just – and the others surrounded him. He sat down, and a circle formed round him. He spoke, and they all listened. When he went off, they still listened. When he had departed, there was a concert. 'What a head', said one. 'He's an Assyrian', said another. 'What a nose', said the first. 'He's a Spaniard', said the second. 'What a mouth', resumed the first. 'He's a Venetian', replied the second. 'What eyes', added a third. 'He's an Indian', put in a fourth. 'What teeth', someone observed. 'He's a Burgundian', everyone answered. 'This Bisontin is quite simply a Byzantine', exclaimed an enthusiast.[34]

Delvau mentions among the artists whom he noted there: A. Guignet; Français, land-scapist of the Seine banks; Staal, 'the most delicate illustrator of all those four-sous or one-sou publications that have flooded France for fifteen or twenty years'; Anastasi, painter of the Meuse's banks; Baron, the Gavarni of painting; Bonvin, the successor of Chardin; Traviès, the Parisian Cruikshank, who invented the satirical character Monsieur Mayeux; Bodmer, painter of forest-depths, a Swiss transplanted into France; Mouilleron, king of lithography; C. Nanteuil, his viceroy; Smithon, the English engraver; Regnier, the French engraver. And among others, Silbermann, chemist and member of the Society of Meteoro-logy; Dupré, professor of anatomy; Furne, editor. Bodmer told travel-stories; Baudelaire tried the effect of his Edgar Poe on the heads of his companions, who thus served him as dynamometer; Français mimed well-known persons, friends and enemies, and told a humorous tale, *The Story of the Great Serpent*; Silbermann advised on the weather; Baron listened a moment, then went to sleep till the next time for drinking came; Traviès talked metaphysics with a sort of serious bantering, capping his maddest paradoxes with the statement, 'That's what Hartmann said' – this authority being his own invention. Smithon, Français, Courbet, Guignet, Anastasi made up a pool at billiards; Baron, exhausted at trying to follow the paradoxes of the big table, came to join them, chose a cue, and was asleep when his turn arrived.

There was much singing. Staal sang Swiss and Tirolese airs; Mme Andler looked happy when he sang the 'Ranz des Vaches' or some such song in German; Français sang a song of 'Sawyers' and Guignet sang 'Strawberries'; Promayet sang de Nerval's version of Goethe's 'King of Thule'. When Courbet's turn came, he leant back and sang in his 'Bisontin but agreeable voice' the songs already cited, or else:

> When I drink, I drink,
> And time goes hurrying by,
> And there I smoke my pipe,
> An old friend at my side,
> And time goes hurrying by.
> *And la la la la etc. etc.* . . . .
>
> Now marriage, all my friends,
> Is a very precious affair
> For a loving pair. . . .
> The Moon that goes that way
> Bursts laughing out once more,
> And the Moon remarks:
> I've seen all that before. . . .

Also an old ballad, which 'he sang, Silvestre declares, before the honest bourgeois and respectable bourgeoises of Pontoise':

> Coming home from Lille in Flanders one day
> *Tra la la, tra la la, la la ;*
> Coming back from Lille in Flanders one day:
> Hey, there's my heart, hey, there's my heart, I say.
>
> I met some pretty Flemish girls on my way . . .
> I didn't choose, but I took the biggest one . . .
> Into the highest-up chamber I led her then . . .

We can guess what happened in the next four or five stanzas; the Pontoise bourgeois wanted an encore, and so did the inhabitants of the Andler. Champfleury described the brasserie in its rustic manners and conviviality as a Protestant Village; here was the natural breeding-ground for the ideas of Realism.[35]

About 1855 Courbet painted a portrait of Mme Andler, known as *La Mère Grégoire*. She is shown as a plump woman in black, with white embroidered collar and cuffs. She sits behind a marble-topped counter on which is a vase of flowers, some coins, and a big flat book. One hand rests on the ledger, the other delicately detaches a flower from the bunch. She is shown as the rather formidable woman who could overawe students that were flush for the moment, and who did not approve of mistresses. But as usual with Courbet's works the adverse critics hurried to find something objectionable in the work. Silvestre said that the woman's 'hideousness makes one forget the witches and the dwarfs which the most brutal painters have sometimes introduced into their compositions for the sake of contrast', and G. Randon in the *Journal Amusant* in 1867 wondered if anyone could see in this hag 'that good and amiable *commère* with brilliant eyes, blooming complexion, and laughing mouth, whom we all know'.[36]

The year 1848 was decisive in almost all ways for Courbet's maturing. The political events came just at the moment when he was searching round for the themes which would most fully express his revolt; he met the men who were to help him forwards by clarifying his thought; his love-affair with Virginie Binet was reaching a point of conflict and un-happiness which precipitated his decision to expel all romantic ideas and emotions from his being. Thus, driven along three main lines, artistic, political and psychological, he was driven to his goal of Realism.

Champfleury (Jules-François-Félix Husson) had been born at Laon in 1821; his father, a printer, directed the *Journal de l'Aisne*. From the local college he went to Paris in 1838, worked in a bookshop on the Quais des Grands-Augustins; returned home and worked at printing; then moved again in 1843 to Paris, where he came to know dissidents like Dupont, Baudelaire, Murger, Bonvin, Journet, Courbet. His *Chien-Caillou* of 1847 was the tale of a poor etcher Bresdin, in which appears a sort of embryonic realist manifesto. Bresdin runs away from his brutal father and falls in with a group of *rapins*, art students. 'He was only ten years old; he drew in so naïve a fashion that they hung up all his works in the studio.' He tried engravings, but they too had 'something of the primitive German, the Gothic, the naïve and the religious which made the whole studio laugh'. Thus early Champfleury showed his interest in the naïve and the popular tradition. Later (in his 1867 notice on Buchon) he declared: 'Realism was a democratic aspiration, latent or unconscious in certain spirits; for towards 1848 we were driven on by a specific breath which made us act without any obvious reason.' Only now he understood what was meant when Thoré stopped him in the street and cried, 'Don't you see new horizons opening up?' He did much in working out the theory of Realism in its first phases and was thus of great value to Courbet for the clari-fication of his impulses. He was deeply interested, like Buchon, in popular art and poetry, but with a wider range; his researches in these fields again helped Courbet to strengthen his concepts and give them a deeper root than he could have given them alone. He had admired Courbet's work in the Salon of 1848, and about this time came to know him. Till about 1855 he was his chief defender, then began to sheer away from him and his work, dis-turbed by his political views.[37]

Proudhon, as we have seen, was a native of Courbet's own area, some ten years older, of the same peasant-mountaineer stock, but at a poorer level. First taught by his mother, he entered the college of Besançon with a bursary, early resisted religion, and had to have his first communion forced on him. His family's poverty prevented him from taking the baccalauréat and near the end of 1827 he became apprentice to a printer at Besançon, and saw the printing-stick (as the symbol and instrument of his freedom). Though he loved the printing shop, he at times grew weary, especially after reading endless proofs of theological works; he felt the need to get back to nature.

To find the purest air I would scale the high hills bordering the valley of the Doubs, and I did not fail, whenever there was a storm, to treat myself to the spectacle. Crouching in a hole on the rocks, I loved to stare into the face of flashing Jove, without either defying or fearing him. . . . I told myself that the lightning and the thunder, the winds, the clouds, and the rain, were all one with me.[38]

After he passed his apprenticeship, he had a period of unemployment, even being forced to sell his college prizes, his whole library; he left Besançon and tried teaching at Gray not far off, then walked through the Jura to Neufchâtel, where he stayed half a year; then went back to Besançon and printing. A friend, Fallot, succeeded in drawing him to Paris, and in 1832 he walked there. He nursed Fallot who fell ill with cholera, then tramped all the way from Paris down the Rhône valley to Lyon, and on to Marseille, a journeyman companion of the tour de France. Inspired by an uprising of workers in Paris, who had raised barricades with a demand for work, he went to the mayor's office at Toulon and formally asked for work. He was told to get off, and the experience remained with him, helping him to his revolutionary viewpoint and his total distrust of the state as such. Returning to Besançon, he was asked by Just Muiron, a disciple of Fourier, to edit *L'Impartiel*. He took the job on, but resigned on the first day when he learned that the article he had written would have to be passed by the Prefect. So he went to work for a printer of Arbois, refusing the offer of a coach for the thirty-odd miles. Instead, he walked. Back in Besançon in early 1835, he heard that his brother had died during military training. 'That death finally made an irreconcilable enemy of the existing order.' (Later he told the Russian exile, Herzen, that the brother had been pestered by an embezzling captain, who wanted him as accomplice, and finally committed suicide.)

The next few years were taken up with work in the printing trade, illness, another trip to Paris (1838); he was upset by another suicide, that of a partner in a printing venture. In November 1838 he again went to Paris, where he worked hard at developing his thought, attending public lectures at the Sorbonne, the Collège de France, and the Conservatoire des Arts et Métiers. Back in Besançon again, he printed an essay *On the Utility of the Celebration of Sunday* on his own press. He was worried at the discontent among the workers in Paris, who might rise at any moment though 'they know that the plan of Paris is drawn by the government in such a way that it can suddenly occupy all the points of the town at the first rising; they know they cannot rise today without being massacred in thousands'. Indeed, a few months later the uprising called the Conspiracy of the Seasons broke down for the reasons he had sketched out. He was at work on a book, *What is Property?* in which he set out his position in the aphorism, 'Property is theft'. It appeared in 1840.

We need not here examine his thought in detail. It is enough to point out that his strength lay in his destructive analysis of the State and everything connected with it; this analysis he often made with acuteness and insight. But his positive schemes were feeble; they amounted to little more than a liberal faith that the workings of contract would bring about a just and harmonious world. He opposed the union of workers for political purposes since such union interfered with the free working of contract; he wanted Association solely for the sake of pure mutuality. In 1848:

My spirit was in agony: I carried in advance the weight of the sorrows of the Republic and the burden of the calumnies that were going to strike socialism. On the evening of 21 February I again exhorted my friends not to fight. On the 22nd I breathed with relief on learning of the retreat of the opposition. I thought myself at the end of my martyrdom. The 23rd dissipated my illusions....[39]

On the day of the Republic's establishment he wrote, 'The mess is going to be inextricable. . . . I have no place in it'. He was thus an odd mixture of sheer egoism and selfless dedication, of inflexible dogma and great mobility of mind. Marx put his finger on the hard core of petty-bourgeois illusions inside his anarchist critiques when he pointed out that he could not rise to the concept of the resolution of opposites in a higher unity. But Proudhon's position was not one of ignorance; he rejected the Hegelian system of logic root and branch:

The Hegelian formula is a triad only by the sweet will or an error of the master, who counts three terms where only two exist, and who has not seen that an antinomy cannot be resolved, but that it indicates an oscillation or an antagonism susceptible only of equilibrium. (*De la Justice*)

This position he consistently held; hence his rejection of any direct forms of struggle, which upset the movement towards the hoped-for harmonious balance. It gave him in practical politics a devious, wily and apparently confused course, though in fact all his contradictions derived logically from his notion that somehow out of the inherent development of extending social and economic factors the State would be eliminated. 'In the place of laws we will put contracts. . . . In the place of political centralisation, we will put economic centralisation.' He was terrified of the proletariat; in 1860 he noted with dismay, 'The petty-bourgeoisie declines, declines, towards the gulf of the proletariat; it's the great wound of France.' He always sought compromise and collaboration with the capitalists and ruling class. In 1847 he noted: 'Try to come to an understanding with the *Moniteur universel*, journal of the masters while the *People* will be the journal of the workers.' He declared that the Tsar Alexander II was setting alight 'a hope of liberty' and initiating a progressive policy; he wrote a book against Poland in honour of the Tsar. He kept on trying to collaborate with Louis Napoleon; he called on him to take the lead of the revolutionary movement; he wrote a book to show that '2 December is the symbol of a movement ahead along the revolutionary path. . . . Louis Napoleon is its general'. The emperor was presented as 'the first of revolutionaries, the last of government-men'. Somehow Courbet and Buchon managed to ignore these traits and see him only as the critic of State-power; in no sense can Courbet be called a disciple of his except in this aspect of his thought. True, Courbet had his petty-bourgeois weaknesses, allied to those of Proudhon, but he had a true instinct for the enemy and his whole concept of struggle denied Proudhonian gradualism and compromise. (The final nemesis of Proudhon's readiness to compromise, his exaltation of petty-bourgeois pre-industrial France, came when he was taken up by the theoreticians of Vichy Fascism after the fall of France.)

He matured during the 1840s. In 1842 he was arrested for his work, *Avertissement aux Propriétaires*, and tried at Besançon, but acquitted. Now in June 1848 he was elected deputy in the new republican Assembly, but though he put forward proposals for the reform of taxes and banking, nothing came of them. Hugo watched him address the Assembly on 31 July and described him as 'a man of about forty-five [actually thirty-nine], fair, with scanty hair and abundant whiskers. He wore a black tailcoat and waistcoat'. (He was not very prepossessing, and disliked being painted.) Perhaps it was his Franc-Comtois accent that Hugo referred to in remarking that 'his voice had a vulgar intonation, his enunciation was common and guttural, and he wore spectacles'. He was strict and puritan in his personal behaviour and it is strange that he and Courbet managed to get along; he was hostile to all forms of bohemianism or sexual looseness. Somehow their strong elements of sympathy overcame such differences. Thoré tried to bring out certain similarities:

Father Fourier, whom I knew, was a man of metal, not at all malleable. Proudhon, also my friend and comrade – what stubbornness, despite his apparent changes.
  The talents of Courbet and Proudhon are not unlike; both show unusually forceful characters and a bold sincerity to such an extent that they seem deliberately to seek out anything that will offend sensitive tastes. Through their horror of banality they seem to plunge wantonly into coarse uncouthness. Yet both . . . have exquisite delicacy. There are pages of Proudhon that are airy, flowing, witty, with that silvery flame found in Voltaire and Diderot; there are paintings by Courbet with a quality of tone that recalls Velasquez, Metsu, Watteau, Reynolds, and the most refined colourists.[40]

Certain aspects of Proudhon's thought profoundly affected Courbet, especially the destructive analyses of authority; but, as we noted, there was no question of Courbet tamely taking over all his ideas. Courbet simply ignored or did not register the weaker aspects, as did Buchon. True, in the political system which he worked out decentralisation and free co-operation were the key-elements, and he wanted to see these put into action from the outset of the successful revolution; but he did not take over the Proudhonian illusions which rejected struggle and distrusted the working class. He knew that collaboration with reaction was disastrous. Further, certain aspects of Proudhon's thought took on new colorations and emphases when applied to, and developed concretely in, art. (These new angles were only imperfectly and crudely reflected in Proudhon's own book on art.)

Just what Buchon got from Proudhon is well summed up in his remarks on the latter's first book, *Qu'est-ce que la Propriété?* The work's style is 'powerfully muscular, and it's the style which in my opinion gives it its great merit'. He explains:

The provocative boldness with which he lays his hand on the economic holy-of-holies, the witty paradoxes with which he mocks at the flat commonsense of the bourgeois, the corrosive critique, the bitter irony, with here and there a feeling of deep and true revolt against the infamies of the established order, the revolutionary spirit: that is what electrified the readers of *What is Property?* and imprinted a strong impulsion from its first appearance.

Courbet could have said much the same.

The early years of Courbet's life had been years of uprisings and struggles of the emerging working class:

Although he was some years younger than Stendhal's hero, what he has seen around him since he exercised judgment and began to understand things, was the landscape of that society one sees in *Lucien Leuwen*, 1830 . . . the standard of famine raised at Lyon from November 1831, the plots of 1832, cholera, the insurrection of Paris at the obsequies of General Lamarque, the extraordinary growth of strikes in 1833, and there it was that the great cry of 1831, 'Live working or die fighting', rose up afresh among the silk-weavers of Lyon. This time, Carbonarism, the Republicans of the League of Rights of Man, the first working-class associations, *mutuellistes* gathering the heads of workshops, the *compagnons* united in the association of silk-weavers, the Society of the Friends of the People (where the influence of Babœuf comes out and where Auguste Blanqui was found), mingled their banners. The insurrection at Lyon in 1831 had been the product of the workers alone before repression. At Lyon, in 1834, for the first time a section of the middle class allied itself with the proletarians. . . .[41]

But how far did such matters echo in the houses at Ornans and Flagey, in the college of Besançon? Courbet was not so isolated from industrial matters as might be thought. He and his friends like Buchon could see, opposite the Roche Founèche, under the château,

the sombre barrier of the Ornans tanneries on the banks of the Loue. However, six leagues away, at Besançon where Gilbert called Miran published *Le Patriote Franc-Comtois*, one learned through small handwritten posters of the Lyon insurrection and that in Paris. Pontarlier, on the other side of Ornans, was steeped in the *mutuelliste* plot. The rumour came from Belfort that King Charles Albert had just invaded Switzerland. In the countryside of Max Buchon, at Salins-de-Jura, on the Furieuse, where the father of Gustave, mayor of Flagey, went to the Fair, everyone shuddered at the neighbourhood of insurgent Arbois; people awaited the Arboisiens, tried to persuade the commandant of the fort Saint-André to surrender without a blow, and passed on the *Patriote Franc-Comtois* which wrote: 'Insurrection is a Duty' (ARAGON).

Courbet, as schoolboy and student, was clearly not concerned about such matters; but he must have heard them talked about; and as he later began to attempt to make political sense of his world, the memories would to some extent return. They must have revived when he heard of the spontaneous *jacqueries* that swept the French countryside in the bad harvests of 1847 and 1848. His friend Max definitely tried to resume and develop the local traditions of struggle, and Courbet shared his hopes. In 1848–9, as he matured artistically, the wider relations of his struggle for independence asserted themselves in his mind, above all in the formulation that Realism was the art-creed of Democracy and Socialism. Such formulations did not arise out of an abstract line of argument; they gathered together, in a new dynamic unity, a multiple series of experiences, emotions, thoughts.

There is a further point to be borne in mind when we are considering Courbet's relations to the revolutionary spirit of his times. His own arrival in Paris had occurred at about the same date as the beginning of the railway boom which brought a new wave of peasants into the city. This invasion was not just part of the general movement from the countryside into the developing towns of Europe; it involved large numbers of temporary workers, peasants who swarmed in during the summer to live in the *taudis* or hovels on the Île de la Cité or in the expanding industrial sprawl outside the new *barrières*. The older working class was thus entangled with raw peasants who had not been tamed to city ways and factory controls. In 1848 the most ardent rebels, those most responsive to the call for revolt, were the new peasant recruits; the older sections had been to a considerable extent broken down and weakened both physically and politically. So, when the workers in the suburbs started blowing up the railway lines in June 1848, to prevent the arrival of the trainloads of National Guards (called in by the central government), they were men who usually still wore the peasant smock. In this situation we see peasants on the verge of proletarianisation fighting peasants who had had no experience of the city and who were still subservient to their provincial masters. (Indeed Paris was permeated at most levels with the newly-arrived peasant; some had even in the not-too-distant past made enough money to penetrate into the financial aristocracy. We have only to look at Daumier's caricatures to see the prominence of Parisian bourgeois whose fathers had been peasants, but who, after immigrating to Paris, had managed by luck, hard work, a little capital, or a lucky marriage, to rise in the world.)

Courbet with his mountaineer's-independence may then be said to have been undergoing, at the intellectual level, the same experiences as the peasant labourers had been undergoing in Paris at the level of crude exploitation. His distrust of all gentlemanly pretences, of all falsity in art which had the aim of veiling the facts of life and of producing a comfortable and 'elevating' background for the bourgeoisie, was at root not so different from the recoil of the peasant who found he was losing his last poor hold on the land in order to toil for the enrichment of a class full of fine phrases but in fact ruthless in its demands. Courbet was thus the opposite of the peasant who managed one way or another to cash in on the situation and climb up on the backs of his fellows. He resisted and fought back, just as the peasant-worker did in his riots and uprisings.

His friendship with Baudelaire about this time also helped his intellectual development, though the link was not as simple as that with Champfleury, Buchon, and Proudhon. The poet was two years younger than Courbet, and at this time was often without money or bed. Courbet was always ready to let him sleep on a made-up bed on the studio floor. One night Baudelaire got him to write down his dreams or visions; but the result was a series of frightening images that made Courbet's flesh creep. Gros-Kost gives a heightened version: Courbet, 'one evening of drunkenness, was engaged unfortunately, under oath, to note down on a big blackboard all the obscure and incoherent ramblings of the starry Bohemian. Write! Do you understand? What a torture! On his waking, Baudelaire found, rearing up before him, the colossal height of a wrathful man, regarding him with eyes of fire and holding a bit of chalk.' (We know how readily Courbet wrote long letters; but Gros-Kost was determined to depict him as anti-literary.)

Later writers refer to a quarrel or some sort of break. Possibly Baudelaire was annoyed by the portrait which Courbet painted, which is often dated 1853 but was probably done in

1848. The poet, in a brown suit, blue shirt, yellow cravat, reads a book stuck up on a table where stands an ink-bottle and quill; behind him is a pile of red cushions. The lighting, which picks out the end of his nose, gives an informal effect which finely summons up the image of the concentrated poet in the dim studio. Baudelaire seems to have disliked the work, though others who knew him considered it a good likeness. Courbet himself said, 'I don't know how to finish Baudelaire's portrait; his face changes daily.' Champfleury comments:

It is true that Baudelaire had the power to alter his appearance like an escaped convict seeking to avoid recapture. Sometimes his hair would hang over his collar in graceful scented ringlets; the next day his bare scalp would have a bluish tint from the barber's razor. One morning he would turn up smiling with a big bouquet in hand. . . . Two days afterwards, with drooping head and bent shoulders, he might be taken for a Carthusian friar digging his own grave.[42]

We have seen that the young Courbet was certainly interested in poetry. In his post–48 life he probably did not read much prose or verse, and gained his sense of what was going in culture, in all the fields, from conversations in his brasserie or elsewhere. In his polemics against all the complacencies of the cultural establishment, he had no more time for poetic shams than for artistic ones. Gros-Kost in his rhetorical, superficial way writes:

To make verses, he used to say, is dishonest; to speak differently from everyone else is to pose for the aristocracy. But Baudelaire found grace with him, as well as Max Buchon. . . . Baudelaire had for him his *Charogne*; this residue of deliquescent matters infecting the ditch testified to a great talent and a great boldness. Courbet gave hospitality to the author in his studio. In a corner clothes were heaped up, a pair of cloths were laid above; the bed was improvised. Henceforth the poet had a domicile. While one man painted, the other rhymed. The long sessions were ended in front of a good beer-mug brought in from the nearest bar. The only thing that the realist reproached Baudelaire for was the abuse of opium that carried him off.[43]

But Courbet made fun of the term 'artist' as of 'poet'. 'Artists, I despise them'.[44] He himself took the title of 'Master Painter' – thus equating himself with craftsmen.

His friends, indeed, stressed that he did little reading, at least in his later years. Max Buchon said, 'As an instrument of education and study, Courbet never had anything but his magnificent eye, and that was enough.' Castagnary repeated the idea. 'As for reading, he did not over-indulge in it. By not reading, he remained closer to instinct. The idea escaped him; he grasped the world through form and colour.' To some degree or other, such comments must be true of any great artist, since all his intellectual ideas, whether born from reading, conversation, or ponderings on his own experiences, must be reborn in the sensuous form of art, which has its own immediacy like any other art-expression, poetry or music. In Courbet, it is true, the turning-away from literature has a particular emphasis; for it was implicated in his whole rejection of ready-made ideas, reactions, interpretations. But when this turning-away is used to define him as a man without ideas, 'this bull of a Courbet' (in Manet's phrase), it ends by completely distorting and devaluing his art. It was precisely because he had so many ideas, which the cultural establishment did not like, and still largely does not like, that he has been presented as a sort of spontaneous eye, responding to certain aspects of nature but ignorant of what he was doing. In fact there have been few artists with such a clear and consistent, explicit as well as implicit, development of an ordered world-view in their art; and this was a world-view which he achieved by hard thinking as well as by abundant feeling.

How well up in literary niceties Courbet in fact was, is exemplified by the account of Trapadoux made in his last years in exile. Looking some thirty years back, he remarked that that eccentric had been 'of the type of Gérard de Nerval, Privat d'Anglemont, Poterel, and others'. Or take the following anecdote recorded by Castagnary: 'He attributed to Arsène Houssaye this affected phrase, which is sufficiently in that writer's style, "If Realism is victorious on earth, what will become of the roses?" He cited and recited it, accompanying each citation with a burst of prolonged laughter.'

Apparently there was no definite disagreement between him and Baudelaire; the two men simply drifted apart, though they felt friendly enough when they chanced to encounter one another later. What Courbet gained from the relationship is hard to define, though we can feel its subtle presence. On the one hand the whole concept of the 'heroism of modern life', which was to some extent carried on by Champfleury – the call for a painter who would show us 'how much we are great and political in our cravats and halfboots', and the comment that 'we celebrate, all of us, some burial'. But beyond that, the general stimulation of Baudelaire's comments, his insight into the alienating pressures of the new industrial cities, his cruel ironies. There were elements in his world-view, which, at the pre-1848 phase, must have been of great value in enabling Courbet, less analytic and learned, but with an intuitive acuteness capable of seizing on the essence of a social or cultural situation through an incident, a single word, a conversation, to get rapidly to grips with the Parisian world in all its aspects. But the value of this relationship could only have lessened after 1848; if Courbet had continued at all under the spell of Baudelaire he would have been unable to make the great break of 1849–50 in the clean way he did; the romantic and rebellious pathos of the bohemian outlook, evident in the self-portraits of the 1840s, was something which Courbet had to discard if he were to mature. The break with romanticism was also a break with Baudelaire; after 1848 Courbet went a very different route from that of Baudelaire though without discarding the positive aspects of what he learned from the poet, his deep insights into the fragmenting and desolating nature of bourgeois society.[45]

His friendship with Baudelaire was supplemented by that with the poet Pierre Dupont, whom Baudelaire at this phase deeply admired. Courbet and Dupont had been close friends since 1846 and holidayed together in the country. Dupont wrote many strong political poems, but he also had a pastoral side; the sophisticated literary world considered him rough, rustic, too realist – though with his mixture of the idyllic and the revolutionary he inspired Baudelaire with the idea that all poetry was in essence a utopian protest against injustice, a desire for freedom and happiness. He composed the music for his songs, basing himself on folk melodies. Indeed his poems are throughout derived from the folksong without any effect of pastiche; they remain fresh and unforced – qualities appreciated by

Gautier as well as Baudelaire. The latter called his 'Song of the Workers' the 'Marseillaise of Labour'. With such a kindred spirit, gay and resilient, Courbet could not but feel his popular sympathies strengthened and deepened. He later painted his portrait, as also that of Gustave Mathieu, a poet close to both him and Dupont.[46] We see Dupont with cravat negligently knotted over his half-open shirt, robust, with dark hair.

Much later, in 1884, Jean Gigoux recorded a visit he paid to Courbet in 1848. He tells of the odd painting that Courbet had made of Apollo chasing Daphne, a sort of parody of a common academic theme. Courbet and Bonvin were busy all the evening, sometimes well into the night; and Courbet worked on a large canvas, some four by three metres. He called on Gigoux, asked him 'with his accent' to come and see the finished work. 'Sir, I come to ask if you could come and see my picture.' In the studio stood the vast canvas showing a Nymph pursued by 'a sort of Apollo, his arms outstretched, running with gymnastic steps, and, as a final touch, wearing a frockcoat, of which the floating tails accompanied the movement of his legs, a big felt hat on the side of his head in the prevailing fashion'. Gigoux felt that he shouldn't comment on these oddities; he hadn't come to give the painter a course in mythology. Still, he observed that Courbet might have used a brush to bind his colours; the impasto was thick and lumpy. 'Oh, but the paste is roughcast', Courbet replied. Gigoux adds:

That happened in 1848. The picture was at first refused; but immediately the Revolution burst out, all Frenchmen became equals before the law and rejected pictures went in like the others. Poor Courbet then had an access of mad laughter, but a laughter such that, supposing a thousand men had gathered for the same end of amusement and gaiety, never could the laughter have come from so good a heart.[1]

Gigoux may have got his facts and chronology mixed up, but we may assume that he had seen this canvas in the studio.

The years 1848–9 were crucial for Courbet's development. He at last found fully and squarely what he wanted to do. Between late 1848 and mid-1850, apart from many lesser works, he produced four major canvases which clearly revealed his break from the past and his creation of a new outlook in art. As always with such a break, we can trace its antecedents. Courbet was picking up afresh a tradition that went back to David and had been powerfully developed by Gros and Géricault: the fusion of the heroic with the everyday. Delacroix, despite his strong romantic trend, had in many respects derived from this tradition, which in his work came to a head in *Liberty on the Barricades*. But in the late 1840s the vital elements of the Davidian school and its closely-linked offshoots had died out. What came directly from that school was arid and flat in the extreme. Delacroix had no effective disciples; there were many weak romantic sentimentalists like Scheffer, and hosts of painters attempting to catch the colour of the East. Though capable painters like Couture came up, they sought only to cash in on the vogue for the large pseudo-classical fabrication. The high bourgeoisie who had triumphed with Louis-Philippe in 1830 wanted no exploration of the real world; they asked from art a false picture of the past which could be used to decorate their own existence with various glamourisings. Literature in Stendhal and Balzac had broken through such fetters; but art, granted its Salon by the king and dependent on rich patrons, was on the whole obedient to the demand for flattering portraits and the pseudo-heroic. True, certain contrary trends had been quietly at work in the field of landscape.[2] Théodore Rousseau had settled at Barbizon in 1844; and Corot for some time had been building his work on a direct vision where his treatment of light, form and space was dependent on his strong sense of tonal values – though he went much further along this line in his sketches than in his exhibited work. Millet had shown in 1848 a genuine peasant-subject, *The Winnower*, and next year he moved from Paris to Barbizon. But these trends, though looking in the direction that Courbet now began decisively to take, had not matured sufficiently to provide an effective challenge to the established systems – though *The Winnower* did come in for some attacks as socialist in outlook. The four great works that Courbet now painted provided the definitive shock and break-through: *Afterdinner at Ornans, Stone-Breakers, Burial at Ornans, Peasants of Flagey Returning from the Fair*.

The jury for the 1849 Salon, which opened on 15 June, was not the usual set of men from the hidebound Academy, but was chosen from the exhibiting artists. It included Delaroche, Decamps, Delacroix, Verney, Ingres, Robert-Fleury, Isabey, Meissonier, and Corot. Courbet had sent in seven works; they were all accepted. Four were landscapes: *Grape-picking at Ornans* (under the Roche-du-Mont), *Valley of the Loue, Château of Saint-Denis* (near the village of Scey-en-Varais), *Communal Pasture at Chassagne*. The other three paintings were the portrait of Trapadoux, a self-portrait (presumably the work known as *The Man with the Leather Belt*: Courbet wearing a belted smock, his cheek on his hand), and *Afterdinner*.[3]

Castagnary later claimed that it was with the *Man with the Leather Belt* that Courbet matured. 'There is in the ensemble a nobility, a harmony, a distinction which denote the master.'[4] The work is indeed a fine piece of painting, with a glance back at the Venetians, and it does show how Courbet was now mastering the handling of paint; but by itself it does not reveal the new direction he was taking. *Afterdinner*, though less finely painted as a whole, makes the direction clear. It attracted much attention and almost all the critics mentioned it. They found much to praise, though many objected to the unprecedented size and importance given to what they considered a *genre* picture. The figures were almost life-size. We see a group in front of a big kitchen fireplace at Ornans; the table has been cleared but for a dish of fruit, three bottles of wine, four tumblers. On the left Régis is dozing in his chair; Gustave sits on the other side of the table. Adolphe Marlet has his back turned as he lights his pipe with a bit of wood from the hearth; under his chair sleeps a bulldog. On the right sits Promayet, playing his violin. The evening shadows are thickening; and there is an afterdinner atmosphere of drowsy repletion and relaxation, half-dreamy absorption in the music. The kitchen is not in the Courbet house, as is often assumed. In the description contributed by Courbet to the Salon we are told: 'It was in the month of November, we were at the house of our friend Cuénot, Marlet was returning from the hunt, and we had engaged Promayet to play his violin before my father.' The return-to-roots in the painting is also to be found in its link with the *Family Meal* by Louis le Nain (1642), which had probably been brought to his notice by Champfleury. The latter had discovered the Le Nains (artists from his own home town of Laon) about 1845, and in 1850 he printed a brochure which described them as painters of reality.

The critics who felt uneasy at the size, at the insistence that this moment of everyday life should be treated with full seriousness, were the ones who had correctly surmised the path now taken by Courbet. But the unchallenging nature of the subject masked the significance of the work. Courbet was awarded a second-class gold medal (with T. Rousseau and Préault); Bonvin, who was steadily following his course of reviving a Chardin-like sense of the materiality of objects, gained a third-class award. Charles Blanc, now director of the Beaux-Arts, bought the picture for the government at 1,500 francs; he had meant to hang it in the Luxembourg, but on second considerations, or under pressure brought on him by the more academic artists, he handed it over to the museum at Lille. He was not very sympathetic to Courbet.[5]

Champfleury wrote enthusiastically of the picture. 'Courbet forces the doors of the Salon. For a long time there has not been so abrupt a success. . . . Before many years he will be one of our greatest artists.' But other critics were more guarded:

(HAUSSARD) This lifesize interior, these family-portraits in the guise of a colossal *genre*-picture, are of a strange novelty; all that has never been done before, but therein lies precisely the singular merit of M. Courbet and the bold stroke of his rude and naïve talent.

(T. GAUTIER) M. Courbet can be ranged on that class of realists who take advice only from nature. His temperament is male, robust, a little heavy and rustic, but with all the peasant's healthy qualities.

(PEISSE) The technical cleverness in the *Afterdinner* is at least equalled by the absence of taste, the lack of distinction, and that's to make a by no means small charge. One could not degrade [*encanailler*] art with more technical ability, be more of a painter and less of an artist.

(LAGENEVAIS in the *Revue des Deux-mondes*) M. Courbet paints well, that's true, he renders perfectly what he has under his eyes. This exactitude, however, produces only a trivial truth. . . . The impression of boredom that the *Afterdinner* causes.[6]

The notes of disquiet reveal the sort of thing that was to be said, with increasing sharpness and violence, of the works to come. The key-attitude has already been set: a capable painter, but a boor, a mere peasant, who lacks all taste and all response to the finer things of life.

Champfleury had asked Wey, after their visit to the studio, to put in a word for Courbet with the critics of leading journals, who were 'liable to make mistakes about pieces too new' for them. Above all, he wanted Théophile Gautier interested. 'It's not worth the bother', Courbet put in. 'He'll understand nothing and it'll be a nuisance for him; that fellow is doomed to spoil his reputation before my painting.' Gautier wasn't helpful. He told Wey 'You'll take under wing something with no resemblance to yourself. You'll see. That man will do you harm.' Then, in the Tuileries, from which the king had fled and which was used this year for the exhibition, Wey met Delacroix, who took him by the arm and showed him the *Afterdinner*, remarking with his usual vivacity, 'Have you ever seen anything like it, anything so strong, with no dependence on anyone else? There's an innovator, a revolutionary too; he bursts out all of a sudden, without precedent; he's an unknown.'

Then as Delacroix went off, Wey saw Ingres come up. He was less responsive. 'How does it come about', he cried, 'that nature herself ruins her finest creations? She has endowed this young man with the rarest gifts. Born with qualities that so many others so rarely acquire, he possesses them full-grown at his first brush-stroke. This prelude throws out with a sort of bravado a work that's masterly in the most difficult aspects; the rest, which is art, totally evades him. He has given nothing of himself and he has received everything. What lost values! what sacrificed gifts! Is that remarkable and depressing enough? Nothing as composition, nothing as drawing; exaggerations, almost a parody. This fellow is an eye; he sees, with a perception very distinctly his own, into a harmony of which the tonality is a convention, realities so homogeneous in themselves that he improvises a nature more energetic in appearance than the truth is, and what he presents is, as artistic talent, of a perfect nullity. This new revolutionary will be a dangerous example.'

The eye of hatred can sometimes see with a surprising clarity the nature of a threatening force. In saying that Courbet 'improvises a nature more energetic in appearance than the truth is', Ingres was paying him the highest possible tribute. He too seems to have realised, as no one else did, that it was not merely a case of a clever rustic who could only paint his own coarse world, but that here was a dangerous example that could overthrow art as he knew it. Wey appears to feel that Ingres's remarks were all-too-percipient, for he adds:

This sally, of which I have retained the smallest details, was not taken in by me alone; a group of friends surrounded M. Ingres, too academic for me to know any of them personally, with the exception of the engraver Henriquel Dupont, one of our most sympathetic artists. M. Henriquel did not understand a great deal. A man of style, a virtuoso in drawing, he found all that too dark and very ugly.

As for the smoky scale, I thought the same and spoke of it to Courbet. 'I see like that', replied the *master painter* (he had applied this title to himself like a peasant). 'One can't render a factitious colour, the reality of which escapes us. That would be adulterated [*frelaté*] art like Ingres and the others. If I want a livelier one, I'll think of it, and when I see it, the thing will be done without my willing it.'[7]

We have another nude by a woodland stream that is dated 1849. Here the girl seems certainly Virginie. The skill with which the luminous flesh is rendered against the dark background shows how far Courbet had come since the somewhat similar subject of 1845; it shows also his study of Rembrandt and other Dutch masters in 1847.[8] As an example of the sort of landscape he was painting at this phase we may take *The Valley of the Loue in time of Storm*, which is probably the picture of the Valley exhibited in 1849; it still shows the detailed treatment of the foreground, which would have pleased an orthodox jury of the time. For some years T. Rousseau had already been making the foreground less definite, less a sort of barrier cutting across the front of a scene, so as to lead the eye at once into the distance. A sense of space was thus created, not by a succession of planes organised in terms of perspective, but by atmospheric effect and a feeling of light-depth. Courbet soon took over this new way of dealing with the foreground, which was one of the preconditions of Impressionism.[9]

In the spring of 1849 he had made many excursions with friends into the countryside round Paris: to the woods of Marnes where were the hazelnuts and rabbit-stews of *mère* Pihan, to the woods of Fleury where were the thrushes and cutlets of *père* Bazin, to the Pool of Plessis-Piquet where swam the ducks of *père* Cense. The Pool was the best-liked spot: a simple cottage with thatched roof with the murmur of poplars behind it. Here they were all at home, shook hands with *père* Cense and his dog, even kissed *mère* Cense, talking of rainy or fine weather, the rain bringing up the asparagus and the fine weather making ideas sprout. 'And while chattering away and ordering a lard omelette, one even went to choose the rabbit destined for the sorrowful honours of the casserole', says Delvau. 'Then one sat in the shadow of the great poplars, before a table of true old wood, on benches uncertain in their intentions of balance, and drank amid a gossip of love and poetry, according to the moment and the guests.' Delvau recalled as members of the parties that sought to escape the Parisian Sunday, Courbet, Banville, Bonvin, Murger, Bodmer, Champfleury, Baudelaire, Schanne, Promayet. Mistresses were changed too often for their names to be recalled.[10] We have no indication that Virginie shared any of Courbet's pleasures; her child was in his second year.

In early summer he visited Wey at Louveciennes near Marly-le-Roy. Invited to dinner, he stayed on for about two months, returning to Paris once a week for fresh clothes. The change of air did him good; he had been suffering from the kind of ailment that kept recurring all his life.

He was just recovering from an attack of cholera [European cholera, enteritis] and he needed (as he used to say) to feather again. Rawboned and paler than ever, he who later became so fat was a pitiful object, though he had become the most vigorous of wraiths and acquired a good appetite. His conversation, inexhaustibly loquacious and with a cutting crudity . . . was at bottom devoid of wit, but it was variegated with sallies so unpredictable and of such an original nature that our neighbours and friends came to dine with us out of curiosity, well warned that at each encounter they'd be treated as idiots with all affability. Courbet saved everything by his good nature; he repaired everything with his bursts of gaiety. He never thanked us for the hospitality he had himself solicited, and nothing seemed to us more natural.[11]

One day, going to his studio for more paraphernalia and a little linen, he remarked on his return that the place was full of vagabonds who used his bed and other furniture to escape having to pay rent elsewhere. The Weys were indignant, but he cut them short, 'I left them the key for that purpose'. Wey mentions also that Courbet told them how Champfleury had been ill some six months before and the doctor had blamed the periods when he had been too poor to buy food. During this tale 'Courbet could not refrain from bitter sobs at the thought that he hadn't guessed his friend suffered from hunger without coming to him for help. The painter was very poor; his susceptibility touched our hearts.'

He spent his mornings at landscapes in the open air, working quickly; for he 'painted the earth-planes with the palette-knife, and sometimes even the leaves on the tree. He did not ever set to work on canvases or white panels. He daubed beforehand in strong tints any odd scrap he meant to use; he has left many sketches painted on the sections of cigar-boxes.' One afternoon he went out with Corot, who had come to lunch, to sketch in the forest of Marly. Corot looked around quite a while before he settled on a view to paint; Courbet set himself wherever he happened to be. 'Where I place myself is all the same to me. Any location is good as long as I have nature before my eyes.'[12] There was an element of truth in his claim; but in fact he did care what he painted, and was attracted by particular sorts of scenery. And he didn't keep at all slavishly to what was before him. His act and comment was rather a manifesto; he had broken from the conventional views as to what constituted a paintable motive; he could, if put to it, find valuable elements of colour and structure in any aspect of nature.

This clear country, with effaced contrasts, surprised him greatly after our mountains; he returned continually to his 'Marly', not to retouch them, but to make others of them, with a remarkable persistence and a similar facility. I recall that one day, before the slope with the hillock of Marcil rising beyond, he pointed out a distant object, commenting, 'Look down there, what I've just done! I haven't the least idea what it is.'

It was a certain greyish block, which, at the distance, I couldn't define; but, turning my eyes on the canvas, I saw it was a mass of faggots. 'I didn't need to know it', he said. 'I put down what I saw without considering what it was.' Then, drawing back before his picture, he added, 'Yes, it's a fact, it was faggots.' – I guarantee that he was sincere, sharing my own nature, which was as *montagnard* as he.

Wey says that it was Corot who inspired his skies. One morning he painted on a very small canvas a wooded hillock in a rainy atmosphere. 'Mme Wey was convalescing after a long illness: it was this somewhat sad memory he wanted to set down. A miniature of this sort with broad brushwork is, in his work as in its manner, a unique piece.'

On 13 September Courbet was presented with his medal in the hall of the Orangerie at the Louvre by the Prince-President, the nephew of Napoleon I, who had been elected president for four years in December 1848.[13] In October he went off to Ornans to be lavishly welcomed for his success. From Besançon he continued on foot, escorted by friends who came to meet him on the road. That night, after the dinner at the Courbet house, Promayet carried out an impromptu serenade outside the windows, playing music which he had composed for lyrics by Courbet. The latter gave a speech of thanks and invited the musicians inside. They all sang and danced till 5 a.m.[14] 'I leave you to imagine', he told Wey, 'how, many people I had to embrace and how many compliments I had to accept all over the town. It seems I've brought great honour to Ornans.'

He was determined to follow up the *Afterdinner* with something yet more striking; and for work at Ornans he thus needed a larger studio than the family-house could provide. His mother had inherited from her father two houses at Ornans: the one where Gustave was born, another near the old gate, on the road leading to the quarter of the Îles-Basses, which included a big two-storey structure where laundry was hung out to dry. He persuaded his father to turn this structure into a studio. He had a big window opened in the north side and painted the walls greenish yellow and dark red; the window-embrasures were white, the ceiling and upper fourth of the walls sky-blue; on the blue he painted swallows in flight. Thus he could feel even in the studio that he was under the open sky: 'That makes a fantastic effect.'[15]

He had found the idea for his next big work, which was to be ten feet wide, more than seven high. A letter to Wey told the story:

As I had taken our carriage and was driving on the way to the Château at St-Denis to paint a landscape; near Maisières, I stopped to consider two men breaking stones on the highway. It's rare to meet the most complete expression of poverty, so an idea for a picture came to me on the spot. I made an appointment with them at my studio for the next day, and since then I've been working on the picture. It's of the same size as *Evening at Ornans*. Would you like me to give you a description? On the one side is an old man, seventy, bent over his task, sledge-hammer in air, he is tanned by the sun, his head shaded by a straw hat; his trousers of poor material are all patched; in the cracked sabots torn stockings, once blue, show his bare heels.

On the other side is a young fellow with dusty head and swarthy skin; his back and arms show through the holes in his filthy tattered shirt; one leather brace holds up the remnant of his trousers, and his leather boots, caked with mud, gape dismally in many places. The old man is kneeling; the young one stands behind him, holding a basket of broken rock. Alas, in labour such as this, one's life begins that way, it ends the same way. Here and there is scattered their gear: a basket, a stretcher, a hoe, a country boiler, etc. All this happens in the blazing sun, in the open countryside; at the edge of a highway ditch; the landscape fills the canvas. Yes, M. Peisse, it's necessary to *encanailler* art. For long the painters, my contemporaries, have produced art from an idea and cartoons.[16]

In a novel, *Biez de Serine*, which Wey wrote soon after this, Courbet's account of the stone-breakers is used, almost word for word. That such a fastidious character as Wey should use thus the exact phrases of Courbet hardly fits in with the efforts to depict the latter as anti-literary, hating anything to do with the word. Indeed one striking thing about Courbet is the fullness of his correspondence; if he isn't reporting at length to the family, he writes detailed accounts of his work and activity to the person who is most in his thoughts at the time: Wey, Champfleury, Bruyas, Castagnary.[17]

He posed the two models separately. The old man, Gagey, had spent his whole life on the roads around Ornans, and was a well-known character. The painting was much admired by local folk, who, according to Proudhon, proposed to buy and hang it over the altar in the parish church, as it pointed so strong a moral. That was no doubt a tale told him by Courbet, based on some semi-jesting remarks made by friends. Proudhon later also called it the first socialist picture ever painted.

Others before Courbet have attempted socialist painting and have not succeeded. That was because the wish was not enough; one had to be an artist. . . . *The Stone-Breakers* is a satire on our industrial civilisation, which continually invents wonderful machines to perform all kinds of labour . . . yet is unable to liberate man from the most backbreaking toil.[18]

We must leave for the moment the full discussion of the relation of Courbet's socialism and his art; but we may note that most of the arguments at the time, and indeed most of those since, have been on a low level of understanding. It has too often been assumed that a socialist painting means a piece of obvious propaganda approximating to a political cartoon. The question is rather whether Courbet's art was affected in any essential way by his socialist convictions and whether he would have painted in much the same way if he had merely carried on in a vague general form his independent ethic. Here we may cite the exchange between him and Ideville in 1866: Ideville asked, 'Did you mean to make a social protest out of those two men bent under the inexorable compulsion of toil?' 'I see in them, on the contrary, a poem of gentle resignation, and they inspire in me a feeling of pity.' Courbet answered, 'But that pity springs from the injustice, and that is how I stirred up, not deliberately, but simply by painting what I saw, what they call the social question.' He means that he has not invented or exaggerated anything for partisan purposes; he has set down, as truly as he could, the things he saw. Yet the desire to paint that patch of roadway with its two stone-breakers came originally from his feeling of the completeness with which they summed up injustice. His remarks during the work on the canvas to Wey and Champfleury show that he particularly felt this emotion because of the way in which the working-together of the old man and the youth expressed the cycle of unending misery that the system around him perpetuated. He was painting not two workers doing a specially back-breaking job and getting a poor reward for it, but the whole endless repetition of hopeless toil among large sections of his people, the whole endless cycle of exploitation. The strength and fullness with which he felt the nature of the image was determined by the movement to socialism which was going on inside him.[19]

As soon as he had finished *The Stone-Breakers* he began on a yet more ambitious and exacting work, *The Burial at Ornans*; and then, for the rest of his stay at Ornans, he worked on another big canvas, *The Return from the Fair*.

The death of his grandfather in 1848, at the age of 81, so soon after the death of his wife had deeply moved Courbet; the death of the veteran of 1793 in the revolutionary year of 1848 must have also had its symbolic touch for him. Besides, had he not witnessed the death of one form of society and the advent of another? and in the period of change, many deaths? The relation of life and death had been powerfully raised in his mind. From the endless cycle of youth-age, victim following on victim, in *The Stone-Breakers*, he came to the point of break. The cycles, the patterns of change went on, but the individual death was irrevocable. So the idea of the *Burial* came to him.

He decided on a vast canvas in which all the mourners and officiants connected with the burial would be shown; in the end there were more than forty life-sized figures. His family and its friends were well represented. At the extreme left the old man is grandfather Oudot adapted from a portrait of him made in 1844. Next come four men carrying the pall-covered coffin; they turn their faces away from the smell of the corpse. They are *père* Crevot, Alphonse Promayet, Etienne Nodier, Alphonse Bon; above Nodier's broad-brimmed black hat is the head of Max Buchon, in front of him is the sacristan Cauchi blocking out an unidentified mourner. After the two choirboys stands the *vigneron* Colart holding up the cross. The curé Bonnet in black and silver vestments reads out the prayers for the dead;

above him is the surpliced organist, father of Promayet. Two beadles wear flaring red hats and red robes trimmed with black velvet; their reddish faces chime with their robes: Pierre Clément with bizarre fiery nose and *vigneron* J. B. Muselier. In front of them kneels on one knee the gravedigger Cassard by the open grave; his head is half-turned round, as he waits, listening to the curé; at the head of the grave is a skull he has turned up. The central group consists of Sage (profile with tall hat); the mayor's deputy, Tony Marlet, in front of his elder brother Adolphe; Bertin with handkerchief to face; and to his rear Régis Courbet in the tall hat. More to the foreground stand the notary and deputy J. P., Proudhon (cousin of the philosopher), whose central position and formal dress suggest the chief mourner; the bulky mayor, Prosper Teste de Sagey, and two veterans of 1793, Cardet and Secrétan, in old-fashioned clothes. Then comes the group of women on the right. Above the mayor in black hood is Joséphine Bocquet, drying her tears; one of the women in big white bonnets is Promayet's mother; on the extreme right Mme Courbet holds the hand of the mayor's little daughter. On the side away from the two veterans are the three Courbet girls: Juliette pressing a handkerchief to her mouth, Zoé hiding her face, Zélie in profile. Others of the women are not identified but include Célestine Garmont, Félicité Bon, and Gagey's wife.[20]

Along the back run level lines of cliffs characteristic of the area, the Roche du Mont and the Roche du Château, with a gap over the priest and beadles into which the staff of the Cross reaches. A dull heavy sky weighs down over all. The great weight of the blacks in the rows of people, hardly affected by the reds and whites, seems to bear everyone down, to lock them in the grief of the shared occasion. Well might Manet joke that here the whole world is buried, even the horizon is buried ten feet deep; and the caricaturists depict the scene as a solid blackness lighted only by the burning noses of the beadles and a white toy-dog. Though some mourners stand behind others, the primary effect is of a row of figures more or less on the same level. Mary Cassatt, on seeing the work, cried out, 'Why, it's Greek!' We are reminded of the way in which David was attacked for the same sort of effect in a less drastic way and the suggestion that by keeping the heads thus at the same level the artist was setting out a democratic view in place of an hierarchical one. (We noted the frieze-row in Baud's painting of his pupils.) This frieze-equality of the figures is not without its reference to the levelling power of death, the democracy of the grave. But we shall deal more fully with the work's significance in a moment.[21] There were Flemish elements, as well as Spanish, in the work's realism; but we do not need to turn to the paintings of Companies by Hals, van der Helst and Rembrandt for the inspiration.

In completing it, Courbet had to solve many practical problems. The size was 23 feet long, 11 feet high; and the studio was only about 16 feet longer than the canvas. Also it was only 14 feet wide. There was little room in which to muster the models; Courbet painted them one at a time. Since winning his medal, it was easy for him to get local folk to pose for him. He wrote to Champfleury:

Here models are to be had for the asking; everyone wants to appear in the *Burial*; I'll never be able to satisfy them all; I'll make plenty of enemies. Those who've already posed are the mayor who weighs 400, the curé, the J.P., the cross-bearer, the notary, Marlet the deputy, my friends, my father, the choirboys, the gravedigger, two veterans of the Revolution 1793 in their clothes of that time, a dog, the corpse and the coffin-bearers, the beadles – one of them has a nose like a cherry, but five thumbs long and thick in proportion – my sisters, other women, etc. I'd hoped to pass over the two precentors of the parish, but it couldn't be done. I was warned they felt upset as the only church-persons I hadn't 'taken'. They complained bitterly, saying they hadn't done me any harm and didn't deserve such an affront. Only a madman could work under the conditions in which I find myself. I am working blindly, I've got no room to step back. Will I never be installed as I should be? As things are, I'm just about to finish fifty lifesized figures with a background of landscape and sky on a canvas 20 feet long and 6 high; it's enough to kill one; you must gather that I haven't had much sleep.[22]

Luckily we have an important document telling us what was in his mind at this time. This was the *annonce* composed by Max Buchon to publicise the exhibitions which Courbet put on at Besançon in May and at Dijon in July 1850. The exhibitions themselves showed how he felt about his new paintings; they represented a sort of appeal to the people ahead of the Salon, and he felt very strongly about them. In asking Buchon to write the *annonce*, he must have known that his friend would sum up what they had said about the paintings in their discussions; and so, though the particular phrases may be Buchon's own way of interpreting those discussions, the general points must refer to what Courbet himself felt. We happen to have a letter from Courbet to Buchon (probably of 1851) in which he says, 'I felicitate you on your article, I am deeply grateful to to you for it, it perfectly reflects the nature of my talent and it belongs to that art I love so much.' He may be referring to the *annonce* or to the notice of the *Return from the Fair* in *L'Impartial de Besançon* on 17 January 1851; but in any event it testifies to the closeness of thought between the two friends at this time (as indeed at all times). Buchon revised the text of the *annonce* for Dijon, presumably after he and Courbet had seen and estimated the effect of the works on the people at Besançon. After a few remarks about Courbet and his successes, he turns to the pictures.

The *Stone-Breakers* is a picture of two lifesize persons, a child and an old man, the alpha and the omega, the dawn and the dusk of this life of convicts. A poor young fellow, of twelve to fifteen years, with shorn head, scurfy and stupid, as poverty too often fashions the children of the poor; a lad of fifteen years lifts up with effort a huge basket of stones ready to be measured or powdered on the road; shirt in rags, trousers held up by a trace of rope, patched at the knees, torn at the ends and tattered everywhere; shoes red with use, trodden at heel, twisted and lamentable, like those of such and such a poor man of your knowledge: there is the child.

On the right comes the poor breaker, in old sabots bound with copper, in old hat of straw worn by time, rain, sun and dust, his knees tremulous on a pad of straw, and raising a smasher-hammer with all the automatic precision given by long habit, but also with all the feebleness that such an age suggests. Amid so much hardship, however, the physiognomy remains tranquil, sympathetic, and resigned. In his waistcoat pocket doesn't he have, poor old fellow, his old snuffbox of horn rimmed with copper, with which he offers, when he wishes, the *pinch* of friendship to all the comers and goers who cross his way on the road, his domain?

The soup-pot is there always ready, with the spoon, the basket, the crust of black bread.

And this man is there always to lift his goodnatured club; always, from the New Year up to St Sylvestre's Day; always, to smooth out the way for passing humanity, to earn enough to save him from starving to death; and yet this man, who is not at all an imagination of the painter, this man who really lives in flesh and bones at Ornans, just as you see him there, this man with his old age, his crude labour, with his poverty and his gentle old-man's face, this man is not yet the last word in human distress. If the poor devil had the least thought of turning to the left [*au rouge*], he could be feared, denounced, expelled, destituted. Just ask M. the Prefect.[23]

The text here is that of Dijon; in the earliest text the Prefect was specified 'of the Jura', and a weaker phrase was used at the end of the first sentence: 'human life' instead of 'convicts' – the word is better in French, 'forçats', suggesting slave-labour. Turning 'au rouge' means turning into a socialist or a *montagnard* republican. Bouchon continues:

From this page, which, to be so gripping, needed only to remain imperturbably sincere and faithful: from this page, before which one feels so distanced from all whining tendencies and from all melodramatic stage-tricks, let us pass to the principal piece of M. Courbet this year: *A Burial at Ornans* . . .

For him who, like ourselves, has the honour of knowing a little this good population of Ornans, it is at first a meeting with a naïve enough effect – this picture where are grouped, aligned, and disposed in rows these figures that you have just saluted a moment ago in the street and who are gathered together there by the master's brush in so natural a way, with such intelligence and *bonhomie*. M. the curé, M. the mayor, M. the deputy, nothing is lacking. They are there, I say, to the number of fifty, all in their own character, in their traditional deportment, in their specific preoccupations.

And yet, when your eyes have finished running through this vast composition, they come down on the gravedigger, who is there, knees on the earth, on the edge of the grave into which he is going to make the corpse descend, I don't know what austere thought detaches itself suddenly from that gaping grave, flashes like a lightning over these physiognomies, and, thanks to the great landscape distances, those mournful and greyish skies and the air of contemplation that hovers over everything, makes it into a veritable synthesis of human life.

Formerly, in the old macabre dances, it was Death personified who made kings, popes, emperors, the great ones of the earth, the oppressors of the poor, dance, whether they liked or not.

M. Courbet seems to us to have gained, with his gravedigger, an effect quite as energetic and significant, without having in the least departed from his complete realism, which is henceforth as indispensable in painting as in politics, and which the good women of Ornans appreciate in anticipation, just as the *Presse* and the *National* will be able to do at the forthcoming Exposition.

These paragraphs about the old Dance of Death do not appear in the Besançon text. Either Buchon had not yet fully thought out the logic of his interpretation of the gravedigger, or he and Courbet did not want to define the local bourgeoisie (who include Régis Courbet) as oppressors who would in due time be made to dance to the gravedigger's tune. Not that the words would have lacked considerable support in Besançon, where the workers of the northern parts of the city, mainly *agriculteurs*, gave Louis Napoleon a violent reception when he visited the town this very year, 1850. Ornans on the other hand was largely conservative, always rallying behind the Party of Order at elections.

At bottom, this man, this gravedigger, indicates nothing spiteful in his robust build. He also is on his knees in this immense gathering, and yet, look! he alone carries his head high, he alone commands.

Tomorrow, this man who is in the vigour of his years will return calmly to his *vigneron's* hut, which he has left yesterday; today only he feels himself the final link of things here below, the gate-keeper of another world.

And yet, must we say it? across the oppression into which his vague contemplation throws you, you return involuntarily, doubtless by thought of compensation, to our poor breaker of stones, of whom this gravedigger could well be, in the painter's mind, only the psychological antithesis, the counterweight; I should almost say, the avenger.

This paragraph about the avenger also did not appear in the Besançon text. Buchon is saying that the picture defines what Blake would call a Last Judgment in which a reversal of values will come about; the first will be the last, and the last first. The old labourer bent on his knee has turned into the stalwart worker who rests on his knee beside the grave, which becomes the grave of all the oppressors. We may note that his white sleeves provide a dominant note in the picture's centre, one arm giving a straight line that parallels the cross-staff, the other bent in a line that leads up to the image of Christ. The cross-staff with its Christ is the only thing that breaks the heavy down-pressing weight of colour and form. It is paired off on the other side of the gravedigger by the two revolutionary veterans, who could not but have been used by Courbet to represent all that his grandfather had meant for him. The one at the front, whose full body we see in detached action – unlike the bourgeois proper, who are merged in a black mass – has lighter-coloured garments, which again distinguish him from the bourgeois black. Thus, the gravedigger, the Christ of resurrection, and the revolutionary veteran stand out as expressing something lost or unknown to the officiants and the mourning bourgeoisie.

In Buchon's choice of the Dance of Death to bring out the popular basis and the revolutionary significance of the painting, there was perhaps a recollection of Courbet's participation in the Carnival at Ornans while he was at work on the canvas. The connection of the ancient revelry that followed on the celebration of Christ's death-and-resurrection and the dearth-days of Lent, with the painter of the collective death-rite, may have helped to make Buchon think of Courbet, and so the gravedigger, as a figure of death–rebirth. For the idea of the socialist confronting the upholders of the class-world as the living man confronting the dead, Courbet may well have had in mind at least the title of a work by his compatriot Considérant: *Socialism before the Old World or the Living before the Dead* (1838) – the living man (singular) before the dead (plural).

The idea of a Dance of Death in connection with revolutionary 1848 may well have been suggested to Buchon and Courbet by the Dance-of-Death woodcuts by the German artist Rethel (issued in 1849), which sought to show the futility, the disaster, of all revolutionary activity. Champfleury ended his *Histoire de l'imagerie populaire* with an account of them; Buchon with his keen interest in German culture may have known them soon after their publication. He and Courbet would have disliked the ideas of Rethel but may have been struck by his revival of the medieval theme.

It is unlikely that Courbet began the picture with anything like the intentions that Buchon finds in it; but that does not mean that Buchon is wrong. Starting with the desire to do a large-scale depiction of common life, with the hopes and disasters of the 1848 revolutions at the back of his mind, and with the ghosts of his grandparents haunting him, he found himself shaping the picture, and colouring it, with a multiple set of meanings. That was the way he always worked. He found the significance of his material by penetrating ever deeper into it, not by setting out with an already-defined idea which he proceeded to interpret or express. His whole concept of realism implied this line of approach and development.

We may say that his return to Ornans in 1850, with the long stay in which he produced such decisive works, was a return to the family, a return to roots. He had made such visits before, and would make them again; but this one had a special force behind it: the experiences of 1848, the quest for the realist themes that would be truly of his age, the struggle to repudiate the last elements of romanticism, to overcome the anguish which his conflicts with Virginie Binet were causing him. He wanted to have an end of all uncertainties and probings; to find himself by finding his full expression in art, to stand at last wholly on his own feet. In the *Afterdinner* he had announced the return to the family in a minor key, intimate, richly personal; now from the drowsy kitchen of contentment, lulled with familiar music, he had to break out into the wider world. He found a secure point in *The Stone-Breakers*, the picture of the unending cycle of toil. But that cycle was just what he wanted to break, so that men might move into a fuller life, a life of freedom and brotherhood. The toilers were held to their task by invisible forces, those of power and money, which had their seat outside them; those forces entered into everyone in varying degrees and in criss-crossing entanglements. The united family was real and he could not live without it; but the family was also rent by the forces that rent society; it was part of society. In the *Burial* we see the Courbet family both united in a shared act of grief, a rite of the Church, and broken up inside the rural bourgeoisie of which it is a part. And this wider grouping is in turn rent by social differentiations, by the network ensnaring both exploiter and exploited. And so the painting gradually evolved into the Last Judgment that Buchon found in it. Not 'deliberately', as Courbet said to Ideville about *The Stone-breakers*, 'but simply by painting what I saw'. For 'what he saw' was not only the figures or things before him, but also their *social nature*, their relationship to one another in the full context of the invisible forces. What probably began in his mind as a picture of social concord, an extension of the *After-dinner* to take in friends and acquaintances on an important occasion, ended as a picture of the processes of differentiation and conflict inside the rural population – all because of 'what he saw'.[24]

The exclusiveness of the event intrudes on what was meant to express an all-inclusive gathering. Not all men could afford a proper funeral. In the years 1839–47, 78.8 per cent of Parisians were dumped when dead in the *fosse commune*; and the refusal of the Paris clergy to administer their rites to men who had not received extreme unction sparked off popular uprisings in Paris on several occasions. When we read of the peasant hatred of the black-clad bourgeoisie in these years, the massed blacks of Courbet's painting take on a new significance. In 1849 the Prefect of the Drôme reported:

The bourgeoisie having sold its lands and become creditors of the peasants, the demolishers [the republican and socialist propagandists] have made the bourgeois suspect to the peasants, because they have said to them that the bourgeois do all they can to stop the peasant from being able to free himself, so that they can keep him in some sort of servitude. Thus it is that a war has been declared by the *veste* on the *habit*[25]

– a war of the peasant short-jacket on the tailored dark clothes of the bourgeois. Durrieux in 1865 wrote that one of the principal traits of the peasant is to be found in the fact that 'black clothes are an enemy for the man of the fields'. It has been well remarked:

Courbet's black is not the old drama of light and shade from which figures emerge, or by which they are swallowed; the black and the descriptive colour of hands and faces exist in an unstable equilibrium, since one is the *matter* to the other. In spite of Courbet's 1847 visit to Holland, and the depth of his enthusiasm for Rembrandt, the drama is not in the ebb or flow of light, or a sudden mimetic leap of space: Courbet's achievement was to assimilate Rembrandt's handling to a totally different attitude to form. The drama in a Courbet of this period is in the interplay between the basic anonymity of matter and the perceived individuality of another person or even another thing.

What is important is that, in the *Burial*, ground and image are in conflict – each is given an equal and opposite pictorial weight. A head in the *Burial* exists clearly against the dense blackness of the bodies, and yet by the very method of painting we feel the way in which the blackness informs and defines it. This blackness is also its terror. At this point materiality is not neutral in Courbet; it is taken as the *essential*, with a kind of horror. This may be the reason why the handkerchief which masks the face of Courbet's sister Zoé is so disturbing: underneath the handkerchief, instead of an imaginable face and features, is blackness, and that is both 'matter of fact' and also terrible. Elsewhere in the picture the conflict of matter and individuality, anonymous community and asserted 'personality' reaches no such conclusion. As a whole, the conflict is unresolved. (CLARK) [26]

But Buchon might reply that it is indeed resolved in the gravedigger with his assured personality: that is, his assured social role (as leveller, commander, avenger). Bourgeois individuality evokes unresolved conflicts, for that is its nature. Courbet is at once realistically defining his rural-bourgeois origin, his sense of community, and his achievement of individuality, his resolution of the conflict which the bourgeois cannot realise, by his emotional identification of himself with the gravedigger, the old stone-breaker transformed and given an awakening strength in place of social passivity. The two heads that successfully emerge from the black anonymity are those of the revolutionary veteran and the gravedigger. The painting thus appears as an affirmation of Courbet's family and class origins, and also of a new consciousness of struggle which transcends them. Only because of the transcending vision can he achieve the realistic definition of things as they are.

We see, then, that all Courbet's great pictures are Real Allegories as he later called *The Studio*. Buchon accepts without question that *Stone-Breakers* and *Burial* are linked in a series, and Courbet certainly thought so himself. His realism was inseparable from a philosophical understanding, in which there are many elements of Proudhon but also something that goes far beyond the concept of reconciled opposites that was central for the philosopher.

There is yet another angle from which we can approach this fruitful picture. An early stage, perhaps the first, of the Burial-image can be found in a sketch on paper, which shows the mourners in funeral procession to the cemetery; they move from right to left, and the gravedigger is on the extreme left. In the middle is, not a grave, but a flat gravestone. The landscape is vague, but seems of a rocky cliff-background. The concept here is close to a popular woodcut, *Souvenir Mortuaire*, produced about 1830 at Montbéliard, only a few miles from Ornans. This was a cut which the peasants stuck up on the wall after a funeral and inscribed with the dead person's name. Courbet would certainly have encountered it, perhaps many times. It depicted the mourners entering the cemetery from the right, with the gravedigger on the extreme left and an acolyte lifting the cross above the skyline at his side; gravestones lie in the foreground. The coffin and its bearers hold the main part of the composition, with an open grave before them. The whole is enclosed within the cemetery walls, of which we see three sides in naïve perspective, with some mountains looming up at the back. In Courbet's painting the gravedigger, not the dead man, has become the central point of interest; and the mourners are arranged so that the youngest is on the extreme right and the oldest, the revolutionary veterans, nearest to the grave. This notion of age-gradations has also its echo in popular prints. 'Les Degrés des Ages' ('the Steps of Life') was a common theme, with the mourners set in their age-grades in a semi-circle round the scene of burial. Before the French Revolution the central space was filled with a Last Judgment; it was at times later given more secular emblems; a hearse, a rose-bush, a sheaf, a vine (plants at the various stages of the year's growth).

The importance of these relations between the painting and the prints is that the deliberacy of the setting of the gravedigger in the centre is established; the painting shows a deep rethinking of the whole motive after the first sketch with its similarity to the print. And secondly we find a definite link of the theme in the popular mind with the Last Judgment and with imagery of rebirth that is not specifically Christian.

An amusing link of the officiants of funerals with such imagery occurs in Champfleury's *Les Excentriques* (1852). He tells how Bug-Jugal leads his fellow *croque-morts* (undertakers' mutes) to pay a tribute to the bizarre poet Pétrus Borel; and he ends his sketch:

He sees nature only across a sepulchral prism. He was looking at a plantation of young trees that workers were making on the boulevard d'Enfer [Hell]. 'Those trees there,' he said, 'they're coffins sprouting.'

With the impetus that Courbet had now gained he started on a fourth large work, *The Peasants of Flagey Returning from the Fair of Salins*. When it was shown, Geoffroy jeered at the precision of the title: 'It's a question of the peasants of Flagey in the Doubs, and not of Pontoise.' Pontoise had long been a catchword in Paris for a specially bumpkin place. But Courbet's point was precisely that the Flagey peasants were not those of Pontoise or anywhere else; they were first of all themselves, and only when realised in their particularity could they be generalised as peasants. In the picture we see some peasants with cattle and loads passing along the Ornans highway, on top of the Mont des Feuilles, in a mixed group. Régis Courbet dominates the composition, with his tall hat over his swathed head like a sort of bourgeois crown strongly outlined against the glowing sunset-sky. At his side a rider of lesser status is trying with affable earnestness to gain his attention; but Régis sits rather stiffly uninterested, with his long whip sticking up like his sceptre of power, and stares ahead. Behind, two stolid women march along abreast like some kind of attendants, one leading a cow, the other (Josette d'Arbon) with a basket on her head. A young farmhand walks to the rear of two oxen in the foreground, who seem to have been bought cheap for fattening up. On the right, a man with an oil-keg on his back and a long baggy umbrella in his hand cuts across the highway verge, holding the cord of a lank pig who browses ahead of him. Here, in a much smaller grouping, we have the mixture of community and differentiation that we found in the *Burial*, but without the apocalyptic setting. Régis is linked with the others by his blue smock, but cut off by his manner and his pompous hat. The effect of exploitation is conveyed mainly by the scraggy nature of the animals which have presumably been bought from poor peasants who could not keep them in proper condition and who would be forced to sell at low prices. We may recall the peasant insurrections of 1847 and 1848 as a result of bad harvests.

The picture which we have is not the 1850 work, which has a somewhat different arrangement. On the farther side of the man with the pig there was a woman with a basket; she appears in a caricature of the work. Our copy of 1855 has a strip fixed on the right; but this does not mean that Courbet has cut off the woman. We can see the faint shadow of a basket still left on the canvas; and radiography has revealed the woman underneath the man. Also, the caricature shows Régis over on the left, not in the central place. In making his changes Courbet may have wanted to strengthen the effect of varying social layers in the peasantry; for the new relation of the two riders does in fact do that, as does the placing of the two women behind them. He also put in a couple of walkers in the distance to give a stronger feeling of people straggling home after a strenuous market-day of haggling. In making the copy he carefully reverted to the style of the period, which he had outgrown; he used the rather hard and solid treatment of individual figures which provoked critics into seeing him as a primitive craftsman, a painter of inn-signs, a fashioner of marionettes in wood. This method came from his anxiety to depict each person as an individual complete in himself as well as a member of a social group; it was part of his anti-romantic reaction and led at times to the stressing of idiosyncrasies to a point that appeared caricature to the idealising academics just as the carefully worked out and hard-edged way in which the creases and tatters in the stone-breakers' clothes were treated could only seem a dogged clumsiness. Towards 1854 he modified this strongly sculptural approach to figures and objects; and let his natural sense of plastic form find its outlet in broadly rounded brush-strokes or in structures built up richly with the palette-knife.[27]

Especially in the early 1850s Courbet was apt to stress the rusticity of his themes by a certain deliberate naïvety of drawing and grouping: something that goes deep in the whole concept of the image (and which has links with the approach of Van Gogh).

In the *Enterrement* the stark contrast of red and black on the grey background and the clarity of the aligned, recurrent faces with their strong red tones, were conscious departures; before, he had painted similar heads in outdoor scenes with deep shadows and more subdued colours. That is why the portraits in the *Burial* gave the impression of a primitive, rustic taste. The distant heads are almost as bright as the nearer ones. They pleased the people in Ornans who had sat for them, but the Parisian critic, schooled in the contrasted, shadowy, atmospheric painting of the romantics, found the portraits not only ugly as human types, but plebeian in execution. The desire for shadow-less, unatmospheric portraits was a typical petit-bourgeois taste, like the frontality, which had been ridiculed by Monnier in his play *Le Peintre et les Bourgeois*. (SCHAPIRO)

Fournel in his *What one sees in the streets of Paris* (1858) expatiated on the petit-bourgeois fear of shadows as spots on the face. The critical attacks on Courbet for primitive and popu-lar traits thus had a considerable element of truth in them; but they lacked any under-standing of what he was aiming at or achieving. The peasant-popular character of the *Burial* was above all what horrified the Parisian bourgeoisie. (An anticipation of the line taken by Courbet appears in a milder form in David's late painting, *The Three Ladies of Ghent*, with its frontality, its comparatively unshadowed faces, its effect of gawky casualness, as if in a photo-sitting.)

While Courbet learnt much from the Spanish and Venetian masters as well as various other painters, he felt his deepest kinship with Rembrandt, whose attitude to people and reality had a fundamental effect on him. It is of interest, then, to note that Rembrandt was in his own times attacked in much the same terms as Courbet was. The following poem by Andreas Pels was cited with approval by his biographer Houbraken (1718):

> If he painted, as sometimes happened, a nude woman,
> then no Greek Venus was the model for him,
> but a washerwoman, a peat-treader from the barn;
> and Imitation of Nature he called his whim.
>
> What a loss for Art that such a masterly hand
> didn't use its native strength for finer creations.
> Who above Art in painting itself could stand?
> But the greater the talent, the larger the aberrations,
> when attached to no principles, no rules, it goes,
> and imagines that everything of itself it knows.

This tradition was still alive. L. Viardot wrote of the *Night Round*: 'The subject requires only true verity, without nobility, without ideal, without expression . . . pure and simple reproduction of material things.' All this is extremely close to what was said of Courbet.

Before we deal with the effects of the three big pictures, we must go back and examine Courbet's activities during 1850. On 12 December 1849 he had written to Wey to announce that he was sending a superb fish, 'one of the kings of La Loue', caught in the deep waters along the estate of M. Ordinaire at Maisières by Jean-Jean de la Male-Côte, professional angler. 'At this moment I'm composing my picture on the canvas. I have not only got burial clothes from the curé, I've also persuaded him to pose, as well as his *vicaire*. I've had some truly side-splitting moral and philosophic discussions with him. I've had to rest some days after the picture I've just done; my head had had enough of it.' No wonder he told Champfleury that, 'since I left you, I've already done more painting than a bishop could bless'.[28]

In March 1850 he again wrote to Wey:

I'm still working like a *nègre*. . . . I've worked with perseverance and tenacity, and now I feel more satisfied than I could have thought possible; what tires me most is that the last fortnight has been like summer, and after such a fine winter you can imagine how delightful it is to ramble amid the beauties of nature, especially in one's own country when one hasn't seen the spring for twelve years.

He also remarked:

In our over civilised society, it's necessary for me to lead a savage's life; it's necessary for me to free myself even from governments. The people enjoy my sympathies; it's necessary for me to address myself to them directly, that I may draw my knowledge from them and that they give me life. For that reason I have just now started off on the great vagabond and independent life of the bohemian.[29]

Ever since he went to Paris in 1840 he had been living that bohemian life: why does he feel the need to protest about it at this point? As we have seen, even while reasserting his sense of the family bond in the *Burial* he is expressing a new detachment. But some personal emotion is urgent behind the statement to Wey, which cannot be reduced to the deepened social sense and revolt born through 1848. We can only surmise that his long stay in Ornans is stimulating his sense of guilt for, in effect, abandoning Virginie and his son. A certain falsity also rings in his complaint that he has been long in hearing from Wey and fears that this silence comes from his failure to send condolences on the death of Wey's father. For excuse he declares that he doesn't weep for the dead, for he is sure that tears come only from egoism. The life of one man is not 'directly useful to the life of another'; it is better to make use of time than to regret the dead; sorrow is a good thing, but one must associate oneself in it by person, not by letter; if he wasn't afraid of boring Wey, he'd write four pages on it; his abstention is not the result of forgetfulness; he must be taken for what he is, not for what he should be. All this reads like the casting-about for excuses by a man with a bad conscience. We must remember that he is thus repudiating all piety to the dead with the *Burial* strong in his mind; his comments make nonsense of the painting. Some strong emotion lies behind his uneasy words, driving him to deny all bonds of responsibility, including all family bonds.

The conflicts going on between the Prince-President and the Assembly led to delays in arranging the Salon, which did not finally open till 30 October 1850. In this situation Courbet, impatient to find out the reaction to his big canvases and feeling that the moment was ripe for an appeal to the people, decided to exhibit the *Stone-breakers*, the *Burial*, and two landscapes (of which one may have been *Rocks at Ornans*), in the concert room of the Besançon market place. The mayor placed the room at his disposal gratis. Courbet placarded the town with announcements and the show opened on 7 May.[30] One-man shows were almost unknown; but it was not the rarity that made the show a success. Rather it was the considerable gossip that must have been going on for some time about Courbet, his Paris exploits, and his work at Ornans. However, he was highly pleased. The unpopularity of Louis Napoleon among the lower classes at Besançon may also have helped to swell his audience. He charged a fee of fifty centimes, and told Wey that he had done so since the

Ornans folk thought him a fool when earlier that spring he had let them in free to see the works displayed in the seminary chapel, 'which proves it's silly to have a kind heart, for it merely deprives one of funds without enriching others in spirit or purse. To be free, people want to pay, so that their judgment won't be warped by gratitude; they are right. I want to learn and so I'll be so grasping that I'll give everyone the right to tell me the most cruel truths.'[31] Again he argues his case over-vehemently. To Max Buchon he wrote about the show: 'There is *no retouching* to be done; I must admit I do not go in much for retouching. . . .' Like his remark about not choosing what he painted, this statement has a broad truth about his method and aims; but is not strictly correct.[32] Perhaps for cheapness, perhaps to stress the specific local quality of the *Burial*, he had had the canvas put in a frame made of plain boards of local fir.

He did not repeat his success at Dijon. The political crisis was worsening; troops were billeted in public buildings; and he could not find a suitable hall. He was forced to rent, for ten francs a day, a room in a house with a café on the ground floor. Dijon was torn by factions, the Reds and the Whites; and the café belonged to a radical. There seems to have been no reaction at all to the exhibition, but the cause for this was no doubt the distractions of the political conflict. Courbet failed to cover his expenses; he closed the show and went off to Paris in early August. A letter gave instructions for a new big canvas to be got ready.[33] As soon as he arrived, artists 'of all sorts' as well as men of the world came to see his new works and agreed they'd have a big effect on the Salon. 'Their fame runs through all Paris; wherever I go, people speak of me.'

He had just painted a picture, one metre square, 'the historical portrait of an eccentric man of our time, the Apostle Jean Journet. Journet is so well known in Paris that it'd be necessary to put a policeman by this picture during the exposition.' Champfleury knew Journet, and with his interest in odd characters, especially those who had links with popular culture in some form or another, he wrote an account of him in *Les Excentriques*. Born at Carcassonne in 1799, Journet became entangled in insurrectionary movements in 1819 and fled to Spain. Returning, he worked as a chemist at Limoux near his home town; then he joined the disciples of Fourier (who had preached the setting up of communistic colonies or phalansteries) and decided to popularise the Fourierist theories. As the Apostle for Universal Harmony, he began his evangelising in Paris. He attracted attention on 8 March 1841 at the Opéra, where *Robert le Diable* was being played, by flooding the place with pamphlets. Arrested and brought before the police commissioner, he explained his motive:

the irresistible need to announce to the world in general and to the rich in particular the Advent of the Law of Justice and Truth, and the hope that among so many individuals, society's élite, there would be some who'd deign to turn aside a moment to judge, with knowledge of the case, if that event, miraculous as it might seem, is found really justified by the works of the immortal Fourier.

He was sent on to the prefect of police, who committed him to a lunatic asylum, the Bicêtre. 'Third Division Third Room, Tenth Bed, and that Thirty-Three years after the appearance of the Theory of the Four Movements: I was taken into a dormitory occupied by a hundred madmen; I was completely stripped of my clothes, which were replaced by garments very old but very appropriate.' The doctor recognised him as a Fourierist, but diagnosed mono-mania of grandeur. The cure was 'three-hour baths, aspersion of cold water on the head'; his beard was shaven. However, he was put in the *admission*, a tree-planted court with small lodges for single persons; but the doctor, angered by a discussion on poetry in which he was told he knew nothing about it, had all paper, ink and pens, as well as tobacco, taken from him; instead Journet was prescribed assafetida to drive out his socialism. He grew weak, but some friends intervened, and M. de Montgolfier got him out.

Thereafter he was the centre of one strange encounter after another. For a while he took part in the phalanstery set up by John Young and Mme Gati de Gramont with an eclectic set of ideas from Saint-Simon, Babœuf, Restif de la Bretonne, Campanella. Then he decided to attack the leading figures in the cultural world as well as ministers. Many received him and listened, though he complained that he had called twenty times in vain on George Sand. He felt there was hope in Hugo; Lamartine he accused of smugness and hypocrisy; he told the Academy, 'You sleep, slack sentinels'. His words to Lamartine are characteristic of his message:

Poet, you have eyes for seeing nothing. The cry of children, the groans of the aged find you deaf. The tears of woman, the despair of man find you blind. Poet, down with hypocrisy. Enough of religious pretence. The farce is played out. Nebulous star, it must be eclipsed. The sun of intelligence floods the horizon. The Last Judgment will precede the social resurrection. All is stirred, all is agitated, all prepared; future, future. God enlighten you!

Courbet's strong response to such a character, with his prophecy of an impending Last Judgment in the Blakean sense, supports the interpretation we have made of the *Burial*.

Journet went on upsetting various gatherings. He scared Hugo's guests and told the poet, 'Fifteen days of strong and conscientious study and you will see. But please don't forget the apostle when, saintly Sibylline, you fulminate the Song of Songs. I love you.' At Toulouse his diatribes in a café upset the domino-players and he was carried to the jail called the Capitole by four men and a corporal. But the prefect, to whom Fourierists appealed, freed him on condition that he preached no more. So Journet went to Montpellier and assailed the bishop, walking into an ecclesiastical gathering with the chant:

Sacrilegious Levites, wake today!
Incense-drunken, sunken in purple, held fast,
The Holy Spirit has bared your snares, I say,
And whited sepulchres will be cleansed at last.

And so on. In Belgium he called on the great and the little, importuning the Queen. Back in Paris, he rejoined his family and took work as a florist, then he was off again. At the Congress of Peace on 21 August 1849 he rose after Hugo had scarcely finished his opening remarks. 'I ask the floor for an important communication. It is not enough to give fine speeches; we must seek the means of arriving at our desires. . . . I know that my position is terrible and I have need of your encouragements. Encourage me. Encourage me.' He asked who Christ was. 'The son of a carpenter. Ah, well, in what position do I find myself? We know nothing of it. Perhaps we'll know it later on.' Striking his chest, he raised his eyes to the skies. 'I am on the cross, and if I had the happiness to rouse your sympathies . . .' Someone shouted for him to expound his idea. 'My idea, I have a hundred thousand ideas. I'd have betrayed my apostolic mission if I'd neglected to announce to you the supreme event. Reflect on what I've said, and you'll soon see the grateful Universe rise up to shout Universal Peace, Universal Association, Universal Harmony.' He stepped down from the tribunal and went out.

Champfleury says that in 1847 he applied at the Odéon for a part as a tragic actor and was rejected. 'His project was to make his debut in Paris, gain the great success of which he felt certain, then carry into the provinces the word of Racine and Fourier. He wanted with the help of *Britannicus* to put over the Theory of the Four Movements.' He did at last somehow get together a troop of actors at the Châteleine; but the audience found his southern accent so comical that the play could not proceed after the first act. He also failed to recruit sub-apostles; the only one he found broke away after a while and founded a rival utopia. His difference with the Fourierists lay largely in his demand for immediate results; they were ready to rely on a slow change. He had a vast treasury of abuse: Cosmopolitan Vampire, Patron of Impiety, Omniarch of Rebuttal, Abortion of Science, Gulf of Humanity, Hardened Fascinator, Subversive Magnetiser, Material Mercantiser, Pygmy of Perversity, Beggarly Fetish, Pimp of Proserpine, Omnivorous Omniarch, Fascinating Serpent. 'The vertigo increases from hour to hour. The abyss awaits all its prey. The cataclysm is imminent. It is imminent and not one of you does not know it.' A chaste man, he was once terrified when Champfleury and Murger got a tart (Musetta of the *Vie de Bohème*) to sit on his lap; he dropped her on the floor and fled.[34]

When Courbet proclaimed himself to Wey as a follower of the savage's life of vagabondage, he was in fact thinking of men like Journet. Flora Tristan likewise decided on the trek across France that ended in her death. She was propaganding for the Union Ouvrière. Looking out from her window at the towers of Saint-Sulpice, she had meditated: 'One solitary priest had made it his mission in life to have that church built. He had gone on foot, begging from door to door to gather the necessary money. Could I not follow his example?'[35] On a broader scale, the cult of nature was leading to much hiking on foot. Courbet and Buchon were great walkers.

Courbet's response to popular art appeared further in the lithograph he made, which showed the Fourierist missionary setting out to warn the world of the coming Last Judgment, staff in hand, hung with his satchels of pamphlets and spare clothes: *the Apostle Jean Journet setting out for the Conquest of Universal Harmony*. The lithograph is surrounded on three sides by a *Complainte*, the author of which is unknown.

> Soon, apostle bold and tried,
> Myself I guide

By truth's strong torch; and see,
I plunge, fall flat in mire
    In my desire
To save humanity. . . .

God gives me confidence
    And I advance
To the Infernal City at last,
The modern Babylon,
    The cavern wan,
Evil's volcano-blast.

What in this filth have I
    Seen mingled lie,
Where crimes in myriads swell,
The gulf of poverty,
    Of wrath, I see
And recognise as Hell.

I've seen this base example,
    The fine-built Temple
Invaded by the thieves . . . [36]

Here is the Baudelairean vision at the popular level; and again, looking back, we feel more than ever that the space of the *Burial* is this *caverne* of the death of man, presided over by the black and pompous bourgeoisie, out of which, in a flash of judgment – the austere thought detaching itself from the gaping grave to play like lightning over the faces, in Buchon's phrase – we see also the possibility of new systems, new values.

The verse-framed lithograph belonged to the broadside tradition of the early nineteenth century; we may especially compare the religious broadsides of the pilgrim St-Jacques. It was printed by Vion, 27 rue St-Jacques, Paris – a street that since the seventeenth century had been one of the main centres for turning out popular imagery. Its copper engravings provided the models for many woodcuts. In the second third of the nineteenth century it became the centre for a semi-popular lithographic imagery. It is also of interest that the painting of Journet (now lost) belonged to J. P. Mazaroz, who came from Lons-le-Saunier and was a friend of Courbet; he was well known for his art-furniture and his radical ideas; he made some furniture for Courbet. His father, a bookbinder, had made popular images at Lons in the early part of the century.

In the autumn of 1850 Courbet was introduced to Berlioz. Wey wanted him to show some portraits of famous persons, and he thought Berlioz a good choice, 'a controversial figure, in perpetual struggle' like Courbet himself. So he pleaded with Berlioz, whom he knew well.

The illustrious composer only understood it was a chance of doing a service to a man of merit who found obstacles in his road; and a day was fixed. It was less by his art than by music that the painter damaged himself. He had a mania for singing songs in his own way, without rhyming the words or keeping any rhythm as another example of his disregard. It was the vilest and most incoherent prose a shepherd could have devised. These formless melodies he presumed to bawl out to Hector Berlioz while he painted. At first Berlioz thought he was being made fun of; then, seeing that this was not the case, he took Courbet for an idiot. And as he understood absolutely nothing about painting, he let himself be convinced by his wife (the second) that the portrait was worthless, that she knew far more of the matter than I, as she had made little pencil-drawings of landscapes and miniature portraits of finesse, of finish!

These poor folk thus ended by refusing a head offered as a pure gift. This portrait has now been seen by all and exhibited everywhere; it's the best portrait by Courbet, the best of Berlioz.[37]

Courbet didn't want to do the framing, so Wey did it for him. Courbet then offered him the work, but Wey had scruples in accepting it, so it was given to Chenavard, an odd forceful character, a follower of Comte, who denounced colour in art and whom Courbet had probably met in 1848–9.[38] Other works, probably of 1850, are the *Head of a Woman* and *Village-Girl with Goat*, both of which show his liking for fleshy faces and plump bodies. The more plastic handling and the chiaroscuro, as well as the pastoral feeling of the second canvas, suggest a somewhat earlier date; but it is possible that Courbet might paint in this style with smaller works, while turning to comparatively hard and cut-out forms for his big works with popular and political motives.[39]

The long-deferred Salon had two juries. The exhibiting artists elected one, which dealt with admissions; the other, made up of 13 elected members and 17 appointed by the Minister of the Interior, dealt with awards. Courbet, as a medal-winner, was *hors concours*; he had the right to exhibit unjudged. He sent in four portraits (Wey, Berlioz, Journet, himself as the *Man with the Pipe*), two landscapes (*View of the Ruins of the Château of Scey-en-Varais* and *The Banks of the Loue on the Maisières Road*), and the *Burial, The Stone-Breakers*, and the *Return from the Fair*. Because of the delay, the Salon was to serve for both 1850 and 1851. Courbet's works had a varied reception; only the *Man with the Pipe* was approved. As the three big works absorbed the critics' and the public's attention, the landscapes were more or less ignored. But before we come to the reactions in detail we can take the account by Jules Vallès (written long after in 1867), which corrects the violent abuse of the orthodox by showing how the vigorous young responded.

It was, I think, in 1850. We were strolling, some friends and I (the oldest might indeed have been 18 years old) through the galleries of the Exposition. Suddenly we halted before a canvas which in the catalogue was listed as *The Stone-Breakers* and which was signed in red letters: 'G. Courbet'. Our emotion was profound. We were all enthusiasts. It was the period when heads were fermenting. We had in our hearts respect for all that was suffering or conquered, and demanded of the new art that it should serve also in the triumph of justice and truth. This grey-toned picture, with its two men with calloused hands and sunburnt necks, was like a mirror reflecting the dull and painful life of the poor. The awkward stiffness of the persons helped the illusion; and the lack of skill, or the genius, of the painter had in a single gesture shown the fatal immobility to which under an ungrateful heaven is condemned the whole breed of wage-earners.

Some steps further on we saw, under the same signature, a burial followed by beadles with rough veined noses, with phizes like the knots of trees; behind, sublime in grace and grief, women dressed in black were weeping. One felt oneself in the very cemetery, and recognised the drunken chanters who, before putting on their surplices, had elbowed you in the exit from the pothouse. The work had a terrible fidelity. Here, indifferent cynicism, there, dumb grief. In two strokes of the brush the artist had traced the comedy, the drama, and painted with a horrible sincerity these contrasts, this irony and this despair.

The crowd was stopping before these canvases, but with more stupor than emotion; and next day, instead of reassuring this crowd, criticism joined in their chorus; it excited indignation against the audacities of the painter. Courbet was treated as a man of ferocious vanity and comic charlatanry. When he had added to *The Stone-Breakers* and the *Burial* the *Wrestlers* and the *Baigneuses*, all was said. For a dozen years he had to be called an eccentric and to pass in the crowd's eyes as a braggart of vulgarity.[40]

Now let us turn to the reaction of the bourgeois critics and public. Typical was the notice by Claude Vignon:

A great black canvas, which takes up much space, sharply strikes the attention; it is entitled *A Burial at Ornans*, and incontestably has a strong effect. One has never seen, and never could see, anything so frightful and so eccentric. So this picture gains its author, M. Courbet, at least a success of shock. One looks at it, one even examines it for a long time under all its appearances and in all its aspects; but no matter what the long-suffering and benevolence of the spectator, the impression produced is the same on all; each, from the most whimsical artist to the most simple bourgeois, cries out as he makes off: Good God, how ugly it is!

It is in fact abominably ugly. Imagine a canvas of eight to ten metres that seems cut into one of fifty, because all the persons, ranged in a line in the foreground, are on the same plane and seem to form only a single episode of an immense decoration; there is no perspective, no arrangement, no composition; all the rules of art are overthrown and despised; we see black men laid on black women, and behind, beadles and gravediggers with ignoble shape, four black bearers favoured with a democ-soc beard, a mountaineer's cast, and hats *à la Caussidière*. There! Good God, how ugly it is.[41]

He adds that *The Stone-Breakers* and the *Return* represent 'in the most grossly possibly way whatever is grossest and most unclean'. P. de Chennevières remarks that Courbet has been called the Holbein of nineteenth-century art, the Messiah of Democratic Art: which 'convulses one with laughter'. Courbet shows 'hatred even of art'.[42] Even a progressive like P. Haussard of the *National*, a republican-socialist paper (20 February 1851), couldn't stomach the man with the pig and umbrella in the *Return*; and this was the paper that Buchon had declared would approve of the paintings.

The caricaturists had a fine time. We have already noted the image of the *Burial* as sheer blackness lighted by the beadles' noses and a dog that is shown as a toy-dog, to express Courbet's primitivism. The text says that Courbet 'has not accepted worm-eaten tradition and does not march in trodden paths; he has combined his *Burial* in such a way that one is seized with a mad gaiety in looking at it; it's a trait of genius.' Cham in 1851 has a boy looking at *The Stone-Breakers*. 'But why, papa, do they call that socialist painting?' The father answers, 'Why, don't you see, it's not rich painting, it's poor painting.' We find Courbet consulting a *croque-mort* on his picture of a 'Breton burial'. A Zouave, accustomed to the horrors of war, recoils. Again Cham shows Courbet saying, 'There's a bourgeois stopping to look at my picture. He hasn't an attack of nerves. The show's a failure.' And we read elsewhere, 'A respectable member of society has to get himself up as a peasant before M. Courbet will paint his portrait.' The *sabots* in *The Stone-Breakers* attracted much hostility. Cham shows the jury presenting Courbet with a pair of them as his prize.

This sort of satire went on a long time. In *L'Illustration*, 21 July 1855, Quillenbois showed a pair of bourgeois looking at the *Burial*, in which only sabots and hobnailed boots appear. In caricatures of *The Stone-Breakers* the sabots are vastly enlarged. In *La Lune*, 12 August 1866, Gill drew the Candlestick of Realism, where the candle has the heads of Champfleury and Courbet, with *sabot* and hobnailed boot underneath. An accompanying poem by Lux has a final chorus:

> Against Art, Spirit, Fantasy,
> Realists off to war go we,
> Sending up heavenhigh our cry:
> Long live Courbet and Champfleury!

And V. Fournel remarked, 'You needed to hear him trample with his big *sabots* on the idealist and spiritualist schools.' The *Return from the Fair* was caricatured in *Le Journal pour Rire* as entirely composed of wooden toys or dolls, the trees shown as a child's scribbles. The text underlines the point: 'Nothing equals the enthusiasm produced on the public by Courbet's picture. There is the *true Truth* without chic or trick. One does not feel the style of the school and the absurd tradition of the antique. All is naïve, happy, and gay. Courbet was eighteen months old when he painted this picture.'[43]

In the shock felt by people accustomed to the idealised forms of the academics, the naïve or popular elements were felt to a degree that it is hard to recapture today. We must remember that the intrusion of naïvety had been begun by David, whose political attitudes led him in his own way to a break with convention, both in composition and the treatment of the individual. Courbet never seems to have recognised his considerable debt to David, probably being prejudiced against him through his dislike of the etiolated Davidians of his own day, though he did see how he followed on Gros and Géricault.[44] If we can trust the comment of Audebrand, he himself said of David's forms that they were '*bonhommes* [rough drawings or effigies] to amuse children on the same level as the imagery of Épinal'.[45] T. Gautier had in turn mocked at Courbet's art as like the signs of tobacconists and the *images d'Épinal*; it was the 'painting of an Auvergnat', a coarse peasant. Fournel later used the term 'peinture d'Auvergnat' in terms of praise; he had a wide and loving knowledge of street-songs and popular spectacles in Paris. L. Geoffroy on 1 March 1851 in the *Revue des Deux-Mondes* wrote, 'Evidently M. Courbet is a man who looks on himself as having tried out a great renovation, and doesn't notice at all that he brings art back quite simply to its point of departure in the coarse industry of the image-makers.'[46] Banville in a poem of 1852 wrote:

> A realist am I,
> Against the ideal I've reared my catapult high,
> I've created the art *bonhomme*, childish and naïve.

A caricature of 1853, from *Le Journal pour Rire*, shows a child at a gingerbread stall, who calls to his mother, 'O, *maman*, look at those fine *courbets*! Buy me some! Four for a *sou*!' Another, from the same journal, makes Courbet a bogy-man for children. A father threatens a naughty boy: 'I'll tell Courbet to carry you off' – the boy is scared.[47] Baudelaire with one of his keen insights pointed out that such charges were commonly levelled at innovators: 'Many people have accused of barbarism all painters whose vision is synthetic and simplifying, for example Corot, who begins by tracing first all the main lines of a landscape, its framework and physiognomy.'[48]

Vignon and the caricaturists expressed the general view; but Courbet had a few defenders. F. Méry made a witty but shallow defence in *La Mode* on 26 January 1851; and Champfluery did his utmost to expound his positions in an effective way. But he was hampered by the fact that he could not follow Courbet into socialism and wanted him to work as a direct expounder and depicter of rural life, using the perspective of the country bourgeoisie. His view of Realism was thus superficial, despite the considerable knowledge he had of popular imagery and folklore; and he could not correctly interpret the new works of Courbet. First he hoped to break down Parisian opposition by stressing the bourgeois nature of Courbet's outlook – country bourgeois, yes, but something that the Parisians should recognise as their kin under the less elegant exterior:

It is the death of a bourgeois who is followed to his last dwelling by other bourgeois. . . . Is it the fault of the painter if the material interests, if smalltown life, if sordid egoisms, if provincial pettiness leave their claw-marks on the countenance, extinguish the eyes, furrow the brow, stupefy the mouth. The bourgeois are like that; M. Courbet has painted bourgeois. . . . It is not austerity; it is the modern bourgeois, with his ridiculous aspects, his ugliness and his beauties. . . . It has pleased the painter to show us the domestic life of a small town; he has said that gowns of printed linen and black clothes are as good as Spanish costumes, the lace and plumes of Louis XIII. . . . The modern costume is in harmony with modern beauty. . . . As to the alleged ugliness of the Ornans townspeople, there is nothing exaggerated about it; it is the ugliness of the provinces, which must be differentiated from the ugliness of Paris. . . . In our times when political economy plays a big role, where science expands from day to day, where fantasy will be permitted only to learned spirits, costume must become serious. . . .[49]

And this overstress on the bourgeois character of the work, as if there were no critical aspects in it, is linked with the effort to prove that there is nothing socialist about it. 'There is not a trace of socialism in the *Burial*. . . . Woe to artists who try to teach by their works.' They may appeal 'for five minutes to the passions of the mob; but they express matters of but momentary interest'. But 'fortunately Courbet has not tried to prove anything by his *Burial*'. We see here the usual equation of a socialist viewpoint with cartoon-propaganda, and the idea that such art can only appeal to 'the passions of the mob'. Presumably the endless works of art in the Salons which directly or indirectly supported the bourgeois world-view were not political and not ephemeral because they did not appeal to mob-passions. He says that Courbet is considered as a savage who studied painting while looking after pigs. 'Some declare the painter is the leader of socialist bands; they write that he is the son of the democratic republic of 1848; they'd like to put black mourning on the Belvedere Apollo. If one hearkened to them, the members of the Institute should sit in their armchairs, as the senators once did in their curule chairs, and die proudly, stricken by the muddy *sabots* of the realist savages.' Note the *sabots*.[50]

Thus Champfleury gets more and more away from the real content of the works in question. He was on surer ground when he drew on his deep knowledge of popular imagery. 'From afar, as one enters, the *Burial* appears framed by a door; everyone is surprised by this simple painting, as at the view of those naïve woodcuts, dug out by a clumsy knife, at the head of the *Murders* printed in the rue Gît-le-Cœur. The effect is the same because the execution is so simple. Learned art finds the same accent as naïve art. The aspect is gripping as a picture by a great master. The simplicity of the black costumes possesses the grandeur of the Parliament in red robes painted by Largillière.' Thus he returns to the theme, taken from Baudelaire, of the heroism of modern life, but adapted to his defence of the representation of the provincial petty-bourgeoisie, which he wants to make out as Courbet's main aim and achievement.[51]

In the particular emphases which Champfleury is making we can see the seed of the disagreements that finally parted him and Courbet; but for the moment Courbet was ready enough to accept this defence against the serried attacks. To estimate the full nature of the shock administered by the paintings, however, we must go beyond the question of ugliness, of naïvety, and so on. Champfleury in his efforts to disprove any socialist element gives us one main clue; but we must see more specifically what was the socialism detected and detested by the critics and the bourgeois public in 1850–1. Clearly behind the fear of innovation lay the fear of the revolutionary forces of June 1848; but why did these pictures so precisely trigger off a correlation of the rural workers and farmers with the forces that had been beaten down but not destroyed?

Castagnary comes close to the answer:

There was a tremor of indignation and anger. What! One had dissolved the national workshops; one had conquered the proletariat in the streets of Paris; one had got mastery of the republican bourgeoisie of the Conservatoire of Arts and Trades; one had sealed in the cabals of the rue de Poitiers the alliance of the old parties; one had purged universal suffrage by scratching out, in the law of 31 May, three million electors—and here is the 'vile multitude', hunted out of politics, reappearing in painting! What did such audacity mean? Whence came these peasants, these stone-breakers, these hunger-stricken and tattered folk, who were seen for the first time advancing silently between the naked divinities of Greece and the plumed gentlemen of the Middle Ages? Was it not already the vanguard of those *Jacques*, whom public anxiety, fed by the criminal acts of some, the imbecility of others, depicted with a torch in hand, a wallet on back, mounting to the assault of the elections of 1852?

> When will the glorious appear
> For which Jean-in-Gaiters waits
> Thousands and hundreds of years:
> The Republic of the Peasants?

The clamour was immense, continual, irresistible. It was impossible to discuss, reason, present arguments drawn from aesthetics or history. No one wanted to listen or understand. The indignant articles rain down like squalls in March. Courbet was a charlatan, a pistol-shooter, a barbarian alien to all delicacies, an ignorant uncouth being, incapable of sentiment and poetry, a drunken helot who had to be displayed to the youth so that they might learn how not to paint. He was put in songs and caricatures. The vaudevillists seized on to him as they had done with Proudhon and Socrates, and handed him over on the stage to the guffaws of the crowd. In art records there is no example of worse insults.[52]

But surely, it may be asked, it was the conservative provinces that had voted Louis Napoleon into power in 1848: why should the peasantry be feared? The answer is that after the failure of the Parisian uprising of 1849 the revolutionary initiative had passed to the peasants; and a highly complex situation emerged, with uncertain balances and sudden resurgences of revolt. The spirit of resistance was especially strong in Courbet's native Alpine regions.

By December 1851 when Louis Napoleon staged his *coup d'état* against a demoralised Parisian working-class, all eyes were on the response from the provinces. And the peasantry was, in fact, the only class to mount an organised and coherent resistance to the *coup* – in the Alpine departments 25,000–30,000 peasants took up arms; there was insurrection in the Var, in the Lyon countryside and the Rhône valley, and elsewhere. More important, the resistance to the *coup d'état* had a real political and social programme: in three years the peasantry had moved from the spontaneous *jacqueries* which swept the French countryside in the bad harvests of 1847 and 1848, towards full political consciousness, a determination to forge and this time to *control* the *République des Paysans*, the *République Démocratique et Sociale*.

The process which ended with the resistance of December 1851 is complex, and the story of the Republican secret societies in the countryside is still being written. But two things are clear. First, the idea of the peasantry as immutable supporters of the *parti de l'ordre* was in disarray – and news of its breakdown reached and excited Paris. Attention in the capital – on both Right and Left – was focused on the struggle in the provinces, and on the magical date of 1852, the year, so it was rumoured, of the peasant revolution. Secondly, the focus of that conflict was the intensifying hostility between the peasantry and the rural *bourgeoisie*. (CLARK)[53]

This is the situation in which we must evaluate the enraged and even panicky response of the Parisian bourgeoisie to Courbet's works. Was Courbet himself at all involved in the agitation carried on by many of his friends? That is unlikely in view of his extremely busy preoccupations as a painter over this period; but we can be sure that through Buchon, Cuénot, and others he knew a great deal of what was going on.

We are still not clear, however, as to the ways in which Courbet's imagery was felt and understood apart from creating a general mood of disquiet. *The Stone-Breakers* was seen as a fairly direct piece of accusation and menace. In such a situation as that of December 1850, it posed the question: How long will the blind cycle of submission to exploitation go on? By painting the man and lad life-size, and thus arrogating to them the dimensions and dignity of History-Painting, Courbet stressed this question; for, in terms of the period's sensibilities, he was saying that these men had as much right to consideration as gods and the great ones of the earth. But how did the *Burial* and the *Return* have so sharp an effect? It has been argued that in the *Burial*, by showing the differentiation of rural society, he was shattering a myth dear to Parisians, that rural society did not suffer from the class-conflicts which rent the towns – that peasant and master worked in harmony. The peasant-world was thus seen as somehow quite different from the bourgeois one. If one peasant was greedier than another and acquired more land, that was a blind sort of process which hardly affected the over-all community-sense. A bourgeois was a different sort of person; he made himself by an act of will, which severed him from the blind peasant-cycles, and he inhabited the world of history, not that of nature in which the peasant with his unconscious responses and compulsions was buried.[54]

That such a myth potently existed is true; but Balzac and George Sand had already shown its weak and untrue aspects, as Flaubert and Zola were to do further. Certainly one aspect of the shock of Courbet's pictures was to give it a severe blow; and that blow, coming at a moment of very strong political tension in which the role of the peasant was crucial, must indeed have played a considerable part in the impact of the works. But we must see this aspect in terms of the total shock, which may be summed up as the effect of a powerful vision of social reality and of individual existence. What the Parisians came up against like a brick wall was this vision of *reality*, and by knocking their heads on it they felt dazed. The reality included the facts of social differentiation among the peasantry, but it also included the assertion of individual human rights; and these two aspects of the definition were inseparable from the form, the challenging life-size largeness, the popular elements concentrated in the shapes and the central ideas, the sculptural solidity of each item, the sheer weight and clarity of the image which was felt as outrage and ugliness. Nobody in Paris seems to have realised the role of the *Burial*'s grave-digger in the terms felt by Courbet and defined by Buchon; but that does not mean they failed to discern some sort of dark menace in the work. Buchon, well read in dissident literature, may have known the *Communist Manifesto* and its metaphor of the proletariat as the gravedigger of the bourgeoisie; if so, he would have cited it to Courbet.

On 13 February 1851 Cuénot wrote from Paris to Juliette Courbet:

Gustave is always the theme of all the conversations in the artistic world. The most contradictory rumours about him come up, and the most amusing news. In some salons it's asserted he was a carpenter or mason who one fine day, pushed by his genius, set himself to try painting and achieved masterpieces with the first attempt. In others it's stated that he is a terrible socialist who is at the head of a band of conspirators. All that can be guessed from his painting, they assert; the man's a savage. . . . No day goes past but further foolishnesses are credited to his account.[1]

In view of the discussion of the *Burial* in the last chapter, we may note the words, 'All this can be guessed from his painting.'

As we saw, he later claimed to have founded a socialist club in 1848; but apart from propounding the necessary link between democracy or socialism and realism at Andler's and such places, it seems unlikely that he had any direct political affiliations till the later 1860s. That does not mean that he did not know and encourage the activities of men like Buchon. Proudhon had been arrested after March 1849 when the reactionaries were firmly in control. In Sainte-Pélagie and the Conciergerie he went on writing pamphlets and doing editorial work till he was freed in June 1852. The tales about wild bands owing allegiance to Courbet went on being told, however. Even Wey declares that in 1850 he showed 'that vast canvas, darker still [than *Afterdinner*] of the *Burial at Ornans*. I do not have to describe it: it was the most violent manifestation of his natural qualities and his natural infirmities. An undisciplined band, recruited from the lower depths of the studios, threw themselves on his faults to assimilate them, and, more master than ever, our man had fanatical partisans [*séides*], not being able to create a school.'[2] Elisa de Mirabel in *La Revolution Littéraire*, a magazine where the notion of revolution was wholly literary, wrote confusedly of a *populaire aviné*, a drink-sodden lower-class audience; and this image of his followers became fixed.[3] We hear of peasants among the crowds that pressed in to see David's *Horatii* just before the Revolution; how far did peasants and workers ever look in at a Salon, even when rumours of a socialist artist had percolated to the more politically-developed among them? Daumier in a caricature of 1853 depicts stupefied peasants before Courbet's work, with the text: 'Great admirers of the pictures of M. Courbet'. But we do not know if this is a mere joke or whether such people did intrude on the Salon. Certainly at Ornans he showed the big canvases to *vignerons* and *cultivateurs*, who were much impressed.[4]

In early September 1851 he was invited by Clément Laurier, a young barrister, to spend a week or two at his country house near Le Blanc (Indre). Dupont was there too. Ideville tells us that Laurier had recently inherited the estate from a rich eccentric father, who had hidden coins and banknotes in odd parts of the house. The old housekeeper Brigitte now kept finding these and handing them over to her master. Soon after his arrival Courbet showed much agitation and declared that he must go at once to Paris. His dismay was explained when Brigitte brought Laurier a gold-hoard in a sock she had found. Laurier discovered Courbet's gold medal of 1849 among the coins, and realised that the hoard was his. Courbet had been ashamed to mention his loss because he had refused Dupont a loan of fifteen francs on the grounds that he'd brought no money. But when Laurier returned the sock with a mild twinkle, he was relieved and said that he need not depart after all, and gave Dupont fifteen francs as a present. A mixture of generous carelessness about money, and an extreme peasant meanness, accompanied him through life.[5] Castagnary tells us:

Generosity mixed with avarice: he had a peasant's habits. The painters of today have a current bank account and a chequebook at the Crédit Foncier. It was only when he made large sales to Khalil Bey that Courbet put money in railway stocks and at the bank. He knew nothing of ways of increasing money, and in the way of peasants he kept it in a sock. His pinching habits did not stop him from having a feeling heart, and then he knew how to put his hand in his pocket.

After returning to Paris, Courbet went on to Belgium, stopping to have a look at his *Afterdinner* in the Lille Museum. At Brussels his *Stone-Breakers* and his self-portrait as a *Cellist* were on show, praised by the young critics and studied by the artists. Some of his other works were on show at Munich, and he may have paid a visit there.[6] In Paris he found himself accused by the *Messager*, under the signature of M. Garcin, of attending a meeting held by the reactionary Friends of the Constitution at the Salle Saint-Spire. In a letter of 10 November he defended himself. He wrote, he said, not to clear his name, but for the sake of the truth. He has been called the socialist painter; he gladly accepts the term. For he is 'not only a socialist, but indeed further a democrat and republican – in a word, partisan of the whole revolution – and above all, a realist: that is, a sincere friend of the real truth.'[7]

Back in Ornans, he did not find the enthusiastic welcome that he had had in 1849. The abuse of the papers had worried and confused those who had sat for him. The notary Proudhon feared that he had compromised his official prestige; the curé was infuriated at the jeers and merriment over his beadles, 'for they belong a little to the Church, and what touches the clergy must not be ridiculed'. Alphonse Bon and Célestine were angry at having been, as they thought, made to look ugly; Marlet complained, 'As Courbet knows how to embellish himself in his portraits, why didn't he treat us as he does himself?' Only the grave-digger Cassart was reserved. The three Courbet girls went round with journals at all favourable to those who had been spared by the critics, while they hid the journals expatiating on the sitters' ugliness. *La Fili* Caillot and Joséphine Bocquet, who had been found pretty, aided them. Finally Courbet with his boisterous reassurances managed to appease the disgruntled.[8]

On 2 December 1851 came the *coup d'état* when Louis Napoleon seized power. Courbet and his friends were at once exposed to more serious attacks. Perhaps because of his well-known position as an artist, Courbet escaped; but others suffered. Buchon's position had, indeed, been precarious since June 1848. He had then retired to his home, where he was left for a while in peace; but he was finally tracked down and arrested by the local police. Our main source for information about him is the letter that Courbet wrote to Castagnary after Buchon's death in 1869. We cannot trust Courbet's memory for details, especially after such an interval; in his effervescent way he always wanted to make strong points, and when time had blurred things a little, he could easily reshape them. But we may trust in general what he says. Buchon spent a year in jail awaiting trial, then was

conducted, with a chain round his neck, from Besançon to Lons-le-Saunier to be tried. He travelled twenty leagues on foot, between two mounted policemen, under these conditions, by the orders of Napoleon II, that is Cavaignac. After 2 December [1851] Napoleon [III] went after him again. A warrant for his arrest was issued, he was hunted like a wild beast. During this time he hid in a secret place under the floor, where he stayed for a long while; then he escaped dressed as a plasterer. He hid in the house of a poor old man, a bachelor, in the neighbourhood; then one fine night he turned up in quest of me and took refuge at my place [Flagey or Ornans?]; he spent two days concealed by us. My mother had had trapdoors cut to provide lairs for us. In his attempt to run away, Buchon had fallen into the wolf's jaws, as a warrant for my arrest had also been issued. The position wasn't tenable. Urbain Cuénot was shut up at Marseille. We decided to escape, he to Switzerland, I to Paris under a false name. His father died while all this was happening. There was an odd episode. The elder Buchon had been an infantry captain. His sabre and his sword had been put in a cross on his coffin, and when the body was in the street, the police seized both sabre and sword. Buchon spent eight or nine years in exile at Berne. His small fortune diminished daily after his father's death and [at last] his friends had him brought back to France, where he remained under police surveillance till his death.[9]

Courbet probably exaggerates in saying there was a warrant out against himself; but he was certainly watched and even harried by the police. In January 1852 he wrote to Wey from Ornans that his letters were being intercepted and opened; that one of the officers at Ornans kept him under surveillance and had denounced him to the prefecture. He asked Wey if he could safely return to Paris. 'For I'm not anxious to be deported to Guyane at the moment; I can't say how I might feel about it later on.'[10]

The situation was in fact grave and liable to erupt. The prefect of the Basses-Alpes had stated in a report of 1850: 'The struggle has settled down between the capitalist and the debt-encumbered landowner.' The peasants were more enraged against the bourgeois of town or borough than against the local rich farmer who resided on his estate and at times gave them hired jobs. On 7 December 1851 the folk of Chavannes marched on the château of a man who had been their mayor, but not because he had inherited the lordship; they hated him as a man who had been a notary and held a large number of them in debt. Régis Courbet seems rather of the type of resident-farmer than that of creditor; but we see that there was enough tension between the peasantry and the bourgeoisie of the boroughs to warrant Courbet's picture of social differentiation and tension in the *Return*.[11] As noted above, the Alpine areas were especially in a state of ferment:

There was no question of a Jacquerie, nor of a simple movement of spontaneous resistance to the fortuitous action of a man. The breadth of these movements, the fanaticism manifested by the combatants of Crest des Mées are the result of a tireless propaganda carried on for three years among peasants and artisans of the rural boroughs who were registered in very large numbers in the secret republican societies, the considerable extent of which was revealed by the events. . . . This movement of resistance had only as a secondary characteristic the negative aspect of a protest against Louis Napoleon's act; he was much less detested than the conservative notables. . . . The insurrection often, especially in the Basses-Alpes, took on the positive aspect of a veritable new Revolution, who needed to found the democratic and social Republic. . . . It is indeed a political matter; but who would think of risking his life to defend an unanimously decried regime? The men fought to install a new one, that which one had hoped to start off in 1852: a regime that would give a large place to social reforms and popular demands. (VIGIER)[12]

Much of the peasantry of northern France, however, took no action; the army was able to isolate and crush the risings. Buchon had been one of the most active propagandists for the movement; and Courbet's claim that he had founded a socialist club in 1848 might well refer to a certain amount of implication in the work of Buchon and other friends. This conjecture is much strengthened by a fact that comes out in the police files kept on him in 1868: 'The *Français* speaks also of a picture which has been previously mentioned by one of our Parisian correspondents: It is announced that M. Courbet will send this year to the Salon a picture representing Martin Bidauré, the peasant of the Var, twice shot.' The man must be Martin Bidoure, who was the most famous of the insurgents of the Var. We do not know if Courbet ever carried out his intention of painting a picture of Bidoure; but the fact that he was recalling the 1851 revolts as late as 1868 and thinking of using them as a theme of protest against the Empire, is proof that they had deeply impressed him.[13]

Strangely, in this very disturbed situation, he turned to a work which, while again stressing social differentiation in the countryside, did so in an amiable and even idyllic way: *Young Women of the Village*. In an upland pasture near Ornans, with a wall of cliff at the back and a stream winding through, the three Courbet girls stand in the centre – Zoé on the right with the big ribboned hat she liked, Juliette in the middle with parasol, Zélie on the left, offering a sweet from her basket to a little cowgirl who stands shyly hesitating. Behind Zoé a bushy-tailed dog keeps watch on the cattle. The work must have been painted in midwinter, between November 1851 and February 1852; but the scene is one of green grass, azure sky, and bright sunlight; foliage is full-grown and the girls wear summer clothes. The work is thus light in tone and lively in feeling, a contrast to the *Burial* with its sense of a descent into the grave, or even the *Return* with its effect of riding rather grimly into a sunset world.

Courbet wrote to Champfleury about this painting in what for him are guarded terms. 'It's difficult to tell you what I've done this year for the Exposition; I'm afraid of expressing myself rather badly. You'll judge better than me if you see the picture. First, I've put my judges off the track; I've put them on to new terrain; I've done something graceful; all that they could say about me till now is quite off the point.' This unusual refusal to describe the work on which he is busy suggests some strong emotion which he cannot quite focus and which he fears. The clue is given in the rest of the letter where he tells how Virginie has definitely left him and taken their son with her.[14]

We have to piece together our picture of that relationship from a number of disconnected facts and records. Here is a good point at which to set them out. We cannot do better than start with considering a work that belongs to his romantic period and has a close connection with Virginie: the *Wounded Man*. He put this painting in each of his own shows, dating it 1844; the catalogue of 1867 adds that it had been rejected at the Salons of 1844, 1845, 1846 and 1847 'by the jury composed of members of the Institute'. In 1882 Castagnary, in view of its 'free and supple craftsmanship' (*facture*), dated it 1854; Riat says it was redone at that time, but accepts its first creation in 1844. If, however, it was indeed sent to the Salon, it must have been in 1845 and under another name; for only in that year is there registered a small canvas. Radiography has shown that the theme of the *Wounded Man* was not the first on the canvas. There were two previous subjects: one was linked with a drawing, *Country Siesta*, and belongs to the same phase as *Lovers in the Country*, a work done at the height of Courbet's youthful romanticism and expressing the first flush of his relations with Virginie. If we may correctly interpret the wound as really that of love, not of a duel, why did he transform the image of happy lovers into that of the desperately wounded lover? Silvestre cites him as saying, 'If I suffered from my passions when younger, I suffer more from them today. I have taken at a pinch one or several years in ridding myself of an attachment or a prejudice. That's how I became free.'[15]

We may, then, surely link with the *Wounded Man* the allegoric work of which we hear: *Man delivered from Love by Death*. There Courbet is shown trying to hold a woman whom Death carries away. Here again death or the wound is a metaphor for the emotion of mortal loss. Courbet effaced the work, crying, 'Why hate woman? It's owing to the ignorance and egoism of man that it's necessary to lay the blame on her. There is no reason for her to identify herself with me, since her character is so different from mine. Let her live. At that moment I entered fully into the tolerance and liberty that are at the root of Realism.'[16]

This statement seems to express, not a liberation from egoism, but the supreme submission to it. If we are right in pointing to Courbet's irresponsible way of wandering about and boozing without any concern for his woman and child, to his failure to stand by her at her hour of need (at the time of his son's birth), to his leaving her alone to bring up the child, as the chronology of his movements seems to show, then it was her effort to assert some claim on him that drove him to desperation. Such an analysis fits in with all we know of his character, with its fierce need to assert complete independence in the face of any external claim, whether from the State or his family. So, after alienating Virginie with his egoism, he declares that it would be egoism to blame her or to try to keep her (that is, to try to find some basis of union in which her claims as well as his could be considered). The final part of his statement given above is even more important for our understanding of his development. 'At that moment I entered fully into the tolerance and liberty that is at the root of Realism.' It pairs off with the remark to Silvestre, 'That's how I became free' – by ridding himself of attachment or prejudice.

We see that three factors came together into a unity to bring about the leap in his art-faculty shown in 1849–50. All three factors worked inside his general need not to conform, not to submit to any sort of dictation or pressure, emotional, intellectual, social, artistic, political. They were: (*a*) his general rebellion against the bourgeois world of Paris which matured politically in 1848; (*b*) his need to overcome the intense suffering caused by his relationship with Virginie, where he sought a close bond, yet refused to consider her needs; (*c*) his growing conviction that he could not adequately express his personality within the bounds laid down by the prevailing art authorities, and that he must somehow break through the classical–romantic impasse, not by an eclectic combination of elements from both schools, but by moving to a synthesis transcending both of them. Out of the fusion of these factors he achieved his new sense of the object as something to which he was powerfully drawn, but which he also held at arm's length, admitting both its inherent forces and its right to exist in its unique nature. The result was his Realism. Though, in his wish to irritate the conventional, he at times spoke as if he meant the unchanged transfer of the object from external space on to the canvas, in fact he was seeking anything rather than a mere naturalist reflection. To define the object with all its own rights to exist as it was, he had to define also its own inner force which made it what it was; he had to define the demands on him simultaneously with his rejection of them. That is, he had to accept the object in its totality and in terms of its own inner formative principle; his rejection of the claims made on him was also a rejection of any effort on his part to assert claims over the object. Thus, his new direct vision in art was dynamically linked with his politics of 'tolerance and liberty' and his struggle to transcend romantic love and its pangs. But though Courbet gives his own twist to the rejection of marriage, we must recognise that his position links with certain dissident trends given voice by his compatriot Considérant in a booklet of 1841 on Fourier's Doctrine, which supported the right to free love. The latter's argument scandalised socialists like Proudhon and Leroux, or communists like Cabet, who all claimed to be defenders of the family.

We can explore further the great importance that the *Wounded Man* had for him. In Autumn 1854 he wrote to Bruyas: 'With this laughing mask that you know on me, I hide inside chagrin, bitterness, and a grief that attaches itself to the heart like a vampire.' In May he had written of a portrait already old, the one before the penultimate one, where he has depicted himself 'laughing and dying', and of the penultimate one, which is that 'of a man in the ideal and in absolute love'. This latter is perhaps *The Happy Lovers*[17]. In any event he seems certainly to have in mind the contradiction-and-unity of that picture and the *Wounded Man*; and the most likely date for the representation of his stricken state is 1851, about the time when Virginie left him or during the strain and conflict leading up to her departure. He seems to have had the work in mind when he asked Proudhon to consider that 'in our days human beauty is worthy, true beauty is met among us only in suffering and sorrow', and when he cited in support of his statement several of his own works including *The Dying Duellist*.[18] The romantic character of the painting is brought out by the fact that it seems clearly related to Delacroix's *St Sebastian Aided by the Holy Women* (1836) in the parish church of Nantua. The connection also brings out the idea of martyrdom: for Courbet, martyrdom by love.

It is of some interest that in 1872 the painting was used to provide an illustration for 'The Death of Musoni' in Bruno's book *Les Misères des Gueux*. Here we see the end of the hero, an architect of Florence, who is condemned for conspiracy and has to leave the city; he does not regret sacrificing a brilliant future to a cause as noble as that 'of snatching his country from the shame of being bent [*courbé*] under the yoke of an abhorred government'; in exile his 'ideas expand' and his solicitude extends to all men. Thus the image of romantic pain is transformed into one of devotion to the cause of 'tolerance and liberty'; romanticism becomes realism.[19]

In the letter to Champfleury written during the winter of 1851–2 Courbet, after mentioning the departure of his mistress, adds, 'May life treat her gently, since she thinks she's acting for the best. I must regret my little lad, but I have enough to do with art without concerning myself with a household; and then a married man is a reactionary.' That rings false, though no doubt he means the good wishes; he falls back on one of his café-quips, which would make Proudhon and Buchon, married men, both reactionaries. Years later, in 1883, his friend Lydie Jolicler, writing to an unnamed friend, mentioned that in November 1872, in one of his many visits to her house, he began painting her; as he worked alone with her, he chatted away and told her that he had recently lost his son, whom he loved dearly, 'a fine lad' aged twenty.[20]

Castagnary, whom we can rely on to set down what Courbet had told him, states: 'The truth is that this son, whom I have seen and who bore little resemblance to his father, was a carver of ivory at Dieppe and had never followed any other profession. He died there before he was twenty years old.' As Castagnary didn't come to know Courbet till about 1860, we see that Courbet must have kept in touch with the Binets fairly regularly. There are two other accounts by people who knew Courbet. Gros-Kost says:

He had a son who died at the age of twenty. This illegitimate son could not be legitimised by law. . . . As he couldn't give the boy his name, he tried to transmit his talent to him. He taught him to paint. The young man worked so hard that one day his proud father told some friends: There's nothing more I can teach him. According to Dr Collin this son was a distinguished writer. That is an error. A writer! His father would have disowned him. He might have had to read the boy's works.

We may disregard the bad joke at the end of that; but it is true that the boy was certainly not a writer. As certainly he was not a painter, taught by Courbet or anyone else. Perhaps Gros-Kost misinterpreted a remark which he or others heard Courbet make about the boy showing progress in his art (carving) – which was taken to refer to painting. The account by Dr Paul Collin was certainly given in good faith; he was attending Courbet in his last days and did his best to glean any information from the dying artist himself or from those about him. Later he communicated his findings to Lemonnier. The story of the son he got from Pata, a glib disciple of Courbet in his last years. Pata was genuinely attached to Courbet, who would indeed have told him endless tales of his earlier days; but, with the best will, he may easily have got much mixed up, and, an amiable fellow who liked to help, he may have elaborated details to provide Collin with a good story. All we can be sure of is that Courbet did talk about the son and that he did express profound sorrow and regret about him.

Courbet had the misfortune to lose a son that he worshipped and in whom he had put his consolations. This son died at the age of twenty. He had had him of a woman whom he had known in the fine time of love and youth, when everything was smiling on him and when good fortune lighted up the road ahead. It's a sorrowful and charming story.

A lady came to sit for her portrait in the young painter's studio. He was then twenty-eight years old [1847]. Love soon followed, and one day the lady fell on her knees before Courbet and begged to be allowed to stay with him, saying, 'I have left my husband and now I want to belong only to you.'

They lived together and a child was pledge of this union. The husband died. Courbet, I am told, recognised the child. This lad, this son, was one of the greatest happinesses of his life. He loved him with a boundless tenderness; and when he lost him, eight months after losing the woman who had given him to him, he felt stricken in the very depths of his being. The young man took up literature; he had published some well-considered articles. What is odd, it doesn't seem that Courbet ever made a portrait of his beloved son. I say what I know, not anything else, and I tell you well because it goes far to explain that passion for drink and night-wandering that has been one of the causes of the death of this poor man of genius.[21]

The general emotion of all that no doubt truly reflects the way in which Courbet spoke to Pata of the matter; but details are certainly confused. How the error about literature crept in, it is hard to say.

The link with Dieppe may well have occurred through Paul Ansout, son of a cloth-merchant of that town, whose portrait we saw painted by Courbet in 1844 (probably the year in which Courbet met Virginie). Ansout had an uncle, Louis Belletete, who died in 1832 and had been an ivory-carver at Dieppe. Perhaps through Ansout the boy was taken on as apprentice to one of the uncle's successors. Researches at Dieppe have established that the municipal records record the death of Désiré-Alfred-Émile Binet on 5 July 1872; he is described as an ivory-carver and his birth is given as 17 September 1847, son of Thérèse-Adelaïde-Virginie Binet. His mother was unmarried and had not been born at Dieppe. No father's name is given. Désiré Binet had been married on 17 August 1868 to Juliette-Léonie Blard, born at Dieppe, daughter of Joseph-Noël Blard, a ropemaker of that city. Virginie had died on 7 May 1865; she was some eleven years older than Courbet, and that discrepancy in their ages may have helped to bring about the break-up of their relationship.[22]

Désiré was about twenty-five at his death, whereas Courbet clearly told friends that his son had died at twenty. But he was not a man for exactitude in such matters; and 'twenty' might well have stuck in his mind as expressive of the young man's untimely death. The weight of the circumstantial evidence leaves no doubt that Désiré Binet was his son. It was in 1872 that he told Lydie of the bereavement. Since Virginie was then dead, he must have had friends in Dieppe who notified him of his son's end. In that troubled year he would hardly have been making inquiries himself at Dieppe – though it is possible that after his release from jail and the sanatorium, he wrote on his return to Ornans to the boy and was told of the death by the widow.

As Courbet's attitudes to women, with their full dramatisation in the case of Virginie, are so important to the understanding of the process that drove him into Realism and Socialism, we may take some more passages which record his utterances. Castagnary says:

He boasted that he had freed himself from women. 'If I suffered from my passions when young,' he used to say, 'I suffer from them no longer today.' Illusion. He had a tender heart and was jealous. He rolled his eyes. Woman in his life never went beyond the second order. She was a companion; she was a model. He has painted the living French woman. No more of a Greek woman with straight nose and thick chin. Nothing of the East.

Silvestre imputes to him much the same point of view; he may be expanding a little what he heard Courbet say, and his own comments are quite superficial, but his account clearly has its factual basis. It needs to be cited at length:

He adores originality of opinions and eccentricity of words, which brings him to believe in the value of certain grotesques, the apostle Jean Journet for example. But these passing infatuations have been no danger for the artist, who is absorbed in the joy of being himself.

'I have found', he says, 'perfect happiness; boredom is unknown to me (so much the worse: without torments, no genius); I love things for what they are, and I make each of them spin to my own profit. Why should I seek to see in the world what isn't there, and to disfigure by efforts of the imagination all that I find there. There are some persons who detest dogs; why? Myself, I judge them by what they are; I recognise in every being its natural function; I give it a just meaning in my pictures; I even make stones think. I don't scorn anything. If I meet today a woman endowed with a quality, I enjoy it; tomorrow I pass on to another with a different quality.'

Then he makes the remark about becoming free, cited above, and adds, 'Every night I go over my ideas, my actions of the day: which teaches me to live logically, rationally. If I feel myself on the wrong road, I change it.' Silvestre goes on:

He believes that he has arrived at the knowledge, the possession of himself, and has got 'to the bottom' of his illusions. 'In losing them I have lost nothing; there always remain enough, and besides, have I not the unknown before me to take the place of them all?' It is thus that he is assured of instructing himself, of watching his personality grow from day to day in geometric progression, of *thinking more and more strongly* about his own genius and our stupidity.

From sixteen to twenty he was distracted by a love which he calls Chivalric Love and which made him shed tears on the ills of humanity. Then a less disinterested love possessed him: Self-love. 'I'd have liked to save from a fire a beloved woman before the eyes of ten thousand astounded spectators; but I wouldn't have been fully satisfied at rescuing her without witnesses.' Then a third variety of Love brought him to ask a woman to sacrifice herself, kill herself for him, to prove to the world at what a price Courbet was to be adored.

He has become more modest, if not more reasonable. 'Impossible', he says, 'to stick to one woman if you want to know woman, and as nothing "belongs" to a man but his ideas (his boots, alas, are not always his) it's only a fool who can say that the least thing, his woman for instance, is exclusively his. She belongs to all men, and all men to her. She plays in the world a mysterious role that one can call an apostolate. If you can seduce her by money, sentiment, or glory, she belongs to you more naturally, more legitimately, than to her husband. She's a bird in passage which stops for a certain time in your place. Love is born to run through the world and not to instal itself in households, like an old domestic; and the artist who gets married isn't an artist; he's a sort of jealous proprietor, always ready to be irritated when you visit his home, and who says, "My wife", as he'd say "My stick" or "My umbrella". If my ideas could prevail, the world wouldn't long delay in seeing things clearly.'

He thus identifies marriage entirely with property and cannot conceive of a permanent love-relationship which rises above the property-sense, jealousy, greed. Such an attitude reveals his own strong property-sense, which imposed on him so intense a feeling of insecurity in his dealings with women that he could not endure the suffering. As Castagnary said, 'Illusion. He had a tender heart and was jealous.' And Champfleury remarks, 'Decidedly Courbet understands nothing of women.' Castagnary further insists; 'Courbet, I must state at once, so that there may be nothing equivocal, was chaste and modest [*pudique*]. His healthy peasant nature had preserved itself as well as his democratic ways of behaviour. He was, if you like, a subtle and crafty peasant, but above all chaste and virtuous. Those who've kept company with him know as I do that indecencies of thought repelled him and that the refined hypocrisy of the Empire-manners made him indignant.' He adds, 'Chaste and modest as he was, he would never have been ready to hold an exhibition of nudes.' He may be overstressing his point; but it seems true that sexual matters on the whole rather frightened Courbet. We may indeed assume that he gave much more of an appearance of being a promiscuous lover than the facts warranted; his increasing indulgence in beer and wine must be seen in part as an escape from the problems of sex. As we shall see, he was extremely timid of approaching women with offers: we have two cases when he used intermediaries in marriage-projects and was quite incapable of speaking to or meeting the women he wanted, and one case where he used intermediaries in vain to win a peasant-girl as mistress.

An interesting sidelight into the world of artists, models and light girls frequenting the cafés of the *vie de Bohème*, is given in a laconic comment of Jongkind's in a letter: 'I add that from 1849 to 1855 in Paris, I could have got four natural children that are dead or didn't live in the world because I didn't have any money to pay out. And that only one child has survived because for three years I have given 20 francs a month to the old nurse. I have never seen mother nor children again but I hope they're getting on all right.'

We can now return to the painting of his three sisters, *Young Women of the Village*. His bond with all three of them was very close; in wanting to paint them in a group after he had suffered from the news of Virginie's departure, he was seeking to find in them a consolation for his loss, a substitute for Virginie, which would lessen his pain. In place of his own newly-established lost family group, Virginie and Désiré, he returns to the bosom of the family from which he had sprung. Virginie has gone, but he still has Zoé, Zélie, Juliette. He still has his *franc-comtois* nature, with which he surrounds the girls in the form of the enclosing cliff-walls and the central nook from which water flows: a landscape-image especially dear to him, with an underlying sexual significance. *Young Women* like the *Burial* has, then, a background of cliffs, but here they have a cosy protective aspect, enclosing the pleasant little pasture where the girls are grouped like the Three Graces or the Three Goddesses in the competition before Paris – whereas in the *Burial* they are obscurely and threateningly shut in. (In the theme of Paris and the Goddesses, the shepherd holds out the golden apple: here one of the trio holds out, not an apple, but some sort of dainty.) An act of charity carries across the class-barriers.[23]

The impulse driving Courbet to this picture was his deep suffering over Virginie and his need to rediscover and affirm his primal family bond. With Zoé and Juliette he felt an intense and enduring bond, though the self-willed Zoé ultimately broke it; of his relations with the more shadowy Zélie we know less. In the last years Juliette stresses how she and Gustave had meant to live for one another, and she writes at his death as if she had lost a husband. We know little of the lives of the girls apart from Zoé's later years. They certainly had to do hard work on the farm and in the kitchen, though they soon developed very different characters, which were well brought out in the painting: Zoé stands a little withdrawn, firmly and proudly posed, her shoulders drawn back and her middle thrust out, 'with her pretty profile and arched nose, her big eyes, her magnificent head of hair half hidden under a broad hat'. Juliette is also a little withdrawn, sheltering under her parasol and turning her head rather than her whole body towards the cowgirl. Zélie alone is out in the open, piously absorbed in the act of charity, gentler than the other two. Zoé's head-strong career we shall trace later; Zélie seems simply to have declined into disease and religion; Juliette thus became the dominant figure in the family as her mother aged, wilful and possessive. Zoé later said of her, 'It is necessary for her to dominate and her alone; having failed to realise her illusions, she has become ferocious and embittered against the whole human race.'[24]

Despite Zélie's ill-health she had to toil on the farm. Gros-Kost describes an encounter with her.

We saw her for the first time on one of our walks at Ornans. She was at her father's house, in the stable. Arms bared, her hands full, she was picking up dung. Our romantic instincts of the epoch – we were young – were at first chilled. The heap stank so badly that it produced a torrid heat. However, when the young girl lifted up her head to speak to us, and when we saw her two eyes, white and long as eggs, we suddenly understood Realism. *That* no longer stank. On all evidence he could find things beautiful in what the fops of letters call rottenness. Courbet had made the portrait of this young woman. The eyes in it are very beautiful.[25]

We may recall the earlier picture of the three girls chatting with an old woman; they are very much farm-girls there.

This farming aspect of family life we must set by the more genteel picture of the musical evenings with Zoé poring over a fashionable novel, especially those of George Sand. The genteel aspects, however, are what dominate in Champfleury's novel already cited. What is stressed there is Zélie's deep withdrawn piety and Zoé's restless feminism. Champfleury was not a novelist of much imagination; we can be sure that, while underlining certain traits, his picture is substantially correct, especially since it harmonises with the other evidence we have about the girls. He may perhaps overstress Zélie's piety; and at one point he makes her try to save her brother's soul by an attempt to destroy his manuscripts (that is, pictures). We have no evidence to support this episode. But Juliette and Zoé certainly seem to have been drawn very close to the facts. Here are some passages, with only the names changed:

With an astonishing flow of words she pestered me with questions about the celebrated Octavie Chaumont [George Sand]: was I a devotee of her novels, had I known her in person, had I loved her, did she really dress as a man, did she smoke, was she beautiful, had I read her last book, *Caressa*, what did I think of its style, etc.

'My dear child,' said Gustave, 'we aren't fanatics of the writings of women who with rare exceptions have something else to do than dirty their fingers with ink.'

Without fear of offending his sister Gustave maliciously added that there were no women famous for the practice of medicine, that history named no more women illustrious for their work in the law, and that poetry could dispense with the cult of giddy young ladies.

'You are a man without ideals,' Zoé replied.

Mme Courbet and her two other daughters listened to this discussion without taking part; but one read in their eyes that they weren't displeased at seeing Zoé being given a little lesson. However, I had pity on her and added that our studies prevented us from reading novels and that the book *Caressa* was as unknown to me as its author.

'What do you spend your time doing then?' Zoé asked ironically. . . .

Saturday evening, M. Courbet didn't appear at table; he had gone to see a property for sale in the neighbourhood. Zoé profited by his absence to return to her favourite theme, the role that woman ought to play in the future. To hear her, woman will have 'superb rights' such as the seigneurs of comic operas enjoy. Woman no longer being the *slave* of man, the conditions of marriage will be entirely changed, and the position of women will correspondingly rise.

'Don't you think, sister, that women should enter the Chamber of Deputies?' said Gustave. . . .

If Courbet were echoing Proudhon's ideas, the raillery of Zoé would be correct enough; for Proudhon was extremely reactionary in his views on women. He declared that woman could be only housewife or courtesan; 'rather seclusion than emancipation. Woman must always be a minor or an apprentice. To give her political rights was profligacy or pornocracy. Only man must have the right to divorce; any woman who complains must be guilty and sent back to her household.' From a different angle Courbet indeed held the same positions. In some notes, apparently written for Proudhon, he makes these aphorisms on women:

Work necessitates the domination of the senses and the conservation of one's authority over woman. That is why marriage should be free.

The man who has consciousness of himself can, I believe, up to a certain point, reproduce himself normally in his children.

Woman, who lacks the aesthetic and dialectic faculties, should be submitted and faithful to man.

The basis of these attitudes in his jealous temperament, his fear that any attempt at an enduring pact with a woman would drive him mad with jealousy, appears in another aphorism:

The extreme love that one can have for a woman is a sickness; it absorbs the thinking faculties, makes man jealous and worse than the beast. Jealousy is misplaced pride.

To return to Champfleury:

Once again Zoé began her diatribes against men, and so sharply that such remarks would make one think her unmarriageable in the country. Zoé had driven off the young men of the town by her pretensions. . . .

Zoé returns unceasingly to the *ideal woman*, and I seek in vain to find out what is the ideal woman she means. Perhaps she regards herself as the ideal woman. . . .

Champfleury adds that all this talk about the Ideal Woman makes him think rather of Juliette with her life of uncomplaining hard work. In another passage he stresses the bond between brother and sisters. 'When he spoke of his sisters, of his father's devotion, I felt the force of the bonds that attached him to his family.'[26] If Zoé indeed kept on talking of the Ideal Woman, she must have been one of the irritants pushing her brother on to his denunciation of the Ideal, which for him came to mean romantic love and illusion, and also all idealised forms in art. This hatred of the Ideal was a necessary aspect of his drive to Realism.

The 1852 Salon opened on 1 April. There was a single jury, made up of seven men chosen by the artists and seven appointed by the director-general of museums. Besides *Young Women*, Courbet showed the *Banks of the Loue* and a portrait of Urbain Cuénot. He did not meet such massive and strident disapproval as in 1850–1; but the critics were mainly antagonistic. The *Demoiselles* was found vulgar, the cattle wooden. Even the cliff-rocks, so true to Franche-Comté, were declared preposterous by G. Planchet, who had never visited the area. L. Esnault grew indignant about the dog: 'Courbet has extended the ridiculous as far as dogs', the creature was 'a frightful little bastard'. E. Loudun declared:

One can't imagine a scene uglier, more deserted, less agreeable; it's one of those withdrawn places where sometimes wanders an emaciated goat seeking a blade of grass. As for the girls, 'the beggar-girl isn't beautiful; she's clad in rags, that's all too correct; but the young ladies! My God! one understands clearly why they've sought out this solitary place! They're so lacking in charms, so ungraceful, with such a common air, so badly dressed, that they can't want to meet anyone. Unquestionably M. Courbet is unlucky in not knowing any prettier girls.

He makes jokes about the perspective, and concludes, 'I am not touched, nor instructed, nor amused. M. Courbet follows this road so as to get himself talked about, he's satisfied; in this I express the general feeling'. T. Gautier in *La Presse* on 12 May liked one of the sisters but said that another had 'the air of a woman-cook in her Sunday best; her flesh is brick-red with shadows of soot, and the rose of her dress turns into wine-dregs'. Still, Courbet 'the rustic, the wild man, the realist all the same has sacrificed to the Graces in his own fashion.' C. de Ris in the *Artiste*, however, found the work full of energy, truth, and life, though he apologised for small-town girls who would not be expected to show the easy graces of Parisians.[27]

It is usually considered that Courbet had sheered off political themes in a failure of nerve after the violent attacks of 1850–1; and his comment that he would put the critics 'off the track' might seem to support this view. But, as we saw, the remark occurred in a letter where he was oddly shy about explaining his subject, and was the sort of thing he thought up with a chuckle during work. What he was avoiding was not politics, but his pain over Virginie; or rather he was trying to resolve that pain in a definition of the family bond that had not proved a snare and a delusion. That he was even more ready to make a political affirmation in the Salon is shown by his putting in the portrait of Cuénot – especially as it seems that this work had already been shown in 1848. The point of putting forward this work lay in the fact that Cuénot was in jail at the time, one of the men arrested during the purge after the *coup*; to show the portrait at this moment was a bold act. (We may note that Cuénot had once been mayor of Ornans, so that there may well have been a stronger radical section there than election results generally showed).[28] Proudhon was still in jail and Max Buchon was in exile.

Courbet had on his hands a work which he had begun the previous summer before going to Belgium, on a theme said to have been suggested by Proudhon: *Departure of the Fire-brigade*. Here, as in *The Stone-Breakers*, he was taking up a popular art-system, that of the Trades or *Métiers*. The handicrafts of the village had appeared in small *genre*-pictures; he gave the theme a monumental form in *The Stone-Breakers*, which had been to a slight extent foreshadowed by his earlier (unexhibited) *Knife-Grinders*. In the 1840s there had been published a book by De la Bédollière, *Les industriels métiers et professions en France*, with engravings after Monnier; its picture of knife-grinders reminds one of the work by Courbet and also one by Decamps.[29] Indeed in this matter Courbet had many predecessors besides Decamps. The Leleux brothers had been depicting road-workers and woodcutters; and we often meet the rebel figures of poacher and smuggler. Industrial work proper, which Courbet never attempted, had been treated by Bonhommé in the Salons of 1838 and 1840, while Chassériau had painted the Le Creusot mill in 1836 and Géricault *The Lime-Kiln* in 1823. Millet, as we noted, had begun realistically on the country workers in the fields. But, apart from certain aspects of Millet's work, none of these developments had the challenging character or the monumental assertion of Courbet.[30] He alone made his work seem as aggressive in the world of art as did the workers with their demands for the Right to Work, the revolutionary slogan of 1848. It is noteworthy that a leading theoretician of this movement was the Fourierist Victor Considérant, compatriot of Courbet and Buchon, having been born at Salins.[31]

However, Courbet had no luck with his *Firemen*. The work showed the brigade setting out to deal with a night-fire. Awakened householders lean from windows; the uniformed firemen with their engines, followed by an excited crowd, race to the burning house; on one side a bourgeois couple are caught up, yet isolated; on the other a woman of the people is seen with a child. Courbet, we are told, began the canvas in the large hall of the *caserne* which the commandant had put at his disposal. The latter even sounded the alarm one night to let him see the men in action. An order came that such favours must stop, but a lieutenant, a friend of Courbet, was accused of telling his men to throw vitriol on buildings to produce a better fire, and was condemned to be deported. The canvas was returned to Courbet, who rolled it up. Exactly when these events occurred is not clear; but it seems clear that the *coup d'état* ended the favours and brought disaster on the heads of Courbet's friends among the *pompiers*.[32]

As with the *Burial* there is a certain link with the Dutch paintings of Companies (which range from Van der Helst's *Captain Bicker's Company* to Rembrandt's *Nightwatch*); but in both his works the whole concept of the big group-composition has been metamorphosed. In the *Burial* the group engaged in a ceremony are given symbolic depth; in the *Firemen* the civic organisation is shown dramatically at work.

Courbet has reduced and simplified the formal and expressive complexity of Rembrandt's group-portrait, lining up his figures across the surface of the canvas rather than having them emerge from an evocative shadow-filled background.

The reductive tendency in the composition, as well as the iconography of the *Firemen*, may be due to the intervention of popular, or more accurately, semi-popular, art. The theme of fires and firemen, while hardly touched on by major artists, had long been a favourite of their more popular counterparts, especially of the *canardiers*, those creators of broadsides consisting of crude wood-cuts accompanied by simple commentaries, dealing with crimes of passion, disasters, and other *épouvantables catastrophes*; on a more elevated level, publications, like *L'illustration* or the *Magasin pittoresque*, used more accurate, circumstantial, and realistic wood-engravings, often with nocturnal settings. . . . (SCHAPIRO).

Also, *L'Illustration* in 1843 had printed a long article on the work of the fireman and the up-to-date techniques of fire-fighting; and one of the engravings may well have served Courbet as the starting-point for his work. Finally he may well have been stimulated by a song, *L'Incendie* (published in 1851), by his friend Dupont, which has much the same material and feeling, with the firemen as *soldats pacifiques*.

In January 1852 Courbet had written to Wey, 'I paint stonebreakers; Murillo did a flea-cracker. I'm a socialist and Murillo an honest man. It's unbelievable.' He was complaining of police-surveillance. Perhaps he had drawn attention to himself by visiting Proudhon in jail. In 1874 the Italian Ferrari, in an article in the *Nuova Antologia*, mentions Courbet among the friends received by Proudhon in the prison-parlour; Proudhon at that time was wearing the blouse in which Courbet painted him and which a peasant of Beauce had given him. In his notebook Proudhon mentions under 4 June that he was set free and on that day went for a walk with Courbet and some others to Meudon. Later, in the summer, he went with Courbet and Champfleury to visit Chenavard in the studios in the Louvre. Carrying heavy vinestocks as sticks, the visitors wrote their names on a piece of paper. The guards, we are told, were scared and stupefied; they ran left and right with an air of wanting to pass on the responsibility of letting in such dangerous persons. At last permission was given. They found Chenavard meditating a pastoral letter from the Archbishop of Paris, which condemned his decorations prepared for the Panthéon as guilty of humanitarian and palingenesiac trends. Champfleury notes, 'Though Chenavard was one of the most seditious spirits in Paris, I think he cursed us for thinking of this visit.' Still, he and Chenavard engaged in a learned discussion. Suddenly Proudhon noticed a cartoon that depicted the burning of the Alexandrian Library by Omar. 'Then you don't know that's a legend?' Chenavard was put out of countenance. The talk turned on marriage, and Chenavard got his own back on Proudhon by accusing him of inconsistency in marrying when his theories were a negation of marriage. Courbet agreed. Champfleury, though still celibate, disagreed. 'For me you're all wrong. A celibate is hardly interesting. It's certain that in the arts and letters he finds too many reasons for growing old and corrupt.' For a while the talk was envenomed. But at last it was cut short. Proudhon was pleased at the visit. 'Your *paintings* have interested me; at least I'm not bothered with *colour*.' Chenavard painted *en grisaille*, grey. Later Proudhon used the discussion for a chapter in his book on art: 'Opinion of M. Chenavard on the Degeneration of the Arts.'[33]

On 5 September, Champfleury wrote to Max Buchon (whom he had not yet met but with whom he had begun an extensive correspondence): 'I have been to see Courbet who was leaving for some days at Dieppe, and who will send you your manuscripts on his return, unless he takes them to you personally.' No doubt Courbet was off to see Virginie and his son. How often he paid such visits we do not know; this is the only one that we definitely know about. An undated letter, perhaps written about this time, mentions that many meetings were going on. 'I'd like to have the time to tell you the adventures of a barrister who is at bay and who made the mistake of bringing us together, once a week, Courbet, Dupont, Mathieu, Français, Schann[e], Murger and me. What this unfortunate man has already suffered from having us with him would require two or three pages.'[34]

In September Théodore de Banville and Philoxène Boyen put on at the Odéon a revue, *Le Feuilleton d'Aristophane*, in one scene of which Réaliste, made up to look like Courbet, recites his creed:

> It's not enough for a Realist to paint the truth;
> One must paint ugliness. So, if you please,
> Whatever I draw is horrible to excess.
> My painting's frightful. To ensure its utter truth
> I tear out Beauty as you pull up weeds.
> I love the colour of mud and cardboard noses.
> I love the dainty maids with bearded chins,
> The features of scarecrows and of nonsense-bogies,
> Bunions and corns and plenty of warts as well.
> Such is the Truth.[35]

Aristophanes, revolted, summons a Muse whose verses in praise of Beauty send the Realist fleeing in dismay.

Courbet's ideas had now fully crystallised; he was to refine and expand them, but what he had arrived at was the clear basis on which he built henceforth. As we have seen, from one aspect his breakthrough into Realism belonged to a wide trend which embraced many other artists and many writers; it expressed something that had to happen one way or another as a result of the thinning-out of the classical and romantic schools. But it happened as it did, not only because of general trends, but also because of the specific character of Courbet, his ingrained spirit of *montagnard* independence reacting from the given situation and acting in turn upon it. In literature with Stendhal and Balzac a powerful movement towards Realism in Courbet's sense had already come about. That is, these novelists depicted social reality with great faithfulness, but they also realised the social forces embedded in the individuals they depicted. With Balzac a new sense of energy entered literature, a complex dialectic of the new bourgeois individual (self-made in a literal sense in that he has built himself up in a world of ruthless competition) and the society of which he was a refraction and an expression, and which heightened its inner drive with the myth of the bourgeois as the first creators of history. But despite Géricault, paint-ing lagged behind till Courbet burst into the new dimension. Balzac had defined with end-less variety and depth the new individual convinced of his existence as a self-made force, but as artist he defined also his social essence; and he maintained this dual vision (brought together in a single focus in the creative act) by his critical position as a defender of the earlier bonds and solidarities that the bourgeois order was destroying. For Courbet such a position was no longer tenable. He needed to find his critical position in terms of the future, not the past; in terms of what man should, would, and must be, not of what he had been. The Balzacian vision of energy (derived from a man who himself was a dynamo of activity) thus worked on a new level, in a new field. Courbet the *montagnard* in a sense was a more archaic figure than Balzac the Parisian with his intricate awareness of what was happening in society at all levels; and yet by virtue of his new allegiance, which could only have been achieved by a man in his particular class-situation, with his particular peasant-bourgeois basis, he drove forward to perspectives impossible to Balzac, or glimpsed by him only in passing intuitions.

In considering these points we can come closer to understanding Courbet's Realism (inseparable from his socialist views and his desperate personal need to transcend romantic-ism) than by any amount of analysis of the state of the artistic world in the 1840s – with its lack of inner drive or purpose, its inability to find any way of developing on Delacroix, and its schools derelict of vitality. The picture of an emptiness has significance only in terms of the new outlooks coming up to fill it with life and purpose; and that life and purpose could not but be the intrusion in some shape of the Balzacian world of vehement energy, self-absorbed and opening up a new sense of the social whole. Although Champfleury, Max Buchon and others had been moving towards some sort of more realistic outlook, it was Courbet who alone had the comprehensive grasp and drive that created Realism as an aesthetic concept. Similarly, while Corot and the Barbizon school, Millet, Decamps and others, did important work in leading in the same direction or in strengthening the trend as it clearly emerged, it was Courbet who made the definitive breakthrough, so that the potential of these other expressions could be realised. It was essentially in connection with his work that the term 'Realism' came into use. When we consider the gigantic contribution by Balzac, the so-called realist novels of Champfleury and Buchon are very slight stuff. These works had their links rather with the work of George Sand; their affinity with Courbet lay in their rusticity, their interest in popular levels of culture and manners. They thus reflected certain elements that went to make up the full composition of Courbet, but with incomparably less intensity; and they lacked his large-scale synthesis. A new breakthrough in the novel at all commensurate with Courbet's achievement came with Zola, whose work had its links with both Courbet and Cézanne.[36]

Though Courbet now had his course definitely set, it is not for some years yet that we shall meet his mature statements of the nature of his Realism – in part because he had to absorb much of Proudhon's philosophy before he had the words for those declarations.

There is thus a certain amount of truth in Lemonnier's statement:

Realism was both a rallying-point and an expression of defiance. It was like a blast of trumpets, sounding a flourish in the ears of the timid with a bellicose uproar; on the contrary it had for others the sonority and the precision of a watchword, and Courbet was the leader who directed both attack and defence. The disputes of the spirit need a banner, as the battles of the body need *panache*; it is good to know where one marches and behind whom one marches.[37]

But one has to add what one rallies for and what one defies.

We may pause here to consider some of the many accounts we have of Courbet at work. Castagnary tells us:

Towards three o'clock, 'Must work', he said. We went up. I sat on the divan. He lit his pipe, set himself before his easel, threw out some words in his high voice, and then, seizing his palette and knife, he began to paint, all the while talking, laughing, smoking, sometimes getting up and going back a step or two to see the effect of his work. He painted with a marvellous precision. I followed the movements of his arms. His hands were long, elegant, and of a rare beauty. I felt an extreme pleasure in watching him work. For the first time I saw how he used the knife and what marvellous effects he got with it.[38]

But with all his interruptions of jokes, stories, laughter, and bursts of songs of his own invention, 'his hand was so agile and sure that he ended by doing a lot of work'.

With his quick attack he needed the use of the palette-knife, which he was the first painter to use on such a grand scale and for such a variety of effects. With a driving impulse which insisted on breaking down the old barriers of life and art, he needed a method that both enabled him to do a great deal of work, some of it big in form, and at the same time to spend much time in the business of living: talking, drinking, moving about, making love to models. By his talking and singing at work he to some extent broke down those barriers even during the act of creation. And yet his particularising vision prevented him from scamping work, from brushing wildly and lavishly in over-generalised or abstracted forms. His method had to combine speed, precision, breadth and clarity of individual form. While he developed much control of the brush for the purposes of quickly defining and moulding a form in terms of its rhythmical nature, he went further and learned how to use the palette-knife for the same purposes at an even greater speed. Here lay his one great technical innovation; and its implications led on to both the fresh direct attack of impressionism and to the expressionist rhythms of Van Gogh. It was typical of him that while his drawing with pencil and pen was at times clumsy and rarely distinguished, with brush or knife he seldom failed to express form with power, fullness and truth. Thus, we can see that his approach was essentially plastic; he needed the sense of directly moulding and building up his forms. His more successful drawings are those which rely least on line and most on tone and mass: for example, the charcoal-study of the heads of two sleeping girls which has been taken as a first idea for the *Demoiselles of the Seine* (interestingly the girls here have a rustic quality, and nothing of the ingrained heavy 'vice' of the *demoiselles* of the painting).

After he broke from the old methods of chiaroscuro, he turned more to local colour, but always with a rich effect of underlying harmonies. His visits to the sea and the South gave him an increased sense of atmospherics and of strong sunlight; his colours became higher and lighter, subtler in their tonal variations. To some extent he was carrying on the work of Rousseau and the Barbizon painters, of Boudin, but once again he was the one that made the decisive break with academic notions of colour-harmony and opened the way to Monet and Cézanne.[39]

It is of interest to glance across the channel at the advent of the Pre-Raphaelites, which was synchronous with the advent of Courbet's Realism. Certain similarities are at once evident: the rejection of academic norms and traditions (Courbet was even more scornful of Raphael than was any pre-Raphaelite), the aim of capturing directly the form and nature of the object, the use of local colour, and the turning to the world of work for themes. Ruskin rejected school-teaching in favour of the direct study of nature. 'No one had ever told me to draw what was really there.' In 1842 in the Forest of Fontainebleau, when drawing a tree, he found 'the beautiful lines insisted on being traced. . . . I saw they "composed" themselves, by finer laws than any known of men. At last, the tree was there, and everything that I had thought before about trees, nowhere'. This is the essential Courbet-experience. Ford Madox Brown in the later 1840s, as he himself said, 'endeavoured to carry out the notion of treating the light and shade absolutely as it exists at any one moment instead of approximately or in a general style'. At the Pre-Raphaelite exhibition in April 1850 the reaction of critics and public was close to that which Courbet aroused. Hunt was criticised for 'abruptness, singularity, uncouthness'; the *Art Journal* said that 'the manner and drawing of the figures show all the objectionable peculiarities of the infancy of Art' – exactly the sort of thing said of Courbet. Of Millais's *Christ in the House of his Parents*, *The Times* declared: 'The picture is plainly revolting', and the *Literary Gazette* saw it as 'a nameless atrocity . . . in which there is neither taste, drawing, expression, or genius'. Dickens in *Household Words* launched a vicious attack, ending with the statement that the mother was 'so horrible in her ugliness that (supposing it were possible for any human creature to exist for a moment with that dislocated throat) she would stand out from the rest of the company as a monster in the vilest cabaret in France or in the lowest gin-shop in England'. But what was truly revolutionary in the school was soon lost; the impact weakened and faded out; the main stream (of Rossetti) went on to cherish dissidence only on the level of aestheticism: a rebuke of bourgeois ugliness that could be tolerated or absorbed – or it accommodated itself to the demand for sentimental anecdote. Millais, who in his way could have become an English Courbet, steadily lost his force. Only with Morris, in the later stages, was the original revolutionary impulse belatedly regained – and then it took the form of Ruskinian critique and craft-applications. There was no great artist such as Courbet, or as Millais might have been, to provide a rallying-point in the sphere of practising art itself. (Henry Wallis in 1858 showed a *Stonebreaker* as a protest against crushing physical labour and John Brett painted a youth at the backbreaking toil; but no one took the works to heart. Wallis's *Chatterton* of 1856 was the popular work.)[40]

Why did this happen? No doubt we must seek the answer in a number of converging factors. After 1848 there was no such radical resistance among the people as in France led in time to the Paris Commune; the response which Rossetti and others confusedly gave to 1848 had no staying-power; there was no *montagnard* Courbet; the issues were blurred whereas in France the fight against Salon-controls and Napoleon's imperial State kept them sharp and urgent. But only a detailed analysis of the protagonists and their situation could help to explain the divergent tracks taken by French Realism and English Pre-Raphaelitism. Still, the fact that similar choices did appear in the art of England and France in 1848–50 is highly significant, and brings out the role of socialist convictions in Courbet's break-through.

It is instructive too to compare the fortunes in France and in England of the large-scale (History) painting with a contemporary subject. In France, Courbet combined his realism with this form of direct attack on the ruling idealist themes. In England the transition from the old type of *genre*-painting to a big canvas with a considered representation of contemporary society was slower, with many transitions. The man who made the final leap was W. P. Frith, and his work gained immediate acceptance because of its complete conformity to the ideas that bourgeois society had of itself. In 1851, on holiday at Ramsgate, he 'determined to try my hand on modern life, with all its drawbacks of unpicturesque dress'. But 'so novel was the attempt to deal with modern life that I felt it very necessary to be able to show to those whose advice I valued the clearest possible indication of my new venture'. Then after the success of his modest *Ramsgate Sands*, he grew more ambitious; he sought 'a theme capable of affording me the opportunity of showing an appreciation of the infinite variety of everyday life', and found it in his *Derby Day*, exhibited in 1858.[41]

In his *Méthodes et Entretiens sur l'Art* in 1867 T. Couture declared that 'the year 1848 had given a new impetus to sales; fear of confiscation had caused many persons to dispose of their pictures'. A vogue for small works set in. Couture adds, 'Great art should be as true to the creations of the spirit as *genre*-painting should be to reality.' Thus he allows *genre* its claims to realism but banishes it to a lower level than the big picture of serious art. That was the attitude that Courbet had challenged with his treatment of everyday life as History; he thus annoyed both the academic world and the expanding bourgeois audience that wanted small works for its walls. However, the Comte de Morny bought *Demoiselles de Village*.[1]

The Salon of 1853 opened on 15 May. In the catalogue Courbet was listed as a pupil of Hesse; he repudiated the description in a letter written on 18 May and published two days later in *La Presse*. He protested that he was self-taught; but when he exhibited at the 1844 Salon he had been obliged, like all new applicants, to register as the pupil of some well-known painter and had asked Hesse for leave to use his name.[2] He had now sent in three works: *Wrestlers, The Sleeping Spinner*, and *The Bathers*. *Wrestlers* was not one of his more successful large pictures. Painted over his romantic *Walpurgis Night*, it showed a pair of massive wrestlers in a tense grapple; their muscles are as painstakingly depicted as in a work by Pollaiuolo; indeed a somewhat academic effect is perhaps due to the debt that the picture owes to Guido Reni's *Hercules and Achelous* in the Louvre.[3] The background is quite out of proportion, enhancing the effect of studio-figures imposed on an out-of-doors sketch. And yet the painting is not such a failure as has been often stated. Courbet certainly admired it and kept on exhibiting it. And:

The picture astonished me for several reasons: the realism of this struggle that assumes a universal significance and took me by the throat; the plasticity of the muscles and its compact rhythm. All that can be said to me on the composition, and that Delacroix has already said, relates to the middle-ground. It's not that, however, which is important for Courbet. And still that sunny sward which gives the painter, through light, the possibility of achieving this plastic quality by means of the play of shadows, has for me a meaning. The pavilion which appears in the background is indeed far off with its elegant spectators. The action of the *Wrestlers* carries on far off from their interests and their life. They lack any true interest in what happens, as they have lacked interest in the struggle of Courbet (M. VISSER).

The Sleeping Spinner must have been painted at Ornans; a fattish girl in a flowered dress and shawl striped white and blue sprawls asleep, the wheel still attached to the fallen distaff by a thread. *The Bathers* showed a heavily built woman, naked save for a towel held across her buttocks, stepping from a shallow pool; her right arm is raised to greet a second woman, dressed and sitting by the water; there is a background of trees and shrubs.

All three works were derided in various ways. The *Wrestlers* were called wooden; a caricature showed the painting on a fair-booth behind the strong-man and the flautist: 'Who then asks what use M. Courbet's painting can have?' Delacroix noted that the work 'lacked action'. The *Spinner* was widely attacked as the picture of a filthy girl. 'A spinner who has never washed herself [*débarbouillée*]': *L'Illustration*. 'The freshness of this village-girl tends to prove to us that slovenliness is not so harmful to the health as is generally thought in society': Cham in *Charivari*. One joker puns on *peindre* (paint) and *peigner* (comb), *filer* (spin) and *filer* (slip by): 'While Courbet was painting her, we see clearly that she was combing out her hair; when she'll wake up, it would be a bad idea for her to slip off to the bath.' It became fashionable to regard Courbet's paintings as stinking. We see a man asphyxiated by his palette on entering the studio without precautions; Cham in 1855 showed the jurors of the Salon in a fainting condition.[4]

But all this was mild fun in comparison with the attacks made on *The Bathers*. Chenavard tells how he heard Delécluze, standing before the canvas, mutter between his teeth, 'These creatures are such that a crocodile wouldn't want to eat them.' Mérimée jested about Courbet sending his works to New Zealand where the cannibals judged how appetising a captive is by his or her weight. Gautier in *La Presse* wrote of a 'Hottentot Venus', a 'bourgeoise Calli-pyge'; Courbet was 'the Watteau of the Ugly'; the *Spinner* had hands like spatulas of wood. P. Mantz in *Revue de Paris* was all for Courbet's protest against the pseudo-classical, but thought he had gone too far; ugliness should be the means, not the end; the *Wrestlers* in its tones was a sad imitation of Guercino; but the broadly-painted *Spinner* was of a luminous reality. However, Edmond About, who had not been friendly to Courbet, praised the sheer animal force of *The Bathers*:

She is not so much a woman as a column of flesh, a rough-hewn tree-trunk, a solid. The artist has handled a human figure like a still-life. He has constructed this brawny mass with a power worthy of Giorgione or Tintoretto. The most surprising thing about it is that this ponderous woman of bronze, articulated in layers like a rhinoceros, has faultlessly delicate knees, ankles, and all joints in general.[5]

This last observation was correct enough; Courbet uniformly painted hands with much delicacy and made them fine objects. Cham described the naked woman as one of 'forty-five years old on the point of washing herself for the first time in her life in the hope of relieving her varicose veins'. C. Perrier called Courbet the 'Antichrist of physical and moral beauty' in *L'Artiste* of October.

Before the public opening came the private show for the imperial family. Napoleon was so shocked that he hit *The Bathers* with his riding-crop. 'If I had only foreseen this spank-ing', said Courbet, 'I'd have used a thin canvas; he'd have torn a hole in it and we should have had a splendid lawsuit.' The empress, who had been admiring the big heavy Percherons in Rosa Bonheur's *Horsefair*, asked, 'Is she a Percheron mare too?'[6]

In *Les Doctrines de G. Courbet* (1862), Guichard, who himself admired the *Baigneuses*, says that he had had many disputes about it. 'The irritation got to the point that the police commissioner of the Quarter wanted to drive it out of the Exhibition, as injuring proprieties and manners. Ladies turned away in disgust, grave men shrugged their shoulders, young fellows laughed and were captivated by the young girls' embarrassment; there was a chorus of condemnation.'[7]

The model for the *Spinner* has been often identified as Zélie; but this is unlikely. She seems to be the girl whom Courbet painted with a goat in her arms; he himself tells us, 'I've taken a cowgirl for my spinner.' And the portraits we have of Zélie are not at all like the spinner. Riat says that the huge *baigneuse* was a model named Joséphine, who was also his mistress. Silvestre says of a *Study of a Woman* bought by Bruyas that the model of the nude was a thirty-year-old woman, bourgeoise and *franc-comtoise*, who early in 1853 came daily to pose in his studio; he adds that this Joséphine left her husband to follow Courbet. (It seems that in the gossip handed on among Courbet's friends there was some confusion between this Joséphine and Virginie Binet.)[8] Apart from the portraits, and the two pictures with the three girls in a group, Zoé seems to have been the sister whom Courbet used as a model. She appeared in *Winnowers*; and she may have been, it is suggested, the nude bather of 1866, in which the head is clearly not that of the model, and the inspiring Muse-model of the big *Studio*. We cannot prove this point, though it is plausible; and if Zoé did indeed pose naked for these works, we have a further insight into the hidden complexity of Courbet's relations with his sisters. From what we know of Zoé's bold character, such posing is not at all unlikely.[9]

We have a letter of Courbet's, written home on 13 May, just before the Salon opened:

My life here is a ceaseless tribulation of comings and goings, of visits; in short, my head's in a ˙ʅɹᴉɥʍ My pictures have been taken by the jury some days ago without any kind of objection; I have been considered, as it were, admitted by the public and *hors de jugement*. They have finally left me the responsibility for my own works. I make a bit of money every day. All Paris gets ready to see them and hear the noise they'll start off. I've just heard from Français that they're well hung. It's the *Spinner* that wins most admirers. As for *The Bathers*, it causes a bit of a scare, though, since you saw it, I've added a cloth across the buttocks. This picture's landscape has a general success. As for the *Wrestlers*, nobody has so far said anything good or bad. M. de Morny lent me the frame of the *Demoiselles de Village*, which means a saving of 200 francs. I've been offered 2,000 for the *Spinner*; I haven't accepted as I hope for 3,000 at least. According to what is coming out, I take a risk. I've sold recently a small landscape of L'Essard-Cendrin, a foot square, to M. Demandre, an iron-master of our region. . . . The biographical notice done on me by Silvestre will soon appear. We've been very taken up, these last days, in getting the photograph of the *Wrestlers*, the *Spinner*, the *Bathers*, and my own likeness. There's nothing more difficult than these operations. We've tried out three or four photographs, which didn't come off. My own portrait is superb; when I have some copies, I'll send you some as well as of my pictures.[10]

A few days later the storm burst. It is a pity that his way of always insisting on his successes in his letters does not enable us to get any idea of how he himself estimated or described his attackers; he of course linked them with the establishment, artistic and political, but a more precise analysis on his part of the role of the attackers, their social bases, and so on, would have been valuable. It is of interest that Delacroix was disquieted and yet fascinated by the *Baigneuses*:

I was amazed by the vigour and depth [*saillie*] of the principal picture; but what a picture! what a subject! The vulgarity of the forms would not matter; what is abominable is the vulgarity and use-lessness of the idea; and moreover, if only that idea, such as it is, was clear! What do these two figures mean? A fat bourgeoise, seen from the back and quite naked but for a strip of cloth, negligently painted, which covers the lower part of the buttocks, emerges from a little sheet of water that seems deep enough only for a footbath. She makes a gesture that expresses nothing, and another woman, whom one supposes a servant, is seated on the earth, busily taking off her shoes. We see stockings just removed; one of them I think is only half done. There is between these figures an exchange of thoughts that one can't comprehend.

The landscape is extraordinarily vigorous, but Courbet has done nothing more than enlarge a sketch we see there near his canvas; the result is that the figures were added later without being corrected in terms of what surrounds them. This brings up the question of harmony between the accessories and the main subject, in which most great painters are deficient. That is not Courbet's worst fault. There is also a *Sleeping Spinner* which displays the qualities of vigour as well as of imitation. The wheel, the distaff, admirable; the dress, the armchair, heavy and graceless. The *Two Wrestlers* show insufficient movement and confirm his poverty of invention. The background kills the figures, and more than three feet of it should be lopped off all round.[11]

He returned to the *Baigneuses* on 17 October. 'It is the cruel reality of things I flee, when I take refuge in the creations of art.' Here he sharply admits the new thing that Courbet has brought into art: a directness of vision which creates an immediate and overwhelming impact. What is involved is not the naturalistic reflection of persons and objects, but the realisation of their individual existence in all its force and weight. Where the artist comes in is in his joyous acclamation of life, his total acceptance: Blake's 'Everything that lives is holy.' There is thus both a passionate unity between artist and image, and a pellucid object-ivity. This relationship rules in all Courbet's work, whatever the theme; and so it is right that his work should be described as essentially 'erotic' – in the sense that he is deeply and sensuously in love with all that he paints.[12] Something of this relationship, indeed, must appear in all vital art; but in Courbet there is a peculiar intensity of contradiction-and-unity between the acceptance of the object in all its rights of individual existence and the aggres-sive act of taking possession. His obsession with hunting, which was soon to appear in his art, had an emotional link with his omnivorous attitude to all objects – persons and things alike.

Champfleury in a letter to Buchon shows that he had anticipated something of the uproar about the *Baigneuses*: 'I think he will have a great success this year; in particular he has a *Spinner* that I rank as a masterpiece. The *Wrestlers* won't be questioned; I won't say the same about a certain nude bourgeoise coming out of the water and showing her behind to the public. You may expect a big scandal if the picture is accepted; for already opinions are heated.' We see here his predilections; and in fact he was beginning to be upset by Courbet's refusal to settle down into a painter of the rural bourgeoisie and their world.[13]

What, then, are we to say of the exhibits? The *Spinner* belongs to the series of *métier*-pictures; and also to Courbet's sleep-series. The sleeper, as we noted, sinks down into the unconscious life of nature; and perhaps what stirred Courbet in part was the effect of vulnerability. For it was almost always a woman that he showed resting and slumbering.

The sleeping woman, absorbed into the life of nature, was no longer the woman with a sharp tongue and demands of her own; in her was then resolved the conflict which we traced above in Courbet's sexual life. He wanted the woman to be a totally free agent, existing in her own right; he wanted her to fall into his arms without bargaining and complaints; but he could not bear the situation when her needs and demands began to conflict with his own and when the ethic of entire independence showed up its egoist basis.

The *Wrestlers* shows in a sense an attempt to carry on the popular-art line which, despite its power and suggestiveness, does not succeed in establishing a style of modelling developed from that of *Stonebreakers* and *Burial*. But the *Baigneuses* was a more complex work. The extent to which it was hated showed that it belonged to the line of the *Burial* and the *Return*; but here it is not a social grouping which is explored. The nude, when effective, has a close relation always to the inner life; for it suggests sexuality and the endless fantasies or experiences connected with nakedness. The naked body suggests a solitude of one or two, in opposition to the clothed body of social intercourse; it symbolically suggests the stripping of pretences and lies. Truth is naked. The approach to the nude thus gives away much about an artist and his society. The smooth graceful nude of the academics, in which sexual life was minimised or diverted slyly into innuendo, represented for Courbet an important aspect of the bourgeois lie and distortion he was attacking all along the line. His big naked woman was an anti-academic image, directed against all the prevailing hypocrisies. From one angle it says: This is the truth you are hiding behind the prettifications, this gross and monstrous body which exposes all the indulgences and greeds in your petty lives. But because of Courbet's love of life the image is ambivalent; he glories in every crease and ounce of the huge body. (We may note how Champfleury and Delacroix agree in calling her 'bourgeoise'; she typifies the gross existence of the bourgeois world. The hostile confrontation of Napoleon and his empress with the work brings out the political point.)

We see then that the work proceeds naturally from that of the previous years: the *Stonebreakers*, the *Burial* and the *Return* giving his post-1848 vision of the rural bourgeoisie and labourers, and the *Demoiselles de Village* expressing his effort to find a sustaining element in the family bond after the blow of Virginie's departure. The *Demoiselles* had its social reference, but also raised for him the question: Where now do I find my sexual point of rest? Thus he moved on to a work which contained both a powerful image of desire and a strong social criticism.

It may be argued that all this is very devious. Why did not Courbet, with his conviction of Realism as the expression of Democracy and Socialism, paint obviously political pictures? This point came up earlier when we noted that Champfleury denied the socialism of his art. We might answer first by asking how much of the art that Courbet looked on as bourgeois and reactionary consisted of works with a directly political defence of the capitalist system? We are not concerned with journalistic cartoons but with the deep and complex ways in which a world-view reveals itself in art. David had built his art on neoclassic History because that style of painting was at its height and he was a partisan in a struggle where the transfer of State power was on the agenda; the conflict *inside* History-painting was the most forceful way of giving an artistic expression to that struggle. Courbet lived at a period when History-painting was in extreme decline and there was no question of a revolutionary taking-over of State power. The art which reflected the ruling class and its allies was the academic art of his attack. What he felt from the outset as the key-thing was a different attitude to people and nature; he fought for a sensibility which outraged the prevailing sensibility because of its values, human and artistic. His great effect lay precisely in the fact that he did not try to short-circuit the process by painting works with a strong overt political content, but in which the new sensibility was poorly realised. What we have to look for is, indeed, many direct political aspects, but, surrounding and penetrating them, the new feeling for people and nature which we have been analysing in his work ever since *Afterdinner at Ornans*. We cannot expect such a deep and complex matter to reveal itself at a glance; we have seen the immediate effect of the new feeling in the violent reaction against his work by those imbued with the old sensibility; but what they were reacting against in all its fullness can only be distinguished by a careful sounding of the depths in his expression. In the same way the involved tangle of personal, social, political and aesthetic elements in his development, in his choice of themes at any given moment, cannot be expected to yield up its secrets to any simple or one-track inquiry. It was the deep tension between his intellectual and political views on the one hand, and his personal conflicts and experiences on the other, which gave his work its great power. Only such a tension could have created a body of art works truly based in a sensibility which broke away from the prevailing values and successfully embodied a socialist world-view.

The 1853 Salon had one useful result for Courbet; it brought him into contact with Jacques-Louis-Alfred Bruyas, who was strongly affected by the works there. Bruyas promptly bought the *Spinner* and the *Baigneuses*, as well as the *Man with the Pipe*, and commissioned a portrait of himself, which Courbet at once painted. In the next four years he bought eight more Courbets. He had been born on 16 August 1821 at Montpellier, his father being a rich easy-going banker. He studied under Matet (then at the head of the Musée Fabre in Montpellier), but gave up the practice of art for the collecting of pictures, drawings, bronzes. In 1846 he had visited Rome to study the paintings there. His health was always delicate; he became tubercular, though he didn't behave as an invalid till he was almost fifty. 'Slim and distinguished in appearance', says Borel, 'there was nothing particularly remarkable about his looks, but one was at once attracted by his eyes'; they were of an unusual colour, 'in which a mysterious fire seemed to glow and which caught and held one like a magnet'. He had a charming voice; introspective, he liked to give an effect of not being quite of this world, a mystic, a saint. But he could be a warm and generous host, and got on well with the noisy chattering Courbet. He had a daughter by a mistress, but did not marry. Having considerable wealth, he commissioned portraits of himself by the most celebrated artists; we know of at least sixteen. The artists included Cabanel, G. Ricard, Diaz (his work later destroyed), Couture (twice), Glaize (thrice), Courbet (thrice), Tassaërt (four times). His characteristic mood appears thoughtful; his features long and thin, his nose bony, his eyes sorrowful, his beard and hair reddish brown. Silvestre, a friend, says that he had so many portraits painted so as to get to know contemporary art and artists. 'A sort of Hamlet, pensive, suffering, but energetic and tenacious, such as Delacroix has translated him in his own ideal, and showing his spirit even when hiding his life.' One small canvas showed him wearing a crown of thorns. In 1868 he gave his whole collection to the Musée Fabre; in 1872 his mother added his fine library of books on art.[14]

In Courbet's first portrait the left hand rests on a green book, *Studies of Modern Art: Solution: Alfred Bruyas*. That expressed the enthusiasm Courbet felt on meeting this patron who suddenly stood by him at a moment of loud obloquy. Bruyas's health did not allow him to stay long in Paris, but he asked Courbet to visit him at Montpellier.

During this year occurred a dispute between Courbet and Couture at the Divan in rue Lepeletier, a café frequented for some years by poets like Baudelaire, de Musset, Banville, de Nerval, Pétrus Borel, artists like Chenavard, Daumier, Delacroix, Gavarni, and saunterers like Wey.[15] Jongkind was not present during the argument between Courbet and Couture, but he wrote an account of it on 7 June 1853 in his bad French:

I have learned that M. Decamps has visited the exposition and said that he finds among all the pictures there that there is in Courbet's pictures *le plus artiste*, only the painter (M. Courbet) mistakes himself [*se méprends*]. Also there has been an encounter between MM. Courbet and Couture at the Divan, where Stevens Willems was, and some good scholars or men of letters, but I wasn't present. But from what I've been told the conversation got so worked up that the public filled the door and the street was crammed with the crowd, I believe that the result is that M. Courbet and M. Couture said they will speak again together at the end of a century.[16]

An account published in *Le Figaro* in 1859 stated that Couture called Courbet a 'cutter of dogs' tails', and was himself called an 'illuminator of boudoirs'. Couture, a small man, got up on a table; Courbet did the same so as to keep his advantage; Diaz, abusing them both, tried to climb up despite his wooden leg. From insult the conflict led on to injury, with Chenavard sitting gravely unconcerned all the while. In the following January, Guichardet with the famous red nose, poking about in the two-*sous* shops, bought for Couture a Harlequin's wooden sword and for Courbet a cardboard turd, 'which is Realistic enough'.[17] Couture was a short-tempered man; after he became court painter, he finally wrecked his own position by answering Napoleon sharply, 'Sire, is it your majesty or me painting this picture?' Among the drawings left in his studio were some for a painting, *Le Réaliste*, satirical of Courbet. The picture he painted showed a realist drawing a pig-snout.

This year Courbet painted a portrait of Champfleury in profile which portrays a rather grim face and was found far from flattering.[18] We do not know in which month the return to Ornans occurred; late in the year Courbet wrote a long letter to Bruyas. He said he had been working very hard or would have written earlier. When he arrived at Ornans, 'I was obliged to go to Berne and Fribourg on business, which was inconvenient' and held up work on the pictures he had in mind. He was sorry he hadn't gone to Montpellier after all, as he wouldn't have lost any more time and it would been more beneficial and pleasant.

One must have courage. I have burned my boats. I have declared war on society. I have insulted everyone who treated me scurvily. And now I am alone against society. One must conquer or die. If I am beaten, it will cost them dear, I promise you. But I am growing more and more certain that I'll triumph; for there are two of us, and at the present time perhaps only six or eight [others] that I know of, all young, all energetic workers, all arriving at the same conclusion by different paths. My friend . . . I am as certain as I am of my own existence that within a year we shall number a million.

It is odd that he should so confidently include the rich connoisseur Bruyas among the devoted band sworn to realism and socialism; but apparently Bruyas's financial backing of his work makes him a solid adherent of realism, and by supporting that creed he is supporting all the causes involved in it.

He goes on to tell proudly of his encounter with Count de Nieuwerkerke, in whom he was at length able to confront and rebuke directly the embodiment of the State and the Institute:

I want to tell you about an incident. Before I left Paris, M. Nieuwerkerke, Director of the Beaux-Arts, invited me to luncheon in the name of the Government; and fearing I might refuse the invitation, he chose as his ambassadors C[henavard] and F[rançais], both *won over*, both *decorated*. I must say to their shame that they played an official role against me. They got me into a favourable mood and supported the Director's wishes. Also, they'd have been happy to see me sell myself as they had.

This is the sort of not-so-creditable way in which Courbet often writes when describing his triumphs. He would certainly have known all along what Chenavard and Français were proposing, and he obviously jumped at the chance of discomfiting the Director. The two artists were not men who had sold out; they lacked Courbet's political convictions, but in this matter they were merely trying to help him according to their own lights.

After they had earnestly begged me to be what they called a 'good fellow', we went to lunch at the Restaurant Douix in the Palais-Royal where M. de Nieuwerkerke was awaiting us. The moment he saw me, he hurried forward, shook my hand, and said he was delighted at my acceptance, that he wanted to be frank with me, and that he wouldn't hide the fact he had come to convert me. (The two others exchanged glances as if to say: What tactlessness! He has just spoiled everything.)

I replied that I was already converted, but that if he could make me change my viewpoint, I asked nothing better than to be taught. He went on to say that the Government regretted to see me going my way on my own, that I must modify my ideas, put water in my wine, that everyone wished me well, that I must not be so quarrelsome, and all kinds of nonsense of that sort. Then he ended his introductory remarks by telling me the Government would like me to paint a picture in my most vigorous style for the Exposition of 1855, that I could rely on his word, and that he would ask condition my presenting of a sketch, and that when the picture was done it would be submitted to a committee of artists chosen by me and a committee selected by himself.

I leave you to imagine the anger which such a proposal roused in me. I replied at once that I didn't understand a word he'd just said, since he was a Government and I did not consider myself in any way included in that Government, that I too was a Government, and that I challenged his to do anything whatever for mine that I could accept. I went on to say that for me his Government seemed just like any private citizen, that if my pictures pleased it, it was free to buy them from me, and that I asked only one thing: that it should grant freedom to art in its Exposition and not use its budget of 300,000 francs to favour 3,000 artists opposed to me. I added that I was the only judge of my own work, that I was not only a painter but also a man, that I painted not to produce art for art's sake, but rather to win my intellectual freedom, that I had used the study of traditional art to liberate myself from it, and I alone, of all contemporary artists had the ability to express and represent in an original way both my personality and my society, etc. etc.

Though Courbet is recording the interview in as favourable a light for himself as his considerable eloquence permits, he had every reason to feel pride. No artist had ever before talked to a high government official in these terms. He could justly feel that the conversation marked an epoch; and so he went to much pains to write out what had happened, for a man whom he wanted to impress and who would be sure to preserve such a document. We may recall how he told Silvestre he had dreamed of rescuing his beloved from a burning house – but with a vast host of spectators.

To this he replied, 'M. Courbet, you are very proud!'
'I'm surprised', I told him, 'that you've only just come to realise that. Sir, I am the most arrogant man in France.'
This fellow, perhaps the most inept I've ever met in my life, looked at me with bewildered eyes. He was all the more confounded because he must have promised his masters and the court ladies that he was going to show them how to buy a man for twenty or thirty thousand francs. He asked me again if I meant to send nothing to the Exposition. I answered that I never entered competitions, because I did not recognise judges, but all the same, out of cynicism, I might send my *Burial*, which was my beginning and my declaration of principles, that they would have to deal with that picture as they could, but that I hoped (perhaps) to have the honour of organising an exhibition of my own, as a rival to theirs, which would bring in 40,000 francs in cash, a sum I certainly wouldn't earn at theirs. I also reminded him that he owed me 15,000 francs for the entrance-fees they had collected on my pictures at previous Salons. that the attendants had informed me they personally conducted 200 people a day to look at my *Bathers*.
To which he gave the idiotic reply, 'Those people didn't go to admire it.' It was easy for me to retort by questioning the value of his personal opinion and by saying that that was not the point: whether visitors came to criticise or admire, the fact remained that they'd pocketed the fees and that half the reviews in the press were devoted to my works.
He went on to remark that it was very unfortunate there were people like me in the world who were born to destroy the finest institutions, and that I was a striking example. I laughed till I cried, and assured him the only people to suffer would be himself and the academies. I daren't say any more of the fellow for fear of boring you too much.
To conclude, he at last went off from the table, leaving us stranded in the middle of the restaurant. As he was passing through the door I took his hand and said, 'Sir, I ask you to believe that we're still as friendly as ever.' Then I returned to C[henavard] and F[rançais], and begged *them* to believe they were a brace of idiots. After that we went out to drink beer.
Here's another comment by M. de Nieuwerkerke I recall: 'I hope, M. Courbet,' he said, 'that you've nothing to complain of, the Government is paying enough court to you, no one can flatter himself at receiving so much attention as you have. Bear in mind that it's the Government and not I that invited you to lunch today.' So I'm indebted to the Government for a lunch. I wanted to pay him for it, but that suggestion made C[henavard] and F[rançais] angry.

Courbet goes on to say that he has begun five or six works that he expects to finish by the spring. As he is relying on Bruyas, he says:

I am delighted that you rely on me. I won't fail you, be sure. Do me that honour; for I offer you as pledge my hatred of men and of our society, a hatred that'll be extinguished only when I am. It's not a question of time, so you are more important than I am, you possess the means I've always lacked and always will. With your background, your intelligence, your courage and your financial resources, you can rescue us while we're alive, and enable us to save a century of time.

On his way back to Paris he means to call in at Montpellier. 'When you're in Paris, we'll look for a gallery together, if we decide to hold an exhibition.'[19]

What Courbet wanted was 46,000 francs out of Bruyas so that he could stage his own show in opposition to the Exposition Universelle of 1855.

We have no comment by Chenavard on the meal with the Director; but an abridged account of Français's impressions has been published. It hardly gives the same impression of Courbet's total domination of the proceedings as the letter to Bruyas. 'Courbet, despite the efforts of the other guests, plunged into politics'; he said the aim was 'to corrupt artists and a thousand other polite remarks'. After the dinner, 'Français did his best to counteract the bad impression produced on the Superintendant of the Fine Arts, but was not able to dispel it entirely.'[20]

We know four of the works he painted during the winter of 1853–4 at Ornans. There were three landscapes: the *Roche de Dix Heures*, the *Château of Ornans* (a cluster of houses on the site of the ancient ruin above the town), and the *Rivulet of the Puits Noir* (a shaded well-spring). The Black Well was a site that fascinated him; it was his chief source for the image of the central orifice with water flowing out, flanked with rocks, which we noted in *Demoiselles de Village*. The fourth work was *Winnowers*, in which a girl in a red-brown dress, with her back turned, kneels on a white cloth and sifts grain through a big winnowing-basket. On the left are grain-sacks against which another young woman (perhaps Juliette) in a small cap leans as she sorts kernels on a platter; on the right a boy looks into a wooden grain-bin. On the wall enclosing the yard the sun casts the shadows of a vine-hung trellis; and baskets and bowls lie around. The girl with her back turned is probably Zoé; this identification was confirmed by her son later on. There is a strong sensual impact from the image: the girl's legs are wide open and we feel a sort of circular swing in her body as she moves the sieve to bring the grain through its mesh; the swing, expressed by the two ovals (of her arms with the sieve, and of the sieve itself) is communicated to the rest of the body by the tension of her open-legged pose and the lines of her dress – the downflow ending in two more *rondures*, especially that on the right. Altogether a very effective pattern of tension and movement is created by the lines and forms: the long out-thrust arms and the long shapes of the shoes, the curve in and out to the small of her back, with the frill of her jacket as the balance between the upper and lower halves of her stable, yet agitated body. We may note the small-of-the-back curve and out-thrust belly here as in the Zoé of the *Demoiselles*: which in turn helps towards the identification of the model in the *Studio* with her. The various utensils with rounded tops help to stress the rotary movement of the sieve and of Zoé's body. If we now look at the *Spinner* again, keeping in mind the strong union of rhythms of work and sex in the *Winnowers*, we cannot but be struck with the presence of the same union. The wheel, which has here the role of the circularly-swung sieve, is quiescent, for the girl is relaxed, asleep. But its rounded pattern stands over against the bunched rounded body, the fatly rounded face, as a sort of repetition in simpler form. The arms, stretched out in a rough parallel, do not actively complete the oval as in *Winnowers* – though the inert fingers send their lines on into a fold in the material which does provide a linking curve. Between them lies the distaff over the hidden thighs as a magnified genital emblem. In short, the *Spinner* shows the same elements as the *Winnowers*; but where Zoé in the latter is richly awake and active, here all is lulled in a sensuous sleep which is the dream of the total body.[21]

With the insight these two works give us into the strong sexual element in Courbet's organisation of forms, we can now look at the enigmatic gestures of the *Bathers* which disquieted Delacroix. Here both women have their arms flung out in parallel systems that again repeat what we see in *Spinner* and *Winnowers*. One of the arms of the naked woman is hidden behind her, but the hand holding the cloth shows that it comes down in the rhythmic sympathy with its fellow which we see in the other two paintings. A slight realistic explanation is given by the act of holding the cloth in the case of the bather, by the act of holding the bough in the case of the sitting woman. But these acts fail to explain the gestures and the parallelisms. The naked woman's arms are roughly parallel with the rift of blue sky in the leaves, with a line of rocks on her left, and with the other woman's arms; the second woman repeats the out-thrust gesture at a lower level, and there is a system of balances and unbalances between the main components of her form and those of the naked woman. We can only surmise that Courbet has been deeply impressed by the work-rhythms of his sisters when spinning, sifting, making dough, stirring food in the kitchen and so on; we meet the same sort of up-and-down, in-and-out, rhythm in the picture that Gros-Kost gives of Zélie delving in the dung. This rhythm fascinates Courbet on account of its sensuous effect of the body revolving on its axis, opening and closing; and he transfers it to the *Bathers* even though there is no ostensible basis for it in what the women are doing. It here has merely a sort of magical evocation for him of sensuous movement and contact – an effect increased by the strained position of the two heads, the glances which link the two women emotionally as well as formally – the line of the lower woman's head and her left arm leading up to the other's averted head. Though there is no question here of sleep, the lolling and hanging pose of the heads has its affinity with that of the sleeping spinner, the enclosing green darkness provides a metaphor of dream-sleep to support the magical strangeness of the gestures.

An interesting early variant of the gestures appears in *Woman Brushing her Hair* (dated about 1847), in which the hand of the out-thrust left arm turns up and leads on rhythmically to the uplifted bent right arm. The arms thus give an effect of forms revolving round the bared shoulders and down-slipping white garment in a charming way. (This work also shows in its atmosphere and general character the influence of Vermeer, whom Thoré had done much to publicise.) The strong sexual character of the pose and movement in the *Winnowers*, we may note, was not missed by the critics; About remarked, 'The girl agitating the sieve throws out her arms with a certain grandeur, but the disposition of her legs is more than trivial, it is indecent.'

We may now return to the *Wrestlers*. There seems to be a significance in the fact that it shares with the *Bathers* a strong interest in the plastic modelling of the musculature; the one picture shows two powerfully modelled men, the other a woman with equally detailed and subtle modelling. And the two works must have been painted round about the same time. Looking at the *Wrestlers*, we see that here again we have a variant of the gestures we have been analysing. The man on the left thrusts out his left arm: his right arm goes out into the opposite direction, making with the right arm of his opponent a rough oval. This is the sort of thing we get if we draw together the gestures of the two women in the *Bathers* instead of keeping them apart in parallel rhythms. The embrace of the *Wrestlers* is one of conflict; but it shows how the patterns in question could also compose an embrace of love. (Note the four parallel lines of the legs of the *Wrestlers*, which gives stability to the tensions of arms and torsos.) Formally, in all the works considered, the relation of verticals and horizontals provides a strong balance of forms; but the particular way in which the relation is worked out has its links with Courbet's emotional response to people, especially to women. A gesture of repudiation, of repulse, is linked with one of embracing; and the whole complex is related to the to-and-fro, the circle, of work-rhythms.

The work-significance of the out-thrust arm is brought home to us if we look at a painting by Velasquez, *Spinners*, which Courbet certainly had in mind when he composed the *Winnowers*, and which he knew no doubt from an engraving in the well-circulated *Musée de peinture* by E. A. Réveil. We know that he admired Velasquez; and without understanding much about the iconography of the *Spinners* he would have liked the contrast between the working women in the foreground and the idling courtiers at the back. There are four women at work; on the right is one winding wool with her arm held out in a way that reminds one of the *Winnowers*; on one side of her is a boy and on the other a crouching woman with her hand down at floor level – these two figures Courbet seems to have had in mind and to have used, with modifications, in the *Winnowers*. On the left is a woman with a spinning-wheel in front of her, so that its whirling motion is superimposed on part of her body. A woman standing at her side and leaning down has her arms thrust out in very much the same way as those in the *Bathers*, and the angles at which the heads are inclined, as they exchange some remark, suggests the way in which the heads of the two women in the *Bathers* are inclined obliquely to one another – though the relationship is not identical. We can only assume that Courbet had long pondered the composition of the *Spinners*, linking it with his own observations of his sisters at work, and using elements of it in the three pictures we have discussed. The elements of sensuous impact, the absorption of the imagery of rotation into the bodies of the women, is, however, all his own. The more one looks at the two women on the left of Velasquez's picture the more one feels that they underlie the two women in the *Bathers*, different as the situation is, and that it is the fusion of the work-scene and the private nook of nakedness which creates the enigmatic quality of the gestures in the *Bathers*, their strangely intent relationship.[22]

In the work-relation there is yet another picture we can look back to: *Stonebreakers*. There both workers have arms out-thrust, the old man clasping the hammer-handle with both hands, the boy holding the basket with both hands as he lifts it on to his knee. The link with *Winnowers* is masked by the fact the parallel arms in each case are in profile or partly hidden; and the weight of the basket means that it lacks the mobility of the sieve. But the circling rhythms are present. The curve up and round of the boy's body, leading to the rounded basket, gives an effect of a certain resilient resistance, as if he is not yet mastered by his heavy fate. Via the strong horizontals and the diagonals, the pattern here moves over and breaks up into that of the old man, who is built like a sort of swastika. In his body there is both an element of sculptural arrest and an effect of revolving movement. The picture as a whole thus has its link with the others in which work-rhythms are invoked. In it the artist powerfully discovers his own characteristic structures of composition.

Courbet was not under the usual pressure to complete his winter work; the Salon for 1854 had been cancelled so that preparations for a very large and comprehensive art-show at the Exposition Universelle might go on. Courbet felt he had more free time for hunting and spent days with his friends on the wintry hills. At times he was up to his belly in snow, chasing hares and wolves. The hungry hunters had voracious meals, probably at Levier's inn for the most part. Then Courbet found himself confronted with a police charge for hunting with prohibited snares. 'I had gone hunting, my head was all abuzz, I needed fresh air and exercise, the snow was superb. But it happened to be illegal. When I came back to our town, I received a summons that made me lose three days as I had to go to Besançon to hear the indictment and avoid jail. Long live liberty!' He had to meet a fine of 100 francs, but it was no loss as he sold a picture at Besançon for 400.[22] 'I've begun two pictures that I'll soon finish.' The first was the *Winnowers*; the second was to show a gypsy and her children – 'part of my roadside series, a sequel to the *Stonebreakers*.' He did not finish the gypsy-painting, but fifteen years later used the group as a basis for his *Beggar's Alms*.

He was writing to Bruyas and seized the chance to press yet again his project of a one-man show as a rival to the State's exhibition. 'So we'll set up our artillery and proceed to the great burial.' The phrase is significant; here he means the burial of academic art, in the *Burial* he had from one aspect been burying his own bourgeois world. 'You must admit the role of gravedigger is a congenial one and that to clear away the dirt from all that litter of bric-à-brac will not be unpleasant.' He thus reinforces the image, seeing himself as the gravedigger of all that is outworn and unnecessary – exactly in the way that Buchon saw the gravedigger of the *Burial*.

The sum of 40,000 francs is something to dream about. We'll have to lease a plot of ground from the city of Paris opposite their big exposition. I can already see my huge tent with a single column in the middle, frame-walls covered with painted canvas, the whole thing mounted on a platform, also hired guards, a man dressed in black for the ticket-office, a cloakroom for canes and umbrellas on the opposite side, and two or three attendants in the gallery. I believe we'll get back our 40,000 francs (even though we're counting solely on hatred and jealousy). Subject to change, this will be the title: *Exhibition of Paintings by the Artist Courbet and from the Bruyas Gallery*. That will really be something to turn Paris upside down. Beyond doubt it'll be the greatest joke ever played in our time. It'll cause some people to fall ill, I'm certain.[23]

This winter he had some works exhibited at Frankfurt. He delightedly told Marlet they had provoked such furious arguments that 'at the Casino they were forced to put up a notice to this effect: "In this Club it's forbidden to mention M. Courbet's pictures." At the house of a very rich banker, who'd invited a large party to dinner, each guest found tucked in his napkin a little note thus inscribed: "Tonight nobody will talk about M. Courbet".'[24] Gorchakov, Russian minister in Frankfurt, wanted to buy the *Man with the Pipe*, but Courbet had promised it to Bruyas. In May 1854, just before leaving for Montpellier, he sent a letter ahead, saying that the painting had arrived.

It is not only my portrait; it's yours. When I saw it, I was impressed; it's a crucial element in our solution. It's the portrait of a fanatic, of an ascetic, a man without illusions as to the nonsense that made up his education, one who's trying to establish himself in harmony with his principles. I've painted many self-portraits in my life, corresponding to the changes in my state of mind; in short I've written my autobiography. The third most recent was that of a gasping and dying man, the second was the portrait of a man filled with ideals and love in the manner of Goethe, George Sand, etc. And now this one. One more remains to be done, that of the man firm in his beliefs, the free man.[25]

The reference to 'our solution' recalls the book on which Bruyas rests his hand in the portrait; Courbet had made up his mind that he had found a fellow-spirit in Bruyas, who with his sensibility and money would make the perfect combination with the painter, who had artistic ability and no money. Bruyas seems to have been flattered and made no effort to define what separated him from Courbet; his letters show that he could be extremely confused in his thinking – or rather could get intellectually lost in the grip of a strong diffuse emotion. (We have already referred to this letter in connection with the *Wounded Man*; the man of ideals is probably the *Man with the Leather Belt*.)

Yes, my dear friend, I hope to realise a unique miracle in my life. I hope to live by my art all my life without ever deviating by a fraction from my principles, without ever lying to my conscience for a single instant, without ever painting a picture even as big as my hand to please anyone whatever or to ensure its sale.
  I have always told my friends, who were frightened by my fortitude and afraid for me: Have no fear – though I might have to search all over the world, I'm sure to find men who will understand me; if I find only five or six, they'll keep me alive, they'll find me out. I am right, I am right! I have found you. It was inevitable; for it was not we ourselves who met, it was our solutions. I'm overjoyed you'll own my portrait. At last it has escaped the barbarians. It's a miracle, for during a period of extreme poverty I had the courage to refuse an offer of 2,000 francs for it from Napoleon, and later one from insistent dealers acting for Gorchakov.

Proud words, and without precedent up to this date. Many other painters such as his own beloved Rembrandt had acted on similar principles of integrity; but those principles now reach a new level of consciousness, of coherent affirmation, because Courbet is the first who sees that they imply a ceaseless vigilance against State power, a ceaseless rejection of every insidious advance which in any way is linked with that power. Artistic integrity reaches a new level because it is bound up with a new depth of political insight and penetration.
  In his excitement he interprets events in the way most effective for the case he is making

out. He didn't sell to Napoleon because the offer fell through; a reduction of revenues (in 1850) made the latter give up the project. But at that time Courbet would gladly have sold the work to anyone with the necessary cash. I take it that he is not now consciously lying; he feels so strongly that the painting was fated for Bruyas that the failure of the deal with Napoleon is seen as a decision on his part. What he feels as his compact with Bruyas has deeply moved him; it helps him to see his destiny more clearly, to take his oath of integrity with sharper purpose; it even gives him an illusion of stable inner tranquillity:

Dear friend, how much trouble one has in life to keep faith with oneself. In this charming country of France, when a man who has something to contribute finally reaches his goal, he arrives like the Greek soldier [who ran from Marathon] *dead*. But as there's always something new under the sun we'll show them an example of two individuals who do not mean to die. I beg you, my dear friend, not to fret yourself any longer over such people. . . .

For my part, I confess that I look at a human being with curiosity just as I look at a horse, a tree, any natural object, and that is all. And for a long time I have ceased to feel anger, I assure you I have recovered my tranquillity in that direction. I go a step further. They have even become of value to me because I study men attentively, the more I see the different aspects I encounter: which fills me with joy, and that is what demonstrates to me the superiority of men over horses. . . .

Yes, I have understood you, and you have a living proof of that in your possession: your portrait. I am ready to depart for Montpellier; I shall leave Ornans next Monday, spend a day or two at Besançon, and after that I don't know how many days it will take me to reach you. When I arrive I shall do anything you wish and all that is necessary. I am impatient to be off, for I'm eagerly looking forward to this journey, to the meeting with you, and to the work we'll do together.[26]

Behind these protestations we feel the extreme pain he has suffered over the attacks on his Salon pictures – all his remarks about 'they'. We see that much of his warm embracing of Bruyas derives from the great consolation he found in his appreciation (backed by the buying of the maligned works); he feels that a new phase of his art is opening up as a result of Bruyas's aid and praise. This new phase is 'our solution'. We must remember the intensity of emotion shown in this letter when we come to the meeting he forecasts, and its results. It is also probably correct to see in this passionate turning to Bruyas 'with tranquillity recovered', a release of the tensions of loneliness and guilt he has felt since Virginie left him; where the oath of love has failed, the oath of artistic integrity is born – an oath which is also the oath of comradeship, as he insists. We feel that the 'compact' with Bruyas has filled a deep emotional gap, which he is now able to face.

He stayed at Montpellier from late May to September 1854. The region was a revelation to him of fiery sun, azure depth of sky, lucid air, and clarity of shadows. He had never been so far south before; and this experience of a new sunny world, linked with the sense of release he had found through Bruyas, had a profound effect on him, lightening the key of his palette and giving it a luminous intensity which it had lacked. The deepened colour-sense was to be of great value to him throughout his future work, both in his treatment of sea-scapes and of his own familiar uplands; among other things it gave freshness and subtlety to his treatment of forest-depths and enabled him to paint the fierce reflecting whites of snow as they had never been painted.[27]

S. Courbet.

7 *Man with the Pipe.* 1846–47. 45 × 137 cm.
Musée Fabre, Montpellier (see pages 31–32).

38 *Peasants of Flagey Returning from the Fair*. 1850. 206 × 275 cm.
Musée de Besançon (see page 67).

39 *The Stone-Breakers*. 1851. 91 × 115 cm. (destroyed 1945)
(see pages 59–61).

10 *The Firemen* (author's title: *Departure of the Fire Brigade*). 1850–51. 388 × 550 cm. Musée du Petit Palais, Paris (see page 95).

11 *Girls Sifting Corn* (author's title: *Winnowers*). 1853–54. 131 × 167 cm. Musée de Nantes (see pages 111–114).

42 *The Seaside at Palavas.* 1854. 39 × 46 cm.
Musée Fabre, Montpellier.

43 *Courbet in a Striped Collar.* 1854. 46 × 37 cm.
Musée Fabre, Montpellier (see page 117).

44 *The Meeting* or *Bonjour M. Courbet*. 1854. 120 × 149 cm.
Musée Fabre, Montpellier (see page 117).

45 *Girls Beside the Seine* (author's title: *Young Women on the Seine Banks*). 1856. 174 × 200 cm. Musée du Petit Palais, Paris (see pages 148–152).

46 *Spring Vase of Flowers*. 1855. 60 × 82 cm. Kunsthalle, Hamburg (see page 148).

47 *The Lady of Frankfurt.*
1858–59. 103 × 138 cm.
Wallraf-Richartz-Museum,
Cologne (see page 161).

48 *The Trellis* or *Girl Arranging
Flowers.* 1863. 109 × 135 cm.
Gift of Edward Drummond
Libbey
Museum of Art, Toledo, USA
(see page 203).

49 *Women Bathing.* 1853. 227 × 193 cm.
Musée Fabre, Montpellier (see pages 102–107).

Always ready to relax and enjoy himself, Courbet was able to combine work and pleasure in a highly satisfying manner. Through Wey and some others he had known something of the life of the well-off and cultured bourgeoisie, but not to anything like the extent he now encountered it with Bruyas and his friends. He was soon popular with the more easy-going members of Bruyas's circle. In the late afternoon he played at *mail* (a sort of croquet) at which he quickly became proficient; and he was able to spend the long evenings he loved at café-tables with tankards of beer and carafes of local wine. During the summer he painted two more portraits of Bruyas, both smaller than that of Paris; also a self-portrait known as *Courbet in Striped Collar*. But the new big work he achieved was *The Meeting*, later nick-named *Good-day, M. Courbet* or *Fortune Bowing before Genius*. Here we see his arrival. He stands in the hot dusty road with the diligence in the distance going off round a turn. He wears white shirt, blue duck trousers, buttoned gaiters; in one hand he holds his staff, in the other his hat; and on his back is a heavy box of painting materials wrapt in his coat. His dark beard is lifted, jutting out against the sky. A short way over to the left stands Bruyas in his gentle courtesy, wearing blue trousers and short green jacket with striped collar and piping; he holds his cane and brings down his hat in a sweeping gesture of welcome. Behind him is his servant Calas in russet tailcoat, carrying a red shawl and bowing with a very discreet respect. To the back of Bruyas is his dog Breton. Under the cloudless blue sky the earth is flat and burning.

This picture, when shown, appeared a ridiculous piece of self-glorification. About wrote:

M. Courbet has carefully stressed all the perfections of his own person, even his shadow is graceful and full of vigour; it displays a pair of calves such as are seldom met with in the world of shades. M. Bruyas is not so flattered; he is a bourgeois. The poor servant is humble and self-effacing as if he were serving at mass. Neither master nor valet casts a shadow on the ground; there is no shadow except for M. Courbet; he alone can stop the rays of the sun.[28]

There are other shadows, those of the foliage cast on Bruyas and Calas; but the point has a certain validity. The tree-shadows over the welcomers mark them as inhabitants of a sheltered world; Courbet is out in the light-blown open. He holds a pilgrim-staff; Bruyas holds an elegant cane. Again the remark that the reverence is such as would suit a mass is not altogether amiss. *L'Illustration* referred to 'the adoration of M. Courbet, realist imitation of the Adoration of the Magi'.[29] We shall deal with this point in a moment; but first we must note certain other aspects.

First, the technical and formal aspects. Here for the first time Courbet fully expresses all he has learned from the impact of southern light, a new sparkling tonality which is opening the way to the Impressionists, Cézanne, and Van Gogh. The picture has simultaneously a wonderful depth of crystalline air and light, and a sculptural clarity of pattern. The frieze-effect used massively and heavily in the *Burial* is here used for three detached figures; and whereas in the *Burial* people were sunken deep under a lowering horizon, here the figures loom upwards. There is thus a semi-photographic effect, as if the scene were taken from low down with a camera looking up at them; and the relations of the figures are at once solidly meditated and snapped at a casual moment of encounter.[30]

But this effect of human solidity and purpose in an excess of light and an earth dominated by the human presence is not merely an aesthetic effect; it merges with the whole purpose of the picture. In showing the meeting of himself and Bruyas, Courbet is setting out to express and symbolise all that he struggled to put into words in the letter analysed above. It is the meeting of Artist and Patron, Artist and Audience; and the starkness of the setting is used to stress this meaning, to show the event in a sort of apocalyptic clarity and vastness. To take the lesser aspect first: the relation of artist and patron. We note earlier that in the nineteenth century the successful artist sloughed the last of his attributes as a craftsman and met his bourgeois patron on an equal footing. This position was one both of liberation and enslavement. The artist was honoured – but only in so far as he entered the money-market and showed himself as good a money-maker as his buyers. The superficial side of the rise in status appeared in works such as Ingres's *Death of Leonardo da Vinci* (where the artist is supported in the arms of Francis I) or Robert-Fleury's *Charles V Picking up Titian's Paint-brush.*[31] The deeper aspect appeared in Beethoven's behaviour when, with Goethe, he met the Imperial Family; Goethe let go Beethoven's arm and stood respectfully at the side of the road, but Beethoven walked on pushing his way through the nobles. 'Princes and courtiers parted and stood aside, the Archduke Rudolph took off his hat to me, the Empress was the first to salute me; their lordships *know* me.'[31] We are reminded of Courbet's account of his meal with M. de Nieuwerkerke.

But though in the picture the Artist is receiving homage from the Patron, there is also a wider meaning. Bruyas is friend and comrade working with Courbet on 'our solution'. 'When I have decided to love someone, it is for life. You are my friend, you cannot doubt it.'[32] The meeting is thus more than that of arrogant artist and admiring patron; it is of two friends, who have different roles. To realise just what Courbet stands for in the picture we must see that the pattern of the picture is derived from a popular print, or series of prints, connected with the legend of the Wandering Jew, the eternal witness of history and of man's sufferings. Courbet had been meditating in Paris, as we saw from his letter, on the meeting and its importance for him; he must have pondered during his journey how best to record the moment. At some point the memory of the woodcut showing the Wandering Jew being welcomed by Two Burghers flashed upon him. Champfleury made a thorough examination of the tradition in his *Imagerie Populaire*, and he remarks of this episode that in the variants different provinces of France were shown as 'having the honour of giving a cordial reception to such an unfortunate being. Many editions tell of the Jew's arrival "in Paris the great city," where "some bourgeois passing by, with a very tractable [*docile*] humour, accosted him a moment." The South did not remain any less sympathetic than the North.'[33]

Champfleury had not yet published his study of the theme in 1853–4; but he must have worked on it for a long time and Courbet would have heard him discuss it. Dupont too had been working on the theme, perhaps also hearing of it from Champfleury, though he had his own less systematic knowledge of popular poetry. Béranger had published, far back in 1831, an extremely popular song, 'The Wandering Jew'; and Dupont reworked an old *complainte* and tried to infuse the legend with his feeling for human brotherhood. His *Légende* was published in 1856 with wood engravings by Gustave Doré (then unknown), but he may well have recited it earlier. In prose there was the famous work by Eugène Sue (published serially in *Le Constitutionnel* from 25 June 1844 to 12 July 1845) which made the Jew, Ahasuerus, the champion of labour; the poor shoemaker of Jerusalem becomes the symbol of the exploited classes over the ages and the mouthpiece of their protest.[34]

Courbet must, then, have known the theme well; and for him Ahasuerus would have been merged with figures like Jean Journet. We must recall his own statement that in his reaction against all governments, all state-power, he had turned to vagabondage. The image of the free wanderer was strong in his mind, and it linked with the fact of the Compagnonnage, the system whereby journeymen workers wandered all over France. In 1840 Agricol Perdiguier (Avignonnais-la-Vertu), carpenter *compagnon*, published a book on the *tour*, which had a vast success; George Sand took the theme up and created a *compagnon* hero, Pierre Huguenin; the roaming worker became a romantic character, handsome, young, winning the heart of a high-born girl. We see how Courbet equated himself with the craftsman rather than the artist, he was the *maistre peintre*; he went on to equate the school of Realism with the Compagnonnage, for he called Mme Buchon the *Mère* of Realism, meaning, not that she had in any way originated the school, but that she was one of the *Mères* who arranged for the *compagnons* to find food and shelter on their arrival at a strange town. One of his own songs that he sang ran thus:

> I have no fatherland
> The earth is my abode
> I must end my life on a great road
> O tra la-la, la-la, la-la, hola.[35]

Behind such ideas lay on one hand the cult of nature which had for some time begotten the idea of hiking through the countryside; and the romantic concept of the poet as *vates*, prophet, priest of a universal humanity. The Saint-Simonians had developed a semi-mystical notion of the poet as priest or messiah, who was to carry on a 'veritable priesthood'; one of them, E. Barrault in *L'Appel aux Artistes* of 1830, had declared that only the artist, duly absorbing Saint-Simonian ideas, was worthy of guiding mankind.[36] Victor Hugo flamboyantly saw the poet as the prophet who led forward and lighted up the future by his torch; Baudelaire in his days as a Dupont-admirer saw the poet as the man who used the critique of utopian hopes and aspirations to bring out the truth of the present.[37]

Courbet as the Wandering Jew is thus also the Artist as Prophet, as the eternal witness of the wrongs done to man, and the leader into a future harmony. Hence the way in which the personal aspect of vaunting, which was all the critics of his day could see, is absorbed by the larger image of the artist as prophet, Courbet being only the incidental embodiment of the principle. And so the attitudes of Bruyas and Calas are robbed of abasement; for in so far as they recognise the spirit of prophecy they become part of it, and their passive reception of the message becomes capable of turning into an active participation. Thus the mockers who saw a sort of religious exaltation of Courbet in the painting had glimpsed a portion of the truth, though they distorted the application. When Baudelaire, reacting against 1848, jeered in 1855 at Realism as 'Courbet saving the World', he was correct enough in recognising the messianic impulse or rather the revolutionary fervour which saw in Realism a way of changing the world by accepting it – by seeing the full truth, which therefore included the elements making for the transformation of the present. In the same year Courbet, writing to Bruyas, called Realism 'a holy and sacred cause, which is the cause of Liberty and Independence'.[38]

Courbet also helped to lighten his palette by visiting the seaside at Palavas, some seven miles from Montpellier. There on the flat Mediterranean coast he painted his first seascape, recording his awed sense of the vastness communicated by sea and sky; only a few rocks in the foreground and some distant sails against the horizon modify the sense of sheer space. Something of this sense of the immensity of pure sea and sky had been defined by romantic painters; but Courbet gave the image a new austerity and completeness.[39]

Among the new friends with whom he felt most at home was Pierre-Auguste Fajon. Born in 1820, Fajon had recently come back from Paris, having failed to make the fortune he hoped for. In a few weeks he was brought so low as to go peddling in the streets with various goods, especially some sticky jam made of grapes and other fruits, dressed in an Arab's burnous and headwrap, and shouting in a hoarse monotone. But his spirits were unquenched and Courbet liked his gift for clowning and tricks. He painted his portrait in Paris in 1862 and gave it to him; when years later Fajon appealed to Bruyas for help he described this painting as his sole asset.[40]

A more important friend was François Sabatier, the wealthy owner of the Tour de Farges, a large château near Lunel (halfway between Nîmes and Montpellier), who was a Fourierist socialist, poet and translator of poetry (Lessing, Schiller, Grillparzer, Goethe's *Faust*), and patron of the arts. His character and activities help us to understand how Courbet could transform the amiably well-intentioned Bruyas into something of a Fourierist organiser of an art-phalanstery; for Sabatier came close to that role. Born at Montpellier in 1818, he began as a romantic poet, encouraged by de Vigny, with a vision of the world to come in which beauty and love would reign. He attempted drawing and from 1851 wrote art-criticism in the *Démocratie Pacifique*; and he was friendly with Devéria, Hébert, Chenavard, Ricard, Papety. Papety, author of *Dream of Happiness*, was also a Fourierist and travelled with him in Greece, dying of cholera in 1849.

Sabatier married the coloratura contralto, Caroline Unger, who had been taught piano-playing by Mozart's son, singing by his sister-in-law; Beethoven praised her for her interpretation of the very difficult contralto part in the last movement of the Ninth Symphony; she was also successful in *opéra bouffe*. Sabatier and his wife were keen republicans; they welcomed 1848; and till the *coup d'état* they held a brilliant political salon in Paris. After that they moved between the Palazzo Renai near Florence, under San Miniato, a villa at Trespiano, and the Tour de Farges. At their country house they received their friends, composers, virtuosos, historians, philosophers, poets, painters; and while Sabatier painted, read, mused, and looked after his vineyards, his wife rested under the laurels, fostering young singers of promise. We have a good account of the place, written by Moritz Hartmann, a German poet, socialist and revolutionary, who, after being a deputy at the Parliament of Frankfurt, had to flee on the triumph of reaction; he went to Montpellier where lived his translator Saint-René Taillandier, professor in the Faculty of Letters. With Sabatier's help he published in 1853 the *Journal de Languedoc et de Provence*, in the first issue of which he described the Tour de Farges. Only three towers of the ancient château remained, a mere 'feudal grimace' transformed happily into dovecotes, rabbit-warrens, and an aviary for a golden eagle. Before the house had been a garden of pines, cypress, laurels, with ornamental shrubs and baskets of acanthus, iris, stocks; ivy covered the walls and provided nests for nightingales. Inside were vaulted halls for music; a tapestried library; on the first floor a studio called La Cambuse, with drawings by Bouquet and Papety on the walls. Sabatier himself in his red *béret*, with glasses perched on a small nose, and a heavy beard (like Marx and Proudhon), was studying Sanskrit and considering a plan for a phalanstery in Texas to take refugees from the *coup d'état* – a project in which Considérant played a large part.

Courbet painted at least two landscapes here, a *View* of the house and *The Bridge of Ambrussum*, a Roman ruin; a drawing of Sabatier reading has often been reproduced as a portrait of Proudhon.[41] He must have been much at home with the Sabatiers, and his approval of their Fourierist principles would have increased his feeling that Bruyas would help him towards the 'solution'.

He was so taken up with his new friends that he neglected to send his usual letter-record home. Zoé, piqued at the thought of him among such rich and distinguished society, could not resist writing to Bruyas. Perhaps she hoped to draw attention to herself and gain Bruyas's interest, even an invitation; perhaps she merely could not control her resentment. She complained that Courbet had been away six weeks and had written nothing; and she showed some insight into her brother's character in her bitterness. 'There are some people for whom the absent are always in the wrong; my brother is of this number. . . . I understand, sirs, that the good friendship that unites you can fill in a great deal of leisure time; but, without changing this sentiment, I still feel that one can have a thought for those who love you. My brother is going to find me very presumptuous, so that I don't address myself to him, but to you, M. Bruyas, while making my apologies and sending my best wishes. . . . Here is my address: Mlle Zoé Courbet, care of his father, at Ornans.'[42] Bruyas showed Courbet the letter, or told him of Zoé's wish to hear from him; and he wrote an account of his works and pleasures, stressing his prowess at *mail*, which had gained him the title Knight of the Rolling Wooden Balls. Bruyas later sent her photos taken at the Tour de Farges, and Zoé, delighted, sent him her thanks.[43] Zoe's behaviour in all this is very much in the key of *Les Demoiselles Tourangeau*.

But Courbet's stay was not to be all pleasure. A bad outbreak of cholera had occurred at Montpellier this summer; he was stricken down at a dinner-party and was very ill for some time. In the postscript of a letter to Buchon he described his attack:

I was forgetting to tell you I've just been stricken by cholera. I've stayed four or five days in bed, I took all the herbs of St John and I've thrown it off. After all the only ones who die of it are those who take no care of themselves, and the poor. This illness has lost much of its character and intensity. At Montpellier almost fifteen hundred persons have died; today it's over and I am better in so far as I've thinned a little. I had become disgusting. And then I've been purged, my digestion works better. When the pains of colic begin, one takes twelve drops of laudanum in a linseed enema; that stops them almost at once from carrying on. *Au revoir.*[44]

We see that he is already suffering from digestive troubles, and probably as an after-result of the cholera and its treatment he began to suffer from haemorrhoids, which plagued him thereafter. Such was the nemesis of his good-living, together with the fatness which was soon once more upon him. In the letter to Buchon of which the above was a postscript he gives further news:

Write to Champfleury to come. I'll be at Berne I hope on the 15th, 18th, 20th at latest. But above all don't wait for me, don't hold me to an exact time. Don't worry, I'll come to see you. Sleep on your feet, on your bottom, on your head, on both your ears, but above all don't wait for me. On arrival I'll go to M. Poiterlin's; he'll point out where you roost. If I arrive late, I'll put up at the Hotel de la Poste.

Urbain has only to keep on at Ornans in this cholera-time. As for hunting, he'll pay out forty or fifty francs to kill a lark or a partridge. True, that's not worth the voyage; he doesn't know how to stay where he's well-off. I'd have been already at your side if Bruyas hadn't commissioned yet another portrait from me. You must understand that when opportunity comes along, one must take advantage of it. As for your portrait, it's a good idea. You could write to my sister to have it packed and sent to you. It'd give me the greatest pleasure to finish it for you. Urbain, who is strong for beauty, asserts that you are on the point of bringing the hair round from your nape in a latticework over your brow.

Here there's a setback in my loves. Jealousy from Camélia, young girl from Noucy; disclosure of our sallies [*sorties*]. Rose in prison. Blanche is to replace her. The commissioner annoyed [*emmerdé*, shat on] by Blanche. Blanche exiled to Cette [Sète]. Tears, visits to the prison, vows of love, voyage to Cette on my part. Camélia in prison, *mère* Cadet at her wits' end. Love-making of *mère* Cadet with my person. Mina in her anguish takes a new lover. I still have Rose. Rose wants to go to Switzerland with me, saying that I may drop her where I please. My love doesn't stretch as far as a voyage with a woman. Knowing that there are women all over the earth, I feel it's unnecessary to take one with me. Besides there's one who's been waiting for me at Lyon for fifteen months.

When I've done this portrait I'll go to Marseille to see *mère* Blavet and buy some of Urbain's true moka coffee. Thence Lyon, on to Geneva and Berne. Write to Champfleury, I beg you, for me and press him on my behalf to come to Berne, we'll take him after that to Ornans; and then we'll have so many things to tell you. I'll bring photos of my portrait with the pipe.

The paragraph about the girls is very mysterious. If we are to take it at its face value, it suggests a brothel in trouble with the police; the *dénonciation* would then refer to some police charge, not to a quarrel among the girls themselves. If it was all as serious as it sounds, we'd expect more details; and yet it is circumstantial enough, though concise, to have more than the ring of some joke, such as he seems to have got up with the aid of Fajon. And the girl at Lyon appears to have existed; for Courbet wrote later to Bruyas: 'When I left you I was still suffering from cholera. Luckily at Lyon I met a Spanish lady of my acquaintance; she suggested a remedy that completely cured me.'[45]

But he could not have reached Buchon by 18 September; presumably he was speaking of October in his letter; for on 18 September he wrote in the album of some lady-admirer of Montpellier:

Woman,
I know you are keen to desire something from me; you are right and you are within your rights, for you deserve it: my painting is addressed solely to persons of sentiment.
Gustave Courbet
Master Painter
I regret that I can offer you only one photograph of my portrait.

– a very different world from that of Rose, Camélia, Blanche, Mina, and *mère* Cadet.

After Lyon he went on to Buchon, 'a refugee for having wanted to do good to his home-land', who turned out to be 'as gloomy as night'. Courbet stayed six days. 'Switzerland is an exclusively agricultural country; so it's restful, no intellect is called into play. Accept that and one abundantly enjoys nature.' Then, back at Ornans, he hunted for some days: 'an excuse for violent exercise that doesn't displease me.' The result was a relapse into illness: this time jaundice. He had it so badly that he was called the Prince of Orange (he has to excel even in maladies). But now he found himself badly behind with his work for the show. For a month and six days he didn't leave his room, and scared himself with a fortnight's fast. 'So I've lost the *embonpoint* you know.' Still, he managed to sketch out his big picture, 20 ft long and 12 high.

That makes it the most surprising one you can imagine; there are thirty persons life-size. It's the moral and physical history of my studio. There are all the people who serve me and share in my activity. I'll call it: First Series. For I hope to make the whole of society pass into my studio; to reveal also my propensities and my repulsions. I have two and a half months to do it in and I must visit Paris to do some nudes, so I've got two days per person. You see I've no time for amuse-ment.

He was sending fourteen works to the Exposition. 'What a pity we haven't been able to do this show all on our own; it would have been a big and new conception, outside all the old ideas of the past.'

Courbet had perhaps found Buchon too melancholy; for he stayed only six days, but had time to go hunting when back at Ornans. In his exile Buchon had translated the German-Swiss poet J. P. Hebel, the Swiss novelist J. Gotthel (A. Bitzius), and the German novelist B. Auerbach; he also wrote poems, short novels, and tales of his own. Courbet referred, in his letter to Bruyas, to a big literary success in Paris, meaning no doubt the publication of *Le Matachin* and *Le Gouffe-Gourmand* in the *Revue des Deux Mondes*. Buchon was growing restive at his exiled condition, with no outlet save literature; but all applications for an amnesty and safe conduct were refused. Champfleury did his best to use what influence he had on his behalf. In May 1854 he reported that he had difficulty in finding anyone in a high enough position to support the petition. 'But yesterday I hit on the right man: it's Francis Wey', who was president of the Société des Gens de Lettres and so had close contact with the ministries. 'He received my request cordially and now all you have to do is write to him. Be polite.' Buchon had only to explain his position, the reason for his exile, and list his works, etc. 'He will certainly accomplish what you ask.'[46]

Perhaps he would have done so if Buchon had been accommodating; but Buchon shared Courbet's inability to compromise. He refused to make any attempt to be tactful or to ingratiate himself with the authorities. In a few weeks Champfleury was complaining that Wey was displeased. Wey had written to Buchon several times and Champfleury had gone to much trouble. 'All wasted because of a rude letter of yours he turned over to M. Collet-Meygret,' an official of the political police, 'which makes it impossible for your petition to be granted. You did wrong, my friend, in not conforming to diplomatic usage.' At Wey's insistence, the official had explained: 'It's because we should have to send his letter to the prefect of police and we can't with propriety recommend to our subordinates a letter couched in such impolite language.' In July Champfleury tried again. He asked Buchon to write his explanations out again, detailing the rejections of his petition and the officials who had made them. 'I've found a way to get approval of what you ask.' But nothing happened. Buchon stayed at Berne for another five years.[47]

In September, about the time of Courbet's visit to Buchon, Champfleury wrote about the disquiet he felt as to the painter's choice of works for the big Exposition.

If Courbet has turned up, take him up strongly about this. He must know the show is near. Painters have the right to exhibit what they consider as their best works known or not . . . Courbet must send in the *Burial* and make it come back, no matter from where and no matter what it costs. This Universal Exposition is going to attract a vast crowd in 1855. Everyone will be curious to see this *Burial* that there's been such argument about, and it's the picture that best represents Courbet's manner. Let him exhibit with it whatever he judges suitable; but if he doesn't do it, he'll lose. Nothing proves better the value of a man than his work seen afresh after some years. If the system is weak and false, woe to him, but if it's serious and true, then it has gained. . . . I believe that the *Burial* must have gained.[48]

But in October Champfleury felt moved to unburden himself as to the antagonism he had felt towards Courbet and his work for some time, and which was growing worse. 'I think Courbet has a good nature, but you must have noted that I've been perhaps a trifle malicious towards him. However, I should never have seen him again after what he did to me.' Three or four years before he had been sometimes invited by Courbet to dinner. Then Champfleury, on familiar terms with Balzac's widow, took Promayet along to her as a music-teacher; and Promayet introduced Courbet to her. 'What he said, I don't at all know, and I've never wanted to speak to him about it. All I know is that I had a letter from Mme de Balzac, who appreciates what *friendship* means, in which she exhorted me to be on my guard and told me that Courbet had much commiserated my situation and boasted of having *nourished* me.' Champfleury added that he had spoken of the episode to no one but

Buchon, but 'you understand I've kept a little grief about it'. Mme de Balzac's letter had reached Champfleury while he was on his way to Belgium with Courbet; it spoiled the journey and Champfleury returned on his own to Paris. We cannot doubt that Champfleury was telling the truth to Buchon, though Mme de Balzac may easily have taken too seriously a little bragging on Courbet's part about the way he'd given a vocation to Champfleury. Still, even so, the story brings out the bad side of Courbet's need always to shine as the dominant character in any scene or relationship.[49]

Probably about this time he painted a picture, called *La Voyante* or *La Somnambule*, of a woman sleepwalking or caught in some moment of vision-insight. The dating is conjectural. Courbet showed it in 1864 at Munich, in 1868 at Ghent; he sent it to Vienna in 1873. In April 1867 he complained to Bruyas that it was badly placed at the Exposition Universelle. His dating is 1865; but he often signed works in an odd way, with dates that can be refuted by documentary evidence. Silvestre about 1856 noticed *La Voyante* in his studio. What he saw may have been a study; one is mentioned by Juliette in 1897 and now seems lost. But consideration of the style of the work we have makes it likely to have been the one that Silvestre saw; the movement of light and shadow over a surface of paint thickly laid on by brush-point, one stroke set close against another. We see the survival of the earlier Rembrandt influences; and late 1855 is a reasonable date – though the work may be earlier. Anyway, he painted it at Ornans, and the model was certainly Juliette: the prominent brow, the jutting cheekbones, the dimple hollowing the pointed chin, are all characteristics of hers. She was in late 1854 near the end of her twenty-third year; the face of *La Voyante* looks much stronger, worn, and full of experience than we would expect Juliette to look at such an age. But Courbet had a way of making young women look much older than they were, whether because he found it hard to handle young grace, was unattracted by it, or read into a face what he saw was going to develop there: just as he tended to strengthen the structure and features of his male sitters.

We know what an obstinate, hard, and rather strange character Juliette became; it seems certain that here we see her with all the strains already ravaging her young face. Zoé went mad; Juliette had a period of breakdown before her final decline into wilful oddities and dream-union with her brother; Zélie, if we may trust Champfleury's novel, had her moments of religious mania. It seems then that *La Voyante* gives us a glimpse of deep insight into the crushing stresses that weighed on all the Courbets despite the indomitable spirit that carried them along; a glimpse of the other side of the devoted family-bond. The idea of the picture may have been suggested by the opera *La Sonnambula* by Bellini, which the period considered the apex of the pathetic – or the title may have been thought out after the picture was finished; but in any event the reality of the portrayal must lie in a glimpse that Courbet had of his sister at a moment of trial and anguish, when she had retreated deep inside herself.[50]

In the letter to Bruyas about his return to Ornans Courbet showed that the shaken mood from which Bruyas rescued him had returned with renewed force.

I have had so many trials since I left you. My life is so difficult I'm beginning to think my moral faculties are drying out. Under the laughing mask you are familiar with, I hide within myself chagrin, bitterness, and sadness that grips my heart like a vampire. In the society in which we live one doesn't have to dig deep to find a void. Really there are so many blockheads [*bêtes*] that it's discouraging to the point of making one hesitate to develop one's intelligence for fear of feeling oneself absolutely alone.

One could deduce such an inner state from what he calls his laughing mask; but it is nonetheless important to have his confession of the fact. No doubt he could have made it only to a man like Bruyas whom he knew would never use it against him. This is his Baudelairean side: his fear of the inner void, the human desert. But his greatness lies in his incessant struggle against the fear, his peopling of the void with the forms and faces that he truly confronts. Here lies the tension inside his Realism, driving him to define people and things as truly as he can, to hold them at arm's-length, and yet at the same time to fill them with his own deep energy. Thus his fear is overcome and the world of *bêtes*, faced in all its truth, becomes the world of truly human beings – that is, people seen in their full potentiality; nature seen just as it is, and yet also a space in which man can find himself organically at harmony.

Bruyas's father would not advance the needed 40,000 francs. Courbet resigned himself to being one of many artists in the official Exposition. He decided to contribute his *Burial* and the *Man with the Pipe*, plus twelve works not yet exhibited. He asked Bruyas to send his self-portrait in a striped collar, with the two portraits of Bruyas done at Montpellier, and with a photograph of a naked woman that Bruyas had. 'She will stand behind my chair in the middle of the picture.' All these works and the photo he wanted for use in his *Studio*. He promised to keep them as short a time as possible. 'I think the *Meeting* looks scorched and dark. This work is well thought of at Ornans. Tell the Sabatiers how much I like them, if you chance to see them. Many messages too to all our acquaintances. . . . Tell them I have pleasant memories of them and of your country, and that I hope to return there some day and beat them at *mail*.'[1]

A few days afterwards, in late November 1854, he wrote that he was leaving for Paris, where he hoped to see Bruyas after all. 'I hear on all sides I'll be the Exposition's great success, and in the newspapers they're saying Realism is triumphant.'[2] But he had used up so much time in the autumn on travelling, hunting, and lying ill in bed, that he could not hope to deliver the *Studio* on the date specified in the rules. He had to bring himself to ask

Nieuwerkerke for the favour of a postponement, and was given it. 'At last I've got a delay of a fortnight on the plea of three months' illness. It was Français that got it for me.' He had had his frames made at Ornans and sent to the Besançon committee, so as to get the free transport offered by the Government to exhibitors. Now he had only four or five more figures to do in the *Studio*. 'I'd sworn to do it. It's done. You occupy a magnificent place in it. You're in the pose of the *Meeting*, but the conception is different; you're triumphant and dominant. The Besançon painters came to see it; they were overwhelmed.' And he lost no chance of keeping the project of the one-man show before Bruyas, whose place in the *Studio* he much exaggerated. 'If I've troubles with the Government, we can still carry on with our great enterprise, an exhibition of your entire collection combined with my pictures, My dear friend, I'm half dead from work and worry.'[3]

But he hadn't left on 6 December when Zoé wrote to Bruyas a letter which brings out how much she wanted to come close to him. We see here the same sort of attempt to identify herself with her brother that we find later in Juliette.

I would have written sooner if I hadn't been afraid of indiscretion; but I was waiting to join my letter with my brother's. This delay has been occasioned by the attack of very strong jaundice that Gustave has had; now he's in full convalescence and soon he'll write to you. Thanks, Monsieur, for the photos you have sent me. In reading your letter, I've experienced an indefinable happiness. Many times I've looked at your portrait attentively, and I've read there the expression of the affectionate emotion that dictated the various lines you have addressed to me.

Each day I appreciate more the good luck we've had in meeting a friend such as you. I say 'we', Monsieur, because you want indeed to include me in your association; for it's indeed rare in this world to meet a heart so noble and feelings so distinguished as those we appreciate in you since we have had the honour of knowing you.

Allow me to tell you, Monsieur, that henceforth all my affections will be concentrated in our charming trinity.

No one should know of it, for I preciously shut up this sweet thought like a treasure of which I'm the miser.

I have just prepared canvases for Gustave. He is very taken up with beginning his picture of the Painter's Epic. What a work, great God! He'll soon himself give you full details.

All my family has been responsive to your good memory; I offer you my warmest greetings. For my brother and for myself, receive favourably, I beg you, the sincere expression of the profound and lasting feeling that I address to you today.

In a letter to Champfleury he detailed the contents of his work: an important statement that must be read in full:

In spite of being on the verge of hypochrondria I've taken on a vast painting, twenty feet long by twelve high, perhaps bigger than the *Burial*, which will prove to you I'm not dead, or Realism either; for this is Realism. It's the moral and physical history of my studio.

The way he there protests shows how aware he was of Champfleury's slackening support; perhaps he hoped by his description of the work to re-arouse his enthusiasm:

In it are the people who thrive on life and those who thrive on death; it's society at its best, its worst, and its average; in short it's my way of seeing society in its interests and passions; it's the people who come to my studio to be painted. . . .

The scene's laid in my Paris studio. The picture's cut into two parts. I'm in the centre, painting; on the right are all the active participants, that is my friends, the workers, the art collectors. On the left are the others, whose lives are without significance: the common people, the destitute, the poor, the wealthy, the exploited, the exploiters: those who thrive on death. On the wall in the background hang the *Return from the Fair* and the *Bathers*, and [on the easel] the picture I'm working at. . . .

I'll describe the figures starting from the extreme left. At canvas-edge is a Jew I saw in England as he was making his way through the swarming traffic of the London streets, reverently carrying a casket on his right arm and covering it with his left hand; he seemed to be saying: 'It's I who have the best of it'; he had an ivory complexion, a long beard, a turban, and a long black gown that trailed on the ground. Behind him is a self-satisfied curé with a red face. In front of them is a poor weather-beaten old man, a former Republican of '93 . . . ninety years of age, holding a wallet in his hand and dressed in old patched white linen. . . . He's looking at a heap of cast-off garments at his feet (he's pitied by the Jew). Next comes a hunter, . . . a labourer's wife, a labourer, an undertaker's assistant, a skull on a newspaper, an Irishwoman suckling a child, a lay figure. The Irishwoman is also a memory from England; I saw this woman in the London streets; her only garments were a black straw hat, a torn green dress, a ragged black shawl under which her arm held a naked baby. The textile pedlar presides over the whole group; he displays his rags to everyone, and all show the utmost interest, each in his own way. In front of him a guitar and a plumed hat occupy the foreground.

Second part: then comes the canvas on my easel and myself painting, showing the Assyrian profile of my head. Behind my chair stands a nude female model; she leans against the back of my chair as she watches me painting for a moment; her clothes are on the floor in the foreground; there's a white cat near my chair. Behind this woman is Promayet with a violin under his arm, as he's posed in the portrait he sent me; next to him are Bruyas, Cuénot, Buchon, Proudhon (I should like you to see the philosopher Proudhon, who looks at things as we do; if he'd sit for me, I'd be pleased; if you see him, ask him if I may count on him). Then comes your turn in the foreground; you sit on a stool with legs crossed and hat on your knees. By you, still nearer the front, is the woman of fashion, elegantly dressed, with her husband. Then at the far back, seated at a table, is Baudelaire reading a big book; next to him is a Negress looking at herself coquettishly in a mirror. At the back in the window embrasure can be seen a pair of lovers whispering to each other of love; one is seated on a hammock. Above the window are voluminous draperies of green cloth; against the wall are some plaster casts, a shelf holding the statue of a little girl, a lamp, and a few pots; also the backs of canvases, a screen, and nothing more except a great bare wall. . . .

The critics who attempt to judge this will have their hands full; they'll have to make what they can of it. For there are people who wake up at night shouting, 'I want to judge, I want to judge!'[4]

There then we have the main ideas that came up in Courbet's mind as he designed and painted the work. But first of all we must note that he made many changes as he went on. On the left, the heap of clothes at the veteran's feet was obscured by the introduction of a new figure, a seated poacher with his dog – brought in for a better balance in composition. To limit the self-sufficiency of the central group (easel-picture, Courbet, model, and cat) a boy looking up at the painter working was introduced. The theme of the painting-in-the-painting was changed. At first there was a miller leading his donkey to the mill; now there was a pure landscape of the Loue banks. In front of Champfleury brooding alone (as distinct from the group of Promayet, Bruyas, Cuénot, Proudhon, Buchon) he put a boy lying on the floor and drawing; from the viewpoint of composition this helped to balance the clothes on the floor over on the left. The Negress (Baudelaire's mistress, Jeanne Duval) was painted out, no doubt at Baudelaire's request, though her phantom outlines can still be detected. Further, the background was simplified; much of the litter (bric-à-brac, all the cats but one, the hanging canvases), meant to give an actual effect of Courbet's studio, was omitted; instead some sketchily suggested panels broke the flat expanse. This change was an improvement; the space was already crowded enough. But like most of the other changes it had its emotional and symbolic significance. Over on the left is a dimly indicated landscape with a reddish sunset-flare, which gives an effect of menace above the figures there in contrast with the big window opening out on the right.

There is a great number of angles from which we can approach this rich work; but first we may dispose of a few factual points. Courbet's remark, made twice, about a visit to London is strange; we know nothing of it and he never referred to it again. It is barely possible that he had made a rapid excursion to England when visiting Holland in 1847, Belgium in 1851, or Dieppe in 1852; but his silence about it, except here, is curious. It seems likely, then, that he invented the visit to give force to the figures in question. I suspect that he had recently read (perhaps at Montpellier, in Bruyas's library) Flora Tristan's *Les Promenades dans Londres* (1840) of which a popular edition was published in 1842 with the title *La Ville Monstre* and the dedication: 'Workers, it is to you of both sexes that I dedicate my book; it is to make you aware of your position in modern society that I have written it.' She makes a strong distinction between the two halves of the nation, the rich and powerful, and the poor and toiling; and in her account of the worst-downtrodden groups she lays much stress on the Jews and the Irish. She draws a harrowing picture of the filth and poverty of the Irish in their hovels near the bottom of Tottenham Court Road. 'Their skins were so grimy, their hair so dishevelled that they looked like Negroes. They glared savagely at me, but when I stared back with assurance, they lowered their eyes and begged me to spare them a coin.' From the age of nine the boys stole; the girls, when between eleven and twelve, were sold to brothels; the older people were professional beggars. The largest pocket of Jews was in the parish of St Giles; but in all their quarters there was feverish selling of 'old clothes exuding the smell of sweat and stale wine, of ancient vomit, of human decay.'

Here are the passages which I think stirred Courbet in chapters X–XI of Flora Tristan's work. In the Irish quarter, '*I saw* children entirely naked, young girls, breast-feeding women *barefooted*, wearing only a chemise that fell in rags and left their bare body almost wholly exposed.' The stress on actually seeing the degradations may well have led Courbet to speak of having seen them himself. 'No, without having *seen* it, it's impossible to conjure up so hideous a poverty! so profound an abasement! a more complete degradation of the human being!!!' That sentence comes before the account of the suckling women. In the Jewish section Flora stresses the pariah aspect. 'The Jew loves money *as money*, and not for making a parade of luxury-objects. Little it matters to him if he's ill clad, ill lodged, ill fed, as long as he has in his possession a *little hoard* hidden away or sheltered from bankruptcies and revolutions: that is enough for his inner satisfaction.' The box clutched by the

Jew in the *Studio* is surely this little *magot*. The French term 'par devers' suggests a closer contact than 'in possession of'.

Courbet, then, may well have been inspired by Flora Tristan to make the haggling over old clothes the main activity among his group on the left, and to introduce the Jew and the Irishwoman, whom he felt as specifically London characters in this context. More, he may even have got the idea of a large-scale work that expresses his awareness of his own 'position in modern society'. As a socialist artist, he would feel that he was like Flora at the same time expressing the socialist awareness of all that went to make up that society.[5] In view of the complex undertones of the painting we must remember that 'atelier' meant both artist's studio and workshop; in 1848 the core of the struggle had been the National Ateliers and the declaration of the Right to Work. From Courbet's viewpoint his private studio is also the *atelier* of socialist consciousness. The full title of the painting was *The Painter's Atelier, a True Allegory Summarising a Period of Seven Years in my Life as an Artist* – that is from 1847 to 1854.

We saw in dealing with the *Burial* that all his main works were in fact both Realist Representations and Allegorical (or Symbolic) Visions. But previously all the persons shown could have actually been brought together in the spot depicted; except by deliberate contrivance and posing, the groups of the *Studio* could never have been assembled. Hence his dilemma, since for the purpose of polemics he had declared that he painted only what he saw, in the places where he saw it, without invention or manipulation. The dilemma was increased by the fact that his friends on the right could be imagined as gathered in his studio for some celebration or other, but the persons on the left had no connection with him except that he might have asked one or other of them at various times to sit for him. The disparity remains though Courbet could have argued that the persons on the left, while primarily social types, might have sat for him as individual models, while his friends were introduced partly in their role as intellectual types.

In its general form the *Studio* looks back to the triptych of the Christian tradition (with ancient pagan originals) in which the Virgin or Christ at the centre is flanked by worshipping groups. The *Studio* carries this tradition on in the sense that Courbet the artist is the person giving meaning and life to the two groups; and also in the sense that he stands for a secular evangel, a creed looking to paradise restored on earth, and he has displaced Christ, now a lay-figure obscured behind the canvas. There is also a more specific sense in which he has taken over the role of Christ. Very probably he is thinking of the etching by Rembrandt (called the *Hundred Florins*) in which we see the flanking groups composed of pharisees and philanthropists arguing on one side, and the Poor of Christ on the other; a deep gap separates the two groups, one struggling with ideas and the other sunk in inert misery.[6] Christ alone can unite the abstract idea and the human fact; the Artist alone can mediate the world of culture and intellect and that of human suffering and exploitation.

Courbet may also well have had in mind in framing his conception such a work as Ingres's *Apotheosis of Homer*. There we see the supreme poet or creative worker in the centre of symmetrical groups of hierarchically posed and lesser intellects. Courbet with his infinitely more complex systems of groupings, with their involved internal relations and their opposed relation to one another, sets out to smash the concept of an artificial deodorised structure of culture and its reflection in pseudo-classic art. He seeks to substitute the real world and the artist in his living connection with that world. For a false concept of harmony he substitutes the real struggle that alone can lead to a stable and true harmony.

We can now better grasp why Courbet dropped the idea of depicting his studio in detail. Creating instead a background of shifting planes and misty depths of colour he gave something of a dream-effect, which makes more acceptable the motley crowd he has gathered. Geometric perspective fades out in place of the indeterminate masses and merging planes of a world in process of change, where the choices lie between the menacing sunset of decay and the outmovement into light. But the outmovement is not stressed; if he brought in a strong luminosity round the lovers he would destroy the centralisation of colour, structure, and meaning on the landscape-canvas. There, in that canvas, lie the values that will determine what happens to a world balanced between doom and salvation. The key to all that is happening lies in the painting on which Courbet is engaged. He alone is working, though the thinkers on his right are musing and Baudelaire as the Poet is truly concentrated. Only the model and the small shepherd-boy are fully aware of the central act.

The isolation of the thinkers from one another, except in the sense that they share a certain meditative mood, and the isolation of the common folk on the left from the artist and the thinkers, brings out the aspect of Baudelairean thought in the conception. Alienation reigns, and yet the interconnections are there, waiting to be realised. The artist is cut off, and yet he is carrying out the action necessary for the defeat of alienation. He is regaining his unity with nature. The creative act, in so far as it is successful, re-achieves the unity of man and nature, and thus makes possible the unity of man with man. Delacroix was right when he saw the ambiguity of lighting in the landscape and the surrounding scene. The landscape, indeed, makes a hole in that scene, but unless it did so it would not have its significance. The whole conception of the work would be changed. We should merely have a picture of the artist in the midst of his material. As things are, we have a picture of the artist as the leader into a new unity with nature, a realism which is also democracy and socialism. As with the *Meeting* the work is robbed of egoism at the very point where we seem to see egoism enthroned.[7]

We may note that Courbet's hand and brush are touching the valley-landscape at the point which we earlier noted as having a sexual significance for him: the point where two slopes come together and water flows out.[8] His outthrust arm, with the other curving below as it holds the palette, reminds us of the arms in the *Winnowers* and the *Bathers*: the gesture that combined work and the stirring of the whole body. The model at his side is in one sense the Muse of classical and romantic fantasies; she inspires him both as Mistress and as Nature. She is the Truth which is naked. Who posed for him is not clear. We saw him writing to Bruyas for a photograph; he talked of going to Paris so as to paint the nude. But it is possible that after all he fell back on Zoé as the model; the girl has her characteristic curve at the back. If we could be sure on this matter, it would help both to clarify and to deepen the mystery of Courbet's intense relationship with his sisters.[9] (I had written this passage when I saw a study for the Model, in the possession of Henry Moore. In this work, charmingly fresh in colour and handling, the girl reveals herself as certainly Zoé. The eyes have a more ravaged look than in the earlier portraits, but the resemblance is clear. It seems, then, that Courbet used her for the figure, but got rid of the likeness either by generalising the face or working from someone else.)

For himself he used the portrait with the striped collar done at Montpellier; and for his friends (apart from Proudhon, who refused to sit) he used various portraits he had made. Champfleury acutely disliked the version of himself. 'I dare not tell you what I think of the *Studio*,' he wrote to Buchon, 'for I'm appalled by my own likeness that makes me look like a general of the Jesuits. I don't know where he could have seen me with such features. . . . Yet the resemblance is close enough for me to be recognised; and without fatuity, without conceit, I shouldn't be pleased to have anyone see me in that guise.'[10]

The limitations of Courbet's social outlook appear when we consider the range of social types he displays. We might criticise the inclusion of the nameless bourgeois in the right foreground, a highly important area in the composition. In his letter he called this pair 'a woman of fashion with her husband'. By what right can they hold such a place on the positive side of the canvas? In Bruyas he has embodied the enlightened collector; there was no need for a purely modish couple, who could only stand for all that Courbet most detested in the Salon and its frequenters. If he had thought of Sabatier and his wife, there would have been some virtue in the inclusion – though he should have put Buchon or someone like that at this point, to express the movement from thought into action. Further there is much confusion of concept in describing the left section as that of society at its worst, the thrivers-on-death. How can he with his views lump together exploited and exploiter as equally negative factors? And what an extraordinarily narrow and trivial notion he shows of exploitation. He omits the landed proprietors, the financiers, the factory-owners, the functionaries of the State; all he shows is a petty pedlar of clothes. And though he does add a labourer and his wife, he does not relate them to the actual exploiting classes. He does make an attack on religion via the Jew, the curé, and the dummy-Christ; but the attack lacks any incisive point through its lack of correlation with the State and money-power. His sympathies appear in the old revolutionary, the poacher, the hunter, the beggar-woman, but again the lack of correlation makes them objects of pity rather than forms embodying an accusation of the system that has created them. The rejection of established art – romanticism in the guitar and other furbishings; academic classicism in the lay-figure – also lacks force for the same reason. The skull on the newspapers is an emblem which stresses the general deathliness of the scene, but has a specific reference to the press, which Proudhon had called the cemetery of ideas. The setting of this emblem of bourgeois propaganda or brain-washing beside the *croque-mort*, between the peddling scene and the beggar-woman, increases its suggestiveness; but the intrusion of a touch of allegory in the old sense hardly harmonises with Real Allegory (a wider significance emerging from the social essence of an individual form).[11]

We may note further that, apart from the central group, the only fully painted characters are the bourgeois couple on the right and the poacher on the left – the others are put in more loosely, so as to provide the transition to the vague space of the background. Yet the couple and the poacher could hardly be called the most significant characters. One would expect some factory and farm workers at the front on the left, and men like Buchon and Proudhon at the front on the right. Perhaps, as I have said, Courbet was thinking of the Sabatiers in the couple, but lacked studies of them and could not anyway have given them such prominence without hurting Bruyas; as for the poacher, such a figure combined his own damnall independence and the open-air life which he had come more and more to cherish.

There are yet other angles however from which we can view this fruitful work. We can see it as expressing the Ages of Man. There is the baby suckled by the Irishwoman; the children drawing or watching; the young lovers; the married couple; the various phases of adulthood; the old man; the hearse-mourner and the skull. The artist is surveying all the phases of individual development as well as a panorama of society with its varying levels. Again, there is the important role of the two children. Apart from the model, only the young shepherd-boy looks at the painting and enjoys it. No doubt this act of his is meant to stress the aspect of nature-return in the painting; he alone is near enough to nature to see the creative process without veils or mediating arguments; he sees it simply and spontaneously. Further, the only other person involved in creative process apart from Courbet (and perhaps the concentrated Baudelaire) is the boy lying on the floor and making drawings. Here again the stress is on spontaneity.

It is not by accident that the boy is so close to Champfleury. For though Baudelaire wrote powerfully of the child as the prototype of the true painter and poet, as he did of certain forms of primitive or archaic art, in the last resort he always remained tethered to various aspects of the conventional art of the period. He could write very sympathetically of a minor modish artist like Guys; only very imperfectly could he see how Courbet was carrying out certain essential lines of his own programme as to the heroisation of everyday life. Champfleury on the other hand, drawing some of his strengths from Baudelaire, was able more uncompromisingly to see the virtues of popular and children's art. In his view:

The lower classes were the most important in society and it was in their life that the underlying social mechanism could be revealed. They were, moreover, a new and unlimited subject, more attractive than the rich and and the elite by their great sincerity, a virtue which for the realists was almost the whole of art. Finally, their own literature is valuable and suggestive; their songs and legends include masterpieces of realism. Champfleury admired the inherent good taste of the people and imagined that they would be spontaneous allies and appreciate the sincerity and vigour of modern realist works. (SCHAPIRO)[12]

Thus he had no idea of what industrialisation did to people; he relied on the romantic notion of the People which had been current for some decades; he thought that Realism and the revival of popular elements in song and art could help to reconcile the classes in a Proudhonian way. He lacked altogether Courbet's revolutionary application of such ideas. It was above all his concept of the reconciling of opposites, as against Courbet's need to drive all contradictions and oppositions to their extreme, which finally broke their friendship. And strangely he was unable to realise the function of the boy at his side in the *Studio*. The boy is drawing a manikin figure of the kind to which the caricaturists were always ready to reduce the persons in Courbet's paintings; he is thus Courbet's retort to those belittlers. He takes up their mockery and replies: Yes, that is the basis – of my work and of all true art. But Champfleury in a letter to Buchon describes the boy as playing with some prints. And he even adds the stupid comment, which shows that he has no idea of the nature of the painting at all, 'Is M. Courbet really certain that the child of a rich bourgeois would enter the studio with his parents when there is a nude woman present?' He converts the boy from the primary artist to the wealthy collector.[13] Like so many of the rebels of his generation, Courbet had no sense of the class-structure of society. Naturally he realised the existence of deep divisions; and at times he used terms like 'workers' or 'exploiters', but he had no clear sense of what they implied. At root he saw a general force, which was that of the People, and he considered Democracy and Socialism to represent somehow the rule of the People with the role of the State reduced to a minimum. He to some extent mistook his own capacity to meet any member of society on his own ground, whether the person was a humble country-worker or the comte de Choiseul, as a sort of political solution for the existence of social differences. To maintain his character as a Man of the People in all circumstances was one aspect of his moral and political integrity, but it solved nothing as far as society was concerned. He told Bruyas in 1854 how he had informed the comte de Nieuwerkerke, 'I alone, of all the French artists, my contemporaries, had the power to render both my own personality and my Society.' That was true, and pointed to his depth and comprehension as an artist; but he did not clearly grasp that the artist takes into himself the whole of society in order to contain and express the fullness of its inner conflicts, its essential patterns of conflict. He knew all that deep down; but he found himself in his formulations at the mercy of the Proudhonian concept (carried on from the eighteenth-century radicals) that the principle of association would somehow by its own workings break down divisions and differences, and also the conflicts they bred. When this principle was seen to beget large-scale capitalist combinations, the dissidents did not realise they were watching something new, the embryonic formations of monopolistic capitalism, but interpreted the phenomenon as a reassertion of *féodalité*, of a brigandage holding the people to ransom. Their lack of any clear sense of the proletariat was what gave them the blithe confidence in a spontaneous uprising of the people as capable of breaking through into a 'free' world.

The period had seen the semi-mystical notion of the People set out enthusiastically by Michelet. Despite the vaguenesses, which could have the effect of veiling and confusing the realities of struggle, there were many vital elements in the turning to the People as a source of values, moral and artistic. In 1856 Buchon succinctly expressed what was positive in those attitudes (found in both his own and in Champfleury's researches into popular art and imagery): 'The most inexorable protest against professors and pastiches is popular art. To approach our popular literature is to ascend once more to our authentic origins, is to get back into possession of our spontaneity, the only creator of living productions.' And Proudhon had made the same point in stressing the creative potentialities of the productive classes: 'No more confidence in the upper levels of society! Let the worker go forward on the same footing as the scholar and the artist. . . . There is no one in reality more a scholar, and more an artist, than the people.'

The *Studio* then, while a brave and indeed magnificent attempt to show the artist at work in a real world with his multiple connections, brings out the limitations of Courbet's socialist views at this stage. But while noting those limitations we must grasp also the strengths. No one had dreamed of such a conception before. Any previous attempts to show the artist at work or to express his functions within the terms of a painting had been so much more limited in their range and their understanding of the complex situation that we cannot even compare them with the *Studio*. Together with *Afterdinner*, it further leads on both to the paintings by artists of their own or someone else's studio, such as Bazille's *The Artist's Studio, rue de la Condamine* (1870) or Fantin-Latour's *Homage to Delacroix* (1864) and *Studio in the Batignolles Quarter* (1870), and to those of more casual gatherings, such as Renoir's *At the Inn of Mother Antony* (1866).

A jury of 30, presided over by Nieuwerkerke, chose the works for the French section of the Exposition. The voting began on 19 March and ended 11 April. Some 6,504 art works were sent in; 2,730 were accepted. Courbet sent in fourteen, but had changed his mind about having few earlier works. He included *Stonebreakers*, *Young Village-Girls*, *Spinner* as well as the *Burial* and *Man with the Pipe*. New were the *Château of Ornans*, *Roche des Dix Heures*, *Rivulet of Puits Noir*, *Winnowers*, *Spanish Lady*, the *Meeting*, portrait of Champfleury, self-portrait in striped collar, *Studio*. Three paintings were rejected, but these included *Burial* and *Studio*. All the jurors but Français and Rousseau agreed. In such a show wall-space had to be conserved; but Courbet was not likely to listen to such a plea.

He mustered his supporters. He probably got help from the iron-master de Mandre (whom he had known since 1850) and from Wey, who had kept connections with the engineering and industrial world through his period at the École Centrale. Courbet was introduced to P. Picard who had married the daughter of Boulard, the Director of the Company of the Audincourt Ironworks; according to the custom of Saint-Simonians, Picard had added his wife's name to his own, so that he was Picard-Boulard. He had reached an important place in the world of iron-works and wire-mills; and the companies he represented had just built a depot at 64 rue Amelot. (We must also recall the bronze-worker Nicolle, whose portrait Courbet painted later in 1862; he had his workshop in one of the blind alleys which cut off the building of the Forges d'Audincourt.) At 64 rue Amelot there was a façade with a large door, surmounted with a triangular pediment; the hall, lighted through its glass roof,

offered a good site for showing pictures. Probably Courbet was going to take the forepart
of the building, with a partition cutting off the rear; entry to the works would not be
obstructed since on each side were two deep blind-alleys into which it opened.[14]

Courbet liked the idea, since it would mean little expense for him. He went to the prefect
of police for the necessary authorisation for a show to which a charge was made for admission.
He was referred to M. de Mercey, who on 26 April agreed to the site; the prefect advised
Courbet that he could go ahead. But meanwhile Courbet had changed his mind. Though
the quarter had many craftsmen who cast art-objects, it was far from the Exposition. So
he returned to the prefect and pretended that the latter had got things wrong; he said that
he had not in fact chosen a site and that 64 rue Amelot was the residence of Picard, who was
assisting him in the project of his show. (In fact Picard lived at 24 rue Saint-Sébastien.) In
his conversation Courbet must have suggested areas that he was considering; for a pencil-
correction in the prefect's letter to the Minister reads 'Avenue d'Antin or faubourg Montmartre'. M. de Mercey noted on the margin that the authorisation still held, but it would
not be convenient 'for this show to be held at the door of the Universal Exposition. No
objection to the Champs-Elysées.' These comments were expanded in an official letter.
Courbet had already dreamed of a site 'right opposite' the great exposition; now he set to
work to come as close as possible to the Palais Lefuel, where the Exposition was.[15]

The official show was not yet open. It had been ready by 1 May; but on 28 April Prince
Napoleon, in view of delays in handing over the Palais de l'Industrie to the organisers,
obtained from the emperor the fixing of 15 May for the opening of all the sections together.
We have some letters written to Bruyas during this period; but they are undated. The following seems composed with the shock of the rejection of his two big works still recent:

I'm almost frantic. Terrible things have happened to me. They've just refused my *Burial* and my
last picture as well as the portrait of Champfleury. They declared it was necessary to arrest at any
cost the progress of my tendencies in art, which were disastrous to French art. Eleven of my works
are taken. The *Meeting* is taken with reluctance; they consider it too personal and too pretentious.

I'll open a separate show of twenty-seven of my pictures, new and old, with the explanation I'm
taking advantage of the favour shown me by the Government in accepting eleven paintings for
their own show. To prepare an exhibition of pictures from my studio will cost me 10,000 or 12,000
francs. I've already leased the site for 2,000 francs for six months. The construction will cost me
6,000 or 8,000 francs. The strange thing is that the site is actually enclosed within the area of their
show. At the moment I'm negotiating with the prefect of police for the completion of the necessary
finalities. I've already got the 6,000 francs you paid me. If you care to pay off the rest of what you
owe me, and to lend me the *Bathers*, I'm saved. I'll make 100,000 francs at one stroke. . . . Paris
is furious at my rejection. I'm on the go from morn to night.[16]

His new site was 17 Avenue Montaigne. On 16 May the builder Legros signed the contract
for building the gallery 'according to the plans prepared by M. Isabey, architect'. The
materials were to be wood panels with a lining of hollow brick, covered outside with plaster;
canvas-door and grey wallpaper inside. There was to be a solid roof covered with zinc, a
glazed skylight, pine-floors, an office and vestibule covered with tarred paper. The cost
3,500 francs – 1,000 on completion of framework, 1,500 when the job was done between

1 and 8 June, 1,000 three months later. Legros was to forfeit 100 francs a day for any delays after 8 June or get a bonus of 50 francs a day if he finished earlier.[17] Courbet had at first wanted only a round tent set up with a central mast: 'the whole mounted on a stage'. But Félix Isabey, nephew of the recently dead miniaturist, preferred the rectangular buildings, of which we have no drawing or trace.[18]

He had met Isabey, a compatriot born at Besançon in 1821, through Wey. Living at 25 Quai des Grands-Augustins, Isabey was taken up with big constructions of a social type: crèches, public baths, workers' houses. But he accepted the unusual commission and quickly worked out the plans. Courbet was delighted, particularly at being almost in the big Exposition's area. He grew more ebullient as the number of his pictures for the show increased. 'After two months of negotiations with all sorts of ministries and two interviews with the minister M. Fould, I've at last got permission to hold a show for which I may charge an entrance-fee. It'll be organised under extraordinarily independent conditions. . . . I'll be considered a monster, but I expect to make 100,000 francs. At present I'm busy with the building. I'll have thirty pictures at this private show.' The police prefect Prémorin had received him with much kindness and predicted a big financial success; so there would be a municipal guard in view of the probable inrush of money. He seems to have doubted the amiability of M. de Mercey and reassured himself with the thought of the eleven works in the official show. 'I am covered against all protest by this fact, and against all blame.' He didn't know that, as well as paintings of the rejected and relief-plans of Sebastopol being shown at the Jardin d'Hiver, in the very same street as his own show, at 66 Avenue de Montaigne, J. G. Houssaye was displaying, with permission, Chinese objects almost identical with those in the Palais Lefuel.[19]

Promayet was to be in charge of the cash; M. Crétin would look after sticks and umbrellas, his son would take the tickets. He himself was busy getting photos of his works for selling; he retouched all his pictures, sure that Paris talked of nothing else and waited for the opening with impatience. 'My pictures at the Exposition are miserably placed and I couldn't get them hung together, despite the regulations. In short, they want to be done with me, they want to annihilate me. I've been in despair a month. They deliberately rejected my large pictures, declaring it wasn't the works they rejected, but the man. My enemies will make my fortune. This has given me the courage to carry out my own ideas. . . . I shall win freedom, I shall save the independence of art. They're reeling under the blow I've struck at them; but my barriers were so well placed, they couldn't retreat. Your picture of the *Meeting* has made an extraordinary impression. In Paris they call it *Bonjour, M. Courbet!* and the attendants are busy guiding strangers to my pictures [at the Exposition]. *Bonjour, M. Courbet!* is having widespread success. Very odd! from all quarters I get suggestions and letters encouraging me in my project. The public expects it of me. I'm going to ask every owner of my works to be kind enough to lend them to me; I've just written to the Lille Museum for my *Afterdinner at Ornans!*' (This request was refused, though most private owners agreed. By 28 June, when he opened he had forty paintings and four drawings.)

At moments his sense of being persecuted hovers on the edge of paranoia. But while he thus invented motives and speeches for his enemies, the malicious enemies were real enough, even if they didn't always do what he suspected. To keep his spirits up, it was a habit of his to say that his enemies were helping him in their own despite. This time at least he was wrong, except that by having his own independent show like this he did make an important gesture. The Exposition Universelle des Beaux-Arts had cost 120,000,000 francs, and the Government relied on at least a million visitors to cover the costs. The charge per head was 5 francs for the first two weeks and all following Thursdays, with Sundays at 20 centimes; 900,000 visitors did come, but mostly on the Sundays; on the expensive days there were never more than 700; the final deficit was given as 450,000 francs. Courbet had paid out about 12,000 francs; he counted on 100,000 visitors, paying each 20 sous. 'Champfleury will do me an annotated booklet sold (at 10 centimes) and I'll also sell photos of my pictures.' Bad rains held up the building work and he was late in opening. At the end of a fortnight he lowered the entry-charge to 15 centimes; but this still did not attract a crowd, though we are told that his 'defiance' excited the *lycéens* who gathered on Sundays before the *Burial* in loud discussion, 'for the first duty of the good realist was then to show he was a powerful talker'.[20]

The manifesto in the catalogue was his first important statement at length of his principles. Critics often say that no doubt Champfleury wrote or rewrote it; but there is no reason to doubt it is Courbet's own work, no doubt looked over by Champfleury and perhaps pruned by him:

The title of realist has been imposed on me as that of romantic was imposed on the men of 1830. At no time have titles given a just idea of things; if they did, the works would be superfluous.

Without explaining myself as to the correctness, more or less great, of a qualification that no one, it is to be hoped, is required to understand well, I shall confine myself to some words of elucidation so as to cut misunderstandings short.

I have studied, without recourse to any system and preconceived position, the art of the ancients and the art of the moderns. I have not wanted to imitate one any more than to copy the other; nor has my thought been any more aimed at reaching the trifling [*oiseux*] goal of art for art's sake. No, I have wanted quite simply to draw from the total knowledge of tradition the reasoned and independent sentiment of my own individuality.

To know so as to have the power: that was my thought. To be in a position to translate the manners, the ideas, the aspect of my epoch, according to my own estimation; to be not only a painter but a man as well; in a word, to create living art – that has been my aim.[21]

The key-term there is 'living art': a phrase used in a new sense. An art based on the past in so far as it sums up its achievement for the artist's particular purposes, but at the same time free from the past; an art at all points vitally linked with the historical process and with the people who embody that process; an art which expresses the whole man.

Champfleury, home from a visit to Buchon at Berne, attended the opening. He wrote back to say that he did well to return, 'for truly I'd have missed one of the most amusing spectacles of my life. At midday Courbet in a black suit was awaiting his guests. I think the first arrival was Théophile Gautier, who took a seat and inspected the pictures for an hour-

and-a-half, now and then glancing out of the corner of his eye at Courbet, who for his part didn't dare approach his enemy.' Then Gautier went off to relieve his feelings at a café with a group of recalcitrants, including Chenavard and Peisse, official critics attached to the École des Beaux-Arts. (Champfleury is not, however, fair in putting Chenavard thus among the 'anti' group.) Next came the *chansonnier* Gustave Mathieu 'with some Friends of Nature, his pupils, he brought along two quite charming little tarts'. Then Grassot in person. 'Do you know this grotesque of the Palais-Royal, the man who made a success with debilitated hats and mad gestures? The frenetic Grassot, whom I didn't at all know, hung on my arm, spoke as a bosom friend, and explained the drama of the *Burial* figure by figure.' Then in came Proudhon in a broadbrimmed hat of white rabbit-skin. 'Never will one invent a more comic session than that which linked Grassot and Proudhon, Grassot quizzing the pale sun or rather brie-cheese that served as the philosopher's headgear. Two old ladies of fashion came in, severe and curious, a little astonished at the painting and at the Friends of Nature, also at the head of the boozers' party [Guichardet] who cried out without looking, 'It's superb, my dear Courbet, superb! Can't one get a drink here?' Champfleury does not seem to know that this year for the first time, in imitation of English exhibitions, a buffet had been attached to the official picture-show. Not that it was a success; de Mercey in his accounts stated that it never made more than 400–500 francs daily, and in the end it showed a loss. 'The hussies, introduced by the Friends of Nature, behaved indifferently, laughed, ran about, and completely scandalised the fashionable ladies. After Grassot, Proudhon explained the *Burial* to me in his way.' In the evening Champfleury returned home, 'no longer understanding anything about art. All I could be sure of was that the general effect was good and that Courbet's older pictures have grown in stature. After a week's light-hearted comedy of arguments there'll remain only the counting-up of the costs.'[22]

For a few days a handful of curious visitors wandered in, getting fewer all the time. People were too tired of pictures after the vast Exposition to face yet another show. Courbet's wild dreams of success collapsed, but as always he put on a brave face. Though now lacking all enthusiasm for Courbet's work, Champfleury was drawn in, no doubt having been appealed to, and wrote an article. To Buchon he admitted that the show was a financial failure and 'no reviews except derisive ones. I hadn't meant to contribute anything but in the end I wrote an article that doesn't satisfy me, and I did it only to provide, as well as I can, publicity for this experiment so as to make it possible for Courbet to recoup his losses.' The article (in *L'Artiste* of 2 September) was in the form of an open letter to George Sand, who in 1854 had expressed some doubts as to realism's validity. Champfleury too has his doubts. 'The name horrifies me with its pedantic terminology; I fear schools like cholera.' He added that all men with a decisive character were accused of realism, for example Wagner and Gérard de Nerval (an odd pair). 'I won't define for you, Madame, realism; I don't know where it comes from, where it goes, what it is. Homer would be a realist since he observed and described with exactitude his epoch's manners.' These comments have their truth; but if we admit that Courbet was reasserting realism in a situation of enervated tendencies and productions, what was there against redefining the creed in terms of that situation and the lines taken by the struggle against it?

Some people say that it is incredibly courageous, it is the overthrow of all institutions subject to the decision of juries, it is a direct appeal to the public, it is liberty. Others say it's a scandal, it is anarchy, it is art dragged through the mire, it is the platform of a street-fair. I confess, Madame, I agree with the first group. . . . If there's one quality that M. Courbet owns in the highest degree, it is conviction. . . . He advances in art with a sure tread, he displays proudly his point of departure and the goal he has reached, thus resembling the rich manufacturer who hung from his ceiling the wooden sabots in which he once walked to Paris.[23]

(Note the 'platform of a street-fair,' the *sabots*, and the manufacturer as a peasant who has come up in Paris.) Champfleury dealt rather with Courbet's gesture of the one-man show than with his art; and he had to force his tone. Probably in the hope of recouping his losses Courbet had sinned against his socialist convictions by gambling on the Bourse; one is pleased to learn that he lost. For a while he seems confused and lost, though Champfleury may well exaggerate his condition. 'After the loss has come revulsion from work. Criticism knocks him down. Since his exhibition began he has done nothing than run about the cafés, preach, stay up at nights. He should have left Paris long ago and should steep himself again in his homeland. I deplore his lack of commonsense because I love the man a lot, but advice has no effect on him and I see him in Paris like a leaf driven about in a whirlwind.' To Buchon on 1 October Champfleury wrote that he hadn't hidden 'what I think of his future, though I restrained myself a little this year because of the ill-will he's encountered; but in a few years hence, when I publish a serious book on him, I won't beat about the bush; I'll state frankly what I've seen in his works that I don't like.' Three weeks later he declared, 'The fury directed against Courbet is caused by a perfectly legitimate reaction against his exaggerated vanity, and I suffer a little from the rebound.'[24]

The usual abuse was directed at the *Studio* and the whole show.

God save us from dwelling on those painters known in Greece as Rhyparographists, painters of filth. . . . What M. Courbet is trying to do is to represent people as they are, as ugly and coarse as he finds them. . . . But it is all at the tip of his brush; there is nothing noble, pure or moral in the head that controls the hand; he invents nothing, he has no imagination; he knows nothing but his craft; he is an artisan in painting as others are in furniture or shoemaking. (EUGÈNE LOUDUN)

A. J. de Rays in *L'Illustration* (28 July) stated: 'Courbet – that is vulgarity', though he added, 'his popularity reverberates all the more'. The public had now been thoroughly indoctrinated by the critics. Thus in the register of comments at the Exposition we read on 12 July, 'One begs M. Courbet to wish to have his Stonebreakers' shirt well mended and their feet washed.' Auguste Villemot in the *Figaro* wrote that 'Courbet has built a little barrack, which represents well enough the Théâtre de Guignol beside the Scala of Milan'; and he took more space in jeering at the 20-sous charge than in discussing the pictures. Gautier had some good words for the landscapes but said that Courbet was 'systematically throwing away a real talent for painting', and that 'under the pretext of realism he horribly calumniates nature'. As for the *Spanish Lady*, he declared that Léal, painter of corpses in the Hospital of Charity at Seville, 'does not have a palette more gamey (*faisandée*), more charged with green and putrid nuances'. Maxime du Camp wrote that 'we like artists who carry their banner high, and we feel nothing but contempt for those waving them at street-corners'. Courbet has chosen

the place he wants to occupy in the press; he has put his name and his *bombast* on the fourth page of the papers between the [advertisements for] worm-killing pills and essence of sarsaparilla. This is no longer within our province. In our department we are concerned exclusively with art, and now in any event we have nothing more to do with M. Courbet.[25]

Delacroix, however, recognised the importance of the *Studio* even if he could not enter fully into the artist's aims. 'They have rejected one of the most outstanding paintings of the times; but he is too sturdy to be discouraged by so slight a setback.'[26]

Two poets wrote on the *Meeting*. Mathieu tried a quatrain:

> Pause, passer-by. Courbet's before your eyes,
> He whose pure brow awaits the crown at ease.
> That thus he looks at you, feel no surprise.
> Looking at you, it is himself he sees.

De Banville in one of his *Odes Funambulesques* describes a walk in the countryside; for the first time he finds nature horrible, the willows show 'so many gibbosities, goitres too, and bellies, I took them all for ancient baritones', and so on. He asks Cybele who has thus distorted her. She says, 'If you see me made so ugly and so sad, it's because Master Courbet's passed this way.' The leaves, boughs, grasses all chant: 'Good-day, M. Courbet! How do you do?' A far voice of joy and pride replies; and he sees on that side Courbet, his beard 'scaling the skies', get back into a diligence.[27]

A certain admiration of Courbet's tenacity had appeared in the comments, and P. Mantz in the *Revue française* was on the whole favourable, though he thought the *Studio* bizarrely lighted and unhappy in its perspective. Baudelaire, who wrote at length on the Exposition, dealt with Courbet in his section on Ingres:

However enormous a paradox it may seem, it is in this particular that he comes near to a young painter whose remarkable début took place recently and with all the violence of an armed revolt. I refer of course to M. Courbet, who is also a mighty workman, a man of fierce and indomitable will; and the results that he has achieved – results that for certain minds have more charm than those of the great master of the Raphaelesque tradition, owing doubtless to their positive solidity and their unabashed indelicacy – have just the same peculiarity, in that they also reveal a dissenting spirit, a massacrer of faculties. Politics and literature, no less, produce robust temperaments like these – protestants, anti-supernaturalists, whose sole justification is a spirit of reaction which is sometimes salutary. The providence which presides over the affairs of painting gives them as confederates all those whom the ideas of the prevailing opposition have worn down or oppressed. But the difference is that the heroic sacrifice offered by M. Ingres in honour of the idea and the tradition of Raphaelesque Beauty is performed by M. Courbet on behalf of external, positive and immediate Nature. In their war against the imagination they are obedient to different motives; but their two opposing varieties of fanaticism lead them to the same immolation.[28]

This is a piece of Baudelaire's malice. The comparison is false; one cannot in any way compare an artist imposing rigid intellectual formulas and an artist who seeks to grasp the multiplicity of real life, to express the whole man. Baudelaire sees only one aspect of Courbet's work: its protest, its massacre of the ideal in so far as the ideal consists of predetermined forms and categories. Its positive aspects, its release of a host of living forms, its deep joy in life, he totally ignores.

An undated letter shows that Courbet's sisters came to see his show, and gives news of Zoé:

My dear Father, I've just got your letter and reply at once. I've found two rooms in my street with beds; the [female] travellers can arrive, there's one of the rooms for the ladies Boutet if they like. I'm going to find Paul and let him know. As for Zoé, she is excellently placed by chance, for all her choices don't always have a good success. She can say to the innocents etc. She's with Mme Castelli, a rich Italian lady in effect who has taken her into her friendship. I am again pleased to see her there. . . .

He says that his show has suffered through his following the Government's example; he should have built on the boulevards, everyone says so, he'd have taken 100,000 francs. He is getting 100 people a day at 50 centimes. If he had to choose again, he'd have spent less. Nobody believes any longer in the Exposition, and at times like the present, labour, sites, materials are very costly.

Two letters from Zoé to Bruyas around this time bring out further how keen she was to meet him; perhaps in her daydreaming way she hoped to attract him and become his wife, taking Gustave's place in his affections. On 22 July she wrote:

Learning from Gustave that you propose to come soon to Paris, I take the liberty of writing: here's the reason. I am at the moment in Paris at the house of a lady, one of my friends, who is ill and who has begged me to take her place in running the place. This lady has a house very near the Champs-Elysées (avenue Matignon, 4) and just now there are three furnished suites to let, which are as comfortable as elegant, and in a fine quarter.

Hearing of your coming, and in my role as friend of Mme Castelli who is Italian and as amiable as *spirituelle*, I am wholly happy at the idea that's come to me of offering you a suite; that would be a truly great pleasure for me, Monsieur, if you put up at this house; I'd have the advantage of making your acquaintance, which I desire very keenly, and, in my role of mistress of the house, I'd feel a great happiness in surrounding you with a friendly solicitude.

Your strong friendship for my brother, which has extended itself to me, has made me quite confiding; so, Monsieur, I don't excuse myself with you for taking this step, and I hope to have the honour of receiving you. Please, I beg you, reply to this and allow me to offer you my warmest greetings.

Bruyas was far too canny to let himself get into Zoé's clutches. He gave some excuse for dropping his visit; and on 1 September Zoé made the best of a bad job:

Allow me to be indiscreet, I beg you, for I couldn't resist the desire to answer your letter. The affectionate expressions with which it is filled have made me very happy, I am writing to tell you and to thank you for them. Gustave is upset at your absence, he always hopes to see you come. I've told him I was going to write you; he charges me to tell you that he's engaged in looking on the boulevards for a site to which to transfer his gallery, for the bad season is going to make the Champs-Elysées deserted. How are you, Monsieur? In your letter you don't speak of your health, and yet that interests us singularly.

She carries on in this vein, begging him to write to her. She apologises for the liberty she takes in thus speaking, 'but it reminds you of the good friendship you have offered me; I'm happy and proud of it. Your portrait has taught me to know you, and your relations with my brother and me have taught me to love you.' She adds she is soon to leave Paris and regrets not having met him.

The activities and stresses of the show had exhausted Courbet. Late in August he wrote home, 'I'm so tired out I can no longer keep on my feet, I feel a terrible longing for Ornans.'[29] But an invitation took him off to Ghent; and in Belgium, where his reputation was high, he recovered health and spirits. 'I'm welcomed like a prince,' he wrote in early September, 'which isn't surprising as I'm surrounded by counts, barons, princes etc. Some of the time we're entertained at dinners, other times we ride in carriages or on horseback through the streets of Ghent. As for the dinners, I daren't mention them any more; I don't believe we are away from the table four hours a day. I think if I stayed longer, I'd come home as round as a tower. Despite all this I've already done two portraits.' He had been to Brussels, Malines, Antwerp, Termonde, and was about to visit Louvain, Liége, Dinant, Cologne, Mainz, Strasbourg, Mulhouse. He welcomed the chance to see many of the pictures of the great Dutch artists 'who are very useful'.[30]

He must have been moving fast; for he meant to arrive home by 15 September. He seems to have spent most of the autumn at Ornans, but had to go to Paris in December to close his show. On 9 December he wrote to Bruyas that he was dismantling the thing. 'I must vacate the site, my head is spinning.' He was going to Ornans 'for three weeks, reluctantly, as I have work to do in Paris'.[31] On 10 December Champfleury wrote to Buchon, 'Yesterday we went to the *Varieties* to see a play about Courbet; there's nothing duller or sillier than these revues of the end of the year; but just the same it made us laugh.' The revue, by Théodore Cogniard and L. F. Clairville, was *Le Royaume du calembour*. Courbet was shown as the painter Dutoupet (*toupet* as presumption or effrontery). A sitter arrives for her portrait; but the realist is horrified to find she is a lovely young woman; unwilling to soil his muddy brushes with clear fresh colours, he sends for a sooty charcoal-burner; but the man washes himself first and so is also turned away. In the end Dutoupet repents and seeks the Ideal.[32]

This year Courbet went to the monster concert given by Berlioz at the Palais de l'Industrie. It was also in this year that Buchon wrote his song *La Soupe au Fromage*, which became a warsong of the Realists, their *Marseillaise*, it was called. Schanne set it to music, and it was heartily sung at Andlers; it praised Cheese Soup (a variety of Onion Soup), the special delicacy of Franche-Comté.

The pot is on the fire,
Put butter in to stew,
More than enough to spare,
When the butter's melting there,
Add onions and flour too,
And tend with loving care
    The Cheese Soup! the Cheese Soup![33]

There was to be no Salon in 1856 after the giant effort of the Exposition Universelle. Courbet must have been pleased, since he needed a quiet period in which to recoup and to gather fresh energies. He spent 1856 at Ornans or Paris, painting much of the time. This year saw him begin on hunting scenes in the familiar mountains around him. He probably produced this winter or early spring 1856 his first two works in this series: *Fox in the Snow* and the *Dying Stag*, though he may have finished them off in his Paris studio. Into these and the following works he put his expert sense of the hunt; he combined his painter's-eye and his keen observation of the animals in their lairs or in flight. At times he used sketches made on the spot; and often he used the carcasses of slain animals for details, texture, and so on. When no carcass fresh from the hunt was available, he was ready to use the deer or other game from the butchers' stalls in the rue Montorgeuil near the Halles Centrales.[1]

In late winter or early spring he had hopes that Buchon would be allowed to return. 'The empress will soon give birth to a young emperor; here everyone is offering prayers; and the stock market is rising. I must tell you I'm gambling on the Bourse. I've bought twenty-five Austrian bonds; the arrival of the new emperor should bring me some profit. . . . To you it will bring your release.' He mentions too that Silvestre is going to put an account of him in his forthcoming book. He appears to have no sense that gambling on the Bourse runs counter to his socialist creed; if he had the least idea of what he was doing, he would hardly have boasted to the stern-minded Buchon. And he does not seem to have attempted to bring any new pressures to bear on Buchon's behalf. The prince was born on 16 March 1856, with no benefit to the latter.[2]

Courbet made a charcoal drawing of Pierrot to illustrate a pantomime in verse by Fernand Desnoyers, *Le Bras Noir*. The work was staged at the Folies-Nouvelles on 8 February with the drawing reproduced by woodcut on the programme. Pierrot was shown terrified at a large arm rising from the ground.[3]

Champfleury kept on drifting away, setting out his doubts and rationalisations to Buchon in the distance as he found himself incapable of doing to Courbet in the flesh.

As for *Realism*, I regard the word as one of the best jokes of the epoch. Courbet alone has made use of it with the robust faith he happily possesses and which doesn't allow him to doubt. My sincerity long made me struggle before using the word, for I no longer believe in it. Realism is as old as the world; at all times there have been realists. . . . Realism makes progress, I feel, but it would need much effrontery to spread it. Unhappily I have too much good faith, sincerity, to attach myself to a word Courbet was more crafty and more naïve when he spoke of it. I believe he was both those things together. . . .[4]

But doubts of Realism as a creed gave way to doubts of Courbet.

Neither doctrines nor explanations of his system can alter the fact that Courbet has gone off the track since the *Burial* and *After dinner*. Ever since he did those two works, I've regarded him as a man gone astray, influenced by public opinion, by criticism, trying to compromise, not succeeding, determined to cause a sensation and no longer faithful to his own temperament. You know I defended him this year, but I based my plea solely on the *Burial*. I see in him plenty of talent, a craftsman-painter's talent, but nothing more. He is selling nothing, he is being attacked, but what great artist has not been made to die over a slow fire? If the outcries, the advices, made you change your route, it's that you haven't a line settled in your head. What, then, are systems? Lies, since they seek to deceive the public as to the lack of rectitude in a spirit gone astray.[5]

Champfleury wanted Courbet to be a sort of *genre*-painter of the rural petty-bourgeoisie; he overvalued the aspects in his work that seemed to fit in with this role, then resented every movement in a new direction. But it is hard to see how Courbet's refusal to compromise is taken to represent an unsuccessful effort of compromise.

When Silvestre's book appeared, the painter must have been gratified by the length of the account of himself, but he resented much of the tone.[6] 'He has taken from my notes what was substantial there,' he complained to Buchon, 'then has put the whole thing in semi-buffoon tone, so as to turn the question and avoid responsibility for a thing he couldn't do. I don't refer to all the foolish things he makes me say. That belongs to his place of origin; all the folk of the Midi are like that.'[7] Silvestre's tone is exemplified by sentences like these: 'He feels only self-love violently; he holds the soul of Narcissus in its last migration. He paints himself in his pictures always with rapture [*volupté*], and swoons in admiration for his work. No one is capable of making him the tenth of the compliments he addresses to himself from morning to evening.' But his samples of Courbet's talk are clearly close to the facts:

I am Courbetist, that's all. My painting is the only true one. I am the first and the unique artist of the century; the others are students or drivellers . . . I'm not only a *painter*, but a *man*. I can give my reasons in ethics, in philosophy, in politics, in poetry, as in painting. I am *objective* and *subjective*, I have made my synthesis. I laugh at one and all, without being disturbed by opinion any more than by the water passing under the Pont-Neuf. Above all I do what I have to do. I'm accused of vanity. I am indeed the proudest man on earth.

Silvestre adds here, 'His vanity, which people have wanted to impute to him as a crime, is naïve and courageous; that of many others is dissimulated, full of venom.' And he cites Courbet again, 'I have gone through tradition as a good swimmer might cross a river; the academicians drown in it.'

Courbet must have been more pleased with *Receuil de dissertations sur le Réalisme*, which Buchon published this year, 1856, at Neuchâtel. 'The most inexorable protest against the professors and the pastiche is popular art.' Such art speaks only when it has something to say, and what it thinks it says squarely. Buchon linked Courbet and Proudhon; he saw in Courbet the movement of spontaneity; there was no question of depending on inspiration (which meant a method of intermittent work). To watch him at work made one think he produced his paintings 'as simply as an appletree its apples'. His rapidity of production was matched by his abundant powers of sleeping. Based and statured as he was in force, 'put him at table, on horseback, at hunting, at swimming, at canoeing, at skating, at billiards, at *mail*, or in a good bed, and you'll see if he does magnificent honour to the situation'. To his spontaneity was added 'the subtlety of his moral flair, his capacity to follow and even dominate the movement of healthy ideas in his environment, with the aid only of his enormous powers of intuition'. Thus, while stressing the spontaneous and intuitive aspect in his being, Buchon links it with an intellectual grasp. He sums up: 'To live with an energetic and always taut life, to see with a piercing and sovran view, that's the whole secret of this fine intelligence at the service of a great heart.' Moral depth is the other side of the boisterous love of life. 'For my part, I have always kept from Courbet's conversation a beneficent after-echo, analogous to the grave impression left by the contemplation of his pictures.'[8]

Silvestre's book had appeared in August. In the previous month had been launched the short-lived periodical *Réalisme* (three times a month, four pages, fifteen centimes) under the editorship of Duranty and Jules Assézat. A combative article-manifesto declared:

The truth of colour and light is so powerful, so important, that the greatest can scarcely arrive at it. In art an immense genius is needed to reproduce simply and sincerely what one sees before one's eyes, from an earthenware pot up to the face of the most august of kings. . . . The best draughtsman is the colourist. . . . Drawing is not the exterior contour of a form; it is everywhere, in the middle, above, below, everywhere where there's light and shadow. . . . The other day a friend who descends from Herostratos said to me: I've come from the Louvre, if I'd had matches I'd have set that catacomb on fire with the deep conviction that I was serving the cause of future art.

We see what new conceptions were gaining strength under the aegis of Courbet, richly fruitful for the future.

Champfleury tells us a tale about a side-effect of Sylvestre's book. The latter as an advertisement had had photographs of the painters it described, set up in bookshops; among them was Courbet, '*in black clothes* and looking a fine fellow'. Some wag told him that a *grande dame* had gone to the publisher to buy a copy of his photograph, making a great fuss over his looks. Courbet couldn't sleep. 'When will she return? where does she live? how is she? if I only knew where to meet her!' Three days later the wag told him that the publisher had pretended to be Courbet in person and had seduced the lady. Courbet went rushing round, complaining bitterly at the way the lady had been deceived, 'while he himself, Courbet, lost the fruit of his labours, his fortune perhaps, important commissions'. Sylvestre ended by being bored with the joke and told Courbet the lady never existed and the *éditeur* hadn't even seen her garter. Courbet was unconvinced; he went to 'find the philosopher Bellegarrique [literary eccentric and southerner, chief editor of the *Grocers' Journal*] and complained of Sylvestre who, he said, was jealous of his conquest'. Champfleury says that everyone was laughing. Courbet himself told the story. 'The pith of the matter is that he recounts things in so clumsy a way that one at once sees, despite the fine role he gives himself, how he has been duped.' He adds that he always listens to Courbet without contradicting him; 'I even let him launch into the most daring literary theories.'

All that we know of Courbet's love-affairs, apart from his relation with Virginie, tends to the ludicrous. We have a polite note of his, but do not know to whom it was addressed:

M. Courbet has had the indiscretion to penetrate into the apartment of Mlle Octavie who no longer comes to see him. He salutes this *demoiselle* as graciously as is possible for him.

Among the landscapes painted this year were two of the Forest of Fontainebleau; and in his homeland the *Banks of the Loue*. Two more hunt-scenes were the *Quarry* and the *Doe Exhausted in the Snow*. The first shows the end of the hunt in a pine-forest; the carcass of a buck hangs by one leg from a tree-trunk, with two hounds impatient for their share; Courbet leans tired against a tree; a second hunter, seated, blows a horn. The second work shows the fallen doe with only its terrified eyes alive, five hounds closing in, two hunters behind them; under the dark wintry sky we see the spread of snow marred only by a few wind-tossed bushes.

In turning afresh to landscape and to the hunt, Courbet was certainly expressing a weariness with the human scene, a recoil from the brave failure of his one-man show. This year too he seems to have done his first still-life, *Vase of Flowers*. In part he was recruiting his strength, but he had also taken a turn which had permanent effects on his art.[9]

He may have travelled to Belgium this year; for it was now he seems to have done *La Roche à Bayard*, painted near Dinant, and also the *Meuse at Freyr* with its overhanging rocks. The area interested him; for we have other canvases showing the same site from different angles. Perhaps he liked to study rocky cliffs, so familiar in his home-region, in terms of a different climate and light. He had developed a power to define varying atmospheric effects, linked with the kind of country that produced them. In carrying further the attempt to translate specific light-qualities he formed the bridge between Corot and the men of Barbizon, and Pissarro and Monet.[10]

But he did not give the year up wholly to landscape, hunting-scenes and portraits. He painted *Young Women on the Seine Banks*. We see here two richly-dressed young women resting on the banks under some trees; the boat in which they have come is moored at the back. One girl, a brunette, lies flat, asleep on the grass; the other, a blonde in a big hat, rests on one elbow and contemplates the world, with some fresh-picked flowers held loosely in her free arm. The effect of a shady nook in the noon-heat, with the blue water sliding by, is finely achieved; and the two girls are first-rate character-studies, especially the brooding one. We feel the hardening of her face, its pathos, its mixture of desperation and calm acceptance. The two girls are caught off their guard in this retreat, one sleep-relaxed in her fattening charms, the other looking out at the world with tired eyes that have lost all illusions. (The sleeping girl has the out-thrust parallel arms we have discussed above; here, as she lies on the grass, the arms stretch up and beyond her head.) The return-to-nature, expressed in other works by a girl, clothed or naked, asleep among trees, has here the effect of showing up remorselessly all that is artificial, soiled, dehumanised, in the *Demoiselles*. Their rich clothes resist the flowers and foliage, and obliterate the humanity of their bodies. And yet the penetration into their being, ruthless as it is, is made with entire sympathy. Here was another great triumph of his realism: a revelation of individual character and social essence in perfect fusion.

In the title he gave the work in the Salon catalogue he added the word, 'Summer'. In his landscapes he was concerned with a precise seasonal phase, even with the hour of the day – an attitude leading to the Impressionists, just as this and others of his works lead on to Manet's *Déjeuner sur l'Herbe* and to Renoir. (Picasso in turn used the painting as an inspiration.) Courbet seems to have taken special care with the *Demoiselles*, making at least two full preliminary studies and several of details. Normally in his haste to get on with big projects he drew directly on the canvas and then set to work.[11]

Why did he choose this theme? So far we have found an internal logic in his main themes, starting with the romantic image of himself and its climax in the wounded or dying lover, and moving in a complex way through the return to family-roots and the expression of a revolutionary attitude to people and things. Here for the first time he takes a Parisian theme. He may have been partly moved by the assumption of the critics that he was a crude rustic, incapable of Parisian urbanity; and by the use of the term *Demoiselles* he deliberately links and contrasts this canvas with the *Demoiselles de Village*. The critics of the latter picture had stressed the rusticity of the girls; now he deals with two very Parisian types, in all their finery. But he makes no attempt to placate the critics. On the contrary he seems to be saying: You insulted my sisters as coarse rustics and you wanted Parisian elegance – well, here is that elegance covering up something truly coarse and ugly, the self-indulgent bodies of the town-girls who are for sale.

The *Studio* had consciously summed up an arc of his development, from 1848 on. Now he was seeking a fresh start, which, from one angle, he was finding in the landscape and hunts of his home-area. The first hunting-pictures thus play, on the new level, the role of the *Burial* in his previous phase. They express a rejection of (bourgeois) society and its rediscovery, just as the *Burial* had done in its different way. The aspects of rejection appear in the return to nature and in the presentation of the hunter as a hero, a man wholly independent of normal relationships and relying solely on his own skill and strength in the sphere of the hunt (man seen in his simplest terms in relation to nature); the aspects of rediscovery appear in the very image of the hunt itself. Predatory man is not, after all, free; he is, in Courbet's world, also bourgeois man, imagining himself alone and the maker of his own fate, existing fully only in the act of destruction, of preying on another life. From the outset this ambiguity is present in Courbet's mind. The *Quarry* shows the successful predator; the *Doe* brings out the anguish inflicted on the hunted creature. Courbet feels the thrill and excitement of the chase; but he cannot help projecting himself into the doomed and harassed animal.

How then is he to return into the social world from a world where he, the hunter, feels himself cut off from all the usual pressures of historical society? It seems that he sought for some image that would link the hunt-world and urban life, and found it in the prostitute, who is a hunted creature, victim of predatory man. The two *Demoiselles* are then like a pair of does sheltering in their thicket of illusory peace; but their return to nature does not work. One of them is flattened out in a rest that is no refreshment of body and spirit; the other, unable to rest at all, stares out at the world with a dulled anxiety, her eyes slitted in her slightly puffy face and her wilful mouth unrelaxed. Thus Courbet is able to link and contrast his *franc-comtois* world with that of Paris. He moves from nature back into society.

He had started to sketch out the work at Ornans, but finished it in Paris, perhaps early 1857. He sent six works to the Salon: the *Quarry* and the *Doe*, *Banks of the Loue*, portraits of Promayet and the singer Gueymard in the title-role of Meyerbeer's *Robert le Diable*, and the *Demoiselles*. The jury awarded him another medal like that of 1849, despite the fact there were no artists on it and Fould, the minister, had explicitly condemned Realism: art was falling away from 'the pure and lofty regions of beauty and the traditional ways of the great masters to follow the teachings of the new school of realism; it seeks no more than a servile imitation of the least poetical and the least elevated that nature offers'.[12]

We may note that there is an emotional link between *Robert le Diable* and the turn-to-nature in works like the *Doe*. The moment chosen from Meyerbeer's opera is when Robert plays dice with two devils, watched by his fiend-father, and sings, 'Yes, gold is a chimera.' Courbet is condemning the world of gold, of the cash-nexus (also in a peasant-way the world of his grasping litigious father), with which he plays the dice of his art. From such a world he turns to the earthly paradise without money and its alienations. Where the two girls succumb to a corrupting world, the defiant artist gambles and becomes free. (There is also no doubt a reference to his Bourse dealings.)

Many critics kept up the old baiting-game. C. de Ris said that Courbet's vocation was to paint signboards. Du Camp, while admitting his technical skill, found the Seine too blue for 'the muddy environs of Paris', and the girls 'a bundle of stuffs from which emerge arms and legs'; Courbet had no soul and painted just as one waxed boots. J. Doucet in the *Monde Illustré*, taking up a popular song, remarked that he would prefer 'two good cows spotted red'. In general he was accused of painting the tarts who on Sundays journeyed to Bougival or Asnières, then went out in boats with their pick-ups; artists should ignore such matters instead of drawing attention to them.[13] Gautier considered that Courbet lacked artistic temperament; he was a born painter with a 'forceful simplicity, but without composition, drawing, or style'. The *Demoiselles* were deliberately grotesque: 'a deafening tattoo on the tomtom of publicity to attract the attention of the unheeding.'[14] E. About was more amiable:

It was permissible to make fun of M. Courbet's paintings in the days when he built platforms, opened shops, and fired pistols out of windows to lure people to his studio. This young artist, a little too young for his age, has scared mothers of families, upset police commissioners, displeased dignified men, and terrified the Academy by the offensive display of certain trivialities; he seems to have realised at last that scandal does nothing useful for the dissemination of his only distinctive quality.[15]

There is something of a sameness about the attacks on Courbet; but we need to keep on reading them as they appear if we are to realise the massiveness of the shock he caused to the prevailing sensibility of his epoch. Also, his is the classic case of the way in which an artist, who both attacks at its core the dominant class-sensibility of his age and links his attack with a profound political understanding, will be continually assailed with various rationalisations – anything rather than the admission of just what he is doing and what his work means humanly and artistically. We must not make Champfleury's mistake of thinking that Courbet ever sought a sensational effect. Certainly he delighted in attacking what he felt was false and reactionary, and he got much fun out of many aspects of the conflict. But as we have seen, he also suffered acutely from his setbacks. In any event the tumults came out of what he wanted to do; he did not want to do something because it would cause the tumults. (The one exception is perhaps the *Return from the Conference*, but even that probably arose from some joke that overwhelmed him with a desire to express it, the sense of scandal coming later.) When he talks about the noise he is going to make, it is only in part through a delighted anticipation; it is much more because he is heartening himself to meet the attacks.

Champfleury had now quite given up his role of champion; he had come over to the enemy viewpoint that Courbet was just a technically gifted painter who didn't know what to do with his talents. In July he wrote to Buchon:

Impossible to tell you what I think of Courbet's pictures; I don't think anything of them, and despite your enthusiasm I see in them nothing but good, purely material painting. As to the *Young Women*, horrible! horrible! Certainly Courbet knows nothing about women. You'll think me embittered. I've always told you that since the *Burial* our friend has gone astray. He has kept his finger too much on the pulse of public opinion; he wants to please it, and he lacks the requisite flexibility. Courbet should remain a solid and honest native of the Franche-Comté.[16]

No doubt in part Champfleury smarted from the feeling, which he expressed to Buchon, that Courbet's friendship was based in his need for a defender; but he also disliked Courbet's efforts to think out his positions, though he rationalised this dislike in a belief that Courbet should remain on a simple rustic spontaneous level. 'Nothing is more dangerous for him than to want to write.' The core of his need to get away from Courbet however derived from his fear and hatred of socialism. 'I was certain of it beforehand. *Realism* scares them like *Socialism* under the Republic. That monster of a Courbet has well understood it. I've been afraid for a long time of making use of this small bit of charlatanism.' On 20 August 1857 he met Baudelaire before the hearing of the prosecution of *Fleurs de Mal*.

'You'll certainly be accused of realism,' he told him.
    The poet gave a cry of anger. Not because he feared the fierce blows and kicks of opinion. On the contrary, he sought them; but he wanted to take the strokes of the rod, *all alone*. Such was his fad.
    Hardly had the imperial prosecutor risen up before he uttered the word 'realism' and held the poet as one of its most ardent sectaries. Baudelaire grimaced on his bench, irritated at the coming true of my prophecy.

However, a new champion was on the way: Jules Antoine Castagnary, born at Saintes on 11 April 1830, who shared Courbet's republican and anticlerical views, though he did not comprehend his socialism; he thus came closer to Courbet than Champfleury did, but their attitudes were not identical. He respected Proudhon, while rejecting his thesis of social significance as the goal and criterion of art. He had not yet met Courbet and his notice of the 1857 Salon takes the conventional position that 'As a genre-painter he may once have believed that painting should have a social meaning; but at present he no longer believes any such thing. As a landscape-painter he has viewed nature only through a tavern-window.' He liked the portraits best.[17] When later Proudhon came to deal with the *Demoiselles*, he contrasted the two wenches in their 'moral misery and its frightful debauchery' with the 'wretched day-labourers' of the *Stone-breakers*, 'who are inoffensive and whose souls are healthy'. But he lays on the moral interpretation with a trowel. The girl on the grass is lost in erotic reverie; the other, mistress of her heart, knows how to control her desires and 'pursues her chimera of cold ambition'. And 'pride, adultery, divorce and suicide flutter round them and accompany them'. That is why 'in the end they appear horrible'. Such a view obliterates all the pathos with which Courbet invests the girls, the deep and sympathetic insight with which he treats them as individuals. Castagnary was on safer ground when, influenced by Proudhon, he commented on the 'evident critical idea' which contrasted the *Demoiselles* of the village with those of the big city.[18]

If we try to summarise the critical reactions to Courbet's work we may say that his early works of the 1850s were damned by critics who one way or another expressed the bourgeois fear of the revolutionary phase through which French society had passed. They could see only a horrible and deliberate ugliness, a defiant addiction to plebeian themes and models. By 1855 the Empire was consolidated, but some doubts and critical attitudes were arising. This modification of the situation appeared in a more varied line of abuse. On the extreme right were men like Maxime du Camp who continued the flat repudiation. (When after the Commune he wrote *Convulsions de Paris* he defined Courbet as mentally unbalanced, a megalomaniac in whose show of 1855, apart from three or four works, only self-portraits were shown – a statement wildly at variance with the facts.) Romantics like Gautier could only mourn over a talent gone wrong; but the de Goncourts, who had defined extreme (Courbetian) realism as a 'daguerrotype' carried out by a blind man who stops to sit down whenever he comes to a dungheap, had begun to favour a milder realism that did not deal only with what was (in their view) the ugly. Something of the dilemma appearing for critics is seen in G. Planche's account (*Revue des Deux Mondes*, 15 September), which lauds Delacroix, Ingres, Decamps, and, while insisting that Courbet has misread tradition, which 'does not authorise the cult of the ugly', admits his 'magnificent and courageous resolution to express his own personality'. By 1857 we see further changes in the critical camp. Champfleury has lost heart; but in general the extreme attacks have ended. While Courbet is accused of many failings, certain aspects of his work come in for praise; and a new radical critic appears in Castagnary, to carry on from where Champfleury gave up. 'The human aspect of art takes the place of the heroic and the divine. . . . The Salon of 1857 marks the glorious date of the arrival of Man as a work of art.' In place of the broad revolutionary movement of 1848, which had broken down in 1851–2, a more limited form of resistance is born, linked with the growth of embryonic dissatisfaction with, or rejection of, the Empire.

In late May or early June 1857 Courbet, this time with Champfleury, Schanne, and Bonaventure Soulas, made a second visit to Bruyas at Montpellier. For the sake of a reduced fare, they travelled in a train with a noisy party of botanical students. Champfleury wrote to Buchon, saying that he went with Courbet, though ill, and that there were some 300 students, of whom not more than thirty were serious. 'Some got drunk, others went chasing after girls. At Montpellier the police started off by hauling a dozen of them to the police-station.' Fêtes were organised for the visitors, 'banquets in honour of realism, splendid dinners. . . . Bruyas did the honours. The room was decorated with our portraits. Toasts, quarrels. North and South face to face. Schanne and Courbet very drunk. Statues thrown out of windows.'[19] Courbet seems to have done little painting during the short stay. He was at his most careless and gay, says Troubat, friend of Bruyas, singing his rhymeless love-songs:

But the bonhomie, full of finesse, the rhythm above all in which he sang them and which was his own invention, the animation he put into repeating the refrains, made of them something altogether original and indescribable. Nothing was less naïve than these musical compositions . . . in appearance so simple; they were in fact most composite: which isn't to say that Courbet could have been a great musician, . . .

As for the painter's boasting, it didn't obtrude yet as it did later; at least it was tolerable. The main fault became accentuated in him, like his bulk, with age. In the years of his youth, if he spoke much of himself, it was more with the conviction of his art and the revolution he was conscious of bringing about in landscape, than of the merits of his person. His speech grew even then soft and persuasive. He dreamed already of political action, and he had long conceived the project of painting a gigantic landscape in which he'd represent Prometheus destroyed not by a vulture but by an eagle [the emblem of Napoleon's Empire].

Courbet in 1857 was tall, slender, straight-built. . . . His eyes were big and gentle like a bull's. This has been already said, but it was a trait so striking in his physiognomy that one can't help repeating it. Long black hair was also one of the most striking features of his comeliness, spoiled only by his teeth, which were very black.

One met him in the Montpellier streets, always the good fellow, escorted by two or three friends; he walked leaning on a huge cane, usually with a pipe in his mouth. When he worked, he was just the opposite of Delacroix at grips with the idea, who shut himself up to struggle victoriously with it. Courbet gladly let himself be surrounded by a numerous company of idlers; he went on painting, smoking his pipe, and drinking beer from time to time.

During his last stay at Montpellier, he was taken by an old painting in the house of a local artist, grandson of the naturalist Magnol, who introduced the '*magnolia*'. The picture represented *Love and Psyche* lifesize. Courbet asked permission to copy it. The canvas was brought and set up in a studio where all the idle young folk of the town gathered. The painter quickly made a copy of the big composition with a palette-knife, which he made supple and handled like a trowel. The arrangement of this picture was not unlike that of the later *Woman with the Parrot*, one of the last pictures that marked his second manner: that in which he began (in the words of his old friends) to sacrifice to the gods of the day.[20]

Armand Gautier had a friend and compatriot, Gachet, who had lodged for some years at his place, rue de Seine, studying medicine; he had now decided to go to Montpellier and pass his doctorate there. In July Gautier wrote, saying that Courbet and Champfleury could put him in touch with Bruyas, a man of much influence, who in turn could introduce him to very wealthy people. He also wanted Gachet to find Courbet and ask him to send a letter authorising him (Gautier) to deal with *L'Artiste*, which wanted a lithograph of the *Exhausted Doe* (*Snow-effect*). 'Tell him too that his success is very great and I rejoice in it; he's expected to get a first medal, as they don't dare to give him the Cross straight out; everyone talks of him and of Daubigny.' Schanne had just turned up, very merry, and made Gautier sorry that he hadn't joined the party. But meanwhile Gachet had met Bruyas through the Librarian of the Medical Faculty. Courbet wrote to Gautier on 23 June with the authorisation for the lithograph, 'I hope to take advantage of my journey by doing some seascapes; I've renounced the advantage offered by the Botanical Congress. I've already been to the sea, made three sketches, return tomorrow and mean to make two serious sketches of a metre and a half length.' Gachet adds a note to say he writes from the Café du Commerce where he has been able to catch Courbet; and he adds a comic P.S. to Courbet's letter:

I break the letter open to tell you that Courbet (who through excess of modesty doesn't dare to tell you himself) has found behind the citadel in front of a grotto a colossal flea, two hands big, supplied, it's said, by gypsies. I've seen it, Champfleury has seen it, and could tell you the whole story. It has been put under the observation of Prof. Martin of Montpellier. If there were only two of them in the Midi of this build, one couldn't stay there. It's always those on whom one counts the least who find the most. In return they wanted to nominate him Member of the Entomological Society. At the moment here Courbet is on the point of discovering a new species of bug – he already has one in a bottle (which he feeds with the greatest care) which is of the size of a man [*une homme*].

In view of the way in which 'homme' is made feminine, there may be a set of puns ('puce', 'pucelle', 'punaise', 'putain'), to say that Courbet has picked up some fat and gross tart. On 4 July Gautier wrote to Gachet, 'Courbet is going to return; tell me what he should say for Bruyas who'll be with him, if you want his recommendation.' But Bruyas had no connections with the Faculty's professors; Gautier tells his friend to rely on hard work. On 7 July he wrote, 'Today, Monday, hoping to see Courbet at Andler's, I found him there. He says you've failed in the first exam and propose to came back. Energy, in God's name, and don't consider yourself beaten. Always struggle.' Still, on 17 July he wrote that Courbet would after all write to Bruyas if it was of use: 'it seems you were taken too late.' And in August he announced that, in part through his lithograph of the *Doe*, he had been commissioned to do one of his own *Madwomen*.

There was however an unpleasant aftermath of the visit. On his return Champfleury showed the unreliable side of his character by publishing in the *Revue des Deux Mondes* a sketch, 'The Story of M. T——,' an episode in a series, *Les Sensations de Josquin*. 'As I was passing through the little town of S——, I was advised to visit the picture gallery of young T——, whose activities were the talk of the region.' T.'s mania consisted of collecting 'nothing but portraits of his own countenance'. Josquin gets into the house and sees T. 'lying languidly on his divan' with the effect rather of 'chronic illness than of convalescence'. In his appearance was 'something of a pretty woman who's bored, a mystic tortured by ecstasy, and the debility of a sensualist'; he thought himself 'the most beautiful of mortals and had never found a painter skilful enough to reproduce his features with a brush's aid'. Josquin sees several portraits which he describes; then his host reverently opens the curtains of a richly ornamented tabernacle and reveals yet another. 'It was the portrait of Christ! Christ crowned with thorns! . . . M. T—— had had himself painted as Christ.' Josquin hurried off.[21]

T. was obviously based on Bruyas, who was deeply hurt. At first he suspected Courbet of aiding or encouraging Champfleury. Fajon wrote, perhaps at Bruyas's request, and Courbet at once protested:

Before answering your letter I'd have liked to read the *Revue des Deux Mondes* so as to understand the situation. But without knowing what happened, if M. Champfleury has in the least degree been offensive to my friend Bruyas, I censure him severely; and I'm deeply hurt that anyone could imagine I had anything to do with it. My dear friend Alfred Bruyas is the most courteous, the most honest, the most charming man I've ever met in my life. More, he's one of the most intelligent men in Montpellier. I don't want him to have thought for a single instant of doubting my friendship and the sincerity of my feelings in this matter. Further, everything in my previous association with him should prove the opposite. . . .

M. Champfleury does just as he pleases, entirely without my co-operation of course; still, on the basis of your letter, I've taken him to task for this exploit. He replied the sketch was written before he went to Montpellier and had been sent to the *Revue* a long time before his journey to the Midi. In short, my dear Fajon, you must remember I'm responsible only for my own works, and other people's thoughts and actions don't concern me at all. Please communicate all I've here written to my dear friend as well as any others who may be interested.[22]

What difference did it make if Champfleury had written the story before the journey? It was still about Bruyas. And how can Courbet consider that it's no concern of his if someone he brings into a friend's house behaves so badly? Besides, there can be no doubt that Champfleury had based the story on tales he had heard from Courbet – not that that excused him; rather it made his action worse as a betrayal of two friends. Champfleury's own defence makes his action look worse, not better:

'The Story of M. T –' does not altogether please you; many people will feel as you do. I knew that would happen, but what does it matter to me? The story had obsessed me for a long time; it poured itself willy-nilly from my pen and I enjoyed writing it so much that the phrases took form by themselves. There were also many considerations that might have prevented me from writing it – the cordial hospitality of M. B., but art is above all that.[23]

So the high name of art is brought in to defend a trivial bit of bad-mannered journalism. Bruyas, as good-natured as he was touchy, exonerated Courbet, and even seems later to have borne no grudge against Champfleury.

A show of Courbet's works was being put on at Brussels. In September he told Fajon, 'In ten days I go to Brussels. My pictures have had a great success and drawn crowds. Now they're in Belgium where they produce the same effect.' But a letter from Brussels to A. Gautier shows him unhappy and brings out how much use he made of this amiable friend:

I've felt very guilty for not writing anything till now, but I'm in a situation where I feel hypochondriac [*esprit de hypocondre*]. I send you the authorisations you asked for, I wanted you to pack up a small picture that's on my console, that sketch of a hippodrome where there's a bull fight. A

Brazilian has bought it and would like to have it at once. If my concierge has letters for me, please make up a packet and send them care of M. Radoux, photographer, Montague de la Cour, 73, Brussels. If there's any money to pay out, please get it from M. Andler in my name. I think there's a small case on my landing that would hold the picture. Tell my concierge also to write if there's any news. I've left a picture at the Exposition, I'd like very much to know what's become of it. If it has to be removed, please tell Lambert the colour-dealer to remove it and keep it at his place. You could also get him to pack up at my cost the small picture I ask for. There's a lot of commissions, my dear friend, I take advantage of your friendship. I lead a boring life here. I'm in the portraits, in the lawsuits. I'm going to send everything to the devil and go off for Frankfort where my pictures are having a big effect. I've seen Champfleury who's at Amsterdam. Write to me. That's all I can say to you today. Write to me.

Presumably it was just before he got this letter that Gautier had written in jest to Gachet, 'Still no reply from Courbet. I've just written him a letter: M. Courbet, Somewhere in Europe.'

On 2 November Kohlbacher, Inspector of the Kunstverein of Frankfurt, recalled his promise to get the Société des Beaux-Arts to send the pictures on from Belgium to his show.[24] This year Jongkind met Courbet at dinner in the house of E. Picard, dentist and collector, in the avenue Frochot, who was friendly also with Corot and Millet.[25]

Castagnary, writing for the Courbet show of May 1882, declared that after 1855 he grew tired of endless battle with the public and the critics, with the production of violently controversial works.

What use to persist obstinately? Courbet felt that he would use up his energy and his youth. He decided, in short, he had better turn his quest in some other direction; without in any way abandoning his ideas, he could avoid clashes and let time the great conciliator get to work. . . . Without exactly fleeing from mankind, he considered more the sky and the sea, greenery and snow, animals and flowers. . . . From the *Bathers* of 1853, accused of being gross and squalid, he climbed to the elegant nudities of the Parisian.[26]

There was certainly much truth in that, though the matter is put too simply. With all his brave front, Courbet was forced to recognise by the failure of his one-man show that he was outrunning his resources and his support. His outpourings on paper give some idea of the vast expense of bodily and spiritual forces needed to carry on as he had done. But beyond all that there were the confusions in his own mind, brought clearly out by the *Studio*, which made it difficult for him to see how best to wage his struggle. The left group in the *Studio* showed a vision of society as composed of petty exploiters and hagglers, lost and hopeless labourers, remnants from the past struggle, and purely individual rebels (the poacher); the group of dissident intellectuals on the right are not gathered in any purposeful way together and make no impact on the left group. Courbet, the artist, draws on both sides; but there is no suggestion of the ways in which his vision (of democratic and socialist realism) is going to affect the struggle in turn, and to bring together and unite hand and brain, individual and group, theory and practice. The 1856 failure had increased his sense of isolation, just at the moment when he needed fresh encouragement, fresh conviction of gathering forces. The Empire seemed secure and triumphant – the situation in which, as Zola, looking back on

1848–52, was to declare, we see 'for a moment, as in a flash of lightning, the future of the Rougon-Macquarts, a pack of ravening beasts unleashed and gorged, in a blaze of blood and gold'.[27] It was no chance that he used the hunting image, which was now to obsess Courbet. The popular resistances that had been turbulent in the early 1850s had died away; he too used the hunting image directly to define the society of the Empire:

Like fat game, this society at bay, with its role played out at last, in a desperate and supreme effort, tries out its final guiles, its tricks, its lies, and, while falsifying the scent, begs for pity, invokes the superannuated silence of its gods, its priests, its old men, then feeling the approach of the death-blast of the horn [*hallali*], burns down its house and slaughters its own children.

A mixed metaphor, but with the hunt at its heart. 'The day of vengeance nears,' he goes on.

This was the situation in which Courbet turned back to nature both for physical and spiritual refreshment, and for imagery that would express what he felt of society. He was not seeking any easy way to popularity; he was following the only course in which he could be true to his convictions and to his aesthetic.

The year 1858 was taken up largely by arranging shows and travelling; he held exhibitions at Bordeaux, Le Havre, Dijon, Besançon; went again to Brussels in the late summer, then went on to Frankfort where he stayed from September till February 1859. During this period he strongly consolidated his grasp of the hunting picture, of the representation of wild creatures in their forest life.

A letter of 26 March gives us an unfavourable glimpse of Courbet; but Champfleury, who wrote it, was now convinced that Courbet had abandoned art for booze and braggadocio. Courbet at the time was in Brussels.

I was almost certain that Courbet was drowned in the depths of a month of *faro* [Belgian beer]. Ten years ago he played a similar trick in the same Brussels where we had to stay for three days. A month later, he still hadn't left the brasseries. A little overdose of beer and discussions will spoil his painting, if he doesn't take care. If you see him, give him my good wishes and tell him that one of his sisters has just become a nun. For the scoundrel doesn't bother about his family or his friends or his letters or his pictures or anything but the terrible ideal.[28]

The sister is not named. We at once think of Zélie, whom Champfleury depicted as extremely pious. In his novel he shows himself rather attracted by her, so that he may have kept in touch with her or at least have tried to learn from Courbet or others of the Ornans region what was happening to her. But we know that Juliette also, in some moment of weakening in her busy domestic round, wanted to become a nun. In any event the episode proves how correct Champfleury had been in giving the female side of the household a strong religious bent. His comment here shows that he has not heard the news through Courbet himself; his source, then, seems most likely to have been Zoé, who, with her vehemence, was apt to exaggerate things. She too became conventionally pious in her later years, but not so much from any religious conviction as because of her social conformism, her Bonapartist connections and her desire to rise in the world.

She had certainly carried out by this date her decision to leave Ornans and make her way in the great world in which she had jealously watched her brother's progress. Probably she had left home in 1856. From this time we find letters from Courbet addressed to Mme Courbet, to M. Courbet, to Juliette at Ornans. Zoé was no longer there. Why Zélie is ignored is not clear. It is hardly likely that she could not read; perhaps Gustave felt out of harmony with her, with her religious views; perhaps she was too ill or had indeed for a while withdrawn into some nunnery. Zoé was keeping herself as a governess. Later (February 1879) she stated, 'I worked to get a position as teacher, *institutrice*, and didn't return to the country till after my marriage.'[29] Somehow she came to know a painter, Eugène-César Reverdy, and on 1 March 1858 she bore him a son, who was registered at the Mairie of the 2nd Arrondissement under the name of Courbet, the father 'unnamed'. Where the child was born is unknown, as the original documents are lost; but it was probably at one of the houses of the numerous *femmes sages* of the Quartier Feydeau or the Faubourg Montmartre. The boy was named Eugène-Jean-Charles.[30]

Reverdy had been born at Paris on 11 July 1822. His father is said to have been of Spanish origin; his mother Marie-Edme Minard most likely came from the valley of the Cure, between Monsauche and Vermenton where Edmes and Minards were numerous. The father, a lieutenant on half-pay, became a shoemaker, then seems to have re-entered the army in 1830, gaining the rank of captain, the Légion d'honneur, and, later, a sufficient pension. His son studied art in the studio of Drolling and on 4 April 1839 was admitted to the École des Beaux Arts. In 1844 he seemed near success; he was one of ten chosen as probables for the Prix de Rome; but his *Cincinnatus receiving the Deputies of the Senate* failed to win. A portrait of a young girl at the Salon attracted no attention. In 1845 he was less to the forefront, and his *Man at the Fountain* was refused for the Salon. Though he did show two portraits in 1847 and one in 1848, he gave up his career as an artist. He was too much of a bourgeois to struggle under difficulties and take the chances of the *vie de bohème*. The advent of the daguerrotype was putting minor portrait-painters out of work. He took a job in charge of the gallery of the Marquis de Saint-Denis, at 72 rue de l'Université, where he became friendly with a member of the family, Marie-Jean-Léon, his junior by a year. This young man worked on Spanish translations, and when he went to Naples for documentation of an historical work (which appeared in 1856) he took Eugène with him.[31]

Such was the man who entered into a liaison with Zoé and finally married her, and who played an obscure role in Courbet's last years. He seems to have been conventional, ambitious, but not ready to take a risk. Yet he was drawn into Zoé's clutches; perhaps they shared something of the same dream of rising in the world. In due time he won Zoé over to the belief that only by supporting the establishment in its most reactionary form could they reach their rightful position. How did he and Zoé meet? We have no evidence. At first Zoé must have based herself on Courbet's studio; we soon meet her in charge there. But that was not a likely place for encountering Reverdy. She probably met him during one of her jobs as a governess. The one member of the family who must have known what happened to her was Gustave; and we see how secretive he could be, for all his loose volubility, when a family matter was concerned. He kept his knowledge from Juliette and the others; and this suggests a particularly close bond between him and Zoé.

During June–July the indefatigable Gautier was trying in vain to find out where Courbet was. 'Impossible to know where to find Courbet; everyone is disquieted. I have written to him to send me a letter so that his photographer may send me copies: I've been commissioned for lithographs after him, and he's nowhere that I write to. I'm kept in suspense on this matter [*suis le bec dans l'eau*].' A little later: 'One can't count on Courbet; first no one knows where he is; one day he's said to be at Brussels, Frankfort, or at the Blanc. I've written everywhere to get a letter out of him for a lithograph I've had commissioned, and for that I need the key of his studio . . . but no reply.' He wanted the address also to send on to Gachet. 'I'll get his address one of these days, and, as I'm going to be useful to him, he'll absolutely need to write to me.' Finally in July, while at le Havre: 'Here's the address of Courbet whom you probably won't find; he lodges on the right, then on the left; he leaves a house and is found no more; for the rest, he never replies to letters: M. Courbet, care of M. Radoux . . . Brussels.'

The trip to Frankfurt was the main event of the year. Just before he left, or during his stay in Germany, he bought at Ornans a plot of ground on which to build a studio. He had been thinking of the project for some time; in 1854 he had told Bruyas, 'I'm about to buy a site for a studio to be built on. The price asked is 4,000 francs; I'm loath to pay so much, I find it dear. Still I must do it, for the property suits me well.' We do not know if the site he bought in 1858 was the one he coveted in 1854; that now in question was on the outskirts of the Besançon highway.[32] (The building wasn't done till 1861.) In going off to Germany he left his Paris studio in charge of Zoé and M. Nicolle. He must have met the latter through Proudhon, who had been jailed with him in Sainte-Pélagie and declared, 'I have found in you a true democrat, a faithful companion, a good friend.' Nicolle, who had been imprisoned in June 1849, was still held when Proudhon was let out in June 1852; we do not know when he was released. (By late 1864 we find him at the head of an industrial establishment in the rue Amelot.) Now he and Zoé were taking over the role that Promayet, who had gone to Russia, used to play. While Courbet was at Frankfurt, they wrote to say that two Russians wanted to buy all the pictures in the studio; delighted, he fixed a price of 76,000 francs; but the Russians faded out with nothing settled. Courbet cursed Zoé and Nicolle as duffers, *deux andouilles* (literally 'pork-sausages'). However as usual, his anger quickly evaporated; in 1862 he painted Nicolle in Paris before leaving for Saintonge.[33] It is possible that Zoé had taken the Russians to the studio; for in *Les Demoiselles Tourangeau* Champfleury depicts her as working with Russians:

A week later, instead of coming as usual to see Gustave, Zoé sent a cold note, in which she apologised for her absence, being much taken up with a brilliant position offered to her. This 'brilliant position' is a place as companion [*demoiselle de compagnie*] to a Russian lady, who has come to spend the summer in Paris, whom Zoé has met and whom she wants to follow out of the country. At first we didn't believe a thing of it; but Zoé, quite enraptured, announced to us the following Sunday her approaching departure. Full of illusions, she saw in Russia a future from which Gustave did not attempt to divert her, saying that perhaps this voyage and the new position would bring some sense into his sister's spirit.[34]

Furthermore, we later find Juliette making accusations against Zoé which imply connections with rich Russians.

In July Proudhon went into exile in Belgium. His book, *Justice*, had been seized by the police; and he found that at the following prosecution he was not going to get a fair trial. Courbet must have been enraged on his friend's behalf, but no record of his reactions survives.

His reputation had been built up in Frankfurt by Victor Müller, pupil of Couture, who lived in Paris during 1849–58, and by Anton Burger who had often visited him in Paris. The invitation was probably the work of Jacob Becker, who had taught at the Kunstinstitut since 1842 and who promptly put a studio at his disposal.[35] Courbet wrote home with the usual flourish, after being banqueted and praised by the local painters:

I ramble in foreign lands to find the independence of mind that's necessary to me, and to get away from that Government with which, as you know, I'm out of favour. My absence has succeeded admirably; my stock is going up in Paris. Letters to me and to my friends from all sources say that my partisans have more than doubled and that in the end I'll be the only one left on the battlefield. I think this year . . . will be a definitive year. It's not so much I want to be a success. Those who succeed at the start are those who batter on open doors. Here in Frankfort a crowd of young people are followers of my doctrine.[36]

Etienne Carjat told later how he came to the town near the end of September 1858, after doing caricatures of Baden-Baden visitors. The Greek consul recommended him to the banker Erlanger. One evening on the *terrasse* of the Café Hollande, in the Goethe square, he was contemplating 'the horrible monument in the form of a hot-air stove set up in memory of *Faust*'s genial author' when he saw looming up the large and robust outline of Courbet. The latter told him of Becker, 'a painter who knows his anatomical figure better than Bandinelli and Michelangelo; he asserts that even clouds have a special anatomy.' Carjat visited the studio and found Courbet perched on a platform, shirt-sleeves rolled up, a big earthen dish of paint at his side, a big trowel in his hand, as he daubed away at a huge white canvas. 'His mason's-work done', he led Carjat into a corner where stood two magnificent stuffed stags. The taxidermist had been a great artist, he insisted, catching nature as it was. Three days later, 'the two animals were painted on the brown canvas with the boldness, the inspiration, and the suppleness you can admire today in the Louvre'. Carjat asked what landscape he meant to put in.

'Not the Academy, sure indeed. Come with me. On the other side of the Main I know a tavern where there's excellent ham and a white wine that's almost our own. At the side there's a little wood I've had my eyes on which will do finely for the job.'

After lunch, in an hour 'he knocked off a ravishing study of the underwood, and four days later, the picture'. Becker came to see, and Courbet asked his opinion. 'Your animals are superb, they really fight, but . . .' 'But what?' 'Your landscape seems to me negligently done. It could have been more studied. Thus the leaves of your trees are a little . . .' 'You'd

have liked them perhaps with the nervures shown. M. Becker, you may be a good professor of anatomy, but in painting you'll never be more than a c—' (it is not clear if Carjat's
bowdlerising covers a 'cul' or a 'conne'). Becker didn't understand the insult, but later in
the day he had it translated. That evening he told Courbet to move. The latter consoled
himself by painting the young wife of Erlanger's son for 6,000 francs. 'Is it worth that?' the
banker asked. Carjat told him he had done well. 'It's not so exact, so fashionable as a
Cabanel or a Dubufe, but it's a bit of painting out of the ordinary. Portrait aside, the work
will triple in value before ten years.'[37]

Courbet had gone off to 44 Kettenhofweg, where his disciple A. Goebel lived and V.
Müller also had a studio. He spent his time hunting in the forests of Frankfort, Wiesbaden,
and Bad Homburg; painting; and helping a group of young disciples. He sold his *Exhausted
Doe* and another hunt-scene to a collector who commissioned a landscape. He painted portraits of Mme Erlanger and of Jules-Isaac Lunteschütz (who, born in Besançon in 1822,
had studied under Flajoulet, then at the Beaux-Arts in Paris, finally settling in Frankfurt as
a painter of decorative murals and portraits, including several of his friend Schopenhauer).
Perhaps Carjat introduced him to the Erlangers. The painting known as the *German Lady*
or the *Lady of Frankfurt* may be Mme Erlanger (or perhaps Mme Goldschmidt). We see
a woman in a grey gown in an armchair by a tea-table on a terrace against a background of
pines and a little lake. Courbet worked a lot on the picture, making many changes: the rail
was once prolonged to the extreme right, the steps were later added, a shadow behind the
round table witnesses to the presence of someone there replaced by the temple. There is a
certain dreamy effect despite the definition of the form, a meditative sense of arrest in the
reddish-yellow sunset-hour. Perhaps Germany stirred some of his romantic embers?[38]
Something of the same mood appears in the *View of the Town* with the old bridge, where a
heavy atmosphere weighs on the bridge-houses and all is modulated on this sombre tone,
under the stormy sky streaked with rich yellow, with violet and yellowish clouds nearer the
front.[39]

Courbet did not leave the Mainz underwood as the setting for his rutting stags. On his
return to Ornans he put in a more suitable spring-scene based on the forest of Levier near
Flagey. Meanwhile on the last day of December he had written home with news of his
hunting. The stag he had killed was the largest brought down in Germany for twenty-five
years.

This aroused the jealousy of all Germany. The Duke of Darmstadt said he wouldn't have had it
happen for a thousand florins. A rich manufacturer of Frankfurt tried to steal it from me; but I
must render justice to the people of Frankfurt; they were all on my side. A petition was drawn up
by the Society of Huntsmen and at its end the signature of forty of the principal (meaning the
richest) huntsmen of the region for the return of the stag to me. It's a splendid story. The whole
city's been on tiptoe for a month. The newspapers took it up. They couldn't give me back the whole
stag; it had been sold by the Society and eaten. But they've given me the teeth and the antlers, and
the Society presented me with a very fine skin, though smaller, to make amends for their error. I was
also given a photograph of the dead stag showing my bullet-holes. . . . After that one of the

huntsmen gave a dinner at which 700 glasses of Bavarian beer were drunk; it went on till morning. I've gone hunting about ten times. I killed that magnificent stag, four or five bucks, about thirty hares. . . . When one's hunted in Germany one no longer wants to hunt near Flagey.[40]

On 19–20 April 1861 he wrote a long letter to Wey which had better be given here; for he packs into it much information about his hunting. The letter shows his full awareness that he had now broken through in a new direction, and that the picture of the rutting stags had now for him the same significance as the *Burial* had had for his first great phase.

The *Battle of Stags* should have, in a different sense, the same importance as the *Burial*. . . . Without setting out to you the value of these pictures, let me explain their place in my idea. This *Rut of Spring* or *Battle of Stags* is something I went to study in Germany. I saw similar battles in the game-preserves at Hamburg [he means Homburg] and Wiesbaden. I followed the German hunts at Frankfort for six months, a whole winter, until I killed a stag which I used, together with those killed by my friends, for this picture. I am absolutely sure of the action.

In these animals no muscle stands out; the battle is cold, the fury overpowering; their thrusts are terrible, though they don't give the impression of touching. That is easily understood when one sees their mighty armature. As well, their blood is as black as ink and their muscular force is such that they cover thirty feet in one leap, as I have seen with my own eyes. The antlers of the one I killed had twelve points (thirteen years) computed in German style, ten points in France.

He gives technical details about his bullet, which hit the stag in the shoulder and went through lungs and heart;

when I fired a second time, six buckshot entered his leg, which didn't prevent him going 150 metres before he fell. Just think how strong he is.

These three pictures form a series for hunters and a theme which belongs to me; they have no fellows in tradition or in modern times; they have not a farthing of the ideal in them; in their values they are as exact as mathematics.

He goes on about the *Hunter* (*Piqueur* or *Le Cheval Dérobé*), for which he had used two horses as models. 'Distrust what is called movement, energy; here we are no longer dealing with Horace Vernet's horse, in which all the muscles start out, and fire jets from the eyes and nostrils. The one here is a trained horse, which, with no impression of such speed, covers a kilometre in two minutes in a carriage. . . .' He gives a detailed account of different hunt-manœuvres to the sound of the horn.

The landscape of the Three Stags is one of the start of spring; it's the moment when what is close to the earth (as at the moment depicted) is already green, when the sap mounts up into the big trees, and only the oaks, which are the most retarded, have still their winter leaves. The picture's action demanded that moment of the year; but in order not to put in all the stript trees found at that season, I preferred to take our country of the Jura, which is always exactly the same, with its mixture of white and black wood. I've introduced, at Reugney [village near Ornans], a forest half bare, half of evergreen.

As for the landscape of the *Stag at Bay*, it's the same moment as that of the *Hunter*, only it's evening, for it's solely at the end of six hours of hunting that one can bring a stag to bay. The day is on its decline, the last rays of the sun graze the countryside, and the smallest objects cast a very long shadow. The way in which the stag is lighted increases its speed and the picture's impression. Its body is wholly in the shade and yet fully modelled, the ray of light striking it is enough to bring out its form; it seems to pass like a *trait* [arrow, bolt, lightning], like a dream. The expression of its head should please the English; it recalls the feeling in Landseer's animals.[41]

He mentions Landseer because his composition was clearly based on an engraving after a painting by that artist showing the death of a stag, which was published in the *Magasin pittoresque* in 1851. In both works the stag's antlered head is lifted in the same pitiful way on high.[42]

The landscape of the *Roche Oraguay* has been done at Ordinaire's place, at Maisières, in a wild spot on the Loue banks. It's in the month of June; it's a plateful of spinach as M. T. Gauthier [Gautier] said when Cabat reacted against a romanticism which made up landscapes by the light of artifice. In this landscape I was too hurried, but still it lacks only arrangement on the right side; the force of the rest was singular in its impression of freshness.

He now launches into a protestation about his integrity. It is odd that he should have to make such an emphatic statement to a man like Wey; and one is tempted to say in such a situation that he protests too much. Yet what Courbet says is true of himself; his outbursts helped to nerve him for the struggle; he needed to project the image of himself into the minds of others, not to convince himself, but to strengthen and clarify his goal. His character was based in the conflict-and-unity of his concept of extreme individual independence and his need to socialise his thoughts and images, to link the lonely quest with a social goal. Some such conflict must appear indeed in all creativity, but with Courbet it has a specially stark form of expression.

I speak to you with bared heart, my dear friends, since I've long known to what point I may trust in you. You know better than any others that I act without speculation, without shame, and that I make the public witness even to all my shortcomings. It is perhaps pride, but in any case it's a praiseworthy pride, since it deprives me through honesty of what my painting could have brought me in. In my poverty I've always had the courage to be only what I am, without pretences, without a got-up affair for anyone. And yet, knowing my art thoroughly as I do, it would have been easy for me to act otherwise – but there are laws of birth that it's difficult to infringe.

Then he makes the remark, quoted earlier, about his grandfather as a revolutionary veteran who always said: 'Shout loud and walk straight on!'

For a month I had the idea of sending only the canvas of the big Stags, but the other pictures were done, and also they were more within the range of the general run of people. I was annoyed also at not appearing in the Salon save in the form of landscape and animals. I'd have liked to send a figure composition if I'd been able to get a delay-permit, but the Government didn't agree. As it's absolutely necessary for me to sell this year, if I want to go on painting, I had to send these works, and I'd even have sent more, if I hadn't broken my thumb this winter, which held up my work for a month and a half. The Government, slave of its institutions, cannot support me; so I must have recourse to individuals if I wish to go on as free as I am. As to the finish of the pictures, that reminds me of a letter of Wagner in the papers: without finish in painting and ballets in operas there's no hope of success.

One gets the impression that he is hoping to stir Wey into buying something of his. As with Bruyas, his self-laudations are often meant to buttress his claims for aid.

In the early spring of 1859 at Ornans Courbet painted two more hunt-scenes: *Stag and Doe in the Forest* and *Stag on the Alert*. He was moving here from the hunt proper to the life of the animals in the wilds.[1] He did not send anything into the Salon, and must have been interested to see that the attack now seemed to have shifted on to Millet, whose *Death and the Woodman* was refused but whose *Woman pasturing her Cow*, commissioned by the Ministry, was shown. Castagnary commented on its mixture of 'Byzantine stiffness and solemn grandeur'. Alexandre Dumas wrote, 'Millet produces at the Salon the effect that Courbet produced there six or seven years ago. It's an outcry of indignation on the part of some, a *hourra* of admiration on the part of others.' Paul de Saint-Victor wrote, 'The artist has set this woman on her *sabots* as on a pedestal; he has draped her in a petticoat with lapidary folds; he has imprinted her mournful profile with a solemn and melancholic crétinism.'[2]

In June Courbet went with Schanne to Le Havre. Schanne described the first meeting with Eugène Boudin, who with his luminous paintings of beach and sea had a crucial effect on young Monet. In the rue de Paris Courbet saw in a stationer's window some seascape-panels and asked for the artist's address. Boudin welcomed the pair and offered to act as guide for the district. Schanne calls him very young, but he was in fact 36 years. 'Next day he took us to Honfleur and installed us in a rustic inn halfway up the cliff': the farm of Saint-Siméon owned by *père* Toutain. Landscapists patronised this spot so much it was called the Barbizon of Normandy. Boudin recorded on 16 June: 'Courbet's visit. He was pleased with everything he saw, I hope. If I were to credit him I'd certainly consider myself one of the most talented men of our era. He thought my paint too weak in tone: which is perhaps true. . . . But he assured me few people paint as well as I do.' Seeing Boudin at work, Courbet cried, 'It's prodigious. In fact, my dear fellow, you're a seraph, there's no one but you that knows the heavens.'[3] Boudin wrote two days after the arrival, 'Returned from Honfleur with Courbet. Spent a fantastic evening at De Dreuil's with Courbet and Schanne; it was monstrously noisy. Heads whirled feverishly, reason tottered, Courbet proclaimed his creed, needless to say in a most unintelligible manner. . . . We sang, shouted, and bellowed for so long that dawn found us with our glasses still in our hands. On our way home we made a din in the streets, which was very undignified.' Next morning their heads felt dull. 'We've watched Courbet at work. He's a valiant fellow; he has a broad conception that one might adopt, but still it seems to me rather coarse, rather careless in details. . . . I find in him great determination; but haven't people turned him into a fanatic by calling it eccentricity?'[4]

Schanne tells how one morning as they strolled round the harbour, they were surprised to meet Baudelaire, who explained that he had to spend some time with his mother in her country house near the town. 'I'll take you home to dinner and introduce you to her.' They felt embarrassed at their lack of proper clothes, but Baudelaire insisted. 'I can still see Courbet bending himself double to offer his arm to the mistress of the house, who was very small.' The dinner was sumptuous and they had coffee on the veranda among rare plants overlooking the sea. They left about nine to catch the night-train to Paris.[5] Baudelaire saw them to the station, then suddenly got into the train with them, saying he hated to waste his time in the country when the weather was fine; the region reminded him of India and he preferred the skies of Paris that didn't keep changing. Perhaps he couldn't bear his mother any longer and wanted to see his mistress Jeanne Duval, with whom he had started off afresh the previous December. One wonders if Courbet took advantage of his visit to the coast to call in at Dieppe and see his son. It must have been during this visit to Le Havre that there occurred the episode he later recounted to Pata, who had pointed out a fine Swiss view. 'You remind me of that poor Baudelaire. One evening in Normandy he led me at sunset to a rock dominating the sea; he drew me to a yawning gap framed by rents in the rocks. "Here's what I want to show you," said Baudelaire, "there's the view." Wasn't he a true bourgeois! What's all this about points of view? Do they really exist?' (But, as we have seen, all that was only a half-truth for Courbet, who was a thorough organiser in his paintings; what he is here rejecting is the romantic rapture over the picturesque.)

Urbain Cuénot wrote from Ornans on 3 July, "I wrote to you more than six weeks ago to tell you to make some money at all costs; I told you that you had to meet a bill of 800 francs for the month of July. Well, nothing from you, no breath, no news. The nonsense [*balivernes*] you utter in the Paris taverns doesn't count as current cash. *Père* Crétin wants to be paid."[6]

When he returned to Paris is not known; but on 1 October he invited a large group of friends and acquaintances (including Baudelaire) to a gala *fête du Réalisme* at his studio. We have the announcement printed on yellow paper:

Today Saturday 1 October 1859 Great Fête of Realism Last Soirée of Summer (The Painter Courbet will not receive this winter) First Performance of *M. and Mme Durand* Comedy in 5 Acts and in Verse, rejected by the Theatre of the Odéon, read by the poet Fernand Desnoyers. The Author of the Bourgeois de Molinchart. Champfleury will execute on the Counter-bass a Symphony of Haydn. The interludes will be performed by MM. C. Monselet, G. Staal, A. Gautier, Bonvin, A. Schann [*sic*], and a crowd of other Notables. Mme Adèle Esquiros will read an epic poem. Titine will dance the cancan. The Chroniqueurs will be able to sit down. Andlers Beer will be drunk. The editor Pick de l'Isère, founder of the *Almanacs Parisiens*, of *Jean Guêtre*, and of *Jean Raisin*, will be present at this Solemnity. The Piano will be held by Someone. Great Surprise White Physique.[7]

This year Astruc showed the growing support that Courbet was gaining. He described a morning visit when Courbet was painting, and thought him like the self-portrait of Giorgione; his handsomeness, 'vigorous and generous, is yet more accentuated by a reflection of sadness and bitterness that give him a fine expression. His manner is noble and severe, full of cordiality, without pose.' In his paintings 'is revealed his soul, ardent, somewhat savage, simple and good, violently smitten by nature'. His admiration was for Velasquez; he was indeed a man of the Renascence, not of the present; he looked to the younger generation. Everything, says Astruc, in France wears out, even jokes, and the jokes at Courbet are at an end. The attacks on him have shown a collapse of taste. His *Burial* expressed the physiognomy of an epoch; the *Return from the Fair* was as good as a Cuyp, but more solid; the *Demoiselles by the Seine* had an unprecedented beauty, a feeling of repose and delicate enervation in the warmth, and the young woman in the hat had the quality of a Gainsborough. What is noteworthy in this account is the degree to which Astruc finds him hurt – full of bitterness, discouraged, eaten by chagrin after all the barriers put in his way, and complaining 'very gently' of the malevolence directed towards him.[8] A description of him by A. Delvau in the *Journal Amusant*, 29 October of this year, compared him to the Black Bear of Louisiana.[9]

Napoleon issued an amnesty. Buchon was able to return to France, as also Théodore Thoré, who had been writing on art under the name of W. Bürger.[10] When Courbet reached Ornans, he found a letter from Buchon, dated 11 October, asking him to come to Salins and taste an assortment of fine wines chosen for the celebration. A few weeks later Courbet went along; and during his visit painted the *Young Girl of Salins*.[11] He stayed on at Ornans right through the spring of 1860, painting, and occasionally hunting. His landscapes included *Oraguay Rock*; and among his hunting scenes was the *Hunter*, in which a rider on a grey horse gallops through a forest – later, on the suggestion of T. Gautier, he painted out the rider and the picture was called *The Runaway Horse*. (He described this work in the letter cited above to Wey.)[12]

One day this winter, while hunting in the Forest of Levier, he saw an accident: a diligence come to disaster in deep snow. He used the scene for his *Wreck in the Snow*: we see the carriage foundered in the drifts under a heavy sky, while oxen from a near-by farm try to drag it out, the terrified horses plunge about, and the passengers plod helplessly along. Knowing the way Courbet's mind worked, he may well have meant this work as a Real Allegory of the imperial war-adventure of this year, the Expedition to Italy. Seeing the accident, he may have reflected: Here's the image of mankind dragged along and wrecked by forces they can't control – thrown out and driven to fend helplessly for themselves in the blizzard of war, of mad State-power.

It was probably in the spring of 1960 that he played a joke on a girl he had known from her early days, Lydie Marthe Chenez, born at Pontarlier in 1840 of a solicitor of that town. Later she told the tale:

In 1860 I was driving to Besançon with my father in a private carriage and we stopped to rest at Ornans. Just as we were going off, Courbet came up to the carriage and begged my father and me to stay overnight, 'We're going to have a concert,' he told us, 'and Lydie will play in it.' I protested, as you can imagine. He insisted. I resisted. At last he persuaded us to go to the house of one of his friends – for five minutes, he assured us. During that time he went back to the carriage, and, to ensure our remaining, he sent it on to Besançon . . . to wait for us, he said.

When we found out the little trick, I wept with disappointment and fury; I didn't want to miss the theatre at Besançon. He consoled me as well as he could, invited us to supper, and escorted us that evening to the concert where I was obliged, whether I liked or not, to play a selection on the piano. He had arranged for flowers to be thrown and bravos shouted, and swore in our friends' presence that as I'd given him my music he'd give me some of his painting.[13]

We do not hear of Zoé at the Fête du Réalisme. Courbet seems careful to keep her out of his Parisian life. In any event, she bore Reverdy a second son, Edmond-Jean-Eugène, on 30 May 1860. Once again no father was named. But if she had begun her liaison in the spirit of Gustave's independence and in the name of Women's Rights (as set out by Emmélina in Champfleury's novel), she now had swung over to the ambitious side of her character, to the Reverdy-world. She did not want to be left out of, or ignored by, his 'very honourable' family – she used the revealing phrase more than once. She was clearly engaged in a duel of wills with Reverdy, demanding to be recognised by his family and refusing marriage until that came about; but the Reverdy family must have been suspicious of an alliance with a sister of the scandalous Courbet. She managed, however, to get herself introduced to the household of the Marquis de Saint-Denis; and when that family went on their travels, she and Reverdy accompanied them. The elder boy was boarded out at Saint-Nicolas. For seven years the connection with the Saint-Denis went on, with voyages in Spain, Italy, perhaps in Austria, with intervals in Paris. Zoé absorbed the Bonapartist principles of her surroundings. How far she kept in contact with her brother during this period we do not know. Perhaps one of the reasons for his spending so much of 1860 in his home-area was to escape all responsibility for Zoé's problems. She, with the Courbet capacity of interpreting events as best suited her, saw him as a painter who kept wrecking his chances of success through being swayed into bad courses by his wicked companions. She may have kept in touch with Champfleury; for his views of what was destroying Courbet were very close to hers. (Later Zoé accused Juliette of having advised her 'to get rid of' her children; but we do not know the date of this advice, which brings out the hard side of the Courbets.)[14]

Courbet was still making use of the painter Amand Gautier as his factotum in Paris – Zoé and Nicolle no longer being available or in favour. Gautier, born in 1825 at Lille, had been the pupil of Souchon, himself a pupil of David and Gros, who did much to start off Daumier, Diaz, C. Duran and others. He was close to Courbet in his opinions; he always wore a red shirt, dressed his daughter in red, and asked to be cremated at a time when cremation was considered a vile offence to religion; he later fought in the ranks of the Commune; and he too had his scandals at the Salon – in 1863 with *Woman taken in Adultery* and with *The Republic* in 1879. He and Courbet no doubt met at Andlers. We find Courbet writing to him, 'I am grateful for your activity; I'm ashamed to ask so much of you.' And adding, 'If we don't want to die of hunger at the end of our days we must carry on and profit from the talent given us.' He not only made use of Gautier; he also offered his intervention to facilitate Gautier's access to the big Parisian or foreign shows; and in his expansive manner he includes him as a disciple in his own successes, 'My dear friend, we get a move on, the articles about us take on a new coloration. M. Castagnary has just done a superb one in the

Opinion Nationale; one more blow and we're there.' And in another letter, 'My dear Gautier, seeing how time slips away, how many pains, torments, one has in life to arrive at a little in the works of the spirit; in short, we must let the water flow by and hold fast in spite of everything.' Gautier became Monet's first master, this year 1860; and Monet held him in affectionate and grateful esteem.[15]

In 1860 Courbet was represented at four shows, at Montpellier, Besançon, Brussels, and in a gallery in the boulevard des Italiens, Paris.[16] This year Castagnary met him in his Paris studio.

At this time there had not been invented the studio-of-parade of the venue de Villiers and the neighbouring streets, waxed, polished, Henri II furniture, Japanese knick-knacks, grand piano, Chinese vases, rare plants: all that's needed to impress the bourgeoisie and keep prices high. One was still at the working studio, drawing its beauty from its size or the quality of the light; but even for these primitive times Courbet's studio was simple as a cenobite's cell.

The painter emerges from a strait little room built in a corner of the studio. He was slipshod and short-sleeved, hair dishevelled, eyes blurred with sleep. Presentations made, he excused himself for not yet being dressed; he had come home late. He asked our permission to finish his toilet, and after a few words went back into the small room, where one saw through the half-open door his small and more than modest couch.

Castagnary looked at the pictures: *Lovers in the Country, Wrestlers, Return from the Fair*. Courbet returned with his pipe and lighted up. 'You want to see my painting?'

'Yes, I'm hungry to see good painting.'

'Oh,' he said with a half-smile, 'no lack of that here.'

He put the *Loue Banks* on the easel, passing a wet sponge over it to revive the tones; then other works. Castagnary studied him. Courbet, now forty-one, was no longer the handsome young man depicted by Silvestre. He was thickening and growing fat.

He was none the less a curious and original figure of an artist. His head was conical in form; will-power was to be read in the jut of his cheek-bones, love of struggle in the development of the cranial base. White threads striped the fan of his black beard; and his hair, flattened on the skull that it moulded in the way of a headband, silvered towards the temples; signs of crow's-feet showed at the corners of the eyes. There was already the touch and the lines engraved by maturity. But if his face had lost in freshness and grace, his physiognomy had gained in accent. What dominated was gaiety, cordiality, gentleness. Whether through awareness of his power or certainty of the future, Courbet had not let himself be impaired by the battle of life.

Castagnary was astounded. Some years earlier, without knowing Courbet and his work, he had announced 'the advent of human painting, that is to say, disengaged from all mysticism and limited to the representation of the surrounding society. And this art, human, democratic, living, which I had dreamed of for my country, was there, before me, or at least a fragment of it. I saw there the glorification of work, the advent of the little democracy, what Gambetta was later to call the new strata [*couches*].' He poured out his feelings. 'Ah', said Courbet in accents of emotion, 'if I had been encouraged!'[17]

This year (1860) M. G. Merlet in the *Revue Européenne* showed that all the old terms of abuse were still alive:

Iconoclasts of Art
They have stamped with their heavy sabots
on the mutilated marble of all the chaste goddesses
and danced a tattered carmagnole
around the crossroad Venus
cut in a milestone
by the hammer of a stonebreaker.

On 9 November Courbet wrote to Gautier with details of the Besançon show. He added, 'Daubigny has come to see me at Ornans; he went off yesterday.' Daubigny had exhibited at Besançon, with Corot, Isabey, Meissonier, Troyon; his work was *Moonrise*. Both in this letter and in another, probably written soon after, Courbet mentions his *Love and Psyche*. In a letter to Champfleury, 'The newspapers of my country can't make anything of my show, they behave like imbeciles with regard to me.' Some time in 1861 the Ornans studio was completed. Max Claudet, sculptor from Salins, described it in 1864:

It was in the most utter disorder: canvases stacked on the walls, newspapers and books on the floor, jars filled with reptiles on the shelves, primitive weapons given by the geologist Marcou hanging on the partitions, paint-boxes, clothing etc., all mixed together. The studio was enormous. On a large flat space connecting wall and ceiling Courbet had painted two superb frescoes: *View of the Escaut* [Schelde] where the river flows into the sea, and *The Seine at Bougival* with fine trees mirrored in the water.[18]

For the Salon this year he sent *Oraguay Rock* and four hunting scenes, including the *Battle of Stags*. As we saw in the letter to Wey, he had broken his thumb, but was refused a postponement in delivery; he said that henceforth he'd rely on private collectors. But his hunting-pictures were widely admired. Old foes like Maxime du Camp recognised the imprint of 'a profound feeling for nature'; Anatole, an attacker of 1855, declared himself won over 'by this strong though brutal talent, adored for this fault by all the long-haired students who clean palettes in the Luxembourg quarter'. And so on.[19] Even Champfleury admired the *Battle of Stags* and *Organon Rock* [*sic*]. Castagnary was so ardent in the *Monde Illustré* that his Courbet advocacy or his general tone brought in shoals of letters 'execrating' his reviews; warned, he didn't mend his ways and was told to write no more on the year's paintings.[20] For the third time the jury awarded Courbet a second-class medal; but what had been an honour in 1849 was now an insult. Thoré protested that Courbet and Doré should have been made Chevaliers of the Legion of Honour – and it is possible that at this phase Courbet would have accepted a decoration from the State.[21]

In a letter to his parents he shows his usual turmoil of high hopes. He has sold *Roe-deer Hung up* (at a private show) for 2,500 francs, the *Roche Oraguay* for 3,500, the *Fox* for 1,800. 'If I'd been in Paris, I'd have sold the *Fox* for 5,600.' The public was forcing the Government's hand. 'All Paris expects me to be decorated and my picture bought for the Luxembourg.' And he recounts one of the manoeuvres which he considered astute and which seldom, if ever, came off. 'Already twice, a price has been asked for the *Big Stags*; I've been adroit in dealing with them. In both cases I replied first to M. de Chenevières, then to

M. de Nieuwerkerke, that, having been deceived as to the price of the *Fox*, I wouldn't put a price on my picture, that I'd leave it entirely to their discretion, but they could be sure I wouldn't fix any price, that I'd refer the matter to their good will, and so they can object to nothing in public, not to the expensiveness of the price, or anything. As a result (so far) the picture goes to the Luxembourg, and I am decorated in all appearance. All this will be known in four days, by Tuesday next, the third of the month; I'll write to you the next day how it's come off; so far I've had nothing official, they hang on till the last moment, they're in a cruel position with regard to me at this moment.' The picture wasn't bought by the State.

In this letter for once we get a reference to Zoé. 'I've seen Zoé a few times; she goes with her lady to Baden Baden or to Spain, she is delighted, she's doing well now, she had fallen ill again through insisting on taking a strong purge.' We see how well he is keeping her secrets from the family.[22]

Some time this year he and Buchon agreed to collaborate on an illustrated book about hunts and hunters; but nothing came of it. On 3 June friends gave him a banquet in Paris to celebrate his Salon success and the triumph of Realism. Desnoyers declaimed a poem on the *Stag Taking to Water*:

> Unhappy Stag at bay, you fall, no mercy for you.
> Up now! the dogs are here. Up, leap and run!
> The landscape like a lighting-flash goes by.
> Weep, foam, but go! Fall down, but still go on.
> Leave skin and blood on the trees; for there behind,
> Behind you, on you, a whole host you'll find,
> Hunters and bloodhounds, horses and loud horns
> Shaking the forest. . . .

Probably some time this year he painted the portrait of a *Woman with Parrot*. The model may be Solange Dudevant, George Sand's daughter, who at this moment had been separated from her husband, the sculptor Clésinger, for some five years. This seems the first of his works in which he associates women with birds; later examples are *Woman with Parrot* (1866), *Venus and Psyche* (1864) where the bird was introduced later, *Young Girl with Gulls* (1865), the *Woman in the Podoscaphe*, the modelling of the woman with a gull on her head. The contrasted softnesses of flesh and feathers attracted him; also no doubt the image of the woman as a bird-of-flight passing across his bed – though perhaps this image is in turn merged with one of himself as the wild creature who is temporarily tamed to the woman's hand. We saw earlier how he described women as birds of passage.

Now more provincial shows were keen to get his works; this year he had pictures at Marseille and Lyon, and the municipality of Nantes bought his *Winnowers*. In August he went to Antwerp for a show of his paintings, which included the *Battle of Stags*.[23]

He came home strengthened in his conviction that Realism was now established on a firm base. In the autumn he got a petition from a group of students who were discontented with the École des Beaux-Arts; they asked him to open an atelier and teach his own system.

Advocate of the self-taught artist, he resisted their plea, then gave in. Castagnary took charge of the arrangements, finding a studio at 83 rue Notre Dame des Champs, on the ground floor; a lease was signed on 6 December 1861 for three months, at 900 francs a year – though the period seems to have been extended to four months. In a few days the students began turning up, there were thirty-one at first, forty-two by the end of the month, each paying twenty francs to cover rent and expenses; Courbet took no money for himself. Only two of the students later made a name, the painter Fantin-Latour and the engraver L. Flameng.[24]

Castagnary wrote a light-hearted account of the event. Late in 1861 all seemed as set as ever; there was a passing excitement over the Salon, then the usual flatness. Prizes were given, artists retreated to their studio waiting for commissions, the École des Beaux-Arts went on with its manufacturing of acceptable artists. Picot was busy fabricating works that would gain big prizes; Couture was making art easy for the daughters of the rich bourgeois. Then an odd noise started up on the Left Bank, spreading over the bridges, up the Montmartre slopes: Courbet was opening a school! In the evening, in all the salons, circles, cafés, nothing else was talked about. Thus: 'A hundred young painters came from all the Paris studios; Courbet had to yield to this unprecedented manifestation.' 'Any from Picot's studio?' 'Of course, the Picot studio renounces the Prix de Rome and goes over in mass to the Courbet studio.' 'You're joking?' 'But how is it that Courbet, who recognises only nature as his master, has decided to open a school?' 'Nature begot him and then rested; while we wait for her to regain fecundity, Courbet's taking her place.' 'What irony! will they paint the nude?' 'They'll do all that lies within painting's domain and falls into the *métier* of the painter.' 'It's all over with the Beautiful,' shouts a dry-fruit of the Rome School whom the exigencies of the time had turned eclectic, 'all over with the Ideal. Materialism enters art by the wide open doors of teaching. Materialism is the cancer of the nineteenth century. After having depraved our philosophy and cheapened our literature, it must, to consummate its work, attack our art.' A voice breaks in with a popular march-refrain. 'Sirs,' says someone, rising, 'there's the watchword of the situation; a revolution begins.'[25]

Courbet drew up a manifesto, which perhaps Castagnary toned down a little. Dated 25 December, it appeared in the *Courrier du Dimanche* four days later.

You have indeed wanted to see a painting studio opened where you could freely carry on your education as artists, and you wanted to put it under my direction. Before I reply, I must first explain myself to you as to this word *direction*. . . . I must set out to you what I recently had occasion to say at the Congress of Antwerp: I have not, I cannot have pupils. Believing that every artist must be his own master, I cannot dream of setting myself up as teacher. I cannot teach my art, nor the art of any school whatever, since I repudiate the teaching of art, or, in other terms, I assert that art is wholly individual and is for each artist only the talent resulting from his own inspiration and his own studies of tradition.

I add that art or talent, in my opinion, can be for an artist only the means of applying his personal faculties to the ideas and things of the epoch in which he lives. Especially art in painting can only consist in the representation of objects visible and tangible for the artist.

Any epoch can be produced only by its own artists, I mean the artists living in it. Historical art is in essence contemporary. Each epoch must have its artists, who express it and reproduce it for the future. A period that has failed to express itself through its own artists has no right to be expressed through later artists. That would be the falsification of history.

The history of an epoch ends with that epoch itself and with those of its representatives who have expressed it. It is not given to new periods to add something to the expression of previous times, to augment or embellish the past. What has been has been. The human spirit has the duty of working always afresh, always in the present, while starting off from results already gained. It must never recommence anything, but must march always from synthesis to synthesis, from conclusion to conclusion.

The true artists are those who take hold of the epoch just at the point to which it has been brought by earlier times. To go back, that is to do nothing, to act in the form of pure loss, it's to have understood nothing and got no profit from the teaching of the past. Thus is explained how archaic schools of all sorts are always reduced to the most useless compilations.

I hold also that painting is an art essentially *concrete* and can consist only in the representation of *real and existent* things. It's a totally physical language which uses for words all visible objects; an *abstract* object, not visible, non-existent, does not lie in painting's domain.

Imagination is art consists in knowing how to find the most complete expression of an existing thing, but never to suppose or create this thing itself.

The beautiful is in nature and is met in reality in the most diverse forms. As soon as one finds it, it belongs to art, or rather to the artist, who knows how to see it. As soon as the beautiful is real and visible, it has itself as its own artistic expression of itself. But artifice has no right to amplify this expression. It cannot touch it without risk of denaturing it and consequently weakening it. The beautiful given by nature is superior to all the artist's conventions.

The beautiful, like the true, is a thing relative to the time in which one lives, and to the individual suited to conceive it. The expression of the beautiful is in direct ratio to the power of perception acquired by the artist.

There is the basis of my ideas on art. With such ideas, to conceive the project of opening a school to teach conventional principles would be to return to the incomplete and banal notions that have so far directed modern art throughout.

There cannot be schools; there are only painters. The schools serve only to seek out the analytic procedures of art. No school could lead in isolation to the synthesis. Painting cannot, without falling into abstraction, let a partial side of art dominate either colour, composition, or any other of the manifold means which alone in their totality constitute this art.

I cannot then make any claim to opening a school, to forming pupils, to teaching such or such a partial tradition of art. I can only explain to artists, who wish to be my collaborators and not my pupils, the method by which, according to me, one becomes a painter – by which I have tried myself to become one since my start – by leaving to each the entire direction of his individuality, the full freedom of his own expression in the application of this method. For this end, the formation of a common studio, recalling the fruitful collaboration of studios in the Renascence, could certainly be useful and could contribute to opening up the phase of modern painting. It will stir my eagerness to bring about all that you desire of me.[26]

Courbet gets very close to a deep comprehension of his whole aesthetic in these formulations, especially in his realisation of art as a concretising activity and of its need to find 'the most complete expression of an existing thing'. Here we see how far in thought he was from those who thought that his Realism meant the direct and simple reflection of an existing object. The complete expression of an object implies a full grasp of its inner and outer relationships, of their dynamic unity; in dealing with a person it involves the dialectic of his individual existence with his social essence (all that has gone to make him what he is);

in aesthetic terms it involves a full grasp of all the tensions operating inside and outside a form, giving it its rich organic nature and setting it in vital tension with its environment, all the other forms around it. And this question of form, as the periodical, *Réalisme*, had pointed out, was a question also of colour, of plasticity, of rhythm. We see how Courbet's concept of art-expression leads directly on to Cézanne's.

He speaks here of the necessary synthesis. To bring his meaning fully out, we need to add the statement cited by Silvestre: 'I am *objective* and *subjective*, I have made my synthesis.' The creation of the art-image was never seen by him as a merely skilful reflection of the existing thing: that would be pure objectivity – and, as we have seen, most critics attributed to him such objectivity as his aim. The subjective artist was emotionally romantic or imposed on nature a pattern derived from his own mind. The Realist sought a living fusion of objective and subjective factors, seeing the object just as it was, in all its unique nature in time and space; and he did not want to distort this nature by subjugating it to his emotional needs or his intellectual preconceptions. What he added was the fuller understanding that transformed the object from an isolated and meaningless unit into a vital part of life, so that it revealed its essential being as well as its individual form. This was the synthesis of objective and subjective in the creative act. (Incidentally we see how far Courbet has advanced from Proudhon, who saw synthesis as a temporary equilibrium between opposites that could never fuse.)

To return to Courbet's *atelier*. He was as unconventional in his choice of models as in his methods. Castagnary described a visit he made with the two editors of *Le Siècle*, E. Pelletan and G. Chaudey:

Standing on spread-out hay, with dilated eye, lowering his black muzzle, and swinging his impatient tail, a red bull, marked with white, was tied by the horns to a ring of iron strongly sealed in the wall. It was the model. The noble animal, disturbed at being the centre of all eyes, moved about on its solid legs and hardly maintained its pose. Did it come from the pastures of Normandy, the plains of Poitou, or the meadows of Saintonge? I don't know, but it had a fine form and its spotted garb pleased the eye. So many easels, so many artists. Each worked in silence. The blackbearded master came and went, distributing his hints, and each time taking up the palette to demonstrate more clearly. He came before us; and after an exchange of greetings he explained with his fine *franc-comtois* bonhomie the new studio's character and the reasons deciding him, Courbet, to yield to the prayers of the youngest generation of artists.[27]

The manifesto led to much discussion. 'Philosophers, aestheticians, critics, collectors, wags, made it a vast theme of conversations, commentaries, observations, reflections, quibbles.' A caricature by Bénassit showed the Master straddling a bull, palette in one hand, brush in the other, marching over the body of the Prix de Rome, to inaugurate, to the great terror of the Greeks and Romans, the studio of Modern Art, followed by a huge train of students lost at the horizon in the fogs of Montmartre.[28] Castagnary did not understand what Courbet was saying, for he himself argued that beauty is wholly in man; and he oversimplified the issue by saying that the question was to make art 'what it should always have been, a social agent'.

Oddly, when so many critics were now looking on Courbet as having got over his more outrageous impulses, Wey thought he was going to the bad. He saw him as surrounded by flattering parasites, becoming daily more bitter and rebellious. 'He worked less, began to drink, and became thenceforth, with wretched [*vilains*] pictures, the precursor of the Impressionists.' He makes 1861 the time of his break from 'the ideas of his time and the traditions of art'. Titian, Raphael, Michelangelo became, with the most scornful irony, *M'ssieu* Raphael, *M'ssieu* Michelangelo, *M'ssieu* Titian. Delacroix, even Titian, were only *corrupted* artists; there existed in the world now only the Master-Painter Courbet.[29]

Round about 1860–1 Andlers began to decline. Andler refused to install beer-pumps as the better-class establishments were doing; Mme Andler disapproved of young folk with their mistresses, who 'had to endure the blaze of her wrathful glance'.[30] Her niece Louise married a man named Schaller and opened a rival place round the corner in the rue de l'École de Médicine, luring many frequenters away. Courbet and others drifted to the brasserie near by run by *père* Laveur at 6 rue des Poitevins. The end came in 1866 when the boulevard Saint-Germain was pushed through the old quarter and the building with the brasserie was demolished.

'*Père* Laveur was a character', says Castagnary. 'Had he been a monk in his youth? Each evening endless discussions on aesthetics and ethics.' Dupont and Mathieu were often there. After dinner Laveur began a game of billiards and forgot his customers' need for beer. 'Courbet cried out in a stentorian voice, "He who pours out for drinking, of what are you thinking?" This drollery made me laugh.'[31] Courbet was also going of an evening to the Brasserie des Martyrs on the lower slopes of Montmartre. Here was nothing of the village-tavern such as one found at Andlers; the frequenters were large numbers of well-known artists, musicians, writers.

There are substantial divans and oak tables of a very happy effect. . . . It's elegant and comfortable: 'pleasing and comfortable' [in English] as says Corporal Trim. But what are much less 'pleasing' are the glasses, the gildings, the colourings, the loud daubings [*peinturlurages*] and other clamorous things that give ophthalmia and shudderings to people who have eyes and taste. There are also lamp-stands which have borrowed their caryatids from the *Three Graces* of the museum of the Renascence and condemn these unfortunates to carry capitals and artificial flowers in the guise of flames. (DELVAU)[32]

Desnoyers was a frequenter, roaming about the place, and always heard even when not seen: 'he has the dragging intonations of Schann[e], Courbet and G. Mathieu; I regret I can't give it in notation.

> There are dead men that we must kill.
> Inhabitants of Le Havre, Havrais,
> I come from Paris with purposive will
> To smash the statue in my way
> Of Delavigne (Casimir).
> I myself am called Clodomir.

Fernand Desnoyers is wholly there: he is the breaker of images, the overthrower of statues, the statues of all the poets past, present and future.'

The Courbet *atelier* did not last long. On 2 February 1962 Castagnary was asked to vacate. 'The wallpaper and the floor are already reduced to such a state I can't decently let it till it's been repaired; if in two months so much damage has been caused by your tenancy, what will it be like at the term's end after two more months!' But Courbet refused to leave. The school went on till the lease ended early in April.[33] Courbet himself had soon been bored, and he found the work tiring and getting in the way of his own projects. But the enterprise had not been wasted time. It did much to spread a liberalising tendency in other *ateliers* and even at the Beaux-Arts; its general principles (no rigid system; development of personality) were taken over by H. Lecoq de Boisbaudran, who taught at the École Impériale, which he directed during 1866–9; among his pupils were Fantin-Latour, L. L'Hermite, Dalou, and Rodin.[34]

Also, near the end, Courbet tried his hand for the first time at sculpture and modelled before his students the *Bullhead-Fisher* (bullheads were small fish with broad flat heads): a naked boy with fish-spear. He decided to have it cast in iron for the fountain in the main Ornans square: a project he had had in mind from 1853–4. As with his later few pieces of sculpture, the work was not of high quality, though with his strong plastic feeling it seems likely that if he had ever thoroughly given himself up to sculpture he would have been more successful at it. When later the statue was installed, the conservative and religious citizens were stirred to protest; a petition was taken to the local Council accusing the work of indecency and of a depraving influence on the youth; and the statue was spattered with filth.

In April 1862 he met Saint-Beuve, who wrote to C. Duveyrier, the dramatist:

The other day I was talking to Courbet. This vigorous and solid painter has ideas as well, and it seems to me he has a great one: to inaugurate a kind of monumental painting appropriate to the new society. . . . He proposes to convert our large railway-stations into modern temples of painting: to çover these huge wall-spaces with a thousand thoroughly suitable scenes, anticipatory views of the main sites through which the traveller will pass; portraits of the great men connected with the towns along the route; picturesque, moral, industrial, metallurgical themes; in short, the saints and miracles of modern society. Isn't that an encyclopedic idea, one that deserves encouragement? But Courbet needs the railway-stations more than quires of paper. MM. Pereire have, it seems to me, one of these as much as the other, and it would be worthy of you to find out what can be done of all this as far as practice goes. You who act as midwife to men and minds, go to see Courbet, if you care to, and force his fine timidity and his naïve and potent pride to clarify and develop themselves.[35]

We may note his insight into Courbet's character, so unlike those who saw only the bluster-ous side. The idea that Courbet was setting out went far back, however, in socialist tradi-tion. Considérant in his *Démocratie pacifique* had propounded it as early as 1848; it thus seems Fourierist in origin – though as far back as 1843 Flora Tristan in her *Union Ouvrière* had suggested the building of Workers' Palaces; artists would be asked to help in building and decorating; actors and actresses could give special shows, musicians give concerts, to raise funds for buying 'blocks of marble, canvases, paint, and all that sculptors and other artists might need for creating statues, etc., to adorn the Palaces'. Champfleury in *Grandes*

Figures (1861) wrote with reference to the *Fire Brigade*: 'The frescoes projected for railway-stations would depict scenes no less unusual. . . . Is not the machine, the place it occupies in the landscape, sufficient to make a fine picture?' But in June 1864 as part of his general disillusion about Courbet he told Buchon, 'In the *Grandes Figures* I outlined for Courbet a programme for the decorating of railway-stations. He has not done it; it will be done.' However the idea was very dear to Courbet, even if circumstances never allowed him to try actualising it; it was an integral part of his whole concept of realist art. We can guess how he would have welcomed the approach of Rivera and the other artists of the Mexican revolution.[36] Though he never worked out his programme systematically, we may say that he considered the first stage to be the triumph of realist painting, which would drive academicism out of the Salon and the Museums; the second stage would come with the victory of socialism, when the artists would find social functions for their work in the decoration of public buildings, etc. The socialist artist would be a realist since in no other way could he make man his key-theme.

His Ornans studio had used up much of his cash; about this time we find him writing to the publisher P.-J. Hetzel (who published three novels by Champfleury and corresponded with him):

I feel the greatest want of money. If you'd pay for the *Stag* you've bought [*achetté*] from me for 200 francs you'd do me the greatest pleasure; for I've just built a studdio [*atelier*] in the country to work there in the peace that was indispensable for me. There's Louis Redout who owes me almost twice as much, of whom I'd be very glad to have news. If he could also pay me it would be equally useful[37]

Champfleury was sending the letter on.

In May 1862 Buchon, now aged 44, was married to Héléna-Félicité Diziain, aged 21, daughter of a proctor at the Besançon Lycée. She was lively, with a downright sense of humour, suitable for offsetting and complementing Buchon with his grave intensity. Courbet does not seem to have attended the ceremony; he was getting ready to go with Castagnary, at Étienne Baudry's invitation, to Saintonge in western France: an area with broad plains and open views, as unlike as could be to Franche-Comté. Castagnary, himself from Saintes, had taken Baudry, a rich dilettante, to Courbet's Paris studio, and Baudry had invited them to Rochemont, his château a mile or two from Saintes. He himself wrote, was a patron of music, and held a patent for a gadget to be fitted to underwater pumps; he dressed in his own style and was considered an eccentric. On 30 May the visitors left Paris by night-train and arrived next morning. A diligence took them in three hours to Saintes, where Baudry met them with a carriage and drove them to his country house on the road to Saint-Jean d'Angely, approached by an avenue of interlaced trees. There was a fine view down on to the Charente; and the big iron gate, the ha-ha, and the woods on either side gave the place a grand air.[38]

It was this residence, very comfortably furnished and recently equipped with a fine studio, that Baudry set at his guest's disposal. While the horse was plodding up the hill, Courbet looked at the landscape with persistent attention as if trying to absorb it through his retina. After lunch, which was long and merry, he asked as he lighted his pipe if there was in the house a piece of canvas on which he might paint. Several were brought. He chose one a metre long and broad in proportion. Then, taking his palette in one hand and his palette-knife in the other, he began painting from memory, out of the elements he'd observed from the road: a landscape which he finished in less than two hours, to the great astonishment of the assembled neighbours. The surprising thing was not so much the rapidity of execution as the character of the work itself. With its superbly modelled clump of young elms it was unmistakably a landscape of the Saintonge; but it was the Saintonge defined by its essential features. Half an hour's drive had been enough for this astounding artist to assimilate the scene, so new to him, and he reproduced its aspect with a sureness of touch that won him the praise of all those present.[39]

Though in his letter to Hetzel he had said he needed peace for work, here at Rochemont he excelled himself as a painter able to work among the noisiest distractions. He painted happily while visitors crowded in to watch him and talk. 'He was the flattered, spoiled and petted guest.' A young cousin of Baudry, Théodore Duret, who was to become an art critic, was one of the visitors; but he failed to penetrate Courbet's character and the unity of his realism and his socialism:

At Saintes the artist, wholly devoted to his art, steeped himself in nature, a simple jovial man on friendly terms with the artists and neighbours; in Paris the artist combined with the leader of the realist school, the politician, the socialist, in which capacities he was constrained to strike attitudes, to write for and harangue the gallery; a great man within the sphere of art, an incompetent in the political sphere.[40]

We can gauge the extent to which Courbet was a new sort of artist by the inability even of those who knew him best, like Champfleury or Castagnary, to understand the springs of his inspiration; Proudhon saw the social core, but in an extremely narrow way. 'While painting,' says Duret, 'he'd smoke, chat, tell tales, burst out laughing, start off a pleasant tune in his head-voice, or strike up a couplet of his own making. His hand was so nimble and sure that he ended by doing a great deal of work, though he set to only after noon and then only for a few hours. But if he didn't withdraw into himself at the easel, still less did he do so at table. The lunches were long, the dinners endless. Merry quips mixed with serious discussions enlivened them. We talk of politics, literature, philosophy. We ran down the Empire, as all thinking persons in France were starting to do. After coffee we lighted pipes or cigarettes; we drank Strasbourg beer that Baudry had brought along in small casks so as to be always available fresh.'[41]

Louis-Augustin Auguin was one of the artists who gathered round. Born in May 1824 at Rochefort-sur-Mer to the wife of a carpenter (who was so interested in drawing that he set up as a teacher, himself self-taught), he set off for Paris in 1842, with a three-year scholarship paid for by the town council. Though J. Coignet was his master, he in fact followed Corot; a supporter of the 1848 Revolution, on its failure he went back home and took to teaching art; then in 1860 he closed his studio and devoted himself to painting in the Forest of Aulnay, then settling at Port-Bertaud.[42] Another artist who became friendly with Courbet was Hippolyte Pradelles, Alsatian portraitist and water-colourist; he too was living at Port-Bertaud on the Charente. Courbet went to and fro in a carriage between that village and Rochefort a great deal; with his careless (and economical) ways he left Baudry to pay the bill for 1,200 francs presented after his departure.

There was also the sculptor Arnold, who 'had all the naïvety of medieval artists and whose pencil designed works of the humblest kind; he worked oftener for churches and cemeteries than for private town houses.' Then in August Corot came for a fortnight. One day he and Courbet both painted a view of the distant town of Saintes from near the highway. 'They worked on small canvases of the same size,' says Duret,' and agreed to finish at the same time. Two or three of us, their friends, watched. They sat close to one another, but far enough apart not to see each other's work, while being able to talk to one another and join in the bystanders' chat.' Corot put Courbet painting in the foreground of his canvas.[43]

It was at this period that Courbet began seriously to paint flowers. Perhaps he found that their bright masses expressed the easy happiness he had found here in the Saintonge, as the rugged or rock-enclosed scenes of his native uplands provided imagery of struggle, hardship, violence (in the form of hunts), or deep refuge. He painted *Myosotis; Young Girl arranging Flowers; The Branch of English Cherry*; and another flower-piece he sold to a local deputy. Also for Fédora Gaudin, earlier a representative of the people, he did two flower-works. 'Gaudin had then a spirit turned to mysticism, and he wanted a sort of allegoric picture with an inner meaning. Courbet, keen to please, did the requested compositions and wrote at the bottom the legends I met again in the catalogue of the Saintes Exhibition of 1863:'

Poppies, legend: *Death triumphs over Desire and the Poppies put the Cares of Life to Sleep. Soucis* (meaning both Cares and Marigolds), legend: *Cares strip the Roses of Life.*[44]

There were some large scale entertainments. On 12 August Baudry invited friends to a big party. Four days later there was a huge fête at Port-Bertaud for Courbet, Auguin, and Pradelles; starting on Saturday evening, it went on all through Sunday. On Saturday 16 August Courbet wrote to Castagnary who had gone off. 'I was carried by the Port-Bertaud ladies before two thousand people.' Steamboats were to bring visitors from Saintes next day; there were concerts, fireworks, dancing in the Place Courbet (the main square renamed to commemorate the occasion). The local paper tells us that Courbet was in an armchair when the ladies lifted his bulky figure.[45] For song there was the Galin-Paris-Chevet school; the Society of Saintes Oarsmen was prominent; the dancing, eating, and singing went on on the green river-banks; complicated fireworks were let off on the roofs of houses. As for the chairing, 'this mighty colossus, the Farnese Hercules of modern art, acclaimed by dainty mouths, was triumphantly uplifted by feminine arms that enthusiasm sustained.' The ladies declared him 'the handsomest man for ten leagues around'.

A fortnight later there was a fête at Rochemont. The journalist describing it said that he would need to 'exhaust all the vocabulary of the East' and evoke the 'faery memories of the Thousand and One Nights'. The gardens were bright as day with thousands of coloured glasses and venetian lanterns; the band of 40 musicians played in dancehall for 300 dancers; vast Bengal Candles burned constantly at the château-windows; the école Chevet sang under the trees; refreshments and cakes were free at a specially-made kiosk; seven hectolitres of punch were made and shared out from a tap put in a big butt. At 3.0 a.m. there were still many of the ten thousand (as estimated by the reporter) asleep on the ground in the woods; and the Saintes firebrigade lost its way when going home. (The drink was brandy-punch, as Saintes was in the midst of the cognac district.)[46]

Another reason for Courbet feeling in the best of spirits was the fact that he seems to have had some affairs. In his home-area he was too well watched to do much philandering; in Paris his mistresses were of the art-world, models and the like; in his Montpellier stay we hear of no affairs of his in Bruyas's somewhat discreet and well-behaved society – apart from the enigmatic brothel-group. But here at Saintes the ladies seem to have opened their bosoms to him. Telling Castagnary of the Port-Bertaud fête, he remarked, 'I am in love with a wonderful woman, who arranged my triumph.' She may or may not have been Mme Laure Borreau of Saintes, who seems to have been his mistress and of whom he painted four portraits, one in a simple black dress, one in a fashionable costume with bouquet. He appears to have come to her aid in some financial difficulty. Shortly before he left in March 1863 he wrote to the photographer Carjat (then editing the weekly *Le Boulevard*). 'The Saintes ladies are insistently demanding copies of my portrait made by you; they have seen a copy and find that the one you made is the only good likeness. Please send me some to fill the void of their hearts; send two large and several small prints of the one with the cane.' His excitement bubbles over, 'I love you as you know, my confidant in love, you are my photographer, you are my biographer, you are my friend.' Perhaps he wanted photos of a lithograph by Carjat published on 7 June, of which he may have seen advance copies. In his PS he adds, 'I'm making pictures that will astound you; I won't say more than that.'[47]

He certainly stayed some of his time with the Borreau family, who arranged a studio for him. He painted the daughter Gabrielle (properly Louise-Laure-Zoïde), who had been born in 1848; the work has been taken as a portrait of the mother, perhaps because he has made her look rather older than she was – a common trick of his with young girls. He liked this girl and called her Briolette; here he gives her a dreamy and yet self-conscious look, hard, satisfied, sly: which makes her indeed the daughter of the woman whom he shows with a calm assurance, refined but with large enigmatic eyes, her features both tight and self-indulgent. But he enshrines the girl in a more sensuous world of luxurious paint, thinking of both Velasquez and the Venetians, even her clothes evoke the Renascence world, as those of her mother do not; poised in her slightly lost way against the rich background of foliage and sky, she provides an image of youth which looks back to his early romantic period but which carries also the weight of his accumulated experience.[48]

In November 1862 he had moved to Port-Bertaud, to a house by that of Auguin, who, as a person of less physical stamina and negligence than Courbet, soon grew worried at his dissipation and apparent frivolity. In January he wrote in alarm to Castagnary:

The Salon was near – and our friend idles about, sleeps, smokes, drinks beer, and does little, very little painting, at least painting for the Salon. I'm more concerned about his fame than he supposes.

His apathy upsets me, all the more because I'm forced to keep silent for fear of my remarks being misinterpreted. Fame means obligations. Well, my wish at the moment is to see him rally the glory that'll abandon him if he treats it so lightly. For him glory is at Paris, in his work, and his work is not in the torpor of provincial life. Further, he lends himself not so badly to that torpor. I tell you, dear friend, what I can't say to Courbet. It does me good and I trust you. As you know, I'm somewhat of an observer. Today I know our friend as much as, or better than, he knows himself.

He is a child, a rather weak woman, who has to be led by the hand. His force is concentrated in his talent; as for the means he's *weakness incarnate*. We've lived as brothers at Port-Berteau [*sic*]. I understand there is today a bond between Courbet and myself, an indissoluble bond. I love him. The proof is I'm interested in everything that touches him. Because of him I feel anger and sadness. One moment I curse his uncertainty, his lack of resolution. *I fear this*: that some day he'll feel a grudge against Saintonge for losing time and fame, and against his friends for not daring to cry out to him: Animal, shake off your fleas! But there's no way. He takes any advice badly. I want, however, to strike a big blow. That would be a great service to render him if I made him understand that he's on the way to suicide. He treats me like a brother: which pleases me in all respects.[49]

This letter eloquently brings out the way in which Courbet could quickly create in others a powerful and complicated response. Such persons, whom he had grappled to him, felt that an eternal bond had been built; and Courbet at the time felt it too. But when he moved on to new spheres, new activities, he as quickly forgot about them, unless they continued to be linked with some aspect of his work. Zoé had put it with bitter insight: For him the absent were always wrong. Only to art and the Franche-Comté earth, to the family in its general bearing as part of the deep early bond, was he consistently true – and to the ideas generated by his art-activity. The way in which the present, its immediate interests and demands, absorbed him, was part of his strength; it also laid down the limits within which his art could develop. Auguin, who had known him a few months, like Champfleury, who had known him many years, could not grasp how the irresponsible and responsible elements in his character were closely entwined. His art and its nodal points of change were linked in the last resort with his deeply held ideas, but they also needed moments of surrender to all the pulls of immediate living.

In January 1863 a joint show was held in three rooms of Saintes Town Hall for the benefit of a local charity, with a charge of a franc for entry (25 centimes on Sunday). Courbet showed 43 works, all done at Saintes, with two sculptures (female heads cast in plaster), and he added 10 more paintings in a fourth room after the opening. Corot showed five works, Pradelles 42, Auguin 64. The show was a success and Courbet sold several works to Baudry and others. In all he painted at least 60 pictures during his stay: many landscapes, seven portraits (including one of Corbinaud, a prominent citizen, the 'first bourgeois of his race', who rejected it as making him uglier than he was); and above all the flower-pieces.[50]

He had found himself in a land 'not easy to come out of'. He liked the place and the people and they all wanted him to stay on. But the too-comfortable way of life begot in him the need to do something disruptive. Sending 200 francs as new-year's gift to Zélie and Juliette, he informed the family that he was at work on a 'subversive' picture, a large canvas 9 or 10 feet long by 7 or 8 high (actually 11 by 7¼): 'satirical and comical to the highest degree; everyone here is delighted with it. I shan't tell you what the subject is; I'll show it at Ornans; it's almost done.'[1] This work was *The Return from the Conference*. We see a group of drunken priests going home from an assembly such as that held every Monday at one of the parishes round Ornans; for the setting Courbet used his memories of the valley of Bonnevaux in that area. A fat priest sits heavily on a small donkey led by a young abbé; an older man supports the rider on the other side. Next comes a seminary student holding up an old priest who stamps his feet and brandishes a cane. Over on the right a curé with an umbrella is about to kick a yapping dog; four women, servants, bring up the rear, two with baskets on their heads. On the left a farm-labourer stands guffawing, while his kneeling wife is horrified. A statuette of the Virgin is set in a shrine-hollow in a tree; in the distance are steep hills and cliffs. The Bonnevaux folk claimed to recognise all the characters and said the peasant was old Poulot, a local rapscallion whose real name was Boillon. Didier, their curé, was the man on the donkey. He was 'an extraordinary man, of Herculean strength with a huge body, huge feet, an enormous belly. A native of Ornans, he possessed to a great extent the characteristics of that region. Courbet and Didier, former schoolmates at the little seminary, were good friends; they both loved the old wine of the valley and drank it.' Courbet is said to have given Didier an inscribed photograph of the picture, and Didier to have replied, 'Gustave, you shouldn't have done this.' However, it is more than unlikely that Courbet would have pilloried his old friend; if Didier made the remark he must have been referring to the picture as a whole.[2]

The studio at Baudry's house was too small, and Courbet felt it unfair to make his host at all responsible for the work. A suitable site, however, was found on the grounds of the imperial stud-farm close to Saintes, where the director, Maillard, had been building a house, but had had to stop through lack of funds. The roof and walls had been completed and Baudry persuaded the director to let Courbet use the big enclosed space. But Courbet was no man to keep secrets. Citizens protested and he was told to go. He moved to the house of a ferryman Faure, at Port-Bertaud, where there was a big upper loft. Here he was again almost thrown out when Faure thought one of the priests based on himself; but Courbet quieted him by pouring two or three bottles of wine down his throat.[3] One day he let some friends in to view the work. They saw a donkey rolling in straw at the foot of Courbet's bed, and a curé's soutane draped over a lay figure in a corner. Mère Faure, finding her ceiling get wet, raged about the madmen upstairs and cried out that she had let the loft to Christians, not to animals. The sculptor Arnold posed for the laughing peasant; Poitiers of Saintes for the small laughing abbé; Gaudin for the fat curé on the donkey, and his dog for the dog. Courbet wrote to his Paris friends that he was working at Saintes because he didn't 'want any indiscretions. I know Paris. I want to arrive with my canvas finished. I'll send it in to the Salon. What they're going to yell! But no one will say it's badly done.' He said he had made concessions. 'It's overfinished; one would speak of Raphael.' He expected a noise, a *potin*.[4]

He hesitated to send it in alone; but when he did send it, he did not add any of his recent landscapes or flower-pieces. Instead he sent the *Fox Hunt*, a portrait, and a plaster cast of the *Bullhead-Fisher*. The *Return* was naturally rejected and he could not even get it hung in the Salon of the Rejected. So he put it on show in his own studio, where for weeks a crowd of critics, collectors, and sensation-mongers came and went.[5] On 23 April he wrote to Albert de la Fizelière of Saintes, 'I wanted to know the degree of freedom that our time accords us.' He adds the motive. 'I made the work to get it refused. I've succeeded. That's the way it'll bring me in money. However, considering the scare it caused, it'd be comical to force the administration's hand.'[6] But in such comments he belittles himself. He could not bear to admit defeat in any respect; so he now pretends that he did the whole thing to send up his prices and gain notoriety. But he gives himself away in the final statement; what he wanted was the confrontation with the State and he still hoped somehow to beat the authorities. On 28 July he sent his father a fine damascened firearm. 'As you can see from the papers I have sold my picture of the *Curés* which has caused a clatter.' The picture had been in London for eight days; he was trying to get to Ornans for a fête of 10 August. 'Perhaps I'll be there.' The casting of the statue would be ready at the end of September, and the statue would be unveiled on 1 October.[7] His venture into sculpture was jeered at. Caricaturists showed people rushing from the sculpture section at the Salon; not even there were they now to be secure; let them go into the architecture section before he invaded that too.[8]

As for the *Return from the Conference*, an American entrepreneur put it on show in England as a scandalous work in August 1863. (Géricault's *Raft of the Medusa* had been similarly displayed.) The American and Courbet were to share the proceeds. In 1868 Courbet showed it with ten other paintings and some drawings; it was sold at the auction on 9 December 1881, and finally about 1900 it was bought by a zealous Catholic who cut it up. So we have only photographs of it; and many of these must also have been destroyed. In April 1867 Courbet told Castagnary, 'The police have just arbitrarily destroyed the negatives of the *Curés*; I don't know by what authority.'[9]

Critics in general treated the three works in the Salon with contempt. Thoré noted that his medals should have saved him from a rejection.

That a painting should deal with contemporary morality is what seems dangerous to the conservatives. To portray stonebreakers, diggers, and others condemned to rough work, is not that already an indirect attack on the classes who own everything and do nothing? And then, after having presented the virtues of the toilers, to dare to display the vices or even the absurdities of the privileged castes![10]

Champfleury in his letters to Buchon continued to abuse Courbet.[11] The Salon works were 'execrable, carelessly painted, without colour or drawing; an abominable hunting-scene. . . . The woman's portrait strange and unpleasant.' He followed up by saying that he had seen Courbet, who was tired out. 'Painting bores him.' He says that he spoke out, 'but the man's fuddled with the chatterers, loungers, jesters, who overwhelm him with compliments to his face and merely buttress more firmly his already exaggerated conceit.' What he needs is 'five or six years of solitude at Ornans to recover from this setback; if he thinks he has saved the world by his painting he is a lost soul.'[12] That was in June; a few weeks later he and Courbet had their open quarrel. Champfleury 'made some observations' on the *Curés*. 'Naturally he said next day I had sold myself to the Government. At that I wrote to him what I thought of his future if he did not curb his monstrous pride, which I foresaw would lead to fatal consequences.'[13] In fact, allowing for Courbet's downright way of putting things, he spoke truly in saying that Champfleury had sold out; he had long wanted to become a respectable man of letters. In many respects he was a disappointed man; by 1860 as a realist novelist he had been dwarfed by Flaubert, and soon the de Goncourts and Zola were to come up. He turned more and more to history in his slightly pottering though often useful way, and recently had been given the direction of the Funambules, famed for its pantomimes; later he was appointed an official of the state-factory at Sèvres. What Courbet had told him a little earlier about his conception of the artist's function provided the real basis of their split. 'Your friends are concerned about the position which you take as a *man* and lose as a *painter*.' Courbet replied that he didn't admit 'a man may withdraw from the common action. Have not the greatest spirits, whom one admires in the tradition, been constantly mixed up in what went on in their own times?' And he declares that his efforts henceforth will aim at seeing that 'France finally gains consciousness of herself and governs herself all on her own'.[14]

Castagnary was the only one, apart from Thoré, who stood up for the *Curés*. 'In this country of invective, laughter, and raillery, satiric painting is accepted with reluctance.' And he went on to praise the colour and composition.[15] As the work has been lost, with only early photographs surviving, we cannot assess it with any certainty; but it seems to have lacked the weight and force of the other big works running from *Afterdinner* to *Demoiselles on the Seine-Banks*. No doubt Castagnary was right enough in praising the colour (of the landscape); but there appears to have been no such aesthetic unity as Courbet had previously achieved. The work seems a halfway-house to the *Beggar's Alms* of 1868. There had been a rumour in Paris that Courbet had had a stroke at Saintonge. Baudry explained later that the story arose from Courbet's fall off a donkey; a few bruises were all his injuries. For an expert horseman like Courbet to have such a fall suggests that he was drunk; and the mishap may well have reminded him of unsteady curés on donkey-back.[16]

He clearly meant to get back his political punch through the picture; but there seems to be here, as there had not been in the other big works, a disproportion between the end and the means used. We may perhaps say that he felt the rising tide of anti-imperial emotion, but did not quite see how to express it in his work.

To the attacks on the *Curés* Courbet riposted by pointing out that lithographs were publishing showing fat curés on horseback, carrying on the crupper girls with dresses pulled up above their garters. So he meant to paint two more canvases: the *Conference Dinner* where one curé throws his comrades out of the window; and *Conference Bedtime* where the servant-women make tea and put the incapable priests to bed. Needless to say, he never painted these works. But he might have pushed his defence further and pointed out that he was carrying on a genuinely popular theme. In French proverbs, even those that come from areas known for their religiosity, the curé is always a subject of humour or attack; the good curé does not exist. The painting thus 'corresponds to the cynical proverbs and tales of the religious peasantry, whose folklore, even in a Catholic country like France, reveals without exception an underlying malice and hostility to the clergy as a class. If one compares Courbet's attitude with the erudite constructions of his admirer, the philosopher-painter, Chenavard, who must locate the church in a vast cycle of world-history, in order to show its historical limitations, it becomes obvious how rustic and popular in feeling was Courbet's satirical image.' (SCHAPIRO). However the uproar brought him into close connection with Proudhon, who, beginning with the intention of a pamphlet on the *Curés*, ended by writing a long work on art, which, though unfinished, was published after his death: *On the Principle of Art and its Social Destination*. There were 25 complete chapters, 15 compiled from his notes by the executors. In a letter to Buchon, Proudhon wrote that 'Champfleury understands nothing', cannot write, and was never a realist. Buchon is to blame; he owns all the qualities that Champfleury lacks, he should have come to Paris to take up the cudgels for realism. But as he has stayed at Salins, Proudhon has decided at Courbet's suggestion to write the needed work on art. With all his worries Courbet has been ill with a return of constipation and haemorrhoids; Proudhon told him to take a ten-day holiday, which he is going to spend at Fouras near Rochefort in sea-bathing.[17]

Courbet took his share in Proudhon's analysis very seriously; hence his delay in returning to Ornans. He considered that the two of them were collaborating. Proudhon, however, minimised his contribution:

One day when I was starting work on this book, I mentioned to Courbet that I thought I knew him better than he knew himself; that I would analyse him, judge, and reveal him as a whole to the public and to himself. That seemed to frighten him; he didn't doubt that I'd make error on error; he wrote me long letters to enlighten me, letters which taught me very little. And he tried to persuade me that I wasn't an artist. To which I replied that I was as much of an artist as he was, not as a painter, but as a writer . . . and that I was perfectly competent in such matters. That seemed to relieve him a little, and he no longer tried to do anything but represent himself to me as he thought he was, not quite the same thing as he really was.[18]

Instead of being pleased at Courbet's aid, he wrote to a friend, 'Courbet is in anguish. He assassinates me with eight-page letters – you know how he writes, how he wrangles!' Again, to Chaudey this time, 'I've had an enormous letter from Courbet. I think he went poking about in the oldest grocer's shop in Ornans for the dirtiest yellowest coarsest exercise-book so as to write to me. You'd believe that letter belonged to Gutenberg's century. Courbet doesn't write often, but when he puts himself to it, beware! This time he covered no less than fourteen pages with the dregs of wine. It'll be a job to answer all that.'[19] It is a pity that we do not have all Courbet's letters to him. In the following, for instance, he seems to be arguing against Proudhon's oversimplified idea of the function of directives in art's development:

Why govern the arts? If the arts can be governed, it's because they don't exist in France. How stamp a direction on art? That seems impossible to me unless there is no genius in France. If one can stamp a direction on art, that comes from the fact that the arts have been governed, that one has accepted as mould the recognised things of tradition.

Government in the arts (by the very meaning of the word) cannot deal with genius; it would be absent from its mission. It can govern the existing thing only by comparison with the past.[20]

As we know from his own writings, he does not mean that tendencies cannot be clarified and the relation of art to reality discussed and understood; he is opposing any directives laid down from outside the creative situation. He enjoyed the stimulus given by his arguments with Proudhon. He told Buchon, 'I've never written so much in my life. If you could see me, you'd die laughing. I'm smothered in papers; every day I send Proudhon five or ten pages on the aesthetics of contemporary art and of my own art that I'm trying to establish. . . . In the end we'll have a definitive treatise on modern art and the direction in which I've led it in accordance with Proudhon's philosophy.'[21]

About this time, in his efforts to explain himself, he seems to have set out a sort of *credo* in the form of a series of aphorisms. He begins, 'My dear friend, I'm going to recite to you certain *litanies* [*litanies, rigmaroles*] of my own fashion, thrown together without order.'

The past can only serve for education.
One must use only the present in one's works.
Banish the mysterious, the marvellous, don't believe in the incomprehensible.
Put feeling, imagination, wit [*esprit*], and the ideal at the service of reason.
Keep one's thinking faculties in equilibrium without respite, affirm oneself constantly, come to conclusions unceasingly, without shame and without departing from one's principle; always belong to oneself.
Set oneself out [*se produire*] to the public (the sole judge) in one's works, without restrictions and in all one's conviction.
Don't observe humility, nor suffering, nor resignation.
A virtuous man is one with the courage of his opinions, who follows undeviatingly the road that he has set himself.
The man who has spent his life in amassing a fortune has no place in the intellectual world.
In the social organisation, a fortune devolves on men in the inverse ratio to what they can produce.
For a man to be able to spend money usefully, and without doing harm, he must have earned it himself.

The intelligent man, who puts himself at the service of society, should live without foresight and use integrally all the resources at his disposition, in the service of what he's undertaken.

Society should be so arranged that a man can't be humiliated by charity and can't die of hunger.

The solicitude that decentralisation should have for the individual would easily abolish the literary and artistic Bohemia, including that of inventors.

Decentralisation should extend to money. M. de Roschild [*sic*] has no special genius; as a result a certain number of men, clubbing together, could carry out his operations, if it's necessary.

The gigantic fortune of M. de R. is a power inside a power, something that shouldn't exist.

Every man will be obliged to work, and no force of society could be lost by this means.

Starting from there, it seems to me that communes by their way of existence, making work indispensable, could also lead to free and compulsory education, and by these two laws already maintain the dignity of man.

A man, who doesn't work, turns in on himself; he cannot progress through lack of anything to compare himself with.

One isn't born with genius, one is born with particular propensities and faculties; it's through will and work that one arrives at being a man.

Work disappears to the extent and degree that the faculties grow; in that they follow the proportions of the mathematical square.

Pride is inseparable from man, but it is justified only by work; pride is the consciousness of oneself, pride is a reward.

Fecundity lies in the variety of conception.

Never work on commission unless one is left in full and entire liberty of expression.

Fecundity doesn't lie in multiplicity of works.

It is useful to live indifferently with all classes of society without taking the side of any of them; it's the way to find out the truth, to strengthen one's judgment, and to get rid of prejudices.

The distinction of one class from another does not exist. What is truly distinguished is only the man who distinguishes himself by his works or by his actions.

In the arts a man must make no concession to the public mind against his own ideas. If he can do it, his originality doesn't exist. He breaks in an open door.

One of the best reasoned and most spiritual things in men is the tenacity they put into being assured of the individual's conviction. A single concession is enough to kill him. Men among themselves recall the ring of wolves: the first who falls is eaten.

The man who belongs to himself can with impunity and without danger enjoy and share in all that life holds of allurement; it is on the contrary the thing considered dangerous which serves him better.

We see him there in all his strengths and his weaknesses.

On 23 September 1863 Lydie Chenoz married Charles Jolicler of Pontarlier, who had studied law in Paris and called on Courbet there in his studio. A taciturn man, eleven years older than Lydie, he seems to have enjoyed having a lively wife. (Courbet painted her portrait in 1864, her three-year-old daughter in 1869, and her husband in November 1872.) She was a staunch friend of Courbet; but it is unlikely, as has been suggested, that she became his mistress. She remained 'a spoilt child, merry, inconsistent; Gustave's visits were occasions for laughter; she'd recall her childhood-years, a thousand nothings that amused her.'[22]

Back in Ornans for the autumn of 1863, Courbet meditated how to carry on the attack. His first idea, we saw, had been to paint more curés in their debauchery; but he did not follow this up – it would have been only a repetition of what he had already done. In

November Champfleury told Buchon, 'Courbet is probably at Ornans now. If you see him, try to keep him in the country as long as you can. He told Sainte-Beuve he wanted to paint another picture of *Curés*.' What he should do is paint simple themes and landscapes of his home-area. 'But great God! let him avoid symbolism and satire for which he has no talent.'[23] In fact Courbet painted about this time a portrait of F. Gaudy, rich landowner and keen huntsman; *Woman at the Spring* (a nude seen from the back); *Towing on the Banks of the Loue*. But he was also meditating or working on large themes, political and symbolic. For Buchon replied to Champfleury.

I went a month ago to Vuillafans to see the sculptor Claudet. There we learned that Courbet had just come to Ornans. We went to see him. He gave us some large photos of his *Curés*, which didn't cheer us up at all, any more than the series he promises us. It is the same with his sculpture, which seems to me below the mediocre to judge by photography. He's going to do a new *Stag in the Snow* which will be worth more, I trust. And the same with the landscapes in hand. He showed us sketches of the *Conscript's Departure* and the *Vigil*, which seemed to me very involved compositions which need too long commentaries. From all that he'll come out as he can. He's going to stay at home till May. He spoke to me in passing of your differences, which have caused me much pain.

The *Conscript's Departure* was to have been an anti-war, anti-empire work, showing the misery caused by conscription. It came to nothing, but we shall hear more of it later. Courbet's effort to devise some such sort of direct political subject shows how he wanted to get back on to some more solid anti-bourgeois themes; but did not know quite how to do it on lines that engaged his full artistic self. The same dissatisfaction and desire to reach out in new polemical ways appeared also in a large symbolic canvas on which he was at work: *The Fountain of Hippocrene*, which satirised romantic poetry and into which he was putting many poet-friends or acquaintances, Baudelaire, Dupont, T. Gautier. On 18 January 1864 he wrote to Castagnary on the disaster which overtook the work.

My life is a tissue of accidents. I'd started an epic picture, a serious though comic satire. I'd done two-thirds of it, meaning to show it at the approaching exhibition [Salon 1864], when yesterday, Sunday, I went to dine with one of my friends at some distance from Ornans. During my absence someone entered my studio; one foot of the easel was touching the door behind it. No sooner is the door opened than the foot is pushed in, the weight of the canvas and the easel takes over, and the chair I sit in goes right through the canvas.

Farewell, picture! I've no time to begin it again. It was an allusion to modern poets. I was portraying them as they go to drink from the fount of Hippocrene in the sacred valley watered by the springs of Castalia and Parnassus. Farewell, Apollo; farewell, Muses; farewell, superb valley I'd already created; farewell, Lamartine with wallet and lyre; farewell, Baudelaire with notes in hand, Dupont drinking, Mathieu with his guitar and sailor-hat. Monselet was with them but stayed sceptical. The fountain, invisible to Apollo's modern host, was in the foreground for the public to see. It was a very beautiful and quite naked woman like the *Springs* of M. Ingres, a fine model coming from Paris, lying on a mossy rock and spitting into the water that was poisoning all the drinkers. Some of them were already hanged, while others drowned. Gautier himself was smoking a chibouk beside an Egyptian dance-girl.

I can't describe it all; for if one could explain pictures, translate them into words, there'd be no need to paint them. Farewell, harsh criticism; farewell, recriminations; farewell, poetry's hatred of realism. The forthcoming show will again lack gaiety. If by chance I do a great wrong to my detractors, it's not my fault. The goodwill was there.[24]

He asks for the last sending-in date. 'I'm going to start something new.' If there wasn't time for a figure-composition, he'd like to send a big landscape. 'Our mountains are covered with snow and I feel full of ardour for work.'

Juliette wept and said she'd knocked the easel over; Courbet consoled her, even swearing she'd done him a service. (If we may trust the *Demoiselles Tourangeau*, the pious Zélie tried at least once to destroy her brother's work; but there seems nothing much in the *Fount* to attract her zeal, unless the spitting nude was particularly provocative.) Since we have only verbal description of the work, it is hard to know if much was lost with it. In many ways Courbet appears to be returning to his early romantic material. From his words it seems that the theme was the way in which a corrupted or false life was poisoning poetry at its spring. The theme thus pairs off with the picture of the Artist saved from Love by Death (Separation). Courbet has saved himself; Baudelaire has not. From Gros-Kost it seems that De Nerval was among the figures. But what were the realist poets Dupont and Mathieu doing among the corrupted? Mathieu is expressly stated to be drinking the poisoned water. However, without the work itself, we cannot be sure just what roles Courbet was distributing among the characters; and though it does not sound the sort of work at which he would have excelled, still it would have been highly interesting to see how such a theme was defined at this mature phase of his development.

But why did he return to the theme of the poisons of romantic love? Had something made him acutely aware of Virginie and his son at Dieppe? Something unfortunate seems indeed to have happened to him; for the next big work he was to attempt was *Venus Pursuing Psyche with her Jealousy*, with its theme of love-torment. As we have seen, he was particularly susceptible to jealousy; he developed his creed of promiscuity because he could not bear either the responsibility of a steady relationship or the jealous fears he felt for the woman close to him.

But for the moment he was finding refuge in nature and in the hunt. In the spring of 1864 he wrote to A. M. Luquet, a Paris dealer:

I've gone to the Loue's source these past days and made four landscapes of 1.40 m. long almost, like those you have, and one of Mouthier, the *Cascade of Siratu*. In passing Mouthier I met that poor Pouchon, the *vigneron* painter. This unfortunate has an odd talent; he's like Holbein for naivety. I bought from him two little pictures of fruit, though I've no need of paintings. One can't let one of one's confreres die of hunger, a fellow-countryman too. I'll send them to you to be sold; I recommend them to you in particular. To shame the rich folk of the valley I paid him 300 francs. It's a very fine action, and you may rest assured that M. Ingres couldn't do it [the still-lifes] and M. Flandrion couldn't do the portraits he does. Only, this man lives on charity, and when he has to pay for dinner, on bread and garlic and the nuts he finds.[25]

Charles Pouchon had been born at Mouthier in August 1814 of poor *vigneron* family; somehow (perhaps through the help of S. de Vermondans, the mayor of the commune) he went to the Ornans seminary and the Besançon college. He painted portraits and still-lifes, even some romantic compositions, in a hard, dry, naïve manner. He and Courbet may have first met in the group under *père* Baud.[26]

On 8 March 1864 Buchon reported that Courbet was building at Ornans a studio for sculpture. 'With all that, an avalanche of domestic dramas: with Proudhon etc. Add to these tales the presence of a blonde Parisian model eighteen years old, big-breasted, who puts all the fops of the countryside to work, while making fools of them, and you'll understand that Courbet leads a busy enough life.' We see again how Courbet, for all his volubility, is generally quite discreet about such matters as this blonde; and one wonders how the family at Ornans and Flagey took his behaviour and what was said and done by the townsfolk.[27]

The new work that he did in time for the Salon was *Venus Pursuing Psyche*. (We may recall how his old teacher Baud had made many paintings on the Eros-and-Psyche theme; and how he, Courbet, had copied a work of *Love and Psyche* at Montpellier in 1857.) For him to turn now to a mythological theme would have been remarkable; but in fact the title is a piece of respectabilising camouflage. Later the work was called *The Awakening*, which suited it better. We see a naked blonde girl (the model who flirted with the local lads?) lying asleep on a big fourposter bed, while a dark-skinned older woman lifts the curtain and stares down with jealous rage and suspicion.[28] The harmonies of the painting are heavy and voluptuous. The character of this work confirms the suggestion that behind the *Fount of Hippocrene* lay a return of romantic sensuous stress, which he wanted to expel. Here he masks his emotion by throwing the jealousy on to a woman and making the love-conflict one between lesbians. At the same time he reveals his disturbed physical state both by this device and by the sudden influx of a strong sensuality into his art. None of his previous nudes have this directly provocative quality.

We have a further clue to the blonde girl in a painting called *La Réflexion*, which the caricatures of Randon show to have been later included in Courbet's private show at the Pavilion de l'Alma with the title *Head of a Young Girl, Ornans* 1864. The girl is shown in a dishevelled tousle-haired state, and so is not likely to have been a local sitter. She is probably the model who appears in *Venus Pursuing Psyche*. (The work sent in for the Salon seems to have been destroyed; what we possess is a variant he painted, in which the likeness of Psyche to the tousled girl is lessened. In the second version he seems to have got rid of a certain artificiality and strengthened both composition and feeling. There is vehemence caught in a more enclosed space, a more confined atmosphere. Another version shows the darker woman trying to wake the blonde by letting rose-petals fall on her: a motif that further brings out the meaning of flowers for Courbet.) The same model seems to appear yet again in *La Femme à la Vague* (dated 1868), in which we see her standing naked in water up to her breasts. She would then appear to have played a fair part in Courbet's life, linked with him over four years.

But how did the sturdy repudiator of bourgeois vice bring himself to paint lesbians, and with such power? Proudhon shrugged the problem aside by seeing the work as an attack on the lubricity of the day; but, as with the poems of Baudelaire, the exposure of vice is linked with an intense curiosity and sympathetically sensuous feeling. One might claim indeed that this work is the logical conclusion of the *Demoiselles by the Seine*; what is veiled inside their eyes or under their eyelids here comes out hotly into the open. Realism must deal with the bedroom as well as with the field, the highway, the woodland. But the question of emotional complicity remains.

The work was rejected as an offence against morals, despite Courbet's three medals. Thoré pointed out cogently the public readiness to accept veiled and titillating immorality while fearing the revelation of the plain truth: 'Yet there are no curés in this new scandal, only women, women of our own day, who are doing – what they want to do. . . . The women of mythology and the Bible have the right to do as they please. . . . But for a mere nothing the young women of the Seine are accused of indecency.' E. Leclerq in the *Gazette des Beaux-Arts* found both the girls ugly.[29]

Among Castagnary's papers is a letter from Millet dated 4 April 1864:

On reaching Rousseau's place the other day, after leaving you, I learned that a picture of naked women by Courbet had been rejected as *improper*. I haven't seen the picture and can't judge the reasons these jurors have had for their action, but it seems to me very difficult to admit that a picture by M. Courbet could be more improper than those by MM. Cabanel and Baudry seen at the last Salon were indecent; for I've never seen anything that seemed to me an appeal so real or so directed at the passions of bankers and stockbrokers. They appeared to me so gross a provocation I was surprised at women daring to stop before them. These pictures have not been less accepted with enthusiasm by *distinguished people* and considered as the expression of supreme grace. Doesn't it seem to you that would be the occasion for a fine comparison? For I admit that, with an equal intention of indecency, Courbet's picture would be at least three times as indecent for the reason that his women could not but be a thousand more times alive than the others. . . .[30]

Buchon in a letter of 23 June tells us, 'I saw Courbet at Ornans near the end of May. He was much taken up with the singular rejection of his last picture. You know without doubt that his curé at Ornans went to denounce him to Cardinal Mathieu, who then went to solicit the Empress's veto. I saw in advance the object in question at Ornans. I found it, except for one picture, at least the most dazzling painting come from Courbet's brush. The jury had accepted it. You know the rest. All that as vengeance for the picture of the *Curés*.'

This story is doubtless true; for certainly the police henceforth kept an eye on the *Curés*. Courbet, we saw, complained of photographs being seized; as late as 1876 Poncet, looking-glass vendor, rue Oberkampf, was fined for showing a photo of the work in his window. In 1871–2 some persons thought Courbet was being hounded because of the *Curés*. What is likely is that the work procured for him an enduring hatred from important ecclesiastical and police dignitaries.

Courbet stayed on in Franche-Comté most of 1864 and worked hard. At least a dozen landscapes of this time are known, and four to five hunting scenes, including *Poachers in the Snow*.[31] We have a long and amusing account of one of his jaunts. Near the end of September 1864 Buchon heard that he was painting near the village of Nans-sous-Sainte-Anne, some ten miles from Salins; he sent Max Claudet and another friend (? Charles Toubin) to invite him along. Late September was the finest time in the Jura; the vintage had begun; crowds of workers animated the countryside. Claudet left at 10 a.m. with his friend. 'We went on foot; it would be a profanation to go in a carriage through such beautiful country where at every step one was compelled to stop and admire *la grande nature*. 'They found Courbet at Nans and he accepted the invitation, but said he must first finish a landscape, *Source of the Lison*, and started off with his donkey Jérôme, whom he had bought to pull a handcart loaded with painting apparatus. The two friends followed him after lunch. They found him in a field before the spring, with canvas on easel and Jérôme placidly grazing. The wind was strong and blew the canvas over, just as they came up. A projection of the easel went right through the painting. 'That's nothing,' said Courbet, who turned the canvas over, smeared pigment on the tear, stuck paper over it. 'It won't show.' Claudet's companion brought up a heavy ladder which they edged in with large stones and bits of wood, to support the easel. 'You're surprised my canvas is dark,' said Courbet. 'Nature without sunlight is dark and dim; I do as light does; I pick out the salient spots and the picture is done.' At 4 p.m. he had finished. 'We felt in it the master's hand and his powerful inspiration; we were astounded at his speed.' The canvas was about a metre wide. 'Now,' said Courbet, 'off to Salins!' The equipment was stowed in the little cart; Jérôme, annoyed at being disturbed, was hitched up; and they set off.

At the village, as the road ahead climbed for six kilometres, they took a second donkey to help Jérôme. Arriving at the highest point, they sent back the other donkey; and as the road wound down for another six kilometres, Courbet said, 'We must all ride in the cart.' The three of them squeezed in 'like herrings, for Courbet took up a lot of room'. The donkey trotted down and night came on. They saw Salins afar. But the road was very difficult, a mountain on the left, a deep ravine on the right. An oxcart with a wine-cask met them. They swerved to the right to pass, but the scared donkey broke into a full gallop. Courbet pulled the reins so hard that one of them snapped; the intact right rein dragged the donkey towards the precipice. The cart swung over but was caught by its two rear-wheels. They hung over the void, then scrambled back and yanked the donkey to safety. After that they proceeded more prudently, on foot, and arrived at Salins as night came fully down. Buchon was waiting with a good supper; and the picture stayed with Buchon till his death, when Courbet reclaimed it.[32]

He was the most casual chap you could find. When arriving at Salins, he meant to stay three days; three months later he was still there. His baggage was composed of the donkey and cart, a shirt and two pairs of socks; as for other clothes, he had only what he stood in. When the cold came, he bought a blanket from a Jew at the market, had a hole cut to put his head through, and that was his winter-overcoat. Castagnary came in search to take him back to Ornans. Otherwise how long would he have stayed?

His father also came twice to find out what he was doing. Courbet remarked, 'He can't paint like me, but he has invented a five-wheeled carriage.'[33]

Gros-Kost adds some amusing details about the relationship of father and son. Régis couldn't stop watching his son at work and giving him advice. 'With a stealthy tread he came behind and took a look. His eyes moved from canvas to landscape, from landscape to canvas.

His brow darkened; his lips stretched out, until at last his indignation burst out.' He interrupted, 'You can plume yourself on knowing how to draw, ah yes, you can plume yourself. Look at that. Is it a rock? Your grass is absurd. My bulls certainly wouldn't want to graze it. As for your water, why speak of it: it's not like anything. Your pebbles have no commonsense. Your sky's like an umbrella.'

Courbet, exasperated, slowly put down his palette and emptied his pipe. Then, little by little, he turned round. Holding up his head so that his beard pointed out, he stared at Régis, who rambled on, 'In your place, do you know what I'd do? I'd take a little of that green and put it there. See, there, on this cluster of hazels.' Courbet burst out in a curse, picked up his paraphernalia, closed his box, took up his stool, and made off, with echoing oaths.[34]

While he was still in the Salins area a letter came (in November) from Victor Hugo in Guernsey to Buchon, congratulating him on his fine translation of Hebel's poems. At the reading of it, Courbet saw in a flash the exile's noble head bearing profound marks of the proscription he had suffered. He felt Hugo to be the external exile, he himself the internal one. In the following correspondence Courbet wrote Hugo an eloquent letter which may have had some touches added by Buchon, but is substantially his:

Dear and Great Poet,
As you've said, I have the fierce independence of the mountain-born. I think one could boldly put on my tomb, in the words of our friend Buchon, *Courbet without Courbettes* [bowing and scraping].
    Better than anyone, Poet, you know that our country is happily in France the reservoir of men given to upheavals like the land to which they belong, but who are also often carved in granite. Don't exaggerate my value. The little I've done was difficult to do. By the time I and my friends arrived, you'd just absorbed the whole world as a human Caesar in due form. In the flower of your age, Delacroix and you, you didn't have, like me, the Empire to tell you: No success without our permission. No warrants for arrest were issued against you; your mothers didn't make cellars in the house, as mine did, to stow you away from the police. Delacroix has never seen soldiers violating his house and effacing his pictures with a bucket of kerosine, by ministerial order. His works weren't arbitrarily shut out from the Exposition [1855]; he didn't make out of his pictures ridiculous chapels outside the Exposition-halls; the official speeches didn't yearly pick him out for adverse comment; he didn't like me have this pack of bastard hounds baying at his heels, doing the job for their masters, bastards themselves. His struggles were those of art; the questions raised were ones of principle; you weren't threatened with proscription. The pigs have wanted to gobble up democratic art in the cradle; despite everything, democratic art will grow up and eat them instead.[35]

These comments show how little Courbet knew of Delacroix's struggles. Apart from continuous obstructions by the academics, on 22 January 1822 the police included him among the seditious whom they were investigating, and he had considerable troubles at the time of the 1830 revolution.[36]

In spite of the oppression weighing on our generation, in spite of my friends hunted down, even by dogs, in the Forests of the Morvan [department of Nièvre], there are four or five of us left. We are strong enough despite the renegades, despite France today and its demented herds, we'll save art, intellect [*esprit*], and honesty in our land.

Yes, I'll come to see you. I owe it to my conscience to make that pilgrimage. With your *Châtiments* [1853] you have half avenged me. Before your sympathetic retreat I'll contemplate the spectacle of your sea. The sites of our mountains also offer us the limitless spectacle of immensity. The void that one cannot fill brings calm. I confess it, Poet, I love dry land [*le plancher des vaches*] and the orchestra of numberless flocks inhabiting our mountains. The sea! the sea! it saddens me with its charms. It gives me in its joy the effect of a laughing tiger; in its melancholy it reminds me of a crocodile's tears; and in its howling fury a caged monster that can't devour me. Yes, yes, I'll come, though I don't know to what extent I'll prove worthy of the honour you'll do me by posing for me. Yours with all my heart.

Hugo was gracious. 'Thank you, dear great painter. I accept your offer. The doors of Hauteville House stand wide open. Come when you please, except in June and July. I entrust you with my head and my thoughts. You will produce a masterpiece, I'm sure. I like your proud brush and your sturdy spirit.' But of course Courbet never went to Guernsey.[37]

Among the works done at Salins was a portrait of Mme Buchon and the *Gours de Conches*; at Pontarlier he painted the *Ferme des Pussets*. We see in the portrait the sharp mobile face of Félicité, with its lurking flicker of a smile: the animation which made Courbet felicitously remark that its little ripples reminded him of 'a swarm of mice'. Buchon wrote of the portrait n 11 March 1865:

Today I find Courbet what he has always been, producing in turn very fine things and debatable things. . . . In an hour he made a charming portrait of my wife. He has similarly improvised a good number of charming little landscapes, and, at the moment, he is finishing at Ornans a portrait of Proudhon surrounded by his family: about which, when leaving him a week ago, I could not arrive at any opinion, good or bad, beforehand.

We shall later consider the *Proudhon*. For the moment we may note again how Courbet called Mme Buchon the *Mère du Réalisme*, referring to the *Mères* of the *Campagnonnage*, the system whereby workers wandered over France. This use of the term shows importantly the basis of his sympathies and the extent to which, as a craftsman, he felt a complete unity with the roaming craftsmen, whose fraternity often had clashes with the authorities. As far back as the seventeenth century the organisation provided the basis for many struggles, including strikes. At the same time the link between Realism and the Campagnonnage shows the archaic element in Courbet's attitudes; for while the system foreshadowed the forms of union that were to grow up out of industrial struggle, it had for some time lost its vigour. Here then, as in the *Studio*, Courbet shows both his intense fellow-feeling for the downtrodden, the labourer, the craftsman, and his inability to grasp what was implied by the struggle against the emerging industrial system and its financial allies.[38]

The Gours de Conches was a cascade not far from Salins, that small town sunk between mountains crowned by two forts. The painting was done wholly on the spot and shows the skill and precision with which, even on a small canvas, he wielded the palette-knife and built up a thick paint-layer. Among his most successful uses of the knife was, as here, in the definition of rocks; he was able to give the effect of directly building the structure out of the paint and to achieve a remarkable solidity, which is one of his qualities leading on to

Cézanne. A friend, who watched him at work on the Gours, noticed that he refashioned some of the elements of the scene, adding foliage and giving the cascade an abundance of water. 'And Realism?' 'Oh, that's nothing, some grains of beauty. It doesn't often happen.'[39] The *Ferme des Poussets* indeed shows a careful construction on the basis of a large triangle, with the point at the bottom; it also shows his mastery of a particular atmosphere and its kind of light-diffusion, linked with a subtle use of colour-modulations – here ranging from lighter greens up to the sombre pine-masses. The total impression is at once objective and intimate.[40]

We may pause here to consider some writings by Courbet on the Hunt. First, he made some *Notes*:

At the seasons when hunting is forbidden, there are pretty girls in the fields, in the hay.

Hunting in a civilised country can't be taken seriously. In our country it's a great game in which one can deploy much talent, instinct, and activity.

Abundance of game is not very necessary for hunters with the spirit of the hunt. Given a hare, the setting can be complete. Nothing gives so good a hunt as the hare. The hunt is less interesting with the big beast.

The hunter is a man of independent character who has a free spirit or at least the feeling for liberty. He's a wounded soul, a heart that goes to stir up its languor in the wasteland and the melancholy of woods.

For many centuries, we can say, roe deer have been shot. They are always as fine, and also the last one killed is always the finest. More, there's always as many: to the point that one could believe the contrary. When there's too many, one has often noted they leave the locality, the males keep together and the bitches, too disturbed, disperse.[41]

And he tells a tale which brings out his sympathy for the poacher, the odd man out, the country scrounger:

One summer day I got up. It was ten in the morning. In July. The sky was blue, cloudless; the light was shimmering. Heat vibrated on the earth. The birds even were absent, they'd gone for shelter under the leafage. I was at my window, considering the countryside, when I saw in my wood, below the rock, an unusually agitated tree-top. It didn't seem natural. I put on my gaiters, saying, 'You're not curious, but we must see that nearer.' I took my walking-stick and went out into the open where all of a sudden I met Lagarde. I said to him, 'Gamekeeper, aren't you as surprised as I when you note that tree-top's agitation, in the midst of the forest?'

He had a look and answered, 'Yes, it's not ordinary.'

'You share my curiosity. We'll take our way there together.'

There we were. We came up cautiously. What was it we saw? A fine genuine thief was stripping the bark from the foot of one of my best limes – to make hives for use at the coming vintages. We appeared. 'Halt there, mister thief, you're known and you're to follow us with your loot, the bits of evidence.'

He made no appeal for mercy. We went down, the thief, Lagarde and I, and on the way we talked of one thing and another. It was getting hot. When we arrived at my house, what could I do but invite them in for refreshments? Humanity is my rule of conduct. I said to them, 'Mister thief, Mister Lagarde, if you'll do me the honour of coming into my house, we'll drink a glass of Chanais together; for you must admit it's the hottest day of the season.' When we went in, we found the cook had set the table. '*Ma foi,*' I said to them, 'as the table's set, you will content yourselves with my poor dinner. Wine will make up for the good cheer.'

We drank not so badly. The gentlemen found the wine good. We took coffee, liqueur, a glass of kirsch; and as it was three p.m., I said to them, 'Gentlemen, I think it's time to appear before higher authority.'

Mister thief took up his loot, which he'd put down, on entering, in the corridor. We all three set out for the Café du Centre, where my friend Prosper, ex-mayor of Ornans, is usually found. We entered. Prosper was there, playing at cards with some frequenters. I said to my companions, 'Of course you'll accept a glass of beer, and when the moment is opportune we'll submit the case to the authority of M. le Maire'. Mister thief put his hives under the table, and when the card-game ended, we went up to the mayor. After he'd had the matter explained, he said to me, 'And so, Gustave, you drink with a thief. As you've been drinking with him since the morning, you must carry on. At this moment you're his accomplice. What arrest do you want me to make? I don't see any other punishment to inflict on you than that of making you sup together this evening as well.'

I found the reply judicious, and indeed, after drinking absinthe, we went back to sup at my place. For the rest this thief wasn't lacking in observations.[42]

If we imagine this tale told in his hearty rough drawling accent, punctuated with bursts of gargantuan laughter, we gain some idea of Courbet the *raconteur*.

A character close to Courbet's heart was Max Claudet, born 1840, who shared his ideas about realism and academicism. He was self-taught, apart from a year's apprenticeship in a Dijon sculptor's studio and a few months study at Paris: 'a practical philosopher who creates art, breeds animals, plants trees, cultivates his garden'. At a later date he set up a small kiln at Salins for making pottery. He made figurines of common folk and attempted revolutionary themes such as *Robespierre Wounded*, *9 Thermidor*, in which he sought to express a courage triumphing over death. While Courbet was at Salins, Claudet did a medallion of him, and he later made the bust of Buchon set on his tomb.[43]

On 8 December 1864 Courbet wrote from Salins to Proudhon. He says that he is sending his friend Dr Blondon along to remind him of the promise to visit Ornans. Blondon had reported that Proudhon was keen to see 'the picture of the women that engross all Paris at this moment', but the work had gone to be shown at Brussels; now it was back. 'And I've written four fruitless letters both to my concierge and to M. Desforges, the correspondant for the Brussels Show, without being able to get it returned to my studio.' He asks Proudhon, when in the boulevard Montmartre, to call in at the shop of Desforges, a colour-merchant at the corner of the Passage Jouffroy, 'for I suspect he is having it shown to collectors.' Better still if Proudhon could get it sent back to Courbet's studio and see it there.

My dear friend, at this moment I'm on the point of making the counterpart of this picture, it shows a strong woman of the people busy at kneading, her children are round the trough [*met ou mai*: he means *maie*], her latest-born is in a box-chair smearing himself in a tinplate dish of hasty-pudding, on the table of *nonnotes*, *tonnoires* [*sic*] and flour. The children are waiting for the cakes, the woman, superb, blonde, fresh, and powerful, has her hair all loose (but not like the fashionable *lionnes*) – all loose through her work. She lifts up with an effort a huge amount of dough that falls heavily back puffing out; the pot is on the cast-iron stove. That's for the foreground. The place is strewn with dog, cat, scoop, poker, in a word all the necessary furnishings. In the background is the opening of the oven with embers glowing and the red smoke escaping; this charming woman listens to everything, for the men are in the fields.[44]

Thus we see that he meant to couple the picture of the *lionnes*, the luxurious perverse women of the Empire, with one of an industrious peasant-housewife. In detailing this project to

Proudhon he is perhaps forestalling criticism for dealing with upper-class immorality in a glamorous way; but it is the sort of picture that might well appeal to him, continuing the series of the *Spinner* and the *Winnowers*. His description gives strength to what was earlier suggested about the fascination he found in watching his sisters knead, spin, winnow. However, he does not seem ever to have attempted the work.

Two days later he wrote to Castagnary, welcoming the news that he was coming to join him. 'On Monday I'm going to do a lady's portrait [that of Mme Bouvet], which will take several days. So, as I can't devote myself to you, come to Salins in four or five days.' Four days later again: 'In two or three days I'll be free. It'll be most convenient for you to come to Salins; the railway will bring you direct.' They'd go on by donkey-cart, with Courbet pointing out the picturesque spots, to Mme Courbet at Flagey, spend the night there, then move to his Ornans studio.[45] On 29 December Courbet wrote to his hunting friend Gaudy that he'd been at Ornans for some days and was holidaying for the Christmas week. Champfleury seems to have left. 'In a few days I'm going back again to Vuillafans, to take advantage of your hospitality. I've done pictures *en masse* since you left.'[46]

50 *Portrait of Alfred Bruyas*. 1853. 91 × 92 cm.
   Musée Fabre, Montpellier (see page 107).

51 *Portrait of Max Buchon*. 1854. 56 × 46 cm.
   Musée National des Beaux Arts, Algiers (see page 122).

52 *La Mère Grégoire*. 1855. 46 × 38 cm.
   Musée du Petit Palais, Paris (see page 43).

53 *Portrait of Madame Borreau*. 1863. 75 × 60 cm.
   Private Collection, Paris (see page 179).

55 *The Dreamer. c.* 1860. 46 × 55 cm.
Collection of Henry Moore.

54 (*left and opposite*) *The Artist's Studio*. 1855.
359 × 595 cm.
Louvre, Paris (see pages 126–135).

56 *Woman with White Stockings.* 1861. 65 × 81 cm.
Barnes Foundation, Merion, Pennsylvania (see page 217).

57 *Women Asleep.* 1862. 75 × 95 cm.
Collection Prince de Wagram, Paris (see pages 216–217).

58 *The Awakening.* 1866. 77 × 100 cm.
Kunstmuseum, Berne (see page 189).

61 *Battle Between Two Stags.* 1861. 356 × 508 cm.
Louvre, Paris (see page 162).

59 *Snowstorm* (author's title: *Wreck in the Snow*). 1860. 139 × 203 cm.
National Gallery, London (see page 166).

60 *Deer Lying Exhausted in the Snow.* 1856–57. 91 × 147 cm.
Collection de la Vicomtesse de Donville-Maillefeu, Paris
(see page 148).

62 *Pierre-Joseph Proudhon and his Children.* 1865.
147 × 198 cm.
Musée du Petit Palais, Paris (see page 193).

63 *The Clairvoyant* or *The Sleep-Walker* (author's title: *La
Voyante*). 1865. 47 × 39 cm.
Musée de Besançon (see page 125).

In mid-January 1865 came the unexpected news of Proudhon's death. On the 20th Courbet wrote at length to Castagnary:

Under the blow of irreparable misfortune that now strikes us, I want despite everything to make an historic portrait of my very intimate friend, the man of the nineteenth century; I shall give my best to it. I have been promising him to do it for ten years.

More correctly, he had been trying to persuade him to sit without success; for Proudhon was all too aware of his uncomely features. 'Nature has made me ungraceful.' For the *Studio* Courbet had had to fall back on an engraving.

Please send me, I beg, for you and for myself, the deathmask mentioned by the *Moniteur*. A sculptor made it. Send me what [the photo] my friend Carjat has made. Ask him in my name. Go to Reutlinger's place and ask on my behalf and on that of Frond for the large portrait he made of the philosopher in the pose I suggested. Send it to me as soon as possible, as agreed. I want to do it as at 146 rue Notre-Dame-des-Champs, with his children, his wife, as suits the sage of that time and the man of genius. I told you at Buchon's place the theme of this picture. For the moment I'm putting everything else aside; I await these documents. If there's a painted portrait, no matter how bad, tell Chaudey or Proudhon's wife to send it to me. She knows my bond with her husband, she knows the boundless devotion I had for him.

He now goes on with a citation from a letter Buchon had sent him:

'It's with a heart broken by the lamentable news of Proudhon's death that I answer your letter. The news came in a letter from Castagnary and in the newspapers. What an immense void, immeasurable, this death will make in the intellectual world. . . . Let this thought of death restore to you all your great abilities and bring off in your lofty struggle your success at the coming Exposition. . . . Happily for such men the hour of death is, for the public, the moment when justice begins. . . . Let us think constantly of this life and of this death.'[1]

On 24 January he wrote to G. Chaudey, one of Proudhon's closest associates, that the century had lost its pilot. 'We remain without a compass; humanity and the revolution, adrift without his leadership, will once more fall into the hands of the military and the barbarians.' He asks urgently for the deathmask. 'Not only do I want to paint a portrait, but I also want to model a statue of him sitting on a bench in the Bois de Boulogne where I used to talk daily with him, and I want to inscribe on the base an epitaph I've composed: Wiser than men, his knowledge and courage were beyond compare.' In describing his own state of prostration he adds a reminiscence: '. . . discouragement such as I've known only once before in my life, on 2 December [the *coup d'état*], when I took to my bed and vomited steadily for three days.'[2]

His high level of emotion was unfortunately rather marred by a sordid dispute he was carrying on at the same time with his old friends the Andlers. He had let his account run on for years at the brasserie without checking items or asking for the total sum. Clearly the Andlers had not wanted to annoy a man who had done so much to make their place a success, and perhaps they thought that the unpaid account would bind him as a customer. As we shall see later, the sum they now asked for was not excessive; but Courbet with his mixture of reckless generosity and meanness became intensely suspicious. He forgot how much the Andlers had done for him over the years and simply didn't want to pay the bill. On 17 January Andler wrote a letter which shows that the wretched wrangle had been going on for some time:

In your letter you accuse me of appearing before you in the guise of a dangerous and formidable man. I don't believe that I deserve such a reproach. I feel no resentment whatever towards you, not even on account of certain people you have brought to my brasserie. . . . Still I am giving you one more proof of my goodwill by asking you to settle only your own account. I shall wait till the next exhibition [Salon to open in May], which will, I hope, furnish a favourable opportunity for the pleasure of seeing you. In any event if you find it possible to send me some money before then, don't fail to do so. . . .[3]

The tone is painfully humble. Courbet's reply, if he bothered to write, is lost.

At Ornans he was anxiously waiting for the material on which to base his painting of Proudhon. Carjat at last sent not only the requested photographs, but also a photograph of the deathmask and another of a portrait of Proudhon done by the Belgian, G. P. A. Bourson, in 1860 or 1861. In thirty-six days he completed his painting, which showed the family as he had seen them in 1853 at 83 rue d'Enfer (now rue Denfert-Rochereau) where they rented the ground floor and had a garden with apricots. 'When it didn't rain,' he told Carjat, 'he had the habit of carrying all his odds and ends out on to the three steps, his papers, his portfolio, and there, in the sunlight, his wife and his children came to work beside him.' Proudhon with his big bearded face stares abstractedly and pedantically through his spectacles, in grey smock and blue trousers, while Cathérine (then three years), in a little chair attempts the alphabet and Marcelle (who died of cholera in 1854) plays on the ground. In the original version Mme Proudhon, pregnant with her third daughter Stéphanie, sits in an armchair at the back, on the right, with some cloth over her middle to minimise her condition. This modest position in the background of her husband's life expresses what Proudhon thought correct and she accepted. In her case Courbet was particularly inhibited by lack of direct material. 'He was unable to do anything without having his model under his eyes,' said Cuénot, watching him at work on this canvas. (Three years later Courbet was to attempt a posthumous portrait of him too.) He called the portrait of Mme P. 'provisional'; and later in Paris, in the spring of 1865 he made a separate portrait of her, meaning to use it for repainting her in the large work; but he decided against a second attempt and painted her out, replacing the wall at the rear with some leafy trees, taking out the top step and in-scribing on the riser of the step where P. sits '*P.J.P. 1853*' – while the lower step has his signature and '*1865*'; but it is incorrect to assume that he began the work in 1853 and com-pleted it in 1865.[4]

He wrote to Luquet, 'My picture pleases me and touches everyone here . . . I'm half dead, I haven't lost a minute, you'll see, it's very original.' He sent it to Paris on 19 March for the Salon, confident of a big success. Champfleury foresaw a failure, and was right. Claretie reproached Courbet for caricaturing his friend and showing his wife as a hunchback. P. de Saint-Victor in the *Presse* (28 May) complained that there was not even a scandal; 'ugliness has become flat and flabby; the energy is gone, only the vulgarity remains.' Paul Mantz noted 'bitter disenchantments'. Beauquier in the *Revue littéraire de Franche-Comté* wrote two articles, citing extracts from Proudhon's book on art. 'Alas, no, M. Courbet, it's not the same original! Proudhon is dead, he won't complain, but the taste of the outraged public will complain for him.' An epigram was published.

> Poor Proudhon, sad your lot. You've lain
> For three months dead – and all in vain:
> Here Courbet kills you off again.

Even Thoré found the work poor, with Proudhon stuck flat against the wall 'of the same floury colour as his philosophic blouse' and his wife 'in a lump, so to speak, in a corner of the picture'. He added, 'I don't think I ever saw such a bad painting by Courbet.' It was indeed a failure, awkward and artificial, without the hard strength needed to convey what Proudhon had meant for men like Courbet and Buchon; indeed it might be said to convey all that was weakest, confused, and most distracted in Proudhon and his thought.[5]

We see then that during these years, despite advances in landscape, hunting-scenes, nudes, and flower-pieces, Courbet had suffered heavy setbacks in his figure-compositions. The *Curés* and *Proudhon* had failed to come off as he meant them, and he had failed to drive through into other works like *Hippocrene*, the *Conscript*, the *Housewife Kneading*. Behind this weakening in an important sector of his work we see the gaps and insufficiencies in his political theory, which left him with a feeling of isolation and a lack of direction under the Empire as the first fierce resistances were dissipated; he could not see where his allies lay or how and where any breakthrough could occur. His search for sources of spontaneous revolt was baffled, and he was driven back on himself as he had not been in the years 1848–55. But what was loss in one branch of his art was gain in another; his inability to find direct human imagery of revolt did not mean that his revolt had slackened; it meant only that he could not see the immediate point of social application. All the stronger then, in his recoil, was the emotion, which in turn meant aesthetic insight and comprehension, now put into landscape, nude, and still-life. The world he defined was still the world of the rebel, with an insistence on the holiness of all that lives; the individual angle gave freshness and energy to the imagery in which he could find a true outlet for his passionate sensibility. Technically the failure of his big figure-works was bound up with a certain increase in skill, which, however, eliminated the elements of popular art, of heavy sculptural form. The very things that his critics had most ridiculed and hated were at the heart of his creative force and gave both monumentality and generalising breadth to the figures he painted. The *Studio* had correctly expressed his sense that he was at the end of the phase based on such popular and plebeian elements; the *Demoiselles on the Seine* had shown him in transition. There was still enough of the earlier phase to maintain breadth, enough of the next phase to give more delicacy and personal sensibility. But he was unable to maintain this balance – for the reasons indicated. With the nude, the forest and its creatures, the flowers, he was able to advance into a new lyrical space, where his objective-subjective synthesis was truly held; but in the process the old plebeian monumentality went. The *Curés* and *Proudhon* were light-weight just where they should have been aggressively heavy and compact.

But because his emotional resistance to the existing world did not slacken, by some law of compensation he infused his landscapes and hunting pieces, still-lifes or scenes of wild animals, with a force that would not have been present if he had been turning to such things merely as an escape, out of a sense of frustration. Sometimes this element, the total imprint of Courbet on the material, can only be felt in a general way; at times it is possible to isolate it more specifically. Thus, he takes up the theme of Remarkable Trees (discussed in a series of articles in *Magasin pittoresque* in the 1850s); he had been particularly struck by the account and illustration of the 'gigantic oak of Montravail near Saintes', and about 1864 he painted *Flagey Oak, called Oak of Vercingetorix, Camp of Caesar, near Alesia, Franche-Comté*. He gave it this title when he exhibited it in 1867, showing how he combined local patriotism and home-feeling with a anti-imperial motive: Napoleon as the modern caricature of Caesar opposed to the Oak of the Hero who fights for national freedom. He was no doubt recalling, and replying to, the giant sculpture of Vercingetorix in the Salon of 1865, which the artist Aimé Millet had tried in his title to link with 'Napoleon III, emperor of France,' as a unifier of the people. As in similar titles or comments by Turner, the title here gives us the clue to the thoughts that ran through Courbet's mind as he painted the great oak, feeling in it a symbol of the strength of the people, of the revolutionary hero, drawing up energy out of the dark earth. His personal identification with it was made all the stronger by his remembering that *Lise* and *Gustave* were carved on it. Again in the *Hunting-Horn* of 1867 he had at the back of his mind a figure from Delacroix's *Massacre of Chios* for the hunter on his horse; an image from the national struggles of a people haunts a scene that seems to have no relation to it, and yet for Courbet the connection is real and important. He *feels* the energy of the man, though expressed only in a hunting-scene (about as far as could be from political struggle), as the energy of the free man which must by its very nature, sooner or later, be directed against the oppressors. The human presence in nature can be defined in many ways, even when no figure of a man appears, as in *Landscape with a Paper-Mill near Ornans* (1869); and again when the absence of man takes on a positive aspect, as in the Edenic idylls of the roedeers, the lack of man the predatory and oppressive creature, the despoiler of the earth, is a sort of rebuke to him, saying: Here is the harmony you reject. It is of little use to insist that these are irrelevant considerations. They were not irrelevant to Courbet, and he could not have painted these works without the thoughts and feelings that fed his aesthetic impulse. To enter into the depth of the picture, into its wholeness, we must enter into the whole-man of its creator, not neglecting the aesthetic aspects (without which it would not be a realised work of art), but seeking to see them in the perspective of the total impulse which moved the man-and-artist. To make this discovery of the whole-man is not to impoverish one's understanding and enjoyment of the aesthetic element, but to enhance it immeasurably.[5]

Art-criticism in general has suffered from a fear of attempting to enter into the whole nature of the creative process; but no artist has suffered more from a blinkered approach than Courbet.

Courbet as a philosopher, a moralist, a politician seems to us a plain fool. . . . Politics has nothing in common with art. (D'IDEVILLE)
   A great harmless fellow intentionally misrepresented as a terrible social revolutionary. (LÉGER)
   His works are as admirable as the man himself is odious and tiresome. (L. BÉNÉDITE)

'The social content of his works was invented by Proudhon' (RIAT). 'He was the naïve victim of politicians using him for their own advantage' (T. DURET). L. de Geoffroy attacked the *Burial* for 'indifferent reproduction of whatever was before the artist's eyes'; Champfleury praised it for the same reason. The recent change in attitude from these childish positions, which have so long dominated Courbet studies, is to be found admirably stated by Michael Laclotte:

Let us imagine for a moment that we knew nothing of the *Demoiselles de la Seine* of Courbet, and that, as sometimes happens with an unknown masterpiece of past centuries, the picture had come abruptly to light. Would one truly see there the image of vice, the record of social corruption, which the commentators have imposed? Certainly not, but primarily a sumptuous spectacle of truth and of the natural, then a dazzling piece of painting, then perhaps a poem slightly mysterious, dense and secret as are the *Tempest* or the *Rural Concert* [of Giorgione]. . . .
   If one keeps, to judge him, to his pictures stript of all the literature which adorns them, and to the best of his pictures – for his production, why not say it? involves some rubbish – Courbet appears indeed as a 'powerful worker', a mason of genius, but truly many other things as well, as one of the most delicate and most refined artists of our [French] school, as much by the subtleties of his craft, the nuances of his chromatism, as by the poetry. That this may be the fruit of instinct or of the subconscious more than an intellectual aim removes none of his suggestive force – which he breathes into so many of his compositions.
   Let one in effect take care: to ignore such and such an historical anecdote or the political and social intentions wrongly lent to the painter, does not mean that to savour Courbet better it is necessary to forget his 'subjects'. There is at times a tendency, above all in our days, to depreciate somewhat his big compositions so as to give more importance to the still-lifes, the landscapes, the portraits, so as to draw the artist more towards impressionism. This interpretation seems to us incorrect. Indeed Courbet was one of the founders, often prophetic, of modern painting. But nothing authorises us to see in him an adept of pure painting. Whether he describes the *Burial at Ornans* or a basket of apples, whether he arranges a scene or sets himself objectively before the motif, he always paints a 'subject', and, to do this, he 'composes' (there again it would be good to give up the prejudice which denies him the gift of constructor and symphonist to see in him only that of a painter of 'pieces'), impregnating his compositions, more or less intensely evident according to the subject and the inspiration, with feelings, sensuality, moral tenderness, lyric exaltation, also at times melancholy – fed by a deep human comprehension and a prodigious cordiality for the things of life. That is to say, it is not enough before his master-works to admire the vigour, the richness of craft, or the enjoyable justice of naturalist observation; we must also seek there the heart, the poetic imagination, and, let us declare it, the intelligence of a man.

The only phrase there at which I would cavil is the comment on social and political aims. If it refers to the superficial interpretations made of such aims, or to the attempts to reduce the complex nature of his art to them, then I agree. But as I have sought to show, the aims, deeply understood, stand at the heart of his imagination and intelligence. They are not abstract ideas imposed on the works or tortured out of them after the event; they are not opposed to the joy-in-life which he manages so often to convey in his imagery, in the rich means of his definition, but are the very core of that joy in their demand for nothing less than a fully human life.

The drawing of Proudhon on his deathbed, which has been taken to prove that Courbet was present, was made after a photograph for a special issue of Vallès's journal *La Rue* dedicated to the philosopher. It was to appear on the anniversary of his death, 20 January 1868; but the authorities vetoed the drawing. After protests, an autograph letter of Courbet's was substituted; but no more than ten issues were printed when the presses were stopped by the printer, and no other firm could be found brave enough to take the job on.[6] Exactly when the portrait of Mme P. was done is not clear, except that it was in 1865. Courbet had expressed his wish for a sitting before he left Ornans. Having done her portrait, 'I'll transfer it to my picture.' But as permission for such repainting was refused, he may not have asked for a sitting till April (as Castagnary says). According to a press-cutting of 11 August he had then just finished the work 'destined to be transferred to the large painting'. Later, in April 1866, he told Cuénot that he was working afresh on the canvas and was going to put in Mme P. from the portrait already done. Finally he decided not to use her at all, perhaps because he was disheartened at the criticisms of her hunched-up body and did not see how to give it a better structure, or because he thought that too much attention to the wife would lessen the concentration on *Proudhon*. Also he may well have found it hard to make her look twelve years younger.[7]

He had not, however, spent all his time this year on the *Proudhon*. In January–March he completed several landscapes he had already started, including one of his many views of the *Rivulet of the Puits Noir* (which he sent with Proudhon to the Salon). Here we see the water emerging from under thick interlaced bough- and rock-masses, out of the gulf. We may compare its dusky sombreness with the luminous depth of the *Brême* at the exit from the *Puits Noir*, to realise how fully Courbet had now set himself to define a particular phase of light and air, of seasonal change. (He was following the lead given by T. Rousseau in showing the same scene under different conditions, but giving the idea his own strength and breadth.) Whereas we go into the dark recesses in the *Rivulet*, we feel an expansion outwards in the *Brême* as if the light was breathing outwards. Again, if we set the *Rivulet* by the *Gour des Conches* we see how well he could now define the structure of rocks by his use of the palette-knife.[8]

Before he left for Paris Courbet had embarked on an adventure, both comic and pathetic, which underlines the correctness of reading a disturbed sensuality in the *Venus-Psyche* picture and in the concept of the destroyed *Hippocrene*. He, the sworn promiscuous bachelor, tried to achieve marriage; but in line with what has been said of his extreme timidity before all but the most brazen hussies, he was unable to approach the lady of his choice and had to fall back on go-betweens. In the spring he had gone to Besançon to contribute a picture to a local lottery (apparently for charity). He saw there in a show a still-life of flowers by Céline N. of Lons-le-Saunier; he may even have met her briefly at the show or had her pointed out to him. Anyhow he decided that he was in love with her. But, scared of speaking to the girl in person, he called on the good offices of his easy-going friend Lydie Jolicler. On 15 April he wrote from Ornans:

Now, my dear Lydie, I confess I see a wholly azure horizon ahead. You, who are my go-between, the custodian of my happiness, you who hold my future in your hands, you who can change the course of my life with a word or a gesture – fly, lovely bird of passage, fly as fast as your wings will take you to Lons-le-Saunier and bring me back a bird-of-paradise like yourself. The season is ripe, every bird is building its nest.

At the show in Besançon I saw the flowers painted by the bird who enchants me by day, who enchants me by night. I shall plant as many groves as I can at Ornans to persuade her to build her nest there. Dear lady, you who can do whatever you please, fly, fly!

Let us hope that we may beget a generation of painters and artists of all kinds, we shall produce a more intelligent race than the one now existing in our country. The activity demanded by the kind of life I have made for myself, exhausts me. I should like someone to help and sustain me. My liberty is very precious; but birds love freedom, it is what gives them their charm, and their adornment is their own plumage so that they owe nothing to anyone. . . .

But go, but go, my beautiful lady, in my impatience it seems that you do not stir. Forgive me for not having come to Pontarlier sooner. *Had I but wings*, as the saying runs, I should have already made a hundred flights to you know where. But how difficult is life, how troublesome and wasteful. I had to go to Besançon, they wanted me to paint a picture for the lottery, I did two or three, now for the moment I'm free, Next Tuesday I'll go to Pontarlier.[9]

This is indeed an astonishing letter. He pours out his eloquence on Lydie, who in her good-natured way would do her best to oblige him without any such cajoling; he does not seem to have written direct at all to the girl. He relies wholly on Lydie to win her over, to do his wooing. What excites him is the image of bird-Lydie wooing bird-Céline. The emotion here is surely that which has flowed into the painting of the two women in *Venus Pursuing Psyche*; and though it was only later, at a buyer's request, that he added a bird to that picture, he must have felt it in harmony with his conception and feeling. (In fact the idea of the bird had been suggested by his own *Woman with Parrot* (1886), so that the connection was not factitious.) Secondly we see how the letter verifies what has been said of his linking of femininity, of soft delicate limbs, with bird-plumage. The first *Woman with Parrot* (1861) gives the woman a love-brooding look as she sensuously fingers the bird's downy plumage. Further, in the letter the bird is linked with flowers; there seems to have been something in Céline's flower-piece which strongly attracted Courbet with its warmth and fineness of texture. The key-work here is the *Trellis, or Girl Arranging Flowers* (1863) done at the height of his happiness in the Saintonge. There the girl stands on the left in profile in a rich flowered dress, with the mass of trellised flowers which she is fingering. Flower–bird–girl: there was a powerful and provocative fusion of imagery for Courbet in this trinity. We may note that the trellis-girl has her two arms out-thrust in the same sort of pattern as we discussed in the *Winnowers*: a gesture which for Courbet suggested the female body in a regular rhythmic movement that stirred it to its depths, a gesture both of love and of work, a gesture that seems to go back to his observations of his sisters at Ornans or Flagey. Another significant picture in this relation is the *Torso of a Woman* (with apple or cherry blossom). Here we see the girl from the front, with her arms raised to form a sort of oval as she catches at the blossom. Her face has some resemblance to that of the peasant-girl with a kerchief (perhaps 1851); but the style, the evocation of fleshiness, suggests around 1862 for the *Torso*. The pattern has a fine balance between the rounded oval of the bosom repeated in the opening-out oval of the arms, with the head nestling on one side to balance the rounded mass of the belly: the whole body in a delicate balance between tree-trunk and blossom-bough, the two stems of which open out between her hands. The girl is both shrined in the tree-space and offering blossoms-and-herself out of it.

About the time that Courbet was engaged in his strange wooing of Céline by proxy, Champfleury was explaining at final length his break with the painter; what he says has in part a certain truth, but only brings out the deep incompatibility of the two men. He says that Buchon has accused him of wanting to *control* Courbet. But

one cannot be associated with a man for fifteen years, spending with him almost eight hours a day, without coming to love and know him. When I lost touch with Courbet, it was to isolate myself reflect, study, work, and try to improve myself. Courbet has continued his night-wandering life which indeed I never shared, and I've come to realise that, endowed with considerable qualities as a painter, he has let them drown in beer. . . . Courbet had a very strong stomach, I a very weak one.[10]

Courbet had an excellent start, but needed to back it up with 'enormous work' and to listen to his colleagues. His life, habits, talk, his lack of respect for others and for himself had led him from success to failure. 'I am driven sometimes to doubt the perfect balance of his brain.' He is like Dupont in his 'fever for banal admirations and his love of the *canaille*'. And indeed it's from comparing the two men that the upset has come between them, making each of them lose a part of his force, though reciprocal interests bade them carry on the bond. Now it's over. Courbet has 'in his depths his generation's instinct of decadence' and 'seeks to recover himself with blustering motifs'. His friends who haven't a material interest in defending him, as, say, Luquet has, are in consternation over *Proudhon*. 'I see no remedy for this sad situation.'

Courbet made no effort to see Céline or himself press his suit. In June from Paris he again wrote to Lydie. The wild raptures of the first letter are not repeated; we see that negotiations have been carried on, though the details are obscure. Stéphanie is perhaps Céline's sister, or else yet another go-between, someone in Lons whom Lydie has recruited.

You'll see how unlucky I am, in the first place because I couldn't see you in Paris, in the second because I've just answered a letter from Stéphanie and in my haste I again forgot to ask for Céline's portrait [? photo]. I forgot to send them mine and to give them my address in Paris; one would think I'd gone completely mad.

Céline is more eager than I am; that is as it should be; she must be the one who wants it if she is to be happy. I am too fat! I am too old! These are awful facts, still . . . I'm one of the youngest of my contemporaries among those well-known or famous. It's impossible to become a success, except as a notary, till one has done some work. But that must be unimportant to her, since she thought of marrying M. de Lamartine. As for my corpulence, alas, marriage will take care of that; the duties of a husband and the lack of opportunities to drink beer will be enough. . . .

I sent these ladies two pictures, one for Stéphanie, the other for Céline; but I want the one from her show and I told them that if our plans should come to nothing, I'd at least have the picture as a souvenir; and I also told them that if this should end in disappointment, I should kill that little devil of a Lydie, because you know you are the scapegoat . . . and there must always be a victim.[11]

Courbet himself was only 46. How Lamartine, the writer, then 75, a widower since 1863, comes into it, is not clear – unless Céline, in reply to some sally from Courbet about his own age, had remarked as an encouraging joke that she had fallen for the old poet. We can see that doubts have already crept into Courbet's mind; he is afraid of making some bad mistake, though he is still attracted by the idea of marrying. To have come to this conclusion, he must have been much shaken. Perhaps his stomachic and anal troubles had been returning; perhaps the blonde was arousing his jealousy too much; perhaps the whole complex of uncertainties that had beset him was making him look for some point of support other than his art, the family-bond, his beer-companions. From now on, however, the Céline-proposal seems to have steadily lost its appeal and to have faded out by the end of the year. He seems never to have met the girl, only to have exchanged photographs.

In June, anyway, he had a new source of self-esteem, Proudhon's posthumous book. He wrote, 'It's the most marvellous thing that it's possible to see; and it's the greatest benefit and the greatest honour a man could desire in his lifetime. Such a thing has never happened to anyone else. Such a volume by a man in connection with an individual. It's overwhelming. All Paris is jealous and dismayed. This is going to swell my enemies and make me into a man without equal. What a misfortune he's dead and can't uphold the principles he advances.'[12]

It is hard to believe that he really read the whole book carefully; it was enough that he had stimulated and contributed to it. Seven chapters dealt with the history of art; much of the later sections dealt with contemporary French art, with special emphasis on Courbet. Courbet is cited, not by strong authority, as saying, 'It's a good book . . . but too long; he put too much into it; I hadn't told him all that.'[13] Still, it sounds like what he may have said. The book was in many respects crude and dogmatic; it oversimplified the social function of art and tended to a moralistic narrowness. But it did not lack its shrewder points. It effectively characterised the romantic attitude towards history, and was not without some subtlety in its attempt to define how strong artistic personalities like Courbet were shaped and driven on by historical forces, while themselves in turn doing much to determine the line of art's development. Some polemical phrases, though one-sided and violent, were striking; thus the art of the Renascence was seen as a counterfeit art and its imitation of antiquity was 'a vampire art which attacked Europe along with syphilis'. He defined art as 'an idealistic representation of nature and of ourselves, having as its goal the material and moral improvement of our species'. Art for art's sake was a degrading theory: a debauchery of the heart and dissolution of the spirit (*esprit*). He issued his call:

Let art become more rational, let it learn how to express the aspirations of our epoch as it has expressed those of past ages. Let it seize upon modern ideas, assimilate them, work in harmony with the universal contemporary movement instead of being discouraged by a sense of inferiority which is only superficial and which really derives from the artist's false claim to independence. Let artists go to work with courage, and a new artistic era can begin for mankind.

He tells the anecdote about Courbet's *Stonebreakers*, already cited: some peasants wanted to use it as an altarpiece for their village church. 'I commend this idea to M. Flandrin,' comments Proudhon. (The tale probably comes from someone like Buchon or Cuénot saying over beer one evening that such a work would do better for the altar than conventional religious works. Interestingly it shows the image of the broken body of work as Christ, as the bread on which mankind subsists.) Courbet's power came from the rightness of realist art as the expression of an age that had seen the growth of positivism in philosophy and politics. Courbet attacked 'imagination' in such ripostes as: 'You who claim to paint Charlemagne, Caesar and Jesus Christ – could you effectively do a portrait of your own father?' But he was himself, Proudhon correctly points out, 'a painter of the imagination, one of the most powerful *idéalisateurs* that we possess.' (Courbet might indeed reject the term *idéalisation*, which lies at the heart of Proudhon's concepts; and this difference in terms reflects a deep contrast between his concrete approach and Proudhon's abstract moralisations. But he based his art on an imaginative realisation of the social essence, the total relations, of an object or person. That he succeeded unequally in this aim does not lessen its significance as his guiding principle.) Proudhon goes on to say that Courbet's work is the expression of an age that has also produced Comte's works, Vacherot's *Positivist Method*, and his own treatises, 'the Right to Work, and the rights of workers, foretelling the end of capitalism and the sovereignty of producers; the phrenology of Gall and of Spurzheim; the physiognomy of Lavater'. An odd eclectic list of typical products of the age, but reflecting truly enough the mixture of elements, forward-looking and archaic, which had gone to create Courbet's world-outlook.

In his account of the *Curés* (the work that had begotten the whole treatise) he says that Courbet's aim was to show not merely the contrast between 'sacerdotal decorum and an infraction of the rules of temperance', but rather 'the complete impotence of religious discipline' to sustain the rigid virtues demanded of a priest so that 'the priest who sins is the victim of his profession rather than a hypocrite or an apostate'. Throughout he is careful not to identify himself too closely with Courbet or to accept the term 'Realism'. He speaks of defects, 'lack of perspective and proportion, certain flat dark tones', carelessness, a tendency to caricature, 'sometimes *brutality*, something shocking that proceeds in my opinion from a lack of complete integrity with respect to his art and its principles'. Courbet is more an artist than a philosopher. He did not have 'all the thoughts I have expressed'. Certainly he wasn't aware of all the 'implications I have seen and pointed out' in his *Curés*. He is a true artist, 'with a vigorous and broad intelligence', with the mind of a man of the world. But he is a painter and nothing else. 'Though he talks a great deal, his thoughts are disconnected; he has realised intuitions, more or less true, sometimes logical, often sophistical. He calls himself "the most independent of artists; yes, independent in temperament, in character, in will, like spoilt children who do only what they please" '.[14]

Zola emerged as an art critic this year. He sided with Proudhon as to the artificiality and uselessness of most of the art exhibited. 'As science and industry develop, artists take refuge in a cheap and meretricious dream of tinsel and tissue paper.' He appealed, 'For heaven's sake, since you are painters, *paint*. Here is flesh, here is light, make an Adam which shall be your own creation. Delacroix and Courbet will survive because they both seize on nature generously with both hands.' He sees all the rigidity and moral abstraction of Proudhon's thesis, and decides that the philosopher betrays Courbet in order to exploit him. 'Courbet is the only painter of our era; he belongs to the group of painters of flesh'; his brothers are Veronese, Rembrandt, Titian. Thus Zola is on much sounder ground than Proudhon, though he has not reached his mature judgment, far more urgent than that of Proudhon, that all writers and artists must play their part at a moment 'when the iniquitous forces of the past offer supreme challenge to the forces of tomorrow.' He thus inclines to a subjective vagueness as Proudhon did to an arid social imperative, defining a work of art as 'a fragment of creation seen through a temperament'. Courbet's art, he declares, 'is a negation of society, an affirmation of the individual, free from all rules and social demands'. Thus Zola was close to the concrete aspect of Courbet's art, its joy in life; Proudhon was raising the question of the dialectic of society and artist, which underlay the equation of socialism and realism. The ungrasped flaw, or the unclosed gap, in the dialectic meant that in fact Courbet continually swung towards the Zola–esque definition of independence, while his fierce reaction against all ruling values drove him back towards the issue of social and political allegiances.[15]

However, we must give Proudhon the credit for the first prolonged analysis of the relation of artist and society, and of the problems of art in a period when the struggle for socialism had actively emerged. He thus started off a debate that is far from being yet closed. In formulations such as: 'What is the mind, if it is not nature conscious of itself?' he opened the way to a discussion of the formative principle in art and nature alike, which, thoroughly pursued, could have broken through his own narrow premises.

In September we find the business of the Andlers still wretchedly dragging on. Andler writes to say that he has called several times but been unable to find Courbet in. 'I hope that before you leave, you'll kindly favour me with a welcome visit, and that you'll meet me either at lunch or at dinner.' Courbet seems to have totally ignored his letters.[16]

Early in September he had gone to Trouville, where he stayed three months and painted thirty-five to forty works. He did many seascapes, entering yet more deeply into the nature of sea and sky; he also painted fashionable women such as Mlle Aubé, the Hungarian princess Károly, the Duchess Colonna di Castiglione (Adèle d'Affry, a sculptress, who used the signature Marcello). On 16 September he wrote to Cuénot to say that he was in 'a ravishing place. The Casino has offered me a superb apartment over the sea and I paint portraits of the prettiest women of Trouville, at 1,500 francs each.' He adds, 'The folk of Besançon are free to say what they like; they're idiots.' Towards 1825 sea-bathing had become a vogue, and now, under the Empire, the Norman coast with sites like Deauville and Trouville was filled in the season with all sorts of celebrities, elegants, and eccentrics. Boudin and the young Monet grew up in this world and left us paintings of the beaches brightened with crinolined ladies.[17] This year Courbet was attracted by a young woman who had become something of a legend in her odd canoe; she was said to have crossed the estuary of the Seine and reached le Havre – an unlikely feat. On 17 November Courbet wrote: 'I've begun at Trouville a new picture with a woman who goes to sea in a boat called a podoscarf [*sic*]. It's two narrow long boxes bound together.' He called her a 'modern Amphitrite'. The picture has the sophisticated-primitive quality of Le Douanier Rousseau, with a technical approach that suggests later artists like Derain. (He knew and liked the plebeian-primitive type of art in the work of Pouchon.) The paint is put on thickly with the knife, in a bright clear tone: greyblue-green sea, white boat with blue lines, the girl in dark blue with her browned skin and red flying chestnut-hair. The girl, whose movement is subtly linked with that of the birds, has her arms out-thrust in the gesture we have discussed as of special significance for Courbet. (The painting seems to have soon become known; for both Thoré and Castagnary mentioned it in their Salon-critiques, though it was not exhibited.) He is said to have posed the girl, in the Seillier house, seated in her podoscaphe and holding the paddles; he worked with great sweeps of the knife, drinking from big cider-pots at his side and remarking from time to time, 'Would you like to drink, madame? It's very good.'[18]

A letter of 8 September to his Paris concierge gives a picture of his wider activities; his compulsive self-praise is such that he writes to a concierge in the same tone as he would report back to his family:

I'm obliged to stay on here for some time. I've an enormous amount of work to do. I've already painted two portraits and started a large picture. I've done two landscapes and will do more. By chance I painted the portrait of an Hungarian princess; it was so successful that now I have so many visitors I can't work. All the other ladies want me to do their portraits. I'll do one or two or three to satisfy the more insistent ones. So you must send me some clothes; I think that under the piano there's a box in which you can pack my black tailcoat, my trousers with small checks, my lilac-tinted waistcoat, my overcoat of Orléans [light wool and cotton], and as many shirts, socks, and handkerchiefs as possible. I'll be much obliged if you'll send these by express tomorrow. I think you need only deliver them to the omnibus in the Place Saint-André-des-Arts [a few yards from the studio]. Greetings to everyone. I expect to stay here three more weeks, the sea is delightful.[19]

He found it hard to go. On 17 November he told his parents, 'My fame has doubled and I've grown acquainted with everyone who might be of use to me. I've received more than two thousand ladies in my studio, all of whom want me to do their portraits after seeing those of Princess Károly and Mlle Aubé. Besides the portraits of women, I've done two of men and many sea-landscapes. In a word I've done 35 canvases: which has astounded everyone. I've bathed 80 times in the sea. Only six days ago we bathed with the painter Whistler who's here;

he's an Englishman who's my pupil.' The American Whistler had arrived in Paris just in time to see the one-man show of 1855; in the following decade he several times met Courbet and was certainly much influenced by him – though a couple of years later he denied the value of the contacts:

Courbet and his influence were disgusting. The regret and rage and even hatred I feel for that now would perhaps astonish you, but here is the explanation. It isn't poor Courbet who's loathsome to me, or his works either. I admit, as always, their qualities. Nor am I complaining of the influence of his painting on mine. It has had none, and none will be found in my canvases. It couldn't be otherwise; for I'm very personal and I was rich in qualities he had not and which were adequate for me. But that was not why all that was extremely harmful to me. It is because that damned Realism made an immense appeal to my painter's vanity, and, disregarding all traditions, cried aloud to me with the assurance of ignorance: 'Long live Nature!' Nature, my dear fellow, that cry was a great misfortune for me.[20]

Whistler had with him his Irish model, the girl with copper-coloured hair, Joanna Heffernan (later Mrs Abbott). She had been his mistress for some five years, so that Courbet had doubtless met her in Paris: for example, in 1861–2, when Whistler was painting her as the *White Girl*. Now she sat for Courbet, regarding herself intently in a mirror with her fine hair displayed. Whistler used the figure of Courbet in one of his seascapes. The latter also did a charming picture of three young English girls. The story is told that they had come with a nurse across the Channel to be painted by Alfred Stevens; Courbet happened to visit the studio while they were there, and was so struck that he asked permission to paint them as well.[21]

From Champfleury we hear of another of Courbet's illusory loves, which came to a head at Trouville. Courbet and a friend were going once to Auteuil in a diligence, on the top of which was a basket of grapes addressed to the Princess K—off, a Russian who had been prominent at the theatre and elsewhere. The friend slipped into the basket a pencilled note: 'Madame, I love you more than life and I cannot live without you: Courbet, master-painter, 32 rue Hautefeuille.' Next day Courbet was woken by loud knocks on the door. A man with a long pointed moustache and a somewhat Cossack nose entered and declared himself to be Prince K—off. Courbet thought he had come to commission his wife's portrait. The Prince accused him of sending a note to his wife; but Courbet denied the writing was his, and at last got rid of the Prince. On reflection he decided that the Prince was the victim of some stragatem of his wife and that the Princess perhaps wanted to meet him, Courbet. But nothing more happened, till he was at Trouville. There one day he received a scented note from the Princess. 'He spent half an hour getting inside his black trousers, which had become clingingly tight, the master-painter having forgotten that in three years he had grown considerably fatter.' He called on the Princess, whose husband had died; she had sold all her property in Russia and now had a large fortune to offer him. She believed that he had truly written the note. 'When the curtains were drawn, Courbet recognised that if the fortune was heavy, the hand was thin. . . . She was a diaphanous princess, with the colour of wax that has stayed twenty years in a shop-window.' She was fifty years old. He fled. (Champfleury may have heard this tale from Courbet himself or from someone else to whom it had been told; but he sets it out in the style of his Josquin stories.)

By 3 January 1866 Courbet was back in Paris, writing of his 'immense reputation' won at Trouville. 'Now I'm enjoying an incredible success in Paris; in the end I'll be without a rival; with determination one can achieve anything. The Comte de Choiseul and his sister the Marquise de Montalembert have just left my studio; they bought some seascapes. Father Hyacinthe has mentioned me in his lectures at Notre-Dame'.[22] Charles Loyson, known as Father Hyacinthe, was a Carmelite friar seeking to harmonise Catholic dogma with modern science; his sermons were very popular, and in 1870 his opposition to papal infallibility earned him excommunication.[23]

About this time Courbet paid a visit perhaps in connection with Zélie's or Juliette's desire to enter her sisterhood to Mlle Antoinette Chapuis, a childhood friend,

now Sister Sainte-Cathérine at the convent Saint-Dominique, avenue de Neuilly, in Paris; it's the third convent she has founded, of this type, under the direction of M. Lacordaire; she is the convent's prioress. I went to see her today, before writing to you. She's as big and fat as I. She appears content with her position. She was pleased to see me and recalls you all with rapture telling me that we're the most distinguished family she's seen in her life. I couldn't embrace her, as she may not embrace men. I thought her position wasn't natural. She told me of the marriages that one wanted to make her accept, and her scant aptitude for that *thing*. She teaches [tells about, *enseigne*] my painting to her pupils and finds that I'm the most celebrated man of this time etc., etc., and asks me to send on to you the warmest of good wishes, and above all to recall her to your memory.[24]

Early in 1866 came the episode of drawing Proudhon on his deathbed for Vallès; and in January he took up his broken correspondence with Bruyas. He asked why he hadn't heard from him, since he had sent Proudhon's book and a photo of the painting of him. 'I might well believe you dead. Fortunately there are travellers who tell me you're living in an Eldorado you've built for youself. Come and tell me you're in love: which would excuse your silence.' Bruyas noted in the letter's margin: 'Received neither letters nor books from this good friend at that time.' One feels a touch of mild sarcasm in the wording. Courbet went on, 'You'd be amazed to know how much painting I've done since our last meeting. I think I've already produced a thousand pictures, if not more, and yet because of ill-will, ignorance, and absurd bureaucracy, I'm still in the same position you found me in. I'd like so much to see you again; I wish I had the time and opportunity to return to Montpellier.' He reminds Bruyas of an offer to exchange a work by Troyon for one of his own landscapes, and takes him up on it; and, as one of the executors of the Proudhon family, he asks for a donation. 'Forgive my presumption, but one can ask such things only from kind-hearted persons.' The amiable Bruyas promptly sent 500 francs.[25]

Later in January Courbet thanked him for the money and said he was sending 'a superb landscape representing profound solitude in the depths of the valleys of my native region. It's certainly the best I have, and perhaps the best I've ever painted.' He adds, 'Now you'll have all my best works.' The picture was *Solitude, Banks of the Loue*, probably started on the spot in 1864–5 and finished in Paris. He was busy with works for the Salon, due in a month and a half. 'I'll show a landscape rather like yours, but with roedeer in it; also a female nude.'[26] In March Ideville visited his studio. 'Without interrupting his work and hardly taking the time to fill up his pipe, the Master-Painter told us of his coming show. "If *they* aren't satisfied this year, *they* will be difficult," he said in his rumbling, bantering voice, with that *franc-comtois* accent he liked to exaggerate. "*They*'ll have two *proper* pictures such as they like, a landscape and an academic study [*une académie*]." ' He showed Ideville the *Covert of Roedeer at the Stream of Plaisir-Fontaine.* Ideville expressed his enthusiasm, and made a typical reactionary comment, 'No one would see a humanitarian manifestation there.' Courbet replied, 'At least *they* won't see a Secret Society of Roedeer gathered in the woods to proclaim the Republic.' Ideville adds, 'That famous *they*, pronounced with so much scorn, signified in his mouth: the Members of the Institute, the Ingrists, the Prix-de-Rome Winners, the Jury, the Government, the Administration, the Beaux-Arts, the Emperor and the Empress, in short all the Bourgeois, that is, who were not Courbet and his court.'[27]

Corot, Français and Daubigny were on the jury, which accepted Courbet's works. The *Covert* so stirred them that at each interval they went to study it afresh. 'I'm happy to have been born in the century where this work appeared,' said Corot with his unjealous character. One of them suggested that they should go and drink some beer with Courbet. They found him and began drinking in a café, growing ever more excited, with toast after toast. Daubigny proposed a toast that was to be the last. 'Bravo,' cried Corot, 'yet another *bock* to the health of Courbet, great as the old masters!' But Français, less volatile, reflected and said, 'Yes, a final health to Courbet despite his faults.' The others were stupefied. Daubigny remained silent but annoyed. Corot, however, leaped up. 'What do you call his faults?' he asked fiercely. 'All right, I, I drink to Courbet because of his faults!' Français had difficulty in calming him down. (Corot in fact had shown a deep insight into Courbet.)[28]

In the *Covert* Courbet had indeed reached the full maturity of his woodland works, one in which his deep sympathy with the wild creatures is richly expressed. On the left an antlered buck munches the tender leaves of a vine that sprouts from the base of a big tree; a doe lies close by at the edge of a shallow mountain-stream. A second buck stands in the water and a doe drinks. The clear-light-bright landscape shows Courbet's mastery of glancing light on leaves and complex transparent shadows. The landscape is an open-air work; the animals were added later in Paris, with carcases as models. The canvas was that which had been used for *Hippocrene*, mended and re-used.[29] The other picture sent in was the *Woman with Parrot*: a fine nude sprawls with loose reddish hair on a fourposter-bed (as in *Venus-Psyche*), and plays with a parrot perched on her raised left hand. The pattern of the arms is the familiar out-thrust gesture in a rounder more lax form.[30] Castagnary's MS has the following explanation: the woman 'is the mystery of the Virgin's conception by the Devil, where in place of the Spirit in Doveform, it is Beastliness [*Bêtise*] that descends in Parrot form. It's for this idiot of the family of parrots [*grimpeurs*], strong of beak and rich in plumage, that the infatuated girl has undone her opulent hair, delivered up all her charms, reserved her smile and caresses.'[31] Certainly here as in *Venus-Psyche* Courbet is consciously entering the Baudelairean world of *femmes damnées*; and, judged by his Proudhonian side, the girl has handed herself over to the forces of evil in her idle sensuality. But, as we have seen, the side of him that is sympathetic is revelling in her softness and abandonment; the bird is the symbol of sheer sensuality. Girl and Bird are only a variant of Venus and Psyche, a Lesbian image or an onanistic one; they are Lydie and Céline afresh. We see in swooning form what appears in the *Dame en Podoscaphe* in braced athletic form.

We may consider afresh the attraction for Courbet of the Lesbian image. Quite apart from any relation to the love-life of the courtesans of the day (for which see *Nana*), he felt a strong personal fascination. We saw how in his relations with Céline he found his greatest excitement in projecting himself into Lydie his proxy-wooer; and it is notable that in this rebellious painter, apart from the early *Lovers in the Country*, the only time he treated directly the theme of love is in the *Studio*, where a pair of lovers are lost in the background. He did not even once paint a husband and wife together, though, as with the Joliclers, he might do them separately. (The sole exception is the nameless pair in the foreground of the *Studio*.) We must find the reason in the intense jealousy we have noted as an essential aspect of his character; he could not bring himself to show another man in an emotional relation to a woman who interested him. When he approached the theme of the embrace, he had to project himself into a woman, as in the Céline-Lydie letter. He could imagine the embrace of two women without feeling himself affronted or displaced; but he turned away from the image of any other man possessing a woman. It is significant that his one picture of lovers is of himself and Virginie in the period before his sufferings made him renounce 'romantic love'. The lost early work of *Lot* showed a seduction-scene (of a father by his daughters); but this too belonged to the phase before his renunciation. Thus the Lesbian image alone allowed him to let loose his strongest sensuous feelings towards woman. For the rest the naked women he painted were drawn apart from the world of men, asleep in bed, or absorbed into woodland-shadows, into the flow of water. (The enigmatic gesture in the *Baigneuses*, which by itself one would shrink from giving too precise a definition, now appears as his first slight step towards the Lesbian theme.)

In connection with all this bird-imagery we must not forget the continual use of birds in the political cartoons and caricatures of the Empire. Napoleon and Bismarck appear as fighting cocks (1867); Napoleon is a melancholy eagle beside the Comtesse de Théba (1853); Prussia and Austria are shown as true eagles, France as a rooster with an eagle's beak stuck on (1853); in *La Belle Alliance* of 1855 the Empress feeds the British Lion, while Victoria feeds the French Eagle; in 1848 Napoleon as Prince-President regards a large eagle squatting on the head of a bust of France; later he appears as an eagle with claws in a Strasbourg sausage. The erotic element appears in a drawing of the imperial eagle straddling the legs of a recumbent woman who lifts up her right arm, her hair outspread; she is ravished France (1851–2). The *lionne* miming the part of Leda, with the bird alighting on her fingers, is in a sense France corrupted and raped by the Empire, its banking and industrial developments.[32] Courbet no doubt was not thinking of such caricatures, which he must often have seen; but in view of Castagnary's definition we must take them into account. He at one time intended to paint a Prometheus devoured, not by a vulture, but by an eagle: this would have been an heroic version of the caricatural theme.

Thoré has a story that Courbet made a sketch of the sleeping girl in *Venus and Psyche*. Chatting before the picture, a friend remarked, 'Ah, if only one woke her up, if she stretched out her legs and raised her arm in the air, with a flower, a bird, what you will, what a charming work it would be.' So Courbet painted the girl with the bird on her raised arm. The story may not be true; but even if it is, Courbet was moved by it because of the peculiar force of the girl–bird image for him.[33]

There were some objectors, but on the whole Courbet had now at last swung the critics and public over to his side. Charles Blanc asked what the fuss was about; the *Covert* was a study without depth, space, perspective, poetry, and the *Woman* was a hollow dummy coifed with serpents and lacking respect for the laws of anatomy; Lagrange said that realism was only a system of the palette, which, instead of imposing impossible subjects, drew on academic or picturesque tradition, so that the only innovation lay in the interpretation; de Saint-Victor found Courbet's success exorbitant, showing how the public came round, if one braved and mystified them long enough, even though one had a limited and very unequal talent.[34] But du Camp, while insisting still that Courbet was only 'a very skilful craftsman', admitted that the *Covert* was 'a remarkable canvas only needing a better grasp of spatial perspective to make it an excellent picture'. And in general there was praise.[35] Castagnary was able to let himself go unreservedly on the *Covert*; he made some criticisms of the drawing of the nude, yet preferred it, as he 'could never admit that a landscape, even a perfect one, might rank above a human figure, even though imperfect'. He regretted that Courbet had not been able to show a big figure-composition like the *Conscript's Departure* or the *Wake of the Dead Woman*. He stressed that the pictures were of a real site, a real woman, with nothing abstract or generalised; and excused himself from mentioning the young painters following Courbet, such as Millet, Bonvin, Vollon, Ribot, Duran, Legros, Fantin, Monet, Manet.[36]

Thoré noted the big shift in public opinion; yet Courbet had not changed.

He has always had this profound and poetic feeling for nature, this expressive execution, this opulent palette, this free touch, which seems to lift the tone and form off objects to transpose it on to canvas. It's necessary to see him paint; he doesn't daub like professional brushers; he doesn't ponder lines while closing his eyes; he looks at nature and tranquilly takes with his brush, sometimes with his palette-knife, a solid bit of paint agreeing with the tone he noted in nature; and he puts down this colour exactly according to the model's form. Procedure of true painters who do not isolate being by contours, in the way of pretended academic draughtsmen, but who decide the outlines [galbes] and model the inner reliefs by the precise relations of the tonality. . . .

Courbet has already painted perhaps a thousand pictures, and I don't think he has ever committed a heresy against his idea, which is to express living nature, *nature naturante*: what he can sieze *de visu*.[37]

At last a critic had seen that Courbet's realism was an attempt to grasp the formative principle at work in all nature, not to reflect things.

Courbet was jubilant. '*They* are slain at last,' he wrote to Cuénot on 6 April. 'All the
painters, all painting, are topsyturvy. The Comte de Nieuwerkerke sent me word I've
produced two masterpieces and he's delighted. All the jurors said the same thing without a
word of dissent. I'm unquestionably the great success of the exhibition. There's talk of a
medal of honour, of the Cross of the Legion of Honour.' We see that he was still ready to
accept a decoration. 'The landscapists are knocked flat. Cabanel has made some compliments
about the woman, as has Pils, also Baudry.' How could he respect compliments from
artists he did not respect? 'I told you some time ago that I'd smack them full in the face
with my fist; they've felt the blow; they're tricked.' The Comte, to prove that all the past
trouble has come from artists, not from the administration, has shown him a drawerful of
more than 300 attacking letters, 'which leave nothing to say'. We learn also that he has been
ill.

In an excited letter to his parents about this time he says, 'I was decorated for a dozen
days before the distribution of awards, then two days before, the Emperor, advised by
someone or other, or by himself, I don't know, scratched my name from the list, and I'm
glad of it, I was in a false position.' He couldn't have worn the decoration with dignity; it
was against his convictions; it'd have done him more harm than good. But people who don't
know his opinion are scandalised, so there's a devil's uproar in Paris, 'so it succeeds admirably
for me'. The award of the second medal is 'utter buffoonery': 'I who have been proclaimed
by all the world without exception the King of the Salon this year.' He is sure his picture
will be bought for the Luxembourg; all the youth of art are on his side. 'I am going to send
you the stereoscope.'[38]

Thoré said the public had changed, not Courbet: how far was that true? Certainly the
public had changed, partly through the continual impact of his work, partly through the
growth of anti-imperial feelings. But while indeed Courbet was still the realist he had long
claimed to be, the change in subject-matter had helped him to this acceptance. A woodland
scene with roedeer, a charming nude playing with a bird on a bed: there was nothing
obviously challenging about such themes. As we have seen, a manifold set of causes had
brought Courbet to these subjects; above all, the way in which he had been driven back
on himself and in the process had lost his earlier plebeian massiveness. He was right not to
attempt to keep on repeating the *Curés*; the *Conscript's Departure* might have been piously
anti-military, but if the forms had lost the weight of those in the works from the *Burial* to
the *Studio*, he would not have been furthering his realist cause; he would have been
weakening it by adulterating it with academic anecdotism and sentimentality.

Millet had not been pleased by Castagnary's reference to him as a disciple of Courbet.
In the 1866 Salon he had only the *End of Gréville Village*; his sister had died and his wife
was ill; he at once sent to his friend Alfred Sensier a draft-reply. In this he pointed out how
the dates contradicted Castagnary; in 1848 he had shown a *Winnower* (male) and had

painted *Haymakers at rest*; the 1849 Salon had his *Shepherdess*; in 1850 beside the *Stone-breakers* and the *Burial* he had shown *Sower* and *Binders*. Here were well-developed works that revealed clearly the course taken by the artist.

Both men have made peasants, but their conclusions are very different; and you feel it so well yourself that it would be impossible to say of Courbet what you have said of Millet. The latter is more particularly rustic in the profound sense of *rus*, and he is, as you have well remarked, above all moved by the man naively vowed to the great work of the earth in the sense of the terrible Biblical verse: You will eat your bread in the sweat of your brow, etc. And the reason for it is easy to grasp, since he has been reared to see only these things and to play his part in them, and he paints only the results and conclusions of his impressions, which he had indeed the time to receive, since he remained labourer till he was twenty-one.

I have no need to tell you this at length since you understand well what I want to tell you: which is that, when one can, as you can, speak effectively to the public, it is better to exalt the fundamental qualities of people who are worth the trouble, than to amuse oneself with things that would become subtleties and trouble opinion instead of guiding it. That should be left to critics who have nothing better to say. . . .

One more point: Millet has no more the pretension of carrying a flag than he thinks of enrolling himself under any whatever. In the matter of works, and from whatever side they come, he loves only those that want to express something. One can indeed believe that a man who keeps to such a stubbornness in seeking to express always the same basis of ideas, who does so while knowing the enmities that it arouses, since it serves a little to trouble the happy in their repose, who does so though he is poor, one can indeed believe that this man finds in himself what gives that stubbornness. Conclusion: that man cannot be assimilated to anyone nor walk in the train of anyone else.[39]

We do not know if Sensier used this material for a letter to Castagnary. Millet makes a dignified protest; and this together with his comment on the banning of *Venus and Psyche* is all we know of his relations with Courbet. Of Courbet's opinion of Millet we know less.

In a poem on the Brasserie Andler, Eugène Vermersch praised Courbet as a painter of earthly paradise:

> Master Courbet with big eyebrows –
> His eyes in clouds are drowned;
> He dreams of the corner of paradise
> Where his great views are found.
> Jules Vallès and Vermorel
> Exalt the great Robespierre on high,
> That democrat, that rebel,
> To Thiers has now closed the sky.[40]

He was still hoping for a medal or the cross; but what happened was that Nieuwerkerke made a tentative offer to buy the *Woman with Parrot* for the State and the *Covert* for the Empress. Soon a furious argument as to conditions of sale burst out. Courbet claimed that the Comte, director of the Beaux-Arts, visiting his studio before the Salon, had made a definite offer for the *Woman* (11,000 francs) so long as he made no alteration to the work, which was then near completion. Now the Comte insisted that no sum was named, but offered 6,000. Courbet on his part had neglected to mention that the *Covert* was already sold to a stockbroker, Lepel-Cointet.[41] He wrote accusing the Comte of bad faith and received a rather crushing reply dated 2 July:

I've just received your extraordinary letter. . . . As I can permit no one to question my integrity, I'll remind you of the facts that you have strangely misrepresented. If you wish you may consult the person who served us as intermediary. This person, M. Frond, called on me one day to ask if I had any prejudice against you and why the Beaux-Arts administration never bought your works. . . . I replied that I had had few personal meetings with you, that our relations were very courteous, that I admired in your talent the elements I thought worthy of admiration, that generally your pictures were not the kind to be encouraged by the Government, but that I should be happy to take advantage of the first opportunity to put one of your works in the Luxembourg.

'I am very glad to find you so well disposed,' said M. Frond, 'for Courbet is in a very difficult position just now. He must sell one of his pictures, and he is painting one that will probably supply the opportunity you're looking for.'

I went to your studio, selected one of your pictures [*Puits Noir, Shaded Stream*], which I did buy for the Empress for 2000 francs and which did not enter into the controversy.[42]

The Comte then says he promised to buy the *Woman with Parrot* after the Salon if it was completed in the same style as it had been begun in. But there was no question of price.

In writing to me, sir, you have distorted the truth; for you have made two entirely false statements. I never told you I would buy the Battle of Stags; and when I asked the price of the landscape you have shown this year [*Covert*], not for the administration of the Beaux-Arts, but for the Empress, I did not know it had been already sold. Such a subterfuge, sir, would have been foreign to my nature, and moreover, why should I have had recourse to it? Am I in debt, that I should have to pretend to be trying to oblige you? You also say that the papers have announced my promise to pay 10,000 francs for your picture, and that since I did not deny this allegation, I tacitly admitted its truth. Do you think, sir, I have time to read every little journal and . . . and note the errors printed there? Come, sir, admit that you were not quite in control of your faculties when you wrote that letter.

The Comte added that he had asked Frond to inform Courbet that he wished to have no further relations with him of any kind whatever.

Courbet however was taking advantage of the interest roused by his nudes to attract a new buyer, Khalil Bey, called a Turk but possibly an Egyptian – Egypt then being under Turkish rule – who had been Ottoman ambassador in St Petersburg. He was a lavish patron of the arts, holding in his collection some hundred works by Ingres, Delacroix, Rousseau, Meissonier, Decams, Gérôme, Fromentin, Chassériau, Diaz, Corot, Greuze, Vernet, Boucher, as well as some Dutch and Flemish masters. But he also loved gambling and all sorts of colourful entertainments, spectacles, fêtes. Courbet probably met him through Sainte-Beuve. We are told that when Khalil Bey arrived in Paris the tale spread that he was myopic as well as amorous, so that slave-traders had several times sold him superannuated sultanas for his harem.[43]

News of the link between Khalil Bey and Courbet reached Besançon quickly enough for C. Beauquier to incorporate it in a notice which also paid tribute to the *Covert*: 'The famous picture of *Two Naked Women*, rejected last year, has been sold by M. Courbet to a Turkish diplomat. Our painter is making at the moment a pendant to this picture. I don't need to tell you that it is as lacking in decency as the first one. *Dame*! for a Turk!'[44] However, the facts of the situation were that Courbet, asked to make a copy of *Venus and Psyche*, preferred to do a new work. This was *Laziness and Luxury*, also called the *Sleepers*, which openly stressed the Lesbian element. Two naked girls, one blonde, one brunette, lie asleep and still embraced on a rumpled bed. The brushwork was superbly sensuous, convincingly fluent and the composition of enlaced limbs highly effective; the comparison of the breadth of smooth form in the raised buttock and thigh, with the compacted twisted-round breasts and torso, in the brunette, came off splendidly. The blonde girl here was Jo, Whistler's mistress.

Courbet also painted for Khalil Bey a vivid picture of a woman's genitals. Khalil kept it locked in a sort of tabernacle or cabinet, on the outer panel of which was painted the landscape of a château under snow. (We may recall that Millet had done much so-called pornographic work, including illustrations to a work *Charlot s'amuse* in manuscript, published later, 1883.)[45] The first provocative nude painted by Courbet, apart from the *Bathers* and girls by woodland streams, was *Woman with White Stockings*. A naked girl is seated, one stocking and shoe on, the other stocking just being put over the bare foot. The foot is pulled up on to the stockinged knee, and, as the angle of vision is from low down, we look straight in on the genitals. The stockinged leg gives a strong diagonal; but the rest of the body is ingeniously foreshortened and compacted; the raised leg and the left arm swing across the torso in a strong horizontal line, echoed by the shoulder with the head turned to one side. The result is a brilliantly original piece of patterning, with the body a single solid mass, yet with the limbs clearly articulated in a rhythmic structure balanced on the slit of the genitals. This is a masterpiece in its organisation of form, making of the nude a compact unity without parallel. The girl is caught at a moment of balance-unbalance as she leans back and presses forwards. We have again the out-thrust arms, though here one of them is lost between the uplifted leg, which takes its place in completing the upper circle. In the *Winnowers* the arms in their circling swing (completed by the sieve) are linked with the strong loins, with the imagined pelvic area as the basis of the gyrating movement; here, in the closed-open system of the compact in-and-out movement of forms, the centre of the balance-unbalance is again the pelvic area. Looking once more at the *Sleepers* we see that the brunette's legs play the role given to the arms in the other works, and that the gyratory effect is gained by the turn of the torso; the right leg is climbing over while the right arm draws the upper part of the body in the opposite direction; again the point of rest is in the (unseen) pelvic area. For the effect of the pivoted body turning in contrasted directions, we may compare the early *Hammock*, though there the effect is gained by different means.[46] For *Woman with White Stockings* the date is given as 1861. If this is correct, the work opens what for want of a better word we may call the erotic series of nudes. It leads us, via the flowers of the Saintonge and the first *Woman with a Parrot*, to the *Venus and Psyche*.

From another angle, if we look at its structure and make a sketch, keeping the essential lay-out but transforming the human sections into rocks, tree-clumps and the like, we arrive at a typical landscape of the kind that deeply stirred Courbet – the vagina forming the cave-entry, the water-grotto, which recurs in his scenes. This point is worth making because it helps us to see how he created the wonderfully compact pattern of the body here, and how a certain symbolism was present in many of the landscapes: for instance, the one in the easel-painting of the *Studio*. In our picture here, the organic symbolism of the landscapes has reacted on his sense of human structure. No doubt he had a sudden sense of a richly signific-ant pattern as he watched one of his models dressing after he had been painting her naked.

Meanwhile, back to Courbet in August 1866. On the 6th he was still in high hope of gaining the Cross of Honour. 'The 15th August will be amusing. If they don't award it, they'll be disgraced [*perdu*] by the newspapers; if they do award it, I'll have the right to refuse it, putting the whole burden on M. de Nieuwerkerke. In any case I wanted to refuse it as I've already done at Besançon. But this move I must refuse publicly: which would have put three quarters and a half of France on my back; but now, however it turns out, I'm reassured and sheltered through the *canaillerie* of these people.' It seems that only now has the idea of rejecting the decoration come up, as part of his campaign against the Comte. He says that he and Castagnary are compiling a pamphlet, which will be highly scandalous, against him; they'll force him to hand in his resignation. 'We've already done some two score pages, which are masterpieces. It'll delight Paris. One of these letters ends with the remark that I'm in no hurry to enter the Luxembourg; I'll have time later on.'[47]

All these pains of his were without point; no offer came. However, he made use of his new esteem this year to exhibit in several shows, at Bordeaux, Lille, Brussels, Frankfurt, and in Holland. Round this time or later in the year he completed or started several works: the portrait of A. Gautier, the *Lady with the Jewels*, the *Seeress*, a *Baigneuse* (stepping into a stream); he probably thought about or worked at some of the big compositions in which he hoped to regain his lost impetus towards social themes, the *Conscript* of which we have heard, the *Funeral Feast* (the wake in a *franc-comtois* village), *Preparations for the Wedding* (bride being washed in the centre, women making bed on left, others setting table). Some of these works may well have gone far back in their origins; for instance *Preparations* (surviv-ing in a sketch) has been dated 1859 but 1865 is more likely. Here we see the out-thrust arms in several forms – in the girl putting a bowl on the table, the girl arranging fruit, the girl leaning down to the oval bathtub, especially the two girls holding a sheet (where we get a strong rhythmic feeling).[48]

In September he accepted the invitation of the Comte de Choiseuil to spend a month or two at Deauville. On the 27th he wrote from there to Juliette, saying that he hadn't stopped working since August 1865.

After my very unpleasant clash with M. de Nieuwerkerke, whom I reduced to silence, I came to Deauville, where M. de Choiseuil has long been urging me to visit him. I yielded to his entreaties as a change was clearly needed, my mind was so upset that I could no longer think clearly [*voir clair*]. Here I am living in an earthly paradise, alone with this young man who is really charming. He has the genuine grand manner and distinction of the most courtly era in France. . . .

The routine of our life here is very simple but extremely luxurious. There are six servants to wait on us. At night the menservants are dressed like prefects in black suits, white cravats, and pumps. The table is laden with dishes and cutlery of chased silver. In the middle of the table is a basket of flowers, at each corner of the basket a bowl of magnificent fruit. Every wine imaginable.

The walls of the salon and other rooms are hung with silk brocade . . . the colour of pearl grey. There are canopies over the beds, toilettes in white marble, with two pairs of water-vases of English porcelain of a huge capacity, basins for hydrotherapy . . .

– and so on: mantelpieces with flowers reaching to the ceiling, grand piano, low divans everywhere, perfumes burned several times a day by a woman throughout the house. Complicated flower-decorations outside. Every morning, as he leaped from bed, he was brought his dressing-gown and ran to bathe in the sea under his window. For the day, a carriage was always ready harnessed to take him on excursions, for instance to the ruins of Jumièges, 'the finest in France'; a steamboat was close to take him to Yvetot and back in time for bed. The Comte threw the villa open to his guest's friends.

My dear Boudin, at M. de Choiseuil's request I invite you to dinner with your wife tomorrow, Wednesday, at six in the evening. I've already asked M. Monet and his wife, who accepted last night at the Casino. I don't doubt you'll do us the pleasure of accepting. All yours, G. Courbet, Chalet Choiseuil. Bring Monet along on your way and please do come, all four of you. I'll expect you without fail.[49]

Monet was living with Camille, whom he married in 1870. Courbet had met him in Paris, admired his work at the Salons of 1865–6, praised him, and helped him with small loans (gifts); for Monet was very hard up.

He also worked at landscapes, seascapes, portraits, a study of his host's finely-groomed greyhounds. By the end of October he was back at Ornans and painted on hard through the winter. Among his works were yet another woodland *Bather*, *Mounted Horseman finding the Trail*; *Siesta* (two teams of harnessed oxen rest in the shade of some trees, with a hay-wagon at the back, a farm-girl asleep under the trees, and two young farm hands stretched out on the right – Marcel and Olivier Ordinaire, sons of his friend Dr Ordinaire of Maisières); and, largest of all, *Hallali of the Stag* (*Stag at Bay*). The last-named (some 15 by 18 feet) shows the death of the stag surrounded and attacked by yelping hounds; one dog goes for its throat, another bites into its hind leg; a hunter (Jules Cuisinier) raises his whip to stop the hounds spoiling the hide; another (Félix Gaudy) watches on horseback; far off on the left a gored dog lies on the snow.[50]

Soon Courbet was entangled in another dispute over buying and selling. The stock-broker Lepel-Cointet, we saw, had bought the *Covert* (10,000 francs) and offered to pay 16,000 for *Venus and Psyche* if a bit more drapery was added to Venus. Courbet put in the drapery, but Lepel-Cointet wanted to withdraw from the agreement. Perhaps he considered the work still rather strong for hanging in his house. Courbet could not get him to accept delivery, and at last brought an action before the Tribunal de la Seine. His most telling point, stressed by his barrister, Chaudey, was that Lepel-Cointet had tried to sell the work to Khalil Bey. A letter from the latter verified that he had been offered it for 25,000 francs, which would have given the stock-broker a profit of 9,000; but he preferred 'to order from M. Courbet a new picture, which he has painted for me'.[51] Finally on 26 July 1867 the court decided in Courbet's favour.

13 TOWARDS A NEW STRUGGLE 1867-9

The Government announced that in 1867 there would be another Exposition Universelle; and Courbet, undeterred as ever, decided that he would hold a private show as in 1855. The official display was partly in the Champs-Elysées, partly in the Champ-de-Mars on the left bank, with an art-section in each region. Courbet leased a piece of land between the two areas, in the Place de l'Alma. The site was not far from his earlier show, and he called again on Léon Isabey for the building. A gallery was raised, which was made more solid than the previous one, since Courbet hoped to keep it for a yearly counterblast to the Salons. He now was better-off and did not need to keep appealing to Bruyas, to whom he wrote on 18 February from Ornans with a statement that the gallery was to be permanent, to last for the rest of his life. He intended to 'send almost nothing to the Government-shows, by which I've been badly treated'.[1] For the big Exposition he however sent in three pictures: the *Seeress*, a hunting scene of hounds and hare, the old portrait of himself in striped collar (lent by Bruyas).

In March he was resisting efforts by Chaudey to get him to Paris for the lawsuit over *Venus and Psyche*. He was busy on the *Hallali*. 'I tried to finish it for the Champs-Elysées show but can't do it before 10 March. I've taken advantage of the metre of snow fallen in my district to carry out this work, which I've had in mind for a long time.' Thus he had meant it for the Salon, but didn't like to ask de Nieuwerkerke for a prolongation of time 'after the dispute between us last year'. Still, he could put it in his own show 'or in one held by the Belgians if they ask for it'. He was extremely fatigued. 'I work by a reflector till 1.30 every morning', but felt that he couldn't go on, 'especially as my mother is very ill'.[2]

Late in the spring he spent a few days at Maisières, visiting Dr Ordinaire, finishing *Siesta*. 'It'll be as good as the Roedeer [*Covert*]; since I saw you [Castagnary] I've painted at Ornans and Maisières the *Death of the Stag* (*Hallali*).' He had also done six more winter scenes, including *Poachers* (perhaps started a couple of years earlier) and *Village-Poverty*, 'the poor old woman leading her goat and begging from door to door'. He calculated that he could get together 300 works for his own show, 'the flower group, the portraits, the animals, *genre* pictures, hunting scenes, pictures of social conditions, *Burial*, and the sketches'. He insisted he was right in sending 'nothing' to the Government-shows; 'I sent only three pictures to the Champ-de-Mars, all poorly hung and hard to see, though they're not large.' He had demanded the showing of 'my famous landscape', *Puits Noir*, according to the rules: the Empress had it in her collection at Saint-Cloud. He expected his gallery to be done by 5 May and opened by the 15th; and himself meant to leave Ornans on the first.[3]

Courbet had now complete mastery of the snow-scene. Snow-scenes went far back to Breughel and others; and a modern treatment had appeared in T. Rousseau's *Givre*, done at l'Isle-Adam in 1846. But Courbet was the first to attempt and achieve fully the harsh brilliance and luminosity of such a scene. He remarked to Castagnary, 'Look at the shadow in snow, how blue; that is what the fabricators of snow in a room don't know.' He began his definition of snow in the *Stag down in the Water* of the 1857 Salon; but now in a painting like the *Poachers* he carried his method to its conclusion, driving up the tonality, with a minimum of objects depicted, and gaining an effect of luminous immensity, of the vast intense vibrancy of sky and snow-earth, with men and dogs both sharply isolated in their dark tones and yet submerged in the sparkling shimmer of the atmosphere. Here, as nowhere else, Courbet freed his colour and tone from all preconceptions, and with the irradiating play of colour in the shadows cleared the ground for the Impressionists, for the winter-scenes of Monet and Sisley, and for their whole new concept of dynamic colour-interrelations.[4]

Round this period he also painted another covert-picture, that of *Stags in the Dusk*. Here the light-bright scene gives way to one of shadowy quiet. This picture and that of 1866 show his turning from the aggressive hunt to an entire sympathy for the harried creatures; behind them lies his own deep yearning for peace and harmony, the weariness he had been feeling at the endless wrangles and bitterness of the art world which he could not do without. In nature he could validly find the release which the self-divided human situation could not give. In this sense the woodland-scenes of peace and harmony have an earthly-paradise aspect which is derived from his social and political struggles. Without the latter he would not have been able to express such an intense self-identification with the roedeer and their lovely world.[5]

Castagnary records a speech of his which shows his early interest in white. Asked how he learned to paint, he replied:

O, that's quite simple. I wasn't rich and models cost a lot. Besides I'd arrived early at the conviction that all models are good for a man who wants to learn. One day I put a white serviette on my night-table, and on this white serviette a white vase. White on white, all the difficulties of painting. My model thus posed, I tried to render it. I indeed painted it fifty times. At the fiftieth, there it was. And it's not M. Ingres [he added in a mocking tone] who'd be able to do as much.[6]

In late April 1867 he asked Bruyas to lend four or five works. 'The last time I'll bother you. This is true for several reasons: one is that it'll be the definitive show of my works, another is that I'm getting old, very old, we're getting old despite our resilience.' He was only 48; and though he is joking, he also is expressing the weariness that has come over him. 'If this isn't a success, I'll be ruined again. That's no joke at my age.' He mused. 'How much work is needed to do anything good! I didn't ask you for the pictures sooner as I wanted to be sure I could arrange the show, which met obstacles on all sides. The Paris municipal authorities kept me in suspense a month and a half, they wanted a bribe of 100,000 francs.' He hoped to see Bruyas at the show. 'My mind's distracted by work and worries.'[7]

Bruyas sent the *Bathers*, *Spinner*, *Man with the Pipe*, a portrait of himself; and Courbet, as usual, buoying himself up with ever-vaster hopes, now wanted him to build next door a gallery for the whole of his collection of modern art. 'I've had a Cathedral built on the most beautiful site in Europe, by the Pont de l'Alma, with a boundless horizon, on Seine-bank and in the centre of Paris; and I've astounded the entire world. You see money can have other functions than to be deposited with notaries for selfish gain.' We may note his notion of what constituted an investment, which was already getting archaic. He goes on:

We're at the second third of our existence; alas, what do we want to do [make, produce] with our money? Always men. Let's do good. . . . Another thing: all the painting in Europe is on show in Paris at this moment. I shall triumph not only over the moderns but even over the old masters.[8]

He urges Bruyas to bring his whole collection. 'We shall earn a million.' And so on in excited calculations.

The remark about notary-investments reappeared in a letter to André Gill, which was printed in facsimile on the cover of *La Lune*, 9 June: 'My dear M. Gill, I'm accused by everyone of spending too much money on my picture-exhibition. The money I earn should be spent by myself; for to deposit it with a notary would be to admit my inability to spend it more usefully.' Above was a large coloured caricature by Gill showing a very fat Courbet with one foot in the thumb-hole of a large palette, holding a number of brushes and regarding a big full-face self-portrait; at the front is a jug and glass of beer.[9]

The building was begun on 15 April. 'M. Courbet is in process of building a personal Louvre,' commented Silvestre. It was finished by 25 May; and two days later Castagnary put an announcement in *La Liberté* that it would open at 10 a.m. on 29 May, entry a franc during the week, 25 centimes Sunday. It had, said Castagnary, 'the importance of a Museum'. Duret in *Les Peintres français* this year declared, 'You find yourself in the presence of the entire man', but added that there is 'an absence of emotion and imagination that leaves us cold and unmoved'. The catalogue stated that scarcely a quarter of Courbet's work was covered by the 115 odd pictures with which he opened (probably referring to the 300 which he had meant to gather). There were nine groups. The first had 18 old and new, ranging from *Hallali* and *Fighting Stags*, the *Burial* and *Return from the Fair*, *Stonebreakers*, to *Bathers*, *Spinner*, *Demoiselles of the Village* and *of the Seine*, the *Woman with Parrot*. The second had 19 landscapes. Then came 7 snow-scenes; 4 Saintonge flower-pieces; 15 studies and sketches, 3 early drawings, 2 sculptures (*Fisher* and medallion of Mme Buchon). The catalogue said that he would keep changing the pictures from time to time, as there was not room for more.[10] He did later add some 20 works, including the altered *Proudhon*. At some time Juliette and Zélie came up to Paris to deal with the cash.[11]

In the *Revue littéraire de la Franche-Comté* (1 July) Beauquier wrote a long review of the show. He noted that Courbet was in his element in a big picture, and says that he tends to blow all objects up; he has 'an excessive nature that sees everything through magnifying glasses', remaking persons in his own burly image. He thought him entirely Spanish in character. 'Franche-Comté for a long time belonged to the government on the other side of the Pyrenees; my grandmother used still to say, "Old as the Cid." M. Courbet has perhaps

Spanish blood in his veins.' But he wrote well of the *Burial*, now become a legendary work for the younger generation:

It's a strange picture, both grotesque and dramatic, which one cannot forget when once seen. You would say it's a page from Shakespeare. There is the same violent feeling of reality allied to a certain epic grandeur. The group of mourning women is wonderful. The men in broad hats who bear the bier have a powerful carriage, full of pride. And the gravedigger on his knees – he comes right out of the frame. As for the beadles clad in red like criminal judges, with noses coloured in the same purple, they represent the gay note equally habitual for Shakespeare in the midst of such a scene of grief.[12]

It is of interest that the gravedigger strikes him so strongly as the figure embodying the energy of life.

But despite the efforts of Thoré and Castagnary the public did not flock in. Most notices were antagonistic or lukewarm; much less attention was paid to the show than to that of 1855. P. Mantz declared he was often the only person there.[13] On 13 July Courbet sent a worried note to Castagnary, 'Tomorrow Monday at 1.30 the students are coming in a body.' He wanted Castagnary to be there. 'I'm afraid their demonstrations might make me lose my lawsuit that's practically won [the Lepel-Cointet case]. They demand to see the *Curés*.' What he feared is not clear; anyhow nothing seems to have happened.[14] But his finances were helped by the sale of *Stonebreakers* for 16,000 francs, and *Village-Poverty* for 4,000. On 16 August he told Castagnary, 'Please see what effect it's having all along the line. It's imperative all papers should announce this event, which is of the utmost important at this time.'[15]

Late in August he visited a friend Fourquet, a Paris chemist on holiday, at the small seaside resort of Saint-Aubin-sur-Mer, some twenty miles west of Trouville. There he painted two views of the beach and a *Waterspout*; and bathed. But he was too excited to rest, and he complained of the lack of trees. After ten days he hurried back to Paris. On 28 September the de Goncourts visited the show and found there 'nothing, nothing, nothing'. Scarcely two sea-skies. 'Apart from that, with this master of Realism, nothing of the study of nature. The body of the *Woman with Parrot* is as far from the truth, from the naked, as any *académie* of the eighteenth century you like. Then the ugly, always the ugly, and the bourgeois ugly, the ugly without its great character, without the beauty of the ugly.' On 22 September Champfleury told Buchon: 'I encountered Courbet at the place of the Hungarian musicians, bohemians with a devil in their body.'[16]

Baudry of Rochemont had been in Paris in 1866 to see about the publication of a work *Les Bras Mercenaires*, which dealt with the difficulty of large landholders in getting workers for their fields on account of the growth of small peasant properties. He came again in the spring of 1867 to see the Exposition and to Courbet's show. At the same time he discussed with the publisher E. Dentu the publication of a new work, *Le Camp des Bourgeois*. Here he was continuing the theme of the first book, drawing an extended picture of the troubles overwhelming a section of the bourgeois, especially the rural landowners without a large fortune. Peasants who hadn't become small landowners were being drawn off to work on railways and new roads, to enter various factories; the smaller bourgeois could get no workers for their lands and were slowly being crushed; those who were able to sell at a good price were likely to go and live in hotels. This thesis was set out with much well-observed details of local character and changing customs.

Baudry wanted Courbet to illustrate the book; perhaps he felt such admiration for the master that he wanted a collaboration, perhaps he hoped to use the latter's notoriety to draw attention to the work. In any event he had not realised Courbet's incapacity for such a job. One day in the autumn he called, with Dentu, at the studio. Dentu pressed Courbet, saying that he had been waiting several months for the illustrations and the text was ready for printing. Courbet replied:

'You find it easy to talk like that, but the thing isn't so easy to do as you imagine. First, I've started nothing and then I don't see what sort of drawings you want me to do, all the more since I've never done pencil drawings. Obviously I draw a bit, since I'm a painter, but painting doesn't oblige me to use any one procedure nor to use a pencil rather than a simple bit of chalk. Besides I've never read the *Camp of the Bourgeois*.'

'Impossible,' said Dentu.

'I see that that astonishes you, but the truth is that what solely interests me in the book is the discussion the author has on art. My personal views are indeed set out there on the opportunity of turning railway waiting-rooms into veritable exhibition halls. As for the illustrations I'm asked to do, I'm ready to carry them out as long as you supply the means. If then you want drawings of bourgeois, you must supply types of bourgeois such as you want me to reproduce. That's all I can do for you.'

So, next day Baudry called on Carjat who put at his disposal a drawerful of photo-proofs; Baudry chose suitable characters and took them to Courbet. He arrived on an icy November afternoon, with the sky dark, though the time was not yet four. Courbet was about to leave, but Baudry held him, quickly lighted the stove and the lamp, set paper and pencil on small table, and looked at Courbet. The latter made no move. So Baudry opened his manuscript and began to read aloud the chapter where Courbet sets out his ideas. When Baudry looked up, he saw the artist at work, with the photos spread out before him. Next day Baudry came back, and the procedure was repeated till all the drawings were done.[17]

Here is the passage in which Courbet speaks. Baudry has posed the question: 'Can art survive when *domesticité* has disappeared?' – when bourgeois home-life with its crowds of servants has broken down? The bourgeois, steadily impoverished, will cease collecting pictures and hanging them on their walls. The only patrons will be millionaires, all the men with millions of dubious origin, the profiteers, parvenus, swindlers, speculators, of the Empire; and even supposing their fortunes to be durable, they are comparatively few and will soon fill up their galleries. There remain the Museums. From this point Baudry goes on to the question of popular education, and sets out the discussion between the spokesmen of academicism and finance, and Courbet, apostle of realist and democratic art. The president asks sarcastically who goes to Museums, since the people, in whose honour they're built, don't have time to go. Durand says that he goes. 'If they didn't exist, they'd have to be invented; besides what would you replace them with?' Courbet breaks in:

By the railway stations (general confusion), yes, sirs, by the stations that are already Churches of Progress and will become Temples of Art. Enter the waiting-halls and look at those admirable vast sites, airy and full of light: you'll agree that we only need to hang pictures there to make, without any expense, the most matchless of museums, the only ones where Art can really live. For where the crowd betakes itself, there is life.

And this idea of appropriation hasn't come to me yesterday; for fifteen years I've been setting it out to those who see great painting threatened in its existence by the growing smallness of apartments. I must tell you, sirs, my programme was enthusiastically welcomed by the highest barons of finance and of the Institute. Soon, I used to say to the late Hittorff, your railways will furrow France; give the artist the mission of depicting the story of our departments. Let one paint the forests, another the plains, others the rivers and sea-shores. This one must ascend the high summits under the dazzling rays of the sun; this other, descend into the dark galleries of coal-mines. He'll tell you of the life of the black toiler. You'll look on the red fire-burst of the furnaces. There'll be no need to impose on them the eternal reproduction of Greek helms and Roman togas. Instead of discouraging the painters with faith in the national genius, stir them to transfer on to canvas the types, the manners, the character, the costumes and the industry of the breed of men whose country stretches from the Alps to the Ocean, from the Channel to the Pyrenees – to teach the people true history while showing them true painting.

Durand: What do you mean by that?

Courbet: I mean by true painting that which escapes from the yoke of all fictions whatever. To paint truly, the artist must have his eye open on the present: that is, he must see by his eyes and not by the back of his neck. He must drop the allegorical fiction which is nothing. The *bonhomme* Mercury, seated on a bale of coffee, cannot represent the trade in colonial wares. (Order! Order! Frightful tumult.)[18]

Durand rushes to the tribune and protests. The waiting-rooms are not bare; they are filled with magnificent advertisements. 'Dagobert indicates to St Louis the best manufacture of breeches. Dugesclin points out to Jean Bart the shop where the best overcoats are made.' Along these lines he parodies Courbet's proposals. Courbet, unmoved, sums up: 'For artists, the salons; for the puffers [*puffistes*] the pavement and the platform.'

Jacques Hittorff, to whom he referred, had died on 25 March 1867; he was an important imperial architect who embellished the Place de la Concorde and the Champs-Elysées, and who built the church of Saint-Vincent de Paul, the Mairie of the Panthéon and the Nord railway-station. Baudry's account of Courbet's advocacy of public art is of interest in showing that he stuck strongly to the idea and talked about it wherever he went.

Few as the admission-fees were, Courbet did not get them all. Radou, who had been a non-commissioned officer in the Zouaves, had been put in charge of the turnstile. He found how to let two visitors through while the mechanism registered only one; he also let visitors in through a back door and pocketed the fees. He was brought before a jury on an embezzlement-charge.

The leader of the realist school appeared as witness. He testified with grave goodhumour. He estimated the amount of Radou's larceny as not less than three or four thousand francs; still he was the first to appeal to the jury for mercy towards this Zouave who had acted bravely on the battle-field, but whom the road to the tavern diverted from the path of duty. The jury, less lenient than M. Courbet, sentenced Michel Radou to two years of jail.[19]

One wonders why he prosecuted; and knowing his sanguine ideas, we may be sure that his estimate of the embezzled fees was a wild guess. Beauquier had the same doubts:

5,000 francs! This sum seems to me so exaggerated that I'd think it an advertisement if the pro-verbial simplicity of Courbet did not shelter him from any suspicion of that sort of gross *trick*. But when did these 5,000 visitors come? I have always found his show in competition with the solitudes of Arabia Petraea. Doubtless they all came together, all in one batch, a band of Orpheonists from the Sandwich Isles. The thief has been arrested. He is in prison. He has alleged in excuse that he saw so often his patron *battre la caisse* [beat the big drum: *caisse*, cashbox] that he took pity on it and rescued it, in the fashion of Bilboquet. (1 December)[20]

Buchon was annoyed at the flippant tone, though Courbet's exaggeration, at the expense of the Zouave, deserved to be attacked. He wrote from Salins on 11 December:

M. Beauquier calls Courbet a *batteur de caisse*. Is he quite sure that the story of the 5,000 stolen francs was the work of Courbet? I was in Paris before and after All Souls Day. According to our conversations with old comrades, I understood that Courbet estimated that the three successive concierges whom he had put at the door of his show must have stolen from him at least 5,000 francs. I had proof that the two francs paid by myself and wife the day we went had vanished. Such an enterprise in the charge of Courbet who is no financier or business-man has always frightened me from the money viewpoint; but to conclude so crudely in public that Courbet thinks only of money, is to give the measure of the complete ignorance one has as to Courbet's character and habits. . . . Courbet, despite all his success and his modest way of life, scarcely holds in liquid capital which is indispensable to save him from being obstructed from day to day in the practice of painting by the need of cash.[21]

He seems to have read too much into Beauquier's joke. Even if there was petty pilfering, Courbet seems to have snatched at the idea of embezzlement to explain away, at least in part, his failure. He had to dismantle his exhibition, but he still hoped to maintain the building for further use.

His volatile spirits quickly revived. On 9 January 1868 he wrote to his sisters. 'Our family is full of news just now. You tell me my sister Zoé is going to marry M. Eugène Reverdy, and that my father and mother are about to share their estate with the children. These are very desirable changes that will contribute to everyone's happiness.' Juliette must now get married. 'Zélie and I will stay single. Her health is too frail for marriage, and I have Art which doesn't mix with Marriage at all.' It seems that Zoé, who had now worn down the resistance of the Reverdys, had informed the family of her coming marriage; and Courbet keeps up the pretence that he has known nothing of her relationship with Eugène. 'My father proposes that I, as eldest of the family, should have the largest share. But that's ridiculous. He hasn't progressed since the Middle Ages; he'd like to establish entailed estates and titles of nobility. If 1793 hadn't already ended such fine ideas, I'd make it my job to end them in the present circumstances. I not only dislike being favoured; I wish on the contrary to get less than my share. Not because I'm in debt to my family. If my education cost more than that of you other children, on the other hand I haven't taken anything from the family purse for more than twenty years: which makes things more or less equal.' He asks only for the assets that the girls didn't want; let them keep the properties earning an immediate profit.

It is hard, however, to see what the fuss was about. Régis had no intention in his strong property-sense of giving anything up; he was too grasping even to give Zoé a dowry or wedding-present. 'Not a *sou*, not a piece of linen,' she later told Champfleury.[22]

Khalil Bey had gone bankrupt; at the sale of his goods on 16 January four of Courbet's works were included and fetched good prices.[23] In February he wrote to Bruyas expressing his gratitude. 'I started off without resources; I'll never forget the clap on the shoulder you gave me. My situation with regard to society is always the same, except that daily I strengthen my manifestation.' He still hoped to set up a permanent exhibition of his work. He was 'in a ridiculous occupation: hunting down thieves. I'm trying to recover pictures stolen from various places. Only yesterday two works, stolen some time ago in London, were sold at auction; they fetched 4,500 francs. It's painful to see the money change hands and not be able to claim it.'[24] He was able to console himself with taking part in several provincial and foreign shows. He had been frequenting a café in the rue Lamartine, where there had met many foreign artists, such as Stevens, Saal, Heilbuth, Knauss, Conrad, Menzel, Meyerheim; and he was now much admired in Germany.[25] His friend C. Chappuis in a letter of 11 February asked him to join a show at Besançon and reproached him for abandoning his homeland, Ornans and the Valley of Gérolstein – 'which has however gained a certain celebrity': an allusion to an electoral pamphlet by Ordinaire, which had caused some stir even in Paris. Courbet sent two works to Besançon, seven to Le Havre, eleven to Ghent, during the year.[26]

In the 1868 Salon he had only two works: *Roebuck on the Alert* and *Beggar's Alms at Ornans*: the latter belonging to his Roadside Series. Some fourteen years earlier he had thought of painting a gypsy and children; now the theme returned in a different form. Under a tree a gypsy sits by a cart suckling a grimy baby; before her is a snarling mongrel. In mid-road a tall thin beggar in rags leans on a crutch and gives a copper to the older child. The theme is the poor supporting the poor. No one liked the work. Even Thoré wrote: 'His friends are surprised that to personify generous poverty, the humanity that valiantly and sturdily survives despite the most extreme indigence, he has deliberately chosen such a horrible and repulsive figure.' J. J. Perraud wrote on 28 March to Claudet: 'All that's human [in the work] is odious. These humans have the air of being in wood, in white walnut that one would have liked to brown with walnut stain. The attitude of this whole world is fantastic. Only, this scene is passed in an atmosphere, a light so extraordinary that the neighbouring pictures are opaque as lacquer.' A caricature had as subtitle, 'The marvellously appropriate tone is composed of Ornans mud skilfully combined with Mouffetard sweepings, the whole relieved by a slight glaze of Macadam.'[27] T. Gautier attacked, saying that earlier realists did not uglify nature; but that is what Courbet does. He 'seems, now, troubled, uncertain, with diminishing popularity, which he seeks to regain with the *Beggar*: it's a muffled pistol-shot. It has no drawing, its colour is livid and chalky; the outlines are gawky, ravelled, smeared. It's pretentiously bad.' Another caricature stated, 'This poor old beggar is deprived of everything, even of the most necessary drawing.'[28]

In returning to his Roadside Series Courbet was certainly trying to pick up afresh his youthful inspiration and regain a direct social force; but what was said of the *Curés* applies here even more strongly. The figures are not successful. The failure does not lie in any question of their 'ugliness' but in their comparative triviality for the burden they bear; they lack the fused individuality and typicality of the people in the earlier big works. They thus tend towards softness, sentimentality, grotesqueness without the great human force that filled the characters of the *Burial*, the *Return from the Fair*, the *Demoiselles of the Seine*. The boy is the best-realised figure, but even he is weak when put by the girl of the *Village-Demoiselles* or the boy looking on in the *Studio*. Cruder paintings like Van Gogh's depiction of the *Potato-Eaters* have the inherent dignity and passionate sympathy which is lacking here; the lack of force therefore tends to reduce the work to an anecdotal level. The Real Allegory which underlay the early works here becomes Proudhonian moralising.[29]

Some feeling of the weakness of the work has driven Courbet here, as also in the *Curés*, to contrast the pitiable humans with the beauty of surrounding nature. Proudhon notes that the deboshery of the *Curés* went on 'in the bosom of a landscape at once charming and grandiose, as if man, in his higher dignity, existed only to soil innocent nature with his indelible corruption'. What validity that point had in the *Curés* is much lessened here, because of the softer, more limited approach. Courbet has fallen back on the contrast because of his inability to typify truly the characters. They are wretched folk; they do not embody Poverty as the stonebreakers embodied Exploitation; the impact is slight, reduced to a mild pathos.[30]

Courbet refused to acknowledge any weakness. He wrote on 12 May to Castagnary:

At last Gauthier [*sic*] is beside himself: which announces definitively the end of romanticism. He explains it himself. It would be cruel to stop a cat from howling when his tail is trodden on. His *feuilleton*, written to order, and official, is illogical throughout. . . . As for drawing, the romantics are expert at it. As for the aesthetic, it's only the romantics who ignore it by nature and on principle; and it's with this weapon that I've killed them. When M. Gauthier says there's no longer any noise around my name, he kids himself; for at the best time of rage there was never written on me so violent an article as this of his. The romanticism and classicism of the administration are dying. The fury is going to reach a paroxysm. It's admirable.[31]

He could, however, crow, for he had just sold *Roebuck on the Alert* for 4,000 francs. After mentioning this and a lady's compliment that the *Beggar* is 'of an absolute delicacy', he returns to Gauthier in his PS: 'Gauthier announcing the death of romanticism, it's amazing. It's the cry of Jeova [*sic*]: To me, my father!'

An artist who had been coming up of recent years, to some extent using the ground cleared by Courbet, was Édouard Manet, whose work at this period was even more based on the Spaniards than Courbet's had ever been. 'What a lot of Spaniards!' he said when entering

64 *Hunted Roe-buck.* 1866. 111 × 85 cm.
Louvre, Paris.

65 *Roe-bucks in Shelter in the Winter.* 1866. 54 × 72 cm.
Musée des Beaux-Arts, Lyon.

66 *The Black Well.*
1865. 94 × 131 cm.
Musée des Beaux-
Arts de Besançon
(see page 216).

68 *The Gour de Conches*. 1864. 74 × 60 cm.
Musée des Beaux-Arts de Besançon (see page 203).

67 *Brook at the Courbon Rocks*. 1862. 38 × 50 cm.
Collection A. Tooth & Sons Ltd., London.

69 *Siesta at Haymaking Time.* 1868.
222 × 272 cm.
Musée du Petit Palais, Paris
(see page 219).

70 *In the Forest.* 1866. 79 × 98 cm.
National Gallery, London
(see page 164).

71 *The Poachers in
the Snow*
(author's title:
*Hallali of the
Stag*). 1867.
63 × 81 cm.
Musée des Beaux-
Arts de Besançon
(see page 220).

72 *Death of a Stag
in the Snow*. 1867.
355 × 505 cm.
Musée des Beaux-
Arts de Besançon
(see page 219).

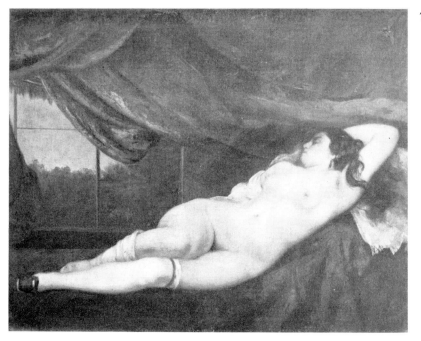

73 *Sleep.* 1866. 135 × 200 cm.
Musée du Petit Palais, Paris
(see page 229).

74 *The Spring* (author's title: *Woman at th
Spring*). 1868. 128 × 97 cm.
Louvre, Paris (see page 187).

75 *The Three Bathers.* 1869.
126 × 96 cm.
Musée de Petit Palais, Paris
(see page 229).

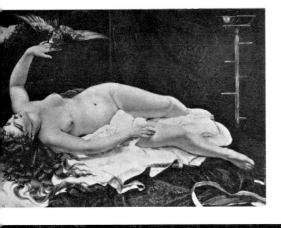

76 *Woman with a Parrot*. 1866. 129 × 195 cm.
Bequest of Mrs H. O. Havemeyer, 1929. The H. O. Havemeyer
Collection. The Metropolitan Museum of Art, New York
(see page 170).

the premises where Manet had put on his own show in 1867, in the Avenue de l'Alma. He remarked of the *clair* in his work, 'I've got to close one eye.' To him also is attributed a comment on Manet painting the Queen of Spades in a card-pack coming out of the bath (a witticism of the sort attributed to many after *Olympia* with its strong flat pattern, 1866). Also: Manet did not invent *le clair* (clear hard tonality rather than highlight, as it can mean in painting), 'but he has given it an enormous strength [*ressort*]. From this viewpoint he has been file-leader. Like me, he wanted the French landscape. He was of his own land; he did not go abroad to seek for *motifs*.' The followers of Courbet, and perhaps Courbet himself, were somewhat suspicious and jealous of him as he struck out on his own; and we know little of the relations between him and Courbet, of whom, however, he made an excellent sketch. In him the large-scale revolt of Courbet, embracing the whole man, begins to be narrowed down, humanly and artistically. In stressing *le clair* in his work Courbet was drawing attention to the way in which he opposed light and shade with as little half-tone as possible. In his way of painting directly from the model and drawing on the everyday life all round him, he was the first painter of importance generally carrying on Courbet's work; and he was at home in the town-scene as Courbet never was. But though he did not lack political ideas (of a republican and democratic kind), he was not concerned to integrate them in his whole art-outlook.[32]

In 1868 Courbet painted several nudes: *Femme à le Vogue*, two versions of a *Sleeping Woman*, the *Three Bathers*; portraits of Dupont and Chaudey, perhaps also of General Cluseret. The latter, a graduate of Saint-Cyr, served in the French army during 1848–55, resigning with a captain's rank; in 1860 he joined Garibaldi as colonel and fought in the Sicilian campaign; then he went to the U.S.A., commanded a body of Federal Troops in the Civil War, ending as a general; in 1866–7 he took part in the Fenian rising in Ireland; returned to France and became a member of the International Working Men's Association (the First International). A leading opponent of the Empire, he was one of those who drew Courbet into direct politics in the late 1860s.[33]

The following account by Zoé may be dated 1867, soon after Cluseret's arrival in France, or early 1868. In either case it shows that she was on fairly close terms with her brother about this time, and it reveals the political attitude she must have been partly hiding from him. She was writing to Champfleury after the Commune, when her attitudes had hardened.

We were at his place when Castagnary brought along Cluseret whom he had known for a long time and who was his friend. He said as he entered Courbet's studio, 'Here is a general who is among my friends and who has just come from the depths of America, drawn by your reputation, and above all by your political worth. He comes to ask you to do his portrait with this shoulder-knot hanging over his chest and this scar on his cheek. As he is an eminent publicist, he purposes to see your pictures and make you known in the world he inhabits.'

Then both of them paid homage to the artist in an exaggerated way. He looked at them sideways, scenting a snare. Whenever Castagnary brought a subject along or wrote an article, the painter knew it was a way of dipping into his purse, proving to him that Courbet would never have been known or had any talent without him. Which evoked the comment from my brother that Castagnary was like a brigand attached to his person and never approached him without the demand: Your money or your life.

The painter did the portrait. During Courbet's arrest, Castagnary forced me to give it to him. While he finished it, Cluseret wrote a filthy article – a sensational article, he said – on the Emperor, on the occasion of Courbet's picture *Beggar's Alms*: which brought him six months in prison and a fine of 3,000 francs, which Castagnary wasn't ashamed of coming to ask my brother for. I was there. He forced him to give it, saying that he'd get as good back, for a personage like his friend knew how to repay those who appreciated him. There's the political life of my brother and the way he availed himself of it.

We see in that account the deeply suspicious eye of Zoé, her continual fear that others were getting out of Courbet the money she couldn't lay hands on, her determination to blame Castagnary and the others for his refusal to build a conventional career. In her view his behaviour was simply imbecile, and so must somehow be blamed on to a naïve inability to understand what he was doing. Cluseret's article appeared in his own *Art*, and it would have been natural for Castagnary to ask Courbet to help in meeting the fine. That he forced her and Reverdy to give up the portrait in 1873 was true; in February Courbet had asked him to get it from the grasping Reverdys and send it to an enameller at Geneva. Zoé inevitably attributed some villainy to Castagnary for carrying out her brother's request.

Among the nudes is *La Source*. The painting in the Louvre seems the same as that shown in Brussels in 1869; but Lemonnier on the same occasion writes of a 'transparent naiad that undulates at the bottom of the picture'. A radiograph shows that in the Louvre-work there has been a second female, somewhat wavy, but in the picture's centre. The title, which seems to have little reference to the picture, may have been given in a challenge to Ingres, recalling how Guichard in 1862, attacking Courbet's definition of art as 'the most complete expression of an existing thing', illustrated his own view from works of Ingres such as *La Source*, which was shown in Martinet's gallery in 1861.[34] Courbet liked this work of his and used to say, 'It's a super-Velasquez.'

Champfleury in June wrote to Buchon about the *Beggar*. 'Courbet has done a humanitarian picture. . . . This show brings him down low. He'll rise up again, we must hope. Unfortunately, he must not hide from himself that the pressure is great today, that there appears a certain number of young folk impatient to make a name for themselves, that some of them possess talent, who ask nothing better than to lay hold on the places due to long labours, and that he must make constant efforts if he is to hold his position.' He seems certainly thinking of Manet.[35]

The Andlers had now lost patience; Courbet clearly had no intention of settling his long-standing bill. On 8 July he wrote to his legal representative Chaudey that he had a number of observations to make about the account, which extended from 1855 to October 1863 and had reached a total of 7,153 francs, 35 centimes. 'From which Andler has deducted, for payments on account, 3,500 francs, which leaves me in debt for 2,553 [*sic*] francs, 35 centimes. I knew I owed Andlers something, but I had no idea it was such a large sum, I'm really justified in questioning his figures.' He admits:

I went to Andlers for a long time; in a way it was my home; I can even claim to have contributed not a little to the establishment's vogue. I allowed everything to be charged . . . without ever verifying anything; and when I paid him something I never thought of asking for a receipt. Today I'm in no position to contest the bill's amount and I don't intend to do so. Let's admit I've paid only 3,500, but am I not justified in demanding information as to my total expenditure? Several good friends have told me that whenever I sat at one of the tables . . . it was known at the cashier's counter as M. Courbet's table and everything ordered there was put on my bill. . . . Very often I admit I had friends lunching or dining with me; but while it's quite fair for me to pay for my guests, I don't see why I should be expected to buy free meals for everybody or be held responsible now for the bills of all unidentified clients in my vicinity. . . . I must insist on the production of his books so that I may examine my account in some detail. I shall be greatly surprised if after the examination I don't reach the conclusion that I don't owe Andler more than 1,500 or 1,800 francs.

This is an example of the worse side of Courbet's nature. We see how he works himself up and grows convinced of the righteousness of his cause. We must remember that for many years he had had his main meal at Andlers and drunk large quantities of beer there; he had many guests and we can be sure that with his careless hospitality he offered drinks to considerable numbers of persons; he used the Andlers to advance money to meet emergencies when he was away from Paris. The sum mentioned as covering 9 years would break down to about 4 francs a day if he went to Andlers for only half of each year. In view of the use he made of the place this does not seem at all excessive. We must recall too that he had been evading the bill from late 1865 at least – probably from shortly after he gave up being a frequenter in 1863. The only conclusion is that he acted with an ungrateful meanness; as soon as he had no more use for the place, he treated the Andlers with contempt.[36]

In the latter part of the year two pamphlets illustrated after his work appeared in Brussels. One, *Les Curés en Goguette* (in merry mood), dealt with clerical gluttony and drunkenness, and had six designs done by an anonymous engraver. *The Return of the Curés* served as frontispiece; and elsewhere we see a curé ringing a bell to call the others to mass, clerics sampling food in the kitchen before dinner, a drunken brawl at table, a maid holding the head of a vomiting curé, two drunken priests riding home in a pig-farmer's cart. The whole thing was cheaply and roughly done.[37]

The other booklet, *The Death of Jeannot*, told of an Hungarian officer Waltzer, called Jeannot, who, blinded in 1814, was sent to a French village where a peasant-woman Jeannette attended to him. Leaving the hospital, he lives with her in a cellar and hawks snuff and rat-poison. Thirty years later, now aged about 80, he lies dying. The curé, using the threat of hell, extorts from Jeannette her life-savings of 1,000 francs. The doctor berates her and sends her to get the money back, but the curé says he's already sent it to a convent for the benefit of the poor. Appealing to the superior, she is thrown out. Peasants pull down the convent-walls till they are stopped by the municipal authorities, who take charge of Jeannot (dying a week later) and of Jeannette for the rest of her life. The drawings show Jeannot as pedlar, and on his deathbed; Jeannot thrown out of the convent, and the peasants attacking.[38]

On 11 August Zoé and Reverdy were married at noon, in the Mairie of the 6th *arrondissement*. The elder Reverdys were present; Zoé's parents assented to the ceremony by *acte authentique*. There were four witnesses, the Marquis of Saint-Denis, two other landowners, and an employee of the Ministry of Finance. Zoé gave her address as 32 rue Hautefeuille (Courbet's studio), but there was no sign of her brother. He may have been at Ghent; but in any event was not likely to attend such a ceremony, even if the Reverdys would have liked it. Zoé and her husband seem now to have taken over the Reverdy house in the rue d'Assas, with the older couple retiring into the country – there is no record of their death in Paris. In January 1869 Eugène and Zoé recognised their two sons before a pair of commissioners.[39]

On 10 September Courbet wrote to Bruyas, 'Tomorrow I go to Le Havre, where I have eight pictures.' On his return he meant to go to Ornans 'and paint some new pictures, heartfelt [*bien sentis*] and socialist'. As things were, 'my head is splitting with worry; my hair is turning white.'[40] There is no need to doubt his suffering. His way of life had undermined his health despite his great strength; he knew that in the line of 'heartfelt and socialist' pictures he had weakened, despite his important gains in other spheres. With his doggedness he kept returning to this problem, yet he could not bring himself to complete some of the big works he had begun: for instance, *Preparations for the Bride*, which, in its unfinished condition, has many fine qualities, incomparably more so than *Beggar's Alms* or *Village-Poverty*. Perhaps he felt that that work lacked the fighting qualities which he wanted. It was this year, as we noted earlier, that the police-spies recorded his intention of painting a work on the peasant revolt of 1851. He was certainly finding a fresh impetus for his political views through men like Cluseret and Vallès; perhaps it was this year he joined the First International. He first appeared in the police-files on 19 January 1868, 'noticed at the cemetery at Passy on the anniversary of J. P. Proudhon's death'. After that he was thoroughly watched and reported on. The files indicate that he was probably by this time a member of the International Working Men's Association, Panthéon section.[41] One part of Courbet would have been delighted to know that he was now considered a serious enough political danger to be so watched and reported on; but he would hardly have been pleased to read the description of him recorded by the spies: 'Gustave Courbet, 48 to 50 years old, big, bulky, bowed, walking with difficulty because of troubles [*douleurs*] in the back, long hair, greying, air of a bantering peasant, badly enough dressed.'

At Le Havre he saw Monet again, and they called on Alexandre Dumas, who, though he had not met them before, received them heartily. The trio spent several days at Etretat. 'When Dumas and Courbet were not talking, they were singing or drinking together.'[42] We may surmise that during these visits to the Normandy coast, Courbet managed to slip away for at least a day's visit to Dieppe.

Early in October Parisian papers falsely reported that Courbet had presented himself as candidate for the chair left vacant by the death in March of F.-E. Picot, a History-painter, one of the forty Immortals of the Académie Française. Now back in Ornans, on the 17th he wrote angrily to Castagnary. He had been annoyed at an article in *Figaro* by P. Arène, which attributed to Castagnary a bad influence on him. 'It's too easy to defend oneself and explain to M. Arène that he was born yesterday.' From the age of fifteen 'I had the independence that I have today; I had the same scorn of rewards of every kind of titles able to replace talent in the public's eyes.' Castagnary, says Arène, had made him lose a decoration and pushed him to political pictures.

That's again admirable. In other terms it means that M. Arène would have been very glad to be decorated. Ah, well, let them decorate him. He must be decorated, all the more since he's of the Midi.

Turn now to the Academy. That's even more side-splitting. This farce is truly funny, one must admit. It's *me who should replace M. Picot* – M. Picot who for seven years by his own action or his influence had me rejected at the exhibitions from 1840 to 1848, and for the best things I've made in my life. Can you grasp, my dear friend, the illogicality in that notion? How can I be expected, when M. Picot has been stupid towards me, to go and carry out reprisals on the martyrs who enter the arts? What I was made to suffer in despair throughout my youth, must I in turn make others suffer? The idea is senseless.

No, established bodies, academies of all sorts, authoritarian *regimentation*, all that denotes a false state of things and constitutes a direct obstacle to progress. Without the February revolution, my painting would perhaps have never been seen. I have established revolt; now one sees the young folk who emerge from it.

An academician is put by our social system in a false position. How do you expect this man to exalt new talent to the detriment of his own values and to kill himself off benevolently when he's still alive? It's to ask of a man more than he can do. Look at Napoleon III: Progress – that's he, and it's by him that France must have genius, without counting that honour must come to him from it.

No, the time has come for someone to have the courage to be honest and and declare the Academy a harmful and all-engrossing institution, unable to fulfil its stated mission. Till now there's never been a national art, there have been only individual attempts and art-exercises in imitation of the past. As everything's centralised, there were some who thought Raphael was art in person and that to do well it was enough to imitate him. At present France seems trying to regain the spirit of art that has been lost. Why? Because she has an idea to uphold and liberty to establish. It's this belief that opposes itself to the old religions that produced the artworks in our museums. To aid a movement, it's necessary to give the national genius a free hand, to do away with commissioners, protectors, academies, and, above all, academicians. Free academies may remain in which young people without funds can work. Open the museums, that's all one can do for art. So I must humbly deny my fitness to be a member of Academies.

In addition to all the reasons given above, there's another which by itself suffices to stop me from accepting, whatever the government may be; and I needn't tell you of all people what it is.[43]

The vehemence with which Courbet here states his opinions arises from the direct involvement in politics we have noted; the struggle for liberty has assumed a new urgency.

A little earlier Courbet had written to Bruyas, who replied on 12 October in a letter which gives some idea of the involved digressive way in which he thought.

I believe that I let you know at the time of my intention, quite definite, to sell or exchange one of my most important Troyons for a more serious subject by F. Millet, on the basis of the proposition which I recall still as come from a word you threw out, and which is quite a revelation for one who judges painting sanely, that is, detached from trickery, if I may thus express myself, and from the procedures of the old masters. Thus, in the sphere to which I refer, T. Rousseau himself leaves something to desire from this angle, being in some degree only a reminiscence of Ruysdael. Now, my dear friend, you know better than anyone that I hold fast to not losing the thread of our ideas though I always am working a great deal; it's urgent you should second me in a matter that would have been more interesting without the obstacles that are numberless and that everyone encounters very regretfully. You've heard of my new installation here. I much doubt that the person who told you, whose name I don't know, can have given you precise information; for with regard to things of art, if there are some exceptions, the largest number is always on the side of the question, you know it! In every case I believe I've acted for the best, in a word: very seriously. And I console myself like you for all the inevitable anxieties as well, as much in the present as in the future.[44]

Some more discoveries were made about the thefts of his pictures. Isabey wrote on 16 November, 'I don't want to bother you to fetch the picture I've recovered from the thieves, so I'm sending it to you.' Courbet had been delaying as long as possible the demolition of his exhibition-building; he still hoped that somehow it might be turned into a permanent site. But now the municipal authorities compelled him to pull down the empty structure, which was in a bad state. Chaudey warned him on 22 December that the roof was gone. 'Don't let the situation deteriorate. If the building isn't demolished at once, you may find yourself involved in extra expense.' So the whole thing was dismantled and Isabey stored the timbers in a warehouse near the Porte de la Chapelle, in the northern outskirts of Paris. Chaudey's portrait had been painted and he told Courbet, 'My portrait hanging in my office stirs up endless argument; the artists and connoisseurs approve; the ladies disapprove. They say you've tried to discredit me in the eyes of the fair sex. . . . It's very amusing.' The Andler dispute was still dragging on. Chaudey notified him:

As for the Andler case, I've been able to have it postponed till now. I've been handed a ledger containing an itemised list, day by day, detail by detail, of all the refreshments for which payment is demanded from you. . . . Being incompetent to question it in detail without you, I shall be unable to do more than challenge the total. . . . The case will not come up again till January.[45]

Courbet stayed on at Ornans through the winter till May or June 1869. But this time he did little painting, unlike the previous occasions when he had recouped his energies after his struggles in Paris. He oddly reverted to an imitation of Régis with his impracticable inventions. He spent much of his time in trying to devise a light carriage of the tilbury type, but running on a single wheel. That at this important phase in his development he pottered about so long on something futile, shows how distracted he had become. Dr Ordinaire wrote to Castagnary on 18 December 1868:

Yesterday I saw Courbet with the Vulcan he is inspiring. They were both in the ardour of planning and execution. The forge glows and the anvil rings. Père Courbet has devised a car with five wheels. The son, shrewder, has invented the *Monocycle*. I'm the one who thought of a name for the vehicle on the spot, even though I'm not much of a Greek scholar. Here is a fine example of the meeting of extremes in the same family.

    At first I teased the inventor cruelly. But he has worked out his scheme so well, designing every part of his one-wheeled carriage and the attachment of his shaft to the horse's flanks, that I've begun to take the thing seriously. The master wants his work to be strong and elegant. Could he neglect the aesthetic aspect? If, as I think he will, he brings it off in all respects, I'm sure that cripples, jockeys, and other lazy folk will use it to circulate like rats along the Champs-Elysées and the boulevards, and the inventor will make money. So I'm urging him to apply for a patent as soon as possible.

One of our manufacturers has already agreed to build them. Don't talk about it. He must first get the patent.

Luckily, the artist has found an exceptional smith, skilful and intelligent. He's known as the Devil and indeed he could effectively play Mephistopheles' role. His volcanic imagination is stimulated by the new invention to such a degree that he'll forget to get drunk till the work's finished.[46]

Courbet was thus seeking to show himself superior to his father by making an invention that would actually bring in money. Fumey gives an amusing account of Régis's carriage. He was accompanying his lawyer-father who had to visit Flagey on the occasion of one of Régis's many lawsuits. Régis offered to drive them back as far as Salins and brought out his *char Suisse*, a high-set carriage with the two back wheels much bigger than those in front; there was only room for two on the lofty seat. 'That's no matter,' said Régis. 'You often hear talk of the fifth wheel of a carriage. Well, I've discovered it.' This fifth wheel was at the back, supporting a sort of wheelbarrow attached to the axle. Fumey was to travel in this wheelbarrow, and at first he was proud of his special seat. They reached Amoncey. Seeing at a crossroads a little oratory surrounded with trees, Régis said, 'My horse has a strong love for the Good God. I'll tie him up there and he won't budge.' They sat down to lunch and had reached the desert when a distracted servant-girl came in to say the horse was loose and trying to force its way, carriage and all, into a near stable. They found the horse stuck in the doorway, pulling and kicking. Régis got in by another door to calm him, but the shafts broke. A smith repaired the carriage and they drove on – now much more fast, to make up for lost time. In his barrow-seat Fumey was bumped about so badly that he arrived at Salins 'with bleeding buttocks; and I suffered for long days from stiffness. It was an experience I can't forget.'

How unusual it was for Courbet to put painting from his mind, even at times when he was socially busy, is brought out in two pleasant anecdotes told by Gros-Kost. One evening they were all talking and drinking, but suddenly Courbet became moody. 'His happiness had lain in working; and he couldn't work'. The others ignored him and went on chatting.

But he was watching us out of the corner of his eye. After dreaming for a good while, he was seen suddenly to stretch out his arm. He brought his hand near the flagon and plunged in his whole fist. It was about eight o'clock. The waiter had just lit the gas jets. Many drinkers had emptied their pipes to go home for dinner. The smoke-clouds thinned. Courbet, taking out his beer-wet fist, raised his elbow, gave a suitable stiffness to his index-finger, and on the oak table, very neat and dry, he began drawing. With two turns of the finger he constructed an elephant; with three turns of his hand he sketched a valley. Then a river; then rocks with brushwood; then an odd building, the character of which escaped us on account of the evaporation. He covered the table's surface with arabesques, starting at one end, finishing at the other. When the masterpiece had vanished in thin air, he began again. He would have stayed all night, plunged in this work, if he had not been reminded that a mountain-sausage, with cummin, warm, was awaiting us.

Another time it was at Maisières. Near mid-meal, Courbet, who had remained silent, folded up his napkin and went off. Nobody gave him much thought till the desert. It was one of those heavy October evenings, when, throwing off jacket and waistcoat, one finds happiness only in going to take the air, in shirt-sleeves, on the doorstep. We were in the garden. The painter, always with his pipe, was leant against an oak. With eyes wide open and staring, he was watching. The sun had just set. The landscape was covered with dark tints. One would have called it a vast charcoal-drawing, a symphony in black, in the style of Gautier. Courbet, studying the transformation of things, under the action of the fading light, was gathering new observations for new pictures.

First of all he found voice to bid us notice how pure and vibrant was the voice of the *bos* croaking by the river. Then he started on his favourite theme: he let himself go on the theme of colours. He pointed out a little cloud, which, darker, stood out strongly against the mass of the others. He made us consider the edges of this cloud, and from minute to minute he described to us in admirable terms the various tones through which they passed before being merged with the environing mists. And similarly with other objects. He took one at chance: a tree, an old house, and, in a brief moment, he made us partake of the multiple metamorphoses which our poor brain would have been hard put to conceive. Some drops of rain fell. We went back in, and he said to us: 'You know now why I've wanted to kill this vile ideal.'

The 'ideal' was for him any kind of abstraction, any weakening in the struggle to wrest the secrets from nature; this attitude Cézanne later shared and carried on. As for the invention, when it had played its part by filling in time, he seems to have forgotten it. However he was still at it on 13 May 1869 when he wrote to Flagey to say that he couldn't come on a visit because of his preoccupation with the carriage, which he meant to send to the Exposition at Longchamps. On 16 April the Andler case had been finally settled. Chaudey reported that the verdict took into consideration the possibility that Courbet had been charged for refreshments consumed by others, 'but taking into account the great length of time the debt has been due and the non-payment of interest for eight to ten years, the verdict has reduced Andler's bill only from 3,500 to 3,000 francs'. He added, 'I think we'll have to be satisfied with that.'[47]

Courbet sent to the Salon only three pictures, which had already been on the walls of his own show: *Siesta, Hallali, Mountains of the Doubs*. This choice reflected his lack of art-activity during the winter.[48] *Siesta* was attacked. E. Roy in *L'Artiste* found it 'bizarre, of an impossible design'. P. Casimir-Périer ranked it among the works to be ignored. P. de Saint-Victor said the bulls were flat and the girl haymaker came from the Opéra Comique. C. Blanc, however, admired the horses, though he disparaged the snow-scene of *Hallali*. Gautier saw the latter picture as a half-faded tapestry and insisted that snow-shadows were brown. P. Mantz called Courbet a fantasist. O. Merson thought the horse good in tonality, though made of cardboard while the rider was of wood. He and Gautier described the drawing as 'chimerical': a term much used in 1868 for Courbet's work. However, de Saint-Victor admired *Hallali*, as did Castagnary. The writer in the *Moniteur Universel* for 22 June suggested that Courbet should decorate the halls of agricultural exhibitions.[49] Both *Siesta* and *Hallali* in their ways were in fact masterpieces: the one in its evocation of drowsy summer-heat, its subtle placing of forms to harmonise with the horizon's line and yet to lead into the open space under the trees, the unity of the heavy foreground planes with the depth of distance. (There was at first another girl sitting near the front, but Courbet painted her out and put a pile of clothes on the grass instead, thus strengthening the lead into the light-distance along the backs of the oxen on the left and the horns of those on the right.) *Hallali* does not show the snow-dazzle of *Poachers*; the sky of mild blue merged with grey clouds gives a more diffused light against which the patterns of the actors, human and animal, stand out starkly, yet are part of the landscape, solidly on the ground and yet afloat in the snow-light. Courbet is in the hunters, but he is also in the splendid beast brought down and doomed.

On 5 July, back in Paris, he suffered another money-blow. 'A terrible disaster has struck me. M. Delaroche [apparently a dealer] has just gone bankrupt and I'm once more reduced to beggary. He owed me 25,000 for my 25 seascapes of Trouville, plus 5,000 I lent him in cash. I must testify at one o'clock at the Chambre de Commerce. I'll collect only one or two per cent. . . . I really have no luck.'[50] About this time Champfleury made a late marriage, to Marie Pierret, goddaughter of Delacroix; but Courbet would hardly have been invited to the ceremony.[51]

In mid-August he was at Etretat, a small seaside place discovered by Isabey and celebrated by A. Carr. He found Narcisse Diaz and his son Eugène there. The latter often swam with him. One day, venturing out too far, he almost drowned, but Courbet, a strong swimmer, brought him in. On 6 September he told Castagnary, 'I've been at Etretat for the last 25 days; if I'd been able to see you before leaving I'd have tried to bring you along with me. This country is charming. There's still time for you to come for a week. It's very hot, the bathing is delightful. I've already done nine seascapes, with which I'm satisfied; tomorrow I'll start one $1 \times \cdot 60$ metres for the Exhibition. I've never shown one of this kind.'[52] He had indeed developed his painting of the sea. *La Vague* was especially successful with its fine depth of colour and its effect of the tremendous force and weight of water. Here, in his different way, he is close to Turner – not to the Impressionists with their stress on momentary appearances of a liquid element.[53]

While still at Etretat he got some good news. His work had gained a first gold-medal at the Internation Show in Brussels; and the young King Ludwig II of Bavaria (not yet mad) had given him the Order of Merit of St Michael for his contribution (*Stonebreakers*, *Hallali*, *Woman with Parrot*, *Oraguay Rock*) to the show in Munich. Despite his objections to official decorations he found reasons for accepting the Bavarian Order:

The situation's saved! By *demand* of the Munich artists and the awards committee I've just been named a Chevalier of the Order of Merit of St Michael by the King of Bavaria. At the Brussels show organised along the same lines – that is, with the artists electing the jury and the jury giving its decisions without governmental interference – I've been unanimously awarded the medal. . . . This gives the lie directly to the regimentation of the arts . . . by the French administration. Here at last are two decorations I can accept because they're given by our competitors of their own free will. More, this decoration (if any decorations are admissible) is more logical than the Cross of [the Legion of] Honour; it is called a Cross of Merit.[54]

He considered that the German and Belgian artists felt 'an overwhelming desire' to follow his example. He asked Castagnary to go with him to Munich, leaving on 20–21 September for celebrations beginning on 1 October. 'If you can give this adequate publicity, it'll be the death of all who've been officially decorated.'

Castagnary could not go. Courbet went alone and stayed some six weeks, the hero of the occasion in an extravagant way that suited even his demands. The King, Wagner's admirer, invited him to paint a scene from *Lohengrin* on the walls of the royal bedchamber; but he had to refuse. However he worked as well as drank. His technical dexterity, especially with the knife, much impressed the Bavarian Academy, including its director Wilhelm von Kaulbach. He painted a forest-scene (from a site near by) in an hour or two. A few days later, mentioning that he'd like to paint a nude, he was supplied by Kaulbach with a servant who often posed for him; and in a few hours he produced *Lady of Munich*: a blonde woman lying with back turned before a window with an autumnal landscape; under the rumpled sheet we see the striped ticking of the mattress; on a chair to the left sleeps a small dog.[55] He also made copies of *Hille Bobbe* by Hals, a portrait by Murillo (?), and a self-portrait of Rembrandt. In doing the last he was returning to early devotion, and while studying the original makes his personal interpretation of it.[56]

Gros-Kost records how Courbet told of his Munich days; and for once his flamboyant style probably catches Courbet's own tone:

He had a way all his own of narrating this voyage. His self-love was so flattered by his success in the brasserie that he sometimes forgot his success on the easel. If he was pushed a little, he would be brought to make more of his bacchic capacities than of his genius in the arts.

Here's his account of his sojourn in Bavaria.

I arrived in Munich, he used to say. A good enough town. Women with real breasts. All fat, all dainty, all blondes. Brasseries everywhere. Tobacco cheap to buy. Unhappily, a crowd of artists. The first thing I was asked: Have you brought pictures?

I answered: I've brought a great thirst. Let's get a beer-mug.

So there we were in a smoky hall where a mob of natives were paying their devotions to Saint Bottle [Canette]. I was told: You want beer. Drink. Our vessels aren't like yours. They aren't women's thimbles out of which you suck a drop of liquid with great difficulty. Our bock deserves a tun.

I drink a mugful, two, three; and as the others get up to go out, I hold them back. It's not late, I tell them, we've still got time to drink a mugful.

Oh, Oh, they cry, we see you're getting a taste for our beer. All right, as you wish. Let's put down a mugful.

I drink a beer, two, three. My good companions begin to talk painting and suggest that I go with them to the house of a famous painter whose name I forget. I'll see there astonishing, admirable landscapes.

I don't want to see astonishing, admirable landscapes, I answer. I make them. I'd rather empty a mug.

Oh, Oh, squeak my Bavarians, you want to challenge us. You're doubtless a good boozer, but you'll get drunk.

Let's bet I don't get drunk.

Let's bet you roll under the table.

We drank for a large part of the night. Every quarter of an hour or so a Bavarian slid down on to the floor. He was carried off opposite on to the yard where the municipality, learning of this great struggle, had had a first-aid station hurriedly set up. After the painters who'd brought me to the tavern came the turn of the collectors.

A hundred and fifty law-students, two hundred medical students, sixty-nine theology-students, two thousand brewers, five hundred merchants of salt pork, three hundred makers of sauerkraut, eighty-two vets, fifty clergymen, eighteen hundred *rentiers* remain on the floor. I must pay homage to the solid value of the clergymen and the theology-students. They gave proof in this dangerous situation of a skill and science that assured them of a great future in the ministry. At one o'clock I got up.

I vainly sought in the hall, in the square, the streets, the houses, the catacombs, everywhere, for someone capable still of drinking with me a stirrup-cup. Nobody. The women had fled with the children. The men lay on the field of battle. I returned to my hotel, and as I was thirsty I sampled one of the bottles of Salins wine I'd had the prudence to put in my trunk, for fear there were no bars in Munich.

Next morning I was woken by loud outcries. A crowd had gathered under my window crying: Long live Courbet! Long live the sublime boozer! I pulled on my trousers. I thanked the people with that particular eloquence which you know is mine. They threw me garlands. They bombarded me with bouquets. My friends of last night, sobered up but suffering from mucus, suggested I should come down so that they could carry me in triumph. I refused.

When I left Munich 422 realist acadamies had been founded.[57]

Just before leaving, he quickly painted as a souvenir for his Bavarian disciples–a picture of his pipe, inscribed: *Courbet, without ideal and without religion.* (He is said to have used the phrase on his notepaper, surmounted by a design of crossed pipes.)[58] On his way home he passed through Switzerland, pausing to do half a dozen pictures, including *Landscape at Interlaken.*[59] Here he showed that he did not need strong contrasts, but could work with a light touch and produce a gentle pervasive effect of autumnal atmosphere. Writing to Castagnary on 20 November, he declared, 'I didn't find it worth the trouble of so long a journey.' He had a low opinion of German painting.

They know almost nothing of good painting; they're all concerned with the negative elements of art. One of the main qualities is perspective: they discuss it all day. Another important quality is accuracy of historical costumes. They're greatly interested in anecdotal painting; and every wall in Munich is covered with frescoes like wallpaper, full of red, blue, green, yellow, pink robes, silk stockings, top-boots, doublets. Here's a king taking an oath, there's a king abdicating, the next is a king signing a treaty etc., etc. As for sculpture, it's incredible. You could easily count 3,000 statues in the town. If the heads were fitted with screws, they could be changed every fortnight, and then ten statues would be enough. A wag has said that a stranger has only one thing to fear among them: to be put up as a statue. Amid all this the Corneliuses, the Kaulbachs, the Schwinds, etc. had their day. Chenavard above all: his picture was the target of general mockery. As the Germans are very strong in that sort of *genre*, they traced all the figures, all the groups, to originals in Italian works. One man was tracking down the figures stolen from old masters in a picture, and said: 'One recognises almost every one.' His neighbour replied, 'Unfortunately, thus treated, one recognises them no longer.'[60]

However, he found kindred spirits among the young artists.

On his way home, he called on the Joliclers and painted the three-year-old daughter; and a family-friend, Mme Sophie Loiseau. Early in December he heard that Buchon was dying, and hurried to Salins. On 8 December he wrote to Gaudy with an account of his triumphs at Etretat, Brussels, Munich; he had spent a fortnight at Interlaken and painted a landscape of glaciers; then at Pontarlier he found Jolicler suffering from erysipelas. After that he mentions how he found his old friend 'suffering from an anthrax [?malignant ulcer or fistula] in his backside. He's in bed, very ill.'[61] On the 14th Max died; and two days later Courbet wrote Castagnary a long letter:

My old friend Buchon, my poor cousin, died in my arms 14 December at 6 a.m. He died of blood-poisoning due to typhoid fever; and with cause enough! During the last fifteen years he'd swallowed so much carrion he'd have the stomach of the Boulogne Eagle to have digested it. This tamer of eagles will end by swallowing up our whole generation.

He tells of Buchon's earlier trials, with which we have dealt above; and sums up:

Buchon was a *grande âme*, unequalled for his disinterested nature, of an extreme humility and sensibility, always working for others and never for himself, never permitting anyone to pay him any honour or compliment. His courage was invincible. Despite all the bad treatment he might be made to suffer, he had the courage of his convictions, a lofty and terrible power of speech. Nobody dared to oppose him, because, with his *franc-comtois* nature, he never acted unless he was right twice over. So his authority in our country was very high. His great intelligence enabled him to nominate the opposition deputies in both the Jura and the Doubs. He was concerned unendingly and tirelessly with the problems of the people.

What brought on his last illness was the defection of a democratic newspaper to the Orléanists. The slightest deviation from probity and honesty wounded him to the quick. Even his poetry was simple and unpretentious. He sought to occupy the least possible amount of space on earth. He would have put himself in a mousehole. It might be thought that he trusted too much in himself. In his mind, without anyone's moral support, he regarded death as a place of arrival, a harbour.[62]

He and Claudet (who had made a bust of Buchon) had been discussing a monument.

A work of Courbet's, long taken as a portrait of Max, has been challenged, on the ground that, though Henner thus identified it when it was found by A. Baud-Bovy in a secondhand-dealer's shop in 1882, nobody at Ornans seemed to know who it was. Claudet made inquiries. L. Proudhon said that his brother, who often visited Courbet's studio, did not know the sitter, and that the work must have been done in Paris. It has further been urged that we see no sign of Buchon's scar and that the person in the painting looks far too jaunty and elegant for the severe Proudhonian. Certainly it is odd that Claudet did not recognise it if it were Buchon. Yet it seems indeed to have been his portrait. From the 1854 letter in which Courbet announced his voyage to Berne he mentions a portrait he had begun; he suggests that Buchon should write to his (Courbet's) sister and ask for it to be sent to Berne, so that it can be finished. The basis of the work would then be a sketch of Buchon made in 1851 when Courbet was in his early thirties, which he finished off rather hastily in 1854. Thus we can explain the simplified background and the rapidly struck-out pattern, which makes the work seem so oddly an anticipation of Manet. A comparison of the head with that of another portrait, painted in 1864, makes the identification very plausible. The jaunty springy effect becomes then the expression of the young Buchon's taut and bouyant energy; the face, examined, has a very serious expression.[63]

With 1870 the Empire's difficulties had come out into the open. Napoleon tried to find a middle course between radicals and reactionaries by calling on a comparatively liberal politician Ollivier (whose portrait Courbet had painted). In February the painter was informed by E. C. J. de la Rochenoire, a landscape-painter who was president of the Association des Artistes-Peintres, that he had been unanimously proposed by a committee as candidate for the jury of the 1870 Salon. He felt that he could not refuse, but urged the setting up of an independent group. 'If I have proved nothing else I've at least demonstrated that without privilege, without protection, and without being a partisan of Napoleon, one can follow an artistic career if one has the right temperament. I have just returned from two countries where I have won outstanding success. Belgium and Bavaria; artists are independent there.'[1]

Next day he wrote to Castagnary that it was the most annoying thing possible, but he must submit and that he had referred the Association to Castagnary for the drawing-up of a petition to the Chamber of Deputies asking that they should be attached to a ministry, not to the imperial house. The Chamber would then turn over to them the Palais de l'Industrie where the Salons had long been held; the entrance-fees would finance the sponsors and pay for the pictures bought by an appointed committee and for the Lottery. If the Emperor wanted to buy anything he'd have to do so from his own funds, not out of the fees. All money got in should be spent at once; no organisation should continue after the show ended – otherwise 'it would ultimately produce a series of little governments'. No existing personnel should be used, 'because all these scoundrels are completely corrupt at heart and swindlers as well'. Not that any of these suggestions will come off. 'Artists don't like independence and the others are too fond of governing.' He says that since Buchon's death he has been unable to work, 'sunk in an overpowering lethargy; I've taken two or three purges but feel my liver's still out of order. I think this is due to previous fatigue.' He will be in Paris a week more, sending pictures to the Salon. (We see that his digestive troubles and constipation are upon him again, the nemesis of his way of life.) He did not, however, serve on the Salon jury; he failed to get enough votes in the final election.[2]

On 10 February, back in Ornans, he wrote to Claudet, with whom he was trying to organise the Buchon monument. 'Since I saw you I've been ill without a break; I've been in a prostrated and over-excited state that didn't allow me to work.' He gave an angry account of a visit to the brother of Mme Buchon's mother.

As soon as I arrived at Ornans, I went, as promised, to Vuillafans, to the house of Uncle Pasteur. I was disillusioned in a way I can't explain to you and you couldn't imagine. Mme Flock had passed that way; you can't conceive the profound blackness, the wickedness, the calumny of this sinister woman.

A series of violent arguments and conflicts broke out, which are hard to follow in detail but which revolve round money and the will. Pasteur spoke of that scamp (*polisson*) of a Buchon and his *vourie* of a wife, and said, 'I've been passed over during his illness, I'll be passed over after his death.' Courbet lost his temper, and tried to hit the Pasteurs' family-pride, 'which is the dominant sentiment'. In vain. He smashed his fist on the table and swore that as a man like Buchon couldn't have any resting-place in his family, 'I charged myself with it and was going to ask the prefecture to accord me the right of taking up the body and transferring it to Ornans on my own terrain, and that there'd be no cost to the family.' Defeated, he wrote a 'terrible letter'. The wranglings over money went on. 'Uncle Pasteur agrees to give 100 francs, and the other uncle as well; but they want to await the result of the subscription.' In the end Pasteur's son went off to Salins for discussion; and Courbet asked Claudet to show Mme Buchon his letter.[3]

Courbet had sent in only two seascapes to the Salon: *The Wave* (or *Stormy Sea*) and one of his versions of *Etretat Cliffs*. Perhaps in the ominous hues and crashing onslaught of the billow of *The Wave* he was packing his own sense of inner and outer crisis. (He dated a *Waterspout* 1870, though he probably did it in 1869; he had used the same theme in 1866 and 1867.) Castagnary wrote, 'I think this year the last remaining detractors will admit defeat, and praise of the great painter will be unanimous.'[4] Indeed, the critics were generally favourable and in April Coubet sold 40 pictures for 52,000 francs as well as getting commissions from ten collectors. One man, Bordet of Dijon, bought five seascapes and the *Woman with Parrot*.

Courbet's unnerved condition appeared in yet another attempt to get married, this time with Bordet's sister, Mme de Villebichot; but nothing came of it. We do not know the details, but we may assume that Courbet did not personally press his suit and the usual absurdity dominated the negotiations. The family, however, remained friendly and later in the year Bordet got him to contribute to a show in aid of the women of La Creusot where a strike in the armaments-works had brought about many hardships.[5]

This spring he painted Castagnary; and he bought for 3,500 francs a large collection of alleged old-masters from Mme de Planhol, who had inherited it from her uncle M. de Naglis, a diplomat under Charles X. The list of 500 works (paintings, objects-of-art, plaster-busts) would have been of vast value, if genuine; it included pictures attributed to Rubens, Holbein, Titian, Veronese, Valasquez and others. They seem all to have been very mediocre copies. It argues a strange blindness in Courbet's critical faculties that he obstinately held them to be originals. On 11 May he wrote to the family on his 'wonderful bargain'. He had rented an apartment at 24 rue du Vieux-Colombier, so as to leave them 'where they are,' and had paid cash down, to get what he estimated at 300,000 francs' worth of art. In fact the works had no value except as prepared canvases for repainting on.[6]

The Borreau family had come from Saintes to Paris about this time.[7] Courbet and Castagnary for some while had frequented the Café de Madrid in the boulevard Montmartre, where were to be found many writers, artists and others of a radical cast: Vallès, Gambetta,

A. Vermorel, Carjat, Paschal Grousset, and Raoul Rigault. At the back of the café was the haunt of the *Purs*, 'old sachems with big beards, solemn and dogmatic ventriloquists', with *Père* Delescluze, who had been sent to Cayenne. After Rochefort founded *La Marseillaise*, the group was reinforced by what the mockers called a 'cloud of students, oldish and pretentious, improvised journalists without wit or orthography, as ignorant of Paris as Patagonians, children with beards who thought themselves called on to regenerate the world, pedants of the Republic, all wearing Robespierre waistcoats and Saint-Just cravats'. Courbet felt thoroughly at home.[8]

We may consider here an account of an outing by Claudet, though the event may have occurred in any of late 1860s. (The account may indeed synthesise several such outings.) The friends had met at St-Lazare station, early in the afternoon. Claudet was one of the first, then Champfleury arrived with Castagnary and Courbet; the latter had brought a young bespectacles man, armed with a large umbrella, whom he introduced as Vermorel. (Champfleury's presence suggests the early 1860s; Vermorel's presence fits better in with a later date.)

We got out at the station of Chatou and went on foot as far as Bougival. When we arrived Courbet found that one dined better at an inn halfway between Bougival and Chatou, on the Seine banks, facing the charming isle of Croissy. We set out for it, skirting the banks by a little roadway worn in the green grass. Courbet spoke of himself and his painting. On reaching the hostelry the painter of Ornans ordered the dinner and we all sat down. And there in the midst of the festivity in came Gambetta. The future Minister of War came to chat with us for a short while, then went back into the neighbouring room.

The dinner was gay. Courbet told droll enough *franc-comtois* tales; the evening passed quickly with such guests; and at night we regained the railway which took us back to Paris. To give the day a proper ending, we went to instal ourselves at the brasseries, where we found the lawyer Chaudey, who upheld with his usual verve that artists were all idiots and didn't know how to settle themselves in a corporation like shoemakers. As antagonist he had Vermorel, as loquacious as he was. Courbet was raging at not being able to talk about his painting. Champfleury listened, and Buchon passed his hand over his moustache as he had a habit of doing when weary of a discussion.

Claudet, looking back, saw the occasion under the shadow of the coming disasters:

You, Chaudey, will be shot by your own partisans; and you, Vermorel, will die a violent death on a barricade, all this amid a Paris in blood and with monuments afire, to the applause of a hundred thousand Germans. As for Courbet, he'll come under a Council of War and go to live sadly in a voluntary exile, saying goodbye to the arts. The lawyer of Cahors will one day be Minister of War and will vainly struggle against the foreigner; unable to drive him from the soil of the fatherland, he'll be forced to use a balloon. And you, Buchon, so strong, so robust, and always ready to sing the old *franc-comtois* Noëls, you'll be the first dead.[9]

If they could have looked ahead, he adds, the dinner would have ended less gaily and Courbet would have got indigestion.

The new Minister for the Fine Arts, Maurice Richard, with whom Courbet was personally friendly, did his best to win him over, inviting him to dinners and receptions. Courbet refused the invitations. In June Richard sounded Dr Ordinaire as to whether

Courbet would accept the Cross of the Legion of Honour. Courbet shrewdly evaded the need to give a direct answer by dodging off to L'Isle-Adam, some twenty miles from Paris, to join the landscapist Jules Dupré. On 22 June the *Journal Officiel* announced the award of the Cross. Courbet was hoping for this situation, in which he could administer a blow to the Government and become the centre of a political uproar. He promptly wrote to Richard:

It was at the house of my friend Jules Dupré at L'Isle-Adam that I learned of the insertion in the *Journal Officiel* of a decree designating me Chevalier of the Legion of Honour. This decree, which my well-known opinions as to artistic awards and noble titles should have spared me, was enacted without my consent, and it was you, *monsieur le Ministre*, who felt the need to take the initiative in it.

Do not fear that I misjudge the sentiments guiding you. Appointed minister of the Beaux-Arts after a baneful administration that seemed devoted to the task of destroying art in our country and which would have succeeded in doing so by corruption and violence if it had not been thwarted by a few honest men who appeared here and there, you have tried to mark your accession by an act contrary to the procedure of your predecessor.

Such behaviour does you honour, *monsieur le Ministre*, but allow me to tell you that it cannot in any way change my attitude or my decisions. My opinions as a citizen forbid me to accept an award that belongs essentially to a monarchical order. My principles reject this decoration of the Legion of Honour you have imposed on me in my absence.

At no time, in no circumstances, for no reason whatever, would I have accepted it. I should be still less likely now when betrayals are multiplying in every direction and human nature is saddened by so many interested palinodes. Honour does not consist in a title or a ribbon; it consists in actions and the motive power of the actions. Respect for oneself and for one's ideas make up its major part. I honour myself by staying true to the principles I have proclaimed all my life; if I were to desert them, I should lose my honour in order to grasp the external form [*signe*].

My sentiments as an artist are no less opposed to my acceptance of an award handed out by the State. The State is incompetent in matters of art. When it undertakes to bestow awards, it usurps the function of popular taste. Its intervention is altogether demoralising, injurious to the artist whom it deceives as to his true worth, injurious to art which it hems in with official conventions and which it condemns to the most sterile mediocrity. The wisest course would be for it to abstain. The day it leaves us free, it will have fulfilled its duties towards us.

So permit me, *monsieur le Ministre*, to decline the honour you've thought fit to offer me. I am fifty years old and I've always lived a free man; let me end my life free; when I'm dead, let this be said of me: He belonged to no school, no church, no institution, no academy, least of all to any regime but the regime of liberty.[10]

The letter was published in *Le Siècle* and reprinted in many Parisian and provincial journals. A furious argument, for and against, burst out. With a document that would receive such scrutiny, Courbet seems to have sent a draft to Castagnary and asked him to supply a more formal version. We have a draft entirely his own composition. While it lacks the coherent and dignified exposition of his position found in the published letter, it is far more vivid and is couched largely in his lively folk-terms:

If I've been decorated without the question put, it's because I belong to the race of artists. But there's artist and artist: just as with a bundle of sticks. I know the moral pitch of the class has been lowered. . . . Today one catches men like frogs with a bit of scarlet; but all the same it's those who want to be caught that let themselves be. I don't understand all these rewards. They establish superiorities that three times out of four are false. A man rewarded is one who has sold out his duty; society no longer owes him anything; they're quits.

Now the number of these decorated persons is enough to abolish their value. A decorated man is amenable to caution. At his appearance everyone grows self-conscious and draws back his horns into his shell as snails do. The need for devotion and for creatures has driven the Empire to distribute this liberty to an endless extent. So it comes about that in a batch of village-townhalls I've known many who'd have been far better in the hulks than decorated. . . .

Look at England, America, Switzerland. A Swiss was asked why there were no decorations in his country. He replied, 'Sir, if one Swiss was decorated, all the others would also have to be; for all the Swiss do their duty.'

PS. The rancour of these gentry and the rigour of their institutions, by killing off all my friends and harming my interests, has only made me grow in public esteem. No, I want to be distinguished among my contemporaries only by my talent, and I'd not know how to keep company with them while wearing a distinctive sign on my person. I also wish to end my life belonging absolutely to myself. . . . If you went to Ornans market, you'd notice all the finest sheep of the market marked with a sign of red chalk on the back. Naive and well-meaning folk, who do not know the laws of agriculture and the arts, imagine in their pastoral candour that it's a homage rendered to their beauty, whereas it's the butcher who's bought them for slaughter.[11]

When one reads such a passage as the last two sentences, or Courbet's description of Buchon ('He sought to occupy the least possible amount of space on earth') or of Mme Buchon's rippling smile like 'a swarm of mice', one wonders at the complacent accounts of his lack of literary or poetic sense.

At Ornans a group of friends got together to send a letter of congratulation on his courage and his democratic principles in rejecting the award.[12] In Paris he was given a banquet at the restaurant Bonvalet in the boulevard du Temple, with Chaudey in the chair. A large number of friends and supporters attended, including Daumier who had refused the Cross with no publicity. Albert Wolff tells us how the two rejectors had met while Courbet was still with Dupré. 'Courbet had come; between lunch and dinner we sauntered in the countryside, Dupré full of enthusiasm for the nature surrounding us, Courbet speaking only of the "slap he'd just given Napoleon". Towards 9 p.m. Dupré led us to the station of L'Isle-Adam. There we met Daumier. At the sight of him a cry of joy escaped from the huge chest of Courbet; he hurled himself into his friend's arms, crushed him to his heart, and cried, "Ah, how I love you, you have refused the Cross like me. Only you were wrong not to refuse it with a loud scandal; it was necessary to make an uproar around this affair." And Daumier, shaking his old head, contemplated Courbet with a profound glance. "What's the use?" he asked in a reproachful tone. "I've done what I thought should be done. I'm satisfied. But that doesn't concern the public." ' Wolff adds, 'I cannot tell you with what exquisite dignity Daumier pronounced these words: his pride seemed revolted at the mere thought that one could suspect him of wanting to exploit his refusal as a means of advertisement.' One can sympathise with Daumier's quiet dignity and recognise the element of self-advertisement in Courbet's action, but Wolff is simply trying to debunk that action; Courbet was right and brave in underlining the full political significance of his position.[13]

Not soon after that Courbet met the historian and politician Thiers. His account is of much interest in showing how much more politically mature he had become:

On my arrival at his house he complimented me on my refusal of the Cross, telling me that he **had**

always had the same idea, despite his many decorations, and even so I must have noticed that he
never wore them except when on a mission in a foreign land. The various remarks and appreciative
comments on this subject over, he asked if I had always been Republican. I replied yes, but there was
no merit in it since I held that one was born Republican; that as for myself, at the age of ten I had
exactly the same frame of mind as today. In this connection I cited a fact: what most tormented me
at that age, what prevented me from sleeping, was the poor folk. I made myself as humble as possible
in their presence to gain forgiveness for my relative well-being, and all day we chatted, we two, my
grandmother and I, to find out what one could do to make all the poor folk of our village rich enough
not to have to go begging any more. I must admit that after considering the social question of our
village from every single angle we didn't reach a solution. Our ages excused us.

'And since then?' asked M. Thiers.

'Since? But I believe we'll arrive at that point soon.'

'You believe it?'

'Yes, I believe it.'

The question was a burning one. I didn't recall that M. Thiers was the Alexander of this Gor-
dian knot, having declared as minister that begging was forbidden. Changing the theme, he said to
me, 'As for the question of popular education: do you find it very necessary? When they know how
to read and write, they'll be much more advanced. They'll become absurd and that's all.'

I objected that he was ungrateful, that he seemed to deny his own origin, and that to be just we
must recognise that three-quarters of those distinguishing themselves in the world were men who
started very low down. Then he went on by asking me how many Republicans I reckoned to exist
at that moment after the elections. I replied, 'Two million five hundred thousand.'

They bandied some figures rather confusedly, but Courbet's point was at root an optimistic
belief in the revolution's power to breed its defenders:

'Guess how many Republicans there were in 1848? Oh well, we were six thousand; the proof is
that the provinces marched on Paris. You see, M. Thiers, they have brought forth young. It's the
days of June and the despotism of the Empire that have made them grow; they're born out of their
ashes like flies.'

'Good luck for the Republic,' he told me, 'since you believe in it. As for me, I think I'll never
be a Republican.'

'You'll do well,' I answered, 'for Brillat-Savarin said, one is born cookshop-keeper and one
becomes a cook. It's the same as to the Republic.' I didn't believe I could speak so to the point.

Some moments later he said to me, 'I can't understand how an artist can be a Republican. It's
not your world.' I answered him that I didn't belong to any class in society, that I belonged only to
the idea, and that when I had reason manifesting itself in me, I had all the classes for me; but that,
independently of that, I had lived very well all this time, resisting openly and not deviating by a
hair from my principles, with my six thousand Republicans.

We talked a good deal more, without understanding one another, about the Republic. Then he
showed me his works of art. His attitude to Art was the same as to the Republic; he was for tradition and aristocracy in art, denying the modern genius. We parted, and as I was leaving his house
I said to him, 'Our temperaments are quite opposed; all my solicitude in life is for the poor, while
all the solicitude of your life is for the rich. That's where we differ. So everything should succeed
for you.'[14]

In denying that he belonged to any class, he was taking a Proudhonian position that, since
his idea went beyond all existing classes to a fully harmonious society, he somehow existed
in the idea rather than in the immediate class-struggle. Here we touch on one of the elements
of confusion in his mind; but his concept of resistance went far beyond Proudhon's preach-
ings.

These last few months seem to have brought the first serious split between Courbet and the Reverdys. Eugène seems to have had a poor opinion of the vast collection of copies that Courbet was keeping in Mme de Planhol's old apartment, and that annoyed Courbet. Also the Reverdys were keen Bonapartists and social-climbers; they were outraged at the affair of the Cross, which Zoé put down to the bad influence of radicals on her simple impressionable brother.[15]

Then suddenly came the war with Prussia. Courbet's Letter became suddenly a slight matter. On 15 July he wrote to his family. 'War is declared. The peasants who voted Yes will pay dear for it. Right at the outset 500,000 men will be killed, and that won't be all. It's said the Prussians are already at Belfort and are marching at once on Besançon. The police and the Government have the cry raised *Vive la guerre* in Paris. It's an infamy. All honest folk are going back home and leaving Paris. In five or six days I'll go to some seaside resort, perhaps to Guernsey to see Victor Hugo, and return by way of Etretat. Despair is general.' If the Germans reach Besançon, he'll go there at once. But even after such news he cannot help launching into an account of his own triumph:

I'm overwhelmed with compliments. I've received 300 flattering letters such as no man in the world has ever received before. In everyone's opinion I'm the greatest man in France. M. Thiers invited me to his house to felicitate me; even princesses come to see me for the same purpose; and a dinner for 80 or 100 people has been given in my honour. All the journalists and men of learning in Paris were there. In the street I have to keep my hat in my hand like a curé. I was delighted by your approval.

Still, he thought the Ornans testimonial 'diplomatic and half-hearted; don't tell anybody I said so'. He considered the Ordinaires had played a shabby role in the affair. 'They didn't come to the banquet; I see them seldom; I let them go their own way. The step I've just taken is a wonderful achievement, it's like a dream, everyone envies me, I haven't a single opponent, I've so many commissions just now I can't meet them. So I'm off. Paris is odious and one can get oneself involved every day. In any event I'll be at Ornans in September.' He seems quite to have forgotten the war; but he returns to it finally; 'My affair lasted three weeks in Paris, in the provinces, and abroad. Now it's over; the war has taken my place.'[16]

He stayed where he was. On 9 August he reported the general disaster. 'I don't know how we'll come out of it.' Napoleon had declared a dynastic war for himself, taken charge with no plan, and proved himself an idiot. 'We're defeated all along the line; our generals are resigning; and we are expecting the enemy in Paris. . . . Today we're marching to the Chamber to declare the Empire's downfall.' But if the defeat rid France of Napoleon, it was worth while. 'I believe we're going to become Frenchmen once more. I can't return home now. My presence is needed here, and besides I've a good deal of property to protect in Paris.' He had nothing to fear from anyone, he said. 'As for you, you've nothing to fear from the Germans; make use of my Cross of Honour of Munich.'[17]

On that day Ollivier had been replaced by Pelikao; on 2 September the emperor surrendered at Sedan; two days later a Republican Government of National Defence was set

up with Gambetta as minister of the interior and J. Simon over the fine arts and education.
On 30 August de Nieuwerkerke had ordered the removal of the most valuable paintings;
two days later the first convoy left the Louvre for Brest, and others followed during the
next three days. Then the removals were halted; it was feared the crates might be seized
and used as material for barricades. When on 4 September the Republic was proclaimed,
de Nieuwerkerke resigned. Many statues or reliefs with imperial associations were taken
down; though nobody asked for action against Napoleon's tomb or the Arc de Triomphe.
On the 6th an unofficial group of artists gathered at the Sorbonne to consider the situation
and set up an art-commission to protect and control art in Paris and the neighbourhood.
Courbet was elected president; others on the commission were Daumier, Veyrassat, Fayen-
Perrin, Lansyer (one of Courbet's former pupils), the sculptors A. Ottin, Moulin, Le Véel,
G. Dechaume, the engraver Bracquemond, the ornamental draughtsman Reiber. They lost
no time and collected works from lesser museums to be stored in the Louvre vaults; they
took steps to deal with fire and theft, had rare MSS and books packed, arranged for the
setting of sandbags around outdoor monuments in case of bombardment.[18]

The family wanted Courbet at home. 'In these critical times and under the shock of
invasion a family should be united,' Régis said. 'You know your mother and I are too old
and your sisters in delicate health.' But Courbet had no intention of leaving Paris. He reiter-
ated that his Bavarian Order was a talisman for the family. 'You'll find it and the certificate
in my room; the Germans have great respect for their institutions.' He had read Régis's
letter 'with great sympathy; but I cannot comply with your desires at the moment. The
Parisian artists as well as the minister Jules Simon have just done me the honour of designating me president of arts in the capital. This pleases me as I didn't know how to serve my
country in this emergency, having no inclination to carry arms.'[19] On 9 September he wrote
again. 'I don't think I have anything to fear. I'll be at the Louvre and I'll be in less danger
in Paris than in the provinces where I'd be obliged to take an active part' in the war. He
wasn't sure if there'd be a siege, but thought communications would be cut. 'In the event
of my death my sisters are to take the money I've deposited with M. Henriot, invested in
the Lyon railway. I'll also leave a note with my concierge or the lawyer Chaudey.' A PS.
clarifies: 'My sisters Zélie and Juliette only.' We see that he has had a definite break with
the Reverdys.

Meanwhile steps were taken to bring down the Colonne Vendôme, the hated symbol of
Napoleonic Imperialism, which were to have fateful effects on Courbet's life. For some sixty
years Republicans had looked on the Column with anger. It had been meant to imitate
Trajan's Column in Rome, but used bronze instead of marble. The order for its erection
was signed 1 October 1803, and Charlemagne was to have stood on the top; but by 1806
he gave way to Napoleon himself. Russian and Austrian cannons were melted down to
provide 150,000 pounds of bronze; and a statue by A. Chaudet depicted Napoleon as a
Roman Emperor. With the Bourbon Restoration of 1814 the statue was melted down and
the white royalist flag substituted. Under Louis Philippe, Napoleon went back, this time

in a modern uniform, designed by G. Seurre. During 1848 many demands, backed by Comte, were made for demolition; but there was no time to get round to the job. Napoleon III had Seurre's statue taken down and Napoleon I reappeared as a Roman (the work of A. Dumont). After Sedan many leading figures and journals called for the destruction of the Column and the re-use of its metal for military purposes. The subject was raised at the meeting on 6 September (setting up the Art Commission) and the artists present unanimously proposed the demolition. Six years later Courbet declared that in his view at the time his function as the protector of art did not involve the destruction of any monument in Paris,

and that the assumption of such a destructive right would make it easy, by the adoption of one aesthetic standard or another, to demolish every monument in existence. I proposed an amendment to the effect that we should transport the Column to the Invalides after unbolting it with care. This proposal was adopted by acclamation. I was instructed to present a petition to the Government of National Defence, who made no response.

He also, he said, suggested the placing on the spot of a large book in which 'citizens would inscribe their names'. But this motion was not adopted. However, it is very unlikely that this is indeed what happened at the meeting; he is probably drawing on ideas he generally held to show himself opposed from the outset to the demolition. The terms of the petition to the Government on 14 September are quite different:

Citizen Courbet, President of the Art Commission charged with the preservation of the national museums and works of art, elected by a general assembly of artists: Whereas the Vendôme Column is a monument devoid of any artistic value, tending by its character to perpetuate the ideas of wars and conquests which were appropriate to the imperial dynasty but which the opinion of a republican nation condemns; whereas it is for the same reason in conflict with the genius of modern civilisation and with the ideal of universal brotherhood that must hereafter prevail among nations; whereas it wounds the natural susceptibilities of European democracy and makes France ridiculous and odious in the eyes of that democracy [*scratched out in draft*: and whereas it is to be feared that the enemy, should misfortune enable him to enter our city, might cause the violent destruction of this monument by inflaming the populace] –
    Resolves: that the Government of National Defence should authorise him to unbolt this Column, or that they should take the initiative themselves by delegating the task to the administration of the Artillery Museum and by ordering the transportation of the construction-materials to the Hôtel de la Monnaie [Mint]. He also desires that the same steps be taken with respect to the statue [of Napoleon by Seurre] which was removed and now stands in the avenue de la Grande-Armée at Courbevoie. Finally he desires that the street-names which recall victories to some people, defeat to others, be eliminated from our capital and replaced by the names of benefactors of humanity or by names appropriate to their topographical locations.

A key-point in this document was the word *déboulonner*, which does not occur in French dictionaries, but can be taken to mean 'unbolt', *boulon* meaning a bolt or large iron pin. In the later defence of Courbet much play was made on it. Gill suggested that Courbet was attracted by the very oddity of the word: 'A new unknown word, slipped into Courbet's head, would cause a disturbance, an obsession, like the humming of a beetle in a jug.' In any event the word suggests a careful dismantling rather than a violent demolition, and this interpretation is supported by the reference to the Artillery Museum – though in turn it is contradicted by bringing-in the Mint (for melting down). Courbet was in fact suggesting an impossible operation; he did not know that the Column consisted of bronze plates firmly attached to a massive stone cylinder which enclosed a circular staircase. But that was irrelevant to the question of intention. We must note, however, that he was only one of many persons who wanted the Column pulled down; and that the demolition would have been carried out, whether he had proposed it or not. The effort to make his proposal the sole or main cause of the action taken was unfair.[20]

On 24 September, Simon set up an agency, the Archives Commission, 'to inspect the Louvre archives and trace to their sources any frauds that may have been committed by functionaries of the fallen Government'. There were at first five members, including the chairman E. Vacherot, the philosopher; but a few days later Courbet and the critic P. Burty were added. No frauds were found, and almost all the curators and museum officials, appointed under the Empire, were left to continue their work. Courbet and Burty resigned on 1 December in disapproval of this policy. Courbet in his letter to Simon pointed out that he could not in any event ratify the acts of the Empire or support men who had served it, 'no matter what appearance of propriety they may have been able to give to their proceedings. Also, by the time we came to close the stable door, the horses had gone; our work could be nothing but a farce.' As the present Government was 'not committed to revolution', the commission's work was condemned to sterility as it could not bring about 'radical reforms in the budget and personnel of the museums. Still, hoping to be of service, I retain with pleasure the mission assigned to me by the group of artists and confirmed by yourself.'[21]

The siege had began on 19 September and conditions steadily worsened, hunger, cold, and confused tumults of the discontented people.

On 5 October Courbet resumed the question of the Vendôme Column in a letter to E. Arago, Mayor of Paris; he declared that his petition had been misunderstood and that he had never advocated destruction. He wanted only

the removal, from the proximity of a street called rue de Paix, of a mass of melted cannon that perpetuates the tradition of conquest, pillage, and murder, and which is as absurdly out of place as a howitzer in a lady's salon among the shops filled with silk frocks, laces, ribbons, fripperies, and diamonds, which adjoin the establishment of Worth, the favourite dressmaker of the Empire's courtesans. Would you preserve in your bedroom the bloodstains of a murder? Let the reliefs be transferred to an historical museum, let them be set up in panels on the walls of the court of the Invalides; I see no harm in that. Those brave men [the maimed veterans] captured these cannon by the sacrifice of their limbs; the sight will remind them of their victories – since they are called victories – and especially of their sufferings.

Perhaps this rather disquieted memorandum was stimulated by the fact that others had been raising the matter and that on 2 October the armaments-committee of the 6th *arrondissement* had unanimously approved the report made by Dr Robinet, one of its members, that the metal of the Column be used for cannons and that the 'odious monument' be got rid of. (We see why Zoé wanted to dissociate her brother from Robinet.) During this month

Courbet composed two *Open Letters* – to the German Army and to German Artists. He
mentioned Victor Considérant as the instigator and may have had some help from him,
but the works have the clear stamp of his own style. He read them at the Athénée on 29
October. The prologue describes a world upside-down, 'everyone gone mad', everyone
doing what he doesn't know how to do, 'we are free men'. The address to the Army is a
mixture of truculent raillery and appeal to democratic and civilised values; he mixes insults
and appeals to brotherhood. France must win because of the revolutionary situation in
which it finds itself. 'Ah, well, famous strategists, the Republic has not sterilely passed forty
years of its life to hold a grudge against you. In forty days it reduces you to impotence, in
forty days this people, whom you are right to envy, has improvised by its activity, its genius,
its resources, what it has taken you forty years to achieve. . . . You won't win, for now we
fight on the terrain of propaganda and the idea, and for civilisation.' In his jeering passages
he calls the Germans 'true patriarchs' who keep their wives in servitude and don't know how
to invite anyone home to dinner. 'I've seen you eating in your homes.' Also 'your peasants
with a spoon in their pocket, a cased fork, a knife on a chain, a porcelain pipe like a cruet-
stand, florins by way of coat-buttons, boots crosswise with mule-irons on the heels, and a
green hat; then each reading the Bible by way of instruction'. He ends with the appeal:

Believe me. Go back home for a little while. I'll come and visit you.
   Go back to your own country. Your women and children call for you and die of hunger. Our
peasants, who've come to struggle against your criminal enterprises, are in the same case as you.
As you return, call out: Long live the Republic. Down with frontiers! You have only to gain by that:
you'll share in our country as brothers.

Turning to the Artists, he calls for Brotherhood and European Unity. He upbraids them for
abandoning their high ideals and succumbing to tyranny.

I've lived with you in thought for twenty-two years and you've compelled me to sympathise with
you and respect you. I've found you tenacious in work, full of prudence and will-power, hostile to
centralisation and the constraint of ideas. When we've met at Frankfurt and Munich, I declared our
common tendencies. Just as I demanded liberty for art, you asked as well for the liberty of the
people. Among you I believed myself in my own land, among my brothers. We drank then to
France and to the advent of the European Republic. At Munich again, last year, you swore by the
most fearful oaths not to be enfeoffed with Prussia. Today you're all registered in the banks of
Bismarck; you bear on your brow a regimenting number [*nombre d'ordre*] and know how to give
the military salute.

They trace humanitarian symbols on their canvases and utter daily hymns to brotherhood,
and yet now 'you forge irons for Germany'. Until 4 September the whole matter was a mere
conflict between tyrants. But now the Republic is born and the situation is radically changed.
'You want to put the Revolution in chains. Poor fools, you're putting the halter round your
own necks.' But 'accumulate soldiers on soldiers, pile up cannons on howitzers, machine-
guns on mortars, the Revolution does not fear you. The Republic, which cannot conceive
of such battles, which has as its resources only the will of the people, the Republic will never
be conquered, I give you my word for it. Pillage, burn, kill: all you'll succeed in doing is to

make France at the most a martyr people. You'll substitute one fetishism for another: the myth of a Nation divinised in the fable of a Man-God.' These last words show a remarkable grasp of German tendencies and may be taken as a prophecy, via Bismarck, of Hitler.

Courbet then makes a powerful appeal to the Germans; he has forgotten that he is speaking specifically to the Artists:

You are said to be needy folk; so much the better. In France poverty is a certificate of honesty. You've dragged with you all your relics, your antiquities, all the chariots of your ancestors, the Cimbri and the Teutons, and the famous battle-tumbril of Arminius. As is right, you don't want to take them back empty when you return over the Rhine. You must have an indemnity. All right. Take it. Load on your vehicles the stones from the walls of Toul and of Strasbourg. We abandon them to you. You can dispose of them in your homeland as heroic souvenirs. Do better. In passing, throw down your citadels. If your heart prompts you to that, we'll give you a handclap for over-throwing altogether those bloody divisions that mark the frontiers and cut in halves groups of people issued from the same blood.
When the frontiers have vanished, no more need of fortresses to guard them. No more frontiers, hence no more armies. No more armies! Only murderers will kill. At least that's our hope.
Do you hold to your nationality? Once you're liberated, we'll help if you ever ask us. Only, in this event, you'll set up Alsace and Lorraine as free and neutral countries, as pledge of our alliance. All those will take refuge there who are horrified at national chauvinism and want a life without political impediments. And in provinces mutilated and crucified, forgetful of wounds that bleed in our side, we'll clasp once more your hand and drink to the United States of Europe.
Salut and Fraternity!
An idea.
Here now. Leave us your Krupp cannons. We'll melt them down with ours all together. The last cannon-muzzle sticking up in air, coifed with a Phrygian bonnet, set upon a pedestal backed on three cannonballs – this colossal monument, which we'll erect together in the Place Vendôme will be your column, yours and ours, the column of the peoples, the column of Germany and France for ever federated.
As once Venus crowned the god Mars, the Goddess of our Liberty will hang on the axles it bears at its sides like arms, garlands of grapes, corn-ears, and hop-flowers.[22]

In looking forward to a United States of Europe, he was carrying on the ideas of men like Considérant, but giving them a more concrete socialist content and allying them with revolu-tionary activity of the masses. (Flora Tristan in *La Ville Montre*, 1842, a book which I have suggested was read by Courbet, stated that she was writing 'from the angle of eventual European unity and universal amity'. Charles Lemonnier, much influenced by her, started with Hugo and Garibaldi the League of Peace – and founded a journal *The United States of Europe*.)

Courbet donated a seascape to a lottery which was to raise money for a cannon cast by the Cail Foundry and named *Le Courbet*. The cannon was to go to the battalion of the National Guard stationed in the Grenelle Quarter of the 15th *arrondissement*. But he objected, in vain, when the Defence Committee under Henri de Rochefort confiscated the building materials left over from his 1867 show and used them for barricades. Many artists were serving in the ranks of the defenders. Chenavard enlisted in the Schaelcher battalions; Reverdy served in the National Guard and was named for his brave conduct under fire.

In September Courbet had sub-let two big rooms of his apartment in the rue du Vieux-Colombier to Dr Robinet for the Republican Circle of the 6th *arrondissement*, the 120 members of which held meetings there. Courbet put many of his treasured copies on the walls; but, according to Zoé, he never attended any meetings. As she was, however, in no position to know, and as she was keen to whitewash Courbet at all costs, her statement has no value. On 2 October the armaments-commission of the 6th, under the mayor Hérisson, with two deputies (A. Rousselle and Dr Robinet), expressed the wish that the bronze of the Colonne Vendôme should be melted down for cannons.[23]

Courbet visited the front line at least once. He was escorted by Pierre Boyer, then a young officer in the medical corps. They went to a point near the bridge over the Bièvre a mile or two south of the city-limits. Some sniping went on; Boyer later wrote, 'I'd known Courbet rather closely. I'd at times accompanied him on his nocturnal prowls', but he met him most often during the siege at *Père* Laveur's. The field-hospital was in a dangerous spot, faced by the Prussian batteries at Bourg-la-Reine, with others on the right at Nagneux and Châtillon, and on the left at L'Hay. 'There was also shooting on the left in the direction of a little grove; we deposited Courbet behind a wall in an armchair', then went to see if there were any wounded. On their return Courbet greeted them with obvious satisfaction. 'I was beginning to get cold here. They've been shooting. . . . I heard the bullets whistle.... Then we'll find the bullets. Come with me.'

For a man with no experience of gunfire, says Boyer, Courbet took it all very calmly; he hadn't even let his pipe go out. The Prussians had in fact been firing near him, but a little to the right. He and Boyer walked towards the walls of a mill, but found nothing. 'While he was puffing away like a seal, bending over to search in the rough grass', Boyer handed him a bullet, then another.

The adventure was a success. Courbet carried away the tangible proofs. That night, detained by my duties, I couldn't go to Laveur's and enjoy listening to the master's account of his expedition. Perhaps that was just as well; for the bullets . . . had certainly been fired by real Prussians, but not on that day. I had a collection of them, and, at the crucial moment, had fished them out of my pocket.[24]

The Government of National Defence, under L. J. Trochu as governor of Paris, had now lost the respect of the radicals and much of the population; it was incapable of effectively carrying on the resistance to the Germans. On 28 January 1871 Robinet gained Courbet's signature to the protest of his Circle against the armistice which had been arranged. In the myth that Zoé sought to build up on the basis of Champfleury's denigrations, Courbet was now the plaything of irresponsible characters who said to him, 'With your name we're going to move the world. We'll act and you'll speak. You'll be the first citizen of our time. We'll make you President of our Republic.'[25] All that was nonsense; Courbet was acting throughout on clearly understood principles. But the myth has had much effect on later writers, who have never paid Courbet the tribute of the hard and consistent thought he put into his art and politics alike.

The seat of government was now at Bordeaux. On 8 February elections were held for a National Assembly. Large numbers of provincial deputies wanted peace at any price; many even supported the restoration of the monarchy. On 12 February Thiers was empowered to negotiate peace-terms; a preliminary pact was signed at Versailles a fortnight later and ratified on 1 March. The government moved back to Paris and on 10 May the Treaty of Frankfurt ended the war. But the people of Paris were not satisfied.

In January Courbet had a pleasant note from a friend, Jules Troubat:

Since July I've had a commission for you. My father, *vigneron* of 71 years, at Montpellier, told me in the midst of his vineyard, 'If Courbet was here, I'd embrace him.' It was at the time of your refusal of the Cross. I haven't found a moment to come and see you, but I'll get along one of these days. The bombardment, which sent an *obus* tonight on to no. 7 (I'm at 11), keeps me in this little house so as to be present for any possible accident. I have the responsibility of wife and children.[26]

This month the Prussians invaded Franche-Comté. Troops were billeted in Courbet's studio at Ornans, damaged the building, and carried off some of the contents. The family was left alone. On 23 February Courbet wrote, 'You give me an account of the scarcities at Ornans, which I had anticipated; I was very uneasy about you all.' Then he hurries on to his own situation. 'The siege was a *farce*, but that wasn't the fault of the inhabitants, who wanted to fight on *to the limit*.' The government gave in because it 'didn't want the Republic to save France'. 'All that crowd of traitors, rogues, and idiots who governed us never fought anything but sham battles, killing a great many men for nothing. These murderers lost not only Paris but France as well by paralysing and discouraging as much as they could.'

These scoundrels used tortures to make the inhabitants surrender. Having resolved on capitulation from the start, they tried to glorify themselves by making it look as if demanded by the people. They stationed 200,000 National Guards at the fortifications where only 25,000 were required. At the municipal butcher-shops they built up queues of 2,000 people, which formed in the afternoon to get a bit of horseflesh half the size on one's fist at ten the next morning. One had to stand in the queue oneself, so that women, old people, and children spent the winter-nights in the open and died of rheumatism. . . .

On the last day there was no bread. That was another fraud. There were warehouses with 400,000 kilos of food left to rot while our bread was made of sawdust and oatstraw. Throughout this whole period M. Trochu, nincompoop, wouldn't try a single determined sortie; and whenever the National Guard gained ground, they were ordered next day to retreat. . . . The real enemies of France weren't the Prussians. They were our friends the French reactionaries aided by the clergy. M. Trochu called for novenas and prayed for a miracle from Ste Geneviève; he proposed a religious procession. You can imagine how we all laughed. . . .

Bombs struck our house and the one opposite. I've had to leave my studio and take lodgings in the Passage du Saumon. Recently the people of Paris proposed to make me deputy, and I received 50,666 votes without making a single move. If my name had been printed on the list and if people had been sure I'd accept, I'd have had at least 100,000.

He says he hasn't suffered. 'I happened to need a good purging and I wasn't hungry. I'm thin now, that's good.' He pacifies the family by saying he'll come when he can; he knew that his Munich Order would be useful. In passing he mentions the project of destroying the Column. 'I wanted to demolish the Vendôme Column. I could not obtain permission from the Government; the people approved.' He uses here the term 'démolir'; but we need not take this passage too seriously. It is a bit of the bombast he uses to make the family feel how important he is.[27]

He had indeed nearly become a deputy. His socialist friends carried on an improvised campaign, in which he took no part. His new lodgings were rented from a dressmaker, Mlle Gérard. On 6 January, fearing more shells on his studio, he had transferred most of his works there; and some weeks later he sent 15–20 important paintings to the dealer Durand-Ruel in rue Lafitte.

The government, highly conservative, was afraid of the National Guard. Thiers, chief of the executive power, with the support of the Assembly, sent a detachment under General J. Vinoy to seize the artillery of the Guard in Montmartre on the night of 17–18 March; but the attack failed and precipitated a revolt. Many of the regulars went over to join the Guard; two generals were killed; the government fled to Versailles. On the 18th the funeral of Victor Hugo's son Charles was being carried out in the Père-Lachaise cemetry. Hugo had now returned to France. He tells us , 'Between the tombstones a large hand was stretched out to me and a voice said, 'I am Courbet.' At the same time I saw an animated and cordial face smiling at me with a tear in the eyes. I clasped his hand warmly. It was the first time I saw Courbet.'[28] On the 19th the elective central committee of the National Guard, now the only effective authority left in Paris, proclaimed the establishment of the Commune. It occupied the Town Hall and with the consent of the *arrondissement*-mayors it organised an election for 26 March. In the 6th *arrondissement* (population 75,438; registered voters 24,807) 9,499 men voted for the election of four delegates. There were nineteen candidates and Courbet came sixth, with 3,242 votes. As two of the winning candidates failed to attend meetings of the Commune, a supplementary election was held on Sunday 16 April for two seats. This time Courbet was chosen (2,418 out of 3,469 votes). His election was validated on 19 April. About this time he wrote a statement of his political faith, addressed to Citizen Vallès.

I have been asked for a profession of faith. After three years of public revolutionary socialist life, I have then not been able to make my ideas understood. However, I must submit to this demand, the language of painting not being familiar to everyone.

I've been constantly concerned with the social question and the philosophies connected with it, marching in my own path parallel to my comrade Proudhon. Denying the false and conventional idea, in 1848 I hoisted the flag of Realism, which alone puts art at the service of man. And so I have logically struggled against all forms of authoritative government and divine right, wanting man to govern himself according to his needs, to his own direct profit and according to his own personal conception.

In 1848 I opened a socialist club in opposition to the clubs of Jacobins, Montagnards, and others whom I qualified as Republicans without the essential nature, Historical Republicans.

The Republic, one, indivisible, authoritative, begot fear. Socialism, not having been sufficiently elaborated, was rejected; and the reaction of 1849 carried the day to the profit of a monstrous regime. Entrenched in my individualism, I struggled without respite against the government of that time, not only without fearing it, but further by provoking it.

To sum up my position in two words:

While keeping in mind the American and Swiss Republics and their organisation, let us consider our own as born yesterday. Today we have a free field. As a result, dropping all revenges, reprisals, violences, let us establish afresh an order of things that belongs to us and depends only on us.

I'm happy to tell you that the painters, at my instigation, have just taken the initiative in this order of ideas. Let all the state-bodies of society follow their example, and in the future no other kind of government can prevail against ours. The associations belong to themselves, and, constituted according to their own proper interests, they will be our *cantons*; and the more they govern themselves, the more they'll lighten the tasks of the Commune. The Commune will then be able to concern itself more with general interests and its relation to the rest of France. So it works out that the existing Commune becomes the Federal Commune of these associations. I take advantage of this occasion to thank the electors for the sympathies they have shown for me in the last two elections.[29]

He speaks of three years of public revolutionary life, which takes us back to 1868. He is presumably thinking of the time when he joined the First International. His remarks show that he sees a socialist France as an interconnected system of self-governing associations with a Federal Commune that coordinates but does not impose any 'Republic, one, indivisible, authoritative'. He was himself much taken up with schemes for reform in the administration of all museums, exhibitions, and institutions of art. *Le Soir* of 6 April published an appeal which he had addressed to his fellow-artists in preparation for a meeting next day at the École de Médecine:

Revenge is ours. Paris has saved France from dishonour and abasement. Ah, Paris! Paris has understood in its genius that one cannot attack a backward enemy with his own arms. Paris has taken its position on its own terrain and the enemy will be conquered as he hasn't been able to conquer us. Today Paris is free and belongs to herself, and the provinces are in slavery. When federated France can understand Paris, Europe will be saved.

He goes on to appeal to the artists, whom 'Paris has nourished like a mother'. The museums must be opened, an exhibition prepared. By starving them out, the Prussians have helped them 'to reconquer our moral life and raise every individual to human dignity'. But now the true and most cruel Prussians were the men at Versailles, 'the exploiters of the poor'. The revolution of Paris has come from the people. 'Its apostles are workers, its Christ has been Proudhon. For eighteen hundred years honest men have died with sighs on their lips; but the heroic people of Paris will defeat the mystagogues and torturers of Versailles, man will govern himself, federation will be understood.' He ends, 'Our era is about to begin. Curious coincidence! Next Sunday is Easter Day. Will our Resurrection take place on that day! Goodbye to the old world and its diplomacy!'

At the meeting next day he submitted proposals for specific reforms 'in the spirit of the Commune'. These covered such matters as the election by the artists of two delegates from each of the 22 *arrondissements*; the handing-over to this committee of all such duties as the appointment of curators and directors of all public museums, the formulation of rules for exhibitions, the abolition of the École des Beaux-Arts, the fine arts section of the Institute, the French Academy in Rome, and all the old awards and medals. Buildings in the School of Fine Arts might stay open for pupils who chose their own teachers and organised their own courses of study. Artists who disagreed with the majority were to be assigned galleries of their own for shows; any awards were to be given by the vote of exhibitors.[30] A temporary commission was elected by acclamation to study the reforms, and brought forward its manifesto at a further meeting on 15 April. The hall was crowded with 400 artists. A Federation of Artists was to be established in Paris on the basis of three principles:

The free expansion of art released from all governmental control and all privilege; equal rights for all members of the federation; the independence and dignity of each artist guaranteed by all, through the creation of a committee elected by universal suffrage of all the artists.

The committee, to be called the Federal Commission of Artists, would preserve past treasures by administering museums and the like; it would support and encourage living art by organising local, national, and international shows; it would stimulate the growth of art by educational reforms; and it would publish a periodical, *Officiel des Arts*.[31]

The committee was to have 47 members (16 painters, 10 sculptors, 5 architects, 6 engravers and lithographers, 10 industrial or decorative artists). At its election on 1 April, Courbet got the highest number of votes, 274 out of 290; and among the others chosen were Bonvin, Corot, Daumier, A. Gautier, Manet, Millet, Bracquemond, Flemeng, Gill. Some had been put forward without their consent; others were away from Paris; a few, like Millet, protested; others ignored the election. But Courbet, Gill, Gautier were active members. Meetings were held in the Louvre, then on 25 April at a place in the rue de Rivoli (formerly occupied by the ministry of Fine Arts). The plans were ambitious, wide in scope, thoroughly argued-out. The Commune did not last long enough for much to be done about them; but the committee tried to get to grips with the Louvre where some galleries were reopened. Courbet later claimed the credit for that, though it has been suggested that the director, Barbet de Jouy, was responsible. On 2 May the various academic institutions were abolished, including the Academy in Athens. On 17 May the directors and deputies of the Louvre and the Luxembourg were dismissed; in their place the committee put some of its own members: A. Oudinot, Jules Héreau, the sculptor Dalou at the Louvre; Gill, J. Chapuy, and Gluck at the Luxembourg.

At some time during the Commune or perhaps a little earlier Courbet had met a woman, Mme G. (with the maiden name of Mathilde Montaigne Carly de Swazema), who claimed to be of noble birth and who offered him 'a chaste heart and a virginity of soul' – commodities he had no interest in. Still, despite her languishing pretences, her practical methods were more direct; and she became his mistress. The whole thing, however, is involved in obscurity except for its disastrous conclusions in 1872–3. But we may give here the first part of Gros-Kost's account, with some passages from her letters:

'I love you and I want to be yours. The man of genius cannot repel the most sincere of his woman admirers, I have had great misfortunes in my life. I have been deceived, calumniated, persecuted. I was disgusted with everything and ready to die when I saw you – don't seek to know who I am.

'I have often met you, but you don't know me. You will never know me.

'I don't want to write to you. Despite all my misfortunes, I offer you a heart still chaste and a *virginity of soul.* . . . I send you, without shame, a confession that you will be able to accept. Receive only my letters and reply to them sometimes.'

There were four pages like that.

The paper was fine, silky, and the envelope smelt nicely; the perfume of woman is a way of caressing from afar that never loses its effect. Courbet, red as a peony, scratched his occiput. He sought in vain in his memory for the features of this woman, doubtless beautiful, certainly young, who came to offer him a chaste heart and a virginity of soul. He read this hysterical declaration to two or three of his friends. What was one to think of it? 'You're dealing with an intriguer. Don't trust her. Don't reply.'

'*Pardieu*, you're right,' said the painter. 'The matter will remain there. And then how amusingly it's written. The little woman can wait for the postman. He won't bring her much consolation.' Another drink was called for and the incident was forgotten.[32]

On 21 April the executive of the Commune set up a committee on public education. There were five members: Courbet, Verdure, Vallès, Jules Miot, J. B. Clément. One of Courbet's first acts after he became formally a member of the Commune was to protest about the arrest of his friend Chaudey, who had been very close to Proudhon. After 4 September Chaudey had served as mayor of the 9th *arrondissement*; in November he failed to get re-elected and was given a lesser post at the Town Hall. But suspicions were somehow aroused that he was working against the Commune. His chief enemies seem to have been Raoul Rigault and Delescluze. The latter had had a fierce polemic with Proudhon, who remained hostile to him. Delescluze had even challenged Proudhon to a duel. (In a letter Proudhon speaks of leaving out the name of Delescluze and another from a committee of May 1863, 'because of their personal animosity against me, and because we must not allow that any of us is open to attack in any way at all in his private life'.) Now Chaudey was being accused of giving the order to 'clean out the square' before the Town Hall on 22 January when a dozen people had been killed. On Vermorel's demand, Courbet made inquiry but could find no verification of the charge. Vermorel then asked for the release of Chaudey, but Delescluze strongly opposed him.[33] At Rigault's order Chaudey had been arrested on 13 April and put in Mazas prison. Courbet's protest occurred on the 23rd.

On 30 April he wrote to his family in tones that show he had carried over into the Commune the extreme optimism that he had always shown in any of his own exploits, however certain to fail.

Here am I, drawn by the people of Paris into political affairs up to my neck. President of the Federation of Artists, Member of the Commune, Delegate to the Mairie [of the 6th *arrondissement*], Delegate for Public Education – the four most important posts in Paris. I get up, I breakfast, I attend and preside a dozen hours a day. My head's beginning to feel like a baked potato. Despite this ache in my head and the difficulty of apprehending affairs to which I'm not accustomed, I'm in a state of enchantment. *Paris is a true paradise*: no police, no nonsense [*sottises*], no extortion of any kind, no disputes. Paris runs on by itself, as if on little wheels. It should be able to stay always like this. In a word it's sheer bliss [*un vrai ravissement*]: all the state-bodies are set in a federation and belong to themselves. It is I who set the pattern with the artists of all sorts.

The notaries and bailiffs belong to the Commune, by which they're paid, also the registrars. As for the curés, if they want to hold services in Paris (though no one wants them to), they'll be allowed to rent churches. In our leisure moments we fight the blackguards [*saligots*] of Versailles.

We all take turns. They can fight on for ten years as they're doing, without being able to get in here, and when we do let them in, it'll be their tomb. We're safe within our walls. We're losing very few men while their losses are tremendous. That's no misfortune; for the whole Versailles crowd . . . will have to be liquidated for the sake of peace. There are gathered all the police spies with their blackjacks, the soldiers of the Pope, the cowards who surrendered at Sedan; and their politicians are the men who betrayed France: Thiers, Jules Favre, Picard and other scoundrels, former lackeys of the tyrants. . . .

I don't know, dear parents, when I'll have the pleasure of seeing you again. I'm obliged to carry out energetically all the tasks entrusted to me, tasks for which I've had so much inclination all my life . . . [though] I've always been isolated within my own individuality. To be in harmony with the Commune of Paris I have no need to ponder, I need only to act instinctively. The Paris Commune is more successful than any other form of government has ever been.

He adds that he's had bad luck in losing his two studios, 'everything I took so much trouble to accumulate': that at Ornans plundered, and the stored building-materials used for barricades.[34]

As April drew on, the Versailles troops went on surrounding Paris; the bombardment grew worse. On 12 April 1871, four days before his election, the Commune had ordered the demolition of the Vendôme Column:

The Commune of Paris: Considering that the imperial column in the Place Vendôme is a monument of barbarism, a symbol of brute force and of false glory, an affirmation of militarism, a negation of international law, a permanent insult by the victors to the vanquished, a perpetual threat to one of the three great principles of the French Republic, Fraternity, *decrees*: First and only article: The Column in the Place Vendôme shall be demolished.[35]

There was no intention of preserving the reliefs. In the *Journal Officiel* for 20 April the point is stressed by a statement that the material will be offered for sale in four lots, two of construction-materials, two of metal; sealed bids were to be sent to the Administration of Engineers, of the War Ministry, 64 rue Saint-Dominique-Saint-Germain. This measure was again passed before Courbet took his seat. On 27 April he made his only contribution as a member of the Commune to the demolition.

Citizen Courbet demanded that the Commune's decree as to the demolition of the Vendôme Column be put into effect. Perhaps it might be advisable to retain the monument's pedestal where the reliefs record the history of the [first] Republic; the imperial column would be replaced by a figure symbolising the revolution of 18 March [1871]. Citizen J. B. Clément insisted that the Column should be wholly broken up and destroyed. Citizen Andrieu said that the executive committee was attending to the decree's carrying-out; the Vendôme Column would be demolished in a few days. Citizen Gambon proposed the appointment of Citizen Courbet to assist the citizens in charge of the operation. Citizen Grousset replied that the executive committee had put the work in the hands of two engineers of the highest standing, who had assumed all responsibility for its carrying-out.[36]

Courbet later held that he had been misreported and that he had asked only for the *déboulonnement*. His remarks may have been overcompressed, as secretaries delivered their notes to the editor of the *Journal* without any checking; but it is likely that the sense of his speech was given correctly enough. What is true is that he was only one of many who had denounced the Column and that there were many others who were much more directly connected with both the decree and its execution. The person mainly responsible for the whole thing seems to have been Félix Pyat, member of the executive committee. Incidentally Courbet was wrong about the pedestal-reliefs, which also represented Napoleonic trophies.

As the situation worsened, the Commune proposed the setting-up of a Committee of Public Safety with unlimited power to act in the Commune's name. On 1 May the proposal was accepted by 45 to 23 votes. Courbet voted with the minority and added his signature to their statement:

Whereas the establishment of a Committee of Public Safety will inevitably entail the creation of a dictatorial power which will contribute nothing to the strength of the Commune: whereas this establishment will be in direct opposition to the political aspirations of the electoral rank-and-file, which the Commune represents; whereas therefore the creation of any dictatorship by the Commune would be in fact a usurpation of the sovereignty of the people, we vote in the negative.[37]

Courbet was entirely logical in taking this course; the question opened was one that is still with us, even if in a much more complicated form. During the debate he announced his resignation as delegate to the Mairie though he does not seem to have sent any formal letter. But he went on carrying out his duties as chairman of the artists' committee till the end. Early in May Thiers had sent from Versailles bundles of anti-Commune posters to be set up on Paris walls; on 10 May the Committee of Public Safety replied with an order for the demolition of his house and the confiscation of its contents, his large collection of art-objects ranging from ancient terracottas to Chinese lacquers and Renascence bronzes. Courbet at the session of 12 May of the Commune expressed his concern as to the fate of these objects, which deserved to be put in a museum. The Committee appointed a committee of five (including Courbet) to take charge of the packing and transport. Finally the Commune decreed that the linen was to go to hospitals, the art-objects to museums, the books to public libraries, the furniture was to be auctioned and the proceeds to go to widows and orphans of the National Guard. It was not known that Thiers had taken the precaution of hiding many of his rarest items in the cellars of the Institute. The demolition of the house took several days, during which Courbet and his colleagues made inventories, super-intended the packing, and sent the crates to a temporary home in a warehouse on the quai d'Orsay. When the bombardment threatened this site, the crates were taken to the Tuileries where a part of them were destroyed during the fires of 24 May.

On 14 May Courbet wrote home. He had been 'charged to demolish the house of Thiers and collect his artworks. The monster won't defeat us.' Commerce (that is, money-values) had taken control of men; it was a monstrosity; but now 'we re-establish the simple life and humanity, while leaving man in his own power [*puissance*] and his own individuality'. The people of Paris has won immense glory, which astounds the whole world. For the third time it wages the only legitimate war on earth. The people of Paris is the greatest people 'that has ever been in the world; and even if one had to die prematurely for this cause, it would be the finest death one could desire'. The provinces can't understand 'the movement we make', for under Napoleon they weren't allowed to meet, form clubs, discuss social questions. He claims that the Commune has 'reason and honesty and nothing will happen outside of that. We haven't shot anyone.'

Meanwhile, on 1 May, the day of the formation of the Committee of Public Safety, the Commune concluded the contract for demolition with Citizen Iribe, civil engineer, member of the Positivist Club; Courbet did not sign the document.[38] The great day was to be 5 May, the anniversary of Napoleon I's death; but Iribe couldn't get things ready in time. After two postponements he declared that all was set for 16 May, at 2 p.m.[39]

At the base of the shaft on the side that faced the rue de la Paix was made a triangular cut extending through about a third of the diameter; on the opposite side at the same level the stone was sawn through and iron wedges inserted, the lowest bronze plates having first been taken off. A very strong cable was looped round the Column's top at the height of the platform and attached to a pulley that was linked, by a cable passing through it three times, to another pulley fixed in the ground. From this the cable was wound round a winch placed opposite the column near the inter-section of the Place and the rue Neuve-des-Petits-Champs. This winch was firmly anchored to the ground. To deaden the fall the ground had been covered by a bed of sand, over which twigs and a thick layer of dung were strewn. . . .

From noon on a large crowd had gathered in the rue de la Paix near the Place, into which access was forbidden to the public. . . . About 3.30 the winch began to turn; the cable stretched and grew taut. . . . After the strain had been applied for several minutes, something was heard to snap; the pulley fixed to the ground . . . had just broken. The contractor sent for a stronger one, which was installed. . . .

About 5.30 several military bands, assembled in the corners of the square on the side nearest the rue Saint-Honoré, played the Marseillaise. All was ready for fresh application of tension to the cable. It had been stretched tight for only a few minutes when the Column was seen to tilt. When it had inclined very slightly from the perpendicular, it suddenly broke into segments, which crashed to the ground, making a tremendous noise and raising a thick cloud of dust. At once the spectators . . . surged forwards to the immense ruin, clambering onto and examining the blocks of stone. Several members of the Commune made brief speeches; red flags were brought from headquarters and set on the Column's pedestal.[40]

The Times correspondent reported that the fall occurred at 5.50. 'The concussion was nothing like what had been expected. No glass was broken or injury done to the Square, excepting that the Column forced itself into the ground. The excitement was intense.' People were searched before leaving the Square, to make sure they were not carrying off any fragments.[41]

Courbet did not speak. Castagnary says, 'Naturally Courbet was there, but merely as a spectator.' Vallès, some years later, wrote:

Poor fool, one doesn't attack fetishes of bronze with impunity. He wasn't such a fool. He knew well what awaited him. The day when the Column was overthrown, he was there, on the Place, with his twenty-franc cane, his four-franc straw hat, his ready-made overcoat bought perhaps at the Reding-gote Grise. 'It'll wipe me out in falling, you'll see,' said he, turning to his friends, and he added, pointing with cane-end at a group in which the faces of some traitors might be seen (I could name them), 'They'd assassinate me like a monarch, hey, if they dared.' He leant on the *â* with all the weight of his *franc-comtois* accent, and shrugged his shoulders with a gesture of *Hercules Goodfellow*.

That night he remarked at table, 'We've done a good deed. There will perhaps no longer be so many soldiers; the sweethearts of conscripts won't wet so many handkerchiefs any more. Come on, drink up and sing a song.'

The bandit struck up a melancholic and simple air, full of naïvety and village-sentiment:

> On the banks of a stream
> I killed my captain.

The cannon of the forts provided the refrain.

He has found, he will find, before his tomb, people to reproach him for passing from the studio into the street and planting his easel in the midst of the barricades. He was not here indeed to take command of an insurrection. But men like Courbet are led despite themselves into the struggle. In our society moulded by Napoleon we have to accept a regimental number, password, discipline. The painters like the footsloggers have their barracks and the generals are called academicians. Courbet, a deserter, wanted to paint living men instead of the dead. He'll end fatally in prison, in exile, in an obscure death, far from his homeland.

Pistol-shots aimed against tradition, when the pistol's butt-end is a brush, upset the tranquillity or the servility of the lickers of pictures, the lickers of ministers. That also irritates the independents, who, upright before men, are cowards before theories.[42]

The Commune did not have long to last. The last session at which Courbet appeared was probably that of 21 May, for the freeing of General Cluseret, who in April had been named Minister of War. That old soldier was a brave man but an incapable organiser; his failure in dealing with the problems of defence had brought about his arrest on 1 May on a charge of treason. Not that he was alone responsible for the chaos that had set in; it was rather the political attitudes which he stood for and which Courbet shared. The latter in his letter to the War Council had reproached the officials of the Commune for lacking in 'spontaneity'. Cluseret represented the 'spontaneous' attitude in army-organisation and battle-methods. On 7 April he had appealed to his soldiers, 'In obeying those you elected [*les élus*, the officers], you obey yourselves.' Excellent principles, but hardly enough in themselves. The result in the end was a vast confusion, a total incapacity for effective defence, merged with much personal heroism of a self-sacrificial kind. The advocates of spontaneity, because of a semi-mystical belief in the energies of the people, maintained a blind faith in victory after all possibility of it had quite gone. On 21 May, Élie Reclus wrote, 'I begin to believe in a victory for Paris, won by high struggle.' By noon that day 60,000 Versaillais were in the city. Courbet had exactly the same wild hopes in a hopeless situation. (It is of interest to note him as a typical *bon garçon* of the spontaneity-school and to recall what Marx wrote to Kugelmann on the same day as Reclus set out his credo: 'If they are defeated, only their *bon-garçon* character will be to blame. They should at once have marched on Versailles.') The breakthrough of 21 May was followed by a week of desperate street-fighting and massacre during which large numbers of men, women and children were killed. On 23 May Claudey was executed by a firing-squad under Rigault's supervision in the courtyard of Sainte-Pélagie; next day Rigault himself was killed in the street-fights. By 29 May the defence had finally ended, and the mass-executions by the triumphant reactionaries began. All Commune-leaders who did not escape were shot or jailed. How did Courbet avoid death?[43]

Courbet could have escaped easily enough to Switzerland via Besançon or Pontarlier; but to flee would be to admit both guilt and defeat – something particularly difficult for him. His optimism probably told him that he had nothing or little to fear. All through the last terrible week he stayed at his post and helped Barbet de Jouy, reinstated at the Louvre, to protect the national collections. Darcel, who published his account of the arts under the Commune in 1872 and who was very hostile to Courbet, has this tale:

Under the pretext that this palace [the Tuileries] could be struck by the bombs of the besiegers, which were already bursting in the Champs-Elyseés, he had engaged M. Barbet de Jouy to have removed from the chapel of the Tuileries very mediocre modern copies of the central and side pictures of the celebrated *Descent from the Cross* by Rubens, which he thought to be originals. One took advantage of the permission to enter the Tuileries for this removal in order to carry away some others works of art and M. G. Courbet was surprised that more had not been taken.
On the other hand he kept saying to anyone who wished to listen, with regard to the Tuileries: 'I'll have all that knocked down' – pointing to the annexes of Louis XIV, on each side of the old ruined palace of Catherine de Médicis – 'and that would be much better. You'd see the greenery either side, and in what remained one could put a museum of tools where workers will study the instruments of their work. One will plant the court of the Carrousel as a garden, but leave the iron-work so that children may play there safely.'[1]

After what we know of his collection of copies, the confusion about the Rubens may well be true; and the comment on the Tuileries sounds authentic but perhaps slightly twisted. Barbet de Jouy sheltered the two delegate artists, knowing that they'd be shot if he let them go; next day, 25 May, he took them out, giving his arm to Mme Dalou, who, with her young daughter, was with her husband, and thus saved them.

Courbet, who, as Vallès remarked, was no fool despite his optimism, had the sense to change his lodgings. He left his possessions in the Passage du Saumon, and moved to 12 rue Saint-Gilles in the 2nd *arrondissement*, the house of an old friend, maker of musical instruments, A. Lecomte, who, after his arrest, said that 'he had no interest in politics', but was unwilling to refuse hospitality to a friend he'd known for twenty years.[2] This move probably saved his life; for he was a marked man. The *Paris-Journal* of 27 May in the section dealing with Executions announced the death of Vallès, who had played as active as odious a part in the Commune, and said that, as for Courbet,

He deserves a special mention. It's indeed an artist we lose, but we must not weep for him; for he's a great rascal that society has got rid of. He was in the Ministry of Marine at the moment our troops took possession of it. Seized with fear, he saved himself; and as people do when they're very scared, he did it clumsily. He was easily discovered in a wall-cupboard too narrow for his large person. The officer marching at the head of his men recognised who it was. Courbet is one of those who first pressed for the demolition of the Column. A soldier couldn't forget him. The officer ordered him to be arrested. Courbet wanted for a moment to resist. One of the soldiers smashed his head in with a shot.

Other journals stated that he was jailed at Satory or died of apoplexy there, was shot at Versailles or on the barricades, fled to Bavaria; he had poisoned himself at Satory. 'His deathpangs were long and terrible. Chance has put us in contact with one of the police on guard at the moment of Courbet's arrival. He was present at his death and has shown us the mound where he sleeps his last sleep.'[3]

By keeping out of the way during the days of worst violence he escaped that sort of fate. On 30 May the police entered the Passage du Saumon and seized a trunk full of his papers. Next day they sequestered in the basement there 106 canvases (already mouldy from damp), two cases of other pictures and an antique panel. On 2 June they searched the studio in the rue Hautefeuille as well as the apartment of a Mme Romenance at the same address, and sealed the studio-door. The pretext given was they had to make sure he hadn't stolen pictures from the public galleries or from Thiers's house. The police commissioner in charge, Gobet, admitted that 'our ignorance in matters pertaining to art did not permit us to decide whether the said canvases were by Courbet or came from galleries'. The only object found that was not Courbet's was a small antique figure and a statuette's head that he had picked up in the debris of Thiers's house, meaning to add them to the rest of the collection as soon as possible.

Meanwhile at Ornans, as soon as the news of the Commune's defeat arrived, the municipality ordered the removal of the *Bullhead-fisher* statue from its fountain. Two days later, 30 May, the statue was wrenched from its stand, with an arm broken off, and given to Régis. In some ways this insult hurt Courbet more than his major disasters. Worse still, a few days later came the news that his mother, perturbed by his setbacks, had died at the age of seventy-seven.

At last, on 7 June, the police tracked him down and he was arrested at Lecomte's apartment. Taken to the prefecture of police, he was interrogated for an hour and locked up for the night. Journals said the house of Lecomte was of 'sinister appearance', and that Courbet hid in a cupboard till he stifled. Bursting out, he cried, 'I was growing old in there; thanks for delivering me.' The facts were that he himself opened the front door in his shirt-sleeves, smoking his pipe. As a matter of form, he contested his identity. 'It's true that without hair and beard you are hardly recognisable,' said the officer, 'but you've kept your accent, which betrays you.'[4] On 8 June in the morning he sent a scribbled note to Castagnary. 'I was arrested last night at eleven. I was taken to the Ministry of Foreign Affairs, then brought on to the police station at midnight. I slept in a corridor piled up with prisoners and now I'm in a cell, no. 24. I expect to be taken to Versailles soon. If you could come and see me, I'd be very happy to talk with you a bit – my situation isn't pleasant. That's what one's heart leads one into.'[5]

On 8 June, again interrogated, he stated that he had become a member of the Commune only to protect the nation's art-treasures and had always opposed the excesses of the extremists. (This was the furthest he went in an effort to exculpate himself; perhaps at this moment he feared that he'd be shot out of hand.) There was no press left that was in the least liberal; journalists, pamphleteers and cartoonists had a free hand in the vilest attacks on him:

H.Morel: That hippopotamus swollen with pride, fattened with folly, besotted with brandy, who with his own weight drags down . . . into the morass a host of insignificant and inoffensive people who try to kiss his feet, the shape of which resembles less that of a horse than that of an ass.

Alexandre Dumas the Younger: The Republic must produce spontaneous generation . . . for example, what fabulous intercourse between a slug and a peacock, what genetic antitheses, what bristly slime, could have spawned the thing called M. Gustave Courbet? In what hothouse, by the use of what dung, as a result of what mixture of wine, beer, corrosive mucus, and flatulent bloating, can have grown this hollow hairy gourd, this aesthetic belly, this imbecile and impotent incarnation of the Ego?[6]

Emile Bergerat wrote a foul poem about him:

> . . . Let him live, before his navel ecstatiated,
> live on his belly, like a Carmelite monk.
> Let him grow fatter, day and night open to the public
> between four policemen, in old age let him be sunk.
> Ah, dead, the bed-shitter's all out, emaciated.
> The baked potato, burst between fingers, flops away.
> The kick-at-the-arse loses its finest object,
> without grace or enthusiasm it wanders astray. . . . [7]

We have to read such things to realise the hatred and fear which Courbet aroused in the respectable classes. In 1849–50 he had been feared as a dangerous disruptive force; now he was feared as an artist, who, having risen high and won every chance to cash in on fortune, money, honours, yet stayed true to his revolutionary creed. About, after the success of his nudes, had told him the moment had come to open one of the luxurious studios affected by the leading artists and to get commissions at big prices; Courbet had ignored the advice. He was thus seen as an incredible traitor, an inexplicable portent, who had to be damned and blasted; only when seen through the veil of foul distorting abuse could he be looked at, considered, accepted as existing at all.

On 14 June Gobet seized two pictures, a flowerpiece and a seascape, 'and an album of the department of the Vosges' at the house of Chappuis, 11 rue du Jardinet; Chappuis was holding them against 330 francs that Courbet owed him for bills at his restaurant. In his extreme need of help, Courbet put aside his differences with the Reverdys. 'I shrink from violence, passion-flares, recriminations, disputes, and all the evil that usually follows from them. I prefer everything in harmony and to be at peace.' That was certainly a cry from the depths. 'I trust that the public, as well as the journalists, will come back from their idea.' Nothing could have pleased Zoé better than such an appeal. She now felt that she had her brother at her mercy, in a situation where he must agree with her thesis of his simple nature led astray by wicked schemers. From now on, while he was in prison, she did all she could to help him – but according to her own lights.[8]

On 11 June he wrote to his family from the Conciergerie prison which adjoined the prefecture of police. He did his best to keep his end up, partly to spare them sufferings, partly because he could not admit what he was up against. (One feels that in his lonely thoughts he faced the facts; but as soon as he had to turn outwards, he instinctively drew on his ingrained systems of self-justification.) 'I can't return home soon because the terrible events that have occurred recently require my presence in Paris.' He turned to the dire insult he had suffered at home. 'As for the municipal authorities of Ornans, who have dared to insult my family as well as myself, I'll have an account to settle with them later.' However, 'at the moment I'm a prisoner until more tranquil times, which will soon follow, enable me to clear myself. I expect to show France the example of a man who has the honour of having done his duty in all circumstances.'[9]

Castagnary was using all his influence as editor of *Le Siècle* to help Courbet. Emile Duriez in the Ministry of Justice wrote to him on 14 June, 'What you ask is very difficult. The unlucky Courbet is one of the most compromised members of the Commune. I shall do what I can, but I don't know that I'll be able to do anything.' The day before, Reverdy had written to him:

I thank you in the name of Gustave's family and in my own for the negotiations you've already opened up and those you propose to start with influential people who may . . . be able to improve his unhappy situation. . . . Certainly my wife and I regret that he has paid no attention to us; for his sister's warm heart and her love for him would have kept him from letting himself get involved so deeply in politics; and we would have saved him and restored him to the arts in which his undisputed pre-eminence should have satisfied him. In spite of his ingratitude towards us . . . we offer him all our devotion. . . . I have asked for a power of attorney . . . so as to be able to safeguard his interests as well as possible, to collect his pictures and possessions that are now scattered all over the world. Very sad news has now been added to our misfortunes: his poor mother, hearing of his predicament and the rumours of his death, could not survive this terrible blow. She died on Saturday 3 June at nine in the evening at Flagey.[10]

We must recall the Reverdys' opinion of Castagnary as a bandit out for Courbet's money and determined to drag him down into the mire. This letter then appears as an attempt to disarm him in the plan now worked out by the Reverdys for getting hold of Courbet's pictures and property. Reverdy remains to the end a man whom it is hard to decipher; in his favour is the fact that Zoé became genuinely devoted to him. Certainly in their self-righteous rage against the bandits who had wrecked the trusting Courbet and prevented him from becoming an honoured member of bourgeois society, the pair were ready to go to any lengths; what is suspicious is the way in which the plans to save Courbet always seem to involve the Reverdys' getting control of his property. No doubt they rationalised their desire to get that control by arguing that it was the only way to keep the bandits like Castagnary away and to stop Courbet himself from wasting his substance on unworthy persons. Zoé added a postscript to her husband's letter:

It is in adversity that one finds one's real friends. I expected no less from you, and I . . . join my husband in thanking you in advance for what I hope you'll do for my luckless brother. . . . Tell him we've forgotten the past, that it is our separation which has caused the damage, since I've been unable to surround him with my devotion. . . . My brother, *in spite of everything*, has lived honourably for fifty years; he has been the pride of his province, his family, and his country.

With such a character, who thinks purely in emotional terms, it is impossible to expect logical formulations; but it would be interesting to know just what period of Courbet's life Zoé thought had been securely surrounded by her devotion. Clearly she was convinced that at one time he and she had been very close together, and that this period was that in which he had creatively blossomed; then, separated from her, he had gone astray, frittering away the successes he had gained.

Other friends were seeking to help Courbet. Bruyas wrote to Régis, expressing his sympathy in the 'sorrowful event' and hoping that the good star of the 'dear great painter' would not abandon him in these 'moments of trouble and agitation'. He declared, 'For those who know the convictions of Gustave Courbet there could not exist two ways of seeing as to his honest and humane sentiments.' We may contrast the letter which Champfleury wrote soon after, saying that Courbet 'has committed a great error in associating himself with this terrible insurrectional movement, of which he hasn't foreseen the consequences'. His friends, while grieving, cannot 'excuse him further'. However, art will get him free better than any lawyer can.[11] Ordinaire, though Courbet had not been friendly with him during 1870, offered to approach a man who'd been a minister in the government of National Defence, and begged Castagnary to pull all possible strings:

I couldn't do so myself because I'd incurred – probably because of my independence – the displeasure of that man who is stuffed with pride and aristocratic ideas. But since he could perhaps do a great deal for our poor friend, I'll write to Dorian to use all his influence with the great Grévy or with anyone else. . . . Let us make every effort to gain for him exile in America or elsewhere. . . . [Gaudy] leaves for Paris tomorrow; he will see you and do whatever he can.

Two busybodies, Champfleury and Reverdy, . . . have written to Courbet's father and asked for powers of attorney to enable them to gather the painter's works in a safe place, and, if necessary, sell them. But his father doesn't think himself justified in disposing of his son's property in the latter's lifetime, and he's right. Moreover he [Courbet] is intensely prejudiced against his brother-in-law and would resent his meddling in his affairs.[12]

Courbet at the Conciergerie was allowed to have his meals brought in from the Brasserie Laveur, at his own charge; but he complained of the deterioration of his health through the dirt, vermin, and enforced confinement. For a restless man such as he had been, who had had to prowl about most of the night through inability to go to bed, jail-life owned a peculiar terror and misery. On 17 June the preliminary charges were drawn up; and at the end of the month he was driven to Versailles in a prison-van with manacled wrists. After a short interrogation he went back to the Conciergerie.[13] In a letter written later to a magistrate dealing with his case, he complained of the *tabatières* (snuffboxes) in which he was confined with his plethoric nature, fits or congestion (*coups de sang*), and intestinal inflammation; of the 'vermin' surrounding him; and of his travel in a police-van, manacled and exhibited in the streets of Paris. It seems that at Versailles he was jeered at by children and struck by a young woman with an umbrella.[14]

An English acquaintance, Robert Reid, tried to help him by forwarding a letter of his to *The Times* (published 27 June) 'in answer to a charge made by the English Press that he personally had destroyed several works of art in the Louvre'. In the letter he insisted on the care he had taken to save all art works, including those of Thiers, and declared that he urged the preservation of the reliefs on the Vendôme Column. 'Knowing the purity of the motives by which I have been actuated, I also know the difficulties one inherits in coming after a *régime* such as the Empire.'[15]

On 4 July he was transferred to Mazas prison. Zoé wrote to Castagnary, 'Since yesterday morning Gustave's been at Mazas; he's been interrogated; he's ill and begs to be moved to a hospital.' She doesn't know whom to apply to, and asks Castagnary's advice. He at once appealed to Duriez in the Ministry of Justice, who replied that a trial in a civil court would be preferable: 'the evidence would be more carefully examined and his resources for defence would be fuller.' But only in cases of absolute necessity would the request for a transfer to hospital be considered. 'In my opinion such a petition would be very ill-advised; a display of resignation would be proper and sensible.'[16] Courbet himself had written in June to Grévy and Jules Simon, Minister of Education. (Zoé may have advised these steps but, as we saw, Ordinaire had written to Dorian in the hope of an approach to Grévy.) Grévy recommended a barrister, Lachaud, for whom Courbet prepared a vast array of notes in vindication of his actions. The authorities refused to consider the idea of a civil tribunal and he was ordered to appear before the Third Council of War of the First Military Division in Versailles, late in July.[17]

In 1951 the manuscript of Courbet's memorandum to Lachaud turned up; it may well be the text which Zoé got hold of and later refused to give up. Written in the third person, it sets out all the points in favour of his actions. It declares:

He entered into the Commune on 23 April. Seeing that this attempt at a commune had no chance of survival [*vitalité*] at the moment, because of the insurmountable difficulties in which it found itself, oppressed by the Prussian invasion, having to combat, despite itself, the army of Versailles, and lacking any communication with its allies in the provinces, he foresaw in advance what would happen, and accepted his role only as peace-maker; and at the same time to have sufficient authority that was necessary for him to carry out his mission without official stamp [*sans contrôle*] with regard to the arts. . . .

He speaks here with hindsight; his letters and behaviour under the Commune show that he did not expect a collapse. He sets out his losses; and recounts a meeting he had with the sculptor Clésinger (some three or four years back) at the latter's place at Enghien, on a Sunday. Clésinger showed him a model of a monument in the garden, 35 feet high, made up of two Corinthian columns, surmounted by a warrior on horseback; the square pedestal had a warrior at each corner backed up against the columns. It was meant to be executed as a monument 160 feet high, in the Place de l'Obelisque, and was being made with the Emperor's close consideration. Courbet asked: Why put there some Greek ruins topped with a rider who looked like Don Quixote and surrounded by four men who looked as if they were sitting on chamber-pots? 'Suppose the Emperor heard you!' cried Clésinger. 'It's all one to me,' said Courbet, and asked who the four men were. 'They are the four Caesars who have saved the world: Julius Caesar, Charlemagne, his uncle, and then he himself [Napoleon III].' Courbet replied, 'Your idea seems to me badly thought-out; and if you consider those four fine lads there saved the world, you're as well up in history and philosophy as the Emperor. As for me, I believe they destroyed it. Do you want to drive France quite dotty? I hope you're not going to put that rubbish on the Place de la Concorde. . . . People will laugh, and what are you going to do with the Obelisk?' 'We'll put it in the Louvre yard.' 'So that's it. You're going to choke up that yard with a bit of stone just as the Place Vendôme has been choked with that other monument of a savage.' Clésinger asked for an alternative idea. In the middle of lunch Courbet cried, 'I've got it. It's the opposite of yours. Here it is, the Last Cannon. Sadly, it's still an allegory. The absurd leads to the absurd. That cannon forming itself a column with its mouth in air, is backed on three balls set on the pedestal' – it was to be flower-decked, capped with a Phrygian bonnet, set with panels representing the triumphs of peace in agriculture, trade, industry, arts. Courbet said he'd made a clay model, to be shown to Napoleon.

He tells this tale to set out his own ideas on public monuments. What he would have liked in the Place Vendôme was 'a low, artistic monument, a woman's figure or a bird or some graceful subject with water and surrounding flowers, related to the elegant world of this quarter'.

He goes on with many statements which would certainly have infuriated his judges. He sets out his own pacific position as an artist and creator,

One realises that a people ignorant of these tactics, these strategies, desperate before certain death, seeks to imitate these lofty facts, this superb science. When one has seen the manner of colonising in Africa and of conquering in Mexico, one is confirmed as to the morality of war and of warmongers. Only, what one doesn't understand is that they may be judged in this matter. . . .

Citizens, if ever you're accused of stealing the towers of Notre-Dame, remember all this, believe me, for if you'll be judged in the way of good politics in the case, you'll be found guilty. Here am I, at the pillory of this Column, like Jesus Christ bearing his cross. Here I am, irrevocably bound to this calendar of war-exploits, for which I have no sympathy, right to the end of my days. . . .

For executioners I have the deepest scorn; in their rage I read their feebleness and their lack of genius. These ignoble hangmen, these revolting cowards, this gross crew, want to remain alone so as to be right; revellers, aristos without lofty conceptions, they monopolise existence while destroying and enslaving the weak, getting rid of those they can't help; so the triumphs of these miserable murderers increase their terrors, and they calm their remorse by centupling their crimes; the unconscious cattle who serve as their instruments, in their ferocious instincts, blindly destructive, dig for themselves an abyss that they can only escape by their death and by the death of their own.

The bourgeois of 93 killed itself, gave way to the bandits of the Empire. A new Nero has just appeared. After burning Paris, he has achieved his dream, he destroys the people and the workers. But he won't destroy modern civilisation, England will give him an asylum.

Courbet has his confusions, but he does not surrender his revolutionary dignity.

During July he was in touch with some friends in Switzerland: Alexandre Daguet, professor of national history at Neuchâtel; the painter Auguste Vachelin, who had been pupil of Gleyre and then of Couture, and his sister Rose, who later married the Alsatian artist T. Schuler. Vachelin was in Switzerland, for the letter to him ends; 'Switzerland is indeed happy.' To Rose, Courbet stressed his mother's death and the desolation of his father and sisters; to Vachelin he stresses the loss of his Ornans studio and the Paris building-materials. To Daguet he wrote:

Our dear friend Buchon, our philosopher-poet, who died in my arms, he too believed in disinterestedness, in duty, in the good for the good's sake. He walked twenty leagues on foot, with a chain round his neck, between two mounted policemen. He did the same when returning to Besançon, in the same conditions. He was going to be tried at Arbois, where he was acquitted; he was acquitted at Besançon also, after nine months of preventive prison.

For forty days, dear friend, I've languished in the same conditions. I trust the result will be the same.

As you say very well, you know my humanity and the horror I have of violence and armed combats, of destruction and capital punishment for any man for whom it looms up. We'll meet again soon, dear friend, or indeed honesty is the crime of modern society.

I remained in Paris, it's true, for several reasons, I couldn't go away to a distance, I'd stay just the same if the situation recurred in the same conditions, without departing one iota from the line of conduct I followed. My artistic position being superior to any sort of employment in a government, I accepted the presidency of the arts on 4 September out of a forecast of a cataclysm, as much to save the arts in Paris as to save my own pictures which are all my existence and all my fortune. I achieved my aim and now I'm waiting for men to become enlightened as to my intentions.

I hope, dear Daguet, that one day we'll resume our pacific philosophy. Many thanks to the persons who are concerned about me; tell them that we have had a good year, to become old in two years.[18]

Some time shortly before the trial Castagnary suggested to Daubigny that an appeal on Courbet's behalf should be signed by leading artists asking Thiers for clemency. He was told: 'We'd collect only three signatures: mine, Daumier's, and Corot's – not one more.'

The indictment was formulated by one of the court-secretaries, M. de Planet, and, considering the counter-revolutionary situation, it was fairly restrained. It admitted that he had opposed the formation of the Committee of Public Safety and that his activities had been mainly concerned with the preservation of art works, that he had conscientiously supervised the removal of Thiers's property, that he had not been a member of the Commune when the decree against the Column was passed and that he had urged the 'unbolting' and preservation of the reliefs.

In consequence we advise that Courbet, Gustave, be tried before the Council of War for (1) participation in a movement designed to change the form of government and to incite the citizens to take up arms against each other, (2) the usurpation of civil functions, (3) complicity in the destruction of the Vendôme Column, erected by public authority, by aiding those who committed this crime in the acts that prepared, facilitated, and consummated it.[19]

Zoé, who was working hard for her brother, wrote to Bruyas on 26 July; he was now a confirmed invalid at Montpellier. The trial was to open on Sunday or Monday 31 July.

'We have seen our poor father, who came to Paris to see our unfortunate brother. . . . I pray you, sir, if you have any friends who might be acquainted with the military authorities who are to try Gustave, ask them to look on him solely as an artist who tried to devote himself to the arts. All deputies, ministers, can be useful. We are knocking at every door, and all the influential and highly placed people are responding cordially. Let us hope. We have seen Gustave. He is very much changed. And we are very sad.' She wrote again in a few days, asking him to come as witness. 'All the eminent people in France and the neighbouring countries have requested seats. It will be almost impossible to get in. Only witnesses have the right. M. Lachaud urges us to appeal to all true friends who are ready to aid my brother. . . . If you could possibly come to Paris and help Gustave on Monday as a friendly witness for the defence, you would render us an immense service.'[20] She clearly enjoys the excitement and the chance of bringing herself to the notice of 'influential and highly placed people' as the Bonapartist sister of a misguided genius whom she is protecting. The comments about the crowded court are in Gustave's own vein and show how much she was his sister.

Bruyas, too ill to visit Paris, wrote to Lachaud. He said that he had held 'with the celebrated painter only an artistic relationship that has enabled me to appreciate the nobility and honesty of his character. So I refuse to believe that he can in any way have been involved in the horrors of Paris.' His remarks could be used in testimony. To Zoé he sent a telegram in very much her own idiom. He was deeply distressed and 'despite the attacks made on him I cannot and will not believe him guilty of the designs of which he is accused. Permit me to express all my hopes that your brother's judges will take into account the subversive influences to which he yielded, and realise they have before them an artist who may have been led astray but has nothing in common with political murderers.'[21] (Zoé in her statement to Champfleury went further; she declared, in words that were either sheer invention or else delusions of her already-stirring paranoia: 'He felt himself menaced during the Commune by those surrounding him. No sooner was he arrested than he felt reassured and used to say to his guards: 'Don't let anyone in to see me, only my sister and my brother-in-law. I'd like to pass my life guarded like this, for, when I'm free, they'll come back. It was useless for me to tell them that I understood nothing of what they were doing and that I didn't want to; that I was only an artist, nothing but that; then they told me that if I drew back, I was a dead man.'[22]

Among other friends whom Courbet asked Zoé to approach was Baudry of Rochemont. She wrote to him on 28 July. He at once made out a deposition in Courbet's favour, which he sent to a journalist friend in Paris, C. Sauvestre, to be read to the tribunal. But notification of the court's sitting was sent to Baudry's Parisian address, too late for him to appear at Versailles on 7 August.

The court did not bully Courbet. The president, Col. Merlin, expressed regret at so talented an artist having blundered into such a predicament. Eighteen other Commune members were also being tried, and Courbet was not called to the stand till 14 August.

The room (the hall of a riding school), heated by sun and crowd, was cooled by heavy rain. Courbet came in last and sat at the end of the fourth bench, near the counsel's stand; Lachaud had him moved to the first bench so that he could communicate more easily with him. The court entered at 12.30. Courbet insisted that his actions under the Commune had all been constructive; he had protected national property, voted against the extremist majority, and saved the Thiers collection. The prosecution called only two witnesses, who were quite ineffective. Mlle Gérard testified that he had been her lodger from 6 January to 23 May, had always behaved with propriety, and had been asked to leave as she didn't want him arrested on her premises. Joseph Duchou, concierge of a building in the Place Vendôme thought he had seen Courbet in a short dark jacket climb up a ladder and strike the first blow against the Column on 16 May. Courbet replied that the only dark clothes he ever wore were long-tailed frock-coats and that his paunch prohibited him from climbing ladders. The defence brought forward more than a dozen witnesses and had a dozen more in reserve. Vialet, president of the Société d'Assistance Publique of the 6th *arrondissement*, deposed that Courbet had restored to him documents confiscated by the National Guard. Cazala, director of the *Magasin pittoresque*, testified to his character and the moderation of his political creed. A. P. de Courteille, professor at the Collège de France, deposed that he was a very good, inoffensive man, incapable of violence, and with opinions more fantastic than radical. Barbet de Jouy of the Louvre and Philippe de Chennevières of the Luxembourg, dismissed by the Commune and now reinstated, declared that he had played an important part in preserving art-treasures in the museums, before and during the Commune, and in the final week of tumult. Dorian described him as an intelligent artist but an inconsistent and inexpert politician. Arago, the former Mayor, somewhat reluctantly agreed that the Art Commission under the Government of National Defence, to the presidency of which Courbet had been elected in September, was an unofficial body, so that there had been no usurpation of civil functions. At the session on 17 August, Paschal Grousset, one of the co-defendants, who had been held in solitary confinement at Versailles and had heard Courbet's charges only at the trial, voluntarily gave evidence that Courbet had had no connection whatever with the decree for the Column's demolition, the contract's negotiation, or the demolition itself. Luckily the contract-draft, prepared by the engineer, had been annexed to his dossier. On 22 August Courbet was accused of the theft or disappearance of a silver statue, two metres high, depicting Peace; but four days later Merlin announced in court that the work had turned up in the Louvre cellars.[23]

Even the prosecutor, Commandant Gaveau, treated Courbet with comparative leniency. While holding him responsible for his support of the Commune and his share in its actions, he declared himself saddened at seeing 'an artist of great talent amid these depraved men whom indolence and envy had turned into criminals'. Courbet was indeed all the less excusable in view of his fortune, talent, and elevated rank in society. On 31 August Lachaud spoke for the defence with much skill. Though his own sympathies were with the Empire, he did his best to show how each detail of the evidence could be interpreted in Courbet's favour. He was proud? Yes, aware of his own value. Jealous – of whom? His only political act had been the refusal of the Cross. All the witnesses agreed that he was no politician. He had suffered enough; his mother was dead and his Ornans statue overthrown. After the pleading, Edgar Monteil saw Courbet at the military hospital. With a bewildered look Courbet asked why he was still pursued. Then he complained of the Bonapartist Lachaud who wouldn't shake his hand. 'When I reach it out, he turns his back. He doesn't want to speak to me. He sends his sons to me to arrange things.' Later, he grew more suspicious, as if Zoé had burdened him with a treacherous pleader. But that was all nonsense. A Bonapartist speaking in his defence was tactically useful. That Lachaud was connected with the Reverdys is made possible by the fact that he lived near them, at 11 rue Bonaparte, but Zoé, if she did play a part in bringing him in, did so because she wanted to link her brother with respectable reactionaries. What the Reverdys were living on at this time is unknown; they seem to have lost touch with the Saint-Denis. (In 1878 Zoé wrote, 'All that world is dead' – though in fact the baron Harvey did not die till 1892.) In a few years it becomes evident that they were extremely hard-up, and there is no doubt that they were hoping both to save Courbet from his friends and themselves from penury. Zoé's dream was of a grateful brother who dispensed his favours on her, not on his boon-companions.[24]

Courbet's health was being badly shattered. He had grown thin and haggard, his hair had whitened, and his haemorrhoids were so severe that he had to sit on a small leather cushion while the court carried on. The reporter of the *Journal de Lyon* noted: 'He has grown completely white. His very short beard, his grey hair, his sickly air make him hardly recognisable. He is broken down, he is suffering, he has quite lost his robust serenity of former times.' Journalists enjoyed themselves making fun of his discomforts, his wasting-away. Victor Fournel wrote: 'During the interminable process Courbet melted visibly away on his bench. Each day a large wet puddle marked the place and reserved it for next day. The guards there showed it to the curious who visited the hall between the sessions, and told them: There's the place where M. Courbet sweats daily, for three weeks, from noon to 6 p.m.'[25]

Shortly after the trial he was taken to the military hospital at Versailles, where he was soon improving in condition. Zoé told Bruyas, 'I go to see him as often as I can. It's so difficult to go to Versailles daily and at the same time do what is necessary in Paris. Though my husband isn't rich, he grudges no sacrifice, and despite our self-denial our expenses are heavy. No matter, we are carrying on bravely; for we must get Gustave out of this fix, whatever it may cost.' Perhaps she hoped to get a contribution from Bruyas; we do not know if he responded. She takes on herself the credit for the removal from the jail. 'As he is ill, I managed his transfer to the military hospital. . . . In the future may he listen only to his true friends and occupy himself with nothing but his painting!' We see that in her tenacity in clinging to her ideas and in carrying them out, she was a true Courbet. 'With a woman like that one could move the world,' commented Lachaud. She added, 'I read to Gustave all the letters received from friends. That is a great pleasure to the poor prisoner.'[26]

On 27 August he wrote to Juliette:

I was very glad to be transferred to this hospital, where I'm very happy. I've entirely recovered from the torment caused by confinement in a cell. Solitude weakens the mind. . . . I'm as thin as I was on the day of my first Communion, you'd be amazed. Sister Clotilde is taking care of me, she's extremely kind and gives me all the food she can, in defiance of the rules.

Solitude has strengthened many characters, who have grown spiritually and morally stronger in confinements worse than Courbet's and much more prolonged. But for a man of his temperament, whose inner life was closely entangled with a continual outer give-and-take, a relaxation in drink, song, and chatter, the imprisonment was peculiarly crushing. Indeed he never recovered from it. To take a contrasting example from among the Communards, Clovis Hugues, sentenced to three years, wrote most of his best poems in Tours jail.

Our causes have been pleaded for several days; the barristers are doing their utmost. I have the best barrister in Paris. Moreover he's on a good footing with all factions. M. Grévy found him for me. If I'm sentenced merely to exile I don't mean to appeal; I'll serve my sentence without asking them for mercy, as I don't want those who've had the impudence to prosecute me, after I'd done such notable services as I did, to be able to get rid of me so easily. I want to retain the right to denounce them at any time.

Here the opinion of most is that I'll be acquitted. If I'm condemned to prison, I'll request the changing of my sentence to exile. If I'm acquitted I think I'll spend a week or two at the seaside before going to see you, for two reasons: I have great need of sea-bathing, I haven't had a bath this year . . . secondly, I want to denounce the municipal authorities of Ornans immediately after the trial, before I return home. . . . Those people, those idiots are nothing but assassins; their decision presupposed my condemnation, and if I hadn't gone into hiding I'd certainly have been shot. The question of the Column has entirely disappeared from my case. . . . The only charge remaining against me is that I joined the Commune in order to carry out my mission. . . .

Further, I'm proud to have been a member of the Commune despite the accusations against it, because that type of government, resembling in principle the Swiss system, is the ideal government; it eliminates ignorance and renders wars and privileges impossible. . . . If I go to Switzerland, I'll have you all join me. I'll go to Neuchâtel. Don't answer this for a week. Anything you write might compromise me, especially [anything from] my father.[27]

On 2 September his sentence was announced: six months in prison in addition to the three already served, together with a fine of 300 francs and his share in the costs of the trial. He was the only person fined. All the convicted men had been made jointly responsible for the total costs; and as Courbet was the only one of them with money, he had to pay for all. Theoretically he could have sued the others; but such a course was unthinkable. He renounced all claims on his fellow-Communards, who were treated far more harshly than he was. On 3 September he reported to the family:

I've been condemned to six months in jail, I still don't know why. These people are trying to please the public. Even after it was proved I had no connection with the Column's destruction they insisted all the same I'd participated in it, despite the assertions of the accused themselves and despite the decree that had been passed before my entry into the Commune. I think they meant to give the impression that everyone was guilty and then to pardon me later. That's not the same for me, as, if it hadn't been for this verdict I could have denounced the municipal authorities of Ornans.

He had tried to raise the Ornans matter during the trial, but Merlin had ruled that it was irrelevant.

I don't know yet whether I'll simply be released or have my sentence changed to exile. . . . I don't propose to appeal, so as not to upset their plan. They've already sentenced me to pay a fine of 500 francs. I don't know why. They think I'm rich. It's a very prevalent notion. It must be that I look rich, perhaps because I'm fat. We'll see how it turns out, but it's almost certain I shan't serve a term in prison. My comrades have got very severe sentences, some to prison, others to deportation, and two of them to death – but that won't be carried out. Everyone thought I'd be acquitted. I didn't think so because I know these people and how irritated they are by the contempt we showed for them in our proceedings in Paris.[28]

In such statements it is always hard to make out if he is trying to keep up his own spirits or those of the persons addressed. As a Proudhonian, he had no conception of the class-struggle; but since 1868 he had associated with men like Vallès and had surely strengthened his antagonism to the State and all its manifestations; the experiences of the Commune had clarified his ideas. Yet he still thinks in terms of abstract justice and of his own good intentions as if they had any relevance to the vengeance which the ruling-class was taking on the men who had thoroughly scared it. Champfleury had spoken the truth when he said that art would free him better than any lawyers; Courbet owed to his European reputation the fact that he was not treated as harshly as the others. However, he had had some grounds for optimism. Gaveau had not tried to upset the defence in his reply to the lawyers (31 August); and next day Lachaud took this point up. 'What I have said is then correct and uncontra-verted.' He ended, 'I am full of confidence; Courbet will be acquitted.'

Behind the comparative lenience with which he was treated, we can probably trace the hand of Thiers, who was surely grateful to him for the preservation of his art works. The fact that Grévy, president of the National Assembly, came to his aid and suggested Lachaud for his defence is practically a proof of this. Grévy was a compatriot, but that would not be enough in the circumstances to make him take strong steps to support Courbet. He was in fact the close friend and confidant of Thiers, with the same sort of political views. Pressure from him (and thus in effect from Thiers) would explain why Lachaud, who had such a keen distaste for Courbet personally and politically, agreed to act for him; and we may be sure that Col. Merlin and the others would be aware that Courbet, if not actually protected by Thiers and Grévy, was enough under their aegis to be treated differently from the other Communards being tried. It was the fall of Thiers that laid Courbet open to further attack.

He was now taken to the temporary jail in the Orangerie at Versailles, where he had to sleep 'in three centimetres of vermin'. Here he had trouble with Captain Serret de Lanoze who accused him of holding secret discussions and threatened to have the disturbers shot. Courbet made a sketch of the yard: an old white wall with flowers at the back, by which the prisoners walked, smoking, reading journals, playing at *bouchon* (tip-penny). After the sentence he had said to Monteil. 'They've killed me, my poor Monteil; they've killed me, these people, I feel it, I'll never do anything good any more.' But his spirits now began to revive, as shown by the sketch.[29] On 22 September he was transferred to the old jail of

Sainte-Pélagie in Paris, rue du Puits-de-l'Ermite, between the rue Monge and the Jardin des Plantes. The building was in a state of decay; there were only dormitories and a few cubicles for prisoners able to pay for meals to be brought in. Normally there was the Pavillon des Princes for political prisoners, but Courbet was not allowed to use it. However he again got meals in from the Brasserie Laveur and was given a cubicle, no. 4, in which was an iron bedstead, two tables, and three chairs. The light there was dim because of pent-roofs built to stop the prisoners from communicating with one another. His door was locked at night, but during the day he could visit other prisoners or walk in the grim yard. To his annoyance he had to wear the grey trousers and jacket of the regulations.[30] A letter is extant in which he asks the Director for leave to have a hip-bath kept in his room 'so that I can continue the treatment laid down by the Paris and Versailles doctors for a haemorrhoidal affliction. I'd also like you to authorise me to have a bottle of beer bought daily, as I can almost not drink wine on account of my malady. Please also let me have the catalogue of your library, plus a cotton night-cap and a large bath.'[31]

On his second day there he wrote to Castagnary. 'They've insisted on treating us like common criminals, not political prisoners; we're among thieves up to our necks. Every effort has been made to humiliate us.' He told Castagnary to ask the police prefect for a permit to visit, and to get permits for the Reverdys; he was worried about the (copies of) old masters in the rue du Vieux-Colombier. 'I'd feel relieved if you could advise my brother-in-law a little in this matter.' He also asked for permits to be got for any friends who wanted to visit him. However, it was not till 15 December that Castagnary himself got a permit for a twice-weekly visit.[32]

For over a year Courbet had done no painting; now with time hanging on his hands, he began to feel the impulse to paint return.

An incomprehensible thing has happened. I'm prevented from working, deliberately. Despite my requests and those of my sister, M. Valentin [General, prefect of police] doesn't want it. Some people are put in jail because they won't work, while as for me I'm in jail to be stopped from working. It upsets me all the more because I've had an idea. It's to paint Paris in a bird's-eye view [*à vol d'oiseau*] with skies like those I do in my seascapes. It's a unique chance. There's a gallery round the building's roof, constructed by M. Ouvrard. It's splendid; it'd be as interesting as my Etretat seascapes. But, a thing unparalleled and of unequalled brutality, I'm not allowed to have my tools of trade; and I'm the only one treated like this at Ste-Pélagie where everyone's forced to work.

I'm compelled to make felt slippers without knowing a thing about it. I pay 5 sous a day out of my 20 francs a week, apart from paying for my dinner etc. You're in touch with Gambetta; explain it to him and ask him to send instructions or a commission that'll oblige me to work. Put it in the *Siècle* if you like. Hurry up, the weather's magnificent, I must take advantage of the chance.[33]

He may have hoped that the complaints, with veiled threats, there would affect General Valentin; for another letter, of 29 September, to Juliette shows that he knew his letters were read.

I don't get a chance to write, my freedom's constricted. I can't write or get letters except through the hands of the prefect, who is very disagreeable. That's why I told you not to write, because things that seem innocent and most natural are interpreted here in a strange way. I'm feeling better and recovering my health. . . . Now I can be in the open air and talk with people, though they've had the effrontery to lump us in with thieves and murderers. All this matters little to me, you know, I defy them to humiliate me.

I get letters of congratulation from everywhere, Germany, England, Switzerland; everybody supports me except the reactionaries and those in the pay of the Government and of Napoleon. . . . My sister [Zoé] is making herself ill with worry, her pride is wounded. As for myself, it's only made me laugh all the time, so don't be uneasy about me. I lack nothing here, I've already served a month; there's only five more. . . .

People here talk so much there's no time to do anything. I'll try to get my paints and work a little. I don't know if my sister will succeed in getting me moved to a nursing home. . . . There I could receive friends and use models. . . .

I'm told you're anxious to come here. I beg you, I pray you, not to come. It would distress me to know you were alone on the way here and in Paris, which is very dangerous. You might be imprisoned. It's almost certain you would be. My sister hasn't, because she's married, but all the sisters, brothers, and fathers of my friends are in jail. The greatest pleasure you and Zélie can give me is to stay at home and above all not to worry. . . . I can't be home this year for the wine-making. I constantly think about what you're doing.[34]

Zoé, with her incessant letters and petitions, certainly did much to help him at this phase; but we must allow for the efforts made by Castagnary and others. Courbet was at last allowed to paint in his cubicle, but not to use living models. On 30 September Zoé wrote to Bruyas:

It's impossible to tell you how much I've done, how much I've suffered. I've followed him step by step and I've seen him several times in a state of despair. Only the results could make you understand. Gustave has suffered a great deal emotionally and physically. Solitary confinement drove him mad.

Zoé again shows her insight here into his character. To be alone for any length of time, especially with no paintbrush in his hand, was sheer hell to Courbet. It seems likely that the panic he showed, when Juliette suggested a visit, derived from his dislike of the family at Ornans seeing and knowing the state to which he'd been reduced. Not so much out of love for them – though that counted – but above all because he had to feel that he was an un-defeated figure in their eyes, whatever happened. Hence his ceaseless rage about the treatment of his statue: in itself a very minor episode at this time of large-scale disasters. Zoé goes on:

Then his health was very poor and I could not arrange to have him cared for. Still, I finally succeeded in convincing them after a fashion. I collected all the documents for the defence, all the decrees related to the Column's demolition. . . . Gustave has never designed any of them. He is not a *destroyer*. . . . He is the only man who at such a time devoted himself completely even when the Commune threatened daily to shoot him as a reactionary. . . . I visit him at Ste-Pélagie twice a week. I've been able to take him his brushes, but alas, two square metres give little space. . . . He's not let work outside his room. Gustave's health has greatly improved since his return to Paris.[35]

Courbet wrote to Lydie Jolicler, one of his most devoted correspondents, a letter in which a great deal of himself is packed.

In these moments of terrible solitude between life and death (for you can never imagine what we've suffered) I involuntarily think of my youthful days, of my parents, my friends; in my thoughts I've run through all the places I traversed as a child with my poor mother whom I'll never see again: my profound and indeed my only sorrow amid all the disasters that had come on me since I saw you. In the mirror of my thoughts I saw again the meadows of Flagey where I wandered with her looking for hazelnuts, the firwoods of Reugney where I went for raspberries. . . . I recalled the cakes she baked for me in her oven. It's strange in these supreme moments one thinks of the most naïve things.

I've been pillaged, ruined, slandered, dragged in the streets of Paris and Versailles, stricken near death by stupidities and insults. I've crouched in cells that made one lose one's reason and physical energies; I've lain on the earth, crammed in with riffraff amid vermin, I've been transported, transported back from prison to prison, in hospitals with men dying all around, in police-vans, in boxes where the body can't squeeze in, with gun or revolver at my throat, for four months.

But alas I'm not the only one. There are two hundred thousand of us, as many dead as alive, ladies, women of the people, children of all ages roaming about Paris without father or mother, jailed by thousands every day. Since the beginning of the world came into existence the earth has never seen such a thing; in no other people, no other history, no other period, has one seen such a massacre, such a vengeance.[36]

Here at last he sees his own experience in some sort of perspective, and the note of egoism in other accounts of his sufferings disappears.

Zoé lost no chance of gathering support in her campaign for de-politicising Courbet. Knowing he was writing to Lydie, she herself wrote on 1 December. 'I'm asking all our friends to use all their powers of persuasion to make my brother promise to occupy himself with nothing but painting; his life will be too short to complete his work; he should turn a deaf ear to, and draw back from, those false friends who seek only to destroy him. . . . Let what I ask seem to originate from you; don't tell my brother or even my sisters that I've requested your intervention. Coming from me it would have no effect.'[37] An odd confession of her inability to move him. She also tried Bruyas. 'Henceforth I hope to have more calm. Rest assured that more than ever Gustave deserves the esteem of his true friends.' But Bruyas was too depressed with his own illness and too well aware of the characters of Courbet and Zoé to attempt interference.[38] She stressed, no doubt truly, what Courbet was suffering: 'That free and independent nature cannot bear seclusion; he must have exercise and liberty. And despite all my efforts to charm and distract that active nature, I foresee death if I don't succeed in shortening the duration' of imprisonment. She wrote again to Lydie on 12 December.

Gustave asks me to thank you for the superb box of Ornans cheese you sent him. He has suffered a good deal for several days. It's so cold he can't take a bath. I am able to bring him all sorts of things, and I try to think of everything possible. I brought him his brushes and canvases; his window is big enough, he's on the second floor facing south. He has a stove in his little room, he keeps a fire burning. I bring him flowers, fruits, as models. I set him off painting them. Also the interior of his room.[39]

Among his visitors was Baudry, as is shown by a letter to him at his Paris address in the rue de Lancry from Castagnary, which deals with the question of getting into the prison. 'Dear friend, Nothing's more easy than to lunch at Sainte-Pélagie, but I'm afraid, my list of names not yet having been approved by the Prefect, of exposing you to a false attempt. I'm waiting for the director, to send him this list. . . .' There is also an obscure reference in a letter of July 1883 from Baudry to Juliette (whose letter had annoyed him): 'as if you don't know what I've been for your brother, deserted by his own, during his illness and his captivity....' At Ste-Pélagie he made several drawings of events that occurred during the breakdown of the Commune; these are the best of his drawings, dramatic and owning a new depth of feeling in the treatment of human beings. They show what he might yet have achieved in paint; for, if we imagine them translated on to canvases, they suggest a regaining of the power of the works done in the early 1850s plus a new richness of sympathy – what he wanted vainly to put into works like *Village-Poverty* or *Beggar's Alms*. They prove that his range of human themes was not limited to the sort of thing he did in the *Burial, Stonebreakers, Return from the Fair*, and that wider type of themes, illustrated by the *Fire-Brigade, Preparations for the Wedding*, and the unachieved political pictures, the *Conscript's Farewell* and the *Death of Bidoure*, were within his scope as he matured.[40]

While in prison he painted a self-portrait. His grossness had kept him for several years from depicting himself; but now, shrunken and marked with his sufferings as a political martyr, he wanted a memorial of his new status, his new self. He leans back by the window, thoughtful, with pipe in hand, beside the window through which we see the prison-yard and some of the overlooking windows. (It has been suggested he did the picture later at Neuilly or even Ornans; but though he may have worked on it later, it seems likely that he set down the main impression in his cell.) There is no attempt at idealisation as in the youthful self-portraits; he shows something of the crushed and bewildered state which Monteil noted earlier, but with a mixture of resignation and doggedness, of slowly awakening strength.[41] He also painted the head of a turnkey; and on the wall next to his bed the head of a girl with a flower in her hair, her head seeming to rest on his pillow; the warden is said to have been deceived for a moment, then to have laughed. He did several still-lifes. But as he liked to make out that works had been done in Ste-Pélagie though he did them a little later at Neuilly or Ornans, it is hard to be sure just what he did in the prison.[42]

His health could not stand up against the strains of even the fairly easy life he was now living. It began to degenerate again. By mid-December he had acute indigestion and was suffering agony from his haemorrhoids. An operation seemed necessary. So, after all, he was let out on parole to a nursing home on 30 December. Zoé had obtained the services of a famous surgeon, Dr Auguste Nélaton. She wrote to Bruyas in the letter cited above:

So I redoubled my efforts. But unfortunately General Valentin, prefect of police in Paris, was violently hostile. . . . He has been replaced none too soon, for he'd have caused a revolution. His successor, M. Renaud, is as polite as the general was brutal. . . . The prefect made a special trip to Versailles, asked for Gustave's parole of honour, and allowed me to move him to the nursing-home of Dr Duval, 34 Avenue du Roule, . . . in Neuilly. This was the advice of Dr Nélaton whom I begged to visit my brother. He found that my brother had . . . an intestinal stricture as well as haemorrhoids. His condition was very grave and needed an operation. . . . Gustave can now receive visitors without difficulty. He is a prisoner on parole and may not leave the premises. But he has a large garden and is very well off. Alas, what will be the end of all this! I tremble. Heavens, what sufferings! I haven't told my poor father about it; he'd be too unhappy. My husband and I will carry on our rescue-work to the end.[43]

It was indeed the replacement of Valentin by L. C. Renault that saved Courbet. He received Zoé in a friendly way and went to see Thiers at Versailles, probably knowing that the latter was disposed towards leniency in the matter; and Thiers permitted him to release Courbet on parole.

Though Zoé undoubtedly felt for her brother, she was also happy to have him at last in what seemed a condition of dependence on her alone. The whole story of Courbet in prison also brings out the weak side of his stamina and morale. He was capable of genuine courage and sustained effort in certain fields; but when cut off from his essential sources of satisfaction and sustaining energy, he was heavily depressed. In such a situation he found further the consequences of his bohemian habits of steady drinking, his restless night-perambulations, his extreme irregularity of life. Stomachic and anal troubles sapped his splendid physique and were linked with the moral stupefaction, the deep sense that the whole basis of his existence had somehow faded out. The rest of his life was to be in many respects the continuation of this story.

While preparing for the operation, he went on painting flowers and fruit. On the first day of the new year Mme Duval gave him an orange with stem and leaves attached; an hour later he gave her a painting of it as a new-year's gift. On 4 January he wrote to the family:

At last, after storms, we have fine weather again. For your New-Year celebrations as well as for my own I must announce I've finished with these miserable jails. I made use of an infallible scheme, which, I think, was impatiently awaited by the rascals who run the Government; for they were as weary as I was of knowing that I was in prison. . . . The method I used will cost me a good deal, but that doesn't matter. When one has spent seven months in a prison-cell, one's had enough. It needs only three months of it to drive a normal person mad. I must tell you I haven't suffered very much. My mind was occupied and I didn't lose my cheerful humour for a moment. The only thing that saddened me was my mother's death.

I also suffered greatly from my haemorrhoids, and it was these that enabled me to free myself from my horrible situation. I thought if I were to engage the greatest surgeon in Paris, M. Nélaton, nobody would dare to refuse him anything, and that's the way it turned out. He had me moved to a nursing home, where I'm in paradise. I have never been so comfortable in my life. I have a big garden to stroll in, a pleasant room. I eat extremely well at the family-table and there are guests almost every day, good friends. I was a friend of the son, who died under the Commune; in fact I had dined at their house in the past. It costs ten francs a day, but that doesn't matter.

My sister Zoé and her husband have gone to an incredible amount of trouble for me. In fact they gave three times as much as was necessary; but that's part of my sister's overzealous character. I should be very grateful to them. While I was in prison they visited me regularly twice a week and supplied me with everything I needed.[1]

On 14 January Zoé wrote to Bruyas that Courbet was much better. This period was the apex of her new friendly relations with him, and she must have imagined that her plans were all coming true.

The operation is absolutely necessary; for if the intestine should fully close up, an opening would have to be made in his side which would be a thousand times worse. . . . As for myself, I've been enduring martyrdom for a year. I trust my fearful sufferings will at least have a happy ending. At present Gustave is painting fruit. He had never done that before. A large picture, a dozen pears, apples etc., heaped attractively on a table, with a fireplace at one end of the room, his dressing-gown on an armchair. . . . Gustave is delighted with himself. He says he's never painted anything with such lovely colours.[2]

It is true that this period saw him fully achieve the fruit still-life as Saintes had seen him master the flower-piece. Again there is a strong emotional and physical impulse behind the turn in his art. His imprisonment has been a sort of death (almost in fact a real death), and he expresses his return to life, to the earth, by the acclamation of apple and pear. These objects are not just the fruit of the earth, the successful new-birth; they express by their simple, solid, satisfying shapes a rediscovery of form – or rather of the principle of the concretion of form, of the life-principle in primary and yet rich formative energy. The womb, the mother's body in its warm rotundities, the suckling breast, the child enclosed in a rondure of satisfaction and security, itself a ball of sensuous happiness: that is the sort of imagery and emotion ultimately underlying and precipitating these fruit-forms. We are coming close to the sort of emotional drive deep in Cézanne as he broke through his romantic immaturities and gradually settled down to his vision of space as made up of colour-structurations and rhythms. On the one hand, Courbet's apples now resume what we may call the Chardin tradition of everyday immediate solidities, familiar by use and yet realised in a new unity of mass, a new concrete simplification; on the other hand, they look forward to Cézanne's space composed of a dynamic interrelation of colour-planes.[3]

Nélaton, helped by his son and Dr Auger, carried out the operation about 20 January. We are told that Courbet refused chloroform and said he could stand the pain. The fear that made it so difficult for him to lie down and go to sleep as an act of will, as a normal moment of choice, made him fear the deliberate application of a drug or gas that would break down his consciousness. Zoé in her letter of 29 January to Bruyas gave full physical details, which can hardly have been appreciated by that fastidious character. 'The patient suffered agonies, but he told them to use all their skill and he would endure the pain until it killed him. It lasted forty-five terrible minutes. . . . So far all is well. Dr Nélaton promises complete elimination of the haemorrhoids . . . and when they are cured, the surgeon will proceed to dilate the intestines. . . . As soon as the operation was over, Gustave, who is very brave, as you know, asked for his pipe, and that same evening he got up, crossed the garden, and went to dinner. He will not stay in bed despite the dreadful pain. . . . He works all day. . . . I hope that as soon as he's well Gustave will take our advice and leave Paris till the turmoil dies down. He will seek repose for his body and his mind among his true friends, and will occupy himself seriously with painting. I'm very annoyed because I can already see the fine fellows [*braves*] who caused all our troubles clustering round Gustave again. It's to their interest to win him to their ways and keep him as scapegoat. Gustave has such a weak character; he doesn't know how to resist. He must be got away.'[4]

Zoé was already feeling her empire begin to crumble. At Neuilly Courbet received meetings or messages from many friends such as Boudin, Monet, Amand Gautier (who had been arrested as a communard), Comte de Choiseuil, the Laveurs. The 'true friend' on whom Zoé seems to have been most relying was Lydie; for she wrote to her, also on 29 January: 'You invite my brother to visit you and go on to Switzerland. The sooner the better, for the poor man has great need of rest and tranquillity. . . . Dismiss politics; they are a noxious quagmire. Persuade Gustave that painting restores the soul and that the creation of a few masterpieces may make him forget the horrors he has just endured. Gustave is exhausted in body and above all in mind. . . . Prison affected him terribly. He'd have lost his morale there if I hadn't followed him step by step, rebuilding his morale and cheering him up.'[5] Zoé was certainly still in her brother's good graces, though every movement he made to better health made him feel her insistent affection oppressive. She was certainly mistaking fantasy for fact when she later told Champfleury: 'Gustave used to say to us that he wanted to pay our debt . . . and to leave half of his fortune to our children.'[6]

That he should paint was in itself good enough advice. But in his worried state he found it hard to settle to anything. His losses weighed on his mind and made him carry on long niggling calculations, count up the money that had vanished, the pictures gone, and discuss trifling details at endless length.[7] On 2 March his sentence ended; he had paid over, ten days before, 6,850 francs. But he still stayed on at Neuilly till May. The intestinal operation was successfully carried out. Zoé told Bruyas that he was completely cured. 'From Dr Nélaton miracles are to be expected.' She added that Durand-Ruel was holding a show of modern art. 'We have just sent about thirty pictures.' The 'we' was ominous. Courbet was not likely to accept such a situation of partnership or control.[8] Nélaton refused any cash-payment but accepted a landscape painted in the Duval garden ('worth 6,000 francs').

A journalist, M. G. Puissant, visited Courbet on 3 March and found him very emaciated. The majesty of his belly had gone, his clothes hung loose and flapped. His skin was saffron and white, with bluish tints, his brow furrowed, the cornea of his eyes scratched with yellowish fibrils, his beard powdered with flour. But he still had his bantering lip, his sonorous laugh, his air of ironic insouciance. His one deep wish was 'to walk, run, breathe with full chest, sprawl in the grass'. He wanted 'to take up earth from fields in a handful, kiss it, smell it, bite it, to slap the bellies of trees, throw stones in waterholes, splash in a stream, eat, devour nature'. It was the same desire to return to childhood that we saw in the letter to Lydie: an expression of the regret he now felt for his wrecked body. True, the experiences of jail had decisively speeded up his breakdown, but he was already old before his time in the late 1860s. We saw how the police-report described him as not only gross but also as 'bowed down' – *voûté*, with stooped or rounded back.[9]

On 3 March he wrote to Juliette, repeating how well he felt at Neuilly where the trees were putting on leaves. He meant to stay there till the noise died down, then paint and sell to recoup his losses, wait till the season was more advanced and suitable for travelling. Many visitors took up his time; some Swiss from Fribourg and Neuchâtel had invited him to come and rest in their land; felicitations kept flowing in. The operation had gone well; he was rid of his trouble for life. But there was bad news. A portion of the works hidden in the cellars at the Passage du Saumon had been stolen. 'The thief is M., the man in charge of the Passage, who took away also 350,000 francs to Nubar-Pacha, the proprietor. For me it's a loss of at least 150,000 francs.' And he had had grievous losses at the rue Hautefeuille and the rue du Vieux-Colombier, la Vilette, Ornans. Add his grief over his mother, the sorrows of his family, his jailing: one would agree he didn't need much more to grow old. 'It's that ignoble Napoleon who is the cause of everything.' Fate was all the more unjust in that he had struggled twenty years to destroy the regime.[10]

Zoé on 10 March lamented to Bruyas that now he was feeling better he didn't want to leave Paris. 'He doesn't want to listen to us any longer. . . . May the cruel lesson he has just received help him for the future. Alas, I'm afraid.'[11] By 25 April Courbet was getting around as usual. That day he called on Victor Hugo. 'Courbet came to talk to me about some pictures which he considers unsaleable. They're by Guignet, pupil of Decamps. "This kind of painting", said Courbet, "no longer has any reason to exist." I don't agree.' He may have painted his portrait of Hugo about this time, though we would expect Hugo to mention it in his notes. He was now drinking with old friends at Frontin's place, the *Cave*.[12]

He had sent in to the Salon only two works, the *Lady of Munich* and *Apples on a Garden Table* (done at Neuilly). Both were thrown out on purely political grounds. Daumier and Puvis de Chavannes were similarly punished. The latter had been on the jury and resigned in protest against the treatment of Courbet. Of the jury of twenty, only two (Fromentin and J. Robert-Fleury) voted for Courbet; the persecutors were led by Meissonier who announced the need to exclude Courbet from exhibitions in perpetuity. Meissonier pointed out that the *Lady* had been painted among the enemies of France and the still-life was falsely dated as from Ste-Pélagie – a piece of bravado on Courbet's part. There was much discussion in the papers, which mostly supported Meissonier, for example by F. Sarcey in an article 'La Grosse Courge' ('The Fat Gourd'). But some critics rallied to Courbet's side: Jules Noriac writing on the Legendary Jury, E. d'Hervilly on the War Council of the Exposition of the Beaux-Arts. Lockroy in the *Rappel* treated Meissonier as a tinter of photographs and recalled that he had been *peintre attitré* of Napoleon. A drawing by Grelot, *No Entry*, showing the panic of the academics as the burly Courbet knocks on the door, was seized. Charles Blanc in the *République française* of 10 April in effect disavowed any official responsibility for the jury's action. Castagnary in the *Siècle* made the strongest blow on Courbet's side. 'The reason why M. Meissonier has chosen to make himself ridiculous is a mystery easily solved by those who know to what extent the moral servitude of Napoleon III's empire has degraded the artists.'[13] However, nobody noted how ominous for the future was the ganging-up of the reactionaries against Courbet. On his part, the naming of his jail as the place where he had produced his glowing apples was a declaration of his unrepentance, of his continuing socialist positions.

Zoé as a last-line of defence for her viewpoint had appealed to Champfleury to write a series of articles for the *Figaro* or some other journal which would recall Courbet's thirty years of service to French art. She knew she could rely on him to take the line that Courbet was a natural painter led astray by clever villains and that his correct course was to drop politics altogether. But Champfleury had no wish to enter the arena against men like Castagnary. He replied that he had recently reprinted three early articles of his in *Souvenirs*:

This means that I have said what I can about Courbet and that a definitive judgment on the man, his work, his art, must now come from the next generation. As to those who steered him into evil ways and made him wander from the path which it would have been easy for him to tread, I cannot follow their manoeuvres. One would have to furnish facts rather than opinions, and I have lost sight of Courbet for ten years, during which I have lived and studied in solitude.[14]

D'Hervilly published in *L'Eclipse* of 14 April an amusing playlet set in the Palais de l'Industrie during a jury-session. Three pictures are brought in. Meissonier orders them to be set with their backs to the jury. 'I repeat that this year we do not scrutinise; we judge.' The first work is by the editor of the *Figaro* (which was violently anti-Courbet); it is at once accepted. The second work is by a chiropodist who was devoted to the Vendôme Column; it is also at once accepted, though Robert-Fleury protests: 'But this picture is repulsive; it depicts a set of toes all covered with corns and looks as if painted with treacle.' Meissonier retorts, 'I love treacle very much. From now on treacle will be my favourite colour.' The third work represents a paper cornucopia filled with fried potatoes. It is rejected as communard propaganda; in Meissonier's opinion it is an obvious allusion to the burning of the Tuileries. The jury then adjourns to judge a horse-show next door.[15]

Some time this spring Zoé wrote to Bruyas with an appeal for Promayet, who, like Bruyas, was dying of tuberculosis – 'one of our friends whom you met long ago at Gustave's. . . . He is from our province, our very devoted, very much loved childhood-friend.' Promayet, hard up as ever, had taken a post as teacher in Russia where he was put in charge of a young pupil. The pair of them left for France and Promayet went on teaching the youth for ten years, making him a prize-scholar. 'His pupil's family is named Romanoff and he's related to the Russian imperial family.' Finally Promayet took him back to Russia, where the family wanted to keep him.

But our friend has an eccentric streak. He insisted it would be wrong to remain after his task was completed, that he'd feel in the way. He left them and took a post with another family, that of the first chamberlain at the Russian court. There he became ill; he lived in a new house and contracted some nervous ailment or other. He came back to Paris to recover, but the Romanoffs watched over him. They sent his former pupil to accompany him; and at the time of Gustave's trial they were in Paris. Then they had to go to Amélie-les-Bains for the winter. Now the doctors are sending him to Montpellier to consult specialists. The Romanoffs wrote to me that Promayet's pupil will go there in June, and his mother, Mme Romanoff, will join him. . . . But I promised them to ask you to be kind enough to visit our poor friend in the meantime and advise him.[16]

Bruyas did what he could, but Promayet died about a month after arrival. Courbet would certainly have blessed any efforts on Promayet's behalf, but Zoé seems acting on her own initiative, proud of any connection with aristocrats. We must recall her Russian associations.

Dupont had died in 1870, but we may insert here a draft-letter that Courbet wrote to him. Its elegiac, slightly embittered tone suits this phase, though it may have been written during 1869–70:

Don't deceive yourself. Life is cruel. Like me you've been able to see Homer, Rembrandt and their fellows . . . all tamers of wild animals: followed, some by Editors, Maecenases [spelt *messènes*], Directors of the Fine Arts; others by Englishmen – all these following them so as to be in at the death. The man who can't do anything wants to enjoy the work of others.

Ah, my dear Dupont, how far-off is this time from us. In our youth we believed in everything. We were in a Republic, we believed that Liberty was close at hand. For the imagination everything was azure, we believed in Love, we wept at Infidelity, we were slight of form and not hard to please in the matter of good cheer [*chère* spelt as *chair*, flesh]. Our needs weren't large. With good shoes and an overcoat of white linen, a big straw hat, a short-petticoated woman with neckerchief and bare head, an umbrella worth three francs in the hand, the heart's desires were filled to the brim. And the whole week one's head was full of the country-excursion to be made on Sunday to the woods of Meudon and of Fleuri, to the Fone-Bazin, the Plessy-Piquet, and of the dinner at the roadside inn, the middle-draught [*coup du milieu*, a term of the Jura: glass of kirsch or marc drunk in mid-meal]. Our band was then still all intact: Monselet, Champfleury, Murger, Baudelaire, Bonvin, Gautier etc., etc. But tossed and knocked about by the hard existence we've had to undergo, all these dreams have fled, and soon we'll be condemned to base our future on memory.[17]

This year the Brussels firm that had used his work for two pamphlets in 1868 issued *Les Misères des gueux* (beggars or tramps) by Dr Blondon of Besançon, who wrote as Jean Bruno. The illustrations, fifty-seven of them, were based on paintings by Courbet, some using the original titles, others with new captions to fit the tales.[18]

At last Courbet decided to go home. 'I had a great success while returning to my country, first at Dijon, then at Dôle. At Besançon I had a mishap. I'd gone to drink at the Cercle des Canotiers (Rowing Club) which has 120 members. While I stood on the pavement, a Bonapartist grocer, who'd stayed at the Club after we left, smashed the mug I'd drunk from. I had a very hard time stopping him from being thrashed; but a week later he was expelled from the Club by 84 votes to 6, and the *Figaro* reported only the broken mug. Later the man was said to have committed suicide.'[19] Courbet reached Ornans on 26 May, escorted by his father, the Ordinaire family, and other friends in four carriages; they went to the café de l'Annette, where others joined them convivially. Beauquier, who directed the *Républicain de l'Est*, tried to draw him out; but Courbet refused to make any statement. 'In the particular situation where circumstances have put me, sacrificed to people who have the habit of saving society, all that I could tell you on this occasion would be interpreted in the sense opposite to my idea.'

He was now quite reconciled to the Ordinaires and spent much time with them at Maisières, where he set up a studio. In July he wrote from there to his sisters at Flagey:

Sometimes I'm at Maisières, sometimes at Ornans. But I can't go to Flagey in this hot weather. . . . I bathe in the Loue. I've also painted four landscapes at the Puits Noir and at Maisières. I haven't been wasting my time. . . . All goes well. If the Commune's caused me unhappiness, it's also increased by a half my sales and my prices: that is, during the past six months I and other owners of my pictures have sold my works to the amount of 180,000 francs. In such circumstances one can afford to let people howl. I've painted some fish caught by the Ordinaire sons. They weighed nine pounds; they were magnificent . . . also some mushrooms (given to Dr Ordinaire). . . . When it's cooler, I'll come to see you. This weather is bad for me. I need complete rest at present because I've suffered too much during the past two years; my liver has been out of order. So you'll forgive me for not coming to see you more often.[20]

In a letter to Castagnary on 14 August he expatiated on his liver-trouble.

I was ill for a month with a swollen liver. The cause of the malady was a fire at Maisières, during which I had to carry hectolitres of water for four hours to put out the flames in a house of some legitimists; and to think I've been called an incendiary makes it all the more disgusting. I've already done five pictures: two landscapes and fish of the Loue of an excessive size. We're always on the look-out, waiting for the growth of the little Republic. . . . It would be a phenomenon if it arrived at this stage [maturity] with such a little president [Thiers]. Painters are arriving in our province. We already have Rapin, Jean-Jean Cornu, some Swiss, and Pata. The last-named told me that one of my pictures has been sold in London for 76,000 francs: which shows that the

Commune has raised my prices. I think it's my *Hunt in the Snow*. I've already sold my *Return from the Fair* to Durand-Ruel for 10,000.[21]

His swollen liver had not been caused by exercise during a fire; it was due to cirrhosis of the liver, the result of excessive drinking of alcohol.

Unable to walk as he used to, Courbet bought a horse and carriage, and drove about, now and then stopping to sketch, but mostly to regain quiet of mind and body by seeing familiar spots again and feeling once more at home in his beloved region. He visited La Glacière de la Grâce-Dieu above a fine valley with an abbey of Trappists; the sources of the Dessoubre at Consolation, in the Bout-du-Monde, a wild scene with a circuit of steep rocks and woodland, with the river Soudre below, flowing out under an arcade like that of the Loue and the Lison, and cascading off into the the narrow valley – marvels 'which I'd never seen before: for which I'm ashamed, and still more ashamed since I've seen them'. At Morteau, an industrial town on the Swiss border, he took part in a banquet with thirty places, arranged by Alexis Chopard, director of the town's musical societies.[22] Chopard had mended the *Fisher* and Courbet handed the statue over to the municipality. (It is still there, with a copy at Ornans.)

He still, however, seems to have used his donkey Jérôme, so called 'out of respect for the painter of that name [Gérôme]', to judge by a story coming from the Ordinaires:

One day when it was very hot, Courbet and Jérôme arrived at Maisières, coming from Ornans. Before entering the house of his friends the Ordinaires he tied Jérôme to the gateway, right out in the sun. After half an hour's chat, Mme Ordinaire asks, 'And Jérôme, is he with you?'
'Of course, he's waiting at the gate.'
'But, dear friend, on such a hot day, you'll kill him off.'
'Do you think so? Jérôme leads a hard life.'
An hour goes by. Mme Ordinaire asks again, 'And Jérôme?'
'He's waiting.'
'Then put him in the stable.'
Courbet doesn't answer or make a move. At the end of the afternoon Courbet's still gossiping and Jérôme's still waiting.
'Courbet,' Mme Ordinaire tells him, this time in tones of authority, 'I'm going to give orders for Jérôme to be put in a sheltered place.'
'Just as you like.'
Mme Ordinaire, who told the story to the *comtois* painter, Louis Baille, added, 'A fortnight later Courbet and Jérôme were still our guests.'[23]

It was probably about this time that he told Lydie of the death of his son. The news of this death, coming on top of so many anxious moments, must have hit him hard. It perhaps explains why he made one more attempt to arrange a stable relationship with a woman: this time a liaison without marriage. Like the other attempts he made to grapple a woman to him, the episode was both ridiculous and pathetic. During his trip to the village of L'Hôpital-du-Gros-Bois and the grotto of La Glacière, he encountered a peasant-girl who strongly attracted him. He decided to make her his mistress, but with his usual timidity before women in a wooing role he asked one Cornuel to act as his intermediary. On 6 October he wrote:

'You can see that with my artist's eye and my great experience of life I guessed in five minutes all that you think of Mlle Léontine. I saw in her an upright nature, honest, sympathetic, natural. It's what I've been looking for for twenty years, because I believe that in the eyes of people who know me I have an exactly similar nature. I found her in a forest, without any frills, busy on some chores that please me. All my family thinks that way. It doesn't go counter to our superior status [*distinction*]. This chance! this encounter, which I had always foreseen, was understood by the friends who were with me. As we came out of La Glacière, they spontaneously said to me, "There's someone who'd suit you. An artist should be surrounded by agreeable and natural persons." I was already of the same opinion before they spoke. On my return to Ornans I consulted my sisters, who agreed with me. I went to Pontarlier. I confided my impression to some ladies there [Lydie], very intelligent and understanding, who wanted to go with me and persuade Mlle Léontine to come and live with me. For I must tell you all. I've suffered so much in my life, I've rendered so many services to everyone, I'd be so inclined to render a service to an honest woman that it's impossible for Mlle Léontine, despite the stupid advice she may get from peasants, not to accept the brilliant position I offer her. She'll be beyond question the most envied woman in France, and could be thrice reborn without ever meeting a position like this one, since I could choose a woman from any level of French society without ever meeting a refusal.'[24]

However that may have been, he was clearly very afraid of meeting a refusal from a simple peasant-girl who couldn't grasp the dazzling offer he was making. He, the advocate of honest simplicity, was afraid that the existence of such simplicity in the village would defeat his plans. He went on to Cornuel. 'Mlle Léontine will be absolutely free with me. She may leave me when she wants, despite me. Money means nothing to me; she'll never regret associating with me. Remember, my dear Cornuel, that out of two days' work I can give a dowry such as no other woman in the village has. In a word, if she comes with me, I declare she'll be the happiest woman to be found in Europe. In this matter let her consult, not the villagers, but intelligent persons (*gens d'esprit*). It's for you, my dear Cornuel, to make this family, who can't know at all who I am, understand all this. I count on you. Write to me what I must do: whether I should go to see her again at La Glacière or at L'Hôpital-du-Gros Bois. Arrange a meeting of some kind and spend whatever money is needed to fix it up as soon as can be, as I must get down to work and go on to Switzerland. If it can be done, I'll take her with me. Orders for pictures await me there, friends of democracy too, and the Berne Exposition.' His many spelling errors in this letter suggest haste and perturbation.

Three days later he wrote again. 'As you know, I wrote Mlle Léontine a very serious letter in which I made offers that many young women of a much superior position than hers would have been enchanted to accept. It seems I was mistaken about this young woman. Instead of replying frankly [*simplement*] to an honestly-made proposition, she thought she should consult, as I predicted to you, her *coco mimi* [village-lad] who gives me the impression of having absorbed all the wit [*esprit*] of Nancray [a village near Besançon] and who answers me with the most sentimental of village-ballads: which might get laughs from the villagebumpkins [*loustics*], but which we could never understand. From this I conclude that Mme Léontine prefers a thatched cottage and the heart of an idiot, who reminds me of a soldier on leave or who's retired, to an established position which would ensure her future as well as mine. Whatever comes of it, my dear Cornuel, I'll always feel grateful to you for the friendly offices you've been good enough to render me in this matter. If this is to be its end, please find out if that reply has been made with her assent or unknown to her. But tell her strongly that all the *coco mimi*, all the *io cou cou* [clods] possess an intellectual value almost equal to that of their oxen, without the same market value. *Salut et fraternité.*'[25]

There is an amusing contrast between his need to use local dialect-terms in his frustrated rage, and his pretences as a fine gentleman whom no lady in France would refuse. This episode shows him at perhaps the lowest moral level that we can trace in his life. But he soon recovered from the blow to his manhood. His bad health, however, persisted, keeping him irritated and unable to throw himself into work in his old way. He had mocked at the Thiers regime, but he now found it was in danger of being overthrown by a far worse faction which considered that no mercy whatever should have been shown to any Communards.

Yet another ridiculous relationship with a woman now crops up: his connection with Mathilde G., which we noted as coming about during the Commune or a little earlier. It was now that things came to a head. On 25 November she approached him about a book that, according to her, they had agreed to write, in the form of letters, which Poulet-Malassis, who had fled to Belgium after the legal action against Baudelaire's *Fleurs de Mal*, was to publish. 'Her letters, set forth in a fine script, crammed with errors in spelling, starred with exclamation marks, dashes, underlined words, capitals where they shouldn't be, and minuscules for proper names, are scarcely ever dated, except by the day when they were written. They are the work of an *exaltée* ready for anything to gratify her vices, and later her rancour, playing with seduction as much as with menaces, but desperately attaching herself, like a shipwrecked person, to the least plank of safety' (Fernier). When put to it, she could at least equal Courbet in physical frankness, but she preferred a lofty tone, a romantic cover. Courbet replied in rage, 'The ideal! the ideal! My God, what in the world is it, this ideal? . . . You think, my dear friend, that by using the words heart, soul, sentiments, aspirations to the infinite, without knowing what goes in the world, you're in a position to control everything. You're mistaken. . . . If you like, I'll show you what love really is. Look at the peasants. I've known them since childhood.'[26] And he goes on to describe without veils the direct physical violence, quite without tenderness or respect for another, which was the way of making love in his home-region.

This is a statement of the utmost importance for the understanding of his psychology, above all his sexual responses, his inability to believe that any woman could be faithful to lover or husband. It further helps us to understand his relationship to his sisters. As we saw, the Courbet household was a mixture of refinement and coarseness. The girls played music, and in Zoé's case at least aspired to all the conventional bourgeois attainments proper to young ladies; but they had to delve elbow-deep in dung and carry out all the duties of a fairly primitive farm. They were close to the animals, to the rutting peasants as to the rutting stags. For the effect of this duality on Courbet we must add the fact of the extremely close inner family-bond, which held them all so tightly that Gustave, Zélie, and Juliette never married, and Zoé had to make her breakaway through Gustave's world of sexual independence – though she finally adhered, perhaps all the more strongly because of her period of rebellion, to the bourgeois family-code. There was certainly a strong sexual link between Courbet and his sisters, expressed in works like the *Winnowers*. If, as is possible, Zoé broke the bourgeois code by sitting naked to him, this point is brought out all the more emphatically. The continuing emotional link with the family, above all with the sisters, was a prime factor inhibiting Courbet from finding a stable relationship with any other woman.

Mathilde offered Courbet 'the most ardent kisses . . . thousand millions of kisses'. Her frankness certainly stirred him: 'I am a man, as everybody knows, who shrinks from nothing provided that I can rationalise it and reconcile it with my conceptions and my logic. Through my efforts to carry this out, life has flung me from the heights into impossible depths. But as I have in my nature the resilience of the mountaineer, I never remain prostrate. I rise from my ashes to defy society and constantly to assert my nature and my own way of living, feeling and maintaining my freedom in spite of men, their spies, and their laws. In short, I am always trying to achieve my independence and my liberty without false shame.'[27] That is a statement with deep truth in it. But while Mathilde aroused desire in him, the element of falsity he could not but detect quenched his impulses and led him into protesting outbursts.

On 25 December he wrote to Pasteur, who had ordered five pictures, that he was behind-hand with his work. There was clear daylight for only one or two hours a day; his painting half-dries out by next day: 'I am ill with a liver-complaint, and I have some sort or other of a *pleurodinie* [pleurodynia], rheumatism in the left side that reaches up to my loins. I've a sister [Zélie] who's ill at my father's place in a village two leagues distant. I have to rebuild my studio devastated by the Prussians. I have to write a pile of letters. I go to bed at 2 or 3 a.m.'

Despite his operation he seems to have trouble still with his haemorrhoids. Gros-Kost says that the instrument used by Nélaton took three-quarters of an hour in application, and Courbet complained bitterly, 'A century wasted for the worker! a century without booze! a century without talk! a century without observation! a century without painting!' If only he could see nature through the privy-door! So, once when he was staying with a friend, he cut down without permission a number of trees that hid the view, so that he could open the door and look out. 'I'll never be one of those base folk who resign themselves to staring a whole hour in such a shed [*cabanon*, also a prison-cell], among spiderwebs and a foul air, arms crossed and eyes empty, *without looking at nature*.' (The tale of actually cutting the trees down probably comes from a joke of his: that he wanted to do so.)

About this time his distracted state of mind, his desire to hit out at someone, led him into three lawsuits. We see him here in a bad state of peasant litigiousness. He brought a suit against the architect Isabey for the loss of his stored material in Paris, claiming 25,000 francs. The tribunal, as anyone could have foreseen, decided that Isabey was not at all responsible for the removal of the materials for the construction of barricades. He sued Dr Robinet for unpaid rent for the use of his rooms in the rue du Vieux-Colombier; and was awarded only 251 francs. As the rooms had been used for a Republican Club, it was unworthy of Courbet to sue. Thirdly he refused to pay Mlle Gérard of the Passage du Saumon her bill of 911 francs for board and lodging; he demanded certain articles of furniture and the like left in her house, with a threat of legal action unless she complied. She at once increased her demand, adding claims for food and loans, plus 1,000 francs for defamation of character – 2,525 francs in full. On 4 April 1873 the Civil Tribunal of the Seine ordered him to pay 1,211 francs, so that he lost 300 francs by his dislike of paying bills. It is hard not to sympathise with Mlle Gérard, whom Riat says was a relation of his – perhaps through marriage.[28]

Meanwhile, as these petty affairs dragged on, Castagnary urged him to send some works to an international show soon to be opened in Vienna. Courbet replied on 16 January; he has had the first wind of the scheme that was finally to destroy him:

I've read in the *Siècle* a proposal by 23 deputies of the Chamber, which is insane beyond parallel. It would merely compel me to set up the Vendôme Column again at my own charge, since I've already paid the costs of the War Council *par solidarité* [accepting the costs of his fellows]. In the War Council I was condemned to a fine of 600 francs and 6 months of jail for my share in this monument's destruction: which is already going too far as the Code doesn't condemn an individual in my case to more than 500 francs' fine and a month in jail. In short, despite all that, the matter is much more serious than it seemed at first. If the Chamber's vote succeeds in condemning me, they're going to confiscate from me my mother's property, then my father's, and worst of all, my pictures. What am I to do? The whole majority will vote, and a part of the left centre.

I'd like you to do me a service and find out about this question in the Chamber, and even from a lawyer of your choice. . . . It costs a good deal of money to register pretended sales. Try to see ahead and let me know so I can arrange them before the Chamber votes. I won't exhibit in Vienna. I wrote to the administration to learn if I could exhibit independently, without the endorsement of a foreign government. They answered that I couldn't exhibit except under the auspices of the French committee headed by M. du Sommerard: which is impossible, because I denounced him and his administration when, in association with M. de Nieuwerkerke, he organised a show in London while the Prussians were in Paris. Nor shall I exhibit in Paris this year. I'm fed up with all these people: all that mob of intriguers and toadies, stupid flunkeys without talent, disgust me. I've been ill all winter with pleurodynia [rheumatic pains in side] and an *enlarged liver: I was afraid of dropsy.*

I've many orders for pictures I haven't been able to meet yet; and now that I'm on the point of being able to work again, along comes another vexation worse than all the others. I was delighted to see *père* Ordinaire, who has helped me greatly and bravely in my distress. We have lived together almost all the time since I left you. I've also engaged a servant who takes care of me and cooks for me. . . .

During the Commune I had a woman in Paris, a noblewoman, who adored me. I don't know what to do with her because she has illusions about me and my financial resources. We're having a frantic correspondence. She's charming. Don't tell anyone about it.[29]

We note how deluded Zoé was in thinking that in Franche-Comté he wouldn't find radicals helping to prick his political conscience. Ordinaire, following the line of Rochefort, had been a vigorous opponent of the Empire; he had read out in the Corps Législatif the declaration made by Rochefort when arrested. Courbet's portrait shows him as a robust man with a high colour and a pensive air of goodness. His wife, quick and imperious, composed music and painted as well as being deeply interested in politics; she was a deputy in 1869 and prefect of the Doubs next year under her husband's name. Her husband wrote, 'If she wanted anything, the powers of heaven and hell couldn't stop her from it.' She wrote articles for journals and became director of a printing firm, founding two organs at Besançon: the *Démocratie* and the *Bon Sens.*[30]

Courbet, however, decided after all to send some pictures to Vienna, in a show arranged by the dealer Durand-Ruel, as long as a scheme could be devised to stop them from being confiscated.

If Durand-Ruel shows me under the auspices of du Sommerand, the pictures must belong to him or *be thought to belong to him* legally. . . . See if it can be arranged. In any event I'll send you a document for Durand-Ruel authorising my brother-in-law, who has my studio's keys, to deliver any picture you and Durand-Ruel choose for the show. You should also notify my lawyer M. Duval, who is prosecuting the thieves that stole my pictures from the Passage du Saumon. . . . Here, to be safe from confiscation by the Chamber, I'm going to a lawyer to register the gift [to Juliette and Zélie] of all I own, my [Ornans] studio and everything else, as well as my share in the property inherited from my mother. Still, I'll stipulate that I may go on enjoying the use of my studio till I die. As to the removal of my pictures from the rue Hautefeuille and the rue du Vieux-Colombier, I think the simplest way would be to send them to M. Jolicler at Pontarlier; from that point I'll have them sent to Switzerland as soon as I find lodgings there. . . . There'll be nothing left but my share of my father's property after his death; but he might be ready to disinherit me as the law allows. . . . I'm still rather ill.[31]

His mind was running more than ever on militant political works. He wrote to the president of Vienna Exhibition (according to Gros-Kost) about two anti-war pictures he proposed to paint – pictures that he had had in mind since 1859–60. The first was the *Conscript's Departure*. 'The slight young man, bag on back, stick on hand, bids farewell to his family. His mother and sisters are in despair; his grandfather, blind and resting his elbows on the table, dreams sadly of the long-past butcheries in which he was one of the actors. The young fellow, who wants to show his courage, holds back his tears for the moment when he'll be far from his folk. . . . In the second canvas the young soldier is transformed. He has profited from the lessons of discipline. He has taken in the good advice of the veterans. The military spirit has breathed on him. There he is at Solferino. He is a zouave. He has fought courageously. The battle is over. The highway is littered with corpses and night comes down. The timid conscript has become a fierce soldier; he is crouching down over one of the dead men and has cut off his head. He swings it in the air with savage cries.' If Courbet had been able to paint such works effectively, he would have resumed the full tradition of Gros and Géricault with a new force, breadth and impact. His achievements of the 1850s and his Commune drawings prove that he had in him the power as well as the will to carry out such projects, not as cartoon-propaganda or well-meaning anecdote, but with all that a complete realisation of the scenes implied. However, his shattered health and

77 *The Charity of a Beggar at Ornans* (author's title: *Beggar's Alms*). 1868. 210 × 175 cm.
Burrell Collection, Glasgow Art Gallery and Museum (see page 227).

78 *Rocks at Ornans.* 1869. 23 × 26 cm.
Musée du Petit Palais, Paris
(see page 70).

79 *The Source* or *Rocks of the Doubs.*
1871. 65 × 81 cm.
Musée des Beaux-Arts de Besançon
(see page 230).

80 *The Valley of the Loue under a Stormy Sky. c.* 1870. 53 × 66 cm.
Civic Museum of Fine Arts, Strasbourg
(see page 54).

81 *The Cliffs at Etretat.* 1869.
130 × 162 cm.
Louvre, Paris (see page 242).

84 *The Lake Leman*. 1874.
50 × 61 cm.
Musée des Beaux-Arts de Besançon
(see page 311).

82 *Stormy Sea* or *The Wave*. 1870.
115 × 160 cm.
Louvre, Paris (see page 242).

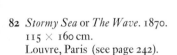

85 *The Trout*. 1871. 55 × 89 cm.
Kunsthaus, Zurich (see page 295).

83 *The Wave*. 1870. 67 × 107 cm.
Kunsthalle, Bremen (see page 237).

86 *The Dead Roe-buck*. 1876.
43 × 33 cm.
Musée du Petit Palais, Paris
(see page 319).

87 *Still Life*. 1871. 45 × 70 cm.
National Gallery, London (see page 278).

88 *Courbet at Ste-Pélagie.* 1871. 92 × 72 cm.
Musée de Courbet, Ornans (see page 279).

89 *Portrait of M. Courbet, Senior.* 1874. 82 × 74 cm.
Musée du Petit Palais, Paris (see page 22).

the new problems he faced did not leave him capable of gathering the strength, moral and physical, for such large and gruelling works.[32]

Yet he never had felt surer of his position; his philosophic and social ideas have matured. We see this in such statements as *The Republican*, and *Society*, which Castagnary preserved. He accepts organisation, but wants a fully democratic basis. 'Authority is not an art that aggrandises man by its practice; there is on the contrary the obligation to use it in such a way as to minimise the effect it can produce.' He shows an acute sense of the way in which human energy has been malformed and distorted. Man

became the executioner for war-leaders under the name of warrior; he became the subject of kings, the invading soldier of emperors, the vassal of nobles; he became the worker of the bourgeois. And [now] he has become a free toiler in the service of progress and civilisation alone. The time of heca-tombs is over. Man is going to conquer the world without cannon and powder, with bread and equality, with common right without charity, with justice without violence and barbarity, with wisdom without religion. . . . It is strange to think that man has lived as if he didn't exist, and that all he has been able to conceive failed to serve him, and only saddened him. Unceasingly reconstituting the past to his own detriment, he could not reach self-government and reveal his individuality; and his end surprised him, leaving of him only his aspirations, confiding to his first-born the execution of his dreams. Labour of Sisyphus, he rolled up his rock without result; like a buffoon, he told and retold the links of this social chain in a vicious circle from which he could not escape. . . . Many men have felt the weight of this march that led to nothingness; some revolted, others submitted. This distrust of nature spoke in an English philosopher, 'The children are our fathers', and mysticism made Bossuet declare without knowing what fly stung him, 'Man marches to the tomb, dragging after him the long chain of his deceived hopes.'

He goes on with a strong attack on the systems of education that rivet men to a false way of life, a dead repetitive pattern.

On 28 January he wrote to Castagnary from Besançon, where he had gone to arrange the transfer of his property. He asked for his pictures in Paris to be packed at once and sent to an address (M. Tramut) at Montbéliard in Doubs:

The first shipment will comprise pictures painted by myself; without delay send after them the old masters. You'll notify me of the departure of each shipment, also M. Viette at Blamont. . . . To advise M. Viette, write him a letter on some trifling matters without mentioning the shipment. . . . Keep this a secret from my brother-in-law. You and Durand-Ruel are to pay all expenses – or you might remove the pictures on the pretext they're to go to the Vienna Exhibition. Let Durand-Ruel into the secret.[33]

He had swung now to total mistrust of the Reverdys. Castagnary had warned him that Reverdy as a strong Bonapartist was working against him. On 16 January he had written to Zoé that he was now 'disgusted with all that's going on'; perhaps his intention was to lull her suspicions and make her feel that she had won him over to her point of view.[34] For on 9 February he unburdened himself to Castagnary: 'I'll tell you something you must keep to yourself. I'm afraid my brother-in-law is a member of the secret police and is specifically assigned to keep me under surveillance. He is impudent, lazy, a man without employment, whose source of income is unknown to me and who is trying to exploit me. By their stupidity he and my sister have done me all the harm that can be done to a man; and I've only one regret in connection with the Commune: that because of our kinship I was obliged to accept their aid. But that is finished. . . . I want to keep only my pictures. . . . I'm giving up my mother's bequest, my studio, and my lands. That's not too dear a price for the fall of the Column.'[35]

He may have gone too far in his doubts; but there is nothing unlikely in his suggestion that Reverdy was a government-agent. Zoé with her outlook would have found no difficulty in reconciling reports to the Government with her aim of saving Courbet from his villainous associates. She could easily have convinced herself that all she and Reverdy were doing was for Courbet's good, the only way of holding him back from even worse disaster. Where Courbet was wrong lay in now thinking the Reverdys wanted to ruin him. They wanted to save him according to their lights; but at the same time, if he proved too lost a soul, they wanted to keep control of his works. Zoé was sure that as her brother's one true friend she had a large claim on his property. As for his turn against the Reverdys we must remember that Juliette now hated Zoé as a renegade from the home. The Commandant Fumey gives us the atmosphere at Flagey and Ornans:

Zoé had married a man named Reverdy who lived in Paris, and she was the mother of two sons about whose birth there hovered a certain mystery. They were mentioned only in veiled words before us, and anyhow we paid little attention to the matter. Father Courbet and his daughter Juliette declared that these children were not Reverdy's and that they showed no signs indicating any kinship with the Courbets. They would have been the sons of a Russian prince who had confided them to Zoé and then disappeared during the Commune.[36]

A letter written on 1 March to Bruyas showed that the Commune had strengthened, not sapped, Courbet's political convictions:

In life there are unfortunate natures: those who are born (one doesn't know why) with the spirit of what is good and just, without any other interest than the love of justice. The devotion I have always felt for the man who suffers has paralysed the well-being that I would have been able to gain myself in life. I regret nothing. I fear only one thing: to end up like Don Quixote; for the lie and egoism are indivisible.

The disinherited in society have yet once again just tried to free themselves from the exploitation and the oppression of their fellows, by violence. But this time, in their despite, I'm a witness of it. The men of 4 September drove them to it, to serve their design and their detestable politics. The revolution was pacific and one of propaganda, which explains my participation. But despite us the massacre took place; that was a part of the plans of this odious government. For the liberals of 1830 wanted the Days of June, which they sought so as to cover up their shame since 1870.

Since I saw you, my dear Alfred, I've gone through the most terrible situations a man can see in life. I've come out of it. Don't let's speak of it further. What is certain in it all is that I saved the arts of the nation.[37]

The question of Vienna was solved by a group of Austrian artists inviting him to take part in a show at a private club. They also asked him to visit Vienna; and he was tempted. On 19 March he wrote suggesting that Castagnary should go with him:

To crush infamy one must have no fear. All the *dirty* press doesn't weigh one ounce. In the foreign world above all I have the whole of democracy for me, all the women of all powers [*puissances*], all the painters, the Swiss, the Germans. In Vienna I'll be in touch with all foreign powers and the whole world – outside France, where I never want to exhibit again as long as I live. At Ornans I already have more orders for pictures than I can complete. I must absolutely take some pupils to get through with them. It's a disagreeable thing to be driven to, but I'm the one who has reaped all the benefit from the Commune. . . . At present I've commissions for more than fifty pictures. . . . If I'd joined the Commune for the very purpose, I couldn't have had a greater success. I'm in an enchanted state. As to my brother-in-law, I'll instruct him through my attorney to hand over the keys of my apartment to the concierge and not to concern himself in future with my affairs. How tired I am of his pretensions! You may be sure, my dear friend, that the Vienna show is the happiest event in my life. . . . I am on friendly terms with all these people and have the same ideas. As to France, I never belonged here. I don't like the people. . . . If you come to Vienna, as I hope you will, we'll amuse ourselves as you've never amused yourself, I promise you. *That is my country.* . . . I've renounced my lands and my studio. I abandon them to the political fury of the majority.[38]

He mentions that Pata was with him, 'making me paint to excess'. He was now one of the pupils whom Courbet was using to finish pictures quickly and fulfil orders.

How was his painting going? We saw that he had poured his sense of release, or renewal, into his still-lifes of fruits. He was maintaining his mastery of paint, expressing it in small themes: for instance, his pictures of trout, already mentioned, in which the texture and the character of the caught fish are richly defined. One *Trout* of his is signed '71, *in vinculis faciebat*' – that is, at Ste-Pélagie. But this was certainly not true; it was merely one of his many defiant attempts to remind people of his captivity, perhaps in a way to date a new start of his work from that experience.[39] We may go further in the case of this work and say that the memory of himself in chains is merged with the image of the snared fish. 'It is a work symbolising his personal situation after the terrible end of the Commune, where he, the friend of liberty, he, the great swimmer, finds himself in the role of this other magnificent creature which, for its misfortune, has snapped at the hook that makes it prisoner; it suffers and sees only obstacles in the red and sombre glimmerings of catastrophe' (Woerler). We must beware, indeed, of too easily reading an artist into his subject-matter but Courbet seems one of those who readily identify themselves with what they paint, and whose minds are active in thought and fantasy as they work. Recall his phrase that spoke of his swimming across the river of tradition where academics drowned, and his act of saving young Diaz. In *Society*, probably written shortly before his Ornans return, he described man in the existing world: 'Like a fish in a cast-net, whatever side he twists and turns in society, he meets a mesh.' He goes on to proclaim the coming change. 'The god of hosts has no more soldiers, the god of the rich has no more poor, and the man who works is going to snatch from its [Society's] hands the wretched ones, its victims, and those who were waiting for help from above will get it from below. The intervention of heaven, as well as the wisdom of nations, is worn out. The man who has so long been abused is going to take things in hand, do his work, and govern himself. But how many centuries he has had to sacrifice to his ignorance in order to reveal himself and recognise his own power.' In the midst of this sense of vast human potentialities Courbet feels himself still the trapped fish. He was also painting some excellent landscapes, such as the *Bridge of the Fleurier* across the Areuse: a site he tackled from several aspects, as did his pupil Marcel Ordinaire, under his directives.[40]

A fresh painting, with all his sympathy for animal life, was the *Calf*, which brings out, as did works like *Siesta*, his kinship with the Dutch tradition, with painters like Potter. Gros-Kost tells us a silly story about Courbet being attracted by the sight of a very dirty calf, asking the farmer for permission to paint it, then next day to his disgust finding that the creature had been carefully cleaned and combed, with pink rosettes on its ears. Apart from the fact that such a tale falls into the obvious pattern of many denigrations and fables, if Courbet had wanted a dirty calf, he could easily have rolled it over in the dirt.[41]

If Courbet thought he could get his pictures away from the Reverdys by simply telling them to give the things up, he was mistaken. They kept on obstructing his plans and trying to keep control of the works. On 5 April the solicitor Charles Duval wrote to Castagnary:

On 1 April I received a letter from M. Courbet asking me to instruct M. Reverdy to turn over the keys of his two apartments to M. Legrand [employee of Durand-Ruel]. I have since heard that MM. Reverdy and Legrand have met and are carrying out M. Courbet's instructions. I cannot and will not do anything more. I shall not take charge of the keys nor be present at the taking of the inventory; such tasks are not fitting to my profession or character. More, I strongly disapprove of all that M. Courbet is doing to safeguard property that is not in danger and will never be seized. I have written to him that I look on the precautions he is taking as neither necessary nor proper.[42]

Duval cannot but be lying in the advice he here gives; anyone could see that Courbet was coming in for further attack. He clearly wanted to be able to say that he had had nothing to do with Courbet's steps and had disapproved of them; but he goes so far that one can accuse him of betraying his client. The Reverdys however were not going to give up easily.

In March Courbet had tried to get a blow back on the Ornans municipality for their treatment of his statue. He wrote to the Prefect of the Doubs, Baron de Sandrans, with a charge of incompetence and vandalism.

At present the trees of the Iles-Basses at Ornans are suffering intolerable mutilation: a mutilation apparently ordered by the administration, which is incompetent in such matters, and carried out by careless workmen who are interested only in the production of firewood. In the name of the district's inhabitants I beg you to be good enough . . . to forbid this vandalism. . . . All that's needed is to lop off the few weak boughs that might fall on passers, to have it done by skilled men.[43]

His correspondence with Mathilde G. was continuing. He had realised that the part of him adored by her was his money. Now he tried to reclaim his letters with their lavish and precise accounts of copulations. Mathilde was forced out into the open. 'What! said I to myself. I, who wouldn't surrender his letters for 100,000 paid in cash down! He asks me that as if it were the simplest thing in the world.' But she wasn't going to be too hard on him. 'However, after all reflection, here is my decision: make it 5,000 francs cash.' Then she makes her idealistic cover-up. 'Only 5,000 francs, that is a slight price. It's my heart I'm giving, it's my soul.' And to scare him further and to provide the chance for the cash payment, she announced that she would soon be arriving in Besançon. She certainly scared him, but she had misread his character if she thought that he'd easily part with 5,000 francs. Courbet rushed off to Ornans; and when she followed him there, he departed for Maisières to the Ordinaire house, where he felt himself secure from attack. Mathilde's movements were linked with a letter-bombardment in which her appeals were merged with high-toned descriptions of her own noble character and her lover's perfidious behaviour. But Courbet was not without his plan of counter-attack. He had talked the matter over with Pata, henceforth a close confidant of his. Mme Pata, living in Paris, was asked to make inquiries and gather facts that could be used against Mathilde to stop her shower of insults, prayers, laments, and threats.[44]

Various factors had driven Courbet into the use of pupils in his artwork: his failing energy, his inability to meet the commissions now coming in, also his extreme resentment against the losses caused by the government, so that he wanted to make a lot of money quickly. True, he did need money for an adequate studio; but he lived for the most part simply enough. His work was fetching good prices and there could have been no real question of money-pressure. From now on, his works have to be scrutinised to make out whether they are wholly his own or works by his disciples which he touched up. The latter section in turn consists of works which are largely his, and of others where a few brush-strokes and the signature are all he added. Of his three aiders, Jean-Jean Cornu is the one we know least of. Marcel Ordinaire was the doctor's son; educated at the Ornans seminary, he had gone to Paris to study law, but had often looked in at Courbet's studio; now, encouraged by the latter and with his parents' approval, he turned to art. Cherubino Pata, the most capable of the three, was Swiss from an Italian-speaking canton: Ticino, says Gros-Kost. In fact he was born in 1827 at Sonogno, in the Valle Verzasca, and had a difficult childhood, but managed to make his first art-studies at the age of twelve, at Locarno, helped by his cousin, Father Nicolas, in a convent where he decorated the chapel for board and lodgings. Next he went to Florence and worked under Ciseri; he returned to Switzerland, then tried Milan; finally, back in Sonogno, he worked at the restoration of the church Santa Maria Lauretana by favour of the priest. But he was a strong radical, joined the carabinieri, and fought with them; at last one night he fled to Lyon, where he married a Schaffhousoise (of the German-speaking area of Switzerland), and went to Paris, where he met Courbet. He grew devoted to him, was with him during the Commune, and later followed him into exile. Light-hearted, active, quick-witted, in some respects unscrupulous, he was just the sort of person to delight Courbet, whose main assistant and agent he became. Now he with the others in the group were painting with much industry; in four days they had produced ten pictures for Americans; in six weeks, forty.[45]

On 26 April Courbet wrote to his sisters:

We have more orders than we can deal with. There are hundreds of pictures to be done. The Commune will make me a millionaire. . . . We've already delivered twenty; we must deliver as many more. Pata and Cornu are doing well; Marcel has come back and will work also, I hope, for I am paying them a commission on the pictures they prepare for me. Pata and Cornu have already had 1,800 francs. But my father must not try to discourage them and meddle with something that doesn't concern him, something he can't understand. . . . My father should mind his own business. We're making 20,000 francs a month.[46]

It is to Régis's credit that he protested against this picture-factory, which cannot be compared with the way in which Renascence and later studios turned out works where master and apprentice collaborated.

Courbet had all too little time left. On 24 May Thiers resigned; the government replacing him was largely Bonapartist and royalist; its president was Marshal MacMahon who had commanded the forces breaking the Commune. But even before Thiers fell, a bill had come before the Assembly for the rebuilding of the Column; on 30 May it was adopted, with an amendment declaring that the whole cost, to be assessed by a civil tribunal, was to be met by Courbet. This was a vindictive piece of legislation without precedent. Never before had any damage to public property, brought about during an insurrection, been laid on the head of an individual or group of individuals. Further, no special responsibility for the demolition had been proved or even argued for Courbet. But he was the only person, ready to hand, for the charge of instigating or carrying out the damage; many persons thought him very rich; he had long been made a scapegoat for all radical tendencies in art and had drawn particular abuse during the trials. One feels too that artists like Meissonier, who had many friends among the worst reactionaries with their programme of establishing the Moral Order, must have helped to keep his name before the authorities as a leading and unrepentant rebel.

Courbet, now fully aware of his danger, vigorously set about disposing of his pictures so as to obstruct their confiscation. He distributed most of his remaining property, even odds and ends of furniture and the few artworks he had at Ornans, among Pata, Cornu, Dr Ordinaire, Dr Blondon; these friends were to hand the things back if he weathered the present storm. He authorised a friend in Paris, Cusenier, to store the furnishings of the studio in the rue Hautefeuille, and instructed Durand-Ruel to send all of his works on show in Belgium, London, Vienna, to Switzerland by routes that did not pass through France. Zoé and her husband did their best to spoil these plans. They kept on trying to get from Duval an authorisation for collecting and disposing of Courbet's works. They seem to have done all they could, at least for a while, to stop Castagnary and Durand-Ruel from getting hold of the works in the rue Hautefeuille. On 15 June Courbet wrote her an enraged letter demanding that she hand the things over immediately; they were to go to Alexis Chopard at Morteau while his 'old masters' went to Blondon at Besançon. 'So nothing short of a legal attachment could get you to let my pictures go. It's incredible a man shouldn't be free to dispose of his own property. I've already issued 40 authorisations in this matter. I'll issue ten more and that's all, since you persist in sacrificing my interests to your own. Against the view of all France, you've succeeded in convincing even M. Duval that it's a crime to protect my interests. . . . You must absolutely consider this letter my final authorisation.'[47] About the same time he wrote to Chopard asking for the name of the agent at La Chaux-de-Fonds in Switzerland with whom his works were to be deposited, and asking if bonds registered in his name could be made 'payable to bearer in Switzerland more safely than in France. The confiscations are beginning.'[48] Many pictures did manage to get deviously through to Switzerland, but others were lost through Zoé's obstructions. Just what she hoped to gain is not clear; perhaps she somehow hoped that she and Reverdy, with government-connections, would be able to claim works and get them excluded from the confiscations. Still, it is only fair to cite her own account to Champfleury, which contradicts that of Juliette to Riat. She says that, when Courbet's authorisation came, she dismantled part of the studio and the whole of the collection of 'Old Masters'. She helped to stack the works in the crates, 'some of which weighed 1,400 kilos'. Reverdy sent them on to Dr Blondon at 26 rue Neuve, Besançon, who transported them to 2 rue du Poteau. 'They were bricked up in a coach-house [*remise*] and the rumour was spread that I hadn't sent them.' She added, 'Luckily we have kept the railway-receipts.' That sounds convincing enough; if it is true, she and not Cusenier sent the cases. She had meant also, we are told, to send the works with Durand-Ruel, who opposed her, so that she suspected a plot to help the sequestration. No doubt there were many misunderstandings on both sides. What seems sure is that the Reverdys were playing a lone hand and wanted to be the sole guardians of Courbet's interests and works.

On 19 June Pierre Magne, the new finance-minister, ordered the sequestration of all Courbet's property in France. Bailiffs were at once swarming round all his premises in Paris, Ornans, Flagey, Besançon, anywhere where property of his might be found; they seized everything in sight. The studio in the rue Hautefeuille was ransacked and the concierge Bain was ordered to let nothing out. Pictures in the galleries of Durand-Ruel and other dealers were taken. The railway companies were forbidden to transport any property of Courbet's. The prefect of the Doubs officially accused two of his friends at Besançon (the painter Jules Arthaud and the accountant Louis Sancey) of fraud in connection with the transfer of railway-bonds by Courbet on 17 June, without waiting for the tribunal to fix the charge for the Column; he also made a tentative estimate of that charge as 500,000 francs. We see by the promptness and the large scale of the operations that Courbet's movements had been thoroughly spied on by the police ever since his release.[49]

Courbet replied with a letter of sarcasm which would have made the Baron de Sandrans all the keener to carry on with his ruin:

In the official writs served by your orders on various inhabitants of the Loue valley you do me the honour of estimating my resources at 500,000 francs: which gives me in the public view a financial status I don't deserve, and which could summon me to high destinies. Note, M. the Prefect, that I've inherited nothing in all my life and that it's by forty years of stubborn toil that, despite my natural independence and outside the ways of routine, I have managed to gain my existence and at the same time render art a service which is as well known in France as abroad.

There was a time when I might have been able to contribute, under constraint, a slight part of the sum you've set on me in the name of the French State for the rebuilding this Column which you lament and which I didn't overthrow, but which went down before public opinion and as the act of a social revolution. Two years of war and revolution, during which I devoted myself disinterestedly to the preservation of artworks (which had taught me so much) have made me lose the little that I'd gained by a lifetime's work, as well as pictures of great value that were stolen from me in the great tumult [*bagarre*].

Amid this shipwreck there remains to me only flotsam, such as the industrial stocks seized by the Government and my studio at Ornans, on which I've had to contract mortgage debts in order to meet my obligations. The rigorous seizures you've made of everything belonging to me or thought to belong to me, in the present or the future, puts me in an exceptional position so obscure that I cannot dispense with addressing you, whom I take to be a competent authority in the matter, for enlightenment.

I think that I have a right to live, at least till the conclusion of the action brought against me, which can last a long time. Well, I can't live without practising my art. Please tell me then if it's still permitted me to make pictures and sell them freely for my profit in France or abroad – or indeed if I am condemned to work like a slave for the benefit of a master, who is the State of France and in whose name you issue writs.[50]

The prefect replied on 17 July that the core of the question was the competence of the tribunals; the measures taken have been regularly practised for the safeguarding of the State's rights. By virtue of an ordinance from the president of the Besançon tribunal, he had issued an injunction to persons who had in their possession objects belonging to Courbet, to yield them up to the extent of the sum laid down in the civil action brought before the Tribunal of the First Instance of the Seine: a reply which blandly ignored Courbet's pertinent question as to whether everything he now produced was to become automatically the State's property.[51]

Clearly his position was untenable. His inability to pay might bring a heavy sentence on his head, and in any event had created an impossible situation. On 23 June, Dr Ordinaire had already written to Castagnary to say that by the time the letter was received Courbet would be in Switzerland. 'This voluntary exile may seem an excessive precaution; but once the State starts off on an arbitrary course, anything may happen.' Zoé was doing all she could 'to sever him from his Republican friends, whom she describes as riff-raff. Only a fortnight ago she wrote that to me, without realising that she was insulting me.' But at that time Courbet was still hoping against hope that something would turn up. He didn't go. Next day Ordinaire wrote that when they'd gone to say goodbye the previous night they found Courbet had changed his mind. 'Notions of chivalry convinced him it would be undignified to flee from an enemy and that it would be nobler to be arrested and jailed.' He added, 'In this affair there are elements as clear as a bottle of ink.'[52] On 28 June Courbet himself wrote to Castagnary, 'Tell me if my liberty is in danger; if so, I'll go to Switzerland. I won't go to jail again; I'm tired of it.' With reference to the studio in the rue Hautefeuille he declared, 'It's my sister who's done all the damage. She has turned all Paris against me because everyone hates her so. *She's a scourge* I can't get rid of.' Certainly she had become an extreme nuisance; what cannot be decided is whether she was acting shortsightedly in the hope of grabbing a lot of the pictures herself, or whether Reverdy was in fact working with the authorities.[53]

All this while, we must recall, Courbet was being persecuted by Mathilde. On 13 June a Besançon solicitor had communicated with him that a lady M., who lived in Paris, had 'read him a passage from one of his letters in which he acknowledged himself in her debt for a sum of 5,000 francs'. He asked how Courbet meant to meet this debt of his.[54] We have a deposition by a bailiff of Ornans, Pannier, which records the steps taken by Mathilde. It states that many letters had been exchanged in 1873 when on 29 April Courbet asked her to send all that he had written, 'with the intention of putting them together and producing a work to be printed by M. Poulet-Malassis, publisher in Belgium, who had offered him for them 5,000 francs, cash down; at the request of M. Courbet, she has come to Besançon, and thence to Ornans, to bring the letters for the revision and correction of this work, and in the hope of receiving the sum promised by M. Courbet in his letter of 29 April. After she has returned to the latter the majority of his letters M. Courbet, who had at first welcomed her, had refused to see her again and has written or had written in the hotels where she lodged several defamatory letters in which he states particularly that he'll pay nobody – this with the aim of having her expelled and of thus forcing her to leave Ornans; she has been obliged to stay for about two months at Besançon and Ornans, without succeeding, despite all her steps, in getting anything from M. Courbet.' So she now asked for the 5,000 francs owed and 2,000 francs for expenses.[55]

But by the time this document reached Courbet he had fled to Switzerland from a more dangerous creditor. On 4 July Planard, delegated by the prefect to search for Courbet's hidden assets, reported:

It's extremely hard to find out precisely if M. Courbet has hidden pictures or furniture in his father's house [Flagey]. According to my information, mainly from the police, his father's house has always been closed to the inquisitive public. Strangers are received only at the door, with great caution. If one's admitted, it's only as far as the kitchen, and one may not stay there long. The only persons let into the interior are those who hold the same views and are very careful not to divulge what is done or said in their hero's house. . . . But it's certain that Courbet a few days ago drove his carriage to his father's domicile and went off on foot. Next day, his father, to satisfy the neighbours' curiosity, claimed he had bought the carriage from his son. Is this true? We don't know, but we know it's at Flagey and may be worth 2,000 to 2,500 francs. . . .[56]

On 16 July Ordinaire told Castagnary that the local prefect was issuing writs against anyone who might hold any article or security of his while the Government was rushing the case on with

unparalleled ardour, so as to reach a verdict before the court's recess. The persecution is ferocious. Courbet's situation is all the more precarious because his sister, meddling in his affairs, has without his consent retained M. Lachaud as his barrister. . . . He resents being defended by this common person who has no conception of distinction and of artistic feelings. Here he is once more thrown to the wolves, he says, and defended by a political enemy. In anticipation of arrest he has decided to take the waters as soon as the doctors tell him to. We're counting on you to advise us as to what precautionary steps to take. . . . Write as soon as you can; he and his family are extremely uneasy.

The reference to the 'waters' (Vichy) was a rather obvious attempt to hide from any interceptor of the letter the project of going to Switzerland.

On Sunday 20 July, Courbet wrote to Lydie. 'The moment for departure has come. Misfortunes are piling on me and going to end in exile. If the tribunal, as everything makes it likely, condemns me for 250,000 francs, it's a way of finishing me off. Now the question is to get adroitly out of France. For after the condemnation it means five years of jail or thirty of exile, if I don't pay up. And so M. O. [Marcel Ordinaire] and I set out for Laverine [La Vrine] and will arrive at 5 p.m. Wednesday. We count on you to meet us there with a closed carriage – Jolicler or else the Doctor [Paul Gindre] and drive us at one fell swoop to Les Verrières [a Swiss village about a mile past the frontier], where we'll dine. In all this there must be absolute secrecy. So we count on one of you being there without any need for a reply. There's no time to lose. The trial comes on Thursday. I address my letter to Mme Pillod in case you're at Morandval.' The trial he mentions must have been a preliminary hearing; the verdict wasn't given till 1874.[57]

On 21 July he wrote to Castagnary, who had suggested the gaining of a delay by the denunciation of a former Commune-member who was safe in America beyond the power of the French courts:

You advise me to accuse Rastoul. Why choose him more than the others? You say because he's in California: which would give me a respite of six months. I'd be glad to do so if I could be sure I couldn't be arrested meanwhile as a precautionary measure. As they're capable of anything, I don't know what to say. The respite of six months might turn out a boomerang, bringing me six extra-months of jail or exile. Still, I leave the decision to you. My family and I would very much like you to serve as an adviser at my trial; you're the only one in Paris who thoroughly knows me. . . . I'm really ill with a liver-complaint and the start of dropsy; and I'm going to take the waters at Vichy. I'll write at once from there. Act as you think best; for you know my incompetence in such matters.[58]

He may have wavered for a moment; but more likely he wrote in order to throw any spy off the scent. On Monday he supped with Jules Cusenier, distiller, at Ornans, and expressed his satisfaction at having given the *Fisher* to Chopard. On Wednesday he lunched with his father and his two sisters at Flagey. At 2 p.m. he drove off with Marcel; three hours later, having passed a forest and La Main, he arrived at La Vrine, a small crossroads-hamlet on the Besançon–Pontarlier highway. Here he stopped for refreshments at a lonely inn, the Hôtel des Voyageurs (owned by Jules-César Fernier). He found Lydie herself waiting in a carriage. Going through the outskirts of Pontarlier, they crossed into Switzerland and slept that night at Fleurier, five miles in. He still didn't feel wholly safe and asked for letters to be addressed '*poste restante* Marcel Ordinaire'.[59]

In Fleurier, Courbet lodged at the house of Mme Schopfer, 16 rue de l'Industrie. But he wanted to get well away from the frontier. He went roaming round: Neuchâtel, Fribourg, Lausanne, Vevey. The last site, near the east end of the Lake of Geneva, suited him. But some of the townsfolk, perhaps worked on by a French secret agent, Jominy, were unpleasant to him. At last he settled, after some weeks, at the small town, La Tour-de-Peilz, close to Vevey, on the lakeside. At first he lodged with the pastor Doulon; but though the respectable address was helpful, he disliked the too frugal meals. So he moved to the pension Bellevue and then to the Café du Centre, run by Budry, a strong man, once a butcher, who soon scared off anyone wanting to pester him.[1] He still feared that somehow French agents would make attempts to seize his pictures; Budry made some secret compartments in a huge wine-cask in the cellar, and in them rolled canvases were stacked. A few gallons of wine filled the rest of the cask. But after a while Courbet lost his fears and put his pictures openly in his studio.

La Tour-de-Peilz was a bourg of the canton of Vaud with some 2,500 folk, largely made up of vignerons and rentiers with modish villas and houses along the Leman's shores. It lay below the vineyards, on the road along the lake. It had fine fountains of fresh water, a promenade of old limes on the ramparts. Before the end of 1873 Courbet leased a fisherman's cottage, 9 rue du Bourg-Dessous, which had once been a tavern with a signboard *Bon-Port*. He liked the old name and revived it, repainting the signboard and setting it over the back-door, on to the street. It was a long narrow structure with one storey, looking over the lake with two windows at one end. In it he had kitchen, dining-room, bedroom, with a combined salon and studio where he showed some of his own works and some of his 'Old Masters'. The furniture was cheap and sparse. The bedroom had a porcelain stove and iron bedstead with single mattress; the studio some stools and easels. A large garden ran along the lakeside with a good view of the mountains of France only a few miles away on the lake's southern shore. He thus had his native land under his eyes. On the right of his house was a refuge for fishermen in bad weather, some shelter for their small boats under the shade of limes and walnuts. Women came down to the shore to wash linen; fishing-boats slid by; at one side was a thick semicircular stone wall, pierced by a door.[2]

Before long he was joined by Auguste Morel and his wife, who lived in a shed or penthouse at one end of the house. Morel, an assayer of precious metals, had been made director of the municipal pawnshop at Marseille during the Commune; escaping to Switzerland, he lived on a small allowance from his more conservative brother, who had taken over his pawnshop-office. Mme Morel did the housework and cooking; and together the pair devotedly attended Courbet till the end. He gave some lessons to Morel, who soon was able to serve as apprentice and do part of the painting on works that Courbet signed. Young Ordinaire stayed on at the same sort of jobs for almost the whole of the first year, with Pata painting but also dodging to and fro across the frontier on various errands.

On 20 August Zoé had written to Bruyas: 'You've doubtless learned from the papers that all the horrors overwhelming us are far from ending. . . . What is going to become of us?' She insists on identifying her fate with that of her brother, who, however, 'has his head in the most melancholy condition'. She still had some hopes of the legal position. 'In November M. Lachaud is going to plead once more.' She unleashed afresh all her hatred of Castagnary. Gustave is, alas, ill.

He has had to leave France to find peace. Ever since he had the misfortune to meet C., that contemptible journalist of the *Siècle*, my brother has been ruined; for this exploiter has lured him away from painting and compelled him to adopt his political doctrines. Oh, sir, if you knew the infamous conduct of this journalist you'd be appalled. He has enlisted the aid of the O[rdinaires] from his own province. They declare that my brother must renounce his family and all who dont share his views, that they alone know the part my brother must be made to play. Since my brother is distracted, these scoundrels write in his name. They try to make him assume responsibility for the acts of their party and to repudiate the Council of War that acquitted him for lack of proof of his guilt. C. claims that this will bring my brother glory and make friends for him, and that he should pay for everybody. Alas, he's been robbed so thoroughly by his friends that he has nothing left. What will become of my father and of our whole family who have sacrificed themselves for him? All his life as an artist must be wrecked by C.'s ridiculous politics, to become the plaything of all these scoundrels.[3]

The key-phrase there is 'pay for everybody'. Above all, Zoe is haunted by the image of the 'false friends' getting from Courbet the money that should, in her opinion, come to her.

In the letter cited above she said hopefully that Lachaud would plead afresh in November. But when, however, he wanted the notes which Courbet had drawn up before the 1871 trial and which she held, she refused to part with them. Since she cannot have imagined Lachaud to be in the plot against her, her motive is hard to make out. Perhaps she felt a desperate need to cling to whatever identified her with her brother and seemed to prove that she alone was his true mouthpiece and defender. In October Dr Ordinaire went to visit Courbet at La Tour:

Courbet has been negotiating to get from Mme Reverdy the memoir and other documents about the affair of the Column that she has in her possession. But after answering more or less evasively, she has recently, at Ornans where she now is, told C.'s family plainly that she has turned everything over to the authorities and that whoever wants those papers can demand them from them. So she has become her brother's implacable enemy, both by the hatred she feels for all his friends (including ourselves) and by her prejudicial actions. She feels that the absolute domination she has tried to exercise over the person, opinions, and activities of our friend has gone from her, which makes her furious.[4]

The act of giving the papers to the authorities may have been blind revenge; it may have been the work of Reverdy who persuaded her that it was the best course. Also, she may have been lying, wanting to keep the papers herself. She had moved to Ornans some time between August and October, no doubt feeling that there she would be able to put pressure on

Gustave, but he had fled. In any event she felt herself badly treated by the family and wanted some return from them. Courbet at La Tour was over-strained, distracted, and above all drinking far too much. Ordinaire went on to Castagnary:

We are here, I, my wife, and Marcel, with C. and I'm trying to help him to rewrite the memoir which we'll send you promptly. . . . The master has painted several excellent pictures at Fleurier, Chillon, and in Valais [canton south-east of Vevey]. At the moment he's painting a sunset over the Lake of Geneva, on the shore of which stands our domicile [Pension Bellevue]. . . . He also has a room at Veytaux-Chillon [some 4 miles south-east] in the house of M. Enoch. . . . He's in good health despite his mishaps. . . . I think it was Signor Cherubino [Pata] who introduced the master to certain dishonest picture-dealers, in particular Berneim [? Bernheim]. . . . As a result so many urgent orders poured in that C., unable to cope with them by himself, had a number painted by Pata, by another young man [? Morel], and a few by Marcel. He then added his brushstrokes and signed them; and Mme Pata delivered them and collected the proceeds, which she sent to the master more or less intact after deducting her commission. But by forgeries Berneim multiplied the output of this factory, and Cherubino is said to be the main author of these forgeries with which Paris and Belgium have been contaminated. . . . Everyone thinks that P. supplied the forgeries; I have very good reason to think him capable of it. . . . He is so dominated by P. that he allowed him to copy [his *Calf*] as soon as it was finished and to sell the copy to Berneim for 500 francs with the signature 'Pata after Courbet'. Now Mme Pata wrote a week ago that Berneim had sold the same picture, 'signed Courbet', for 10,000 francs. . . . Courbet is so infatuated with his *alter ego* that he laughs at his reprehensible speech and conduct and calls him the most honest man in the world.

He adds that Pata at Courbet's instructions has had copies done of his landscapes to be sold at 1,000 francs each, while there are orders at Lausanne, Vevey and Geneva, amounting to 15,000 francs, that he cannot fill. Pata may indeed, as Ordinaire thought, have helped to push Courbet into his dubious practices; with his goodhumoured cynicism he fitted too well into Courbet's frame of mind at this moment. Ordinaire goes on:

I wanted to write an item for the newspapers warning the public against these impudent forgeries; but he wouldn't let me. I'll soon return to France with my wife and Marcel; and I'll bring with me the unhappy knowledge that I've made very devoted but very useless efforts in Courbet's interests. I think you have more influence with him than I. But if you think it necessary to warn him about his commercial *patasseries*, do it carefully; for he's so *empatassé* that perhaps one should not attack him directly on this subject. Please don't drag me into it.

He makes at the end there some puns on 'Pata', 'pâtisseries' (pastries), and 'empâté' (crammed, sticky, impasted in painting).

In December Courbet reported to Castagnary: 'We have never been able to get the memoir from my sister, *who is, I think, demented*.' (He was nearer to the truth in this comment than he perhaps knew.) Ordinaire had clearly felt some revulsion from the situation at La Tour, and had decided to remove his son Marcel from the picture-factory; but his friendship for Courbet drew him back two months after his first visit. By patient pressure he managed to get Courbet to rewrite at least part of his notes. Courbet himself wrote to Castagnary in December, 'My mind has been so confused that neither M. Ordinaire nor I have had the courage to perform this stupid task all over again. We have done it after a fashion, crudely and inadequately.' He complains at having Lachaud to plead his case, but says that he must be accepted: 'He has already been paid 3,000 francs in advance.' He hopes that Lachaud will gain delays, the longer the better. 'We're doing very well here, we're going to have a show in a shop in Geneva. We've produced a great many landscapes; there's nothing else to paint in Switzerland.'[5] Note that it is 'we' who are doing well.

The townsfolk were becoming all too friendly; they drew him into their deadly hospitality and his table at the Café du Centre was always surrounded by boozers. Forbidden beer, he was drinking large quantities of the seemingly light but treacherous white wine of the region, which sapped what was left of his health. Often he drank twelve litres of it a day, as well as absinthe and other liqueurs. On Christmas Day Ordinaire, somewhat annoyed at Courbet's note, wrote his own account to Castagnary:

My dear friend, a few days ago you received at last Courbet's incomplete memoir about the Column. In the covering letter with it our friend gave you to understand that my head is as confused as his own; and this pleasant insinuation will serve as an excuse for telling you about his mode of life, which all attempts have not yet been able to alter. To start with, more than two months ago I managed to pin him down to a few conferences which enabled us to write out most of the documents in question; but since then he's eluded me on the pretext that he couldn't do two things at once: that is, drink and dictate to me what had to be written down for his defence.

Now he has drowned himself with all a savage's perversity in the white wine of the canton of Vaud. The hospitable but dangerous custom of the inhabitants is to invite their friends and acquaintances to drink in their cellars, where superb casks or barrels are stored. One glass is kept constantly filled, and each guest is expected to empty it in turn. C.'s fame and his picturesque and not always rational conversation have won him many invitations to bacchanalian revels, which at times last till 5 a.m. This in addition to the bottles emptied in the café during the day. The need to sleep the wine off generally keeps him in bed till midday; and after that he insists he can't do anything but drink. So he drinks and prides himself on being the foremost drinker in the canton of Vaud, a claim disproved from time to time by his drunken condition.

The most harmful effect of this simple white wine is not immediate drunkenness, which it brings about less readily than our own French wines; but in excess it kills slowly but surely, as is proved by the large number of widows in the canton of Vaud. One of its commonest effects is to produce a palsy in the arms and hands. How Courbet would enjoy that! In vain the folk of the region and even the proprietor of our favourite café himself have co-operated with me to indicate the dangers that threaten him. He pays no heed to experience; he replies that whoever has been inured to drinking will continue to drink, and that after a day or two of abstinence his wine drains off without leaving any trace in his system.

An invitation from friends in Lausanne completed his downfall. Instead of coming back after dinner he disappeared into cellars and stayed there ten days. I went to rescue him from this cesspool and was unceremoniously repulsed. At last sickness carried the day where I had failed; he returned very ill and swearing never to drink again, a drunkard's vow forgotten next day.

To do him justice, I must say that when his father arrived for a few days' stay he summoned up energy to paint his portrait in two sittings. It's a fine work. . . . *Il signore* Cherubino Pata is an astute Italian. . . . It didn't take him long to wind himself round him like an octopus; and since then he's never let him go. His spirits are unshakeably blithe and jaunty. . . . To judge by his own words, he's entirely without morals and capable of anything. Married and father of a family, he enjoys humiliating his wife at every opportunity and showing his contempt for her merely because she's a native of the German part of Switzerland.[6]

He had decisively taken a downward path. Any pauses on it were only temporary and did not affect the general pattern. From one angle we may say that his system of 'free living' was now bringing its nemesis; and that is true enough. His attempt to get hold of Léontine was his last effort to turn aside from it, but it came so late that we may doubt any chance it had of giving him a new start. However, the effects of his drinking and careless habits were certainly sharpened by the experiences he had gone through. He had his triumphs in the 1860s, in flowerpieces, in nudes, in landscapes and in hunting pieces – triumphs more than enough to content and fill the life of a lesser man. But he had consistently failed to find the technical basis for a repetition of the large-scale works with social or human themes which had been his great achievement in the 1850s. One may ask: Did that matter? Was it not enough that he had found important new fields – fields that were in some respects not only new for him, but new for art in general? The answer is that it was not enough for him. He deeply wanted to find ways of expressing more directly his sense of what was happening to men, the full social, political and personal situation realised in its richest pattern of conflict. If we ask what was holding him back, we must again look for a converging set of causes: the difficulty of finding the scene, the particular aspect of struggle, the particular moment that most truly grasped the social essence or condition of man; the confused and often underground forms of struggle against the Empire at that phase; the aesthetic problem of carrying on the monumentality of the great works of the 1850s in a more fluid and enriched form – the *Studio* had here been the point of both summation and impasse. The way in which his sensibility was deeply rooted in the countryside helped to make things more difficult for him. Apart from the night-scene of the unfinished *Firemen*, he never tackled an urban scene. His loose girls, who (from one angle) express the Empire's moral decay, lay about in a bedroom or on the Seine banks of a Sunday outing. With all his sympathy for the workers and the Paris lower class he never depicted them except in the drawing made in Ste-Pélagie of the communards. In the generation of artists who followed him and who made such use of elements of his work, the urban scene presented no trouble – Manet, Renoir, Degas – but they were no longer moved by his fighting spirit, even when their politics were radical; a gap had appeared between art and life which was not present in Courbet for all his limitations. The immediate scene can be taken in, but at the cost of the deeper implications. Courbet could be satisfied with nothing less than both aspects. In discussing, then, his failure – a failure only in terms of the high, arduous, and comprehensive aims he had set himself – we must allow for the part played by his way of life, which after his youthful years became increasingly self-destructive, but we must not see that as itself the cause of his problems and his ultimate breakdown. It had once given him much of his daring impetus; it had fed his conviction of independence, his aesthetic of the object-in-its-own-rights; in turn it became a brake on his progress, intensifying confusions. But it was never a thing-in-itself causing either his triumphs or his defeats.

In January 1874 Dr Ordinaire again wrote to Castagnary, 'Since my last letter C. has worked a little, but he continues to expose himself to the murderous shells from the Swiss cannon. . . . You say you're satisfied with the memoir; so we should be as well.'[7] After returning home, he came back for a few days in March. Pata accompanied him back to France and now produced a more favourable impression:

I fear I've criticised him to you too severely. I've talked with him quite a lot in the last few days while the master was snoring and sleeping off his wine . . . and I think he appears worse than he really is. He realises that the last year's commercial productions have harmed Courbet, but he claims that, like Cornu and Marcel, he never worked for C. save at the latter's request and that my son has done at least as much harm as he has, because his paintings, resembling Courbet's much more closely than his own, were hardly retouched by the master. . . . He denies that he ever produced forged Courbets himself, but admits that his name and his wife's intervention have tended to discredit the genuine ones. . . . He also tells me he has never been paid for certain expensive trips and certain outlays or for his daily services. Courbet would never give it a thought and he hadn't liked to present a bill. He cares as little about that as about morals and conjugal love. This man with his light-hearted frivolity is very odd, but I'm beginning to agree with C. that he is not dishonest. Then why has he such a shifty look? . . . He'll return to La Tour-de-Peils in two months; I don't know where I'll go. . . . False Courbets are also being forged at Geneva and we've identified the forger, a penniless young art-student named Delaunay. He claims that he sells them unsigned for 20 or 25 francs to the dealer Leclerc. The plan is to prosecute the latter, who signs them for exportation to America.[8]

Courbet did paint some works entirely his own, but many of them are mediocre and detract from, rather than add to, his reputation in any respect: views of Bon-Port from his lakeside garden, boats on the lake, various aspects of the Castle of Chillon, the surrounding mountains in sunlight or stormy weather. Some, however, show a fresh and delicate observation. There are a few portraits. The *Vine-tender of Montreux* depicted Cary Blank, a girl of twelve years; she (as usual) looks older than her years and is posed woodenly in regional costume with hoe in hand and basket strapt to shoulder. Some seventy-four years later she remembered him as 'very stout, with big belly, a fine beard covering a round smiling face, and thick grey hair. I heard him whistling and singing continually. When he stopped painting it was to fill his pipe. He was kind and fed me with sweets so that I'd keep my pose.' She said that visitors kept coming into the studio, especially Americans. They 'came in as if it was their own house, watched him paint, went and came, turned round the pictures leant against the wall, chatted in loud voices, and departed a few moments later without the artist giving them the least attention'. They came out of curiosity to see a famous painter who had been a Communard. Cary said she often came to Bon-Port as her sister was engaged to André Slomczynski (called Slom), who lived with Courbet; the sister wanted the portrait to take a long time so that she could keep on seeing Slom. Born in Bordeaux of Polish parents in 1844, he studied drawing at the École des Beaux-Arts in Paris, and under the Commune was secretary to Rigault. He avoided arrest and death by slipping away to Switzerland; now he became one of the members of Courbet's household.[9]

In January Zoé had written to Bruyas:

You'll have seen from the newspapers that this wretched trial will open at the end of February or early March, and we're almost certain he'll lose it. For the isolation in which MM. C. and O. have kept my brother, and their efforts to make him pay for the whole infamous crowd of people to whom we owe the physical and moral destruction of my whole family, have made us give up all hope. C. and the O. are trying to prevent me from supplying the evidence that would liberate my brother, and to force him to take on responsibility for those acts by persuading him that they'll immortalise him. . . . My brother has no idea of what these exploiters are doing to him.

Again we see her anguish at the image of Courbet pouring out money to the scoundrels. Her remark about liberating him by her evidence suggests that she had hung on to his memoir because she now trusted nobody and hoped to find some dramatic way of using it herself.

His curious bad-taste in 'Old Masters' appeared in an episode recounted by Ordinaire to Castagnary on 22 March 1874. He had found a picture in the shop of an Italian junk-dealer at Geneva, which showed a woman in antique clothes, her left breast exposed, dancing in a magic circle with three demons around her. He insisted that it was the work of P. Proudhon, its subject Circe; and he paid 8,000 francs for it, claiming that it was worth 100,000. On his way home, at Lausanne he had raised the value to 200,000; at La Tour the value was 300,000. 'Courbet's excitement over *Circe* is so intense that he declares it the most beautiful work in the world, not excepting any of his own works.' Four days later he wrote to Castagnary, 'I've just discovered something tremendous; it's worth at least 300,000 or 400,000 francs. I think it shows Circe summoning her demons and setting fire to the temples.'[10]

Various visitors called on him, some congenial, others drawn by mere curiosity. The writer Victor Tissot noted a big Alpine canvas on which he was working, the *Dent du Midi*, which was set up in front of the snowy heights on the Savoyard shore. A companion remarked that the landscape lit up the whole studio with its snowy crags. Edgar Monteil, also a refugee, who had shared his imprisonment at Versailles, came and was shown *Hallali*. 'Is it well built [*campé*]? Is it?' He pointed out the hunter with whip: his friend Cusenier. 'And this horse with all the weight of its body on one foot, its muscles all together pressing straight down on the horseshoe. The rider is Félix Gaudy, and those are his dogs.' He was silent a moment to take breath. 'I've done portraits of all my friends. I'll do yours, Monteil, when I'm better.' Monteil came daily, but Courbet couldn't get out of bed. Monteil asked him if Castagnary knew all the stories he told. 'Yes, indeed, he knows them all. As long as he doesn't dress them up. These stories are like a fine plum. In the morning, when it's surrounded with vapour, when it's transparent and savoury to the eye: touch it and the skin is smooth – you'd say it's been polished. You don't dare to bite; and even if you take a taste of it, you spit out the skin.'[11] Before the *Wounded Man* and another self-portrait of twenty-one he remarked, 'Until I'd done these two canvases, I doubted myself; but after that I said: I'm a painter.'

A Munich man with a Bavarian woman-friend described a visit. Pata received them and they went up a shaky staircase, then found themselves confronting 300 pictures, of which Pata gave them a manuscript catalogue. They didn't know where to start; then felt pity at the sight of 'two miserable little rooms, singularly low,' with a dirty floor of firwood, windows almost as low on the floor, so that, despite the bright light outside and the water-reflections no picture had even passable lighting. As for the frames! Then Courbet came in, cordial, unlike what they assumed a fanatical revolutionary to be. He showed them several works. The Bavarian thought the local scenes to be fabrications, symphonies in blue, not true images; but was surprised at their number. Courbet said, 'They've taken all my possessions to rebuild the Column, so I must work to live.' He added that the Germans were to blame, inciting the French by their haste to raise a victory-monument at Berlin. He left a memory of 'urbanity, childish naïvety, and bonhomie'.[12]

The question of money had become an emotional one, not related to facts. True, Courbet had had large losses, which he might justly resent. But with his simple way of living, apart from drink, he did not need big sums; and if he had been ready to drop the white wine, he could easily have made what he needed without recourse to disciples or to dashed-off work. We see that he had 8,000 francs to pay for a worthless 'Old Master'.

After some postponements Courbet's case had come up before the Civil Tribunal of the Seine (Paris) on 19 June. Victor Lefranc, prosecutor for the Administration of the Public Domain, repeated the story of his responsibility for the Column's demolition. He argued that though he hadn't signed the decree of 12 April 1871, the inspiration for the whole project came from his petition of 14 September 1870. Lachaud accepted the legality of the prosecution but argued against the vigorous application of article 55 of the penal code by the state. Félix Pyat, who had escaped to London, denied in *The Times* of 24 June that Courbet had had any connection with the demolition and himself assumed full responsibility; Courbet had only been concerned with artistic aspects; the political decision was made by the Commune, Pyat taking the initiative. 'I make this declaration, as spontaneous as it is sincere, for the benefit of a great painter whom they are trying to ruin after trying to kill him.' On 26 June the court confirmed the validity of the confiscatory steps taken against Courbet, and authorised the further seizure of any overlooked articles; it condemned him to pay the entire costs of the reconstruction, according to the amount found due on completion. An appeal was lodged against the verdict.

Many refugees had gathered in Switzerland. On 23 September Paul Pia, a picture-dealer of Geneva, wrote to Castagnary that on one of his business-trips he met Courbet at La Chaux-de-Fonds. They travelled together to Neuchâtel, 'where I heard of the arrival of H.R. who wanted to see me'. He uses the initials to hide the identity of Rochefort, who had been exiled to the penal colony of New Caledonia, whence he escaped to Switzerland. 'I told Courbet, who at first proposed to return to La Tour, but then made off for Geneva, where he now is. But I think he'll soon return to La Tour.' They were planning a visit there: 'H.R., his daughter, Lockroy, Mme Charles Hugo, and your humble servant.' Courbet wanted to paint Rochefort. Lockroy was the name used by a radical journalist, Édouard Simon.[13] The portrait was painted; but Rochefort disliked it. He refused to accept it; perhaps Courbet had treated too realistically the sallow complexion he had acquired in the tropics.[14]

Courbet was also making some attempts at sculpture. He designed a medallion, the

Lady of the Lake, the head of a young woman with a seagull, spreading out its wings, on her head – an important instance of the way he liked, even identified, bird and woman. The model here seems the marquise Olga de Tallenay, a friend of the sculptress, the duchesse Colonna di Castiglione (painted in 1865). A note of 28 November 1874 seems addressed to her:

It's the ladies' job to correct by their emotions the speculative rationality of men; I'll always be grateful to Mme Colonna, feeling sure she tried to aid me when I was in jail. You came to see me, to see my pictures, to see an exile who misses his family, his country; you came to see a worker who has devoted his life to the services of art in France. . . . Madame, you have enchanted my house; you have enchanted my thoughts, my imagination, by the astonishing beauty of your person, of your kindness, of your sympathetic soul. I can't hope to repay the pleasure you've given me; but allow me to offer you a little souvenir. I thought you were pleased by a small painting of falling snow. I send it to you; just accept it.

A note, dated Sunday, seems her reply. 'I joyfully and gratefully accept the charming souvenir [which was the landscape, *Snowstorm on Lake Leman*]. I'll be at home tomorrow at three; and if you'll be good enough to come at that hour to give me the answer to my request, I'll be delighted to receive you.' What the request was, we do not know. Perhaps he asked her to sit for him. Another undated note seems to refer to the medallion. 'The cast of my head has arrived. Should I send it first to you or have it taken direct to the moulder?'[15]

Certainly the duchesse Colonna and the marquise (a widow, the daughter of a Russian general) had visited Courbet late in 1874. He modelled a head of the marquise, which is far the best work of sculpture that he did, and which shows that if he had worked hard at this medium he could have gone far in it; his painting, we have seen, was essentially plastic, especially when he worked with the knife. But the head does not at all suggest the woman with the seagull. The latter may have been based on the duchesse, or on some third woman.

He also decided to do a bust to be presented to his town of refuge, *Helvetia*, also called *Liberty*, a woman with a Phrygian cap of liberty and the cross of the Swiss Confederation. He is said to have been stirred to do this work after seeing an attempt by a young refugee sculptor at Vevey, Jeunet, to express the allegorical figure (naturally much in vogue among dissident artists). Jeunet asked Courbet's advice; but the latter, on entering his studio, cried out, 'Is that what you call Liberty? But it's an innocent young boarding-school miss that you push on to us there. Give me some clay, I'm going to model you a Liberty, I.' So he set to work. The model is said to have been Lydie; but that is unlikely. The face is too heavy and dull. The craftsmen who cast it in bronze at a Vevey foundry were more used to working in iron; the coarse sand of their mould smudged some of the details. Courbet, however, was pleased. 'It's splendid; everyone's delighted with it.' He asks Castagnary to advise him whether to send a copy to the 1875 Salon. She 'makes a superb effect; she's assertive, resolute, powerful, generous, kind, smiling; she raises her head and gazes at the mountains'.[16]

Despite his drinking and his sluggishness he was restless as ever and travelled a fair amount. He several times visited the Cercle du Leman, at Vevey, in the rue du Lac: a fine

19th-century house with a big garden opening on the lake. Among his friends there were L. Maillard, an architect who had studied in Paris, and Jacques Bercher. The latter put up for renting an apartment at the angle of the Place de l'Hôtel-de-Ville and the rue du Simplon. Courbet said, 'I'm expecting my friend Rochefort who's come to settle in this country; I'll bring him to you in a few days'. In the Cercle it was remarked that Rochefort had come with two ladies *en grande toilette*, 'who didn't quite have the air of being rose-queens'; and Courbet, meeting Bercher, said, 'I understand you, M. Bercher; one isn't used in this country to seeing variety-artists doing their rehearsals on railway-platforms.'[17]

Courbet was keeping in close touch with his family, whom, we must recall, were only a few miles away. He was concerned about the smallest detail of daily life at Flagey. In January 1875 he wrote to Juliette:

You must have been very clever to take out under the eyes of the police the money I'd hidden in the piano. I'll reward you at once. I give you the 480 francs it would earn in interest, for yourself, Zélie, and my father, because you must buy some Burgundy for Zélie [in her illness]. I have a cask of Burgundy in the cellar at Ornans; I authorise you to take it. . . . You can transport it to Flagey without shaking it too much. It'll need two strong men. Let them take it just as it is, and put it in the cart without turning it. You'll let it settle at Flagey. But if our police officers, my custodians, have already drunk it up, forget it.[18]

On 4 February Courbet wrote to Castagnary. 'Now's the time to get rid of M. Reverdy, who is a Bonapartist agent and a great danger to my family and myself as well as to you, Ordinaire, and everyone we know. My sister, who is a monster, wishes to ruin me and is trying to lay hands on my money, through police-action, even in Switzerland. They call everyone thieves.' This allegation was true; the Reverdys were taking more action than appeared in Zoé's letter to Bruyas.[19]

This month Courbet had good news. The rest of his stolen pictures from the Passage du Saumon had been found. On 24 February, a mysterious character, signing 'H.K. 113, Poste Restante, Paris', wrote to Castagnary:

I've just heard you're looking for the pictures painted by Courbet that were stolen from him. It seems you've already found some of these pictures, but don't know where the others are. I know where these pictures are kept, and I'm in a position to tell you in whose hands they are . . . but I want a reward, the amount to be arranged between us if you accept my proposition.

Next day Castagnary agreed to the conditions. Nothing more was heard till 5 March, when the writer demanded 2,500 francs. Negotiations went on, but in the end the canvases were returned. Courbet thought the man 'a lover of the Gérard woman', the landlady.[20]

All this while Mathilde had been struggling to extract her 5,000 francs plus damages from Courbet. She wrote to him repeatedly, from Paris, then from Lyon, trying to make her blackmail-schemes work. She went on dangling before him the ten unreturned letters (once she says 'eleven') which no doubt were the bawdiest or most compromising of the series. But she still mingled threats with flatteries and self-praise. 'Courbet, the poet of realism, Courbet is no more. You are only the ghost of him. . . . Look up at the heaven which has been able to inspire you and make you a man infinitely superior to others. Have courage. Be a man. Be this genius who is called Courbet and who wants still to live again in your despite. In my breast there beats an honest heart. In my head, a firm will. I will sacrifice you wholly, should I say? to go and live on your life, your inspiration, your breath, your art. . . .' 'You'll be my god, my idol, my inspiration.' She assures him, 'Your sacred letters for me are stamped, sealed up, and I'll send them to you. When you wish, you shall have them, and whatever may have happened to me, I've never had a thought of making a bad use of them.'

But Courbet was unmoved, if he ever brought himself to read the outpourings. To her endearments succeeded colder forms of address; for 'my dear lover', 'my dear friend', 'my dear Gustave' gave way to 'M. Courbet', 'my poor Gustave', 'Sir', and finally 'Friend'. Her last letter seems that dated '11 March 1875, Paris'. It contains the sentence: 'Friend, receive the embraces [*embrasses*, actually 'curtain-loops'] of the tenderest lover, the loyallest, the truest, that you have been able to misunderstand and want to crush after having sought to humble her.'[21] Courbet was not her only victim, She was a confidence-trickster working with a male accomplice, a Brazilian; and they ended in disaster, with jail-sentences. According to Gros-Kost, the accomplice had intruded on Courbet's relations with Mathilde, living in the next room to her in an hotel and getting Courbet to pay his bills; he 'found the painter a good fellow and wanted to make a *pal* of him', and so on. All that may be a fiction, but the accomplice certainly existed. Whatever the precise details of Courbet's relations with Mathilde, he certainly made a fool of himself and had a harried and humiliating time through them.

On 1 April Courbet gave Castagnary more news of the Reverdys.

They have caused extraordinary confusion at Ornans and have set up a reign of terror by intimidating people with the support of the Government. . . . They write anonymous letters purporting to come from the police of the town of Besançon. You can't imagine how they've treated my family. They're trying to kill my father during my absence and to terrify my sisters with threats and coarse insults so as to seize our property. . . .

He began by taking possession of our house in a violent way and pocketing the keys of all the rooms, then those of the cellar, so that my poor father, arriving from Flagey with his latchkey, was obliged at his age to sleep two nights on the staircase to avoid a scandal. He has written to me: 'I'm wretchedly unhappy in the presence of people like that; I must have an iron constitution to survive such trials.' Finally he was attacked with violent insults and peremptorily flung out of our house. Now he lodges at the Hôtel de France . . . when he goes to Ornans. And when my sisters go there, they live with friends. Recently my father drove in a carriage to get some wine from his cellar; he found there was none left and had to buy wine.

To buy wine was a terrible comedown for a *vigneron*. Allowing for a little exaggeration Courbet's account is likely enough to be true. Once a property-dispute began among such impulsive and stubborn peasants as the Courbets, any kind of insult and even violence was possible. Also, anonymous letters fit in well enough with the character Zoé has been revealing. About this time Courbet wrote to her:

The judicial authorities in Berne have received through diplomatic channels the denunciations signed by you and transmitted by the French Government, requesting them to make inquiries into my person and my property. The Swiss Government, seeing in the denunciations a manoeuvre absolutely contrary to individual liberty, were alarmed and communicated them to me through the Swiss courts. But the judiciary of this country has been anxious to judge this criminal attack on me as it deserves; and it is all the better placed to unravel the calumny because the magistrates whose duty it would have been to carry out the inquiries are all men who weekly invite me to dine with them. Isn't it enough for you to have scandalised the whole of Franche-Comté by your ignoble conduct, but you must carry the scandal into a country where I am obliged to live?

In view of such an infamous action, coming on top of others, I must warn you to leave the house [at Ornans]. You should leave without regrets this house you've plundered to such a degree that my father is obliged to buy his wine in town and live at an inn. This outrageous behaviour must end, as also the anonymous letters you daily write to my father, my sisters, and myself. These letters are so repellent that they are unreadable. Only persons without honour like yourselves could make use of such means. It's time to bury the countless calumnies you're spreading among my friends, whom you call thieves, and who haven't dragged you into court only out of regard for the family. Now it's gone far enough. Take care your patricidal nature doesn't come to a bad end.[22]

Various friends called on Courbet from time to time: Castagnary, Dr Blondon, Lydie, the attorney Dufay (who later married Max Buchon's widow), refugees like Rochefort, General Cluseret, the geographer Reclus. (This last-named had had his jail-sentence commuted to exile at the appeal of various European geographical societies.) Courbet was generous in his aid to hard-up exiles, gave pictures to be sold for their benefit, and kept on his mantelpiece a cigar-box into which visitors could drop offerings for the poor. Of Cluseret he painted a second portrait in 1876 at Geneva; the proudly bemedalled general had now become a greying and bloused old man. The same year he gave Cluseret a painting, *The Roedeer*.[23] One of the refugees of whom he saw much was Slom, who helped Reclus in maps and drawings for his huge *Nouvelle Géographie universelle*. The story was told that Lydie twice drove across the frontier and brought Courbet back in secret to Pontarlier, where he stayed for a couple of days in her house. But it is highly unlikely that he would have taken such a risk.[24]

Late in May Zélie died. On 29 May Courbet wrote to Juliette:

Your letter and the awful loss we've suffered threw me into deep despair. My poor dear girl, now you alone must bear the burden of saving us all, my father and me. Don't torment yourself, I beg you. I've wept out all the tears in me. My poor Zélie, who never knew any pleasure in all her life but to give pleasure to others and to serve them. What a sad life this sister has had without complaints, always ill, always brave, always good-tempered. Our charming sister will always be engraved in our memories, as will our mother, just as if they were alive.

Only it's of you, my dear, that I'm thinking. What a difficult time you'll have till I come home. I'd have liked to feel you'd be together all my life, and I'd have been happy. For the rest, that would have been the greatest happiness that you could desire. I shouldn't have had to worry about you. I should have needed only to help and live with you. Now you must try to find some needy unfortunate well-bred woman to help you with the work to be done. As for me, my dear, you know we'll always be inseparable and that I'm ready to support you in any way. I worry too about my father, who loved our poor sister so dearly. He has already undergone enough through those monsters who want to destroy our family, who have made our poor sister die.[25]

After the exemplary sense of family-unity expressed in the rest of the letter, it is with something of a shock that one realises the monsters of the last sentence are the other sister Zoé, her husband, and children. He tries indeed to blame Zoé entirely for Zélie's death. 'It is really the persecution to which they've subjected all of you that killed my poor sister; it's the grief that swells the liver which aggravated the disease of that organ from which she was already suffering.' Certainly all the worries of the last few years, with the final misery of the Reverdys, would not have helped poor Zélie.

Ever since the spring of 1873 Courbet had been in touch with Baudry. (On 1 June 1873 he had written to Castagnary, 'Baudry wrote that he wanted to come and see me, bringing you along as well. I've had no news from him.' Later he wrote, 'I'm delighted with all you've done for me.') On 18 June now he wrote a long letter, setting out salient points of his life since war was declared in 1871. Among his mishaps he cites 'the deterioration of pictures, discredit by forged pictures, false signatures that flood and empoison Paris and abroad, commissioned in my absence by a heap of thieving merchants.' He attacks V. Lefranc who had put the State's case against him:

M. Lefranc will gain his end by depriving me of my dues and my affections, he will triumph absolutely when my father who is 77 years old and my last sister who looks after him are dead. He will triumph when my brother-in-law, a miserable Napoleonic adventurer, whom one would think in the service of M. Victor Lefranc, will have taken possession of our goods after a two years' persecution already . . . going so far as to imagine children that my sister hasn't had so as to inherit our fortune. The police of the *moral order* see all that and are not moved, and yet he has put my father to the door of his house, has emptied his cellar, and destroyed, to the detriment of this family, all that doesn't belong to him.

He seems here to be alleging, as Juliette did, that Zoé's children weren't truly hers.

The purpose of this letter was to provide a basis for an appeal by Baudry and Castagnary to their compatriot Jules Dufaure, the new Minister of Justice. This was unsuccessful, and soon afterwards a second appeal was made to Léon Say, Minister of Finance, by Frederic Mestreau, another Saintais, now a member of the National Assembly, who had entertained Courbet during his stay in Saintes. Incidentally, as Juliette made a draft of the letter for Courbet to sign, we see that in July 1875 she was visiting La-Tour-de-Peilz.

On 26 July Courbet told Castagnary, 'I'm beginning to be absolutely ruined; one cannot sell paintings in Switzerland.'[26] Not long after, on 6 August, the Court of Appeals confirmed the verdict against him. Still nine days later he had a local triumph. The bust of *Helvetia* was publicly set in its place, on an ugly pedestal, in front of the Town Hall. On the same day he opened a show of his false Old Masters in his studio, plus some works of his own, at an entry-fee of 50 centimes; the proceeds were to go to 'the relief of the inhabitants of the canton of Geneva whose property was damaged by hail'.[27] Some time later Rochefort, who, like Courbet, frequented the Café du Centre had a fierce political discussion with a *vigneron*, Desplands called Bédoc, who struck him; Rochefort hoisted the man on to his shoulders, ran from the café, and tipped him into the fountain-basin (the shaft of which bore the *Helvetia*).[28]

On 19 November Duval informed him that the properties left by his mother and Zélie could not be distributed; the two estates could not be settled. An indemnity of 400,000–500,000 francs was expected. The only strategy was to gain time and hope the next elections (in February) would help. 'Then we'll decide what steps to take according to circumstances.' Further, Durand-Ruel was liquidating his business. Duval said he'd try to get in what he owed Courbet; the Government would then take the sum and the indemnity would be reduced. The money might even come back if the State ever dropped its claims.[29]

Courbet's interpretation of the events at Ornans was turned exactly upside-down in Zoé's mind. In January 1876 she wrote to Bruyas, 'Poor Zélie, it seems as if the disasters brought on us by my brother will never end; and she was deeply affected by them. They caused her death as well as the sad condition of my father, who is absolutely deaf, stricken with grief by my brother's follies.' If we did not know the facts, how would we guess that she was excluded from the Flagey household and in a state of war with her father?[30] Probably soon after she wrote again:

Alas if my poor brother had been wise enough to rely more on your advice, if he had stayed within the circle of true friends like you, he'd have been happy and at peace today. Instead, he has fallen into the hands of false and dangerous men . . . as well as all those fine fellows who imitated his painting and don't shrink from signing Courbet's name on the most villainous daubs ever seen; these rascals have not only ruined the Man by hurling him into the abyss, from which he cannot save himself, but also have destroyed the Artist by signing their works with his name.

You've no doubt seen in the newspapers that an infamous pamphlet written by his vile friends, which couldn't be printed in France without danger to its authors, has been published in Switzerland over Courbet's signature. It was intercepted and confiscated at the frontier, a further black mark against my brother, whose mind is so disordered that others speak and act in his name without his knowing a thing about it. . . . My poor father is quite prostrated by the various misfortunes my brother has brought upon us.[31]

Bruyas had had enough of her furious letters. A sick man (he died on the first day of 1877), he sent a sample of her remarks to Courbet, who in turn wrote to Juliette on 9 February:

Mme Reverdy has just written a crazy and villainous letter to my friend Bruyas at Montpellier. This is the third letter my outraged friend of that region has written to me. She has written an ignoble letter. She accuses me of every crime. Bruyas is horrified and doesn't mean to answer it. She is an infernal monster. I don't understand how you could let this *canaille* leave your house without taking an inventory of everything in it. So now all my life has disappeared, my manuscripts, my catalogues, my pictures, articles of every kind, everything is gone . . . The Reverdys have robbed me of pictures valued at 100,000 francs. In one of their letters they accused J[olicler] of the thefts; but they have plenty of them. You should have their house searched and recover what they hold belonging to you and me.[32]

In March Duval wrote, 'I've had from the Government a provisional demand for the payment of 286,549 francs 78 centimes.' He added, 'You'll be condemned to pay this. I can see no other way to save you from this fate.'[33] A week or so later Courbet published *An Open Letter to the Deputies and Senators of the New National Assemblies*, in which he recapitulated all the arguments against his being made responsible for the Column's demolition.[34] Needless to say, no notice was taken. (This is the pamphlet to which Zoé referred.)

Zoé seems indeed to have got hold of a number of works by Courbet. He complained on 9 April to Castagnary, 'The Reverdys at Ornans are selling the pictures they stole from the rue du Vieux-Colombier, from my studio, and from the Passage du Saumon.' He presumably means that they were sending them to Paris to be sold, since it is hard to see how they could have found a market at Ornans. On 28 August he wrote again, 'My share in my mother's estate has been sequestered; my sister Juliette has bought it all so as to drive out the Reverdys. But it's impossible; they insist on staying despite everything. They have a storeroom at Ornans filled with my pictures which they're selling off one by one. If I try to claim them, they'll turn them over to the Government.'[35] Included in the property Juliette bought from her brother was his share of the Ornans house; Zélie's share had been extinguished by her death; what had happened to Zoé's share we do not know. Perhaps Juliette had bought it up too. She wrote later (5 February 1878) to Castagnary, 'She has plagued her family all her life; since our mother died she has caused all sorts of difficulties. . . . For four years she has occupied our house at Ornans against our wishes; I have had to buy up the house and lands at the request of Gustave and my father, who didn't want them to pass into the hands of strangers.'[36]

Zoé's psychology helps us to understand her brother. We see in her certain aspects common to the family (omitting Zélie, of whom we know little), which are given a decisively psychotic direction and thus can be seen with an exaggerated clarity. She has Gustave's extreme stubbornness, his complete committal to a line that has been hammered out, his peasant-concern for money, his readiness to inflate a situation and to attribute the worst of motives to any antagonist, to see a particular situation as a sort of world-end. What in him, despite all his limitations, becomes a desire to save the world becomes in her a desire to save Gustave (with whom she identifies herself). There is the same blurring, at a certain point, between personal ambition and general issues. There is the same perpetual revolving round a central aim, a central frustration. And there is the same merging, at a certain level, of the world-situation with the family-situation. The Reverdy-union is a minor matter next to Courbet's vision of a socialist world of harmony; but Zoé throws the same sort of wild energy into her efforts to hold together her Reverdy-family (which she identifies in turn with the 'right-thinking' elements in society) as her brother does in his struggle to maintain and develop his art, his socialism. At moments, as Courbet seems about to lose his balance, we see the Zoé-side begin to dominate; then he pulls himself together and the creative forces are in control again. Thus the glimpse that Zoé gives us of a Courbet breaking down helps us to estimate the inner struggle of Gustave to maintain his balance, the intense strain needed to resist the paranoiac pull and to come out all the more strongly creative – mastering an ever larger section of the unruly and threatening world of experience. Finally, the whole Zoé-episode brings out the strength again of the Courbet family-bond. Gustave has broken away and built his own world, yet he adroitly manages always in the last resort to harmonise that independent existence and his notion of family-harmony, despite the many strains. Zoé got too far outside the magic circle; her attempt to rebuild a new system, which would yet draw in her brother, was a failure. Her fantasy-swing carried her past the dangerous balancing-point where independence and family-unity were somehow synthesised. She, we must note, was the only one of the children who married. The tyranny of the Courbet-concept of loyalty could not allow outsiders in except as allies and friends; Zoé had to try to build her own unit in opposition to the Courbet-unit and to exert a desperate will-power that ended by destroying her as in its failure it turned inwards, against herself.

How many elements in Régis Courbet were akin to the worse elements in Zoé and Gustave comes out in the account of him by the Commandant Fumey, whose father was a Besançon barrister and knew him well:

The *père* Courbet was a handsome old man, of a tall build, vigorous despite his age, his severe face decorated by a magnificent white beard. But he was deaf as a post. And like many persons stricken with this infirmity, he shouted when speaking, so loudly that we, my brothers and I, heard him from our room next to the small room where our father received him. The *père* Courbet used to come to consult him on the subject of numerous lawsuits that he had to carry on before the Besançon Tribunal. This deafness of his led to blunders at which we used to make merry, our age being without pity.

He had a strongly original spirit, a bit cranky, and his language was studded with expressions all his own; his taste for bizarre inventions was well developed. In his role as father of a Communard, he proclaimed a profound scorn for all that was connected with the Church and with religion.

Without being rich, he enjoyed a comfortable affluence, half-bourgeois, half-peasant. He lived on the revenue from his properties and owned a fine enough house at Flagey, several heads of cattle, a horse and a carriage. . . . Litigious in the extreme, he was often in conflict with his neighbours towards whom he was completely lacking in justice.

Régis thus shared in the absolute sense of self-righteousness which we find in Zoé and in Gustave on his weaker sides.

In the letter of 28 August to Castagnary, Courbet showed that he had lost all confidence in Duval. 'I'm still in suspense, so worried I can't work. My father, who's growing very old, writes continually and urges me to leave now that the deputies are no longer in the Chamber. It's heartbreaking.' He is beginning to think Duval is in collusion with Lachaud to keep him in captivity. 'With all the people we know it can't be impossible to get a definite assurance [of safe conduct for a return to France] either from the Ministry of the Interior or the Prefect of Police, with a *certificate in writing* that I can show to the frontier police: so that I can take a holiday in Franche-Comté. You and E. Baudry have told me that the son of M. Dufaure [the premier] could arrange this. If he can't, there are others. I've written about it to my solicitor who's a swine and a thief, I think; but he's done nothing about it. . . . M. Thiers came to see my statue of the Republic at La Tour-de-Peilz; fortunately he didn't call on me. . . . Next Monday or Tuesday I'll go to Vallorbe on the frontier, to see my father. The poor old man is dying of grief and worry. He's coming to discuss our affairs at Ornans.'[37]

Now that the sum he had to pay was more or less settled, he hoped for some system of payment to be reached which would enable him to return to French soil without being arrested. He writes as if he was exiled in some distant land; he was in fact only a few miles from home and his father or Juliette could easily come and stay with him if they wished; he even lived in a region that spoke French. There was never a milder exile; and yet, with his strong home-roots, he suffered as if he were cut away hopelessly in some alien sphere. If he had not been in such a disordered state, he could surely have settled down at La Tour to a programme of work, dismissing the question of the indemnity and finding a satisfying basis of existence, doing his part to keep alive the radical and revolutionary spirit in France, and awaiting the change of political power which would bring an amnesty for the Communards. His utter impatience was a measure of his loss of a clear path in art in these years; and in turn it was linked with his excessive drinking. One of his last paintings reveals what he truly felt: the *Roe-Deer* dedicated to his fellow-victim, 'the Friend Cluseret', and dated 1876. It shows the dead deer, blood dribbling from its throat, hanging head down against a tree-trunk; and with its ochreous tones, broken only by a little red, it is subtly done – though it was doubtless painted from memory, reminding us of the *Dead Roe-deer* (1858) which is itself a copy of the dead deer in *Quarry* (exhibited 1857). It thus looks back to his first hunting-scenes. Now the ambiguity of emotion linked with both hunter and hunted, of excitement in the chase and of sympathy for the animal at bay, is ended; the painter is entirely one with the creature driven to death in the hills and coverts of nature which should have been its happy and peaceful home. In his heart he knows that his time has come.

This year he had received by post the copy of a pamphlet which should have helped to restore his sense of purpose by clarifying what his achievement had been: Duranty's *La Nouvelle Peinture. À propos d'un groupe d'artistes qui expose dans les galeries Durand-Ruel.* Duranty argued that painting has been drawn into its new paths by Courbet's work: 'since Courbet, like Balzac, has traced the furrow in so vigorous a manner.' The origins of the new art were to be found in his studio, in works like the *Burial* and the *Village-Demoiselles.* Duranty referred also to Jongkind and Boudin; and said that out of these predecessors, with Courbet as the great dominant figure, had come Whistler, Fantin, Manet, Degas, Pissarro, Renoir, Monet, Morisot, Sisley.[38]

Here, then, is a good point to pause and briefly review Courbet's achievement. It was true that he had a rich progeny of artists who owed one thing or another to him, and who all owed him one great debt: his smashing through the academic impasses, his opening the way to all kinds of more direct responses to reality. Especially we see his link with Cézanne, who, after his own stormy romantic period, was drawn by Pissarro to absorb many elements from the Impressionists, but who then proceeded to a reintegration of form (his total realisation) which could almost be defined as the rediscovery of Courbet's solidities in a universe made up of dynamic colour-planes. (He carried a small photo of the *Woman with Parrot* about in his wallet, we are told, and took off his hat at Courbet's name.) But we may also note the loyalty to him of Monet: Courbet 'was a giant of nature and a god of painting'. Renoir made him the test of true painting and discarded one of his own nudes 'because it didn't do a Courbet enough'. But unless an artist has a purely historical value, the question of his progeny is of secondary importance; the primary question is what he himself achieved of enduring value: what of his work still can stir us to a deepened vision of ourselves, our place in the world of men and nature, and has an immediate life in our senses, our minds. Like Caravaggio, Courbet threw over the accepted styles of his world, yet often made much use of other painters; he drew from many sources and yet did not beget an eclectic art; he gave the effect of a direct realism, so that his contemporaries mostly could see only a pro- lific reproducing-eye in his activities, yet he often twisted anatomy to suit his purposes and was in the last resort a great constructor; he possessed a dramatic and fervent character that managed to carry an intensely personal quality into works that seemed objective in approach; he conquered the central fields of art in his day, yet in some respects remained a provincial artist – thus carrying on the independent traditions of the Le Nains, of the artists of Tou- louse in the 17th and 18th centuries. His art emerged as a fusion of independent plebeian or popular traditions and the tradition of the great mainstream of art over the centuries.

Thus from the first he had an independent angle of approach, even if it took him some years to find out just where his freedom of spirit was leading him. He responded to Dela- croix and Ingres, but saw the feebleness of their disciples; he turned to the great Spaniards and the Venetians, then to Rembrandt and the Dutch, in his quest for kindred-expressions which satisfied both his sense of living form and his desire for the actual 'feel' of people and things (to use a Keatsian term). From the first he wanted to catch the rich fullness of shapes in their direct impact on his eye, on all his senses, all his emotions. The peasant element appears in his demands for tangibilities, solidities; this element goes back to Chardin and the best Dutch painters, but was reborn in him from its deep original sources. In the best of his early romantic paintings he combines with the sultry emotion and warmth of colour something of an Ingres-sobriety of design. He may force contrasts, but he also deepens and enriches his colour, as if he wants to show that the key to what he is saying does not lie in the subject taken by itself, in any particular aspect of the work, but in the total attack on the theme, the energy of realisation. Rightly did Ingres recognise that *energy* was the essential aspect of his artistic personality, even if he could not accept the forms it took. We see how correct Courbet was in turning later to hunting-themes; for the conflict between hunter and hunted animal was in a sense a continuing allegory of his ardent quest for the satisfying image, for the form or pattern on which he could throw himself with an immediate com- prehension. That is why he wrote in his aphorisms for Proudhon:

Works of art are conceived as totalities, and the composition, well established, well fixed in the brain, in all its parts, throws itself into its frame, on to the paper or on to the canvas, in such a way that it has no need of modification in the course of execution. Beauty of execution results from clarity of conception.

He does not mean that the work was formally fixed in design or sketch before he began to paint; few painters made less preparation in that sort of way for his works large or small. Yet he seems to have pondered many works for a long time. 'He painted only after ripe reflection; he turned a picture over in his head for years before sketching it on canvas,' said Castagnary. But when he felt ready for a work, he set to work confidently, passionately, often with a minimum of preparation on the canvas.

The same sort of attitude is suggested in an anecdote given by Dr Collin of Courbet's last years:

He painted with colour bought at the common shop [*drogiste*], very ordinary and costing little. It was on the chimney-piece in pots. He jeered at painters who ruined themselves to buy fine colours. 'It's in the fingers the skill[*finesse*] lies,' he used to say. . . . His hand had extraordinary elegances. He told me that one day a lady had come to find him and had asked what he did to paint so well. 'I seek my tone,' he replied. 'It's quite simple.' The lady then asked if she could work with him; but she produced nothing of value; and as she was surprised at this, 'Madame, you lack the eye,' he replied, 'everything's in the eye. I've seen my tone, my canvas is done.'

See the tone, find the starting-point, the relevant impulse which ignites the concept in all its aesthetic and emotional aspects; then the image as a whole controls and directs all his actions, his technical methods, his treatment of the parts. Something of this approach must underlie all artistic activity of a profound kind: the question here for Courbet is the particular way in which the approach is made and works out. And his stress on the dynamic unity of the idea in the mind (a unity prepared for a long time but coming into existence only at the moment when 'the tone is found') is not contradicted by his need for a model, for a scene in front of him. 'I am subjective and objective, I am the synthesis.' In the creative act the model or the scene and the idea become one, each modifying the other. In short the 'clarity of conception' from which results 'beauty of conception' is not the sort of clarity which could be expressed by a given set of proportions or colour-relations; it is the clarity and force of the organising impulse as it is set off by the sudden moment of action, the finding of the tone.

Silvestre brings out the directness of his attack and the way in which he built up together his tonality and his colour-system.

He goes by degrees from the strongest shadow to the sharpest light, and he calls his last touch: my dominant. Follow, he says, this comparison: we are enveloped in the morning twilight, objects are scarcely perceptible; the sun comes up, they are lighted and are defined in all their fullness. I do in my pictures what the sun does in nature.

Without pausing at this ambitious and inoffensive comparison, I believe the artist here speaks the truth. An artist who sometimes daubs shadows, sometimes lights, finds himself obliged in the end to have recourse to factitious means: a grain of ivory black, diluted in oil and spread out over the composition, gives it a general tint that appears harmonious. Pure artifice. The harmony of Courbet's pictures is the free result of the tones: relief of objects, depths of space, justness of effect. I bring all that off by force of the wrist. Some of his pictures have the look of masterpieces darkened by time.

He impastes usually the foregrounds, the horizons, the shadows, the lights. It is only by the quality of tone and the precision of modelling that he produces, I repeat, the projections and recessions.

At the core of the Courbetian image is the element of materiality: another way of saying that at the core is the obstinate element of individual existence recognised in the object – an element that must be captured in its totality: just as the animal to be driven to bay and taken is the animal in all its concrete striving existence. Hence the peculiar quality of Courbet's forms: 'Nowhere have volumes been rendered so weightily, so substantially. And yet, this feeling of form in the round is not conveyed by a particularly rich or subtle modelling of volumes. It is conveyed by a generalised sense of density and tangibility – the result of sonority of tone and of the luminous opaqueness of the paint itself, fat, sensuous, somnolent' (Sylvester). In a sense it is his haste that drives him to this sort of effect; but his haste in turn is derived from his whole sensuous response to the life around him. And his haste, his particular comprehensive response, leads him on to his palette-knife technique, with its satisfying effect of building forms up in broad gestures combining structure and texture in a new way.

We can estimate the quality of density in his work by looking at a landscape, *The Glade* or the *Children's Round-dance* of the 1860s. The forest-depths are rendered as a sort of green night, the shadows are deep green, the lights pale-green, the tree-trunks greenish-grey or light-brown; for contrast there are touches of pale pink in the small figures of the dancers swallowed up in the forest-dark and a small patch of blue sky aloft on the left. If we compare this work with woodland scenes by Corot or Daubigny we see how the latter control their system by perspective and tone; the latter aspects are present in the Courbet work but absorbed into the total effect of volume, spatial depth is obtained partly by gradations in the green but more importantly by the placing and relations of the tree-trunks. We thus get something of a Cézanne-depth by means of colour-planes, but not by a complex set of contrasts and mergings of such planes, rather by a bold over-all grasp of volume. In the case of figures the treatment by volume is yet easier to see. In the great works of the early 1850s the definition of each figure in terms of its total volume was linked with the plebeian or popular patterns which gave a monumental quality not without heavy and naïve aspects. These aspects dominated the minds of the viewing public and made the forms seem like those in craft-signs, booth-advertisements, coarse wooden carvings, toys.

The problem of achieving monumentality as the final expression of his sense of volume and of combining it with movement was central for Courbet. In the 1860s he failed to solve it for his social themes such as the *Beggar's Alms*, but he made important advances in tackling it in his hunting scenes, especially when they involved snow. In a work like *Hallali* we have a sort of photographic instantaneousness of a wild scene, yet at the same time the forms are incrusted in the snow-light, caught sculpturally inside their own volumes in a system of patternings. We see here again the conflict of the clarity of the concept, the complete dynamic idea which is present from the first moment of attack, and the often piecemeal method. The *Burial* was put together out of countless sittings of the various characters; for the animals depicted in moments of violent action Courbet often used carcasses in the shops or stuffed specimens. (Sometimes the result was lack of unity in perspective as when he inserted the bull and cow from a study into *Demoiselles of the Village*.) But while we recognise certain weaknesses that result from this contradiction or conflict in his method, we must realise also that his great strengths derive from it. Philosophically and aesthetically the conflict arose from his central conviction that everything had its right to exist in the fullness of its own terms, together with his need to bring the various existences, which included tree, flower, blade of grass, stone, as much as human beings or animals, into the single focus of his realising eye, of his whole sensuous being concentrated in eye and hand. 'I make even stones think.'

We see, then, that his method of handling paint, his use of colour, was all part of the general outlook we are analysing. He avoided the use of lines and brush-strokes, and so the effects of movement and expression by means of paint; he relied primarily on effects gained by the use of colour.

This consisted in making use of 'covering' colours as a rule for reproducing both light and shade, distance and nearness, things clearly recognisable and indistinct things. For the whole surface of his pictures Courbet used the dense, opaque enamel-type, viscous pigment which reflected all light. Ever since the emergence of style in painting, since the days of the Venetians and Rubens, this type of paint had indeed been used for portraying solids on which light shone, while shadows and half-shadows were painted translucently and by applying one translucent hue over another lying below it. This process was not merely incidental, for by means of it he was able to give an intense materiality to things, which was entirely new by comparison with all earlier representations, and to strengthen the force of their 'existence' by giving it uniform significance in every part of the picture. (BADT)

With the broken-up methods of painting used by the Impressionists, the materiality of the object was also broken up; its 'existence' became an aspect or function of the unifying light-impact. Cézanne's problem was to regain materiality without ignoring the impressionist disintegration of forms. In his youth he took over from Courbet the technique of colour-gradations, which was his first step towards the colour-modulations, the colour-structurations, he later evolved. He also took over Courbet's method of putting side by side violently-contrasted colours and of trying out the full potentialities of natural colouration to the limits possible with the pigments at his disposal; and this technique remained of crucial importance to him right to the end. Courbet, however, remained at the phase of using intensified local colours worked up into strong contrasts. Colour, then, was at the heart of his work, but from the angle of producing the maximum effect of materiality, of individual existence.

So we come back to the crucial phase in his development in 1848–51 and when he brought together and fused his revolutionary political ideas and his desperate need to escape from love (in the sense of a stable union with a woman); his struggle synthesised classicism and romanticism by freeing his sense of individual identity in the things depicted – an act that involved making them stand outside his control, his desire to possess, and yet, by realising them in their own essence, their volume, drawing them back into himself in a 'free' world, one from which jealousy and possessive egoism had been obliterated. Not to possess and to possess: that is the question. He puts aside romantic love (love that involves giving someone else the power to make him suffer) in order to love and own the world beyond the bourgeois limitations. That is not to say that he securely inhabits that world. As so often in anarchist positions, one finds both an extreme bourgeois egoism and a concept of pure egalitarian freedom. It is the conflict between these two positions that is resolved in his art. From one angle he sees himself as the totally self-made man, free of all claims, controls, and obligations, ceaselessly reasserting his independence; from another he feels himself vitally a part of the whole social process, deeply involved in sympathy for the oppressed and the exploited, ready to fight for the common cause as artist and as man – the distinction between the two disappearing. His objectivity reflects on the one hand the fragmentation and 'thingification' of man and the universe, everything reduced to a means (a prey, an exploitable victim) by the cash nexus, and on the other hand the total rejection of this process in terms of universal sympathy and communion. He represents thus the completed, the logically final state of bourgeois man, but also the first stage of truly socialist man. The conflict appears throughout his life, driving him along his road of promiscuous sex, drink, and goodfellowship – enjoyment divorced from responsibility – and yet implicating him politically and aesthetically in a devotion to the struggle for the new life of socialist union, where an undeviating responsibility lies at the core. This conflict ended by tearing him to pieces despite his strong frame; but while he was able to sustain it, he found its resolution in his art, where his spontaneous delight in life was fused with his deep social consciousness. Thus he lived constantly at the heart of the central struggles, political, moral, aesthetic, of his age; and because he found a concrete resolution of those struggles, he defined something that went beyond the historical limitations, into the realm of the human universal. All great art, one way or another, penetrates into that realm; what is significant in Courbet is the new way in which he arrives there, the new unity of social and aesthetic positions.

When we grasp these points, we see how inseparably bound up with his aesthetic is his philosophy and his politics. We see what a profound and consistent thinker he was – though a thinker who thought with brush in hand and not in intellectual ratiocination. We see also how important the idea of space was to him, for an individual existence is defined in the last resort by the space it fills. (Note his phrase about Buchon: 'He sought to occupy the least possible amount of space on earth' – thus was defined his spiritual humility.) The idea of irreducible individuality as the living space of a body leads both to the hard patterning and to the vital sense of volume; and the struggle to unite these two elements leads to the characteristic solidity, the direct impact, of Courbet's forms.

Like all artists, Courbet in his development fused the elements of both keen thinking and strong feeling. For the earlier 1850s his feeling, thinking, and the whole aesthetic direction of his craft, were in powerful harmony. He felt the blank wall of enemy resistance; he crashed against it and broke through. Then with the *Studio* and the *Seine-Demoiselles* he felt in some ways unclear as to the next step. There was still plenty of hatred and abuse of his work, as there was to the end in varying degrees; but the blank wall was breached. He needed something to brace himself up against; and in the political situation of those years he felt largely alone. He was too honest to himself, despite all the surface-bluster, to turn to one-track propaganda-work in which he could not feel the flow of his total personality on the one part and a total resistance of the enemy on the other. As a result we find his decisive turning to nature for his material. He feels the need to express his enjoyment of life, not simply as an outlet of personal emotions, but as the pledge of the fullness of freedom which he demands for all men as for himself. (Recall always the great force of his concept of freedom and its limitations, the particular categories through which alone it could express itself adequately.) The ambiguity of the *Seine-Demoiselles* is of the utmost importance here. It is a work of great psychological subtlety; not in any sense a Proudhonian attack on vice, but a picture of rich tenderness and deep insight into all that is slowly poisoning the lives of the girls, the whole pressure of alienation concentrated in the industrial city. The sense of Baudelairean horror at what society is doing to people, softened and muted in the sylvan nook of moment-ary escape, is linked with a pervasive gentle sensuousness; he pities and loves the girls, even if he hates the forces of distortion. He has begun to take an interest in flowers. He wants to express the elements of joy in life which assert themselves despite all the growing hells of exploitation and alienation. This emotion he carries forward now into his nudes and his nature-scenes. Just as nature is the space of violences and cruelties that equal man's bellicose and predatory elements, so it is also the earthly paradise of sheer delight; just as the woman is the spoiled creature of a perverted society, so she is also the source of infinite tenderness and sweetness. At times the two aspects, nature as paradise and woman as the source of release, are merged, when he takes up afresh the theme of the girl in the forest, the girl stepping into water, the girl asleep.

He wants to find the way of turning the spirit of joy against the distorting world, but he has too true a sense of the creative act to force himself beyond a point. The *Curés* fit in well enough with the turn he has taken; for beyond the Proudhonian rebuke of the Church he is also expressing a simple rollicking humour. Why shouldn't the curés get drunk? The duality of response is typified in the two observers, the horrified woman and the merry husband. In his finest landscapes, seascapes and animal-scenes he expresses both his sheer delight in the earth and a symbolic sense of conflict, danger, even doom. It was not by chance that the *Curés* came from the Saintonge period when he fully discovered flowers as direct images of earth-beauty and emblems of sensuous woman. His effort to make a direct symbolic picture of the inner conflict here, the poisoned Fount of Hippocrene, miscarried, but he moved on to an enriched grasp of the nude, which reached its climax in works like *Girl with White Stockings* (where volume, mass, and patterning compose a powerful unity) and the *Sleepers*, where his sense of inclusive volume does not preclude a subtle modelling of contours and breadths of flesh. The last couple of years before the War and the Commune were taken up with works like *Hallali*, *Stags at Dusk*, seascapes in which his sense of the immensity of the universe of change is at times linked with a conviction of tremendous pounding dangers for unprepared man. But he could not find how to transfer the emotions expressed in terms of nature into human themes with an aesthetically satisfying method. His feeling of frustration revealed itself in the waste of so many months in the winter of 1868–9 in playing about with his one-wheel carriage.

After the ordeal of his imprisonment and trial he found a passing release in his splendid still-lifes of the fruits of renewal or rebirth, a bedrock-return to the earth. He had lost nothing of his skill, as we see also in such works as *Trout*. The question which cannot be answered is whether, if he had been left at peace, he would have regathered all his forces for a fresh large-scale attack on the problems before him, political and aesthetic. Probably his ordeal, coming on top of the careless life which had sapped his great strength, had made such a gathering of forces unlikely; but we can only guess. His exile and persecution broke him down. At moments a breath of his old talents passed over his work; but our evaluation of his achievement would have been the same if he had died in 1873. Looking back over his whole career, we may say that his development shows a remarkable consistency. Though he has almost universally been denied intellectuality, it would be hard to find another artist who combined so thoroughly a clear idea (his idea of realism and socialism as freedom) with a direct and spontaneous reaction to the variety of the world. His intellectual vigour appears in the way in which he never let go of the idea; his creative integrity appears in the way in which he never forced the idea in doctrinaire terms on his art, but continued to find the most fruitful fusion of his philosophy of socialism and his immediate sensuous life. He was as much an artist in painting his *Stonebreakers* and *Burial* as he was a socialist in painting his roedeers and his apples. His fidelity to the idea (of freedom) and his integrity as an artist were in the last resort indivisible, and in this above all things he stands out as an example.

Courbet had complained about his legal representatives; but they too had their complaints. Duval on 1 December told Castagnary, 'For two months I've been writing to M. Courbet and asking for answers to very important questions. I haven't had the slightest sign of life from him.'[39] Courbet told Castagnary on 5 December querulously:

I can't supply any more information. In three and a half years I've written more than five volumes. And I've never been able to learn from my solicitor or my barrister why I had to go into exile and what risk of imprisonment I'd run if I couldn't pay. . . . My solicitor gives me no advice, takes no steps whatever; M. Lachaud does even less; as a result I've become, without knowing anything about such matters, the solicitor of my solicitor. . . . With this Sword of Damocles hanging over my head for so long it's impossible to stave off *delirium tremens*, *enervation*, stupefaction, and especially the siren that leads to madness. Impossible to work, and in addition my family in a state of profound sorrow, although they've taken from me securities, pictures (besides destroying studios and materials), far more than I have to pay.

If they insist on my paying this *unjust* indemnity, I must at least – it's what I claim at the very worst – keep my studio at Ornans in any circumstances (it was legally mortgaged before my prosecution) and legally I could never build another. It's too dear and too difficult. If they try to invalidate the mortgage, I think I'll give up painting. I've written to this absurd and dishonest attorney (for a Bonapartist does not undertake the cases of Republicans) to consult you, you and Jourdes.[40]

This comes close to being maudlin. No matter what his legal representatives did, how could they affect a counter-revolutionary government bent on destroying him? At most they could try to get extended terms of payment for the indemnity. But why cannot Courbet construct a good working studio at La Tour and set himself to painting, near enough for

Régis and Juliette, Ordinaire or Lydie, to visit him when they like? Why consider paying the indemnity at all? What better revenge can he take on his enemies than to turn out some powerful works of art? He was free to travel to Vienna, Brussels, Amsterdam, London, with shows. In becoming obsessed with the Government's steps against him, he broke himself down and did the very thing most pleasing to his enemies. (*La charmante*, the siren, may be either absinthe or the wine of Vaud; but in any event his comments in this letter show his awareness that he was liable to destroy himself by drinking.)

Two days later he wrote again, this time jubilantly: 'You won't complain of me. Though no legal expert, I've ended by drawing up an act that no attorney or notary could do, I think. I've found an irrefutable way-out.' Excitedly he discusses who is to take the project up. It's a masterpiece; it will succeed or nothing will. He adds, 'I'm going to send you again the statement of my losses and my distraints as well as what I lost in government-service during the war.' Enclosed was the draft of his proposal, which after a preamble of complaints, suggested that he should pay the indemnity in the form of annual instalments.[41] He thus hoped to be able to return to France – but it was at the cost of heavy payments, and, worse, of accepting the Government's right to fine him. Essentially the project was morally indefensible for a man of Courbet's political position.[42]

He had now got the safe-conduct idea rattling in his head. On 8 January he wrote to Castagnary. 'You know better than anyone I can't pay 333,000 francs. It's hard enough for me to pay the solicitor and barrister; at present I'm utterly ruined and sell no pictures. . . . I think it'll soon be time to put all this out of mind; all these inanities must come to an end, these unending worries, these legal documents of which I understand nothing and against which I can't in any event defend myself, because it's not natural to torment a man in this way for three or four years. . . . You're the only one I know who's helped me in this business. We must get from J. Simon [premier after Dufaure] a safe-conduct allowing me to visit my family, to see how they are, to reassure my old father, to cheer up my sister who has devoted her life to him. In that way I can recover the peace of mind I need so badly to work again.' On the same day he wrote to his father, who kept on asking him to return to Flagey. 'You surprise me by saying the same thing over and over again. It hurts me; one would think you don't understand what I write to you.' (We are reminded of the same sort of protest which he wrote from Besançon as a lad and from Paris as a young man, when Régis repeated himself, no matter what was written to him.) 'Tell me, yes or no, if you want me to cross the frontier and then spend *five years* in prison. I'm doing all I can to reach a solution. . . . The gendarmes are arresting everyone who resembles me at all at the frontiers, especially near Pontarlier. Once when I was at La Chaux-de-Fonds some friends for a joke persuaded me to cross the Doubs. I had nothing to fear; at the first sight of a gendarme I'd have swum back. . . . What happened? Next day French gendarmes arrived on the scene, asked questions, and crossed into Switzerland to interrogate the Swiss police, whom they told I mustn't try that again as they had a warrant for my arrest. If you care to pay 333,000 francs for me, I can return at once. . . . I'm as anxious to come back to Ornans or Flagey as you are; but you must be patient.'[1]

But he had long been in a hopelessly bad physical condition. Morel in his account says that 'after a visit to Geneva for the Federal Fêtes he returned in a piteous state. He had knocked himself, he said, very violently, in darkness, against a half-open door. He had a bad contusion on one leg; it was very swollen. We made Dr Duler come, a friend he'd known in Paris. This doctor told us the leg's condition was only secondary; what was serious was the stomach. He prescribed some remedies', and the Morels hoped for a change for the better. But the doctor didn't come regularly and Courbet gave him up. Then a refugee, Fesnau, at Geneva told them of a doctor from Cette who wanted to see Courbet. The Morels took advantage of the doctor's visit to get his advice, which was that Courbet 'must at once take a firm resolution and seriously look after himself'. He prescribed a regime, which the Morels tried to get Courbet to follow: 'which wasn't very easy'. A third doctor confirmed what the other had said. Fesneau told the Morels that the Cette doctor had said, 'Watch out, Courbet is done-for [*foutu*].' The Morels redoubled their cares, 'myself having hope only in the unknown, my wife in her will and her cares'. All the while Morel tried to persuade him to enter a good sanatorium.

It was not, then, through lack of advice that Courbet neglected himself so badly; he was repeatedly told what he was doing to himself. Finally a fourth doctor, one of his friends, Farvagnie, came. Aged 75, he was in high esteem with Courbet – 'whether from the political or medical point of view'. He came daily. Then, without telling him, Courbet dodged off, as we shall hear later, to the quack at La Chaux-de-Fonds.

On 10 February Duval had reported:

While you haven't answered my letters and seem to take no interest in your situation, I've succeeded in negotiating an arrangement with the Government. I've made an agreement: a verdict will be given condemning you to pay 323,000 francs . . . but you'll be allowed time to pay at the rate of 10,000 a year. . . . It's understood that no prison-sentence will be pronounced against you. Henceforth you'll have entire liberty and be subjected to no more prosecutions and annoyances. I tried to stipulate for yearly payments of less than 10,000 francs, but could get no better terms. The Government was asking for 25,000 or 30,000 francs a year. . . . In about a month all should be settled and you will be able to regain your freedom.[2]

This month the political situation was bettered by the elections which brought about a Republican majority in the Chamber while giving them less of a minority in the Senate. On 4 May the definitive judgment in Courbet's case was pronounced. He received a bill for 286,549.78 francs due to the Ministry of Public Works and 23,420 due to that of Education. There was to be no interest added during the period of liquidation, but 5 per cent was to go on to any overdue instalments. The indemnity was to be paid in half-yearly instalments, the first falling on 1 January 1878. In thirty-two years, if payments were kept up, Courbet would be free. As Castagnary wrote later, 'I can see him on the first day of his ninety-second year, rubbing his hands and saying; At last I've paid for the Column; from now on I work for myself.'[3]

On 16 May Mac-Mahon forced J. Simon to resign as premier and put in his place the monarchist duc de Broglie. The situation was now much worsened for Courbet. But on 14 May Courbet was already expressing doubts about Duval's pact with the Government. 'I still have business to settle here,' he told Castagnary, 'and then I must spend some time at Ornans, where my father awaits me with great impatience. I don't know when all that will be finished. I'll go to Paris as soon as I can.' Such doubts must have been much increased when he heard of de Broglie.[4]

The problem of Zoé was still urgent; but Courbet feared the complications which action against her might create. On 17 May he wrote to Juliette, 'My father writes that he's going to oust the Reverdys. That's dangerous too. They'll take with them everything that belongs to us. You'll have to inspect their trunks; you'll have to do it with official authorisation, as you would if they were servants; for now they no longer have no business to meddle with my things.'[5]

Late in June Mac-Mahon dissolved the Chamber and ruled on his own till October. The Reverdys went on refusing to be pushed out of Ornans. Courbet, still afraid to return, was now for stronger action. 'You must absolutely tell Fumey at once to put seals on our house's contents, to which they have no right. The things belong to my father and me. So write to Fumey. It's my father's duty unless he wants me to be robbed of 30 or 40,000 francs, perhaps 50,000 by these people. And if that should happen, on what would he expect me to live and pay for the Column?'[6] In the political tug-of-war at Paris this month saw a large Republican majority in the Chamber, but Mac-Mahon was hanging on.

On 8 October Courbet was feeling bad. He went to La Chaux-de-Fonds, a mountain-village with 'nothing but snow and clockmakers'. A private hospital there, run by Dr Guerrieri, an Italian, had been recommended to him by friends at La Tour and Vevey. The doctor, at 36a rue Fritz Courvoisier, stated on his note-paper that he was ready to cure 'all kinds of rheumatism, arthritis, sciatica, nervous ailments, glandular diseases, skin diseases, paralysis, neuralgia, heart-diseases'. His methods involved for the most part steam-baths and purges. Whether or not they were likely to aid other sufferers, their effect on Courbet was merely to weaken him. They may thus have hastened his death by a few months, but he had now reached the stage where it is unlikely that anything could have done much good. All the summer the dropsy resulting from his alcoholic cirrhosis of the liver had been growing worse, and now it had reached a hopeless stage.[7]

At first the change seemed to be working well. Leloup, deputy to the Grand Conseil of Neuchâtel and director of La Chaux's radical journal, reported to Castagnary on 31 October that he'd been trying several times to get Courbet to dictate a letter but had failed. 'He would never believe he was ill. Actually he's much better since he came here. . . . We've taken away the little white wine of Vevey and in fact almost all wines; with good care we hope to cure him. His father and sister have come to see him; his morale is excellent.'[8] But on 4 November Auguste Morel wrote that he had found him seriously ill. He had just paid a visit to the hospital with two friends. 'Our first impression was bad. In spite of all our good will and the hope we want to keep of seeing our friend in good health again, we are filled with fears. I've just written to a woman-friend of Mlle Juliette, suggesting a consulta-tion of doctors and the speedy adoption of measures that might increase the chances of saving him. I hope for the best, but not if he goes on with the present treatment, especially in such a cold climate as that where he is. I see that I omitted to mention that his dropsy is very extensive; he has grown tremendously thin, his abdomen is very large and his legs are swollen to above his knees.'[9]

On 10 November Fritz Eberhardt, another friend at La Chaux, wrote to Dr Blondon that the legs were hugely swollen and beginning to exude liquid; the Italian doctor wanted to apply blisters to them. Courbet thought he was a little better. 'He has no appetite but is always very thirsty.'[10] Three days later Juliette wrote to Blondon that Lydie wanted to take Courbet to Pontarlier. 'If he should agree, I think he'd need a safe-conduct from the prefect.'[11] Castagnary meanwhile had appealed to him to come to Paris to be treated at

Dr Dubois's nursing-home; the October elections, he thought, had made it safe to enter France. But now that he could at last return, he didn't want to. Leloup on 16 November wrote that he quite refused to go to Paris, pleading the difficulties of travel, his distended belly, the boredom of the Dubois hospital, etc. 'He is really very ill. My conclusion is that it's high time to act, infringe orders, send him off to the Paris doctor with or without his consent.' Was there a money-problem? 'He repeats all day that he has no money. Is it poverty or mania? His family continues to pay no attention. Oh yes, Mme Reverdy has written to a Catholic curé at La-Chaux-de-Fonds asking him to visit her brother and convert him to a belief in God.' On the same day, Leloup, very worried, wrote again, saying that the steam-baths had not reduced the swelling and that the presence of the Paris doctor mentioned by Castagnary was urgently needed. 'But Courbet won't hear of it. He doesn't want a doctor. Do you know why? He's afraid of being tapped. If one mentions this operation he thinks he's condemned to death.' We may recall his terror of chloroform in 1872, his readiness to suffer terrible pain rather than be made unconscious. Here again this terror asserts itself, linked (as we noted) with the deep ambivalence of the idea of sleep for him: the return to the womb of earth, the loss of individuality. Leloup adds, 'His family at Ornans neglects him completely. His sister doesn't write except to pester him about business-matters, powers of attorney, etc. They are true *franc-comtois* peasants.'[12]

On 17 November Courbet dictated to Leloup a long letter to Castagnary, mainly about his pictures and his legal position. 'Now, as we must speak of business, let's speak of it. I've never been able to get the official report or list of what was distrained in my Paris studio. As a result there'll be a sale, and I, I alone, will know nothing of what's going to be sold. My attorney, who as you know is an impossible man, has written to the Besançon attorney with details that explain nothing. What emerges from it all is that I owe, in costs, 11,750 francs. It's not specified that the fees of lawyers and attorneys on both sides are included in this sum. In my studio are things that are going to be sold and have been deliberately left by Reverdy; they'll go at a low price. Example: Dupont's portrait, a self-portrait, old pictures etc. etc. Also two drawings that I could never do again: the *Painter* and the *Woman in the Cornfields*. I haven't heard anything more said of our friend Étienne Baudry, who would serve finely on this occasion for getting back different things in the public sale, as well buying the *Horse* seized at Durand-Ruel's, if it goes up only to a thousand francs. As for the *Family of Proudhon*, I've always had the intention of presenting it to the town of Besançon; so I can't buy it in. I forgot to mention that it comes out in my Besançon attorney's letter that the objects distrained from me have already realised the sum of 18,521 francs: consult Duval to make sure of the correctness of this figure. One would say the attorney is determined on my utter ruin. Duval in effect recently wrote to me: 'I've sold 600 francs worth of stock [*rente*] to deal with the costs; as for my own account due from you I'm satisfied. . . . Duval wanted to tell me some secrets, once I'm in Paris; what secrets I've no idea. He spoke recently of a demand my Besançon attorney and Lachaud could make on the Government; I think this demand would bear on the remission of costs, as that has been done at all times for those who, like myself, struggle against the iron pot. Now a malady has come on me for the last six months, which has taken away every kind of energy and prevented me from working to reach the first instalment of 5,000 francs for 1 January.' However he was pessimistic about the prices to be got for paintings at the moment. 'Messieurs the painters of the jury have done the opposite of your idea. Instead of taking my pictures, as you thought, the *Hunt in the Snow* and others, they've seized the occasion to show the *Wave* and *Etretat Rocks*, which they know well don't belong to me. I don't know how to react towards these gentlemen.' He had further got into trouble with four pictures sent to an exhibition at Philadelphia. At last he comes back to his dropsy and insists he has consulted all possible doctors. 'What I haven't wanted – I've seen all my friends die with these treatments – is the tapping. You've been told that I had found here an exceptional method treatment, from which I'm doing very well and which will provide an escape from death without the need of tapping.' He insists that he believes he can recover 'despite the unfavourable season' and that apart from the legs he is 'disencumbered'. At the end he adds in his own hand: 'If later this cruel malady gets worse, I'll write at once. I had Leloup write, I've no energy. Many good wishes to friends. I embrace you while again thanking you.'[13]

The doctor whom Castagnary wanted to attend Courbet was Paul Collin, assistant to the surgeon, J. Péan, who had taken over Nélaton's practice. But though Courbet didn't want him to come, he submitted to the pressure of his friends so far as to leave his steambath hospital and go to stay with Eberhardt, who called in a Dr Buchser, who found the sufferer's state much worsened. Eberhardt wrote to Dr Blondon and asked him to come. On 23 November, the day of his move, Courbet dictated a letter to Castagnary, saying that he couldn't follow his excellent advice on account of the cold weather. He seemed more concerned about his finances than his disease:

I've had from Dr Blondon very precise information as to the trial, with details provided by the solicitor Duval. I cite the main passages: 'This is the result of our calculations: (1) the State has already got in from confiscated properties 18,521 francs (2) the trial costs amount to 11,750 francs. Thus 6,800 francs belonging to you remain in the State's hands. . . . Will the State keep the sum as security or as an advance-payment? That is what we must find out. Why . . . does the State claim the right to sell your pictures that are at Durand-Ruel's? This sale doesn't appear to me as necessary or *indispensable* as stipulated in the agreement. All you owe the State at present has been paid, so that, in place of selling up more of your things, the State should repay you 6,800 francs. . . .' You see from this the State has no right to sell my pictures, as it's in debt to me at this moment.[14]

On 26 November the cabinet of de Broglie carried out its last act against Courbet. Ten of his canvases were sold by auction in the Hôtel Druot, Paris. One or two were unfinished, one a sketch, but *Proudhon and Family* was included; the lot fetched 10,000 francs. All these came from the rue Hautefeuille. Various oddments and bric-à-brac from the same studio (mahogany piano, tables, chairs, eight easels, two paintboxes, bedding, unused canvas, and 'a quantity of rubbish') went at very small prices. So the State now held some 18,000 francs, enough to cover almost four half-yearly payments; but Courbet, anxious to leave no pretext for further action against him, instructed Duval to pay 5,000 francs in cash under protest on 1 January if the Government insisted.[15]

On 1 December he somehow got back to Bon-Port, with his girth so blown out that it measured 60 inches. A special railcoach with double doors had to be provided. Two or three days later Dr Blondon, come from Besançon, and an old doctor of Vevey, Farvagnie, tapped him and drew off 20 litres of fluid. For a few hours he was relieved; then the cavities filled up again.

On 12 December he dictated his last letter to Castagnary. The last seven weeks, he said, had cost a great deal. 'In addition, since my return here, I've had to call in two specialists who operated on and tapped me. All this is ruinously expensive, and I assure you my funds are exhausted, quite exhausted. So it will be impossible for me to pay anything to the State at present.' (We have seen who the 'specialists' were.) 'And now, my dear Castagnary, I take leave of you while expressing, both in my own name and in that of some friends, proscribed like myself, the desire that our unhappy country may soon emerge from the terrible crisis it is passing through. One would blush at being French if one did not have the ardent conviction that the last word will belong to Right and Justice. The Swiss are furious at seeing the patience of the French. May the French at least prove to the Swiss that if they are patient, they will be so till the end, but only till the end of Mac-Mahonism.'[16]

On 18 December Dr Collin was sent for; but before he arrived four days later from Paris, Dr Farvagnie tapped Courbet again and drew off 18–20 litres. But Courbet was in such a bad state that the incisions did not heal and for four days the fluid kept on flowing. In spite of an almost constant sponging, he was 'literally bathed in ascitic fluid'.[17]

Morel describes these last days: Courbet had been induced with difficulty to let himself be tapped; he feared the results. But the relief he found raised up his courage seriously. He didn't stop joking with those coming to see him, 'Tell Mister So-and-so who claims to drink a lot, tell him to put down into his stomach a drop like that' – and he showed the bucket in which 20 litres of fluid had just been drained off him. Tranquillity, even hope, came to him with sleep, and next day he went to the café with some friends whom he enlivened with his sallies and gaiety. He sang again. But the terrible malady followed its course. Disquiet returned with the water filling up again in proportion. The swelling went from his legs, but his stomach grew large. He wanted to be tapped daily. 'I'd very much like', he used to say, 'to have some litres drawn off before going to the café.' At last a second tapping was made, which didn't succeed as well as the first, and the doctor left the opening free. Next night Courbet rose and himself drained off 8 litres of water in two operations. Dr Collin arrived three days later. On 19 December Marius Vachon saw him. 'During the twenty minutes I could stay with him he spoke to me of Buchon and some *franc-comtois* friends. He was morally and physically crushed, and seemed above all affected by the fisc's incessant demands with regard to the indemnity.' He said, 'I've saved more than a million for Thiers, more than ten millions for the State; and this is how I'm implacably set upon.

They'll kill me off. I can't work any more. The spirit must be in repose for anything to be produced. I'm lost, etc.' (We see him reduced to a naïvety almost on the level of Zoé's position. He, who had learned from Proudhon and his own bitter experiences the nature of the State, keeps on judging things by some sort of abstract justice. Here it is that his lack of any clear grasp of the class-structure shows up. This point of unclarity was his Achilles'-heel by which the vindictive actions of the post-Commune reaction did achieve just what they sought: his destruction. A little more understanding, much less alcholism, and those actions would have strengthened his morale as man and artist.) Vachon went on, 'It was a harrowing sight. He could scarcely breathe. He painfully raised his arm to eat some grapes and found himself upset by the least movement through the frightening inflammation of stomach and chest. His beard and hair were white; nothing remained of the handsome and powerful Courbet whom I had known but the remarkable Assyrian profile which I saw for the last time and which was outlined against the snow of the Alps. I was sitting on a bench beside him.'[18]

Collin found him much worse than he'd expected or than Courbet himself realised, and at once felt that his condition was hopeless. He lay in bed, and occasionally when the fatigue there grew too much he was carried to a sofa where he lay prostrated. He had only one wish: to bathe in the lake. 'If only I could stretch out in the lake-waters I'd be cured.' Baths gave relief and relaxed him. Two men carried him to the tub and he stayed there till weakness overcame him; only pleadings and long arguments got him out. All the while he asked for his brow to be sponged. Collin saw that the deadly white wine had played a large part in aggravating the illness. Also, he 'had conceived the idea of mixing it with milk, a peasant custom, which gave him violent indigestion'.[19] But all the while he kept on worrying more about money than his health; and despite his weakness he wanted his friends around him. Many refugees came, including Monteil. Morel says that after Collin came, he 'was gay. He told us anecdotes, among others the tale of the portrait of Victor Hugo. . . . He didn't go out any more; he kept to the same room; he took only soups, oysters and drank much milk, which he loved. A friend read him the papers every evening; for he kept up his interest in politics till the last moment. Following his old habits, we kept him company till midnight; we filled his pipe and he went on talking right from the evening to the next morning. Difficult to look after, he stuck to a preconceived idea against doctors; he refused medicines and was persuaded to take them only while he let out ironic complaints. He believed in old wives' remedies, and, when the doctor wasn't there, he begged visiting friends to procure such and such herbs or insects, with which he wanted to make an infusion.' News of the failure of Mac-Mahon's final manoeuvres cheered him; Dufaure had now formed a cabinet. He continued to send optimistic reports to Flagey. On 23 December he declared, 'My dear sister, my dear father, be entirely without anxiety and remain quite tranquilly in the warmth, if it's possible, at Flagey. I'm going to pay the 5,000 francs to the Government, which won't accept less. I've charged Fumey and Blondon with these negotiations as well as Castagnary. I no longer have the head for all these idiocies. I've had enough of it for five years. I embrace you both warmly'.[20] Collin noted, 'He had a wild look in his eyes and his speech became inarticulate; one had to repeat anything said to him.' After the 28th 'he was tormented by hiccups recurring every few moments'.[21]

However, someone must have told his family that things were going badly. On the 29th Régis decided to come to La Tour. On the way he paused at Besançon for some words with Blondon, to whom Juliette wrote the same day, 'I've just packed my father off to La Tour; I didn't know he meant to pass through Besançon. . . . You know more of our dear patient's condition than I do. I don't understand how his malady can have made him, always so strong, in a few months so thin and weak. Is it possible we must lose him? This thought, which grieves me and saps all my courage, is all the more painful to me because all our lives we'd promised each other to remain together. The prospect that rises before me like an unsuspected obstacle will wreck my life.'[22] We see again the strangely strong bond of Courbet with his sisters, which was certainly an important factor in his bachelor status.

Régis arrived on the 29th or early 30th and found his son sitting up but very weak. 'Here, Gustave, I've brought you a little present. It's a dark lantern from our house.' And he added a pound of French tobacco. 'It made Courbet smile.' Régis sat with his son all that day. Things were peaceful enough. Then at nightfall Courbet called for Dr Collin.

He had just felt a tearing sensation in his left side with excruciating pain in his abdomen; it was probably caused by the breaking of a cyst in the spleen that I'd diagnosed. He then made this sadly all-too-true remark, 'I think I won't live through the night.' And he repeated the words to the man who watched at his side. I put on some laudanised cataplasms; but that wasn't enough to calm him. He begged me for a subcutaneous injection in the painful part. By this time his eye was cavernous, his mouth dry and fuliginous. The hiccuping went on. Half an hour after the injection of morphine he went to sleep. It was then about 8 p.m. He woke up towards 10 and stayed for some time in a sort of somnolence. He said a few words, then lost consciousness. The deathpangs began towards 5 a.m. and lasted a little more than half an hour. Courbet died at 6.30.[23]

It was the last day of 1877. The next day the first instalment of the indemnity would have fallen due; and once it was paid, he would have been free to return to Ornans and Paris. An hour or two after his death Collin telegraphed to Castagnary: 'Gustave died six this morning; see Duval immediately family has decided to pay nothing.' Even in the misery of that bleak January morning the question of money wasn't forgotten for a moment. A letter, posted next day, gave details and said that Courbet had died 'without the least suffering'.[24]

Collin wanted a deathmask. 'It's not worth the trouble,' Régis replied, 'He has enough portraits in the house.' He went on repeating that Gustave must be buried in a mill he had near Ornans. 'He'll be there near me.' However, Morel sent a telegram to Louis Niquet, refugee sculptor in Geneva; he arrived on 2 January and took the mask. At first he refused payment as a friend and said that he might earn a few francs from the sale of plaster copies. A few weeks later, being a very poor man and overwhelmed by the death of his wife and child, he asked Régis to pay his expenses (272 francs); Régis refused. Niquet appealed to Blondon, but we do not know if he ever got the money. Here again we see the almost incredible peasant meanness of the family. Yet Régis's grief was extreme. Pata says that he 'wanted to transport the body of his son to Ornans and give him a religious burial. But happily, in the evening, his sister Juliette arrived; she well understood the hope of the entire [local] population: that he should be given a wholly civil burial, and at La Tour.' Juliette herself wrote to Blondon: 'My first thought was to bring my brother home, to his own country, but after thinking it over I feel my brother doesn't belong exclusively to us.' Gustave had wanted 'to be buried in Swiss soil until it could be found whether or not France wanted him'. Further, 'Gustave loved me very much, and his idea of a burial in Switzerland would give me an excuse to avoid a religious funeral; he expected me to see to that. I shall respect my brother's wishes and at the same time do no violence to my own religious convictions.'[25] (She was almost as religious as Zélie and at one time had wanted to enter the Dominicans, but she also had much commonsense.)

The corpse was put in a leaden casket, which in turn went into an oak coffin (to facilitate exhumation, if it was decided on later). On 3 January 1878 a funeral ceremony was held in the mortuary of the cemetery at La Tour. Pata told Castagnary. 'It began at 11.30 in the presence of at least 500 people. The cortège arrived late because so many friends came from La-Chaux-de-Fonds, Fribourg, Lausanne, Geneva, as well as the whole population of Vevey, Montreux, and La Tour. The weather was perfect. A great many persons wanted to give speeches. M. Rochefort spoke first, but his tears choked him and he couldn't finish. Dr Blondon of Besançon came next and he too was interrupted by the weeping of all those present. Later, two speeches were made by gentlemen of this region.'[26] Régis was at last prevailed on to leave the body in Switzerland; he bought a plot in the cemetery, where Courbet was buried on 10 May. Slom designed a monument: a headstone of rough granite with an oval plaque inserted with the name and the dates of birth and death. Around the grave were set eight truncated pyramids of granite linked with heavy chains.

On 11 January Juliette wrote to Castagnary: 'My existence, which was attached to his like ivy to the oak, is broken, and henceforth without hope and support. The affection that united us, my brother and me, had made me gaily accept burying myself alive in the country, thanking every kind of proposal that made me able to stay with him and care for his old age.'[27] The kind of reputation that Régis had is shown by the stories which a friend felt necessary to rebut later (1897): 'We must relegate to the ranks of fable the joyous cries of *pére* Courbet at the sight of the rolls of gold found in his son's house, as also his sleeping on sacks of *écus*. M. Régis Courbet, rich landowner at Flagey, gave money to his unfortunate tenant-farmers rather than asked it from them.'[28] On 8 May, at the demand of Régis and Juliette, L. Ansermet, notary of La Tour-de-Peilz, acting as Registrar and J.P. of the Circle of La Tour, drew up a first inventory of Courbet's goods, with the artists Bocion and Slomczynski acting as experts. According to Courbet's own catalogue, made shortly before his death, '62 pictures by himself and others, 89 pictures by himself and other artists, 3 statues of Liberty (plaster), two medallions of the Lady with the Gull (plaster)'. Among the papers was a small used envelope inscribed *Testament*; inside was a photograph of himself, with his will on its back: 'This is my testament. I bequeath all my property to my sister Juliette.

Written by my hand, Tour-de-Peilz, third of June one thousand eight hundred seventy-seven. G. Courbet.'[29]

Zoé, now in Paris, had little idea of what was going on. She read of her brother's death in the newspapers and produced her own version, garbled as usual. 'They tapped him like a cask and gave him a strong injection of morphia. I read this phrase in a news-sheet. That's how I learned of my brother's death.' She thought the funerary arrangements had all happened at Ornans. 'At Ornans brains are no longer in ebullition, but in explosion.' Her piety was indignant, 'They've dunged [*encrotté*] my brother like a dog.' But she wasn't going to surrender so easily what she considered her heritage. A letter dated 5 October 1878 reached Duval from Lausanne, signed 'Philibert'.

One day at Vevey I met the painter Courbet, He was terribly depressed. 'Anything might happen,' he said. 'I count on you. Promise to carry out my wishes when the time comes and pass them on to my solicitor in Paris, M. Duval, 189 rue Saint-Honoré. He knows everything and will undertake to discharge my obligations.' He told me many things. Emotion overcame him when he spoke to me of his sister Zoé, his brother-in-law Reverdy, and their children. We clasped hands. He asked for paper and wrote what I am sending you. I think the moment has come. . . . In doing my duty I trust you will do yours.

Enclosed was what purported to be Gustave's last will from Vevey: 'This is my only testament: I designate my sister Reverdy Jeanne-Thérèse-Zoé Courbet my sole heir. Written by my hand. GUSTAVE COURBET, painter. 23 November 1877.' In the margin was added, 'Also my mother's house in the Iles-Basses at Ornans, which belongs to me. I acquired it by legal purchase.' In a covering letter Duval told Juliette that he was writing to Mme Reverdy, 'and I am asking her as well as you what I should do about this will. I think someone is trying to play a hoax.'[30] Juliette disputed the authenticity of the document; and her attorney Coulon easily demolished it before the Besançon Tribunal as a very clumsy forgery. The Reverdys could not produce or explain 'Philibert;' and on the day when he was supposed to have met Courbet at Vevey, the latter had been ill in bed at La Chaux. On 2 April 1879 the court pronounced in Juliette's favour.

One can see why Zoé, and nobody else, would think the communication plausible. In her view, Courbet, a weak but reluctant character, was surrounded by bullying villains who signed statements for him and drove him along the radical path. Escaping for a moment from these jailers, he might well seize any chance to express his real self and hand over his property to his one true friend, Zoé.[31] Between August 1878 and April 1879 she was pouring herself out to Champfleury, who seemed the one kindred soul left to her. Here she set out the above thesis. The brutal documents she had received from Gustave in Switzerland were the work of the 'clique', not of him. 'In spite of everything Courbet will be rehabilitated; for he is an artist who belongs to all points of view, to all nations.' The clique had taken their revenge on her 'because I saved Courbet from being shot and pillaged during the Commune'. Juliette was in the plot, preventing the grandchildren from approaching Régis. 'Remaining an old virgin, she takes her revenge.' She suggested to Champfleury that he should collaborate with her in writing Courbet's Life in which 'we'll tell the truth'. Ideville's book was 'only a fantasy'. In a second letter (26 January – 12 February 1879) she told how she had been flung out 'naked' on to the street from her mother's house at Ornans. She had nothing, 'not a picture, not a scrap, nothing, nothing, that recalls Courbet'. (Even the portrait he painted of her was detained by Juliette.)

My husband does painting to provide for all. Gustave used to tell us that he wanted to repay his debt of gratitude, and as for myself I'm absolutely stripped, ruined, as well as my husband who has paid out 23,000 francs from his purse to help Gustave in his law-suit, and as we kept no receipts we can claim nothing.

She then takes up the question of Philibert's letter and says that Juliette demands 20,000 francs damages for her having brought it to light. 'We have two boys' [Edmond-Jean and Eugène-Jean]. 'We work and bring up our children with much trouble. Beg M. Grévy to give us alms . . . the cost of travelling is beyond our means.' She is referring to the testament-case being heard at Besançon. On 21 February she sent the petition she wanted transmitted to Grévy there. In it she imputes all crimes to Juliette and estimates that Courbet left a fortune of two million francs; and she tried to gain the court's sympathy by attacks on the 'commercial travellers of the revolution'. Champfleury probably did not answer or send on the petition. Zoé had no legal representative at the hearing on 2 April 1879.

Mac-Mahon had to resign on 30 January 1879. Jules Grévy, president, brother of the Grévy at Besançon, as one of his first acts granted an amnesty to all former members of the Commune; and a supplementary decree of 14 August 1880 relinquished all claims by the State on those condemned to pay fines or damages. Juliette, who had all along been refusing to accept the indemnity, was now formally notified that Courbet's heirs would not be prosecuted for recovery 'of the civil assessment levied upon him'. As for pictures and other property sequestered by the prefect of the Doubs, 'you and your co-heirs are at liberty to regain possession of them'. But no sums already confiscated, no pictures forcibly sold, were returned. Courbet would only have needed to hang on a few years in Switzerland and all would have been well.[32]

In November 1877, when Courbet's death was becoming likely, Juliette had written to Dr Blondon, 'I rely very much on you. Whatever happens, you are my brother's friend and will take his place in our midst.' It seemed likely that with Courbet gone she would marry Blondon. For five years now he made her interests his main concern, dealing with lawyers and officials for her, helping with inventories, taking a vast amount of business details off her hands. But after awhile her loving gratitude turned into suspicious distrust and she accused him of embezzlement. He died in poverty at Besançon in 1906. Fumey gives a lively and pathetic account of the pair:

She [Juliette] wasn't very big; she had perhaps been pretty in her youth, she kept very regular features. At the time when I knew her, she was massive enough, of a robust health, of a sprightly spirit, but of a stupefying originality. Fashion was the least of her cares, and her toilette defied all laws of good taste and elegance. Above all her hats, which she put together herself, had so comical a stamp that people in the Besançon streets used to laugh openly at them: which didn't at all bother my mother at times when she accompanied her.

Tales were told that when young she had been smitten with love for a singular *bonhomme*, a doctor in medicine, who was named B. and who was a political friend of Courbet. He showed an unimaginable untidiness and dirtiness. I see him still, strolling in the streets with a filthy hat, greying hair that fell to his shoulders, an overcoat in rags, trodden-down shoes – a veritable down-and-out. On what did he live? Nobody could say, for he had no clients whatever. But one whispered that the sale of some pictures by Courbet saved him from dying of hunger. . . .[33]

No doubt this picture of Blondon applies only to his last days after he had been attacked and rejected by Juliette. The trouble seems to have come to a head about the time of Régis's death on 28 May 1882 at the age of 84. He was buried in the churchyard near the village of Chantrans. Fumey tells that after Courbet's death:

The question was to recover the pictures. Certain persons with whom they had been deposited denied having received them. Dr B. admitted that several canvases and some objects of art had been confided to him; but the canvases had been stolen and only the objects of art were left. The matter was very complicated. . . . [Then after Régis's death] the bad faith of B. was so evident that Juliette Courbet attacked him with a lawsuit. But on the eve of the day of its hearing she came to tell my father she had accepted a deal with the doctor. She didn't receive any canvas of her brother's; she received the objects-of-art and some 'rubbish'. My father, who was certain of a favourable decision in the case, showed himself furious at her goings-on. Afterwards he refused to take on any of her cases.

This account is not at all clear. Five years had elapsed between Courbet's death and that of his father; the argument about what canvases Blondon had held could hardly have dragged on all that time, especially as during it he was acting as factotum for Juliette. What seems likely is that anyone handling so much business for a Courbet was liable to bring out the paranoiac streak sooner or later and be suspected of misdealings.

Zoé had been roused afresh by her father's death. Fumey tells us that she took advantage of the occasion to claim once more her share in her brother's property. Juliette retorted by denying that the Reverdy boys were really Zoé's sons; Zoé tried to find the proofs of their birth, but the documents had been lost during the troubles of 1870–1. However, she did regain her own portrait and some other works by her brother. Then, when Reverdy died, she lost the last of her sanity. She refused to believe that he was dead and went roaming about in search of him; finally she was received into the lunatic asylum of Saint-Ylie, near Dôle, on 29 June 1888. She died there on 4 June 1905, aged 81.[34]

Juliette in later years went off to Paris, growing ever more eccentric. She claimed to have been engaged in her days to seven men, whose photos she kept set out on her table. But her main activity lay in her cult of Gustave. She filled her apartment in the rue de Vaugirard with souvenirs and oddments that brought him to mind; she seemed to some extent to have identified herself with him and imagined that she had lived his life, painted his pictures. She died in Paris in 1915, aged 84. Her attitudes are revealed in these passages from letters:

If you know me well, you know I don't need many distractions, a little intimacy and to abide in my memories; I know how to live amid them as in a delightful company, happy and tranquil if those indifferent leave me to enjoy them without troubling me under the pretext of distracting me. . . . Oh, how beautiful our country is, and who'd believe it, yesterday, at table, a traveller was telling us that my land is finer than Switzerland; certainly our valley of the Loue is superb. (17 January 1891)

Soon, as always, I'll go and visit that dear and unfortunate brother and friend who, thanks to memory, that faculty we hold from the Creator, never leaves me any more than the other members of the family. (25 June 1893)

My rooms, all decorated with family-portraits and other canvases by my brother, captivate me absolutely as well as my *bibis*, as you very well call them, which I caress with my glance. (18 January 1895)

Her unrelenting hatred of Zoé (apparently not included in the family) was such that in 1911, to prevent the Reverdys from getting any of the family estates, she gave the Flagey house, with some 50 acres, to a neighbour, Félix Bourgon, and distributed the rest of her farmlands and vineyards among friends of the region. Yet about two years before, she had let one of the Reverdy boys act as temporary curator of a Courbet Museum she meant to set up in the Ornans studio. Léger in 1910 found him full of enthusiasm, modelling a bust of Courbet. He must then have been about forty; and he was still at Ornans in 1922 when Edith Valerio met him and learned that Zoé 'had neglected her two sons, sending them away to be reared by peasants and later placing them in a semi-charitable school'. Zoé had thought her dead husband 'spirited away by enemies. This son made an unfortunate marriage, which ended in a complete separation from wife and children.' He had returned to Ornans some twenty years earlier, that is about 1902.[35] Juliette gave up the Museum a few years before her death. But in 1938 the *Société des Amis de Gustave Courbet* was formed with similar projects. The war interrupted, but in 1947 a small museum was opened in the Town Hall at Ornans under the presidency of Robert Fernier, grandson of the innkeeper at La Vrine where Courbet had stopped for some food on his way out of France in 1873.

In June 1919, on the centenary of Courbet's birth, Juliette's heirs (Mme Lapierre and Mme de Tastes) had the corpse exhumed and reburied at Ornans with Slom's original monument in blocks of granite.

We cannot do better than end with the words Vallès wrote a year after Courbet's death. One became a Communard 'simply because one is a free man, honest, and one follows the the roadway where the sufferers and the poorfolk are. He who painted the *Spinner*, the *Stonebreakers*, the *Burial at Ornans*, had inevitably to find himself, on the day when a choice had to be made, on the side where lay work, poverty, and pavement-stones. After all, don't pity him. He had a finer life than those who from youth on to their day of death smell the reek of ministries, the mustiness of orders. He has crossed the great currents, he has plunged into the ocean of crowds, he has heard beating like cannonfire the heart of a people; and he ended in the midst of nature, amid trees, breathing the scents that inebriated his youth, under a sky untarnished by the steam of great massacres, but which, this evening perhaps, set aglow by the setting sun, will spread itself over the dead man's house like a great red flag.'[36]

NOTES

Where no number is given with an author, the reference is to his first cited work.

The Foreword indicates the writers to whom I feel a special debt; I may add Georges Grimmer for his research into the life of Zoé Courbet.

The following abbreviations are used: A., Louis Aragon; B., Pierre Borel; Box, One of the seven Boxes of Castagnary papers in the Salle des Étampes, Bibliothèque Nationale; *Bull.* (followed by a number), Bulletin of the Société des Amis de Gustave Courbet; C., Courbet; Cast., Castagnary; Ch., Champfleury; Cour., Pierre Courthion; F., Robert Fernier; G., Georges Grimmer; GBA, *Gazette des Beaux-Arts*; GC, Gustave Courbet; GK, E. Gros-Kost; GM, Gerstle Mack; JL, Jack Lindsay; L., Charles Léger; MB, Maximin Buchon; N, Linda Nochlin; R, Georges Riat; S, Meyer Schapiro; Tab., Adolphe Tabarant.

1. *Early Years* (1819–37)

[1] GM, ch. 1; many photos or Ornans etc. in F(1) and issues of *Bull.*, e.g. xli, xxx. Also L(10).

[2] R, 13; Woodcock, 1.

[3] MB(3), intro. by Ch, 142–4; cf. 'Le Vieux Mari', 148f, with C.'s own improvisations. MB asks, 'How explain the perpetual freshness of these *enfantillages*, when so many things, apparently very important, have so quickly aged?'

[4] GM, 4; Cour. (1), i, 63; Ideville; Cast. (1); A. Altheimer, Bull., xl, 3f; birth certificate, *Bull.*, xl, 3f.

[5] Cast. (1), 8.

[6] L(1), 15.

[7] L(2), 15.

[8] Wey, 22.

[9] Cast. Box 4; GM, 6f.

[10] Cour. (1), i, 206–9; to Cast. 20 Feb., 1866.

[11] L(2), 133, to *père* C.: so they were 'cousins gros comme le bras'. The grandmother Sylvie was daughter of Jean-Antoine Oudot, Ornans landowner, and of Thérèse-Josephte (*sic*) Saulnier, also of Ornans; her husband was an orphan; her mother died 1810; her father, J.P. of canton Amancey, died 1814.

[12] R, 2.

[13] Woodcock, 9.

[14] R, 3f: cousin François-Julien Oudot who taught at Faculté de Droit, Paris. For seminary: Dortois.

[15] GM, 10.

[16] Box 1; Cour. (1), i, 206f: letter MB to Cast., 20 Feb., 1866. A fire at Salins, 1825, brought MB's father to his wife's region.

[17] Woodcock, 5.

[18] R, 14–17.

[19] Box 2 (26 Jan. 1874 to Cast. at Vevey); GM, 11; Cour. (1), i, 66–8; dossier Lachaud, Papiers Riat.

[20] GK, 25–8; GM, 12.

[21] Box 3; GM, 11f.

[22] The Petit Séminaire transferred to the Maisonnettes in the vallon of Consolation; the place

left vacant at Ornans was taken over by abbés Pudot and Lemondey as a *pensionnat*: Cast. (1), 12.

[23] Anon (1); R, 4f; Cour. (1), i, 68f; GM, 13. Paintings: F(1), nos. 49f; *Bull.*, xxxvi, 1; xiii. 1–4; *s.v.* in Brune. There is a Baultz under 1828 in list of Gros's pupils (published by J. B. Delestre). C'.s self-portrait at age of 14 at Ornans.

[24] Ideville, 5.

2. *Besançon College* (1837–40)

[1] L. Febvre cited Woodcock, 1. In 1849 most of the population of Bescançon Nord were listed as *agriculteurs*: Clark, 210, n. 13.

[2] L(2), 82f; *Acad. Sc. et B.L. Basançon, Procès-verbal et Bull.* 1947–56: 313–16, Balzac; 309–12, Stendhal; 312, Ste-Beuve; 317, Taine.

[3] Cour. (1), ii, 33–5. GK says that C. boasted, 'I turned everything upside down at the college.' He learned only how to write and read, more or less; talents he disdained. Spelling didn't exist. 'Ideas shouldn't be expressed by words; they should be drawn.' C. may have talked like that at times when drunk; GK, as usual, wildly exaggerates: Cour. (1), i, 71.

[4] Bastide is mentioned; see also Cour. (1), i, 67; Ideville.

[5] R, 6; GM, 14f; Cast. (1), 15.

[6] R, 7f.

[7] R, 7f.

[8] L(2), 21–3; Cour. (1), ii, 69f.

[9] R, 9; GM, 17f.

[10] R, 9; GM, 18; Cour. (1), ii, 69f.

[11] Cast. (1), 15f. For number of house, cf. R, 9; Cour. (1), i, 70f.

[12] R, 9.

[13] Baille became professor of painting at Besançon: Cast. (1), 18–20.

[14] Cast. (1), 20; Baille had gone to Paris this year; it is not certain if he did the drawing at Besançon or Paris; L(2), 26, 32; Cast. (1), 17.

[15] L(2), 23, 22.

[16] Not in Delestre, nor in David lists by Delécluze.

[17] Wey, 12f; GM, 19f.

[18] GM, 20.

[19] R, 9f; two little prospectuses, 'if it doesn't bore you, give one to M. Oudinot *frère*, at the café Pernet'. Among lithos, bridge of Nahin which he painted later. Also *Bull.*, vi, 14.

[20] R, 11; Cast. (1), 18.

[21] Ch. (10), i, 7; Amiel, 383, cf. Cast. (3). A widower with two children, Buchon senior brought them up in army fashion. After supper, he and his servant, La Claude, knelt for prayers, Max and sister prayed in silence, La Claude had to reply to litanies etc. The captain omitted nothing, reciting it all as if giving army instruction. Taking up the prayers for the dead, he turns to La Claude; no reply; in a thundering voice he repeated *De profundis clamavi ad te Domine: Domine, exaudi vocem meam.* The children laughed secretly, seeing La C. still deaf; the enraged father rolled his eyes and yelled straight at La C., '*De profundis*, in God's name!' (This must have been one of Max's tales.): Troubat (1), 83f; L(2), 17f.

[22] L(2), 17, 19f; GM, 21f.

[23] L(2), 24f; GM, 22; Cast. (1), 16. Study of a man by C. at this time: L(2), 25. Date 1839, printed at Besançon.

[24] Cast. (1), 8–10; GM, 9. At Flagey the kitchen was used, by the oven: L(2), 15; the harmonium was given to Flagey church.

[25] Ch. (2), 3f; 2; 4f; 5f; 9f. GM, 8f.

[26] *Bull.*, xxvi, 2.

3. *First Years in Paris* (1840–5)

[1] R, 24; Lemonnier: Cour. (1), i, 73. Other descriptions of C. in Schanne (R, 6of); Gill (1): see *Bull.*, i, 69.

[2] Cast. MS: Cour. (1), i, 73f.

[3] R, 23; GM, 26.

[4] Cast. (1), 8n.

[5] R, 24; Oudot's book and de Velna.

[6] Suisse: see JL (1), 76, 85, 88 – at corner of Quai des Orfèvres and bd. du Palais; Delacroix had worked there.

[7] R, 29; *Metrop.* 119 (? painted 1861); a smaller version once belonged to a Courbet follower, Margottet; the copy, as often with C., was more carefully modelled.

[8] Schanne, 288; GM, 27.

[9] Cast. (1), 11n. (stammer); Hesse: Cour. (1), i, 74f and Anon. (1), 'Hesse gave advice but did not impose himself.' Marlet portrait: *Bull.*, xxxi, 3 (*c.* 1849–50).

[10] R, 26.

[11] *ibid.*

[12] GM, 29f.

[13] L(2), 27.

[14] *ibid.*

[15] R, 27; GM, 30.

[16] Tab., 43–5, 54–6.

[17] GM, 32f; L(2), 28f. Decamps: Tab., 56. Pradier: ib., 45. Cast. MS: Cour. (1), i, 75f. Many early works were painted over or lost. Notebook: A, 208f, Louvre RF 29234, plates 28–60: includes sketches of Ansout (not like the painting), back of hunter, ships and sea, landscapes, study related to *Woman combing hair*, Marly-machines, hills and Loue valley, Source of Lison, Grotto, girl making hat, romantic dreamer with girl downfloating to a kiss, effaced sketches for *Lot.* A. takes drawings of Saintonge and Jura as 1862–3. But oddly the poem has been recopied in the notebook (5th, 7th stanzas) which deals with Alsace, Rhineland, Germany, dated 1856: A., 210f.

[18] R, 52; GK, 75.

[19] GM, 66; Huyghe (1), 16; Schanne, 293. Sons: L(15). Blavet: *Bull.*, vi, 9.

[20] R, 53, also 42–2: Chanson de Valbois and Jeannette.

[21] Cour. (1), ii, 7of. Despair: *Rome*, no. 2, pp. 4f. A replica in private coll. is the first thought; cf. self-portrait at Mesdag (The Hague) known as *Portrait of Hippolyte* (no. 78 cat. of Museum); this seems a little later, with same white blouse but fuller beard.

[22] Dog: cf. *Bull.*, ii (cover). Knife: Cour. (1), i, 75; GM, 34f. etc.

[23] R, 34.

[24] Juliette: *Rome*, p. 6, also for drawing in Louvre; L(2), 32, 29; L(5), 25; GM, 34, 36; F(1), no. 54. Also R, 30.

[25] Father: *Rome*, no. 1, dates in 1840 are Paris; it has also been dated 1844. He did his father many times more (*Afterdinner, Fair-Return, Burial, Return of Hunt* 1857, and in last days).

[26] R, 24: letter 24 Dec. 1842. Anon. (1): Cour. (1), i, 74f. (incorrect date 1842).

[27] Anon. (1).

[28] R, 26; GM, 35; Cour. (1), ii, 71.

[29] *ibid.*

[30] R, 28, also announcing further works; delighted that his grandparents are pleased at his success.

[31] R, 33f; Anon. (1): 'To bring him to the point, his friend Marlet and the painter Hesse went and took from his studio the little self-portrait with his dog', Cour. (1), i, 77f. Salons: see also Clark, 209; P. Grate, 48–50; JL (1).

[32] Tab. 43, 61–3, 70f. The critic Haussard wrote on project to 'abandon the Salon and put the Louvre under interdict', 70. Troyon showed his *Forest of Fontainebleau*.

[33] *ibid.*, 69f.

[34] GM, 34; L(2), 30, also work on Zoé, and Rock of Hautepierre.

[35] R, 36; also called the *Happy Lovers* (Lyon); GM makes the girl Justine and dates 1844–5; R. says '44. Study: *Bull.*, xvi, 14f; A., pls. 2, 3, 7.

[36] R, 34; GM, 37f.

[37] R, 36, 38–40; L(2), 33; Cour. (1), ii, 72 (10 March), he suggests *Man with Pipe* as the admired study of a head. Riat drew on Juliette; if she thought the girl Joséphine, it shows how little C. told the family of intimate matters. Aphorism on sleep: *Bull.*, xxi, 7; *Sculpteur: Bull.*, xxxi, 2. Cast.: Cour. (1), ii, 282. Guillonet on Ansout, who died 1894; had entered Civil Service 1858 and became head of his dept. Vernet: Tab., 74–6. Woman by stream; *Bull.*, v. 9; L(2), no. 2 (Detroit); note *Young Girl Sleeping*. R, 48 (given as 1847). Sylvester sees in *Hammock* and *Lot* the influence of Orazio Gentileschi.

[38] GM, 39; Zahar (3), 2, 8f.

[39] Silvestre: Cour. (1), i, 33–5.

[40] See Boime for case of Ecole des B.-A.; encouragement of sketch by Couture, Decamps, Henne etc.; work from nature encouraged by Valenciennes 1800 in *Elements de la perspective oratique*; Decamps used knife, razor, stones to get rough effect; value of teaching by Couture and Gleyre etc.

4. *To the Year of Revolution* (1846–8)

[1] R, 42.

[2] R, 42f; Cour. (1), i, 72f.

[3] GM, 40f; Tab., 86. But Delacroix had 3 small works and a watercolour (*Lion*) in; Decamps, 4 in, 1 rejected; Corot one Fontainebleau view in. Delaunay attacked Chenavard's *Hell* as capable of giving a woman an abortion, 'as indecent as Delacroix's *Romeo and Juliet*', Tab., 89.

[4] Baudelaire (2), 119.

[5] *ibid.*, 23; cf. Brouwer's *Smoker in Louvre* (N(1), 219); Sylvester.

[6] R, 42f; Cour. (1), ii, 73; R, has: 'towards 16 March', Cour. has: '15'.

[7] R, 44.

[8] R, 45.

[9] GM, 42; R, 44f. Bisontin Gigoux rejected: R, 44. For situation, Tab., 94–102; Thore, *ib.*, 103.

[10] March 1847: R, 46f.

[11] Cour. (1), ii, 73f; L(2), 37; R, 46f.

[12] L(2), 37; Cour. (1), ii, 73f; R, 46f. Also Cast. MS: Cour. (1), i, 84 – but Cour. says he was in Holland 15 March '46 to 15 March '47! Hals was a favourite.

[13] L(2), 38f. For son, see later on 1851, etc.

[14] GM, 43; *Bull.*, iv, 15–17. Later let fall into disrepair, restored 1948. Mayor Monnot of the Commune, 9 Jan. '48, verified the commission; 1850, the Council added the comment: 'The artist has well executed the picture entrusted to his brush.' Note theme of child revived in relation to the birth of his own son: the saint (a man) gives the child life out of the tub (womb): the woman is eliminated. For religious work: the early copy of Guercino's *St Jerome's Vision*, 1840: Estignard, 185; *Bull.*, xxii, 15.

[15] R, 45; Zélie in Florentine pastiche 1845, F(1), no. 53; *Bull.*, xlii, 3; xxvi, 1; vi, 2, 8 (indolence-charm), xxxi, 2. *The Three Girls*: L(2), no. 3, pp. 44f; perhaps for workaday clothes mourning might be forgotten.

[16] R, 47.

[17] Ideville, 84; Schanne, 106; GM, 43–5; Cour. (1), i, 88–90; caricature: L(3). Fine balance of forms: *Bull.*, xxxi, 2.

[18] Schanne, 106; GM, 44f; Delvau.

[19] Cast. Box 1; GM, 45.

[20] R, 47; Tab., 116.

[21] Tab., 117ff.

[22] R, 48f. Peter Hawke: GM, 46 and Box 1.

[23] R, 49f; Larkin (1), 77, fig. 32. R, 53; Cour. (1), ii, 75 (17 April); GM, 51. C. hopes to get a govt. order for one of the 800 copies of the winning pictures to be made.

[24] *Bull.*, iii, 38f; Cour. (1), ii, 45–9; GM, 25f, L(2), 40f; Tab., 114–16. GM says: 'Café de la Rotonde'; Tab.: 'café Aubanel, Place de l'Ecole de Médecine'. Jean Journet as bad poet: Tab., 116. Secret Societies: Cassou, *Le Quarante Huitard*, 22f (1948).

[25] R, 50; Cour. (1), ii, 74.

[26] GM, 25f; Cast. Box 3; Cour. (1), 142f. Torn down 1878.

[27] Cour. (1), i, 183; R, 63f.

[28] Schanne, 195; Ch. (3), 86; GM, 57–60.

[29] Box 3; Cour. (1), i, 150–2; A. Gautier: *Bull.*, xvi, 1–2. Schanne, painter, ended as seller of toys in quartier du Marais: R, 51f. More regulars: R, 55. Gigoux: Cour. (1), i, 85f.

[30] R, 55; L(2), 42; Cour. (1), i, 150f.

[31] Cour. (1), 1, 152f; Ch. (3).

[32] Box 3; Cour. (1), i, 154; Fournel (3).

[33] Delvau, 3–5.

[34] *ibid.*, 6f.

[35] *ibid.*, 7–13; Estignard, 102–4; Schapiro, 170; Ch. (3), 185ff; Audebrand, 72–212 (rue des Martyrs).

[36] GM, 59f; L(3), 69; L(2), 42; Silvestre (2), 68; Cour. (1), i, 58.

[37] R, 56–9; Schapiro, 174, n. 2. Novel: Schapiro, 183 (who compares *Moby Dick* (1851), ch. 57). GM, 97–9; Focillon in Cour. (1), i, 103–7; *Souvenirs*, 171 (article of 28 Sept. '48). Father, sec. to municipality: GM, 170.

[38] Woodcock, 10 (written 1858).

[39] *Essay of a General Grammar*, Besançon, 1837: seven books: 841–7; in '48, *Solution of the Social Problem*. Contract: Woodcock, 171.

[40] *The General Idea of the Revolution*, 1851. For 1948, in the *Peuple*, 19 Feb. '49. Vichy, etc.: Cogniot, 35, 29, 32. Hugo (2), 258. Thoré: GM, 55 and Thoré (1), ii, 277; Cour. (1), i, 215.

[41] A, 10. Buchon: *ibid.*, 14. In general also, Clark, 289; breakdown of old working-class: Chevalier; railways blown up: Molok; all levels: Daumard. For immigration: Chevalier (1) and (2); Daumard. For turbulent Besançon in 1789: A. Young, *Travels in France*, 1792, 27–29 July: 'I do not like the air and manners of the people here – and I should see Besançon swallowed up in an earthquake before I could live in it', with his remarks on the guard bourgeois needed with the regular soldiers who 'would be attacked and knocked on the head'.

[42] GK, 33; GM, 49f; Ch. (3), 135; R, 109–11. Books: Cast. MS (Cour. (1), i, 156). In general: Schaettel, Abe, L(13). Courbet and G. Sand, etc.: A. Bowness in *French 19c. Painting and Literature* (1972) ed. V. Finke. C. and Baudelaux: Bonniot (1) 174f; Léger (2) 80f (no break).

[43] Cour. (1), i, 79f, 150; GK, 31–3; Cour. (1), i, 81–4; Troubat (3). N(1), 217; MB (2); L(4), 14; Cast. (Cour. (1), i, 56).

[44] Cast. MS: Cour. (1), i, 149f. For C.'s style: A. 64. His enemies said, like Péladan, his 'words and writings are those of a crétin', he was of Caliban's race. He didn't read: Silvestre: Cour. (1), i, 57.

[45] Clark, 211; Cour. (1), i, 142.

[46] Shapiro, 172f; Cast. (1), 30; L(2), 142f; Bouvier, 165ff; coll. works, *Muse Populaire* 1861. He wrote poem on Géricault's *Cuirassier of Waterloo*. Ch. attacked C. for 'love of the canaille that makes him a brother of Pierre Dupont'; Troubat (1), 180 (April '65); Gautier, *Histoire du romantisme*, 1872; Baudelaire's preface to *Chants et Chansons*, 1851; *L'Art romantique* (*Œuvres*, ii, 403–13) and second essay, 1861, *ibid.*, 551–7. Portrait: L(2), pl. 51, Mathieu's, *ibid.*, p. 144. Mathieu: Dalligny. He was something of an astrologer. For lively account of meeting: L(2), 144–60.

5. *Turning-point* (1848–50)

[1] Gigoux (1); Cour. (1), i, 85f. Accent: L(3), 64; Collin etc.

[2] Durbé; JL (2) etc.

[3] R, 64; GM, 66f; Tab., 126ff; Corot had five works.

[4] Cast. (1), 491.

[5] GM, 65; R, 67–9; for early attempt at a family gathering (not the Courbets): Meier-Graefe, pl. 1; in letter to Wey, 28 Nov. '49, C. calls the *Afterdinner*, *La Soirée à Ornans*. Schapiro, 174; the Le Nains coming up in 1840s; Ch. Blanc, 1846, compared bros. Laleux with them (L. Rosenthal (3), 383–6); they painted Breton peasants and work-scenes. For family-repast: S. Meltzoff, *Art Bull.*, xxiv (1942), 262.

[6] R, 67; F(11); Tab., 141ff. For Bonvin: Durbé.

[7] F(11), 3f; Wey.

[8] *Rome*, no. 4; it has been dated 1857, but a Louvre drawing of same themes (reversed and clad) is signed and dated 1849. In C.'s show at Pavillon de l'Alma; caricatured then. Cf. *Rome*, no. 12.

[9] *Rome*, no. 5; H. Haug, *Peinture au Mus. des B.A. de Strasbourg*, 1955, no. 627.

[10] R, 62f; GM, 67. Also Mouilleron, Sieurac, Jules de la Madeleine. Marnes, west of Paris; inn near Aulnay-sous-Bois, north-east of Paris.

[11] CM, 67f; Cour. (1), ii, 188ff; Wey. Key: Cour. (1), i, 14f.

[12] R, 72. Note reply to Gigoux, 'Yes, masses, always masses.' Wey cites some sketches.

[13] G(3), 2f suggests Chenavard advised Blanc to give C. the award; C. seems to have met Chenavard 1848–9.

[14] Letter to Wey, 30 Oct. '49; R, 73; GM, 69.

[15] R, 73.

[16] Wey, 17f; Cour. (1), ii, 75f; R, 75f; GM, 69f. Cf. Cour. (1), i, 96n. L. Peisse, born Aix 1803, died Paris about 1860, conservateur of the collections of the Ecole des B.A., wrote or translated works on history and philosophy of medicine; also wrote critiques of Salons. GN says C. would have better addressed F. Pillet, critic of *Moniteur*, or Delécluze, of *Journal des Débats*, but he fails to note what Peisse had said.

[17] R, 74f for citation of novel.

[18] Proudhon, 1865, 236f.

[19] Ideville, 1878, 37f; GM, 70f.

[20] GM, 77–9.

[21] L(3); Cassatt: Duret (2), 32. Manet: A. Vollard, *Souvenirs d'un marchand des tableaux*. David: JL(1). The site is at the bottom of Roche Founèche, a place he liked. Drawing: L(2), 47, in Besançon Mus. Then a canvas (40 cm. by 1 m.), seen by Lèger in 1909 in Juliette's Museum. L(2), 46, recalls long red noses in *Christ at Tomb*; *ibid.*, 46f for instructions to mother. In general: Nochlin (3).

[22] Ch. (3), 194f; Cour. (1), ii, 77; GM, 79f.

[23] *Le Démocrate franc-comtois*, 25 April 1850; (Fourrierist) *Le Peuple, Journal de la Révolution sociale*, no. 18, 7 June 1850. Clark, 211f for collation of texts. Letter: Clark, 209, n.5; Frey, 64, cf. N (2), 106, n.4: not in *La Démocratie jurassienne* (ended 30 July '50). Buchon says 52 persons in *Burial*. Carnival: L(6), 385ff. Rethel: S, 187–91.

[24] Clark, 211, 286. Besançon and Ornans: Clark, 258, and Marlin (1) and, in general (2), also Préclin. Refs. in Clark, to whom I owe most of these sources.

[25] Clark, 286; Daumard, ii, 348.

[26] Clark, 288f. Popular emblems etc., Schapiro, 167, figs. b, d. First drawing: L(2), 47; R, 79. For his interest in folklore, see the tale of the funeral-feast and his relation of the anthropological material to Franche-Comté: Péladan; Cour. (1), ii, 267–80. Gravedigger and cholera: S, 170.

[27] Rome, no. 11; all the persons are locals, though we do not know all the names. C. repeated date '50 on copy (shown at his exhibition '67); description by MB in *L'Impartiel* doesn't mention

distant walkers. In 1855 a reduced version (letter to Bruyas): Mus. of Ornans has a picture of same group of riders (clothing variants): *A Return from the Hunt*, 1857. Letter to Bryuas (B, 42) says first version 'lacked many things' and had 'an error in perspective; I have enlarged it by a fourth' (*L'Olivier*, 483). Cast. MS (Cour. (1), i, 101) says it was natural in 1848 to turn to the 'peasant and the bourgeois' in the milieu of his childhood.

28 R, 76. Schapiro, 166; J. (1). Rembrandt: H. Focillon and L. Goldschneider, and L(2), 38f.

29 R, 79f (10 March '50); Cour. (1), ii, 78.

30 GM, pl. 15, p. 72.

31 R, 82 (undated).

32 *ibid.*

33 R, 83, letter Aug. '50 on preparations.

34 R, 83f; Ch. (11), 38–67; R, 59f; GM, 74. Broadsides: Schapiro, 167f; Duchartre, 29, 33, 58 (combination of *Image* and *complainte*), 87ff; Mazarot, 142f, also L(2), 50f.

35 See her meeting with madman Chabrier in London Bedlam, 'I have come to end all forms of servitude, to free women from slavery to men, the poor from the rich, and the soul from sin.' She thought, 'I was moved; what he said did not suggest madness. Jesus, Saint-Simon, Fourier, had spoken in similar fashion.' The sculptor Ganneau founded *L'Evadisme*, based on equality of sexes; the Saint-Simonians held a woman would regenerate humanity – they asked George Sand to be their Mother; she refused; Père Enfantin and followers went east in quest of Mother.

36 N(1), fig. 20, p. 215. The *Complainte* is to the *Air de Joseph*. The painting is lost. Alexander, 446, has a far-fetched derivation from a relief of Sargon. Schapiro, 166; Fournel (1) & (2); N(1), 214f.

37 L(2); Cour. (1), i, 96. Study in Mus. Oslo. Wey, 9f; GM, 74f. The woman was singer Marie Rocco, married Berlioz later when first wife died, 1854. Probably in 1848 C. had done a small portrait of Chopin (who died Oct. '49), met at house of sculptor Clésinger who had married Solange Dudevant, daughter of G. Sand.

38 G(3), 2. Wey remarks on rich frame, 'a caprice of which Chenavard is little capable'.

39 See *Rome*, no. 6, *Head of Woman* for details; no. 7, *Girl with Goat* – also A, 102, girl asleep.

40 *Lune*, 8 June '67; Cour (1), ii, 223–31: he stresses: 'when C appeared, everything was still stifling in the narrow frame of tradition. That frame he broke into bits; men were woulded by the burst . . .'

41 *Salon de 1850–1* (1851); *Bull.*, ix, 9f; critiques: R, 87f.

42 *Lettres de l'art français*; R, 86. L. Reau, of the Institut, in *Les Arts plastiques: L'Ère romantique*, 175f, says the *Burial* 'ridicules religious ceremonies by representing them as mummeries'. Delacroix: *Bull.*, ix, 11. In general: Weinberg, Tourneaux, Larkin, Grate.

43 L(3), 15 etc. Also Grand-Carteret, 550f. 'Cham' in *Le Courrier de Paris: Album de 60 Caricatures*, 1851; *Le Charivari*, 2 Feb. '51, 4 May '51. Sabots: L(3), 28f; Fournel (1), xx, 366; Cour. (1), i, 154f (tale against angels). *Retour*: L(3), 13.

44 Schapiro in general. C. could hardly have missed the David show of 1845: Tab., 85. Further: Cast. (1), 30. Also Boas, 51–3 (Proudhon); Delécluze, *David* (1855), 176; J. Renouvier, *Hist. de l'art pendant la Révolution* (1863), 77; JL (1). Thackeray in Paris Sketch Boo, drew Horatii as rigid semaphores in a row, 1840; he also compares the new French Catholic school to English playing-cards. For Ingres: Rosenthal (2), 82.

45 Audebrand, some 50 years later, 110; Schapiro, 164.

46 R, 86f; L(3), 34, 37; Estignard, 27–30; Du Val for *Revue des deux Mondes*; Schapiro, 164; Martino, 76. Silvestre (1), 269, classes Ingres and C. as inert and immobile.

47 L(3), 20.

48 Schapiro, 165; Baudelaire on Guys, *Œuvres* (1938), ii, 338.

49 *Le Messager de l'Assemblée*, 25–26 Feb. '51, reprinted with slight changes. Ch. (5). Clark, 211; GM, 8of; Ch. (5), 236–9.

50 Ch. (5); Cour. (1), i, 104f; Cast., *ibid.*, i, 92; Ch. (3), 'speaking of his art with the tenacity of

a peasant, the conviction of a believer, the nuances of a mystic' (Cour. (1), i, 92).

[51] Ch. (5); Cour. (1), i, 92–3; Schapiro, fig. 6; Duchartre, 108, fig. 38b. Ch. on 'a writer who sang of Chinese grotesques, lice-ridden Spaniards, etc.', who was yet 'scared' by *Burial*. Abe on *Burial* 'et l'habit noir Baudelairéen'. Also Schapiro, 177f, on inner conflict in Baudelaire, e.g. in *Salon Caricatural*, 1836.

[52] Cast. (1), 496.

[53] Clark, 287; Marx, *Sel. Works* (1962), i, 233–8; Vigier, ii, 336f; C. Levy for hopes of 1852.

[54] Clark's thesis, 289, n. 22 for refs. I cannot follow him into his stress here, despite the great value of his study. *Bull.*, ix (Focillon and Zahar). See also his *The Absolute Bourgeois* and *Image of the People*.

6. *Wound of Love* (1851–2)

[1] Cour. (1), i, 98f.

[2] *id.*, ii, 188.

[3] *La Rév. litt.*, i, 26f; Clark, 209.

[4] L(2), 57; and (Ornans), Ch. (3), 174; G(2), 3.

[5] *Bull.*, xxxix, 8–10; portrait done 1855 according to inscription and letter. After 1873 he left Republicans for the extreme right; died 1878 at 47 years. Vallès made strong attack on his scorn, mistrust of humanity. 'Snout of rodent, face of rat', a frail build, 'gay and biting, bold even', makes one laugh and fear with his irony that can amuse or draw blood, 'but passion is never mixed with it'. R, 93; GM, 82f; Cast. MS, Cour. (1), i, 157.

[6] GM, 82; R, 93. To thank Belgians he sent *La Signora de la Guerrero* to King Leopold I in 1851: *Rome*, no. 9 – rather hard style, see discussion there, relation to Goya and to Manet's *Lola de Valence*, 1862.

[7] R, 94 (13 Feb. '51); Cour. (1), i, 98; Box 3, GM, 52f.

[8] R, 94.

[9] To Cast. 16 Dec. '69: GM, 51f; Cour. (1), i, 98; Box 2; Troubat (1), 82, as to arrest also R, 100f, which includes a tale of police-spying on C.

[10] R, 100; GM, 52.

[11] Clark, 288; Vigier, i, 73.

[12] Vigier, ii, 336f; Clark, 287.

[13] Clark, 288; Archives de la Préfecture de Police, Courbet file, Ba.1.020 (19 Dec. '68). Maitron, 225 ('the hempcomber Martin de Barjols').

[14] R, 94–6; GM, 52f. Landscape: Meier-Graefe (1), 257, identifies it with that of *Burial*, from a different angle. Thus the two works, so different in emotion, have the same setting: Roche de Dix Heures.

[15] R, 3, 83, 95f, 119, 127f, 146, 158, 252, 298, 368; Estignard, 31f, 77, 155 ('servile imitation of nature'); Ideville, 46, 51, 106, 119; Mantz (1), xvii, 424; Péladan, 409; *Metrop.*, 108f. For the perspective of the cattle, note a previous study incorporated with insufficient care; corrected to some extent in later (Leeds) version. *Rome*, no. 10. *Siesta* in Mus. Besançon, A. pl. 2. Wound: Huyghe.

[16] See further note in *Rome*, no. 10, for the various copies etc.

[17] *ibid.*; F(3). C. himself kept a copy made for Baudry; in Cast. MSS is ref. to a *Man Wounded to Death*, 'not the servile copy of the Louvre canvas', also 'one finds there a different manner of painting', a study also with 'landscape scarcely indicated', signed; also L(2), 35. In general: Proudhon (8), 248; Ideville, 70; Silvestre, 125; Brunesoeur, 32. Caricature, Quillenbois, *L'Illustration*, 21 July '55 (M. Courbet wounded).

[18] J. L. Puech, see *Rome*, p. 23. Delacroix: N(1), 219 and L. Hourtcq, *Delacroix* (1930), 61.

[19] *Rome*, no. 10.

[20] R, 94f; GM, 85–7. Lydie: Bauzon, 238.

[21] Box 3; GK, 68f (Cour. (1), i, 109f); Collin, Lemonnier (1), 87f; Cour. (1), ii, 252. Champfleury

to MB (6 Sept. '52): 'I have been to see Courbet, who was about to go to Dieppe for a few days.' GM, 84; for suppression of the facts, Estignard, 193.

[22] GM, 86; F(4); Guillonet. Women: Cast. MS: Cour. (1), i, 183f; Silvestre: Cour. (1), i, 30–3; Ch: Cour. (1), i, 131; R, 143f. Jongkind: Hefting, 183.

[23] More details: GM, 83f. Landscape around Ornans is now much more wooded, rocks more hidden. Another landscape shows two walkers, perhaps his sisters, sheltered by umbrellas.

[24] G(1), 1f; L(5), 186f; R, 3. Portraits, G(1), 2f.

[25] GK, 22.

[26] Ch (2), 6–8, 12f, 14; ideal woman, 41; Zélie and tale of organist, 18ff; Aphorism: *Bull.*, xxii, 6f. Also Ch. (4), 270ff; Loudun: *Bull.*, xi, 7–9.

[27] GM, 83f; R, 97. More on critics: *Metrop.*, 108; Tab., 212, 216f, 253, 419; MacOrlan, p. 18 etc. Venturi (1), 212; (3), 99, compares central figure with Renoir's *Lise*, cf. Leymarie (2), i, 49.

[28] Clark, 290, n. 27. Also Ideville: Cour. (1), i, 134f; *Bull.*, xviii, 13.

[29] Schapiro, 168f; Bédollière's aim was a philanthropic reconciliation of opposed classes.

[30] Schapiro, 168; Rosenthal (1), 389, 383f; Bénédite, *Chassériau* (1931), 41; Decamps: Durbé, pl. 18. Much more could be said on the work-theme as precipitating new techniques: JL (3).

[31] Schapiro, 169. Considérant, *Théorie du droit au travail et théorie du droit de propriété*, 1839.

[32] R, 100; GM, 84; Schapiro, 172f; N(1), 211f. with refs. and figs.

[33] Troubat (1), 125f; Ch. and marriage, 126ff. R, 98–100. Early relations with Chenavard, G(3), 1–3. Chenavard was ousted from Panthéon by decree. In general: Gautier (2) and Silvestre (1), 105–45; L(2), 146f.

[34] Boyé (2), 7. Balzac: Focillon (Cour. (1), i, 103–7).

[35] GM, 100.

[36] See JL (1); Boas; Nochlin etc. For 1850, Thackeray, *Paris Sketch Book*. Thoré's visit to studio: R, 189f. Zola: GM, 90; *Bull.*, xxxviii–xxxix, xli; N(4), 71–7 etc. G. Sand announced (preface, *Champi* 1850) the need of an art neither classic nor romantic, but responding to the 'modern idea of man'.

[37] Lemonnier: Cour. (1), i, 105f.

[38] Cast. MS: Cour. (1), i, 155f; Gill (2), Cour. (1), i, 147; Astruc (1), Cour. (1), 1, 137–40; Cast. MS: Cour. (1), i, 166f. Delvau calls him the Black Bear of Lousiana, *Le Journal Amusant*, 29 Oct. '59.

[39] Methods: Schanne: Cour. (1), i, 84f; L(1), 27. He prepared three basic tones for light, half-light, shadow; put the unadulterated colours in fan-shape on palette, then painted with brush, knife, rag, thumb, anything.

[40] See for example, T. Hilton, *The Pre-Raphaelites* (1970), 15, 20, 52, 122f; also N(4), 93ff – *Times* attack, 104.

[41] *Autobiography and Reminiscences*, i, 243f, 269 (3rd ed. 1887); Ch. (12) refers at end of preface to the Pre-Raphaelites as seeking a renaissance through scrupulous detail. Millais painted firemen (*The Rescue*, 1855) but in anecdotal way; no generalising force.

7. *The Wandering Jew* (1853–4)

[1] E. P. Spence in Boas, 66f; Marquis of Normandy, *A Year of Revolution* (1857), 145f.

[2] GM, 28.

[3] Schapiro, 165; L(3), 20; Delacroix, *Journal*, 15 April '53; Visser. Reni: C. Gnudi & G. C. Cavalli, *G. Reni* (1955), 71; Alexander, 451.

[4] Quillenbois, *L'Illustration*, 21 July '55; *Charivari Album* 1853. L(3), 29, 24f, 22.

[5] *Bull.* ix, 3; R, 105f; About (1), 150f; L(3), 23f, cf. 30.

[6] R, 104; Ch. (1), 44.

[7] Guichard (1); Cour. (1) i, 111f.

[8] Zélie as model: R, 104; GM, 102f; G(1), 4; L(2), 53–5; *Rome*, no. 7. *Baigneuse*: R, 103; GM, 102f.

[9] G(1), 5.

[10] R, 101f; GM, 104. His first known ref. to photography.

[11] *Journal*, 15 April '53; GM, 105; Cour. (1) i, 110f. Efforts to get C. a medal, foiled by H. de Viel Castel: G(3), 3.

[12] Jouve.

[13] Ch. (1), 44; R, 102; GM, 105.

[14] B(1), 15f; L(2), 111f; GM, 106–8.

[15] G(3), 3f. Balzac, Berlioz etc. used to go to *Divan*.

[16] G(3), 4; Hefting, 18, 63. Studio: *Times*, 23 Nov. 1970; Pool, 136. For his admiring remarks on skilled and organised workers: N(4), 4–9.

[17] Paul d'Ivoi in *Figaro*: G(3), 3.

[18] Troubat 107f; Amiel, 379, called Ch. the 'Courbet of literature'. This year C. saw more of Proudhon, to annoyance of Jules Husson, says Ch.

[19] B, 65–72; *L'Olivier*, 485–90; Troubat, 164–7; R, 128–30; GM, 108–12; Charavay, ii; Cour. (1) ii, 79–84 (giving date Dec. '54). Schapiro, 170n. His business: surely connected with Buchon. The Comte was director-general of the imperial museums and intendant of the B.A. of the emperor's house.

[20] A. Gros: G(3), 6.

[21] GM, 112; Valerio, 251. Château: F(1), no. 26.

[22] N(1), 212, fig. 12; About (1): Cour. (1), i, 116–20. For work: note girl with hat, A. no. 59. Combing Hair: *Bull.*, xiii, 8; Sutton; Sylvester. Genuine? see *Bull.*, xv, 21f, add the proof of the A. drawing, no. 44. Sutton sees Ingres in the arms. The drawing is from the back, but has same circular effect. For *Bathers*, note Meier-Graefe, pl. 98, arm raised, arm tensely down, cf. the Cézanne gesture: JL (1), 191–4.

[23] GM, 113f; B, 41–3; *L'Olivier*, 482; R, 113f. Tent: B, pl. 96.

[24] R, 115 undated.

[25] R, 116; B, 37f; *L'Olivier*, 468–70; Cour. (1), ii, 78f; GM, 114f. 'Ascetic' is at times printed as 'aesthetic'.

[26] B, 39f; *L'Olivier*, 470f.

[27] GM, 116–19.

[28] About (2), 205.

[29] Quillenbois, 21 June '55; L(3), 29, cf. 32.

[30] Anticipation of Degas: *TLS*, 25 June 1952, 414. N(1), 209, 221. Nothing in Alexander's notion of Assyrian relief, 451. N(1), 218f, with more examples.

[31] *Ib.*, 219: see n. 105. Even if tale not authentic, it expresses Beethoven and change in artist's role, to which C. gives final political touch.

[32] B, *Lettres*, 47 (Nov. '54).

[33] Ch. (12), 91f.

[34] Béranger, *Œuvres* (1834), iii, 278–82; Dupont, 1856, in fine folio. Sue: J. L. Bovy, *E. Sue: le Roi du roman populaire*, 1962. Anderson, *Legend of Wandering Jew*; Ch. (12). See N(1), 214; 216 for comparison of Baudelairean wanderer; Hofmann (1), 238f; JL (1), 16–18.

[35] L(2), 177; Cassou, (Le Quarante Huitard) 27; N(1), 216. For hiking, JL note above.

[36] N(1), 217. Saint-Simon, *Dialogue entre l'artiste, le savant et l'industriel*, 1825; Hunt, 18, 34.

[37] Thus, Hugo, *La fonction du poète*, 1839; N(1), 217.

[38] Baudelaire, *Œuvres*, 637; B *Lettres*, 89.

[39] R, 121; GM, 121. Cf. earlier Dutch, van de Velde and van Goyen, but C. fused their sense of the facts of the situation with the romantic emotion: sea and beach crushed by height and mass of atmosphere; the sky takes up two-thirds of canvas.

[40] B(2), 186; GM, 118. 'It's only after exhausting every other available resource I turn to you.'

For the last 12 days I've been in a hopeless position,' etc. Bruyas bought the work.

⁴¹ Claparède.

⁴² GM, 120f; B, 49f.

⁴³ B(1), 58; R, 48.

⁴⁴ *Bull.*, v, 22f; iv, 22. 'Cuénot sets out today, the 13th.' GM, 121f; F(5).

⁴⁵ B, 54–7; *L'Olivier*, 473; Cour. (1), ii, 84–7. Album: F(5), 9.

⁴⁶ Ch. (1), cv, Nov.–Dec. 1913, 213; GM, 122f.

⁴⁷ Ch. (1), 214, 221 (26 July '54); also Troubat, ch. 8, on for steady drifting- away.

⁴⁸ Boyé (2), 7.

⁴⁹ *Ib.*, 5; Boyé (3).

⁵⁰ *Rome*, no. 24, with ref. to study. Estignard, 54, 179, 184, 187; A, 38; Silvestre, 273, 278; *L'Olivier*, 1913, 496; Meier-Graefe (2), 7; B(1), 101; L(4), 118; R, 248, 360.

8. *A Summing-Up* (1854–5)

¹ See n. 45 of previous chapter. 'Most painters are sending, it seems, their entire stock.' 'Best wishes to Mme Bruyas and your sister.'

² GM, 127. 'In our affectionate relationship I should only wound you by paying you compliments.'

³ *L'Olivier*, 376; B, 61–4. Zoé: *Cabinet*, 161f; *Bull*, xvii–xviii, 28.

⁴ GM, 127–30; later critiques, *Bull.*, xxix. Huyghe (1), 23; B(1), 56f. Also letter in L(2), 58f. 'Father Bruyas is afraid of being sent to Cayen (Cayenne).' He calls him *bailleur de fonds*, money-lender, sleeping-partner. 'I'm going to become a maddened poacher.' His picture is 'the history of my studio: what passes there physically and morally; it's passably mysterious. Let him who can guess.'

⁵ She gives a good account of Chartism. Symbolism of Box: *Bull.*, xl, 6–8.

⁶ Hofmann; Leymarie; *Bull.*, xxxiii–xxxiv; Huyghe; Chamson (2).

⁷ Delacroix: *Journal*, 3 Aug. '55; Cour. (1), i, 124f. *Apotheosis of Homer* was shown at the 1855 Exposition: Tab., 215. H. Levin, 70. Later critiques: *Bull.*, xxix.

⁸ JL (3), 40, 162, on sexual aspect of Turner's composition. Note the lovers, the girl is in a *hammock*.

⁹ G(2), 5.

¹⁰ Ch. (1), cxxxiii (Oct. 1919), 532. Letter of Feb.: *Bull.*, xii, 7f; March, 8.

¹¹ Hofmann; also stresses the varying roles of woman.

¹² Schapiro, 174f. (he assumes the shepherd-boy has thrown aside the romantic trappings); Schapiro also for Topffer and his ideas, and Baudelaire in this relation, his contradictions. He notes Delacroix disliked children and showed them as blood-victims. Taine on children: Schapiro, 181. Interest in popular culture, e.g. Balzac, *ib.* 175f. The use of an allegorical object in a realistic scene (e.g. shell) appears in Pre-Raph. works. People: N(1), 210; MB (2); Proudhon (10. i. 349); Schapiro, 170; B(1), 68f. Feudalism: Cassou, 137, 146–54 (*le Quarane-Huitard* 1948).

¹³ *Le Réalisme* (1887), 279f. Letter: 14 April '55: *La Revue Mondiale*, cxxxiii (1919), 532. Ch. in same book criticises the bourgeois as hypocritical and guilty of prudery in disliking song, *La Femme du Roulier*, where the small children of unfaithful waggoner tell the mother what they'll do to him when they grow up: Schapiro, 182. Conciliation: end of (12). Folksongs: Schapiro, 176.

¹⁴ *L'Olivier*, 478f; B, 74–6; GM, 133f; Cour. (1), ii, 87. Rejections and Palais Lefuel: G(2), 4–6, also more details. *L'Illustration*, 21 April '55.

¹⁵ G(2), 6–8. *Archives nat.* F21–521; *Univers*, 4 May; B, 42. Portrait of Ch. engraved by A. Gautier: Troubat (3); Cour. (1), i, 125f.

¹⁶ Box 1; GM, 134f; G(2); R, 131–4; *L'Olivier*, 479–81; B, 78–80, Catalogue: L(2), 60–2. Tab., 217f.

¹⁷ G. Grimmer (2); Bonniot (1), ch. 27.

¹⁸ B, 97. 'It's truly a matter to make Paris dance on its head', and 'It'll be beyond dispute the strongest comedy played in our time.'

¹⁹ G(2), 9f., 5 (Jardin d'Hiver). Houssaye: *Archives*, 26 April. Also n. 17 above.

²⁰ G(2), 10f; Lafenestre, 327, Lycéens. Photos: Laisac, 'He is using a collodion process I don't find very satisfactory.' He had in show portraits of Promayet, Champfleury, Baudelaire, Cuénot, Berlioz, Journet; 3 or 4 self-portraits; *Studio, Burial, Return, Wrestlers*, 4 landscapes near Paris, 9 or 10 from Franche-Comté.

²¹ Cour. (1), ii, 60f; 1855 Catalogue; GM, 136f; R, 132f.

²² Troubat, 108–10; Ch. (1), cxxxiii (1919), 533f; R, 134; GM, 137; G(2), 1f; G(3), 6 for Ch. (28 June '55), but G. makes it A. Gautier.

²³ Ch. *l.c.*, 535. GM, 139; R, 135f; N(4), 36–45. *L'Artiste*, xvi, no. 1, (2 Sept. 1855), 1ff (re-printed *Réalisme*, 270ff). R, 142f: two articles by J. Janin in the *Débats*.

²⁴ Ch. *l.c.* 535, 536; GM, 139f; R, 142; Troubat., 110; Cour. (1), i, 126f; Ch. says: 'He's like a cat dragging at its tail the saucepan of Realism' that 'the *polissons* have tied there.' As soon as he sees Realism getting bad fruits, he'll abandon it, 'free to pass as a reactionary'.

²⁵ Loudun, 139f; G(2), 2f; T. Gautier (1), 155f, and in *J. Officiel*: GM, 138; R, 138; Du Camp (3), 236. Register: *Archives nat.*, F21–519.

²⁶ *Journal*, 3 Aug. '55; G(2), 11f. 'I stayed there alone nearly an hour and discovered a master-piece in the rejected picture; I couldn't snatch myself from the sight. There has been enormous progress and yet that has made me admire his *Burial*.' He dined with Mercey and Mérimée 'The first thinks like me of Courbet; the second doesn't like Michelangelo.'

²⁷ R, 38f; Mantz: R, 137f.

²⁸ Baudelaire (2), 131f. Zoé: *Bull.*, xxiii, 4; xvii–xviii, 29f; *Cabinet*, 172, 180.

²⁹ R. 141.

³⁰ R, 142; GM, 140f. Found it 'a land of Cockaygne' (*Cocagne*).

³¹ *L'Olivier*, 484f; B, 85f.

³² Troubat, 112f; Ch. (1), (Oct.–Dec. 1919), 538; GM, 100f; R, 140.

³³ Amiel, 380; *Réalisme*, no. 3 (15 Jan '57). Buchon was an expert on cheese; he wrote *Les Frommages franc-comtois comparées à celles de La Gruyère* etc., 1869.

9. *Parisian Corruption and Forest Rutting* (1856–8)

¹ GM, 142.

² GM, 123f; R, 144f.

³ GM, 143; L(2), 70. Letter to Gueymard (painted as Robert le Diable) for a Saturday reading of a comedy by Desnoyers. 'The soirée will be very numerous and very animated. We dine at 6 at Andlers, then go up after to my studio,' *Bull.*, xxxi, 13f. Engravings in *L'Artiste*: R, 147.

⁴ R, 142.

⁵ Troubat, 113f; R, 143f GM, 140.

⁶ Silvestre gives list of works litho'd by Masson; Tab., 233. Attitude to classics: Cour. (1), i, 52f; David, Gros, Vernet: *ib.*, 52f. For Silvestre's hard-hitting unscrupulous character: Troubat, 97f. He became friend of Napoleon, later of Gambetta, at whose house he died during a meal.

⁷ R, 148. Silvestre describes C. in the usual way. 'He's obstinate and settles the discussion by mad laughs when he has nothing more to say. For long he's sought to prove to me he's made deep studies in literature, history, philosophy. I've recognised, without contradicting him, that he knows nothing. But he's endowed, like a woman, with a certain instinct, which is sometimes worth more than knowledge.' Stresses his accent, his body bent over an oakstick or vinestock, his long elegant hands, his night-wandering. Cour. (1), i, 28–30.

⁸ MB (2); L(2), 65–7. *Réalisme*: Tab., 232. His loves: Troubat, 97f; F(5), 9f. For moment is interested in spiritualist turning-table; compatriot throws table out of window when he isn't looking: Troubat, 115–17 (clearly a tale told by Ch).

[9] Also portraits of the Lauriers, A.P. (Promayet?), singer Gueymard; Marie Crocq *Woman with glove*; *Amazone*: GM, 142f; L(2), 170. Not Louise Colet, with whom Ch. was very intimate (Amandorine in his *Mascarade de la vie parisienne*); Ch. tells MB of an abortive visit to her with C. See *Metrop.* 113–15. Flowers: L(2), 63. He participated in a London show at Crystal Palace.

[10] *Rome*, no. 13; *Fitzwilliam*, 156f.

[11] L(2), 65; see *Rome*, no. 12 for various studies etc.; *Bull.*, xix, 1–10.

[12] R, 148f; *Robert, Bull.*, xxxi, 14; Salon: Tab., 234ff. At the Palais de l'Industrie, *ib.* 245f. For *Robert* further (painted 1855–6): *Metrop.*, 113. The opera in effect founded the romantic dance, Mayne, 148; it fascinated Degas (contrast of ghostly nuns of corruption and the audience). Silvestre, 278; Estignard, 159; R, 149; L(1), 66, (5), 62; GM, 143.

[13] R, 154–6; *Rome*, no. 12 again.

[14] *L'Artiste*, 20 Sept. '57, 34. For later critiques: *Bull.*, xix, 10–17; Cast., R, 157.

[15] About (1), 141–4, 147.

[16] Ch. (1), cxxxiii, 544; GM, 146f. Baudelaire: Troubat, 88, 110, 95. C. has no sense of reality, one cannot argue with him, 106.

[17] Cast. (2), i, 26–30; A, 33; R, 145f; R, 157–9. Critical changes: Larkin, 54f; de Goncourts, *Etudes d'Art*, 7; Cast. (2), i, 15.

[18] *Rome*, no. 13; R, 157–9. P. de Saint-Victor: material bodies without bodies, hips etc. About says he paints values directly, 'without groping, without transitions', but lacks finesse; all objects equal to him.

[19] Ch. (1), cxxxiii, 543.

[20] Troubat (3): his memories seem confused, treating C. as younger than he was. Cour. (1), i, 128–30. Bonvin, too strict, saw 'a Dubufe'. For A. Gautier: Gachet, 1–4, 8f; L(5), 64f. A. Gautier has seen T. Gautier. C. says he's been asked to sell *Quarry*; message to Promayet. Also the jokes are carried on: C. finds an *araignée maçonne*, and 'hideous monsters pullulating' in the blue sea scare Gachet from bathing: letter of Dr Tailhardat, *ib.* 4.

[21] R, 159–62; GM, 147–9; Toubat (1), 121f. *Revue des Deux Mondes* (15 Aug. '57), 864–70. More works: GM, 150. Statue of C. by Lebœuf, who had had a hard life; C. painted him in '59. L(2), 84; *Bull.*, xvi, 8f; see also n. 5 ch. 12 here.

[22] *L'Olivier*, 490f; B, 88–90.

[23] Ch. (1), cxxxiii, 545. Troubat speaks of Bruyas walking arm in arm with Ch. to concert in Champs Elysées: GM, 149.

[24] R, 149; *Olivier*, 491f; B, 91; GM, 150. *Bull.*, xxxi, 12f—for Gautier, Gachet, 4f. Letter to Mme Joute, 11 Dec. '56 (Cat. Vente Dupont): 'I believe she's undertaken to kill me off . . .' *Bull.*, xvii–xviii, 20n. In 1857: a gouache of Jongkind.

[25] Hefting, 63.

[26] R, 144.

[27] JL (1), 7f.

[28] Chevalier, 20.

[29] G(1), 2.

[30] *Ib.*, 3f. Jean-Baptiste-Eugène-César.

[31] *Ib.*, 6–8, with more details. He had been living at home with his family, rue d'Assas. The Marquis was Messager d'État.

[32] *L'Olivier*, 475; B, 59. Gautier: Gachet, 5f. Also matter of a violin lent to Promayet, who is in Russia. Monet and Gautier: J. Isaacs on, *Monet: Le Déjeuner* (1972), 91–3.

[33] *Bull.*, ii, 6f; Proudhon, *Corresp.* 4 June '55; 1858, on to 31 Oct. '64. He has broad brow, strong nose, beard. R, 163; GM, 153.

[34] Ch. (2), 200f, cf. 203; names changed.

[35] Voss (1); R, 162–5. Becker, genre-painter, born Dittelsheim near Worms, 1810; died Frankfort, 1872.

[36] 21 Dec. '58: R, 163.

37 *Echo littéraire illustré*, 1 May 1892; R, 166–8. Paints: terre d'ambre ou de cassel.

38 GM, 150f; *Rome*, no. 14. A note (by Pata) tells how it was entitled *The Lady with Sherbet* and shown at Trocadéro (doubtless Pavilion de l'Alma) without signature; signed 1877 at same time as *Wounded Man*, which also belonged to Baudry, who probably came to visit C. in exile with the pictures to be signed. From 1889 Juliette pestered him for it, saying how much C. loved it and she'd have no rest till it joined the others that at her death would go to the State; he ended by giving in (23 May '90). Voss (2), 18–20; R, 174, 255, 336; Estignard, 180; L(2), 76, (5), 355; Duret, 76, pl. 23.

39 Voss (1), 10f. For Goebel (born 1821) much influenced in *Poor Folk* by *Stonebreakers*, *ib*. 11; R. mis-spells Lunteschütz: L(2), 77f.

40 Cour. (1), ii, 87–9.

41 *Ib*. ii, 89–94; Delestre (2), 12; Troubat (1), 167f; R, 182ff; *Archives art. et litt*., i (1899–1900), 25. C. says it cost 3000–4000 fr. getting the elements of *Stag Battle* together. Three pictures sold to dealer Detrimont of rue Lafitte.

42 N (1), figs. 16f; *Cerf forcé* bought by Marseille: R, 188.

10. *Difficult Transition* (1859–62)

1 Leboeuf in return for portrait did statuette of C. in painting smock: GM, 154; also on *View of Ornans*.

2 Tab., 259; letter on Promayet's violin (5 May '59): Gachet, 6.

3 Schanne, 229; R, 179f; GM, 154f. Boudin: N(4), 82–6. Four pictures at Honfleur.

4 Jean-Aubry, 39.

5 Schanne, 230f; R, 110; Cour. (1), i, 159.

6 Cour. (1), i, 134.

7 L(2), 79f; GM, 156, pl. 35; R, 176. Drawings by C.: R, 168.

8 Astruc, 371–99; Cour. (1), i, 137–40; R, 169. Waistcoat: Cour. (1), i, 140f.

9 Cour. (1), i, 141f.

10 Tab., 271.

11 R, 177f.

12 Also *Woman with Mirror*.

13 Bauzon, 238; father, Just-Fortuné Chenez. Wreck: L(2), 82. A 70f, citing Léger on Deaths-head at bottom of water: which he relates to expedition to Italy. Fernier denies the attribution on grounds of style. (Note skull in *Studio*.)

14 G(1), 8f. The franc-comtois Firmin Maillard does not report her at the Fête; he is the most detailed reporter. Child born 82 rue de l'Ecole-de-Médecine (close to her brother); her own address, 17 rue Malaquais, at Hôtel de la Bazinière (? domicile de complaisance).

15 F(8), 1–3; also his restless bohemian existence; atheist, he was fascinated by religious apparatus in his pictures. His works: *Bull*., vi, 7; xxxvi, 7. Baudelaire on him, 1859: *Bull*., xvi, 6; Cast. in 1875, *ib*. 4, and Privat, 1881, *ib*. 5. Chenavard at Bougival this year: G(3), 7; presents C. to Mme Jaubert, 7f.

16 GM, 158; Delestre (2). Astruc and Ch. in 1860: R, 181.

17 Cast. MS: Cour. (1), i, 142–6; GM, 160. Merlet and Fournel (1): Cour. For Cast., Badt, 238 (1), ii, 301. Letter to Ch., Oct. '60: Delestre (2), 6–10; to Gautier, 7 Nov., *ib*., 10–12.

18 R, 217f; GM, 153f saw it as wine-warehouse.

19 Tab., 280f; R, 189f; *Bull*., xxvii, 9f. Cast. in *Monde Illustré*, viii, 343ff; R, 190.

20 Ch. (1), cxxxiii, 704; Box 1; GM, 159f.

21 Thoré (1), i, 74 (1870).

22 *Bull*., xx, 20; R, 188f; Delestre (2), 13f: is sending on stereoscope and 60 photos by diligence; will arrive in few days; gives instruction for use. A. Bartet has given him a little enamelled Louis

XV watch. *Woman with Parrot: Rome*, no. 16, note delicacy of hands; Estignard, 178. Still lifes with flowers: *Rome*, p. 88.

[23] GM, 161; L(2), 85; R, 191; GBA, xi, 547; ix, 323. Antwerp: A. Siret, GBA, 1860; Mantz, GBA, xi (1861), 182. Metz diploma: *Bull.*, xxvii, 13.

[24] GM, 161f; R, 193–7 (list of students); *Bull.*, xxvii, 10–12.

[25] Cast. (7); Cour. (1), ii, 199–222. Song: 'Forward the 22nd . . .'

[26] N(4), 34–6; Box 3; Cour. (1), ii, 204–7; R, 86–8. Cf. his formulations in *Précurseur d'Anvers*, 22 Aug. '61: R, 191.

[27] Add to last note Cour. (1), ii, 202f; Cast. wrote in *Siècle*. There was also a horse, a buck (stuffed?), spavined nag held by groom.

[28] *Ib.* Chesnau in *Opinion Nationale* said the Manifesto was 'nebulous, menacing, and of a somewhat ridiculous transcendentalism'; realism continued romanticism. See L(3) for caricatures: *Album Caricatural*, Salon de 1861: man blacks eye of one who calls him Courbet. Cham, Feb. '62, ghastly crippled man, a patient leaving an orthopaedist, gets job as model with C.

[29] Wey; Cour. (1), i, 193. He says the public found the Jura rocks plasterwalls, etc.; forests 'too redoutable by their solitude'.

[30] Schanne, 296; GM, 6of.

[31] Cour. (1), i, 153: Andler in morning, Laveur in evening: scarcely ever a change in programme.

[32] Delvau, 105, lists of frequenters; R, 176. 'All the Parisian schools, the realists and the fantasists, the Ingrists and the colourists . . .': 106; C. among 'pupils of Bougival', 107; Pelloquet, 114f; Desnoyers, 116.

[33] Box 1; GM, 163.

[34] GM, 163f; R, 196f. Statue: F(15), 2f. Upperclass drunks broke it in 1909.

[35] Ste-Beuve, *Corresp.* (1877), i, 189f; GM, 164; Cour. (1), i, 163f. Exposition at Besançon, 30 March–1 June '62, criticism by A. Barthet: *Bull.*, xxx, 15.

[36] GM, 165f; Ch. (5), 266f; Ch. (1), cxxxiii, 708.

[37] Chevalier. C. knew H. well, sends best wishes to his wife.

[38] L(2), 150; GM, 166; Cour. (1), i, 165; Revue de Saintonge et d'Aunis, *Bull. Soc. d'Archives hist.* (Saintes), xxxviii, no. 5 (Aug. 1919), 295; Bonniot (1), for full and detailed account of all the persons and events.

[39] Box 3; Cour. (1), i, 165g; G. 167. For a year or so he had been having an affair with Léontine R. (Rebiquet or Repiquet?), an exuberant rowdy girl (probably a *comédienne*), who gave him much trouble in his jealous fits. A letter dated 4 June Paris from her: 'Fat dog [*gros chien*], you may think it's *gentil*, but you've been away five days and you haven't yet written to me.' She threatens to come to Saintes unless he replies in two days. 'I assure you it isn't necessary to torment me because I love you, besides you know I'm very *méchante* once I'm touched on a sore point, so be *gentil*.' Two drafts of replies to her were kept by Baudry. 'I and my friend have remained prostrated and ill during our voyage, considering the unmentionable brutality of your conduct on Saturday evening; we'd never yet seen anything like it in our life.' He describes her with her 'look that's always oblique and furtive like a scared ostrich, with that dead-calf's head and that white chilly eye with the cowardly and cruel expression of a leashed wild animal. . . . Your treacheries are too childish.' He is jealous of one Tournachon, whom he later said had taken his girl from him. She seems a Jewess as he says that she proposes to come and kiss him 'like Judas who is of your race.' He describes how he has found her bedroom in disorder, and how one night he felt cold in his head and the *foulard* she gave him wasn't his, but fitted someone with a smaller head. At the same time he can't help boasting about the wonderful time he is having, surrounded with charming friends and so on—unlike the deadening time, *temps de bagne abrutissant*, he has just spent with her. In the second letter he says, 'You know how long I've been eagerly looking for the chance to get rid of you.' Apparently she wanted him to take her to the international exhibition in London; he says that Tournachon can do it. Bonniot (1) ch. 12.

40 Box 3; Duret (2), 56; Bonniot (1) Ch. 45.

41 Box 3; Cour. (1), i, 166.

42 Bonniot, esp. (6) & (7).

43 Box 3; Duret (2), 59; GM, 168. Corot: Bonniot (1), ch. 15. He was charmed: 'These places will be my Elysian Fields. When I end my life, it's here that my poor shade will come to roam; it will be my eternal promenade.'

44 Cast. MS; Cour. (1), i, 167f; Mestreau the deputy. flowers: Bonniot (5).

45 Box 1; GM, 169f. Thaumiaux. At Port-B. 'les musiques de Dasque et de Brossard'.

46 L(2), 92f; *Independent de la Charante-Inf.* 21 Aug. & 2 Sept. '62; Thaumiaux. Failure of Poulot-Malessis: Bonniot (1) Ch. 18.

47 To Cast. (Box 1) 16 Aug. '62; GM, 170. Perhaps Carjat made the litho after a successful photo. C.'s address: Saintes, vue Porte-Aiguières.

48 *Rome*, no. 17: she married 1888, died Paris 1918. She visited him in jail; she offered him a small panel of Flowers (Mus. Ornans). Her mother is the *Woman in the Black Hat*. He speaks of a *dame superbe* with whom he is in love on 23 August; Riat says he was held by the fine eyes of a *hotelière* (hostess) 'whose debt-pressed condition he for a moment relieved.' Probably she was Mme Borreau, who kept with her husband Jules a shop of textiles and confections for ladies; Duret in his old age mentioned that 'her charms had exerted their influence' on Courbet. L'*Indépendant* of 13 September mentioned of the B. house in 13 rue Porte-Aiguières; *Liquidation pour cause de cession d'affaires*. A sale was to start on the 16th. Rumours of the family's departure went round, but in the paper on 27 Nov. Jules announced that he wasn't going and his shop would be found full of 'a large assortment of novelties of all kinds at exceptional prices,' Did Courbet come to the B. rescue? It seems likely. Bonniot (1) ch. 18. Also chs. 30 and 46 (relations later in Paris); 'It's love that leads me,' to Isabey, Bonniot 181.

49 Box 1; Cour. (1) i, 172–4; R, 102–4; GM, 171. See Bonniot (a) chs. 29–32. Auguin must have been talking a lot in the same vein, leading to an exhortatory address to C. in the L'*Indépendant*; how far he was directly responsible is not clear. A letter of his, 19 May 1863, seems to show a persisting cordiality. He may have been actuated by jealousy: see repercussions at the Saintes show and Baudry's riposte, chs. 35–6.

50 GM, 171f; R, 200. Duret described the show. L(2), 93–5, anecdote of three peasants. Notices: Anon (1). Pradelles: *Bull.*, xxxvii, 20. Ch. this year and following: Troubat, 175ff.

11. *Drunken Priests and Lesbians* (1863–4)

1 R, 201; GM, 173; L(2), 96f.

2 GM, 175; R, 209; Bonniot; *Bull.*, xxxiv–xxxv, 16f. The woman: Poulot's wife. When Didier left parish, peasants threw small stones (*cailloux*); he shouted, '*Cailloutez*, you are all cuckolds.' The inspiration of the picture was an event in which he himself took part. Actors and actresses, whom he knew at the Café des Variétés, had reached Saintes and he asked them to Rochemond, where after a meal he proposed a donkey procession. He had been taken up with a plump blonde and allotted her the prettiest donkey, 'a little rose-grey Aliborn, the one that sags under the Curé Doyen's weight in the *Return from the Conference*,' Baudry recalled in 1883, Courbet himself had the formidable Balthazar. Somewhat tipsy and preoccupied with his blonde, he fell on his back, spraining a finger and bruising the base of his femur. Rumours of an apopleptic fit reached Paris and Dr H. Thulié, alienist (who had taken part in founding *le Réalisme*), declared that from this date Courbet's decline as artist began: Bonniot (1) ch. 19. On the *Return* Bonniot, chs. 21–2.

3 R, 203f.

4 R, 205; Thaumiaux, 15.

5 GM, 176; for various copies etc. F(17).

6 Cour. (1), ii, 95. He speaks of the emperor's last-year insult.

⁷ L(2), 98; he wants basic construction to be left to his friend C. Lapoir of Ornans; statue will be cast, end of Sept. 'One would like to see an enormous repast in the Iles-Basses.' Collaborating with Proudhon: hence delays in return.

⁸ L(3). Note this year 1863 Manet's *Déjeuner* caused a vast uproar; this must have affected him with a sense of losing his grip and failing to be the prime enemy of the establishment. For attacks on Manet in 1865: N(4), 81f; JL (1); Zola's *L'Œuvre*, etc. For the Salon: Bonniot (1) ch. 42.

⁹ F(17). 21 April '67; Box 1; GM, 177; more details R, 207.

¹⁰ Thoré, i, 382, 417f, 420. GM, 177. Attacks: R, 205f. Desnoyers thought it his liveliest work.

¹¹ Ch. (1), cxxxiii, 705f; GM, 117f; Boyé (2), 8; R, 207.

¹² Ch. (1), 706f.

¹³ *Ib.*, 707; also *Bull.*, xii, 8f.

¹⁴ R, 207; Boyé (2), 8f. R, 217f on Ch.'s self-discontent.

¹⁵ GM, 179; R, 206. He admitted the drawing a bit slack; in *Nord* presented him as a Velasquez of the People.

¹⁶ GM, 178.

¹⁷ R, 208f; L(2), 98–101. Three Curé sketches: L(2), 98–101. Letter on work with Proudhon: GM, 180; R, 208 (undated). Holiday: *Bull.*, ix, 8.

¹⁸ Proudhon (8), 279f; GM, 181.

¹⁹ Woodcock, 257f; to Bergmann and to Chaudey.

²⁰ Cour (i), ii, 63; goes on to argue there are different publics: a point true enough of the existing situation, but he forgets his hope of a mass-audience. Two letters to P., May & June '63: *Bull.* xii, 5f. S, 169.

²¹ R, 209; *Bull.*, xxix, 19–21. Aphorisms: *Bull.*, xxii, 1–7 (a few omitted e.g. on Communes; see those cited elsewhere on Sleep, Love, Art).

²² L(2), 107; GM, 158. He had taken his mother's name: died 1899; she, 1897. Photo and study in L(2).

²³ Ch. (1), cxxxiii, 707f; R, 214f; GM, 186. Ch. says satire of priests is in the French spirit, but on epic scale; let C. return to landscape and domestic themes, and beware of symbolism and satire.

²⁴ To Cast. 18 Jan. '64; Box 1; Cour. (1), ii, 96–8; GM, 186f; R, 215f. Asks how P.'s book is going. Ch. to MB: Troubat, 177.

²⁵ Cour. (1), ii, 95f; R, 217; GM, 189. Pouchon, see also F. in *Bull.*, xliv; L(2), 174.

²⁶ F(6). He died 1882.

²⁷ Boyé (2), 9.

²⁸ R, 216; Cour. (1), i, 189f. Replica: F. in *Bull.*, xlv; versions, L(2), 102.

²⁹ Thoré, ii, 67f; GM, 188; R, 26. *La Réflexion*; *Rome*, no. 21, bought Douai 1870; copy the same size and slightly smaller version. So he rather prized the work.

³⁰ *Femme à la Vague*: *Metrop.*, 130f. Identity of models: R, 264f; *Metrop.* Variants: L(2), 103 (*ib.*, 102, *Femme au Chat*); also *Rome*, no. 30 (Waking); many studies, variants etc. (Coll. Reinhart, Winterthur, Mesdag Mus., Coll. Daber, Birmingham etc.) Meier-Graefe (1), 194f.; (2), 52. For *Woman with Wave*; R, 264 sees her as *Woman with Parrot*; MacOrlan, 42; Fontainas 83; L (2), 138 & 221; Estignard, 166; Lemonnier, pl. 3. For local opinion: V. de Jankovitz in *Annales Fr. Comté*, ii, 143–7, attacks realism as materialism denying the soul and accepting only tangible things; C. likes only 'what is most ordinary in nature'. Cour. (1), i, 190f, from Barbizon; refs. to Cabanel on jury. In general: Marcel; L(2), 115f; conventional account, Focillon (Cour. (1), i, 107–9); Herman for Millet's depth; Durbé, 20–2 etc.

³¹ R, 17. Works: GM, 188f.

³² Boyé (2), 9f. Letter 25 Oct. says he went to Pontarlier and Mortiau (for a doctor's wedding); Claudet, 8–12; Cour. (1), i, 197–202; L(2), 106f (also for studio). R, 218f; GM, 190–2. For Claudet: Box 4; GM, 192; L(2), 105. Claudet says he kept F.C. habit of 6 hours at the table; 'He who pours for drinking . . .'; he spoke of everything. 'In art he had theories that make classics go

bald; in politics he went as far as he could in wicked hits; when one got on to religion, he knocked his adversary down with the *Curés*.'

³³ Claudet, 13; Cour. (1), i, 202f. Ch. to MB, 29 Oct. 1864: Troubat, 177–9, GM, 192; Cf. (1) cxxxiii, 709: 'he should forget saving the world by his painting.'

³⁴ GK; Cour. (1), i, 203f. 'Do you want me *foutre la paix?*'

³⁵ L(2), 110f; Cour. (1), ii, 98f; GM, 193–6.C. may well have been affected by the sound his own name (suggesting to bend or bow) and have resolved not to bend. Hugo dropped the correspondence on the advice of Auguste Vacquerie: Bonniot, GBA Oct. 1972.

³⁶ *Revue de Paris* (1864), 28ff; JL (2); L(2), 110f.

³⁷ L(2), 112; L(7), 359.

³⁸ *Rome*, no. 18; Boyé (2), 10 (letter to Ch., 11 March '65) for a second portrait. Also medallion. L(2), 104f. Campagnonnage: Bruhat, 73ff, 203f.

³⁹ Gours: *Rome*, no. 19. Cafés: L(2), 105; talk, *ib.*, 103f. The cascade falls in three superimposed basins. A Salins *industriel*, Alfred Bouvet, wanted the scene painted; he also bought the *Fort de Joux*: Toubin. *La Roche Pourrie*: L(2), 103.

⁴⁰ *Rome*, no. 20.

⁴¹ Cour. (1), ii, 38–40.

⁴² *Ib*. 36–8. He writes *chair* for *chère*.

⁴³ GM, 192; L(2), 105f; Claudet.

⁴⁴ *Bull*., xxi, 6f

⁴⁵ Box 1; GM, 196; he had just painted Mme Bouvet's three-year-old daughter. Medallion: *Bull*., xxxvi, 3.

⁴⁶ *Bull*. vi, 13. This year 1864 T. Sylvestre published *La Conspiration des Quarantes*, attack on corrupt Academy, seeks to show 'that Letters, Arts and Sciences are stifled by the Empire and that it's impossible for human reason to live at peace with Power'.

12. *Proudhon's Death* (1865–6)

¹ Box 1; GM, 195f; Cour. (1), ii, 102–4; L(2), 112f says he heard 21 Jan. For P.'s face: L(14), 4; *Bull*., ii, 4; he asked Etex to take his plaster bust from the 1850–1 Salon. C.'s Ps says: 'You haven't told me if you saw him before he died.' MB used to read his family some pages of P., always ending with words, 'If we have the misfortune to lose P, we are lost.' (Cf. his father reading prayers etc.) Letter of C. to Luquet: R, 220 (also asking him to get back *Cerf à l'eau*).

² Droz, 255–7. Complains that Nefftzer, director of the *Temps*, in article of 20 Jan., didn't do P. justice: L(2), 113.

³ GM, 61; Box 1.

⁴ *Rome*, no. 58 (Cath. died 1947, aged 97: L(14)—for Bourson, *ib*. 5, 8; R, 256: son of director of *Moniteur belge*). F(16); Ecalle; Fry.

⁵ L(14), 7f; *Rome*, no. 25; GM, 198; R, 224f; P. Mantz, GBA xvii, 517; Challemel-Lacour, *Rev. mod*., 95; C. de. Mouy, *Rev. franc*., 197. L. Avray notes public repulsion. Claretie: *L'Artiste* (1865), i, 415. *Annales F.C.* (1865), 129–31 cites C.'s manifesto and attacks him. Oak: N(1), 213; Cat. G.C. (Philadelphia Mus. of Art, Mus. of Fine Arts, Boston 1959–60, cat. no. 44); *Mag. pitt*., xviii (1850), 220. Statue: *Annales F.C.*, iv (1865), 217f. (criticism of Lebœuf, 220). Note also *Oak of Apremont* by T. Rousseau 1852 (Durbé, pl. 8). *Chasseur*: Kane. Mill: *Mus. Notes* (Mus. of Art Rhode Is. School of Design) iv, no. 5 (May 1946), 2f; *Bull*., xxxvi, 3. For cuts: Larkin, 43; Laclotte, figs. ix–x; Geffroy, *Rev. des Deux Mondes*, ix (1851), 930; Ch. (5), 251. Tribute to the *Oak* by N. de Staël (*Bull*. xlvii, 21f): 'There is a logic in Courbet that supports all the illogicalities . . .' 1954.

⁶ L(14), 11; A, pl. xx. History of P. painting: L(14), 11f. Other portraits, *ib*., 8f; *Rome*, no. 25. Letter to Carjat: R, 223.

⁷ *Rome*, no. 25.

⁸ *Rome*, nos. 22–3; GM, 199. Letter: R, 222 on various works. Photos: F(1), nos. 37f, 23f.

[9] GM, 199f; R, 221; Bauzon, 238f; Cour. (1), ii, 102 (dating letter Nov.). At show of B.A. at Besançon, 1865, C. had four studies of Ornans landscape: *Ann. F.C.*, iii (1865), 301f sees 'no choice or grace of subjects'. Says of *Plaisir-fontaine*, 'a very ungrateful and badly chosen model, in our opinion, but marvellously rendered'. In *Trellis*, though the trellis is at an angle to the girl, C. draws flowers out so as to suggest girl and flowers are on the same plane; this makes the flowers seem alive, bursting out as if to embrace her.

[10] Ch. (1), cxxxiii, 709f; GM, 198f; R, 223f; Troubat, 179–81. Funeral of Troyon, 21 March '65: G(3), 8. Not last letter as GM, 199, thinks: Boyé (2), 10. Torso: *Metrop.*, 120; MacOrlan, pl. 29; Léger (5), 196. For the bird in *Waking*: GM, 213.

[11] Bauzon, 239; GM, 201. All his former pupils have come to invite him to a dinner.

[12] Cour. (1), ii, 105, June '65; R, 227f; Box 1. Also about Fontainebleau races; painting.

[13] Champier, 493f; GM, 182.

[14] Proudhon (8); Max Raphael; Aragon; Larkin (2), 37–62; N(4), 49–53; R, 209–14; Cour. (1), i, 175–82.

[15] *Mes Haines* (1913 ed.), 31–9; GM, 185f; JL (1); Larkin (2), 61f. Zola's Letter to M. le Blond, *c.* 1902.

[16] Box 1; GM, 62.

[17] R, 218f; GM, 202 for works. Colonna: *Bull.*, xiii, 11; Cuénot, *Bull.*, xxiii, 9f: details of pictures, going to write to Fajon; boasts; abuse of Frond. *Bull.*, xxiii, for portraits of Nodlers and Mlle Aubé.

[18] *Rome*, no. 27; Bulls., xxiii & xxxii; *Connaissance des Arts*, no. 149 (July 1864), 30–3; *Bull.*, xxii, 15; L(2), 116f, citing Lermercier de Neuville, *Souvenirs*. Thoré asks, 'Isn't the *Stonebreakers* of C. an allegory of work, rough, unproductive, brutalising? The ancient allegories, stereotyped today, have all their origin in living realities, very significant at the time, but now incomprehensible.' L(2), 219f.

[19] GM, 203 (letter owned by Rewald); R, 228. Cf. letter to Sensier, Sept. R, 228 (GM gives it as to the concierge).

[20] Bénédite (2), 23f (to Fantin-Latour); GM, 204.

[21] R, 219 for portraits. Jo bore Whistler a son. For seascapes: Thoré; L(2), 219. *Metrop.*, 128 for copies etc. of Jo and for suggestion it is Johanne Pfeiffer. L(2), 120. After Whistler's death Jo is said to have set up as dealer and been jailed for selling his works as Raphael's: Hoppe, 80f. The three girls: *Bull.*, vi, 12f; v. 19; A. Ch. at Fantaisies-parisiennes: Troubat, 174.

[22] Cast. Box 1; R, 231f; GM, 205.

[23] GM, 205. R, 231f makes it as to father, as seems correct; requests for work.

[24] R, 232: same letter to family.

[25] GM, 205; *L'Olivier*, 492–4; B, 93–5; R, 229f, 232f.

[26] GM, 207.

[27] Ideville: Cour. (1), i, 212–14. Ideville adds comment as to socialism cited earlier.

[28] *Bull.*, xv, 13f (MS of *Notice sur la vie et les œuvres du peintre C. Dutilleux by Albert Dubuisson*).

[29] *Head of Roedeer*, 1866 (Bayonne): F(1), no. 84 cf. no. 86.

[30] GM, 206; study with arms at side, *Bull.*, xxxix, 15. Manet did a *Woman with Parrot* (1866) in Salon 1868 (*Metrop.*) For Salon 1866: Tab., 181f.

[31] Cour. (1), i, 214f. Jeanne Duval was at first with Baudelaire in *Studio* (but he was taking no notice of her). *Siesta* has both sexes, but apart and asleep.

[32] J. M. Haswell, *The Story of the Life of Napoleon III*, (pt. II, the same story as told by Imperial Caricatures) preface dated 1871: of illustrations, pages 60, 51, 50, 53, 21 and 16, 45; cf. Daumier: Larkin (1), 180.

[33] Cour. (1), i, 215–22; Thoré-Burger Salon de 1866; L(2), 73. Prometheus: Troubat, 118, attributes it to influence of Dr Dupré who gave many ideas to C.

[34] R, 237; GBA (1866), xx, 504, 510; *Correspondant*, 195; *Presse*, 10 June; Challemel-Lacour, *Rev. mod.*, 534; de Sault, *Temps*, 9 & 18 May '66.

[35] Du Camp, *Rev. Deux Mondes* (1866), 511ff; *Les B.A. à l'Exp. Univ.* (1867), 219f. Further R, 237f, also the *Curés* in New York.

[36] Cast. (2), i, 238. Tales: Cour, (1), i, 223; R, 240. Reactions: L. Halévy (*Carnets* 1935: 11 May 1866) and L. Enault in *Rev. illustré des eaux minérales* etc. 27 May '66, praises *Covert*, finds *Woman with Parrot* painted finely in parts but indecent, 'Let's move on, this bitch makes me regret the roe-deers' (*Bull.*, xxxv, 5). C. Beauquier, *Rev. litt. de la FC* (1 Aug. '66)): *Bull.*, xxxv, 3f, on lithos.

[37] Thoré, *Salon de 1866*; Cour. (1), i, 215–22; Thoré, ii, 278 (this has his praise of Fourier, Proudhon, Courbet). He thinks colour decides the 1866 success. C. and sea: Cour. (1), i, 218f.

[38] R, 222f; Cour. (1), i, 215; GM, 207. For Thoré's opinion of Baudry: N(4), 14. To Cuénot, about pictures and the *Burial* 'the statement of the principles of realism,' etc.: R, 236. Letter to parents: *Bull.*, xxiii, 11.

[39] R, 239; Marcel, 77f, his comments on critics who see in background of his *Gleaners* 'the guillotines of '93': 75. Thoré on C. and Millet: N(4), 54–6; see Millet's letter to him, *ib.*, 56–9: 'It's not so much the things represented that create the beautiful and the need one has to represent them; the need itself creates the degree of power with which the task was carried out.'

[40] Cour. (1), i, 222f.

[41] C. was sure de N. was keeping the *Woman* for himself: his letters, 22 March to Alfred Stevens, 6 April to Cuénot; Cast. in *Liberté*, 13 May: R, 241; GM, 208.

[42] GM, 208f; Box 1; R, 241f. Victor Frond was editor of *Panthéon des Illustrations françaises au 19e siècle*.

[43] K.B. ended with 6 Courbets (3 hunts, nude of '66, two done to order). *Bull.*, xxxiii–xxxiv, 16; Cour. (1), i, 191–3 (L. Descaves). Auriant for his mistress Jeanne de Tourney, *la Dame aux violettes*. His favourite author was G. Feydeau (who wrote *Fanny*). *Bull.*, xxxii, 13 (photo); K.B. and Ste-Beuve, Troubat, 119f.

[44] *Bull.*, xxxv, 4; see here n. 36. *Sleepers*: L(2), 118–20.

[45] M.du Camp (2), ii, 263f; Cour. (1), i, 194–6. E. de Goncourt, 29 June '89, says village-church under snow; L says chateau, (2), 115f; GM, 214f. Auction at his bankruptcy, Jan. '68; *Sleepers* and genitals-picture sold separately.

[46] Barnes Foundation. Seems first of his erotica. F(1), no. 46.

[47] Cour. (1), ii, 106.

[48] Works: R, 245–7; *Preparations* (or *Bride at her Toilet*), Smith Coll., Mus. of Art, Northampton, USA: F(1), no. 15; *Bull.*, xvi, 7–9 (J. Seznac), also *Bull.*, xxv–xxvi, 1954–5 of Smith Coll. Mus. (Mass.); N(3). Suggestion again of Velasquez as basis: *Las Meninas* and the *Spinners*. Also rel. to popular prints: N(1), 213. Letter towards Aug., R, 241f. *Siesta*: R, 247f.

[49] Box 3; R, 242–4; GM, 216.

[50] Works: GM, 211; Oct. letter to Luquet: R, 244. *Rome*, no. 29, *Snowscape with Boar*, 1866.

[51] Box 4; GM, 212f.

13. *Towards a New Struggle* (1867–9)

[1] *L'Olivier*, 497; B, 103; R, 248; GM, 215f; details of work for show; *Hallali*. In '67 Ingres died; Manet had his own show; T. Rousseau showed at Cercle de la rue de Choiseul.

[2] Box 1; GM, 216.

[3] Written 21 April '67; Box 1; GM, 217. Makes joke on Napoleon, 'If he insists on inaugurating, he must make a speech on the Luxembourg; for such inaugurations without speeches annoy the folk of Maisières and Ornans.'

[4] *Rome*, no. 32. *Givre*: Walters Art Gall., Balitmore. Besançon has smaller landscape with some figures. Cast. and snow: Cour. (1), ii, 61.

[5] *Rome*, no. 33. Six *Remises* in 1882 show. See *Rome* for details. *Woman with Jewels*: L(2), 127.

[6] As n. 4 above; Cour. (1) ii, 62f, advice on painting. 'Seek the most deep *teinte*, lay on with knife or brush. It will probably show no detail in its *obscurité*. Then attack by gradations the less

intense nuances, trying to put them in their place, then the half-*teintes*; finally you won't have more to do than make *les clairs* glow. There are far less of them than the romantics put in. Your work will grow lighter all of a sudden if you've got the right feeling and the lights seized in midflight will be placed at their true point.'

[7] B, 104f; GM, 217f; estimates Bruyas now has works worth 100,000 fr. R, 248–50 Expos. Univ. opens 1 April: L(2), 131. Daumier's cartoon: Many royal figures present; C. ignores all official events. Larkin (1), 172; Tab., 420.

[8] *L'Olivier*, 499f; B, 100f; R, 251f; GM, 218. 'I've insured for 600,000 fr., I wanted a million' etc.

[9] *La Lune*, iii, no. 66, 9 June '67; GM, 218.

[10] F(14) for lists etc; two letters to P. Bracquemond, *Bull.*, xxvi, 1. GM, 219. Silvestre: *Figaro*, 21 April. Renoir at the show: *Bull.*, xxxix, 6.

[11] Clésinger had a separate show; also Manet: Tab. 416. Sisters: G(1), 10; R, 257; they were told to make up *caisse* every two days.

[12] F(14), 4–7.

[13] R, 255. Notices, *Temps*, 22 June. Visit by E. Monteil: R, 255f. Good notice of *Halali*: J. Buisson, *Rev. de Toulouse et du Midi*: Cour. (1), i, 224f.

[14] Box 1; GM, 220; mentions the altered *Proudhon*.

[15] Box 1; GM, 220.

[16] GM, 221; R, 257f; Goncourts, *Journal*, iii, 164; *Bull.*, xii, 8 (Ch.). Portrait of A. Gautier this year.

[17] Bonniot (3); he announces the age of self-service. L(2), 134–40; GM, 221f. Interview: Letter to Duret (1918, 140f).

[18] Bonniot (3); L(2), 134–7; engravings by E. Bellot. See Bonniot for the characters; also Aragon. Reception of boko: Bonniot, *Bull.*, xxxviii, 22ff; Zola in *L'Evénement illustré*, 5 May, suggests Halles centrales instead of stations, *ib.* 24.

[19] Unidentified newspaper cuttings, Box 4; Cour. (1), i, 227f; GM, 221.

[20] *Rev. litt. de la F.C.* The show is to be permanent to get back the 5000 fr.

[21] F(14), 7f. C. complains of guardians, one drinks too much beer, one too much brandy; they neglect to take addresses of collectors: R, 258. Dec. letter about return of pictures: R, 258.

[22] Box 1; R, 257; G(1), 9f; GM, 223f.

[23] See n. 45 last chapter. *Jeune baigneuse*, 3,000; *Chevreuil chassé aux écartes*, 1800; *Hallali*, 4000; *Fox*, 3400. Three letters from collectors about this time: Cour. (1), i, 228–30 (one of Pontarlier).

[24] *L'Olivier*, 501f; B, 110f; Cour. (1), ii, 110; R, 258.

[25] R, 262, 257. Exception: J. Meyer in *History of Fr. Painting*, 1866–7, criticised him for petrified forms, angular, exaggerated.

[26] R, 262f. Pamphlet: *Une election au Grand-Duché de Gérolstein*. Sent *Beggar's Alms* to Le Havre.

[27] Thoré (1), ii, 490; R, 260; L(3), 80–2; L(2), 138; L(5), 122. Attacks: add R, 260f; Perraut a member of the Institute; Zola didn't like the work: *Bull.*, xl, 15.

[28] *J. Officiel*, 11 May '68; Cour. (1), ii, 108.

[29] Drawing: Schapiro, 166; *Courbet, Album autographique*, 1868; Duret, 138.

[30] Nicholson, 74f.

[31] *Lundi soir*, Cour. (1), ii, 108f. Buyer: Boucicault, house of Bon Marché, rue du Bac, 'The famous dame Cassin, picture-collector', complimented; he replied, 'Courage, all goes well.'

[32] Manet: Cour. (1), ii, 61f (dice image); R. 146f. Juliette said that he went to a show of Manet's: 'I wouldn't like to meet this lad, who is sympathetic hard-working, and who struggles to arrive; I'd be obliged to tell him I understand nothing of his painting, and I don't want to be disagreeable to him.' Manet on *Burial*: *Bull.*, xxxvii, 22; Holleman, for his drawings of C. For card-comparison (Daumier, Cast., Cézanne, C.): Badt, 114f; cf. Zola on Épinal sheets, *Mes Haines* (Manet).

[33] GM, 325; *Bull.*, xxxix, 5. Zoé: G(1), 12; CIuseret: *Bull.*, xxxi, 5.

[34] *Rome*, no. 34 etc. Lemonnier (2), 94. Letter: *Bull.*, xxxi, 15f. 'C'est du sur-Velasquez.'

[35] Boyé (2), 8 (*Bull.*, xii); *La Source, Metrop.*, 121: her bottom is the Source of Life.

[36] Box 1; GM, 62f.

[37] F(17); GM, 226; R, 263f; reprinted (not exactly) Paris, 1884: Duret, GBA, May 1908; 432.

[38] Letter from A. Lacroix, Verboeckhoven et Cie, 19 Aug. '68; reply 21 Aug., *Bull.*, xxxix, 6–8. L(2), 139f.

[39] G(1), 10. Now relation of R.s and Saint-Denis seems to stop.

[40] *Lettres*, 132; *Roman*, 108; *L'Olivier*, 505; Nicholson, 74.

[41] Clark, 208; L(2), 152.

[42] Geffroy (2), 41; GM, 227.

[43] Cour. (1), ii, 110–13; Box 1; GM, 228f; R, 264. First four phrases omitted. Cast. wrote about need to protest.

[44] Cour. (1), i, 233–5; pictures in two consignments sent by C. before he went to Le Havre have arrived.

[45] Box 1; GM, 272, 275, 63. C. at Ornans.

[46] Box 1; Cour. (1), i, 235f; GM, 239; GK, 45–8, for wild version that prolongs it till 1872; also Grand, 84.

[47] GK, 64f; Box 2; GM, 63; R, 265.

[48] F(1), no. 48; GM, 229. Gaudy and Cusenier in *Hallali*.

[49] R, 265f; *L'Artiste*, iii, 373; Blanc in *Temps*, 3 June; Gautier, *J. Officiel*, 16 June. Shadows: *Tableaux à la Plume.* St Victor: *L'Artiste*, iv, 106: Cast. in *Siècle.* For *La Trombe*: *Bull.*, xx, 4; *Metrop.*, 131f; Meier-G. (2), pl. 110.

[50] To Cast. Box 1; GM, 230; *Bull.*, xvii–xviii, 39.

[51] Boyé (2); letter, mardi 27 July '69, a litho of *Girl with Seagulls* painted at Trouville: *Bull.*, xxxi, 15.

[52] Box 2; R, 267f; GM, 230. Before he left he sold five seascapes, 4500 fr.

[53] *Rome*, no. 35; many variants, some done two years later in jail. His Mediterranean seascapes are all calm, bright. For his seascapes: Boat, 78.

[54] Box 2; GM, 230f; says Belgian shows at a loss; Brevet of Order, *Bull.*, xx, 19. Munich: L(2), 147–9.

[55] R, 273; GM, 232; *Bull.*, xxii, 10f.

[56] *Rome*, no. 36. The Rembrandt he used is now seen as a good anon. copy; he took the 'Murillo' for a Velasquez. Collin has tale of him putting his copy in place of original; 'nobody noticed it'.

[57] GK, 89–95; Cour. (1), ii, 238–41.

[58] GM, 273; Ch. (3), 180.

[59] *Rome*, no. 37: for correspondance of Cast. with Stumpf, ceramic worker, on a landscape; 20 Nov. to Cast. 'I've done 6 mountain-scenes in autumn at Interlaken.'

[60] Box 2; Cour. (1), ii, 113–16; GM, 232f. Tells Cast. he can get German papers in Paris; Corot also got order; Cabanel and Doré named. Chenavard, C. Blanc, etc. sit on steps of Glyptothek and bewail state of contemporary art; painted landscape in Tyrol; leaving for Ornans, 21 Nov.

[61] Anthrax (entraxe en derrière). Letter to Gaudy: *Bull.*, vi, 13f, about volumes of *contes* at Vuillifans; clear that C. has not yet reached Ornans, expects to be there in a week. *Bull.*, vi, 13f; L(2), 149.

[62] Box 2; Cour. (1), ii, 116–20; GM, 234, 51f; Cour. (1), i, 98 for earlier life and how 'in this movement he was quite certainly the *homme socialiste* who most clearly understood the social questions that occupy us today'. One of his last projects was drafting a democratic constitution with aid of those of USA and Switzerland.

[63] *Rome*, no. 29, for arguments against; L(2), 150f; F(15), for defence.

14. *War and the Commune* (1870-1)

[1] 4 Feb., L(2), 151.

[2] 5 Feb., Box 2; GM, 236f. There were 18 jurors.

[3] L(3), 121f.

[4] Cast. (2) i, 396; GM, 237. Waterspouts and stormy seas; but in '69 he also did cheerful works, e.g. *Calm Sea, Metrop.*, 131; Venturi (2), 219f.

[5] GM, 237.

[6] R, 277; GM, 238; A. Meinhul introduced C. to the works.

[7] *Rome*, no. 17.

[8] R, 277ff; Cour. (1), i, 249-51.

[9] Claudet: Cour. i, 246-8. Carjat, letter and poem: Cour. (1), i, 251-5.

[10] Cour. (1), ii, 122-5; Ideville, 34-6.

[11] *Ib.* C. had probably anticipated the event, with draft and completed reply ready.

[12] Box 2; GM, 241; Cour. (1), i, 225-7. Ten francs per head at dinner.

[13] Escholier, Daumier 1930; Cour. (1), i, 257f.

[14] Charavay, ii, 279; Cour. (1), ii, 40-3.

[15] G(1), 10f; R, 280. G. Zap in *Le Monde pour Rire*, 3 July '70, 'See then this Courbet who is not only a mighty painter but who troubles himself to be a great character.' Cf. Duret, 85.

[16] R, 280; GM, 241f; Cour. (1), ii, 125.

[17] Box 7; Cour. (1), ii, 127; R, 282.

[18] GM, 243; R, 282-4; Darcel (1), C. inspected cases in de N.'s apartments, thinking they might hold pictures to be secretly sent off, but they held old armour sent from Pierrefonds Mus. for preservation. For statues removed from pedestal etc. GM, 266.

[19] Box 7; GM, 244, He had now convinced himself the Germans wouldn't get to Ornans. 9 Sept., L(3), 123; GM, 244f. Paris-Lyon-Mediterranean railway.

[20] GM, 261f. 6 Sept.; Ideville, 81f; 14 Sept.; R. 157f; *J. des Débats* 29 Sept. '70; Box 2; GM, 263f; Gill, 168; GM, 264f.

[21] Box 2 (draft); Darcel (1), 290. To Arago: R, 289. Robinet: Cast. (4), 21f.

[22] Cour. (1), ii, 128-39; published as pamphlet from his studio-address; GM, 247. Buchon, with his strong idealisation of Germans, was spared 1870-1.

[23] G(3), 8f; G(1), 11 (Zoé to Ch., letter 2).

[24] Boyer, 182-5, 190-2; GM, 247f.

[25] G(1), 11f (letter 2).

[26] 27 Jan. '71: Cour. (1), i, 258f.

[27] Box 7; Cour. (1), ii, 15-16; GM, 250f, 266; L(2), 159f. Disturbed at danger to his studio, was now at 14 passage du S. (rue Bachaumont now) 2nd arrond. Note he keeps calling the Order 'of Honour', though at the time he stressed it was 'for Merit'.

[28] Hugo, ii, 186; GM, 195.

[29] Cour. (1), ii, 45-9.

[30] Darcel (2), 44f.

[31] *Ib.*, 47-9; *J. Officiel*, 15 April; L(2), 161f.

[32] L(2), 188f; GM, 307f; Moreau; F(5), 11f; GK, 51-3.

[33] *Soc. d'émulation du Doubs, Mém.*, 8e sérié, v, 1911; and M. Vuillaume, *Mes cahiers rouges*, vii (*dernier cashier*), 70ff; Proudhon, *Mélanges*, i, 254, and *Mém.* 198 (letter xii).

[34] Box 7; Cour. (1), ii, 140. Jongkind in Paris: Hefting, letters nos. 260-2. L(3), 123.

[35] *J. Officiel*, 13 April; GM, 267.

[36] *Ib.* 28 April; GM, 267f.

[37] *Ib.* 4 May; letter, 14 May, L(2), 163; R, 304 more details.

[38] Box 2.

[39] *Bull.*, xxiv; L(3); GM, 269f; F.

[40] Lanjalley, 486f; cited GM. Vallès's poem, Cour. (1), i, 264: Column to be coined into *sous* for the starving.

[41] *The Times*, 17, 19 May '71; R, 307f.

[42] Cast. (4), 63; Vallès, *Réveil*, 6 Jan. '78; Cour. (1), i, 331–4. Place renamed P. des Piques (Pikes). Statue smashed pavement, head, arm etc. broke off. C. and Tuileries: Darcel (2), 218. Reorganisations: R, 307. For David: JL (2); R, 310; L(2), 157f. See Vallès's *L'Insurgé* for passages where C. speaks in broad patois.

[43] Cluseret: Guillemin, 35f; for odd end of Delécluze, *ib*. 39f.

15. *Trial and Sentence* (1871–2)

[1] Darcel (2), 224; on Dalou, *ib*., 228; Du Camp, *Convulsions*: R, 307f. C. said to be on balcony of Ministry of Justice with others of Commune.

[2] GM, 271f. He spent last days reading and drawing Lecomte.

[3] L(2), 165; R, 309; GM, 273. Satory was a fortress near Versailles.

[4] R, 309f; GM, 271f; mishaps of statue, F(7). Letter of C. to *Gazette de Lausanne* (16 Oct. '73; printed in part 27 Oct.) on house of Thiers, denying charges that he and Rane took part in 'pillaging', he had not seen Rane those days: *Bull*., xxxii, 8f.

[5] Box 2; Cour. (1), ii, 141.

[6] Dumas, *Le Figaro*, 12 June '71; GM, 173f; R, 316f. A Mortier (Cour. (1), ii, 302–5) on C. and Barnum or Tussauds.

[7] L(3), 100, cf. 102; R, 312; two caricatures, *Bull*., xxxii, 2, 5.

[8] R, 311; G(1), 14.

[9] Box 7; GM, 274; R, 313.

[10] Box 2; GM, 274f. Zoé's PS makes it seem that C. had not himself approached them, and as if their relations with the jailed C. began through Cast.'s good offices.

[11] R, 311; G(1), 15.

[12] Box 2; 18 June, Maisières; GM, 276, 22 June.

[13] Letter signed 20 Aug. '71; says he was elected 6 days after vote on the Column. R, 307; GM, 276f.

[14] R, 312.

[15] GM, 276f; R, 307f.

[16] Box 2; GM, 277f. Photo of bust in place: *Bull*., xxxii, 17.

[17] Zoé: G(1), 14, GM, 278. Document: A, 53–63.

[18] *Bull*., iv, 22–4; Daguet (1816–94) wrote *Histoire de la Confédération Suisse*; Bachelin (1830–90) did landscapes and military subjects of his own time. Scheer illustrated Erkmann-Chatrian. Cast. (4), 77.

[19] Box 2; GM, 278f.

[20] B, 115–17, 118; G(1), 15. Lachaud had defended Mme Lafargue.

[21] B, 117–19; GM, 279f; G(1), 15. Bruyas writes on 7 Aug., his letter crossed Zoé's with request to come to trial.

[22] Letter 2; G(1), 14f. Baudry: Bonniot (2), 231.

[23] GM, 281–3; R, 313ff. Monteil: R, 323. Col. Merlin of 1e regiment du génie. The reactionary papers omitted the Grousset testimony. C. was seated on third row between Descamps and Parent, dressed in black and white cravat. Lachaud claimed, 'The horrible Père Duchesne had denounced him at every turn and demanded that he be shot.' C. Pelletan of *Rappel* declared C. said of the majority, 'These people are fools who play odiously roles learned in the repertory of '93.' R, 320. For analysis of the *loi Courbet* : Y. Capron, *Bull*., xlvii.

[24] Baron: G(1), 5; perhaps they had some allowance from the older Reverdys. Letter 21 July, death of mother, anger at Ornans: R, 313.

[25] *Les Artistes contemporains*; Cour. (1), i, 272; R, 317f.

[26] B, 121f. undated; GM, 283.

[27] Box 2; GM, 284f.

[28] Box 7; GM, 285f. Others tried: R, 317.

[29] L(1), 125; R322, 324; St-Pierre jail; Thiers: Zahar (3), but the rest of his argument is too far-fetched. Baudry: Bonniot (2).

[30] Ste-Pélagie: GM, 286; Du Camp (2), i, 204; *Bull.*, xlvi.

[31] *Bull.*, xxxi, 11. Note he says not allowed to send letters out, but see those cited.

[32] 23 Sept '71: Box 2; GM, 287.

[33] Box 2; Cour. (1), ii, 141f; he begins about difficulties of Cast.'s visits as he is a journalist.

[34] Box 7; GM, 288; R, 324.

[35] B, 126 incorrectly given as 30 Nov.; G(1), 17.

[36] L(5), 143; *Bull.*, xlvi.

[37] Bauzon, 239f; R, 325; Cour. (1), ii, 143f; GM, 290f. For Hugues: Varloot, 115–21.

[38] G(1), 17; B dates Aug., but it must be later.

[39] Bauzon, 240; GM, 291. Zoé took a large bunch of red-berried holly to decorate the room. Baudry: Bonniot (2), 231f.

[40] Aragon: R, 326; *Bull.*, xiii, 25, for a couple of drawings probably by Gautier in the notebook.

[41] *Rome*, no. 38.

[42] *Rome*, no. 40, said to be done at request of a Norman collector Jacquette (Caen).

[43] B, 126–8, undated; GM, 292f; G(1), 17. Letter to Mme Dupin, 28 Dec., to whom he has offered *Oranges et Grenades* (done in Ste-Pélagie). 'It'd be bad luck to escape the firing-parties to succumb to surgery', R, 327.

[44] GM, 293f; R, 328f. Further see *Bull.*, xlvii on the Column.

16. *Lull and Renewed Attack* (1872–3)

[1] R, 328f; GM, 294. 'I am loved by the people of Paris' etc.

[2] B, 128f.

[3] *Rome*, no. 39. Perhaps this the one caricatured L(3), 107; *La Chronique illustrée* (6. v. 1871), 'the fruits of reflection.' *Rome* for others; this among largest and best. Fruits outlined by slight circle to sharpen form: an innovation for C., more strongly used in *Fruits in a Basket* (Philadelphia, *Courbet*, 1959–60, no. 79).

[4] B, 129; GM, 294f; G(2), 18.

[5] Bauzon, 240f.

[6] Letter 2; G(1), 18. Probably about this time he painted portrait of Zoé dated by Léger 1873.

[7] R, 329–31; GM, 298.

[8] B, 131 undated. 'We hope this will be helpful to Gustave', so the Rs. have done it or claim to have. We get some idea of number of works he has done at Ste-P. and Neuilly. His passport: *Bull.*, xvii–xviii, 31. Nélaton: Collin to Lemonnier.

[9] R, 332.

[10] R, 332f.

[11] G(1), 18.

[12] Hugo, ii, 205; GM, 296. The *Cave*: R, 338. In May he says he can't go home yet on account of the thefts. 'A formidable reaction' is setting in on his behalf.

[13] R, 374; GM, 299; Cour. (1), i, 282f; Cast. (2), ii, 11–13.

[14] B, 133; GM, 297.

[15] *L'Eclipse*, year 5, no. 181; GM, 299.

[16] B(2), 184f; GM 296f.

[17] Docs. Moreau-Nélaton; Cour. (1), ii, 144f. It is not so much a letter as a meditation; could have been addressed to a dead friend.

¹⁸ For list: R, 335–7. In the book C. appears at end in person to announce the coming marriage of a poet who's resigned to his position, a noble character who has struggled against his passion, and has undergone all possible insults in his village. Beauquier: R, 338f. Tale of procureur-général walking arm in arm with C.: *ibid*.

¹⁹ Box 2; Cour. (1), ii, 147; G, 300.

²⁰ L(3), 123f; GM, 301.

²¹ Box 2; Cour. (1), ii, 146; GM, 301; GK, 167f. Horse: L(2), 170.

²² R, 339f; GM, 301f. Arrival of *Fisher* on 24 Oct.

²³ *Bull.*, xii, 16f. She says he was no boaster and had pleasant tenor voice, 'No man simpler and more attractive.' *Bull.*, xvi, 19f: many spelling and grammatical errors, e.g. *l'oppinion publique*.

²⁴ Box 7; Cour. (1), ii, 147–9; G, 302f. 'In the eyes of the people what difference can it make if she occupies my house or yours, this argument is nothing.'

²⁵ *ibid*; Cour. (1), ii, 150f; GM, 304.

²⁶ F(5), 11; Moreau, 35; L(2), 188f; GM, 307.

²⁷ Moreau, 31; L(2), 188; GM, 307.

²⁸ GK, 83–6; GM, 306. Letter to Pasteur from Ornans: *Bull.*, xxviii, 12f. Riat called Mlle G. his 'cousin,' ? by marriage with Reverdys.

²⁹ Box 2; Cour. (1), ii, 151f; GM, 305f; mentions his three lawsuits.

³⁰ Ordinaire at school with Proudhon: L(2), 113. G(1), 19 citing also Ideville, *Figaro* July '76, on illusion C. would leave politics for art-in-itself. L(2), 176.

³¹ Box 2; GM, 308f. Some stolen pictures found, others didn't turn up for two years more.

³² A, 69f. This an old idea of 1859–60: L(3), 119: letter. Conscript: Cast., Cour. (1), ii, 283 and L(2), 125 (*La Liberté*, May '60).

³³ Box 2; GM, 309.

³⁴ R, 340. Zoé selling works; through her Pasteur gets one; tries to sell the *Promayet*. Letter of 19 Feb by Cast. advises C. that the R.s work against him: G(1), 10; R, 342f.

³⁵ Box 2; GM, 309. C.'s readiness to go to Switzerland: G(1), 19.

³⁶ Grand, 82; probably refers to period 1877–8 but shows Juliette's readiness to malign Zoé.

³⁷ Cour. (1), ii, 152f.

³⁸ Box 2; Cour. (1), ii, 153f; GM, 310.

³⁹ *Trout*: GK, 80–2, with anecdote; Wœrler 6; *ib.* 7 on later *Trout*, 1873, over-lifesize, done as he feels new menaces. *Rome*, no. 42; *Bull.*, xiii, 9. C. Sterling, *La nature morte de l'Antiquité à nos jours*, (1952), 76, 106; M. Faré, *La Nature morte en France* (1962), ii, n. 496.

⁴⁰ *Rome*, no. 43 (bridge now gone). *Bull.*, xii, 13; Fernier (1966), 63, 69, 117.

⁴¹ Pata was let copy *Calf*; *Rome*, no. 41; GK, 77–80; Estignard, 168–85; GM, 101, 311, 324; L(2), 179 – cf. the play by Cogniard, 1855.

⁴² GM, 311f.

⁴³ Box 2; Estignard, 116f.

⁴⁴ F(5), 12.

⁴⁵ GM, 312f; L(2), 177.

⁴⁶ Box 7; R, 343f; L(2), 177; G(1), 21. Letter 26 April '72. Pata: Droz. He was at the event in the café Agostinetti at Locarno. For his presence in Val-de-Traves 1857, *ib.* 14; after 1880 at La Chaux-de-Fonds. Also *Bull.*, xvii–xviii, 33. His portrait of C. (Ornans): *Bull.*, xxv, 15. To Cast.: Cour. (1), i, 302f. Fakes: Isnard; *Bull.*, xxvi, 16f. German and Hungarian disciples, *ib.*, 17; direct disciples, *Bull.*, xxxvi; xxxvii, 16–18 (Bourquet).

⁴⁷ Box 2; GM, 315f; *Bull.*, xxv, 3 for poster of amendment 27 March '73 to be moved by the comte d'Abbadie de Barrau on payment of Column, 'the sieur C. and his accomplices'.

⁴⁸ L(2), 181, Choppard; GM, 316. Zoé: G(1), 21. R, 348 (Cusenier); B, 14.

⁴⁹ GM, 316ff: the Baron to whom C. had complained about trees. For document perhaps part of dossier of defence: *Bull.*, xxvi, 2f; rebuts charge of jealousy. Also *Bull.*, xvi, 18f.

⁵⁰ L(2), 183f, undated; Bonniot (2), 233.

51 L(2), 184: Dossier Blondon.

52 Box 2, 23–4 June; GM, 317.

53 *Ib.*; GM, 318.

54 F(5), 12.

55 F(5), 12f; document costs 5.38 fr.

56 L(9), 10.

57 L(2), 185f; Cour., ii, 154f; Bauzon, 241f; GM, 320.

58 Box 2; GM, 319.

59 GM, 320; L(2), 186 says he left 'mardi matin' without awakening anyone.

17. *Exile* (1873–6)

1 L(9), 12; GM, 321f. La Tour: *Bull.*, xxi; letter to Blondon, 1 Aug. '73: L(3), 124.

2 R, 351f; GM, 322; L(9); Bull., xxi; Collin describes Morels: Cour. (1), i, 336–42.

3 B, 139–41; GM, 343f. Poulet-Malassis wrote to Bruyas, 1 July, that C. was losing his head. Further: B, 143; G(1), 22, on those who 'don't scruple to sign the most unheard-of *croûts* that one could see'. 'They've thrown the Man into the abyss, now thus destroy the Artist.'

4 Box 2; GM, 323–5, 344. Says *Calf* painted some time before departure.

5 Box 2; GM, 325, 345.

6 Box 2; GM, 326f.

7 Box 2; GM, 327.

8 Box 2; GM, 328. Dr Blondon's list of genuine works: *Rome*, no. 44.

9 *Bull.*, iv, 8–10; lived till 1948. Cary by Slom: *Bull.*, xxxvii, 21; *Circe*, Box 2, GM, 332.

10 L(2), 198 (*Circe*). Collin says he attributed it to Watteau and wanted 200,000 fr.; Zoé to Bruyas: B, 141; C. to Cast., Box 2; GM, 345.

11 L(2), 206; R, 361 Letter: L(2), 189.

12 R, 359–61; Cour. (1), i, 303–6; GM, 336f; *Times*, 24 June '74. Article 55 let a debtor choose among his creditors; Dubois for State argued the court only concerned with matter of fact. Collin tells of people taking advantage of his good-nature.

13 Box 2, GM, 337.

14 R, 364; Cast. 14 Feb '75; L(2), 202; two portraits of R. Collin says that R. wanted the Jo painting; C. took down a beach-view and gave it. C. said of R., 'That animal has only one fine thing, his jaw; he's got horse-teeth.' For exile-friends: Fournier-Marcigny of Baud-Bovy, Réclus, Pia; tale of C. playing like giant with small girl.

15 L(9), 18; GM, 330f; Box 2; L(2), 202; F(5), 14 takes the woman to be the countess. F(15) for discussion of all the sculptures. Collin says the medallion was done for 'one of his Vevey friends' and symbolised exile . . .'

16 Box 2; GM, 330; three other copies, Martigny, Besançon, Meudon. L(2), 194–6.

17 L(2), 200f, making arrival of Henri R. late '76. Visit to Lausanne, fête at Morat (June '76): *ib.* 192.

18 L(9), 15; L(2), 194; GM, 334.

19 Box 2; GM, 345.

20 Box 2; GM, 332f. C.'s letter, 22 April.

21 All based on F(5), 13f. GK's account of the whole thing has no doubt a basis in fact but just what cannot be made out. L(3), 124, July '75.

22 Box 2. To Zoé: Cour. (1), ii, 155–7; B, 150–2; GM, 346. L(2), 193: Letter to Régis.

23 *Rome*, no. 45. Letter of thanks to Monselet for article, L(2), 189–91. For the two Réclus under Commune: *Europe*, 282–9. for Nadar, *ib.*, 289–91.

24 C. didn't paint him. In 1879 Slom married Emma Blank; to Paris 1882 after amnesty; died

1909. See L: *Bull.*, iv, 4–8; a drawing of his in Lemonnier, *Habitation de G.C.* is his, not Collin's. He drew C. on deathbed.

[25] GM, 334; from her daughter Henriette (lived till 1948) then only 8 or 9.

[26] Box 2; i, 52f; Cour. (1), ii, 157f; GM, 334f, 347.

[27] Letter 26 July: Box 2; GM, 332. Baudry: Bonniot (2). Also L(3), 124–7 for more details. Mestreau had brought a flower-piece at Saintes.

[28] GM, 331f for text of handbill.

[29] L(2), 202. Slom: L. in *Bull.*, iv, 4–7.

[30] Box 7; GM, 338.

[31] B, 144, 14 Jan. '76, cf. 152; G(1), 22f.

[32] B, 142–4; may be a little earlier; GM, 347f.

[33] B, 153; Cour (1), ii, 158f; GM, 348.

[34] Box 2; Cour. (1), ii, 159; GM, 338.

[35] Cour. (1), ii, 159–66.

[36] Box 2; GM, 348f. Letter 29 Aug. '76: Ideville 80. GK: 'If she was here, I'd shove her into the lake,' Cour. (1), i, 310.

[37] Box 6; GM, 349; Grand, 82; deserted studio: Cour. (1), i, 312–14.

[38] Box 2; GM, 339.

[39] L(2), 197; letter of Bonvin on state of art, 5 Sept. '77: *Bull.*, xxxi, 19. *Roe-deer*: Rome, no. 45; Meier-Graefe, pl. 103.

[40] Box 2; GM, 339. Letter about Whistler: 27 April '76; Cour. (1), i, 306f; 17 Feb. '77 (Bergeron). In general: Bucarelli, Sylvester, Sutton. Cézanne: Anderson, 313. Aphorism: see here n. 21, ch. 11. Cast.: Cour. (1), ii, 282f, cf. Sylvester, Cour. (1), i, 58, slave of model, only paints what he has long known, lack of action, *ib.*, 56f. Ch. also on what he knew well: Cour (1), i, 97. Dice-tail: L(2), 89f. *Glade or Round-Dance*, done at Port-Berteau: Bonniot (1) 104, see also pl. 37 *Underwood. Round-dance* is in Fitzwilliam, Camb., pl. 83, p. 157. Compare with it *Underwood at Port-Berteau*, by Corot, in which Mme Auguin appears. *Knife*, Claudet; L(3); N(4), 49; Badt, see below here. Black basis: Clark, 288 (Monet said when working with C. in 1860s he was advised to start with dark ground so as to establish main masses as quickly as possible.) Stuffed animals: *Metrop.*, 129f. See *Snow-scene* there as fine example of treatment of snow; C. said: 'The painter with power should be able to efface and re-do ten times in succession without hesitation his best picture to prove he is not the slave of chance or of his nerves', Cour. (1), i, 53 (Silvestre). *ib.*, 54 for methods of work.

Cf. vigorous action of Millet's *Sawyers*, or of Daumier in general, with arrested carved image of *Stonebreakers*.

Manet said, 'In a figure look for the greatest light and the greatest shadow; the rest will follow naturally; it is often nothing much': N(4), 7f. Manet used a sort of schematised version that he called concision: this was against C.'s principles.

For casual effect (part of the *Meeting* etc), note the 'monumental informality' of Degas: Mayne, 149f. Degas, notebook of '60s, 'There is sometimes a certain ease in awkwardness which, if I'm not mistaken, is more graceful than the grand manner,' J. S. Boggs, *Portraits by Degas* (1962), 23 (Bibl. Nat. carnet 8, formerly E p. 6).

Fitzwilliam: at Port-Berteau '62 (*Bull.*, xxvii, 4f): ? Mme Auguin and her children. Badt, 244–6, cited and summarised; see 247f for use of palette-knife by Rembrandt, Constable, Courbet and Cézanne—though he does not do justice to Courbet's range or its importance for him in defining the beauty and richness of the material substance. For difference of C. and Cézanne, 249f. For space in C. 253.

'Beyond the bourgeois limitations': I leave the matter at that. One could go further and show how C. has all the typical anarchist virtues and vices. His spontaneous revolt reaches far ahead, but because it has outrun its bases it revives individualism-as-egoism at the heart of its individualism-as-freedom.

Note Manet was said to have declared C.'s ideal was a billiard-ball (Meier-Graefe (3), citing A. Wolff *La Capitale de l'art*): that is, a smooth surface and generalised volume; cf. what is said here of the apples of 1871–2 as images of rebirth, of 'pure form'.

[41] Box 2; Cour. (1), ii, 170f.

[42] Cour. (1), ii, 171–3; 'Try to see Durand-Ruel's liquidation, he owes me 3,000 francs; tell him I'm doing his *Chillon*.'

He claims it is honourable to justice, the government, the police. Morel: Cour. (1), i, 336–42 (6 Jan. 78) to Cast.

18. *The End* (1877)

[1] Boxes 2 and 7; GM, 340f. Morel: Cour. (1), i, 336–42.

[2] Box 2, copied by C. in letter to Cast., 12 Feb. 77: GM, 341. C. Fleury, *Ann. F.C.* ix, 68.

[3] GM, 341f; Cast. (4), 83.

[4] Box 2; GM, 351. Letter of 6 May '77 to Rouberol railway engineer at Ornans on letting house: L(3), 131. 'I am delighted to entrust this house to a sincere republican . . .'

[5] B, 154; Cour. (1), ii, 14; GM, 349.

[6] B, 154.

[7] Lemonnier (1), 86: Collin, 31 Dec. GM, 352.

[8] Box 2; GM, 353. Visit of Juliette and Mme Ordinaire: L(2), 202f.

[9] Box 2; Cour. (1), i, 315f.

[10] *Bull.*, iii, 41f.

[11] *Ib.* 43 (13 Nov. from Flagey).

[12] Box 2; Cour. (1), i, 317; GM, 354.

[13] Cour. (1), ii, 14–18. 'I don't know any more what's become of the cases of Laroche and Gilly.' 'All my friends of F.C. have come to see me as well as Dr Blondon.'

[14] Box 2; GM, 355; Nélaton died 1873.

[15] Box 7; GM, 355f.

[16] Box 2; (1) Cour. (1), ii, 178; GM, 356.

[17] Lemonnier (2), 84.

[18] Cour. (1), i, 322f.

[19] Lemonnier (2), 84–8.

[20] Box 2; Cour. (1), ii, 179; GM, 358.

[21] Lemonnier (1), 96.

[22] *Bull.*, iii, 44; anecdote of Régis on the way (via Fernier family?): *Bull.*, iii, 49f.

[23] Lemonnier (1), 96f; GM, 359.

[24] Cour. (1), i, 327, 324. Anon(1). 'A woman friend of the family had, at his daughter Juliette's request, to bring him back almost by force.'

[25] Pata: Cour. (1), i, 328; GM, 360f; *Bull.*, iii, 45f. Religion: G(1), 24; L(2), 206.

[26] Box 6; GM, 361. Arthur Arnould spoke.

[27] Cour. (1), i, 343.

[28] Anon(1). GK has the tale of the sack of gold found by Régis at La Tour.

[29] Cour. (1), i, 343–5, 348; L(2). *Acte de Décès*: Cour. (1), i, 348.

[30] B, 148f; GM, 363; Duval, 17 Oct. '78 (*Le Xixe Siècle*, Paris, 3 April '79).

[31] G(1), for defence of Zoé; *ib.*, 26f for relations to Champfleury, Eugène-Jean R. became sculptor and showed at Salons 1889, 1890.

[32] Box 6; GM, 365f.

[33] Grand, 83.

[34] G(1), 27; Grand, 83; GM, 364 (who called 10 April 1950, but the rules forbade the giving of information).

35 GM, 364; L(10), 18–20; Valerio, 248, 251. Letters (to Mme Grelet, clos du Ruisseau, La Tour-de-Peilz): *Bull.*, xxxi, 16–18. She was going to visit La Tour, 20 Aug. '93; cf. June '94. Address is 1 rue Notre-Dame-des-Champs. Letter to Cast. (? 1882) on some pictures and project of a Paris apartment, *ib.*, 15f.

Slom's monument: *Bull.*, iv, 6. Ornans Museum: *Bull.*, v, 16–21; xxii, 15f. Grand, 83f for Juliette in Paris (at hotel near church St-Sulpice almost wholly inhabited by ecclesiastics). Once she took Fumey's brother Paul to a restaurant and asked for a private room; the waiter said to Paul, 'M. could choose them younger.'

36 *Réveil*, 6 Jan. '78; Cour. (1), i, 334–6.

BIBLIOGRAPHY

Abe, Y., *Etudes de Langue et Littérature françaises* (Bulletin de la Société japonaise de langue et littérature françaises, no. 1). Tokyo, 1962, esp. pp. 29–41; About, Edmond, (1) *Nos Artistes au Salon de 1857*. Paris, 1888, pp. 141–55, (2) *Voyage à travers l'exposition des Beaux-Arts*. Paris, 1855; Alexander, R. L., *Art Bulletin* (Providence, R.I.), vol. 47 (1965), pp. 447–52; Alméras, Henri d', *La Vie parisienne pendant le siège et sous la Commune*. Paris, 1927; Amiel, J. Henri, 'Un Précurseur du réalisme: Max Buchon.' *Modern Language Quarterly* (Seattle, Wash.), vol. 3, no. 3 (September 1942), pp. 379–90; Anderson, W. V., *Burlington Magazine* (London), vol. 107 (1965), p. 313; Anon., in *Le Petit-Comtois* (Besançon), 13–31 janvier 1897; Aragon, Louis, *L'Exemple de Courbet*. Paris, 1952; Armengaud, André, *Les Populations de l'Est-Aquitain au début de l'époque contemporaine: recherches sur une région moins développée, vers 1845–vers 1871*. Paris/La Haye, 1961; Astruc, Zacharie, *Les 14 Stations du salon 1859, suivies d'un récit douloureux*. With a preface by George Sand. Paris, 1859, esp. pp. 371–99; Audebrand, Philibert, *Derniers jours de La Bohème: souvenirs de la vie littéraire*. Paris, 1905; Auriant (*pseud*. of Alexandre Hadjivassiliou). *Mercure de France*, 1 avril 1939.

Badt, K., *The Art of Cézanne* [*Die Kunst Cézannes*]. Translated by Sheila Ann Ogilvie. London, 1965; Baillods, Jules, *Courbet vivant*. Neuchâtel/Paris, 1940; Bakker-Hefting, Victorine, *Jongkind d'après sa correspondance*. Amsterdam, 1962; Barbey d'Aurevilly, Jules Amédée, *XIX Siècle. Les Œuvres et les hommes*. First series: 'Sensations d'art'. Paris, 1866, esp. pp. 15–29; Baudelaire, Charles, (1) *Curiosités esthétiques, L'Art romantique et autres œuvres critiques*. Paris, 1962, (2) *Art in Paris 1845–62*, ed. Jonathan Mayne. London, 1962; Baudry, Étienne, (1) *Le Camp des bourgeois*. Illustrations de G. Courbet. Paris, 1868, (2) *La Fin du monde*. Paris, 1872; Bauzon, Louis, 'Documents inédits sur Courbet.' *L'Art* (Paris), vol. 40 (1886), pp. 237–42; Bazin, Germain, with A. Albini, *Courbet alla xxvii biennale di Venezia*. 1952; Bellessort, André, *La Société française sous Napoléon III*. Paris, 1932; Benedict, N., *Burlington Magazine*, vol. 104 (1962), pp. 73–5; Bénédite, Léonce, (1) *Gustave Courbet: a biographical and critical study*. With notes by Jean Laran and Ph. Gaston-Dreyfus. London 1912, (2) 'Whistler.' *Gazette des Beaux-Arts* (Paris), année 47, vol. 34, no. 579 (septembre 1905); Benjamin, Walter, (1) *The New Left Review*, no. 48 (1968), (2) 'Some themes in Baudelaire'. *Zeitschrift für Sozialforschung*. January 1940, (3) *Illuminationen. Ausgewählte Schriften* (ed. Siegfried Unseld). Frankfurt-am-Main, 1961; Bérard, J., *La Franche-Comté et quelques-uns de ses enfants*. Besançon, 1888; esp. pp. 158–62; Berger, Klaus, (1) *Gazette des Beaux-Arts*, vol. 30 (juillet 1946), (2) *id.*, vol. 24 (1943), pp. 19–40; Bergerat, Émile, *Sauvons Courbet!* Paris, 1871; Besson, George, *Masters of French Painting 1850–1950*. London, 1958; Boas, George (ed.), *Courbet and the Naturalistic Movement*. Baltimore Md, 1938; Boime, Albert, (1) *The Academy and French Painting in the Nineteenth Century*. London, 1970; (2) *Art Q.*, xxxii (Winter 1969), 411–26 (Salon des Refusés). Bon, J.-E., *A la mémoire de Gustave Courbet*. Paris, n.d.; Bonniot Roger, (1) *Gustave Courbet en Saintonge 1862–3*. 1973, (2) *Gazette des Beaux-Arts*, octobre 1967, pp. 227–44, (3) 'L'illustration du "Camp des Bourgeois".' *Bull*. 37 (1967), pp. 1–9, (4) 'L'illustration du "Camp des Bourgeois" (suite et fin).' *Bull*. 38 (1967), pp. 15–32, (5) *Bulletin de la Société de l'Histoire de l'art française* (1957), pp. 77–88, (6) *Revue de Bas-Poitou et des Provinces de l'Ouest* (1946), vol. 6 ('Auguier'), (7) *Sud-Ouest*, août 1964, (8) Letter in *Bull*. 33–34 (1965), pp. 16f; Borel, Pierre, (1) *Le Roman de Gustave Courbet, d'après une correspondance originale du grand peintre*. Paris, 1922, (2) 'Quatre modèles de Gustave Courbet.' *Revue de France* (Paris), année 5, vol. 2 (mars-avril 1925), pp. 180–6; Bouvier, Émile, *La Bataille réaliste (1844–1857)*. Paris, 1914; Bowness, A.

(C., G. Sand, Champfleury, Le Nain bros.) in *French 19th century Painting and Literature*, ed. U. Finke, 1972; Boyé, Maurice-Pierre, (1) 'Deux letters de P.-J. Proudhon à Max Buchon à propos de Gustave Courbet.' *Bull.* 29 (1961), pp. 17f., (2) 'Gustave Courbet jugé par Champfleury et Max Buchon.' *Bull.* 12 (1952), pp. 1–11, (3) *Arts* (Paris), 21 septembre 1951; Boyer, Pierre, *Les Aventures d'un étudiant 1870–1871*. Paris, 1888; Breton, Jules, *Un Peintre paysan. Souvenirs et impressions*. Paris, 1896; Brière, Gaston, *Catalogue des peintures exposées dans les galeries: I. École française*. Paris, 1924; Brion, Marcel, *Peinture romantique*. Paris, 1967; Bruhat, Jean, *Histoire du mouvement ouvrier français*, vol. 1. Paris, 1952; Brune, Paul, *Dictionnaire des artistes et ouvriers d'art de la Franche-Comté*. Paris, 1912; Brunesœur, R., *Gustave Courbet*. 1866; Bruno, Jean (*pseud.* of Dr Blondon), *Les Misères des gueux*. Ouvrage entièrement illustré par G. Courbet. Paris/Brussels/Leipzig/Leghorn, 1872; Bucarelli, P., in *Rome*, pp. xiii–xxiii; Buchon, Maximin, (1) *Essais poétiques: vignettes par Gust. C—*. Besançon, 1839, (2) *Recueil de dissertations sur le réalisme*. Neuchâtel, 1856, (3) *Chants populaires de la Franche-Comté*. Paris, 1878, (4) *Poésies. Poésies franc-comtoises. Poésies de Hébel*. Paris, 1877; (5) *Romans. Le Matachin*. Paris, 1877, (6) *Le Gouffre-Gourmand: Réminiscences de la vie réelle*. Nouvelle édition. Besançon, 1914; Burlet, M., *L'Est Républicain Dimanche*, 6 avril 1869.

Cabet, Étienne, *Comment je suis communiste*. 1840; *Cabinet=Cabinet Bruyas, Autographes* 1856; Castagnary, Jules-Antoine, (1) 'Fragments d'un livre sur Courbet.' *Gazette des Beaux-Arts*, année 53, vol. 5, no. 643 (janvier 1911), pp. 5–20; vol. 6, no. 654 (décembre 1911), pp. 488–97; année 54, vol. 7, no. 655 (janvier 1912), pp. 19–30, (2) *Salons 1857–1879*. 2 vols. Paris, 1892, (3) Article on Courbet. *L'Opinion nationale* (Paris), 19 mai 1860, (4) *Gustave Courbet et la colonne Vendôme. Plaidoyer pour un ami mort*. Paris, 1883, (5) *Exposition des œuvres de G. Courbet à l'école des Beaux-Arts. Catalogue précédé d'une notice sur sa vie et son œuvre, et supplément*. Paris, 1882, (6) *Philosophie du Salon de 1857*. Paris, 1858, (7) *Les Libres-propos*. Paris, 1864; Castile, H. *L'Artiste* 1856; Champfleury (*pseud.* of Jules-François-Félix Husson), (1) *La Revue mondiale*, vol. 105 (novembre–décembre 1913), pp. 30–49, 213–70; vol. 133 (octobre–décembre 1919), pp. 531–45, (2) *Les Demoiselles Tourangeau*. Paris, 1864, (3) *Souvenir et portraits de jeunesse*. Paris, 1872, (4) *Le Réalisme*. Paris, 1857; esp. pp. 270–86, (5) *Grandes figures d'hier et d'aujourd'hui: Balzac, Gérard de Nerval, Wagner, Courbet, avec quatre portraits gravés a l'eau-forte par Bracquemond*. Paris, 1861; esp. pp. 229–63, (6) 'Du Réalisme. Lettre à Madame Sand.' *L'Artiste* (Paris), série 5, vol. 16, no. 1 (2 septembre 1855), pp. 1–5, (7) *Histoire de la caricature moderne*. Paris, 1878, (8) *Contes vieux et nouveaux*. Paris, 1852, (9) *Les Amis de la nature. Avec un frontispice gravé . . . d'après un dessin de Gustave Courbet*. Paris, 1859, (10) Biographical notice to Maximin Buchon, *Œuvres choisies*, 3 vols. Paris, 1878, (11) *Les Excentriques*. Paris, 1852, (12) *Histoire de l'imagerie populaire*. Paris, 1869; Champier, Victor, *L'Année artistique (1878)*. Paris, 1879; Chamson, André, (1) *Jardin des Arts*, janvier 1964, (2) *Revue du Louvre*, année 18 (1968), no. 1; Charavay, Étienne, *Archives historiques de la littérature*. Paris, 1889–90. Chaudey, Gustave: *see* Droz (1); Chermiss, R.: *see* Boas; Chevalier, Louis, (1) *Classes laborieuses et classes dangéreuses à Paris pendant la première moitié du XIXe siécle*. Paris, 1858, (2) *La Formation de la population parisienne au XIXe siécle*, Paris, 1950, (3) *Les Fondements économiques et sociaux de l'histoire politique de la région parisienne 1848–70*. Paris, 1951; Chevassus, *Max Buchon: sa vie son œuvre*. Paris, 1884; Chirico, Giorgio de. *Gustave Courbet*. Paris, 1925; Claparède, Jean. 'Le séjour de Courbet à la Tour de Farges.' *Bull.* 7 (1950), pp. 1–12; Claretie, Jules, (1) *L'Artiste*, vol. 1 (1865), p. 425, (2) *Peintres et sculpteurs contemporains*. Première série: artistes décédés de 1870 à 1880 (Gustave Courbet, 1819–1878), vol. 1. Paris, 1882; Clark, T. J. *Burlington Magazine*. April/May 1969, pp. 208–12, 282–9; Claudet, Max, *Souvenirs: Gustave Courbet*. Paris, 1878; Clavel, Bernard, *Jardin des Arts*, janvier 1964; Clément de Ris, L., (1) *L'Artiste*, 1851, (2) *id.*, 1853; Cogniot, Georges, *La Pensée*: no. 9 (1946), pp. 27–35; no. 10 (1947), pp. 43–54; Collin, Paul, (1) in Lemonnier (1). (2) in Courthion (1), vol. 2, pp. 245–66; Considérant, Victor Prosper, (1) *Le Socialisme devant le vieux monde, ou le Vivant devant les morts*. Paris, 1838, (2) *Destinée sociale*, vol. 2. Paris, 1838; Cooper, Douglas, (1)

Burlington Magazine, October 1955, (2) *The Times Literary Supplement*, 27 June 1952; Costello, M., in *Marxism Today* (March 1970), pp. 69–75; Courbet, Gustave, (1) 'Lettres inédites.' *L'Olivier. Revue de Nice* (Nice), année 2, no. 8 (septembre–octobre 1913), pp. 468–512, (2) *A l'Armée allemande. Aux Artistes allemands*. Paris, 1870, (3) *Le Réalisme* (catalogue 1855), (4) Letter to his pupils. *Courrier du Dimanche* (Paris), 29 décembre 1861; Courthion, Pierre, (1) *Courbet, raconté par lui-même et par ses amis*: vol. 1: *Sa vie et ses œuvres*. Geneva, 1948. vol. 2: *Ses écrits, ses contemporains, sa postérité*. Geneva, 1950, (2) *Courbet*. Paris, 1931; Couture, Thomas, (1) *Méthode et entretiens d'atelier*. Paris, 1867, (2) *Conversations on Art Methods*. Translated by S. E. Stewart. New York, 1879; Crepet, Jacques (ed.), *Œuvres complètes de Baudelaire*. Paris, 1922–53.

Dallas: Dallas Southern Methodist University. *Landscapes of France in the nineteenth century*. Dallas, Texas, 1966; Dalligny, A., *Jardin des Arts*, 2 décembre 1908; Damé, Frédéric, *Sauvez le peintre!* Paris, 1871; Darcel, Alfred, (1) 'Les Musées, les arts et les artistes pendant le siège de Paris', *Gazette des Beaux-Arts*, année 12, vol. 4, no. 4 (octobre 1871), pp. 285–306; no. 5 (novembre 1871), pp. 414–29, (2) 'Les Musées, les arts et les artistes pendant la Commune.' *Gazette des Beaux-Arts*, année 14, vol. 5, no. 1 (janvier 1872), pp. 41–65; no. 2 (février 1872), pp. 140–50; no. 3 (mars 1872), pp. 210–29; no. 5 (mai 1872), pp. 398–418; no. 6 (juin 1872), pp. 479–90; Daumard, Adeline, *La Bourgeoisie parisienne de 1815 à 1848*. Paris, 1963; Debief, H., *L'Actualité de l'histoire*, vol. 30 (janvier-mars 1960); Delacroix, Eugène, (1) *Journal*. 3 vols. Paris, 1893, 1895, (2) *The Journal of Eugène Delacroix*. Translated by Walter Pack. London, 1938; Delécluze, Étienne-Jean, *Exposition des artistes vivants 1850*. Paris, 1851; Delestre, Gaston, (1) 'Courbet et Corot à Saintes.' *Bull.* 27 (1961), pp. 1–5, (2) 'Courbet à l'Exposition Universelle de Besançon en 1860.' *Bull.* 26 (1960), pp. 5–15; Delpeche-Laborie, M., *Arts*, 23 mars 1850; Delvau, Alfred, *Histoire anecdotique des cafés et cabarets de Paris*. Avec dessins et eaux-fortes de Gustave Courbet, Léopold Flemeng et Félicien Rops. Paris, 1862; Desnoyers, Fernand, *L'Artiste*, 9 décembre 1855; Dolléans, Édouard, & Puech, Jules L., *Proudhon et la révolution de 1848*. Paris, 1948; Dorbec, Prosper, (1) *L'Art du paysage en France*. Paris, 1925, (2) *La Peinture français sous le second empire jugée par les chansons et la caricature*. Gazette des Beaux-Arts, 1918; Dortois, M., *Annales de la Franche-Comté*, vol. 12 (1869), pp. 263–73; Droz, Édouard, *Mémoires de la Société d'Émulation du Doubs* (Besançon), série 8, vol. 5 (1910), pp. 159–257: séance 22 juin 1910; Droz, Georges, 'Un élève de Courbet: Pata (1827–1899).' *Bull.* 14 (1954), pp. 13–15; Du Camp, Maxime, (1) *Le Salon de 1857 : Peinture-sculpture*. Paris, 1857; esp. pp. 99–106, (2) *Les Convulsions de Paris*. 4 vols. Paris, 1878–80, (3) *Les Beaux-arts à l'Exposition Universelle de 1855*. Paris, 1855, (4) *Les Beaux-arts à l'Exposition Universelle et aux Salons de 1863–1864, 1865, 1866 et 1867*. Paris, 1867; Duchartre, Pierre Louis, & Saulnier, René, *L'Imagerie populaire : Les images de toutes les provinces françaises du XVe siècle au Second Empire. Les complaintes, contes, chansons, légendes qui ont inspiré les imagiers*. Paris, 1925; Dupont, Pierre, *Muse populaire . . . Chants et poésies*. Sixième édition. Paris, 1861; Duranty, Edmond, (1) *La Nouvelle peinture. A propos du groupe d'artistes qui expose dans les galeries Durand-Ruel*. Paris, 1876, (2) *Le Réalisme* (Paris), no. 2 (15 décembre 1856); Durbé, D., *Courbet e il realismo*, 1969; Duret, Théodore, (1) *Les Peintres français en 1867*. Paris, 1867, (2) *Courbet*. Paris, 1918.

Écalle, Martine, *Bulletin du Laboratoire du Louvre*, no. 4 (1959), pp. 31ff; Estignard, Alexandre, *Gustave Courbet. Sa vie et ses œuvres*. Besançon, 1897; *Europe*: *Europe*, novembre-décembre 1970;

Fernier, Robert, (1) *Gustave Courbet*. With an Introduction by René Huyghe. Translated from the French by Marcus Bullock. London, 1969, (2) 'En Voyage avec Courbet.' *Bull.* 35 (1966), pp. 9–28, (3) 'Courbet avait un fils.' *Arts*, nouvelle série, no. 310 (11 mai 1951), pp. 1, 3, (4) 'Courbet avait un fils.' *Bull.* 10 (1951), pp. 1–7, (5) 'Courbet et les femmes.' *Bull.* 33–34 (1965), pp. 9–14, (6) 'Un ami de Courbet: Charles Pouchon, le peintre-vigneron.' *Bull.* 43 (1970), pp. 8–11, (7) 'Le pêcheur malchanceux.' *Bull.* 29 (1961), pp. 15f, (8) 'Un ami de Courbet: Amand Gautier.' *Bull.* 16 (1955), pp. 1–5, (9) 'La vigneronne de Montreux.' *Bull.* 4 (1948), pp. 8–10. (10) 'Une œuvre inconnu de Courbet.' *Bull.* 4 (1948), pp. 15–17, (11) 'Courbet au salon de 1849.' *Bull.* 5 (1949), pp. 1–7, (12) 'Courbet sculpteur.' *Bull.* 11 (1952), pp. 1–6, (13) 'Courbet modèle d'un Saint Vernier.' *Bull.* 13 (1953–1954), pp. 1–4, (14) 'Le 29 mai 1867. . . .' *Bull.* 38 (1967), pp. 1–8, (15) 'Tempête sur le Léman.' *Bull.* 44 (1970), pp. 4–6, (16) 'Courbet sculpteur.' *Bull.* 11 (1952), pp. 1–6, (17) *Bull.* 32 (1964), pp. 10–12; *Fitzwilliam*: see Goodison; Fleury, Maurice, & Sonolet, Louis, *La Société du second Empire. D'après les mémoires contemporaines et des documents nouveaux.* 3 vols. Paris, 1913; Focillon, Henri, *La Peinture aux XIXe et XXe siécles. Du rèalisme à nos jours.* Paris, 1928; Fontainas, André, (1) *Courbet.* Paris, 1921, (2) *Les Albums d'art Druet.* VIII: *Courbet.* Notice d'André Fontainas. Paris, 1927; Fosca, François, *Courbet* [Reproductions]. Texte de F.F. Paris, 1940; Fournel, Victor, (1) *Ce qu'on voit dans les rues de Paris.* Paris, 1858, (2) *Tableau du vieux Paris. Les spectacles populaires et les artistes des rues.* Paris, 1863, (3) *Les Artistes français contemporains, peintres-sculpteurs.* Deuxième édition. Tours, 1885; Fournier-Marigny, Fernand, (1) *Ce printemps-la!* Geneva, 1950, (2) *Bull.* 25 pp. 1–6; Fourquet, E. *Les hommes célèbres de la Franche-Comté.* 1929, Frey, H. 'Max Buchon et ses œuvres': Ph.D. dissertation 1940; Fry, Roger. *Apollo* (1969), p. 363.

Gachet, Paul, 'Lettres d'Amand Gautier au Dr Gachet.' *Bull.* 23 (1959), pp. 1–6; Gautier, Théophile, (1) *Les Beaux-Arts en Europe 1855.* Paris, 1855, (2) *L'Art moderne.* Paris, 1856; Gazier, Georges, *Gustave Courbet: l'homme et l'œuvre.* Besançon, 1906; Geffroy, Gustave, (1) *L'art et les artistes*, octobre 1906, (2) *Claude Monet, sa vie, son temps, son œuvre.* Paris, 1922; Gigoux, Jean, (1) *Revue franc-comtoise*, octobre 1884, (2) *Causeries sur les Artistes de mon temps.* Paris, 1885; Gill, André (*pseud.* of Louis-Alexandre Gosset de Guines), *Vingt années de Paris.* Avec une préface par A. Daudet. Paris, 1883; Gooch, George Peabody, *The Second Empire.* London, 1960; Goodison, J. W. & Sutton, Denys. Fitzwilliam Museum, Cambridge. *Catalogue of Paintings:* I *French Schools.* Cambridge, 1960; Grand, G., *Académie des Sciences, Belles Lettres et Arts de Besançon*, vol. 172 (1947–57): 21 février 1953; Grand-Carteret, John, *Les Mœurs et le caricature en France.* Paris, 1888; Grate, Pontus, *Deux critiques d'art de l'époque romantique: Gustave Planche et Théophile Thoré.* Stockholm, 1959; Grimmer, Georges, (1) 'Zoé Courbet.' *Bull.* 17–18 (1956), pp. 1–27, (2) *Bull.* 15 (1954), pp. 1–12, (3) 'Courbet et Chenavard.' *Bull.* 9 (1951), pp. 1–9; Gronkowski, Camille, (1) & Paschal, G. *Catalogue sommaire des Collections municipales.* 1929, (2) *Gazette des Beaux-Arts*, juillet 1929; Gros, A., *Français par un de ses élèves.* 1902; Gros-Kost, E., *Gustave Courbet: souvenirs intimes.* Paris, 1880; Guichard, Marie, *Les Doctrines de M. Gustave Courbet, maître peintre.* Paris, 1862; Guillemin, Henri: see Europe; Guillonet, J., 'Le portrait de Paul Ansout au Musée de Dieppe.' *Bull.* 8 (1950), pp. 9–11.

Hefting: see Bakker-Hefting; Herman, J., *Jewish Quarterly*, vol. 18 (1970), no. 1, p. 28; Hilton, Timothy, *The Pre-Raphaelites.* London, 1970; Hofmann, Werner, (1) *Art in the Nineteenth Century.* [Translation of *Das Irdische Paradies* and *Kunst im neunzehnten Jahrhundert* by Brian Battershaw.] London, 1961, (2) 'Nouvelles analyses et appréciations de L'Atelier' (trans. by Charles Wœrler), *Bull.* 33–34 (1965), pp. 1–8, (3) *Das Irdisches Paradies.* Munich, 1960; Holleman, Barbara A., 'Portrait de Courbet par Manet.' *Bull.* 28 (1961), pp. 1–11; Hoppe, Ragnar, *Honoré Daumier, Gustave Courbet. Tva franska mästare och deras arbeten i Nordisk ägo.* Stockholm, 1929; Houssaye, Édouard, *L'Artiste*, 1885; Hugo, Victor, (1) *Choses vues.* 2 vols. Paris, 1913, (2) *Choses vues.* Paris, 1887; Hunt, Herbert James, *Le Socialisme et le romantisme en France. Étude de la presse Socialiste de 1830 à 1848.* Oxford, 1935; Huyghe, René, (1) with Bazin, Germain, & Adhémar, Hélène. *Courbet. L'Atelier du peintre, allégorie réelle, 1855.* Paris, 1944, (2) Introduction to Robert Fernier, *Gustave Courbet* (1969).

Ideville, Henry d'. (1) *Gustave Courbet, notes et documents sur sa vie et son œuvre.* Paris, 1878, (2) *Vielles maisons et jeunes souvenirs.* Paris, 1878; esp. pp. 165–85; Isaacson, J., *Monet Le Déjeuner*, 1972; Isnard, Guy, *Jardin des Arts*, No. 72 (octobre 1960).

Jean-Aubry, G., *Eugène Boudin d'après des documents inédits. L'homme et l'œuvre*. Paris, 1922; Joubin, André, *Catalogue du Musée Fabre*. Paris, 1926; Jouve, Pierre-Jean, *Tombeau de Baudelaire* (Delacroix – Le Quartier Latin de Meryon – Un Tableau de Courbet). Paris, 1958.

Kahn, Gustave, *Courbet*. 1927; Kahn, Suzanne, & Écalle, Martine, 'Les Demoiselles des bords de la Seine.' *Bull.* 19 (1957), pp. 1–17; Kane, W. M., *Yale University Art Gallery Bulletin*, vol. 25 (1960), pp. 32–4; Kaschnitz, Marie Luise, *Gustave Courbet*. Baden-Baden, 1949.

La Bédollière, Émile Gigault de, *Les Industriels: métiers et professions en France*. Dessins par H. Monnier. Paris, 1842; Laclotte, Michel: in *Rome*; Lafenestre, Georges, *Artistes et Amateurs*. Paris, 1900; La Forge, Anatole de, *La Peinture contemporaine en France*. Paris, 1856; esp. pp. 253–80; Lanjalley, Paul, & Corriez, Paul, *Histoire de la Révolution du 18 mars*. Paris/Brussels/Leipzig/ Leghorn, 1871; Larkin, Oliver, (1) *Daumier: Man of his Time*. London, 1967, (2) 'Courbet and his contemporaries, 1848–1867.' *Science and Society* (New York), vol. 3, no. 1 (winter 1939), pp. 42–63; Lázár, Bela, *Courbet et son influence à l'étranger*. Paris, 1911; Lecoq de Boisbaudran, Horace, (1) *Enseignement artistique*. Paris, 1879, (2) *The Training of the Memory in Art and the Education of the Artist* (trans. by L. D. Luard). London, 1911; Léger, Charles, (1) *Courbet*. Paris, 1925, (2) *Courbet*. Paris, 1929, (3) *Courbet selon les caricatures et les images*. Paris, 1920, (4) in *Mercure de France*, vol. 201, 1 janvier, (5) *Courbet et son temps*. Paris, 1948, (6) in *L'Amour de l'Art*, no. 10 (octobre 1931), (7) 'Courbet et Victor Hugo d'après les lettres inédites.' *Gazette des Beaux-Arts*, année 63, vol. 4, no. 722 (décembre 1921), pp. 353–63, (8) *Courbet à Pontarlier*. Paris, 1948, (9) *Courbet en exil (d'après des documents inédits)*. Pontarlier, 1943, (10) *Au Pays de Gustave Courbet*. Meudon, 1910, (11) 'Lettres inédites de quelques peintres. Gustave Courbet.' *L'Olivier. Revue de Nice* (Nice), année 2, no. 8 (septembre–octobre 1913), pp. 468–512, (12) 'Un ami méconnu de Courbet: André Slom.' *Bull.* 4 (1948), pp. 4–7, (13) in *Mercure de France*, vol. 290 (1939), pp. 721–7, (14) 'Proudhon et Courbet: histoire des portraits de Proudhon'. *Bull.* 2 (1947), pp. 3–13, (15) *Arts*, 24 octobre 1947; Lemonnier, Camille, (1) *Les Peintres de la vie*: 'Courbet et son œuvre'. Paris, 1888, (2) *Salon de Paris*. 1870; *Lettres Françaises, Les*; 9 janvier 1958; Levin, Harry, *The Gates of Horn*. Oxford, 1966; Levy, C., *L'Information historique*, no. 4 (1954), p. 143; Leymarie, Jean, (1) *La Peinture française au XIXe siècle*. Geneva, 1962, (2) *L'Impressionisme: Étude biographique et critique*. 2 vols. Geneva, 1955; Lindsay, Jack, (1) *Cézanne: his Life and Art*. London, 1969, (2) *Death of the Hero*. London, 1960, (3) *J. M. W. Turner: a critical biography*. London 1966; Loudun, Eugène, *Le Salon de 1855*. Paris, 1855.

Mack, Gerstle, (1) *Gustave Courbet*. London, 1951, (2) *Paul Cézanne*. London, 1935; MacOrlan, Pierre (*pseud.* of Pierre Dumarchey), *Courbet*. Biographie et notices par Anna Marsan. Paris, 1951; Maillard, L. V., *Les Villageois*. 1848; Maitron, Jean (ed.), *Dictionnaire biographique du mouvement ouvrier français*. Paris, 1964 on; Malvane, L., (1) *Courbet*, 1966, (2) French edition; Mantz, Paul, 'Gustave Courbet.' *Gazette des Beaux-Arts*, année 20, vol. 17, no. 6 (juin 1878), pp. 514–27; vol. 18, no. 1 (juillet 1878), pp. 17–30; no. 6 (décembre 1878), pp. 371–84; Marcel, H., 'Quelques lettres inédites de J.-F. Millet.' *Gazette des Beaux-Arts*, juillet 1901, pp. 69–78; Marlin, Roger, (1) *Annuaire littéraire de l'université de Besançon, histoire*. 1955, (2) *L'Épuration politique dans le Doubs à la suite du coup de 1851*, 1958; Martino, Pierre, *Le Roman réaliste sous le Second Empire*. Paris, 1913; Marx, Karl, *The Eighteenth Brumaire of Louis Bonaparte*; Mayne, Jonathan, *Victoria and Albert Museum Bulletin*, no. 2 (4 October 1966), pp. 148–56; Meier-Graefe, Julius, (1) *Corot und Courbet*. Leipzig, 1905, (2) *Courbet*. Munich, 1921, (3) *Entwicklungsgeschichte der modernen Kunst*. Munich, 1915; Mendès, Catulle, (1) *L'Artiste*. 1861, (2) *Glatigny* (3rd edition). Paris, 1906; Méry, Pierre, *La Mode* (26 janvier 1851), pp. 206f. *Metrop.*: see C. Sterling (2); Michel, André, (1) *Histoire de l'art*, vol. 8, part 2. 1926, (2) *Journal des Débats*, 10 janvier 1920; Molok, Aleksandr Ivanovich, *Annuaire d'études françaises*. Moscow, 1964; Moreau, Pierre, Académie des Sciences, Belles Lettres et Arts de Besançon. *Bulletin Trimestriel* (Besançon), trimestre 1 (1936), p. 35; Muller, Georges,

'Courbet et la colonne Vendôme.' *Bull.* 24 (1959), pp. 1–11; Muther, Richard. *Courbet.* Munich, 1908.

Naef, Hans, *Courbet.* Berne, 1947; Nicoll, John Stewart, *The Pre-Raphaelites.* London, 1970; Nochlin, Linda, (1) *Art Bulletin*, vol. 49 (September 1967), (2) 'Development and Nature of Realism: the work of Gustave Courbet' (New York University, Ph.D. dissertation, 1963), (3) in *Essays in honour of W. Friedlaender* (1965), pp. 119–26, (4) *Realism and Tradition in Art 1848–1900*, (5) *Art Q.* xxxiv (1) 1971 (Props. for Brise). Englewood Cliffs, N.J., 1960.

Oudot, Julien, *Conscience et science du devoir.* Introduction à une explication nouvelle du code Napoléon. 2 vols. Paris, 1855–6.

Peillex, Georges, *Gustave Courbet à La Tour-de-Peilz.* 1950; Péladan, Josephin, (1) *L'Artiste*, vol. 2 (1884), (2) in Courthion (1), vol. 2, pp. 267–80; Perruche de Velna, Paul, *Annales franc-comtoises*, vol. 6 (1866), pp. 221–9; Pool, Phoebe, *Impressionism.* London, 1967; Préclin, Edmond, *Études d'histoire moderne et contemporaine*, vol. 2 (1948); Proudhon, Pierre-Joseph, (1) *Œuvres complètes.* 26 vols. Paris/Brussels, 1867–70, (2) *Correspondance.* 14 vols. Paris, 1875, (3) *Œuvres.* 1920–39, (4) *Lettres*, ed. D. Halévy & L. Guilloux. Paris, 1929, (5) *Contradictions politiques.* Paris, 1870, (6) *La Pornocratie, ou Les Femmes dans les temps modernes.* Paris, 1875, (7) *Les Confessions d'un Révolutionnaire, pour servir à l'histoire de la Révolution de février.* Bruxelles, 1849, (8) *Du Principe de l'art et de sa destination sociale.* Paris, 1865, (9) *id.*, ed. J.-L. Puech. Paris, 1939, (10) *Carnets*, ed. Pierre Haubtmann etc. 2 vols. Paris, 1960–1.

Raphael, Max, *Proudhon, Marx, Picasso: trois études.* Paris, 1933; Rewald, John, (1) *The History of Impressionism.* New York, 1946, (2) *Histoire de l'Impressionisme.* Paris, 1953; Riat, Georges, *Gustave Courbet, peintre.* Paris, 1906; Rioux de Maillon, P., *Souvenir des autres.* Paris, 1918; Robert, Guy, '*La terre' d'Émile Zola: Étude historique et critique.* Paris, 1952; Robin, M., *G. Courbet.* 1909; Rochefort, Henri, 'Dumas jugé par Rochefort.' *Le Reveil* (Paris), 19 février 1882; *Rome: Gustave Courbet, Mostra all' Accademia di Francia Villa Medici 1969–70.* Rosenthal, Léon, (1) *Gazette des Beaux-Arts*, vol. 43 (1910), pp. 93–114, 227–41, 322–54, (2) *La Peinture romantique: Essai sur l'évolution de la peinture française de 1815 à 1830.* Paris, 1903, (3) *Du Romantisme au réalisme: Essai sur l'évolution de la peinture française de 1830 à 1848.* Paris, 1914; Rostrup, H., *Trois tableaux de Courbet.* Copenhagen, 1931.

Schaettel, Marcel, 'Baudelaire et Courbet.' *Bull.* 43 (1970), pp. 1–7; Schanne, Alexandre-Louis, *Souvenirs de Schaunard.* Paris, 1886; Schapiro, Meyer, 'Courbet and Popular Imagery: An Essay on Realism and Naïveté.' *Journal of the Warburg and Courtauld Institute*, vol. 4 (1940–1), pp. 164–91; Schroder, M. Z., *Icarus.* 1961; Schwerz, H., *Museum Notes* (Museum of Art, Rhode Island School of Design), vol. 4, no. 5 (May 1946), pp. 2f; Sensier, Alfred, *Souvenirs sur Th. Rousseau.* Paris, 1872; Signac, Paul, *D'Eugène Delacroix au néo-impressionisme.* Paris, 1899; Silvestre, Théophile, (1) *Histoire des artistes vivants français et étrangers. Études d'après nature.* 1re série. Paris, 1856, (2) *Les Artistes français. Etude d'après nature.* Brussels, 1861; Soboul, Albert, (1) *La Pensée*, vol. 39 (1948), nos. 18–20, (2) *id.*, nos. 1–20, 39–61; Somaré, Enrico, *Courbet.* Bergamo, 1934; Soria, G.: in *Europe*, pp. 237–56; Sterling, Charles, (1) with Adhémar, Hélène. *Musée National du Louvre. Peintures de l'école française du XIXe siècle.* Paris, 1958, (2) with Margaretta M. Salinger. *French Paintings: A Catalogue of the Collection of the Metropolitan Museum of Art.* II: *XIX Century.* Courbet. pp. 104–32; Sudan, E., *L'Activite d'un socialiste de 1848.* 1921; Sulzberger, Max, *Le Réalisme en France et en Belgique.* Brussels, 1874; Sutton, Denys. (1) *Country Life* (London), 6 June 1953, (2) 'Le Réalisme de Courbet'. *Bull.* 13 (1953–1954), pp. 9–13; Sylvester, David. *Listener*, 11 June 1953.

Tabarant, Adolphe, *La Vie artistique au temps de Baudelaire.* Paris, 1963; Talmeyr, Maurice, *Souvenirs d'avant le déluge, 1870–1914.* Paris, 1927; Tenot, Eugène, *La Province en décembre 1851:*

étude historique. Paris, 1865; Thaumiaux, Jean, 'Courbet en Saintonge: I. Les deux fêtes du 15 août 1862 à Saintes' (extract from *Sud-Ouest*, 27 septembre 1957), reprinted in *Bull*. 20 (1957), pp. 13–15; Thiesson, Gaston, 'Le Peintre Gustave Courbet en 1870–1871.' *Demain. Pages et Documents* (Geneva), année 1, no. 3 (15 mars 1916), pp. 152–7; Thoré, Théophile, (1) *Salons de W. Bürger, 1861 à 1868*. 2 vols. Paris, 1870, (2) *Gazette des Beaux-Arts*, vol. 8; Thuriet, C., *La dernier voyage de Proudhon à Besançon*. Besançon, 1896; Tixomirov, A. N., *Gustave Courbet*. Moscow, 1965; Toubin, Charles, *Souvenirs*; Tourneaux, M., *Salons et expositions d'art à Paris*. Paris, 1919; Toussaint, Maurice: in *Rome*; Troubat, Jules, (1) *Une Amitié à la d'Arthez : Champfleury, Courbet, Max Buchon*. Paris, 1900, (2) *Le Correspondant*, 26 janvier 1878, (3) *Plume et Pinceau : Étude de Littérature et d'Art*. Paris, 1878.

Valerio, Edith, 'Gustave Courbet and his Country.' *Art in America* (New York), vol. 10, no. 6 (October 1922), pp. 246–54; Vallès, Jules, (1) *La Rue*. Paris, 1866, (2) *Jacques Vingtras*; esp. *L'Insurgé*. Paris, 1886; Vandérem, Fernand (ed.), *Le Salut Public* (facsimile reprint). Paris, n.d.; Velna: *see* Perruche de Velna; Venturi, Lionello, (1) *Les Peintres modernes*. Paris, 1941, (2) *Modern Painters*. New York/London, 1947, (3) *Impressionists and Symbolists*. 1950; Vergnet-Ruez, Jean, & Laclotte, Michel, *Petits et grands musées de France*. 1962; Vigier, Philippe, *La Seconde République dans la région alpine. Étude politique et sociale*. 2 pt. Paris, 1956; Vignon, Claude, *Exposition universelle de 1855. Beaux-Arts*. Paris, 1855; Visser, Mathilde, Letter on *Les Lutteurs. Bull*. 42 (1969), p. 13; Voss, Hans, (1) 'Courbet à Francfort-sur-le-Main.' *Bull*. 21 (1958), pp. 9–11, (2) 'Courbet, der französischer Maler in Frankfurt', in *Frankfurt-Lebendige Stadt* (1958).

Waldmann, Emil, *Die Kunst des Realismus und des Impressionismus im 19. Jahrhundert*. Berlin, 1927; Weinberg, Bernard, *French Realism : the Critical Reaction, 1830–70*. New York/London, 1937; Wey, Francis, 'Extrait des mémoires inédits de feu Francis Wey. Notre maître-peintre G. Courbet.' MS. (35 pages) in Salle des Estampes, Bibliothéque Nationale, Paris; Wœrler, Charles, 'Gustave Courbet à Berne.' *Bull*. 31 (1964), pp. 1–7; Woodcock, George, *Pierre-Joseph Proudhon. A biography*. London, 1956.

Zahar, Marcel, (1) *Gustave Courbet*. [Reproductions with an introduction] Paris, 1950, (2) *Gustave Courbet*. Geneva, 1952, (3) 'Le Retour de Courbet.' *Bull*. 6 (1949), pp. 1–8, (4) *Bull*. 32 (1960), pp. 1–7; Zola, Émile, (1) *Mes Haines : Causeries littéraires et artistiques*. Paris, 1866, (2) *Salons* [Articles originally published in periodicals] Recueillis, annotés et présentés par F. W. J. Hemmings et Robert J. Neiss et précédés d'une étude sur Émile Zola critique d'art de F. W. J. Hemmings. Geneva/Paris, 1959.

INDEX

WORKS BY COURBET